HOW TO READ MANGA!

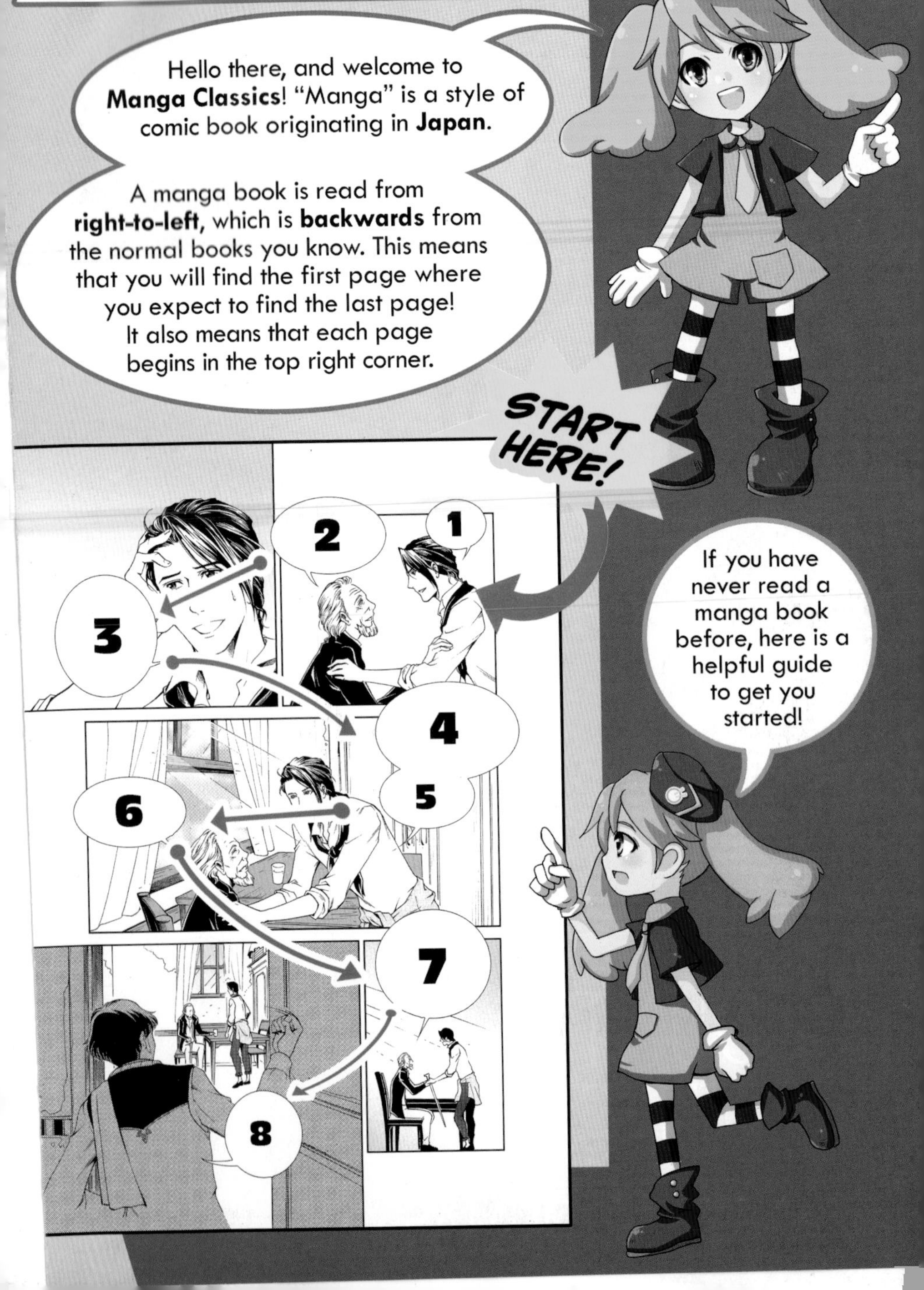
Hello there, and welcome to **Manga Classics**! "Manga" is a style of comic book originating in **Japan**.
A manga book is read from **right-to-left**, which is **backwards** from the normal books you know. This means that you will find the first page where you expect to find the last page! It also means that each page begins in the top right corner.
If you have never read a manga book before, here is a helpful guide to get you started!
START HERE!
1
2
3
4
5
6
7
8

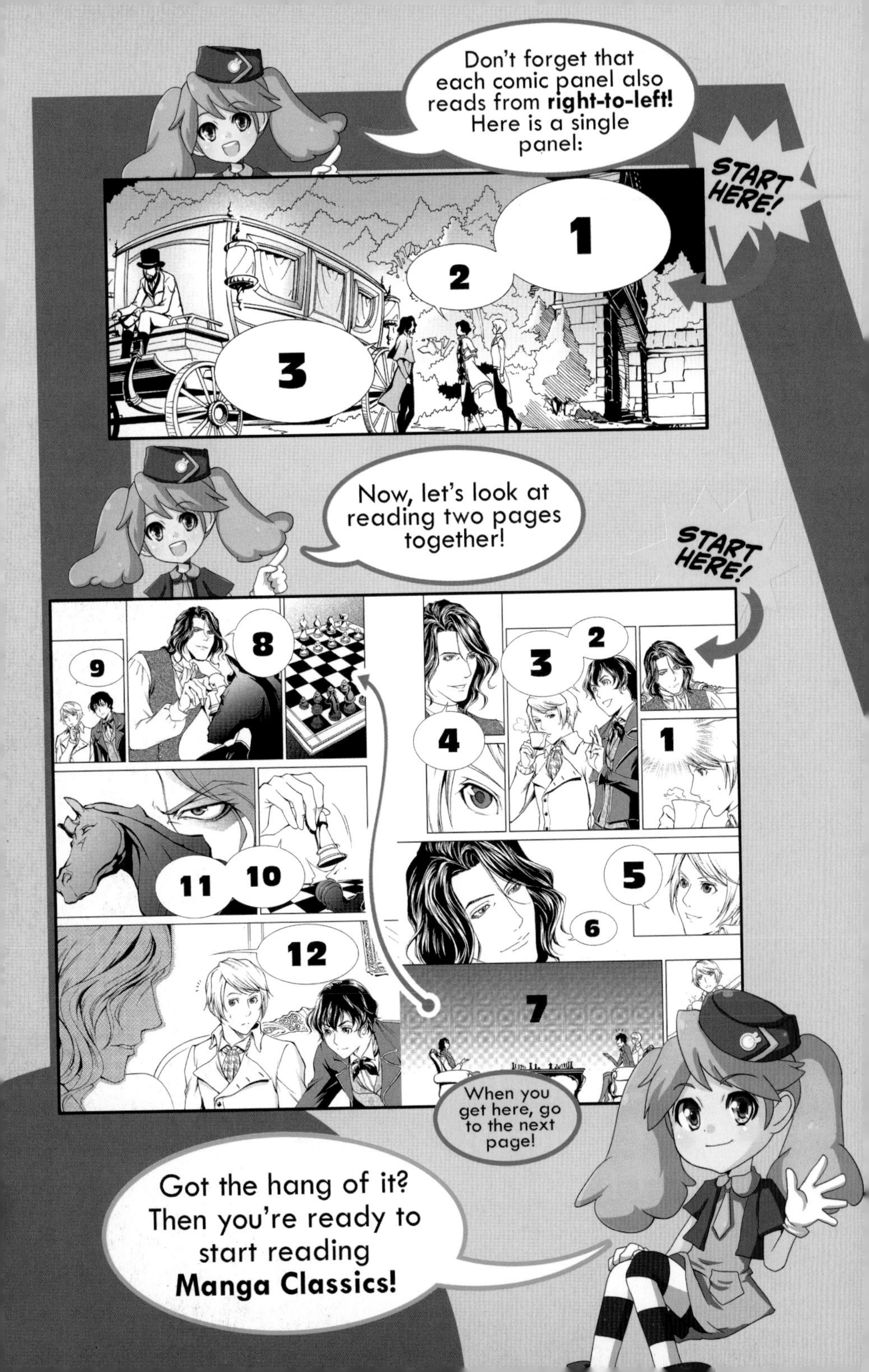
Don't forget that each comic panel also reads from **right-to-left!** Here is a single panel:
START HERE!
1
2
3
Now, let's look at reading two pages together!
START HERE!
1
2
3
4
5
6
7
8
9
10
11
12
When you get here, go to the next page!
Got the hang of it? Then you're ready to start reading **Manga Classics!**

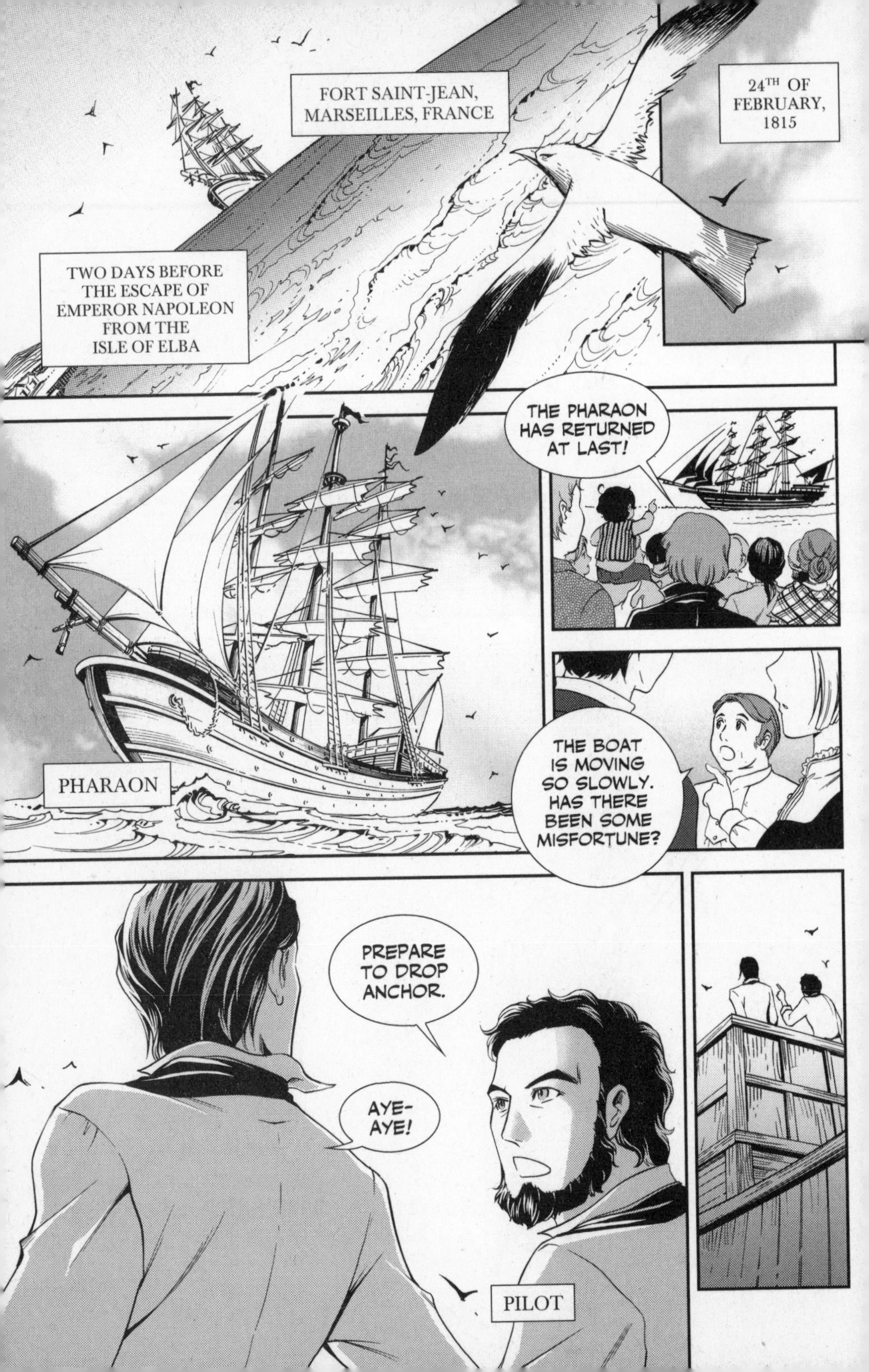
24TH OF FEBRUARY, 1815
FORT SAINT-JEAN, MARSEILLES, FRANCE
TWO DAYS BEFORE THE ESCAPE OF EMPEROR NAPOLEON FROM THE ISLE OF ELBA
THE PHARAON HAS RETURNED AT LAST!
THE BOAT IS MOVING SO SLOWLY. HAS THERE BEEN SOME MISFORTUNE?
PHARAON
PREPARE TO DROP ANCHOR.
AYE-AYE!
PILOT

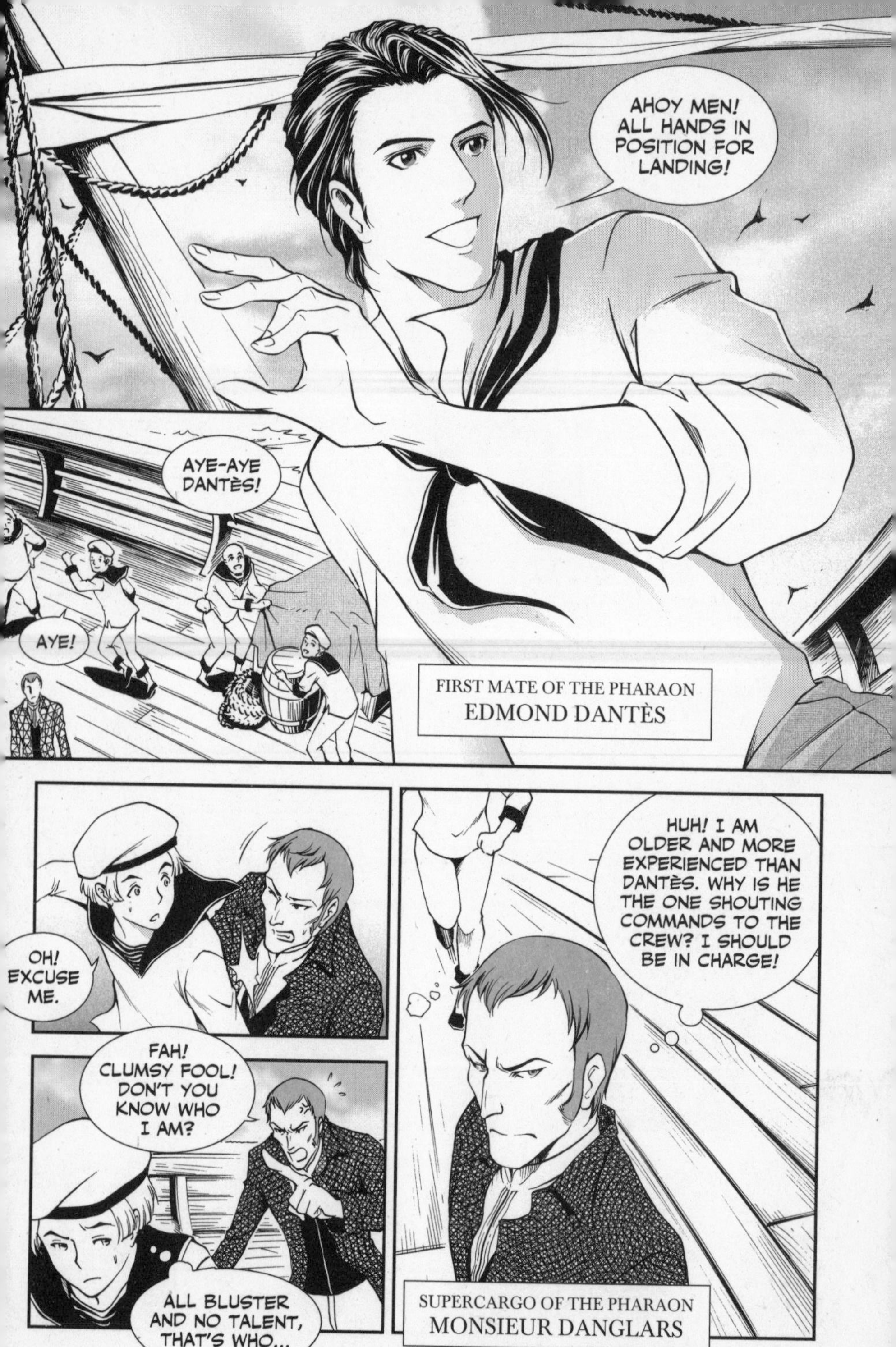
AHOY MEN! ALL HANDS IN POSITION FOR LANDING!
AYE-AYE DANTÈS!
AYE!
FIRST MATE OF THE PHARAON EDMOND DANTÈS
HUH! I AM OLDER AND MORE EXPERIENCED THAN DANTÈS. WHY IS HE THE ONE SHOUTING COMMANDS TO THE CREW? I SHOULD BE IN CHARGE!
SUPERCARGO OF THE PHARAON MONSIEUR DANGLARS
OH! EXCUSE ME.
FAH! CLUMSY FOOL! DON'T YOU KNOW WHO I AM?
ALL BLUSTER AND NO TALENT, THAT'S WHO...

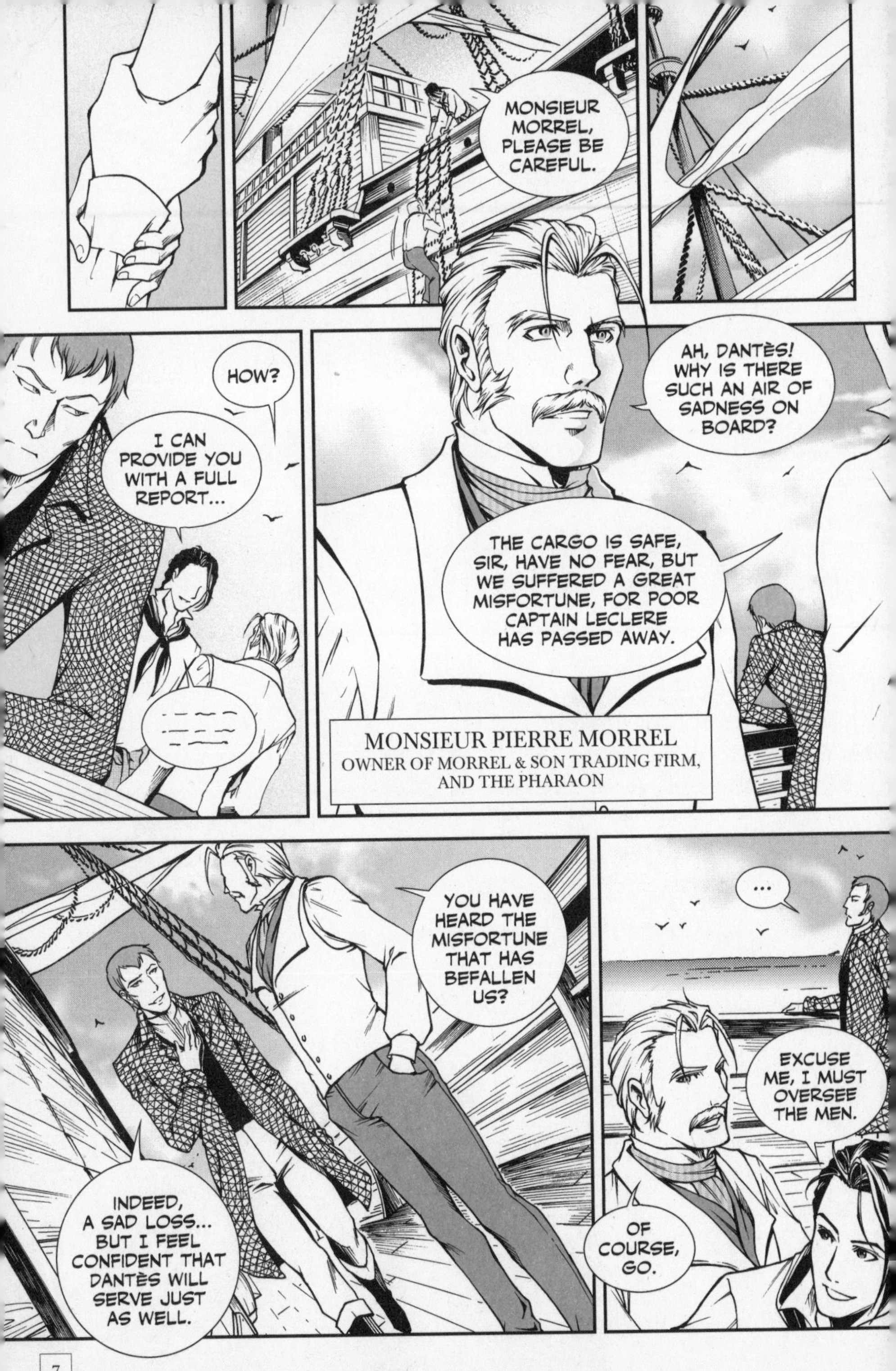
MONSIEUR MORREL, PLEASE BE CAREFUL.
AH, DANTÈS! WHY IS THERE SUCH AN AIR OF SADNESS ON BOARD?
THE CARGO IS SAFE, SIR, HAVE NO FEAR, BUT WE SUFFERED A GREAT MISFORTUNE, FOR POOR CAPTAIN LECLERE HAS PASSED AWAY.
MONSIEUR PIERRE MORREL
OWNER OF MORREL & SON TRADING FIRM, AND THE PHARAON
HOW?
I CAN PROVIDE YOU WITH A FULL REPORT...
...
EXCUSE ME, I MUST OVERSEE THE MEN.
OF COURSE, GO.
YOU HAVE HEARD THE MISFORTUNE THAT HAS BEFALLEN US?
INDEED, A SAD LOSS... BUT I FEEL CONFIDENT THAT DANTÈS WILL SERVE JUST AS WELL.

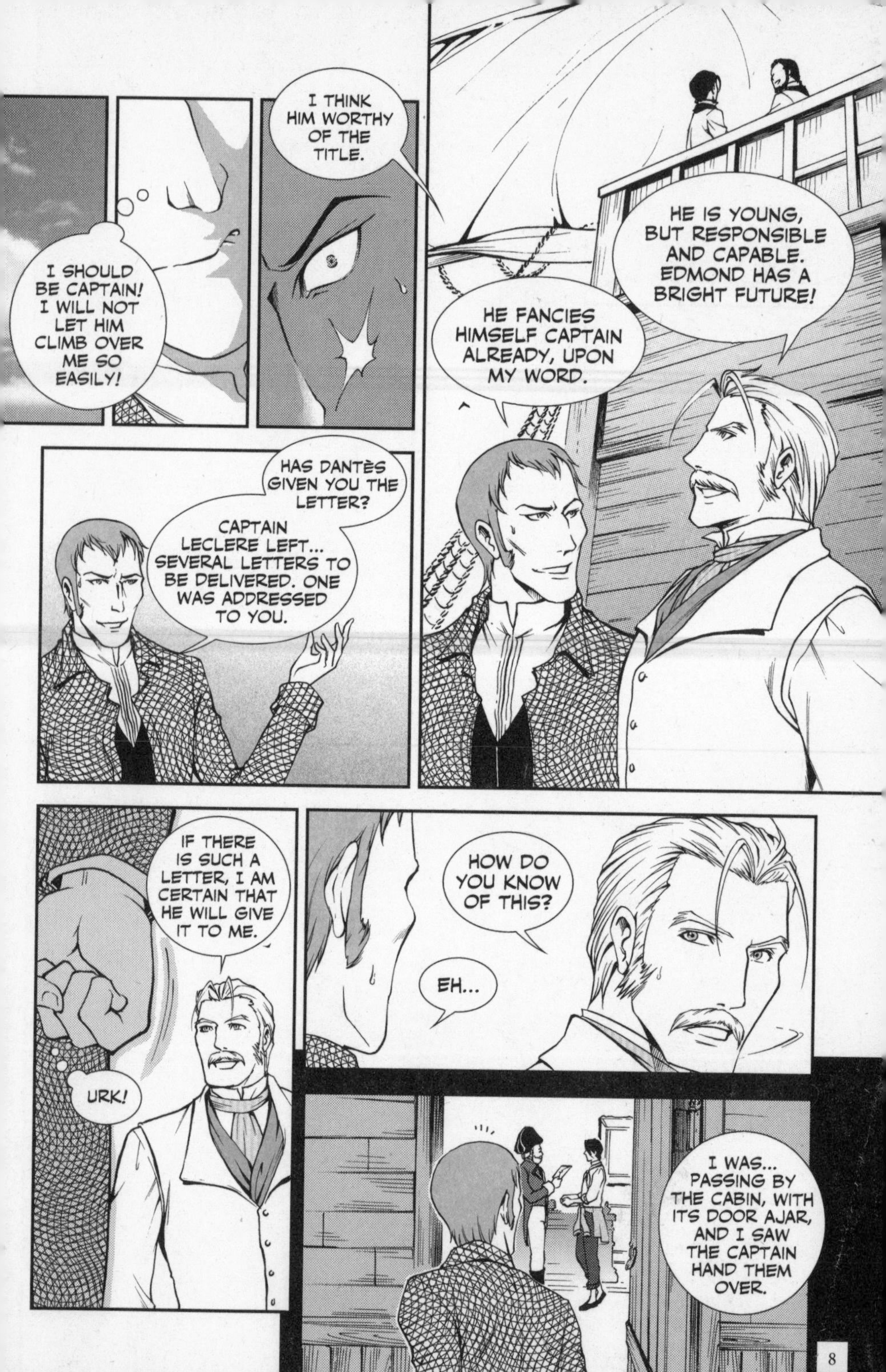
HE IS YOUNG, BUT RESPONSIBLE AND CAPABLE. EDMOND HAS A BRIGHT FUTURE!
HE FANCIES HIMSELF CAPTAIN ALREADY, UPON MY WORD.
I THINK HIM WORTHY OF THE TITLE.
I SHOULD BE CAPTAIN! I WILL NOT LET HIM CLIMB OVER ME SO EASILY!
HAS DANTÈS GIVEN YOU THE LETTER?
CAPTAIN LECLERE LEFT... SEVERAL LETTERS TO BE DELIVERED. ONE WAS ADDRESSED TO YOU.
HOW DO YOU KNOW OF THIS?
EH...
I WAS... PASSING BY THE CABIN, WITH ITS DOOR AJAR, AND I SAW THE CAPTAIN HAND THEM OVER.
IF THERE IS SUCH A LETTER, I AM CERTAIN THAT HE WILL GIVE IT TO ME.
URK!

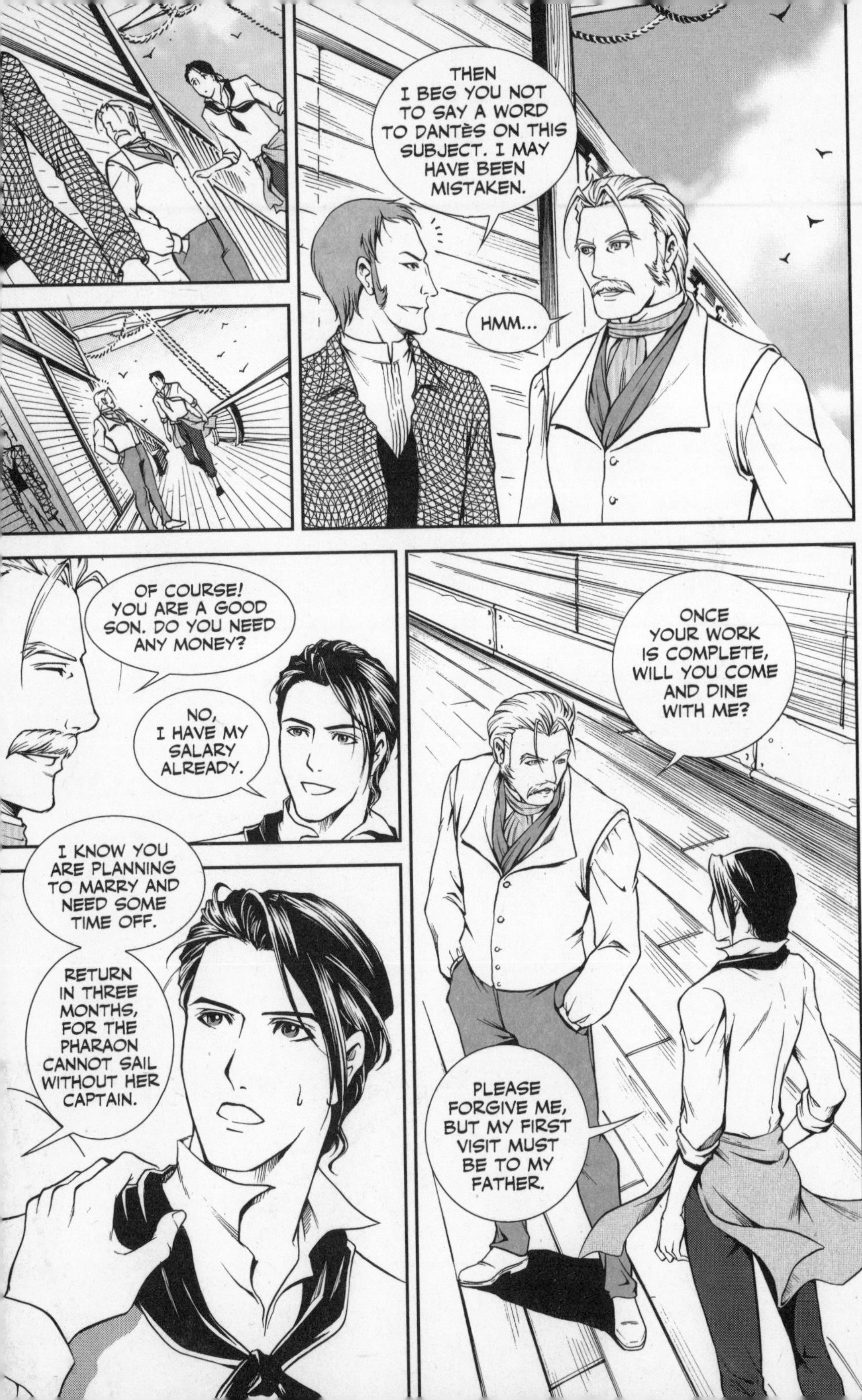
THEN I BEG YOU NOT TO SAY A WORD TO DANTÈS ON THIS SUBJECT. I MAY HAVE BEEN MISTAKEN.
HMM...
ONCE YOUR WORK IS COMPLETE, WILL YOU COME AND DINE WITH ME?
PLEASE FORGIVE ME, BUT MY FIRST VISIT MUST BE TO MY FATHER.
OF COURSE! YOU ARE A GOOD SON. DO YOU NEED ANY MONEY?
NO, I HAVE MY SALARY ALREADY.
I KNOW YOU ARE PLANNING TO MARRY AND NEED SOME TIME OFF.
RETURN IN THREE MONTHS, FOR THE PHARAON CANNOT SAIL WITHOUT HER CAPTAIN.

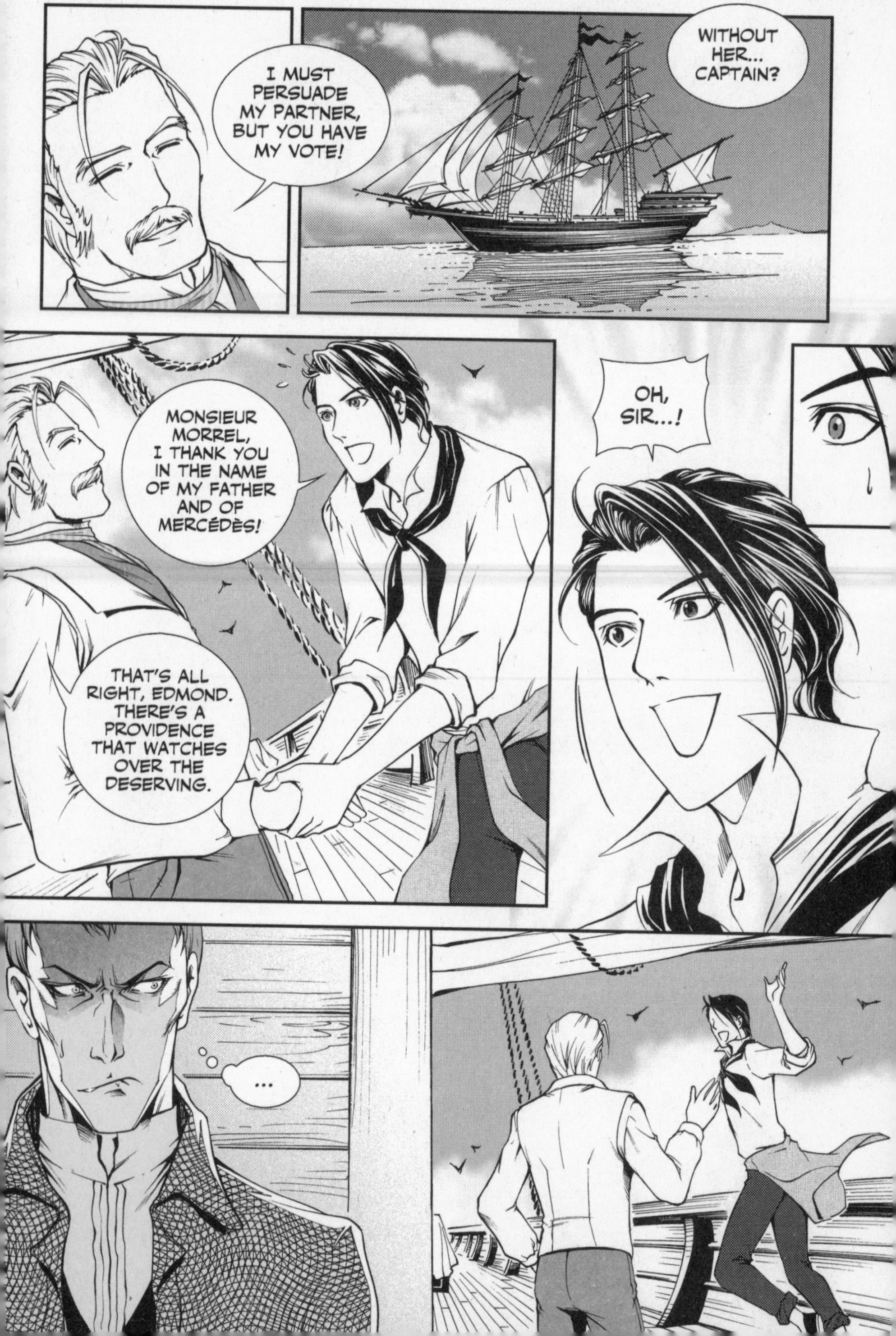
WITHOUT HER... CAPTAIN?
I MUST PERSUADE MY PARTNER, BUT YOU HAVE MY VOTE!
OH, SIR...!
MONSIEUR MORREL, I THANK YOU IN THE NAME OF MY FATHER AND OF MERCÉDÈS!
THAT'S ALL RIGHT, EDMOND. THERE'S A PROVIDENCE THAT WATCHES OVER THE DESERVING.
...

CHAPTER 1
CONSPIRACY

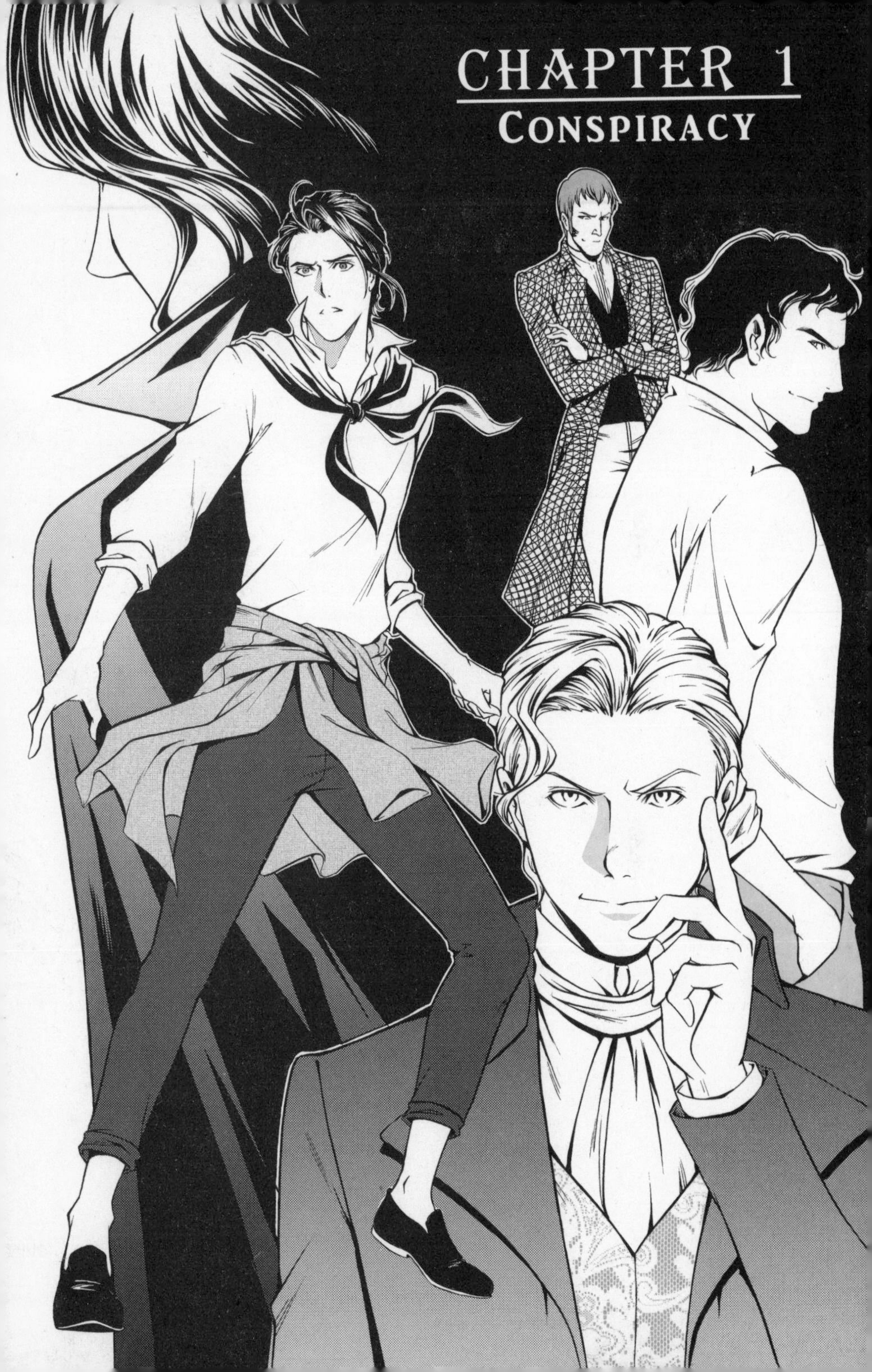

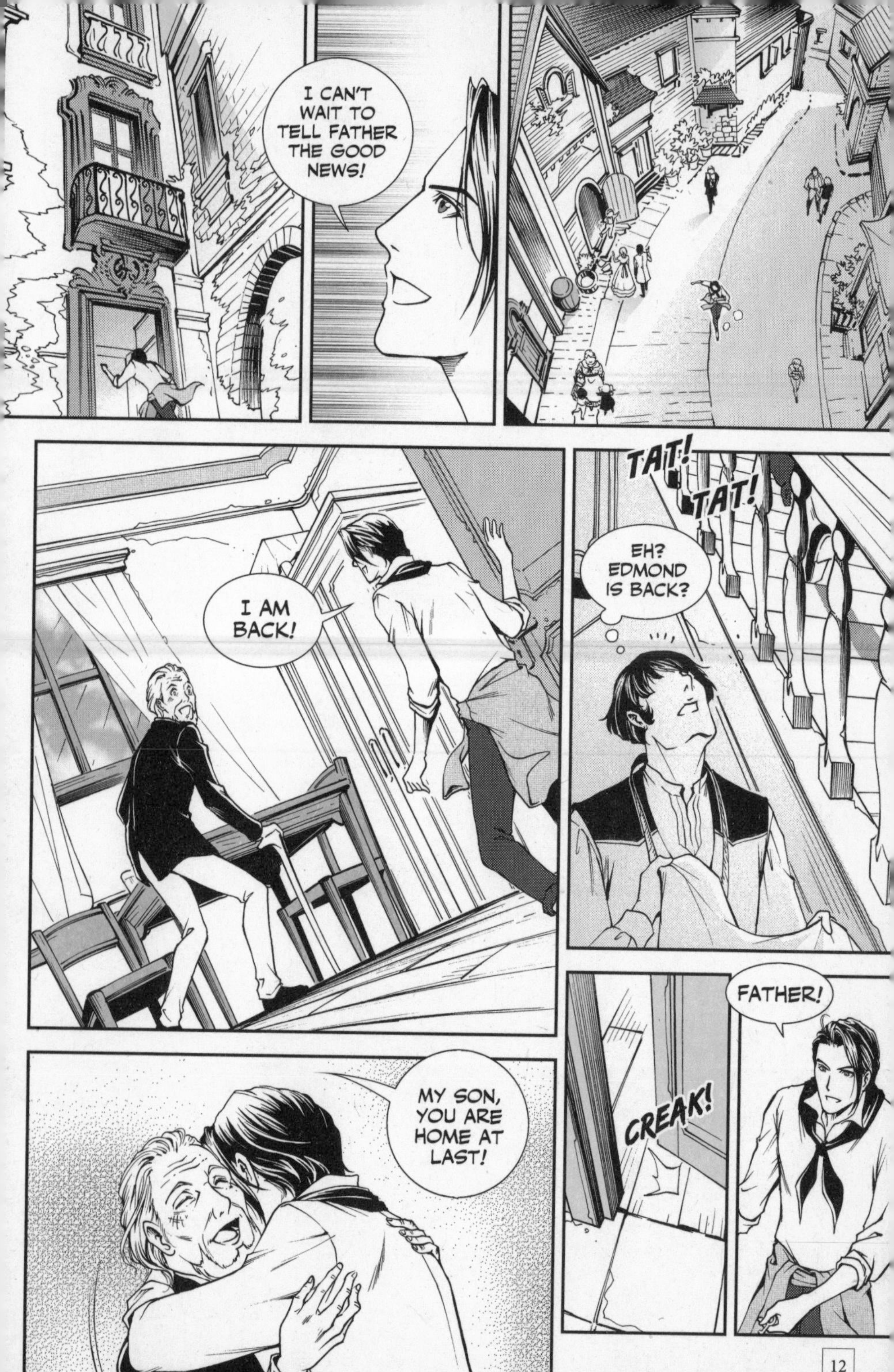
I CAN'T WAIT TO TELL FATHER THE GOOD NEWS!
TAT! TAT!
EH? EDMOND IS BACK?
I AM BACK!
FATHER!
CREAK!
MY SON, YOU ARE HOME AT LAST!

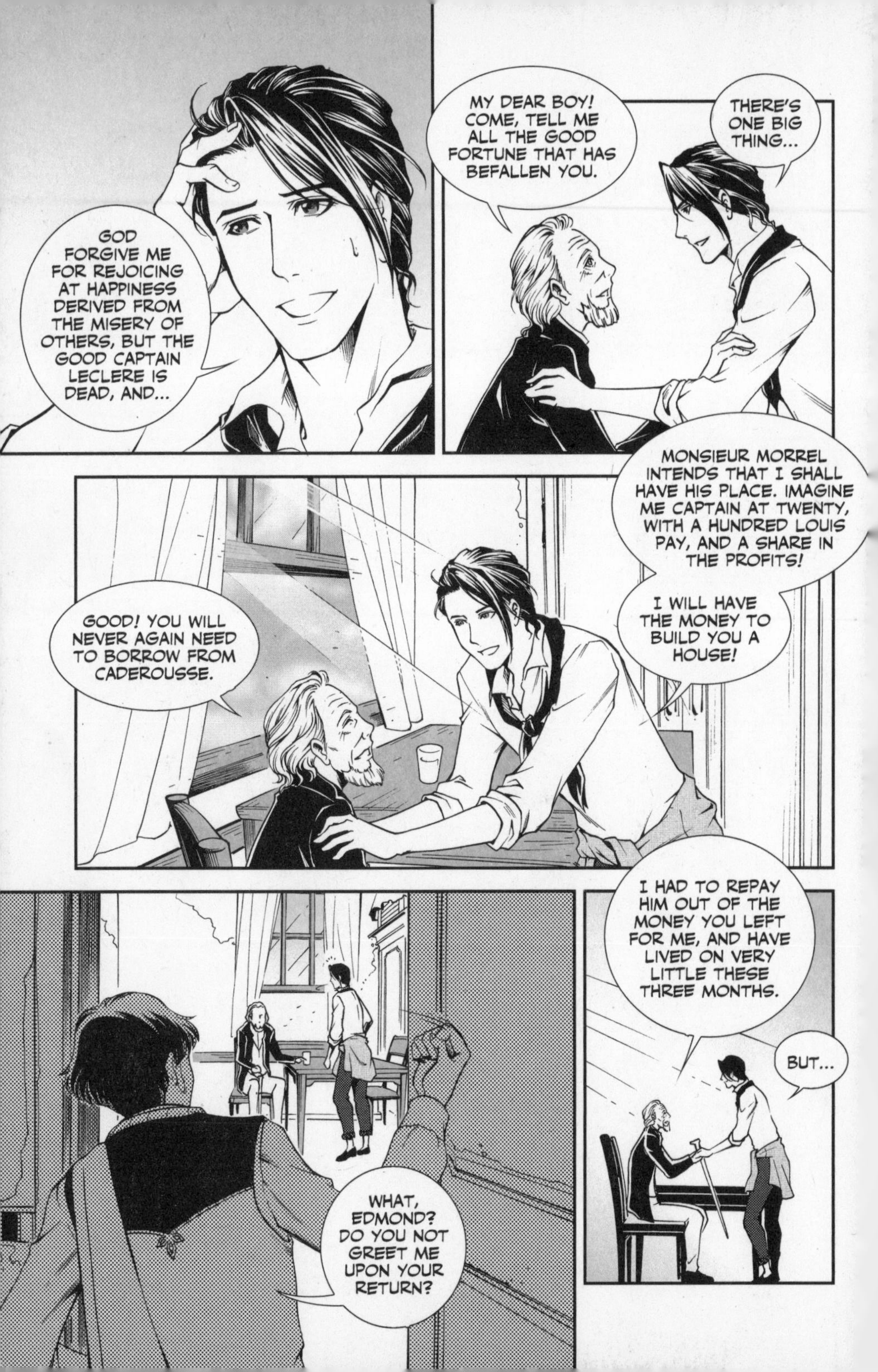
MY DEAR BOY! COME, TELL ME ALL THE GOOD FORTUNE THAT HAS BEFALLEN YOU.
THERE'S ONE BIG THING...
GOD FORGIVE ME FOR REJOICING AT HAPPINESS DERIVED FROM THE MISERY OF OTHERS, BUT THE GOOD CAPTAIN LECLERE IS DEAD, AND...
MONSIEUR MORREL INTENDS THAT I SHALL HAVE HIS PLACE. IMAGINE ME CAPTAIN AT TWENTY, WITH A HUNDRED LOUIS PAY, AND A SHARE IN THE PROFITS!
I WILL HAVE THE MONEY TO BUILD YOU A HOUSE!
GOOD! YOU WILL NEVER AGAIN NEED TO BORROW FROM CADEROUSSE.
I HAD TO REPAY HIM OUT OF THE MONEY YOU LEFT FOR ME, AND HAVE LIVED ON VERY LITTLE THESE THREE MONTHS.
BUT...
WHAT, EDMOND? DO YOU NOT GREET ME UPON YOUR RETURN?

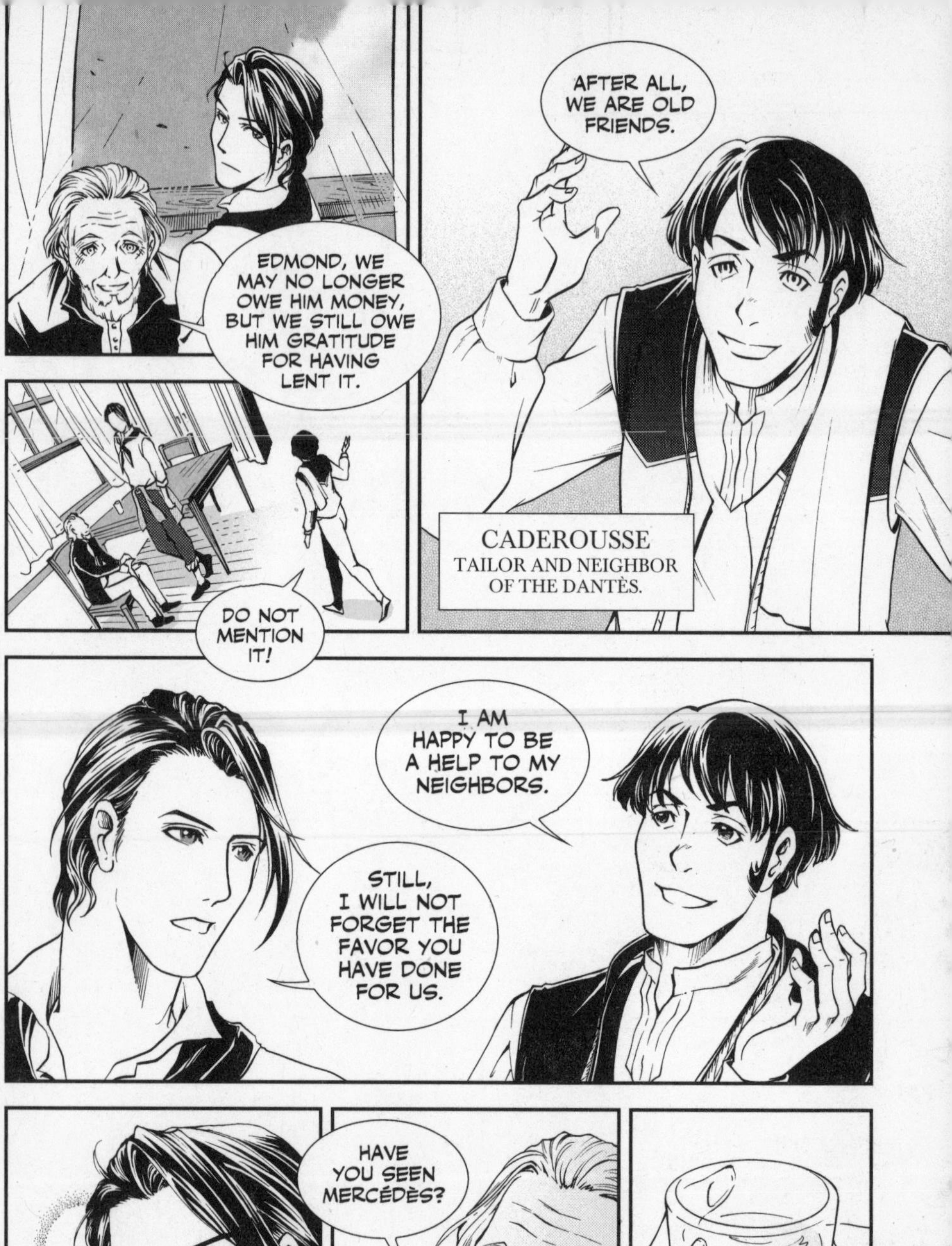
EDMOND, WE MAY NO LONGER OWE HIM MONEY, BUT WE STILL OWE HIM GRATITUDE FOR HAVING LENT IT.
DO NOT MENTION IT!
AFTER ALL, WE ARE OLD FRIENDS.
CADEROUSSE
TAILOR AND NEIGHBOR OF THE DANTÈS.
I AM HAPPY TO BE A HELP TO MY NEIGHBORS.
STILL, I WILL NOT FORGET THE FAVOR YOU HAVE DONE FOR US.
EH...
HAVE YOU SEEN MERCÉDÈS?
THAT'S MY GOOD SON.

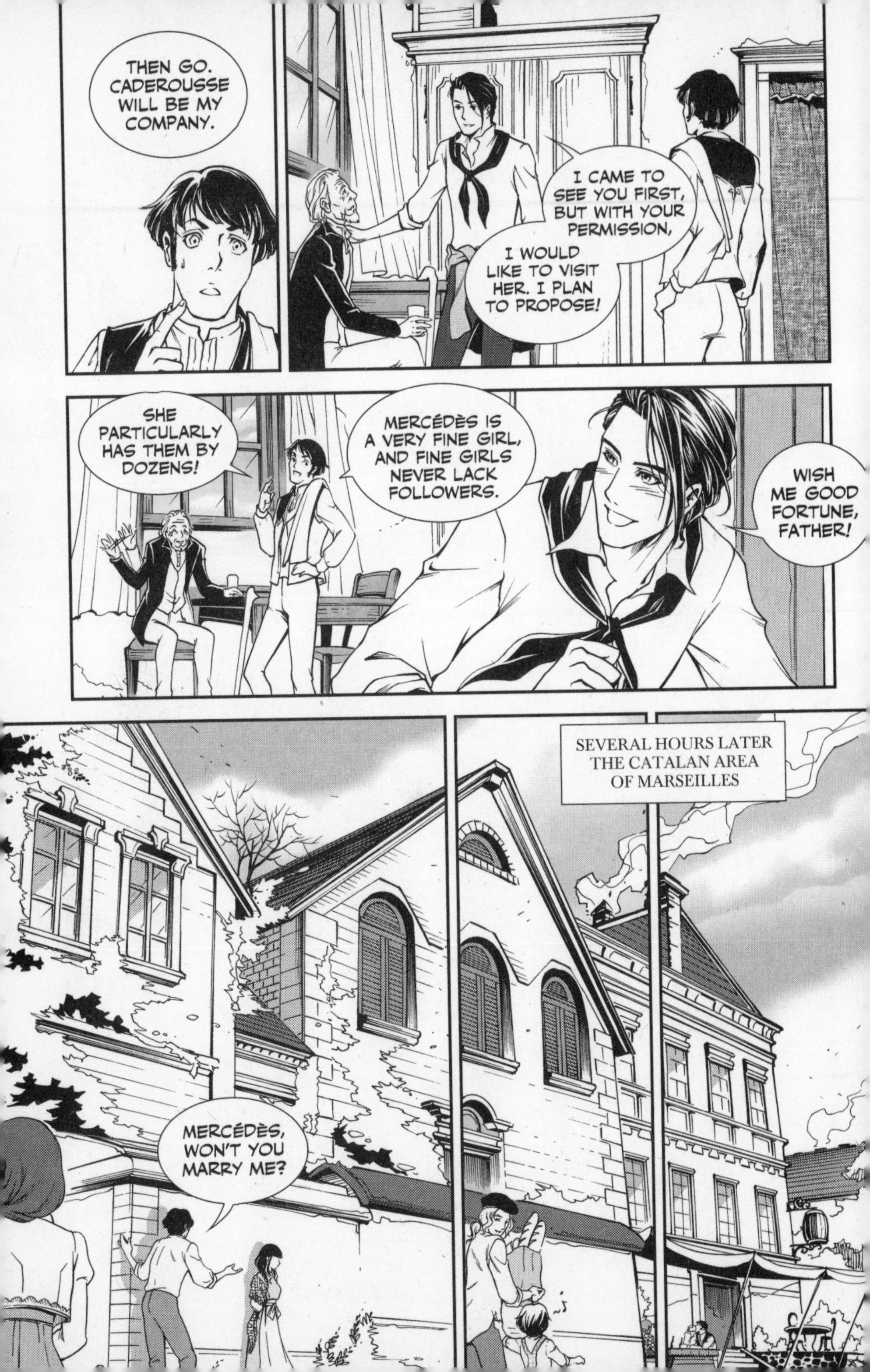
I CAME TO SEE YOU FIRST, BUT WITH YOUR PERMISSION,
I WOULD LIKE TO VISIT HER. I PLAN TO PROPOSE!
THEN GO. CADEROUSSE WILL BE MY COMPANY.
WISH ME GOOD FORTUNE, FATHER!
MERCÉDÈS IS A VERY FINE GIRL, AND FINE GIRLS NEVER LACK FOLLOWERS.
SHE PARTICULARLY HAS THEM BY DOZENS!
SEVERAL HOURS LATER THE CATALAN AREA OF MARSEILLES
MERCÉDÈS, WON'T YOU MARRY ME?

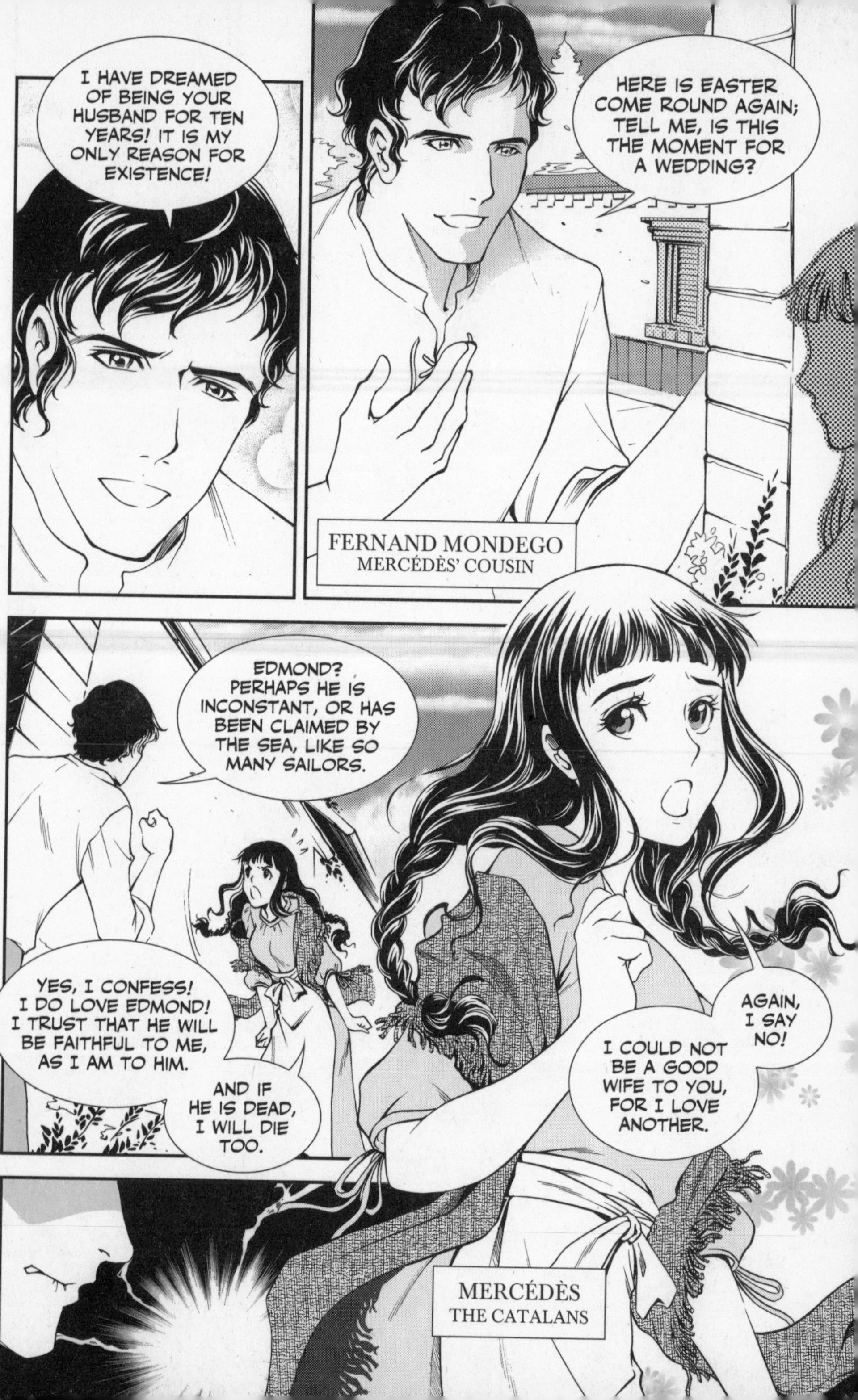
HERE IS EASTER COME ROUND AGAIN; TELL ME, IS THIS THE MOMENT FOR A WEDDING?
FERNAND MONDEGO
MERCÉDÈS' COUSIN
I HAVE DREAMED OF BEING YOUR HUSBAND FOR TEN YEARS! IT IS MY ONLY REASON FOR EXISTENCE!
AGAIN, I SAY NO!
I COULD NOT BE A GOOD WIFE TO YOU, FOR I LOVE ANOTHER.
MERCÉDÈS
THE CATALANS
EDMOND? PERHAPS HE IS INCONSTANT, OR HAS BEEN CLAIMED BY THE SEA, LIKE SO MANY SAILORS.
YES, I CONFESS! I DO LOVE EDMOND! I TRUST THAT HE WILL BE FAITHFUL TO ME, AS I AM TO HIM.
AND IF HE IS DEAD, I WILL DIE TOO.

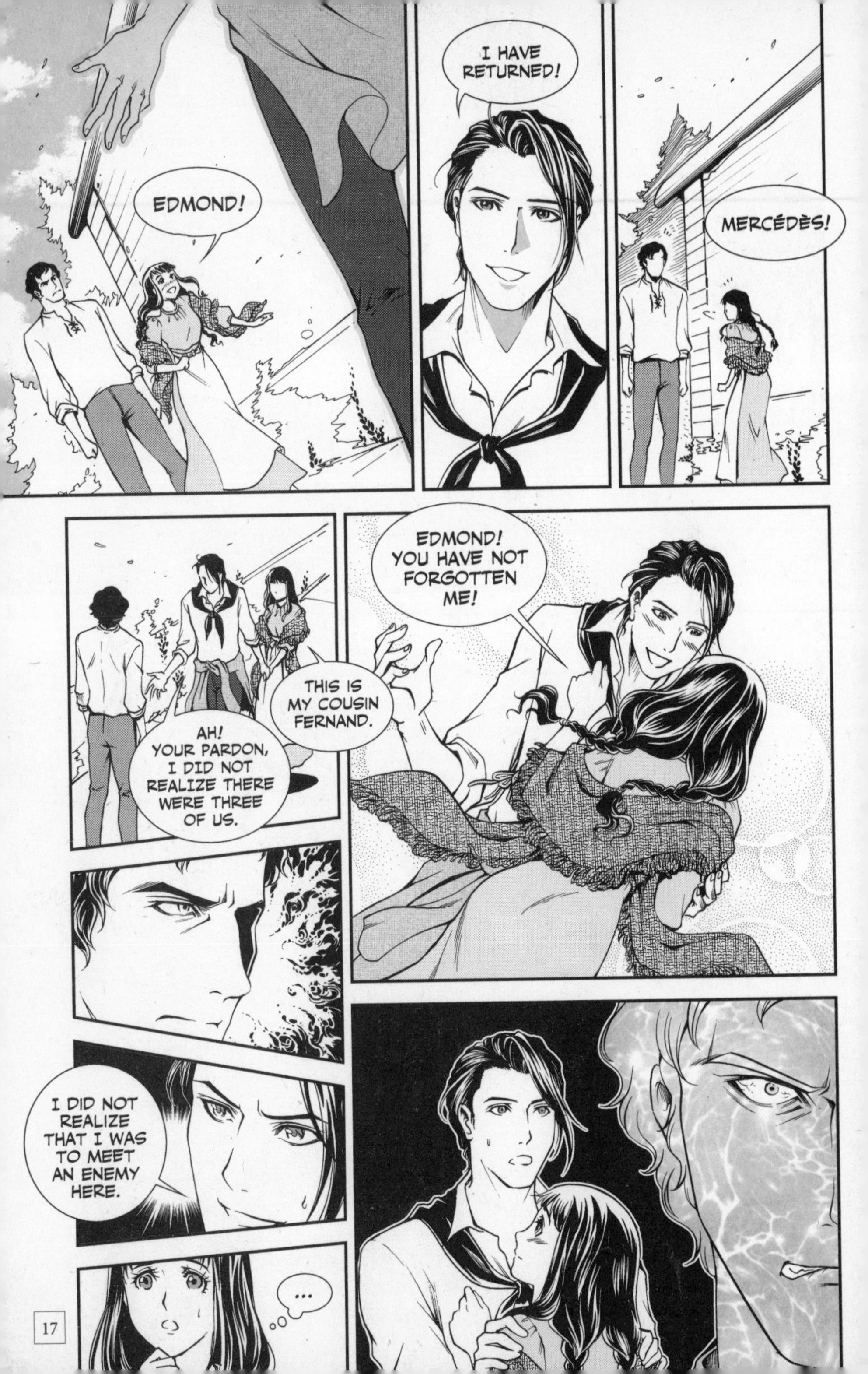
MERCÉDÈS!
I HAVE RETURNED!
EDMOND!
EDMOND! YOU HAVE NOT FORGOTTEN ME!
THIS IS MY COUSIN FERNAND.
AH! YOUR PARDON, I DID NOT REALIZE THERE WERE THREE OF US.
I DID NOT REALIZE THAT I WAS TO MEET AN ENEMY HERE.
...

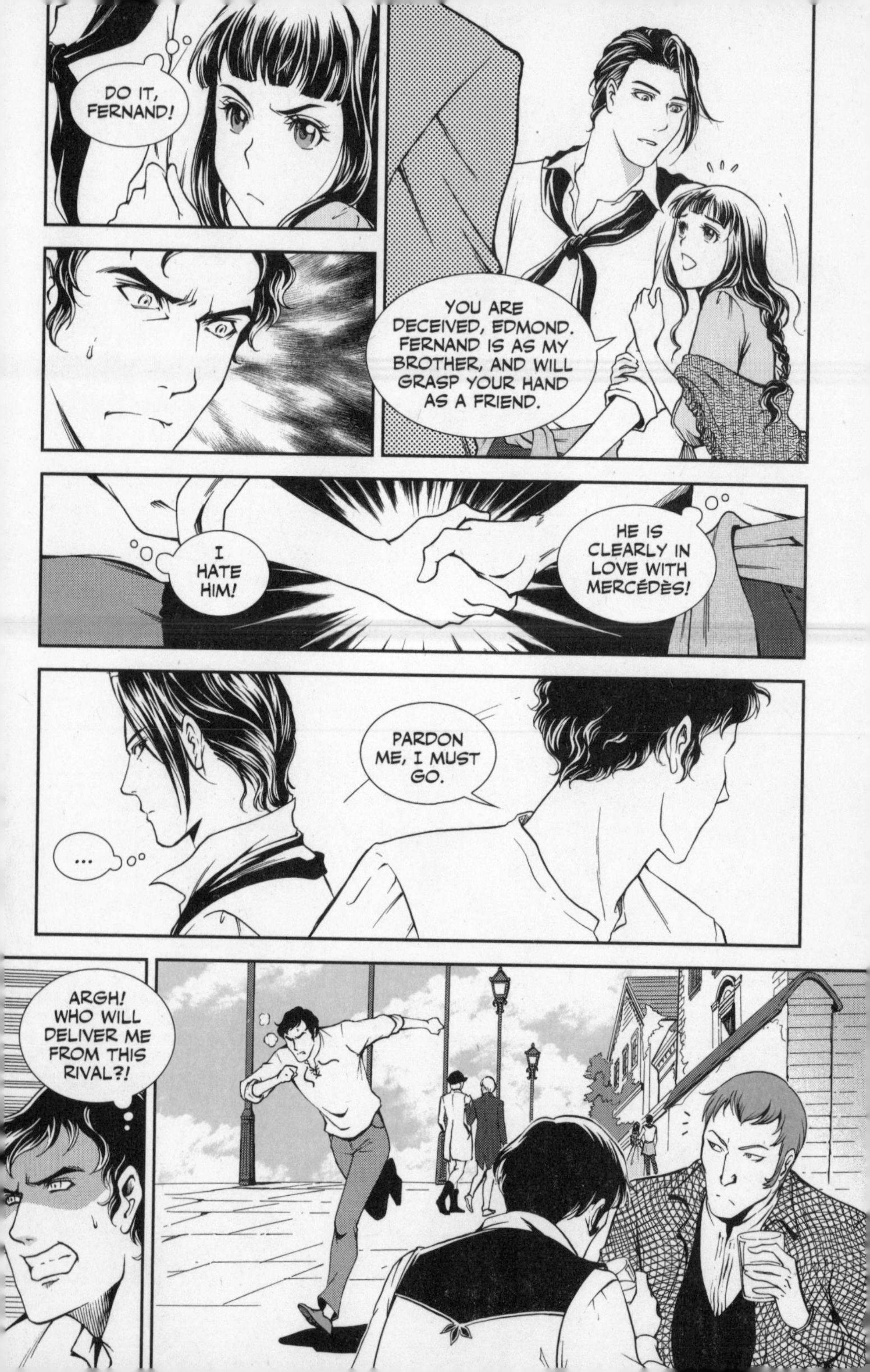
YOU ARE DECEIVED, EDMOND. FERNAND IS AS MY BROTHER, AND WILL GRASP YOUR HAND AS A FRIEND.
DO IT, FERNAND!
HE IS CLEARLY IN LOVE WITH MERCÉDÈS!
I HATE HIM!
PARDON ME, I MUST GO.
...
ARGH! WHO WILL DELIVER ME FROM THIS RIVAL?!

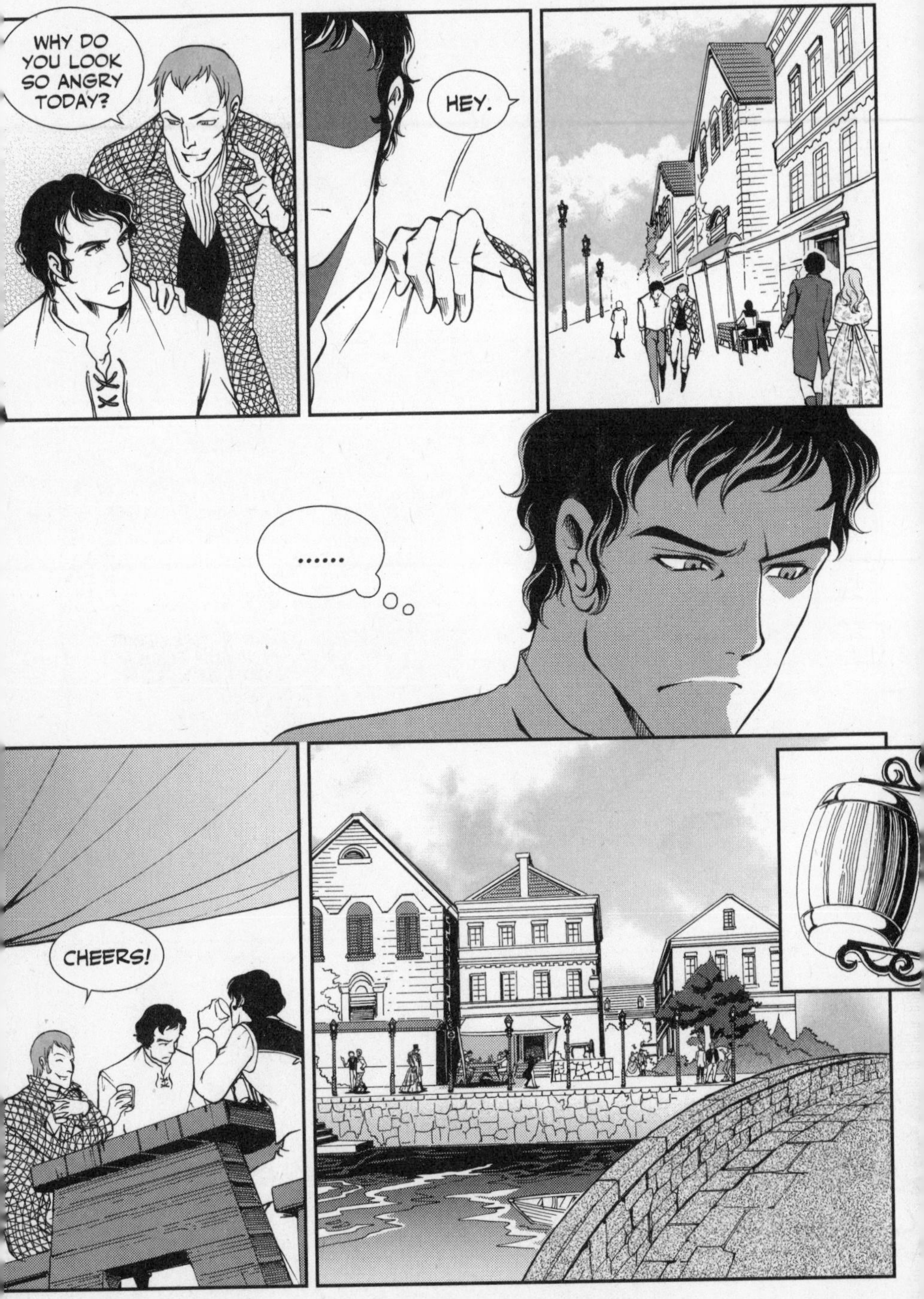
HEY.
WHY DO YOU LOOK SO ANGRY TODAY?
......
CHEERS!

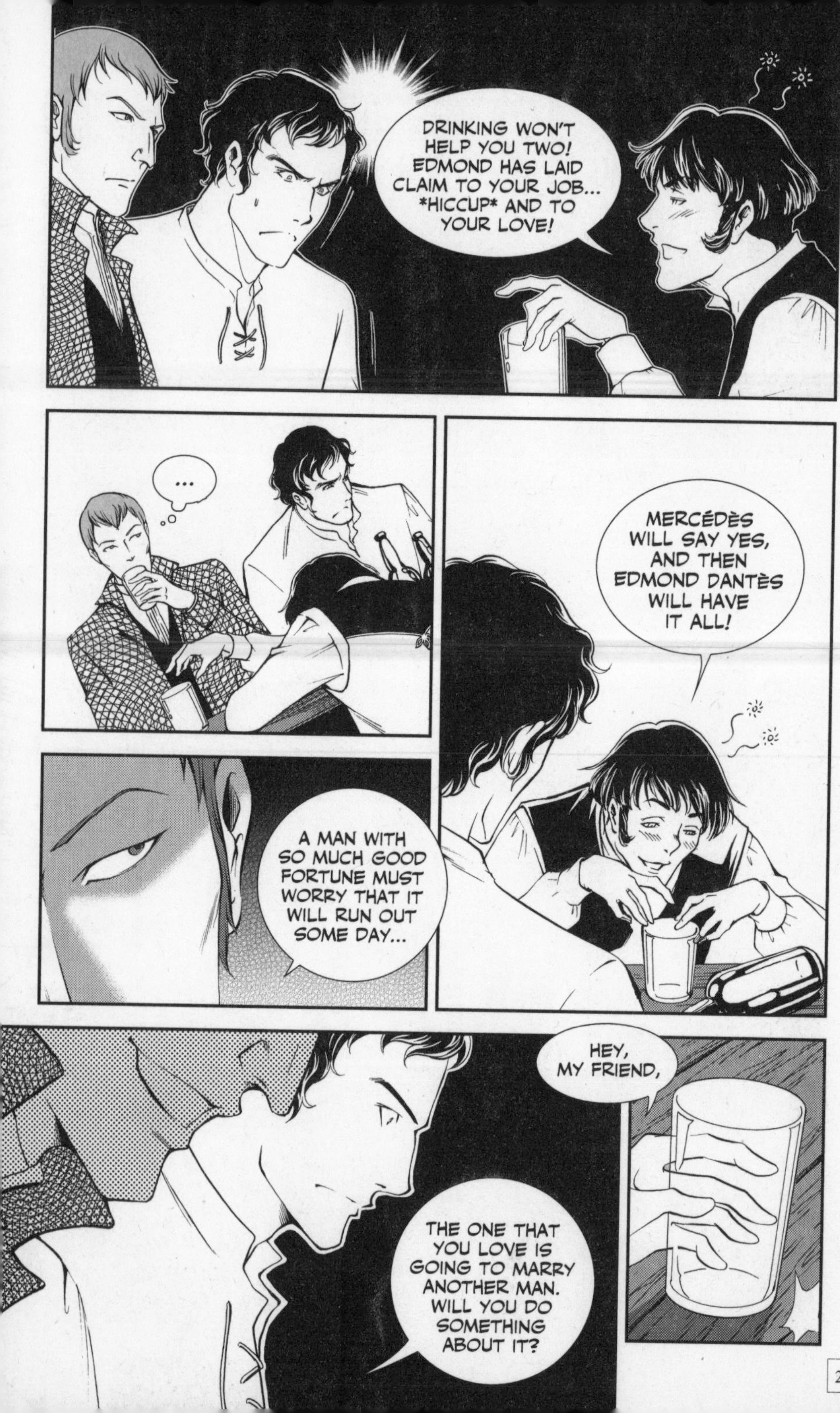
DRINKING WON'T HELP YOU TWO! EDMOND HAS LAID CLAIM TO YOUR JOB... *HICCUP* AND TO YOUR LOVE!
MERCÉDÈS WILL SAY YES, AND THEN EDMOND DANTÈS WILL HAVE IT ALL!
...
A MAN WITH SO MUCH GOOD FORTUNE MUST WORRY THAT IT WILL RUN OUT SOME DAY...
HEY, MY FRIEND,
THE ONE THAT YOU LOVE IS GOING TO MARRY ANOTHER MAN. WILL YOU DO SOMETHING ABOUT IT?

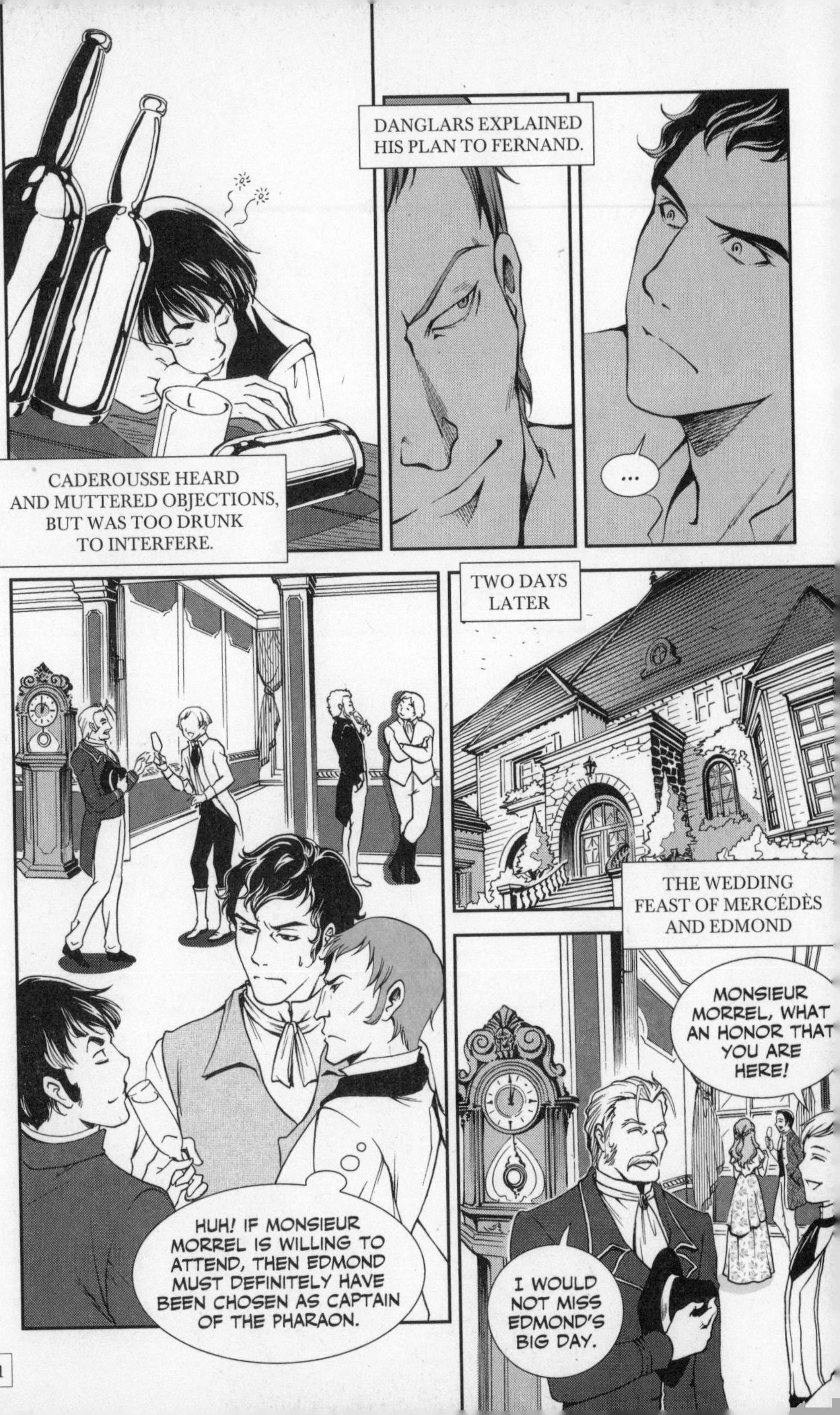
DANGLARS EXPLAINED HIS PLAN TO FERNAND.
...
CADEROUSSE HEARD AND MUTTERED OBJECTIONS, BUT WAS TOO DRUNK TO INTERFERE.
TWO DAYS LATER
THE WEDDING FEAST OF MERCÉDÈS AND EDMOND
MONSIEUR MORREL, WHAT AN HONOR THAT YOU ARE HERE!
I WOULD NOT MISS EDMOND'S BIG DAY.
HUH! IF MONSIEUR MORREL IS WILLING TO ATTEND, THEN EDMOND MUST DEFINITELY HAVE BEEN CHOSEN AS CAPTAIN OF THE PHARAON.

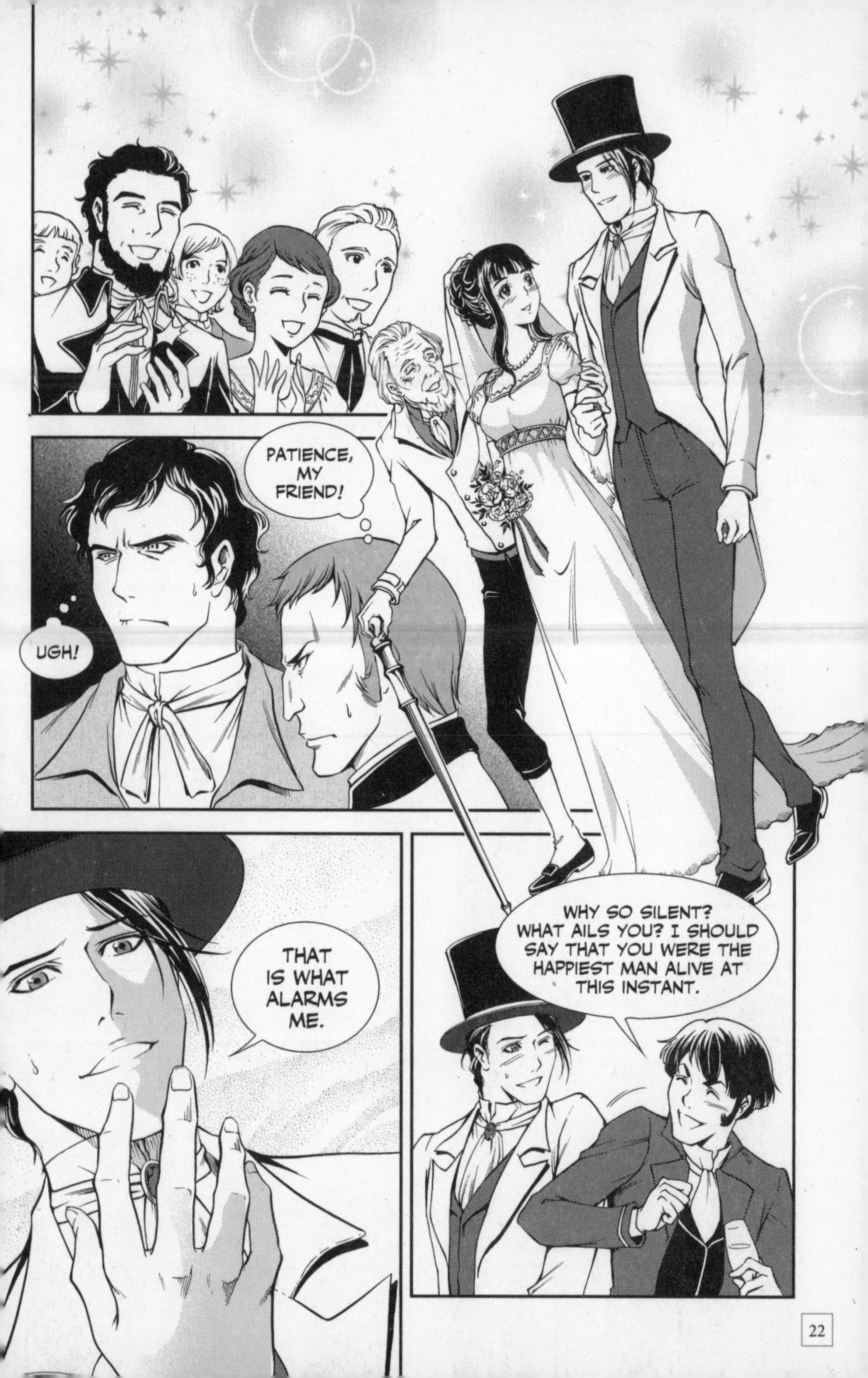
PATIENCE, MY FRIEND!
UGH!
WHY SO SILENT? WHAT AILS YOU? I SHOULD SAY THAT YOU WERE THE HAPPIEST MAN ALIVE AT THIS INSTANT.
THAT IS WHAT ALARMS ME.

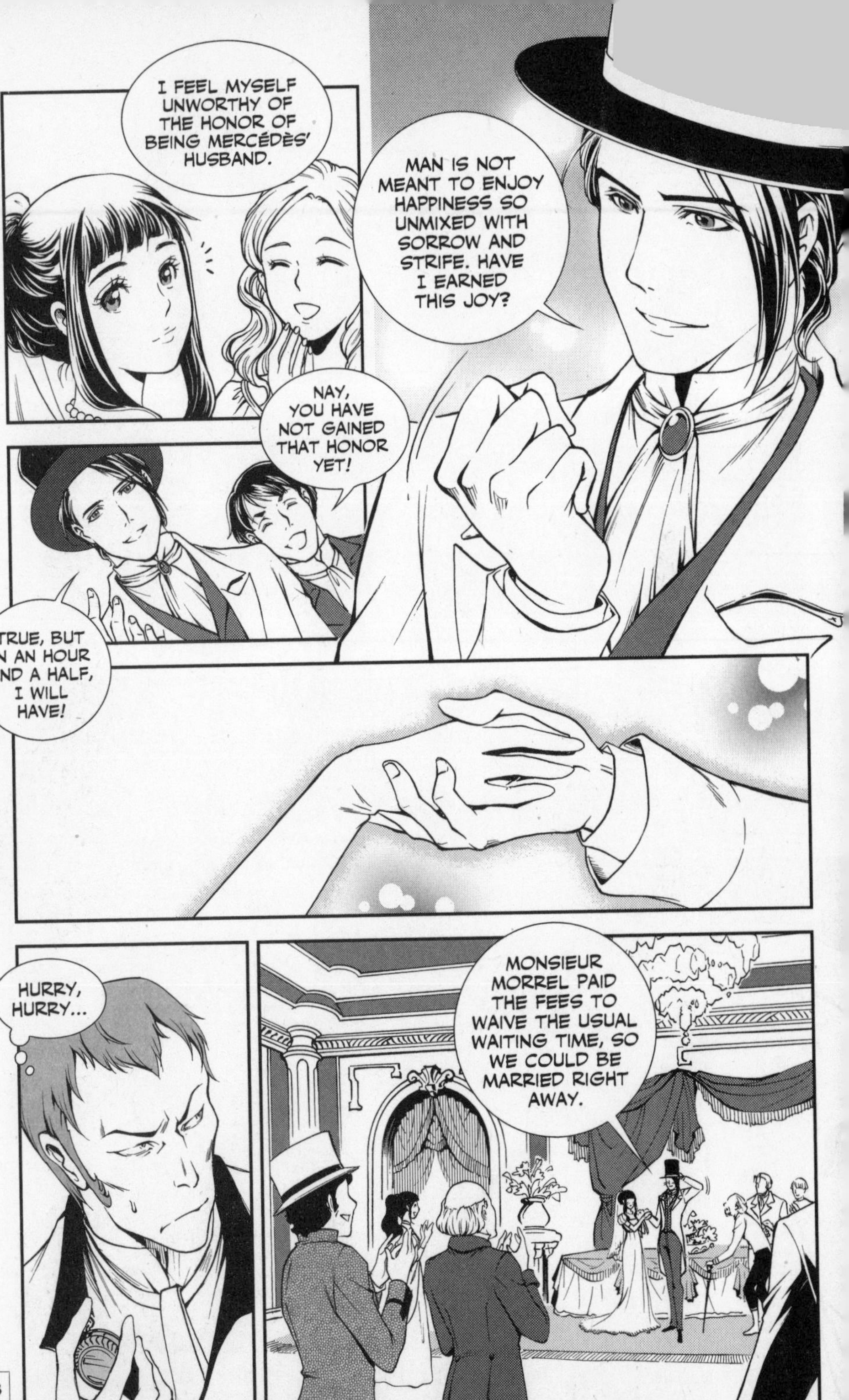
MAN IS NOT MEANT TO ENJOY HAPPINESS SO UNMIXED WITH SORROW AND STRIFE. HAVE I EARNED THIS JOY?
I FEEL MYSELF UNWORTHY OF THE HONOR OF BEING MERCÉDÈS' HUSBAND.
NAY, YOU HAVE NOT GAINED THAT HONOR YET!
TRUE, BUT IN AN HOUR AND A HALF, I WILL HAVE!
MONSIEUR MORREL PAID THE FEES TO WAIVE THE USUAL WAITING TIME, SO WE COULD BE MARRIED RIGHT AWAY.
HURRY, HURRY...

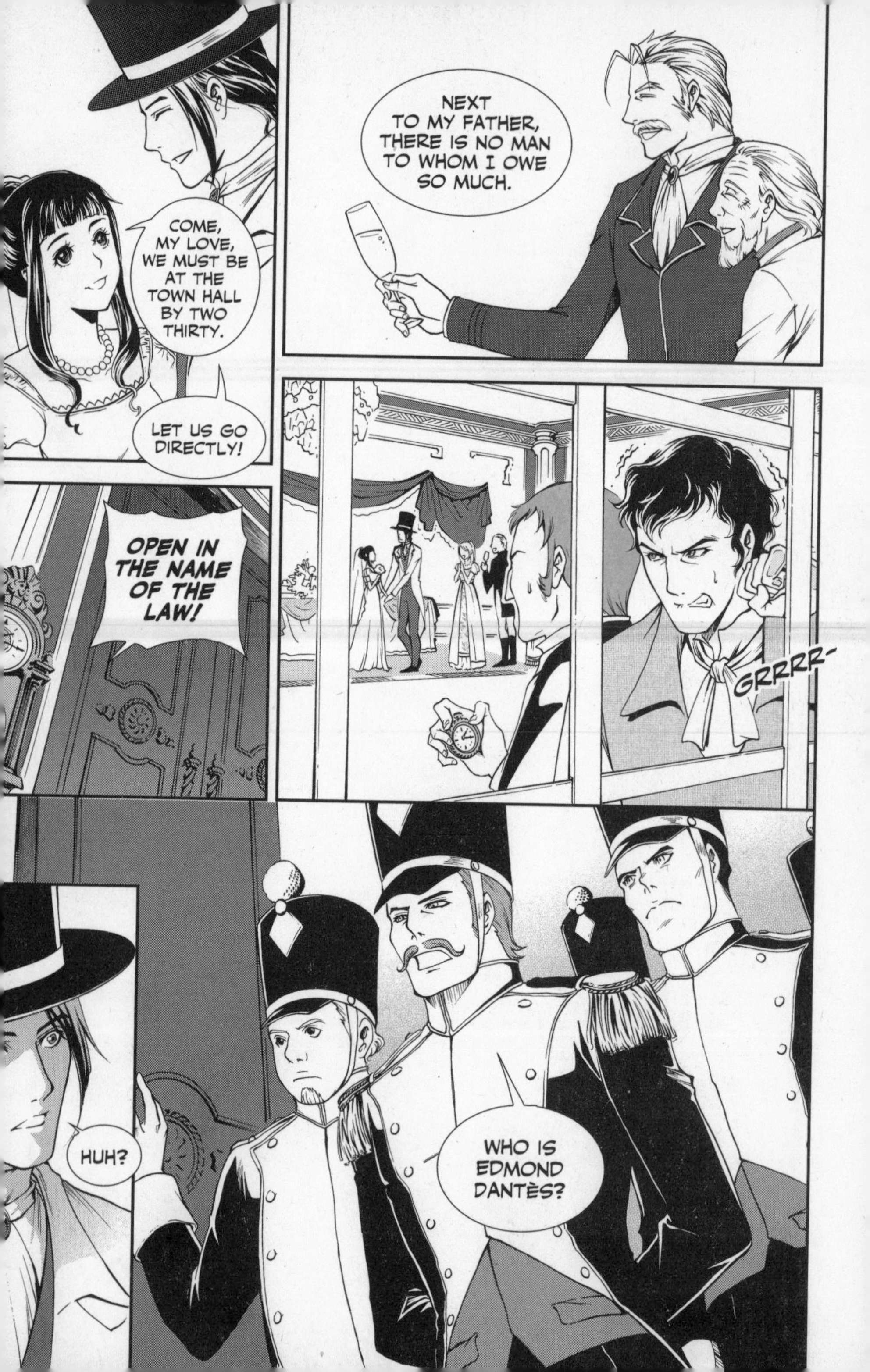
NEXT TO MY FATHER, THERE IS NO MAN TO WHOM I OWE SO MUCH.
COME, MY LOVE, WE MUST BE AT THE TOWN HALL BY TWO THIRTY.
LET US GO DIRECTLY!
GRRRR-
OPEN IN THE NAME OF THE LAW!
WHO IS EDMOND DANTÈS?
HUH?

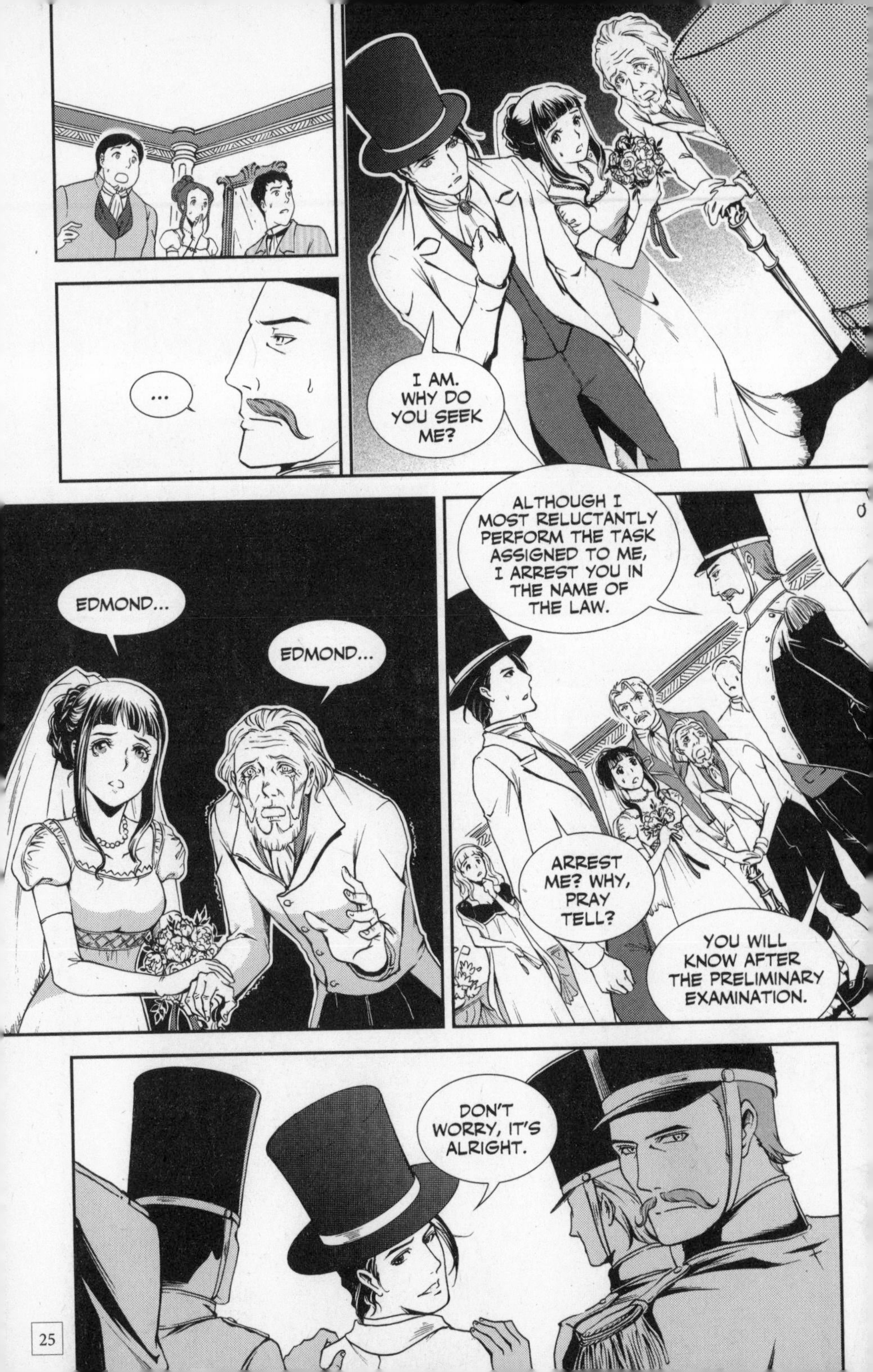
I AM. WHY DO YOU SEEK ME?
...
ALTHOUGH I MOST RELUCTANTLY PERFORM THE TASK ASSIGNED TO ME, I ARREST YOU IN THE NAME OF THE LAW.
ARREST ME? WHY, PRAY TELL?
YOU WILL KNOW AFTER THE PRELIMINARY EXAMINATION.
EDMOND...
EDMOND...
DON'T WORRY, IT'S ALRIGHT.

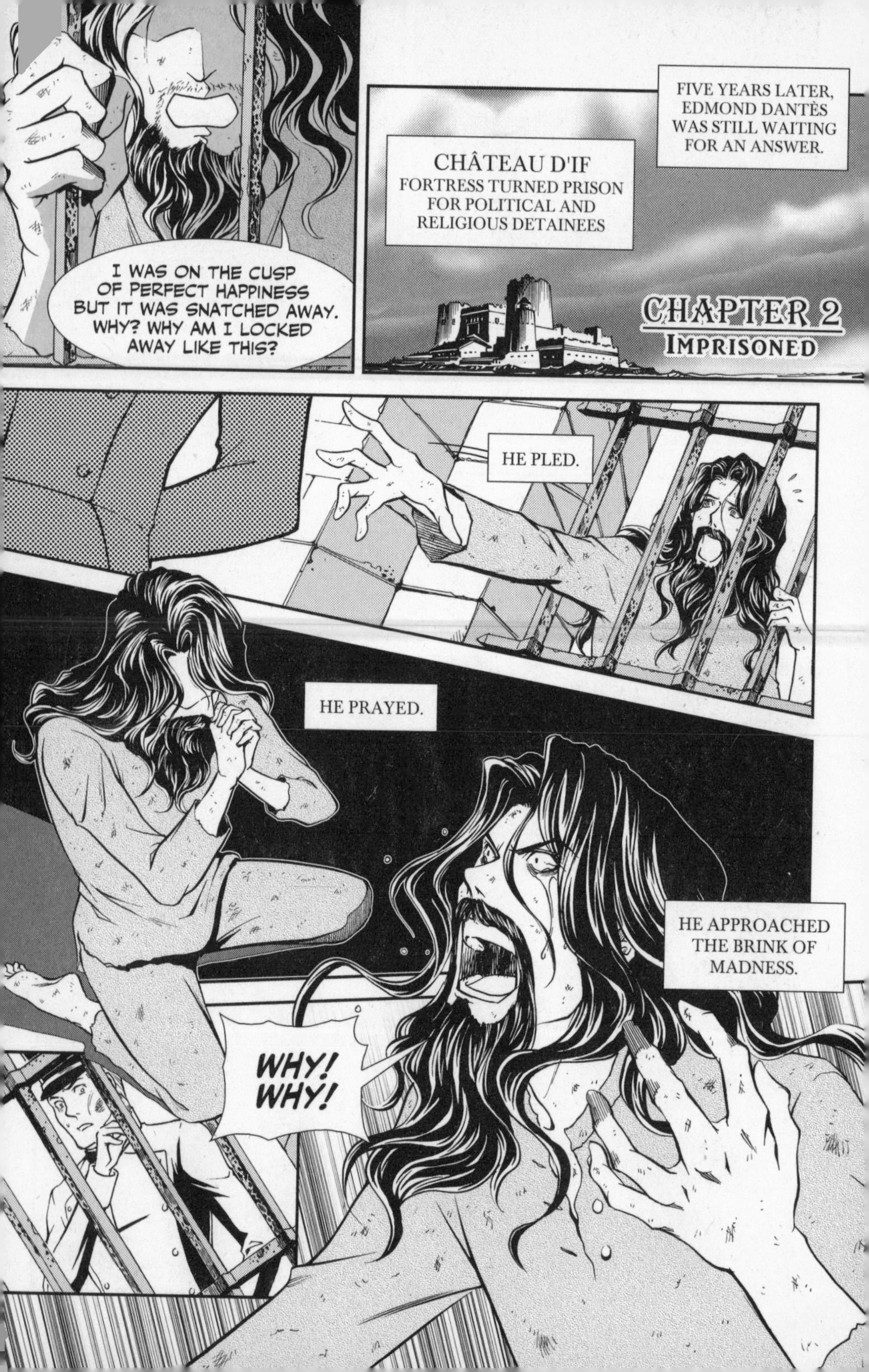
FIVE YEARS LATER, EDMOND DANTÈS WAS STILL WAITING FOR AN ANSWER.
CHÂTEAU D'IF
FORTRESS TURNED PRISON FOR POLITICAL AND RELIGIOUS DETAINEES
CHAPTER 2
IMPRISONED
I WAS ON THE CUSP OF PERFECT HAPPINESS BUT IT WAS SNATCHED AWAY. WHY? WHY AM I LOCKED AWAY LIKE THIS?
HE PLED.
HE PRAYED.
HE APPROACHED THE BRINK OF MADNESS.
WHY! WHY!

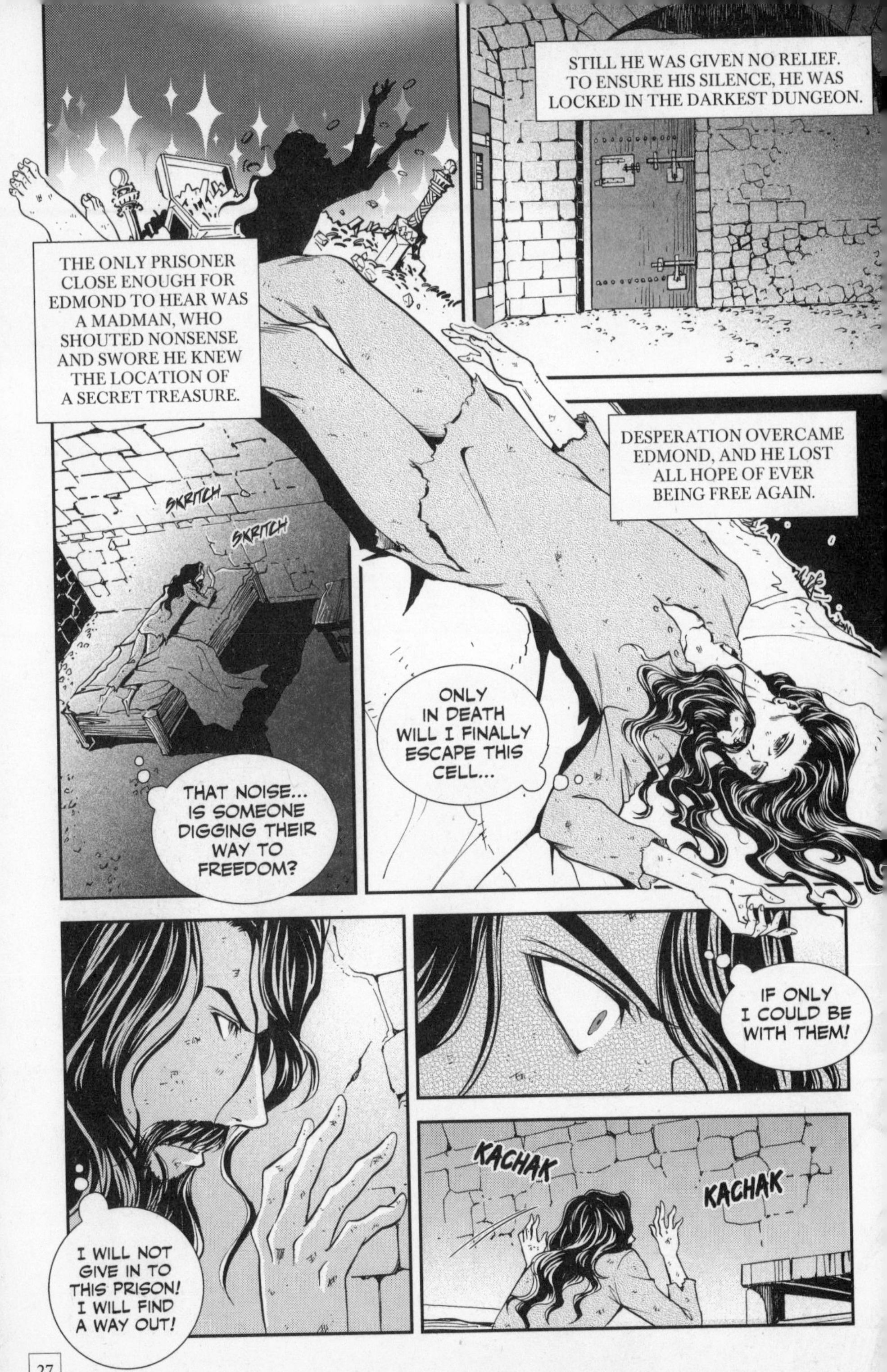
STILL HE WAS GIVEN NO RELIEF. TO ENSURE HIS SILENCE, HE WAS LOCKED IN THE DARKEST DUNGEON.
THE ONLY PRISONER CLOSE ENOUGH FOR EDMOND TO HEAR WAS A MADMAN, WHO SHOUTED NONSENSE AND SWORE HE KNEW THE LOCATION OF A SECRET TREASURE.
DESPERATION OVERCAME EDMOND, AND HE LOST ALL HOPE OF EVER BEING FREE AGAIN.
ONLY IN DEATH WILL I FINALLY ESCAPE THIS CELL...
SKRITCH
SKRITCH
THAT NOISE... IS SOMEONE DIGGING THEIR WAY TO FREEDOM?
IF ONLY I COULD BE WITH THEM!
KACHAK
KACHAK
I WILL NOT GIVE IN TO THIS PRISON! I WILL FIND A WAY OUT!

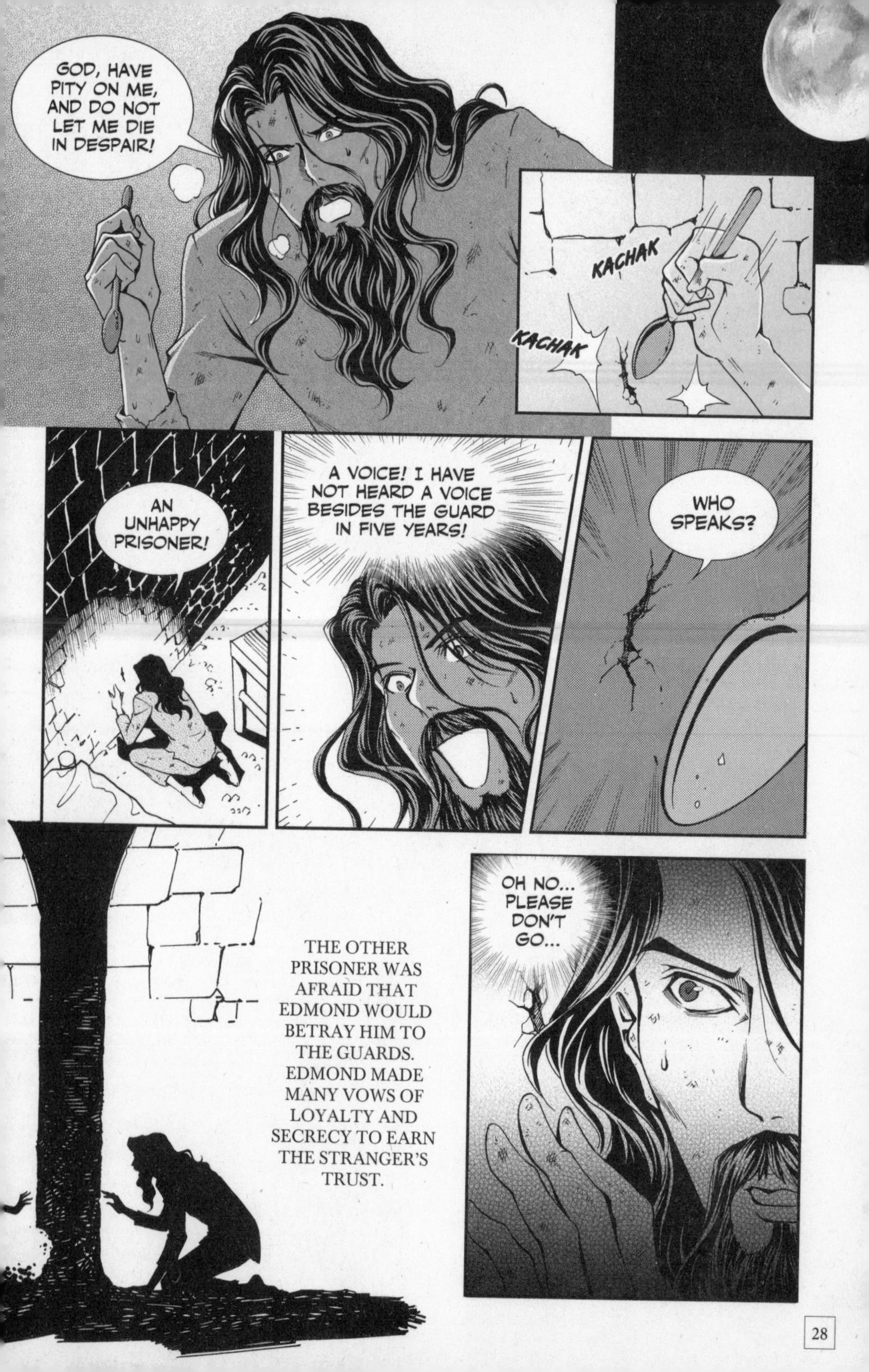
GOD, HAVE PITY ON ME, AND DO NOT LET ME DIE IN DESPAIR!
KACHAK
KACHAK
WHO SPEAKS?
A VOICE! I HAVE NOT HEARD A VOICE BESIDES THE GUARD IN FIVE YEARS!
AN UNHAPPY PRISONER!
OH NO... PLEASE DON'T GO...
THE OTHER PRISONER WAS AFRAID THAT EDMOND WOULD BETRAY HIM TO THE GUARDS. EDMOND MADE MANY VOWS OF LOYALTY AND SECRECY TO EARN THE STRANGER'S TRUST.

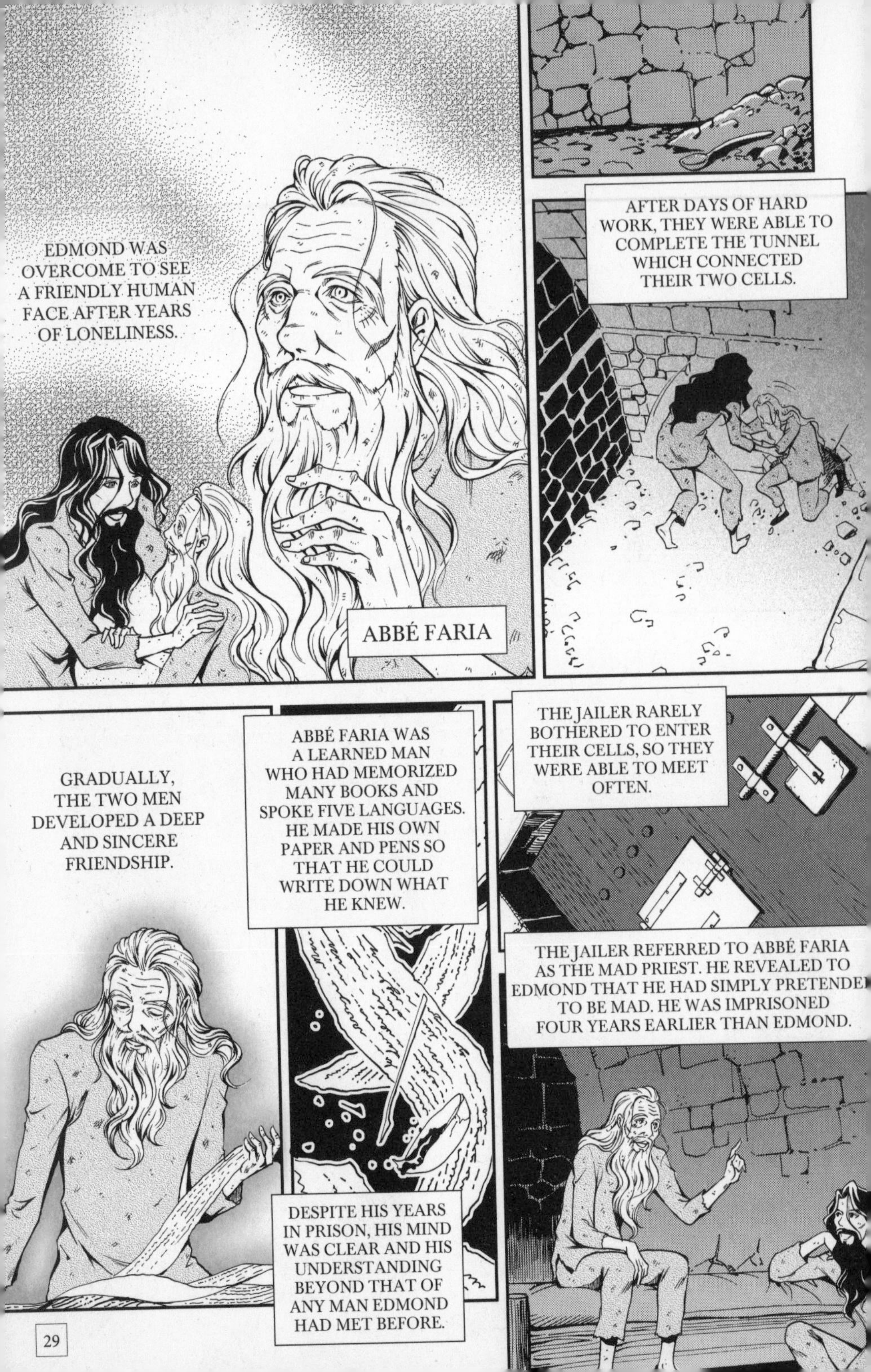
AFTER DAYS OF HARD WORK, THEY WERE ABLE TO COMPLETE THE TUNNEL WHICH CONNECTED THEIR TWO CELLS.
EDMOND WAS OVERCOME TO SEE A FRIENDLY HUMAN FACE AFTER YEARS OF LONELINESS.
ABBÉ FARIA
THE JAILER RARELY BOTHERED TO ENTER THEIR CELLS, SO THEY WERE ABLE TO MEET OFTEN.
THE JAILER REFERRED TO ABBÉ FARIA AS THE MAD PRIEST. HE REVEALED TO EDMOND THAT HE HAD SIMPLY PRETENDE TO BE MAD. HE WAS IMPRISONED FOUR YEARS EARLIER THAN EDMOND.
ABBÉ FARIA WAS A LEARNED MAN WHO HAD MEMORIZED MANY BOOKS AND SPOKE FIVE LANGUAGES. HE MADE HIS OWN PAPER AND PENS SO THAT HE COULD WRITE DOWN WHAT HE KNEW.
DESPITE HIS YEARS IN PRISON, HIS MIND WAS CLEAR AND HIS UNDERSTANDING BEYOND THAT OF ANY MAN EDMOND HAD MET BEFORE.
GRADUALLY, THE TWO MEN DEVELOPED A DEEP AND SINCERE FRIENDSHIP.

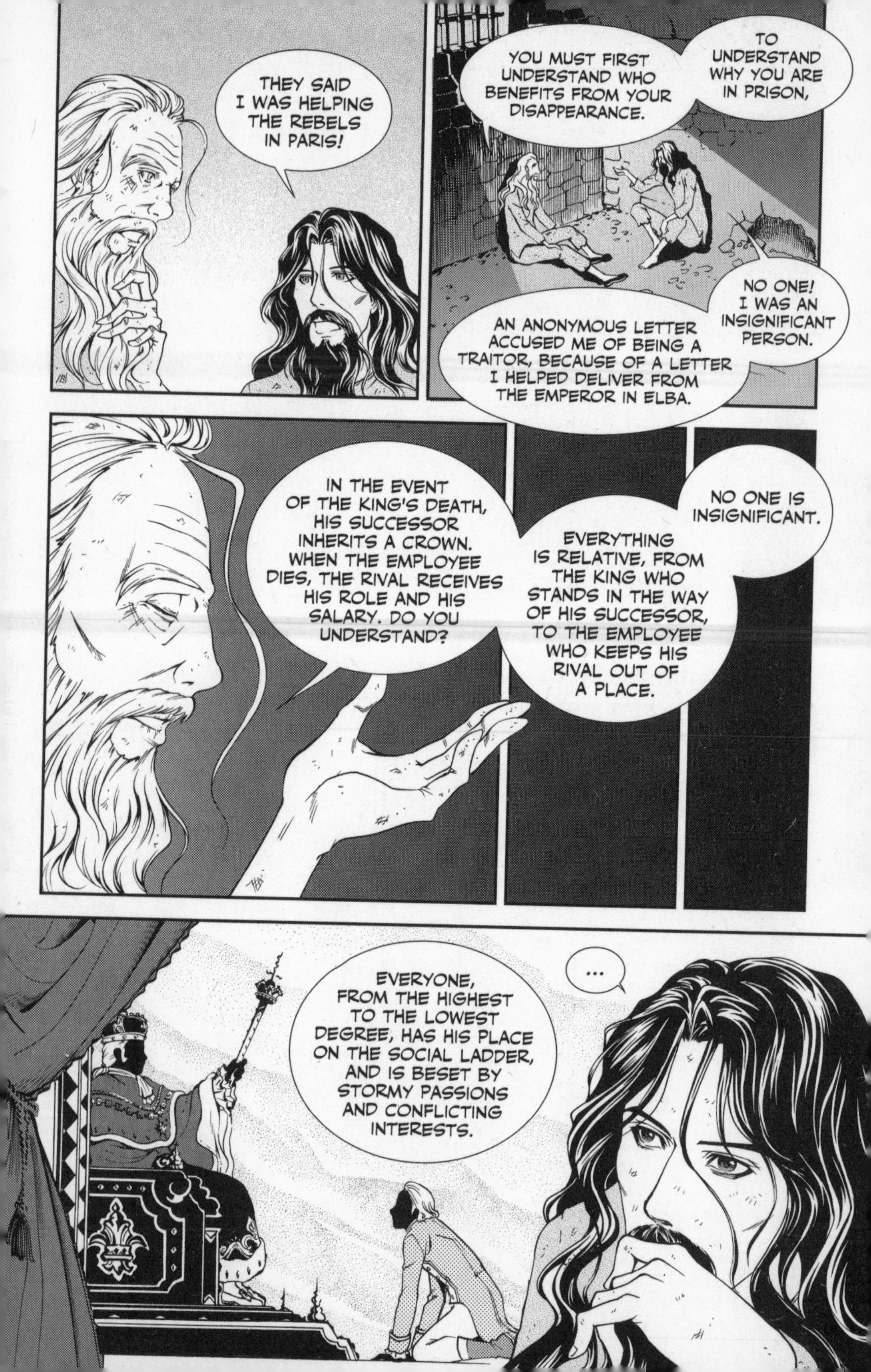

TO UNDERSTAND WHY YOU ARE IN PRISON,
YOU MUST FIRST UNDERSTAND WHO BENEFITS FROM YOUR DISAPPEARANCE.
NO ONE! I WAS AN INSIGNIFICANT PERSON.
AN ANONYMOUS LETTER ACCUSED ME OF BEING A TRAITOR, BECAUSE OF A LETTER I HELPED DELIVER FROM THE EMPEROR IN ELBA.
THEY SAID I WAS HELPING THE REBELS IN PARIS!
NO ONE IS INSIGNIFICANT.
EVERYTHING IS RELATIVE, FROM THE KING WHO STANDS IN THE WAY OF HIS SUCCESSOR, TO THE EMPLOYEE WHO KEEPS HIS RIVAL OUT OF A PLACE.
IN THE EVENT OF THE KING'S DEATH, HIS SUCCESSOR INHERITS A CROWN. WHEN THE EMPLOYEE DIES, THE RIVAL RECEIVES HIS ROLE AND HIS SALARY. DO YOU UNDERSTAND?
...
EVERYONE, FROM THE HIGHEST TO THE LOWEST DEGREE, HAS HIS PLACE ON THE SOCIAL LADDER, AND IS BESET BY STORMY PASSIONS AND CONFLICTING INTERESTS.

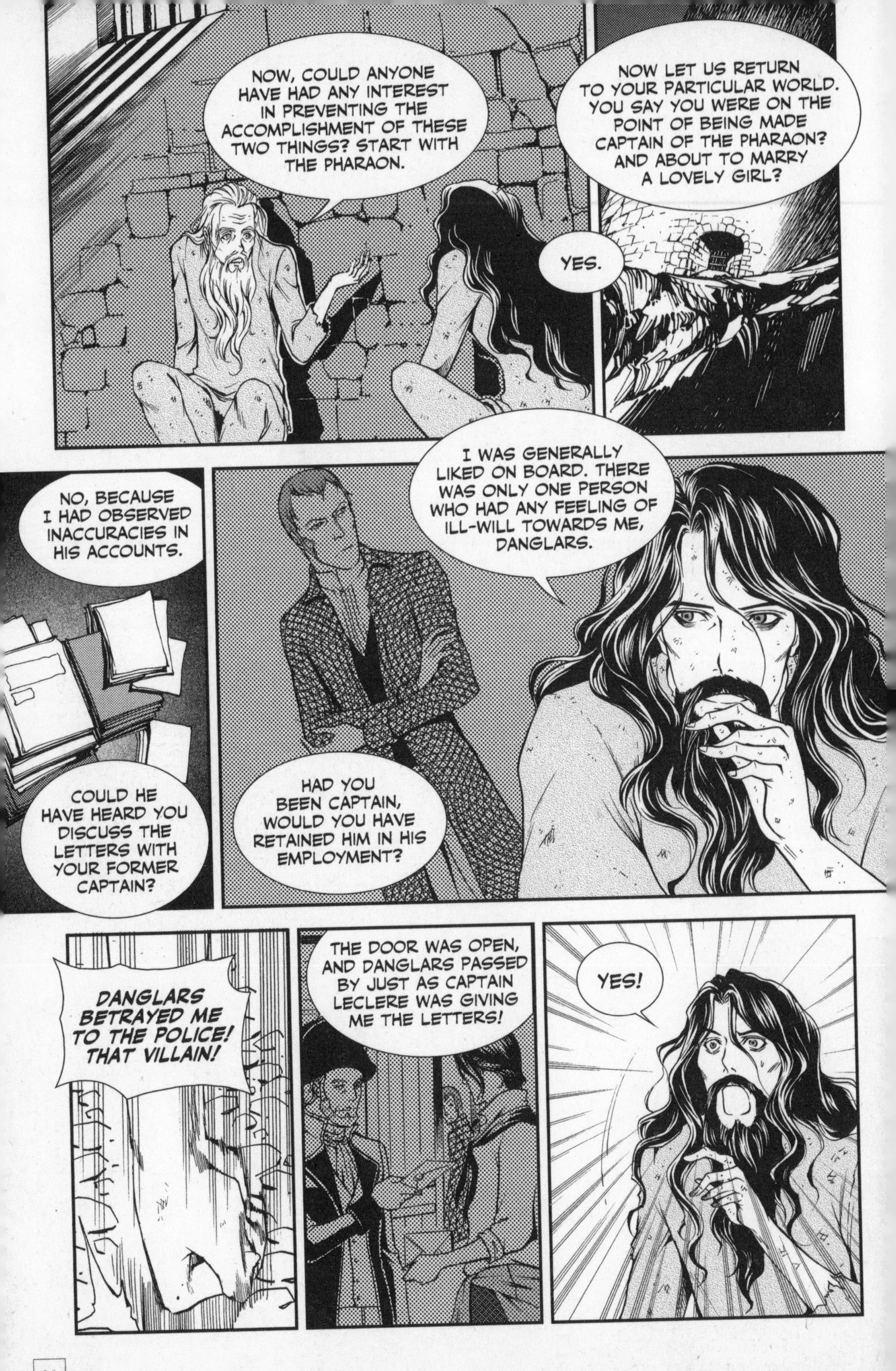
NOW LET US RETURN TO YOUR PARTICULAR WORLD. YOU SAY YOU WERE ON THE POINT OF BEING MADE CAPTAIN OF THE PHARAON? AND ABOUT TO MARRY A LOVELY GIRL?
YES.
NOW, COULD ANYONE HAVE HAD ANY INTEREST IN PREVENTING THE ACCOMPLISHMENT OF THESE TWO THINGS? START WITH THE PHARAON.
I WAS GENERALLY LIKED ON BOARD. THERE WAS ONLY ONE PERSON WHO HAD ANY FEELING OF ILL-WILL TOWARDS ME, DANGLARS.
HAD YOU BEEN CAPTAIN, WOULD YOU HAVE RETAINED HIM IN HIS EMPLOYMENT?
NO, BECAUSE I HAD OBSERVED INACCURACIES IN HIS ACCOUNTS.
COULD HE HAVE HEARD YOU DISCUSS THE LETTERS WITH YOUR FORMER CAPTAIN?
YES!
THE DOOR WAS OPEN, AND DANGLARS PASSED BY JUST AS CAPTAIN LECLERE WAS GIVING ME THE LETTERS!
DANGLARS BETRAYED ME TO THE POLICE! THAT VILLAIN!

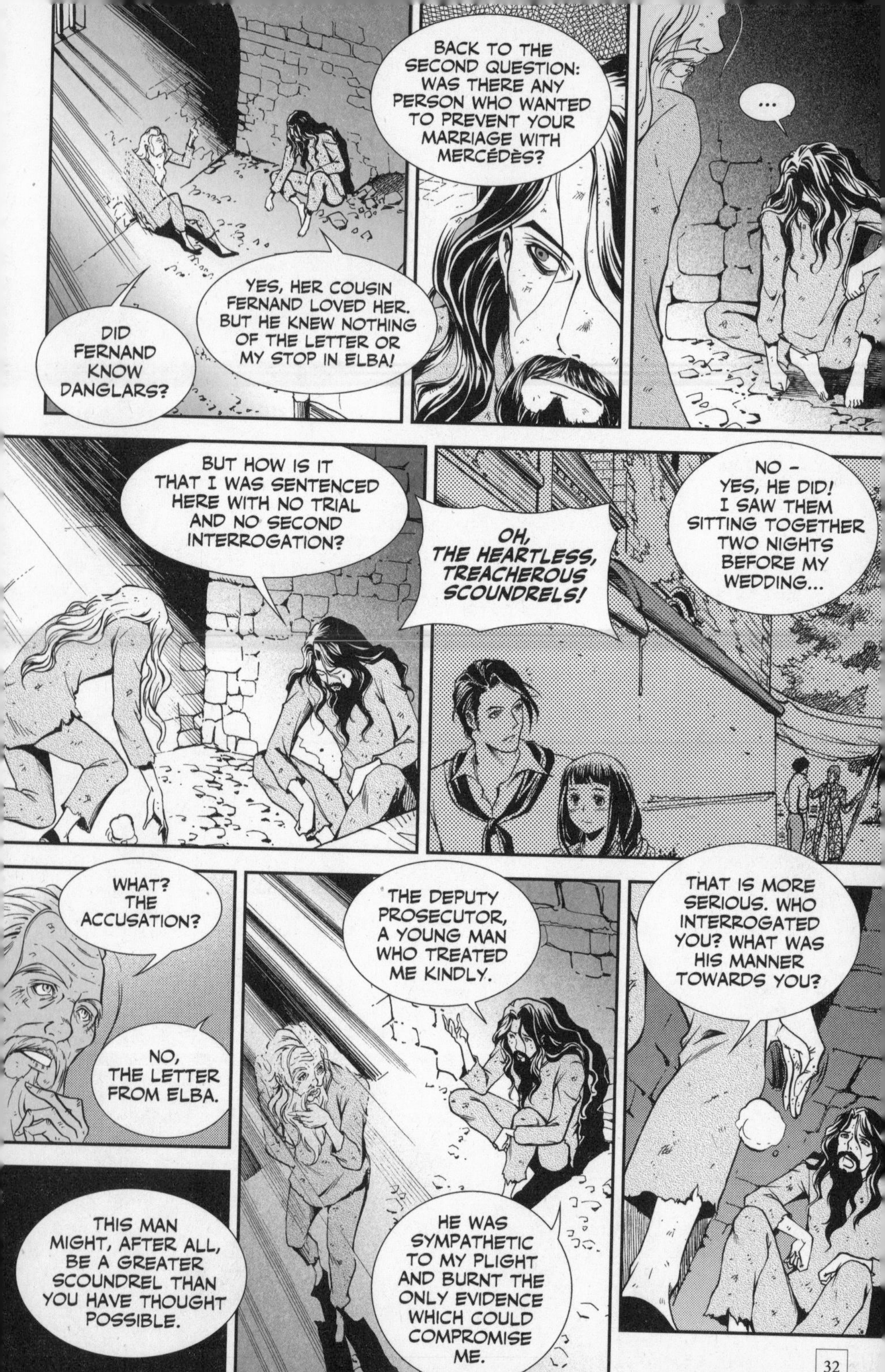
...
BACK TO THE SECOND QUESTION: WAS THERE ANY PERSON WHO WANTED TO PREVENT YOUR MARRIAGE WITH MERCÉDÈS?
YES, HER COUSIN FERNAND LOVED HER. BUT HE KNEW NOTHING OF THE LETTER OR MY STOP IN ELBA!
DID FERNAND KNOW DANGLARS?
NO – YES, HE DID! I SAW THEM SITTING TOGETHER TWO NIGHTS BEFORE MY WEDDING...
OH, THE HEARTLESS, TREACHEROUS SCOUNDRELS!
BUT HOW IS IT THAT I WAS SENTENCED HERE WITH NO TRIAL AND NO SECOND INTERROGATION?
THAT IS MORE SERIOUS. WHO INTERROGATED YOU? WHAT WAS HIS MANNER TOWARDS YOU?
THE DEPUTY PROSECUTOR, A YOUNG MAN WHO TREATED ME KINDLY.
HE WAS SYMPATHETIC TO MY PLIGHT AND BURNT THE ONLY EVIDENCE WHICH COULD COMPROMISE ME.
WHAT? THE ACCUSATION?
NO, THE LETTER FROM ELBA.
THIS MAN MIGHT, AFTER ALL, BE A GREATER SCOUNDREL THAN YOU HAVE THOUGHT POSSIBLE.

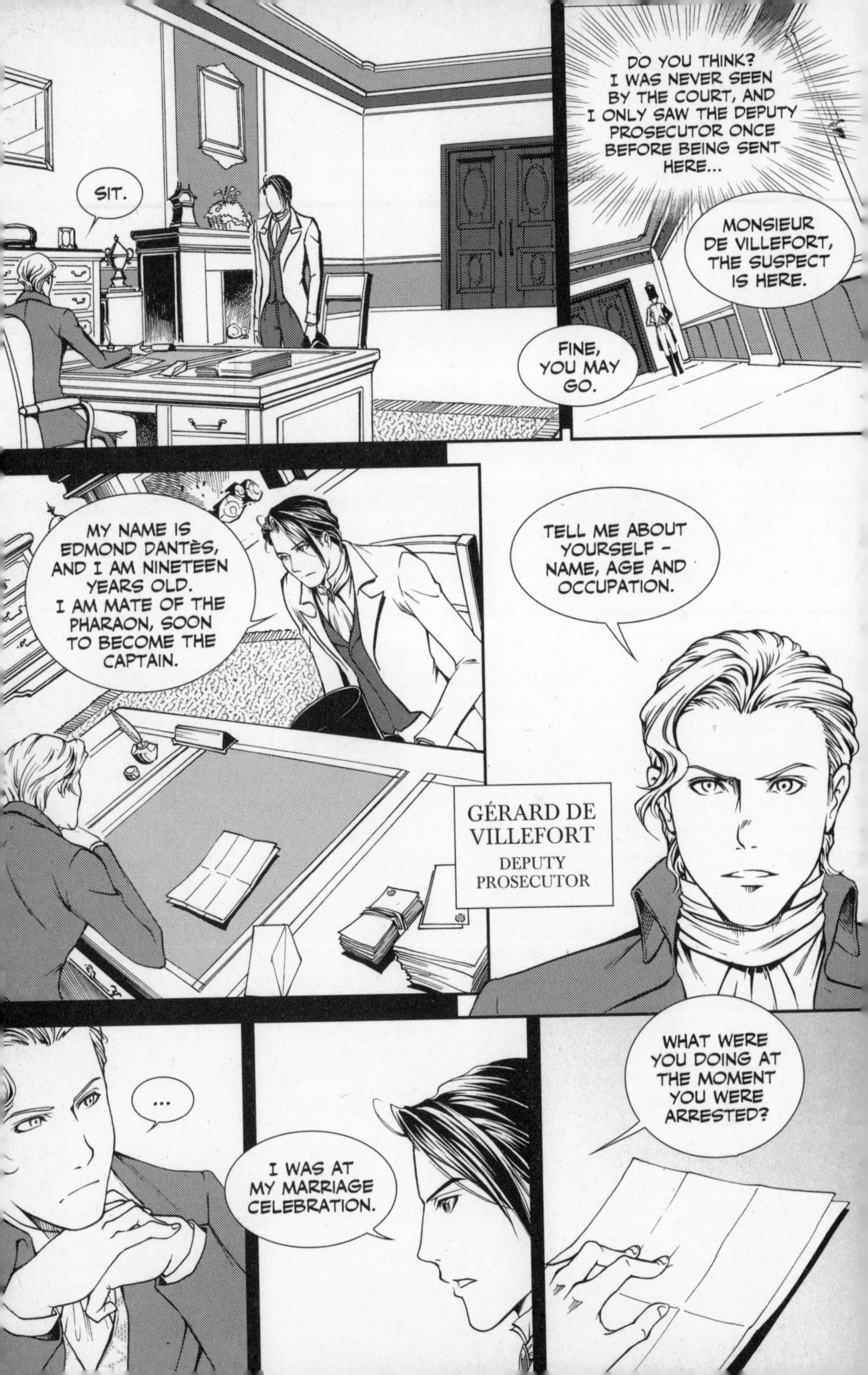
DO YOU THINK? I WAS NEVER SEEN BY THE COURT, AND I ONLY SAW THE DEPUTY PROSECUTOR ONCE BEFORE BEING SENT HERE...
MONSIEUR DE VILLEFORT, THE SUSPECT IS HERE.
FINE, YOU MAY GO.
SIT.
TELL ME ABOUT YOURSELF - NAME, AGE AND OCCUPATION.
GÉRARD DE VILLEFORT
DEPUTY PROSECUTOR
MY NAME IS EDMOND DANTÈS, AND I AM NINETEEN YEARS OLD. I AM MATE OF THE PHARAON, SOON TO BECOME THE CAPTAIN.
WHAT WERE YOU DOING AT THE MOMENT YOU WERE ARRESTED?
I WAS AT MY MARRIAGE CELEBRATION.
...

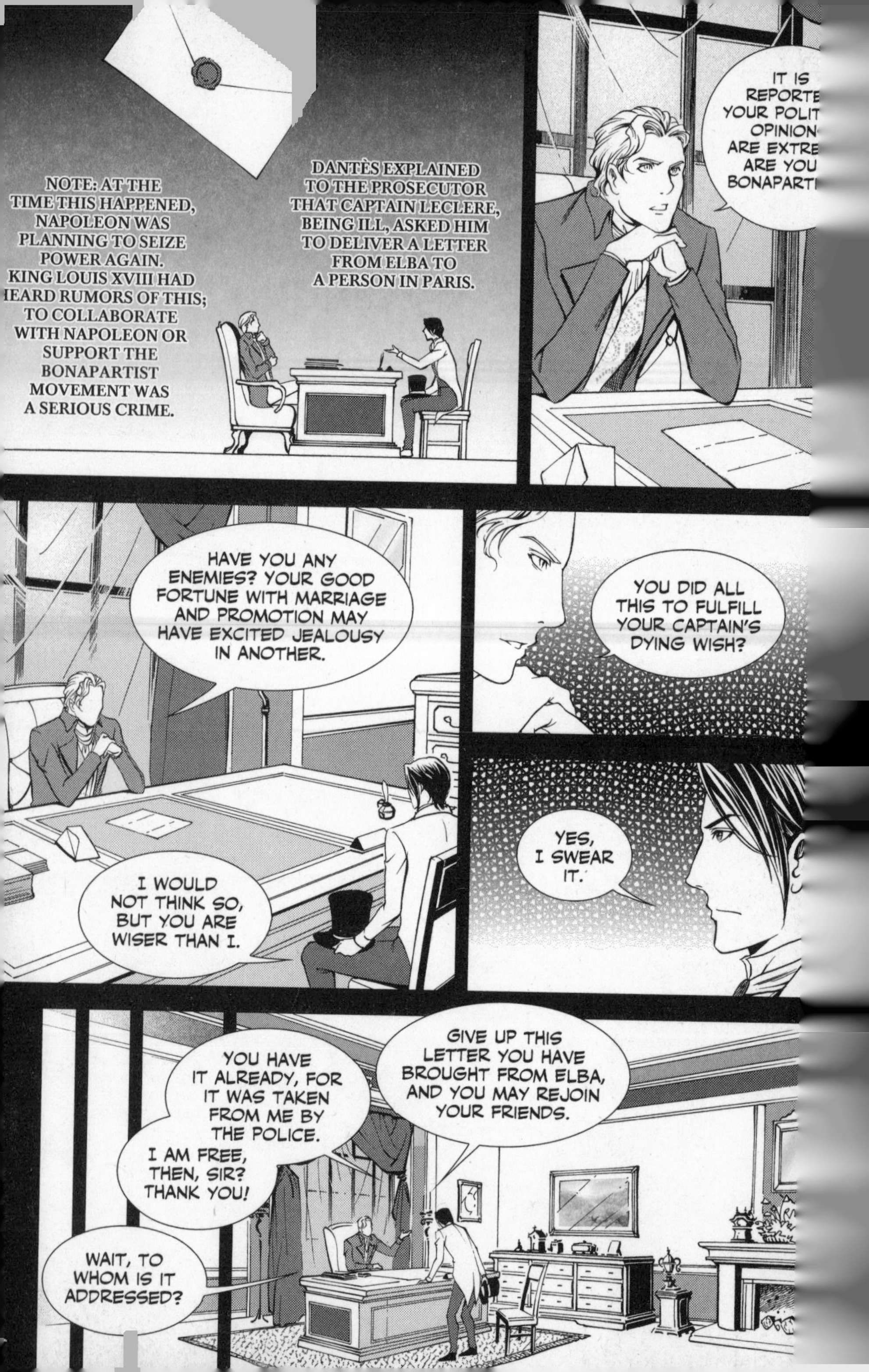
IT IS REPORTE YOUR POLIT OPINION ARE EXTRE ARE YOU BONAPARTI
DANTÈS EXPLAINED TO THE PROSECUTOR THAT CAPTAIN LECLERE, BEING ILL, ASKED HIM TO DELIVER A LETTER FROM ELBA TO A PERSON IN PARIS.
NOTE: AT THE TIME THIS HAPPENED, NAPOLEON WAS PLANNING TO SEIZE POWER AGAIN. KING LOUIS XVIII HAD HEARD RUMORS OF THIS; TO COLLABORATE WITH NAPOLEON OR SUPPORT THE BONAPARTIST MOVEMENT WAS A SERIOUS CRIME.
YOU DID ALL THIS TO FULFILL YOUR CAPTAIN'S DYING WISH?
YES, I SWEAR IT.
HAVE YOU ANY ENEMIES? YOUR GOOD FORTUNE WITH MARRIAGE AND PROMOTION MAY HAVE EXCITED JEALOUSY IN ANOTHER.
I WOULD NOT THINK SO, BUT YOU ARE WISER THAN I.
GIVE UP THIS LETTER YOU HAVE BROUGHT FROM ELBA, AND YOU MAY REJOIN YOUR FRIENDS.
YOU HAVE IT ALREADY, FOR IT WAS TAKEN FROM ME BY THE POLICE.
I AM FREE, THEN, SIR? THANK YOU!
WAIT, TO WHOM IS IT ADDRESSED?

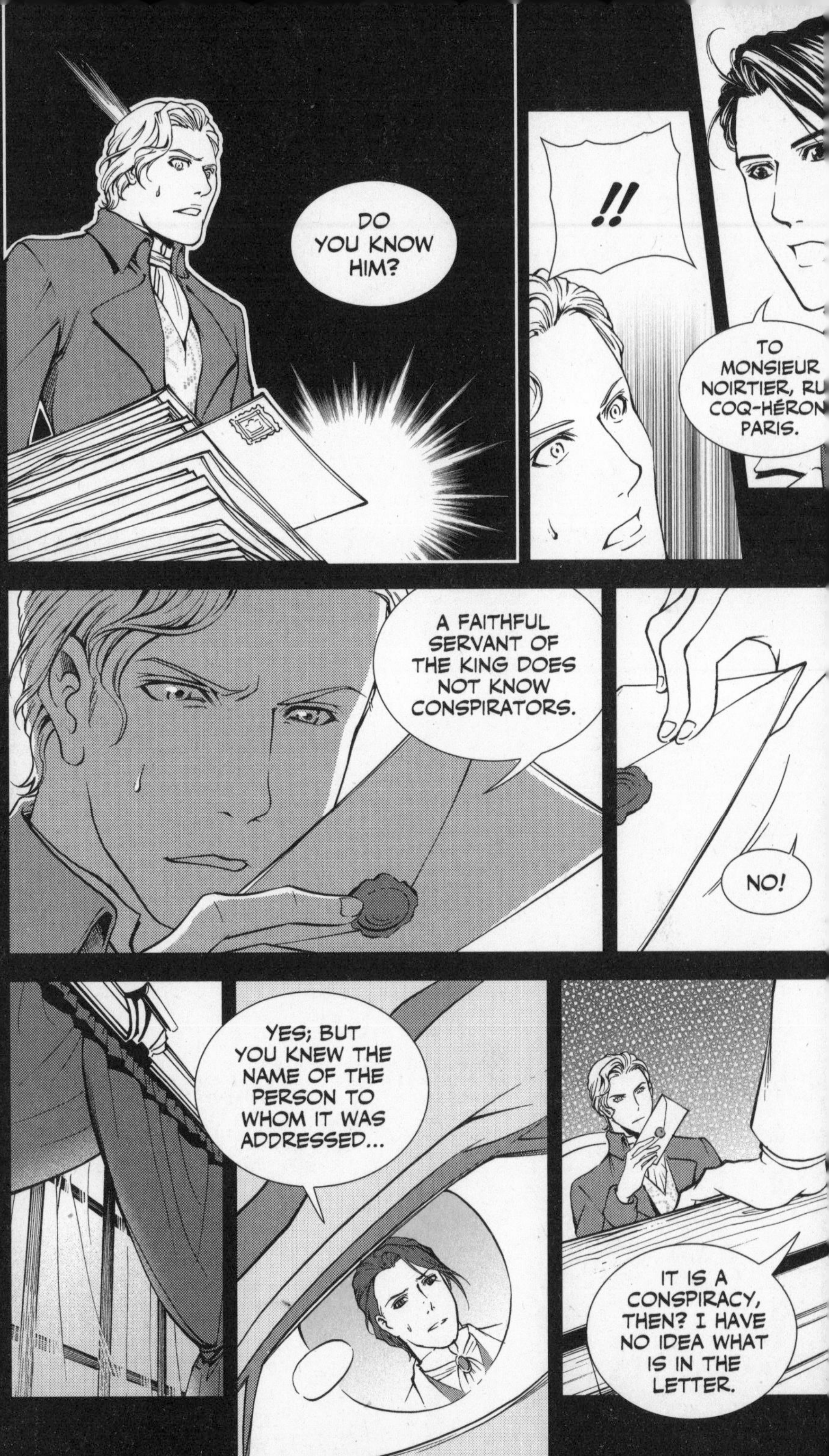
TO MONSIEUR NOIRTIER, RU COQ-HÉRON PARIS.
!!
DO YOU KNOW HIM?
NO!
A FAITHFUL SERVANT OF THE KING DOES NOT KNOW CONSPIRATORS.
IT IS A CONSPIRACY, THEN? I HAVE NO IDEA WHAT IS IN THE LETTER.
YES; BUT YOU KNEW THE NAME OF THE PERSON TO WHOM IT WAS ADDRESSED...

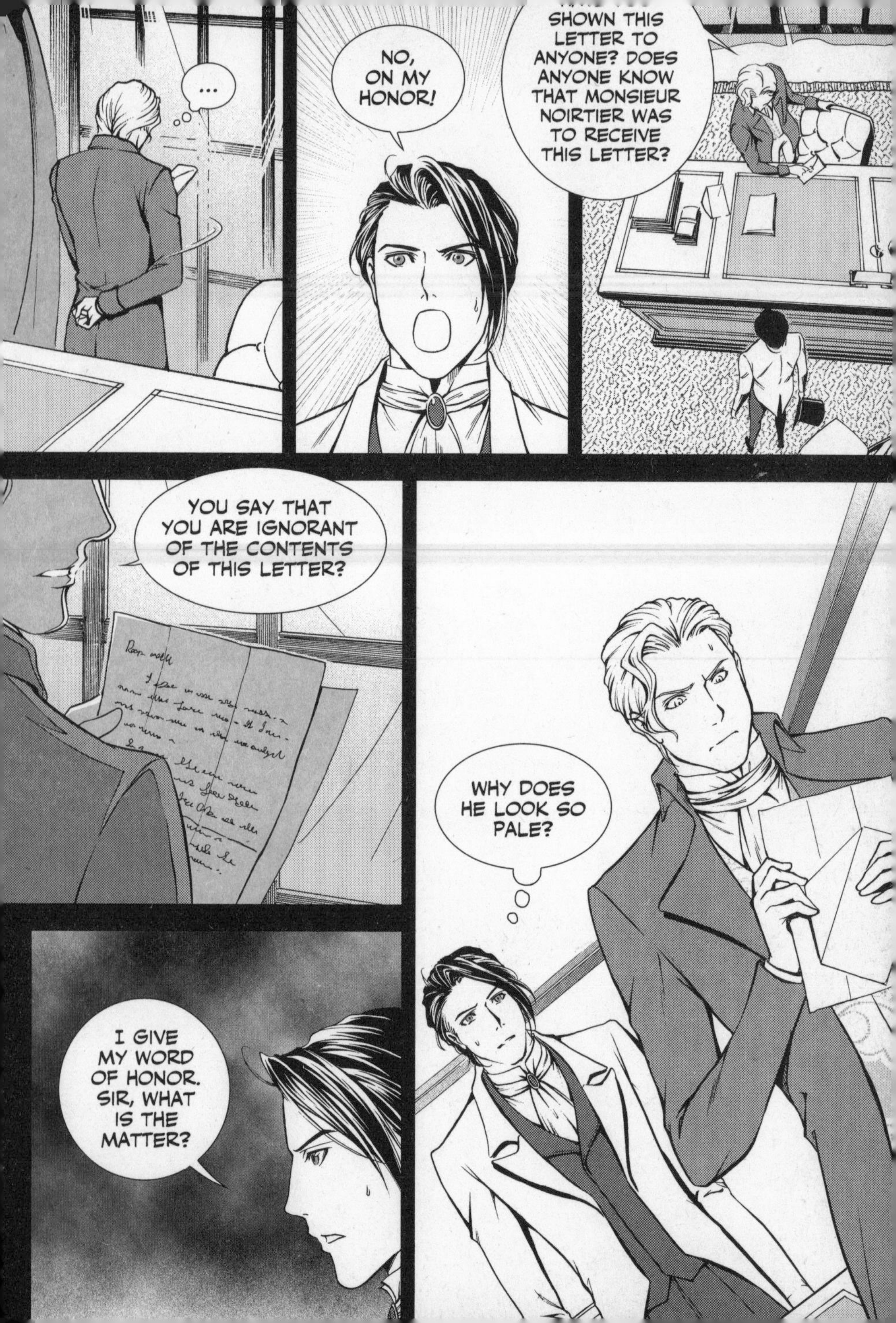
SHOWN THIS LETTER TO ANYONE? DOES ANYONE KNOW THAT MONSIEUR NOIRTIER WAS TO RECEIVE THIS LETTER?
NO, ON MY HONOR!
...
WHY DOES HE LOOK SO PALE?
YOU SAY THAT YOU ARE IGNORANT OF THE CONTENTS OF THIS LETTER?
I GIVE MY WORD OF HONOR. SIR, WHAT IS THE MATTER?

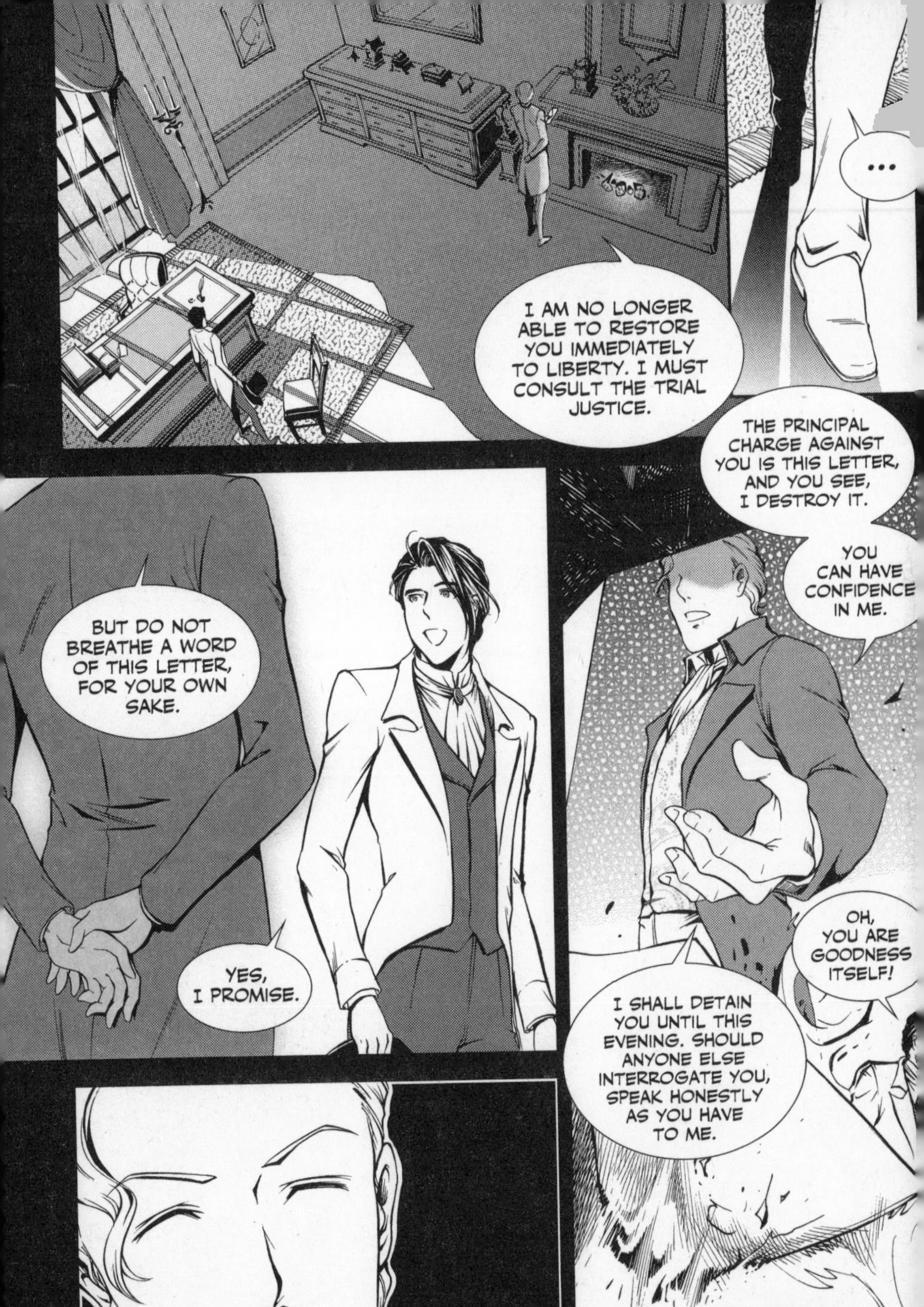
...
I AM NO LONGER ABLE TO RESTORE YOU IMMEDIATELY TO LIBERTY. I MUST CONSULT THE TRIAL JUSTICE.
THE PRINCIPAL CHARGE AGAINST YOU IS THIS LETTER, AND YOU SEE, I DESTROY IT.
YOU CAN HAVE CONFIDENCE IN ME.
OH, YOU ARE GOODNESS ITSELF!
I SHALL DETAIN YOU UNTIL THIS EVENING. SHOULD ANYONE ELSE INTERROGATE YOU, SPEAK HONESTLY AS YOU HAVE TO ME.
BUT DO NOT BREATHE A WORD OF THIS LETTER, FOR YOUR OWN SAKE.
YES, I PROMISE.

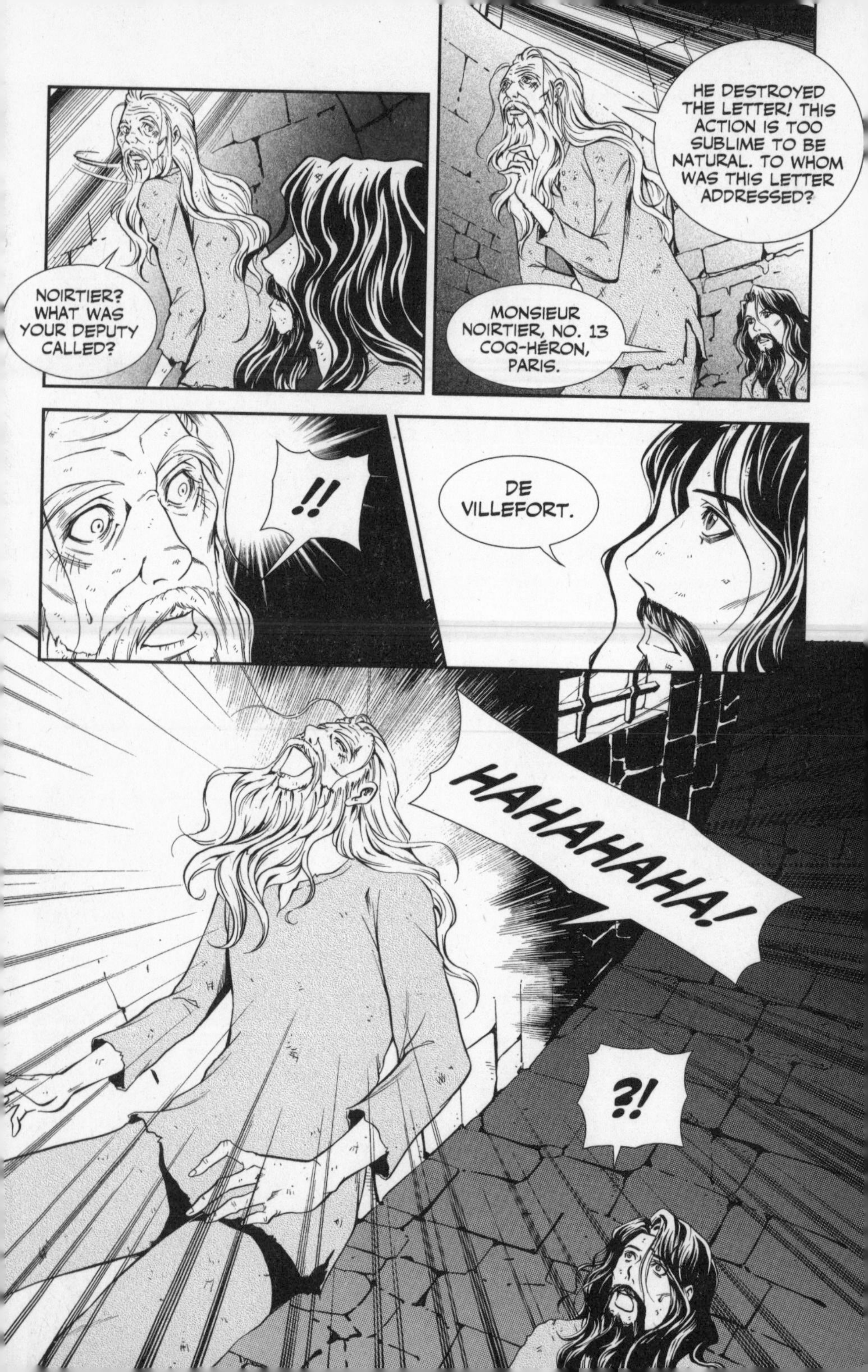
HE DESTROYED THE LETTER! THIS ACTION IS TOO SUBLIME TO BE NATURAL. TO WHOM WAS THIS LETTER ADDRESSED?
MONSIEUR NOIRTIER, NO. 13 COQ-HÉRON, PARIS.
NOIRTIER? WHAT WAS YOUR DEPUTY CALLED?
DE VILLEFORT.
!!
HAHAHAHA!
?!

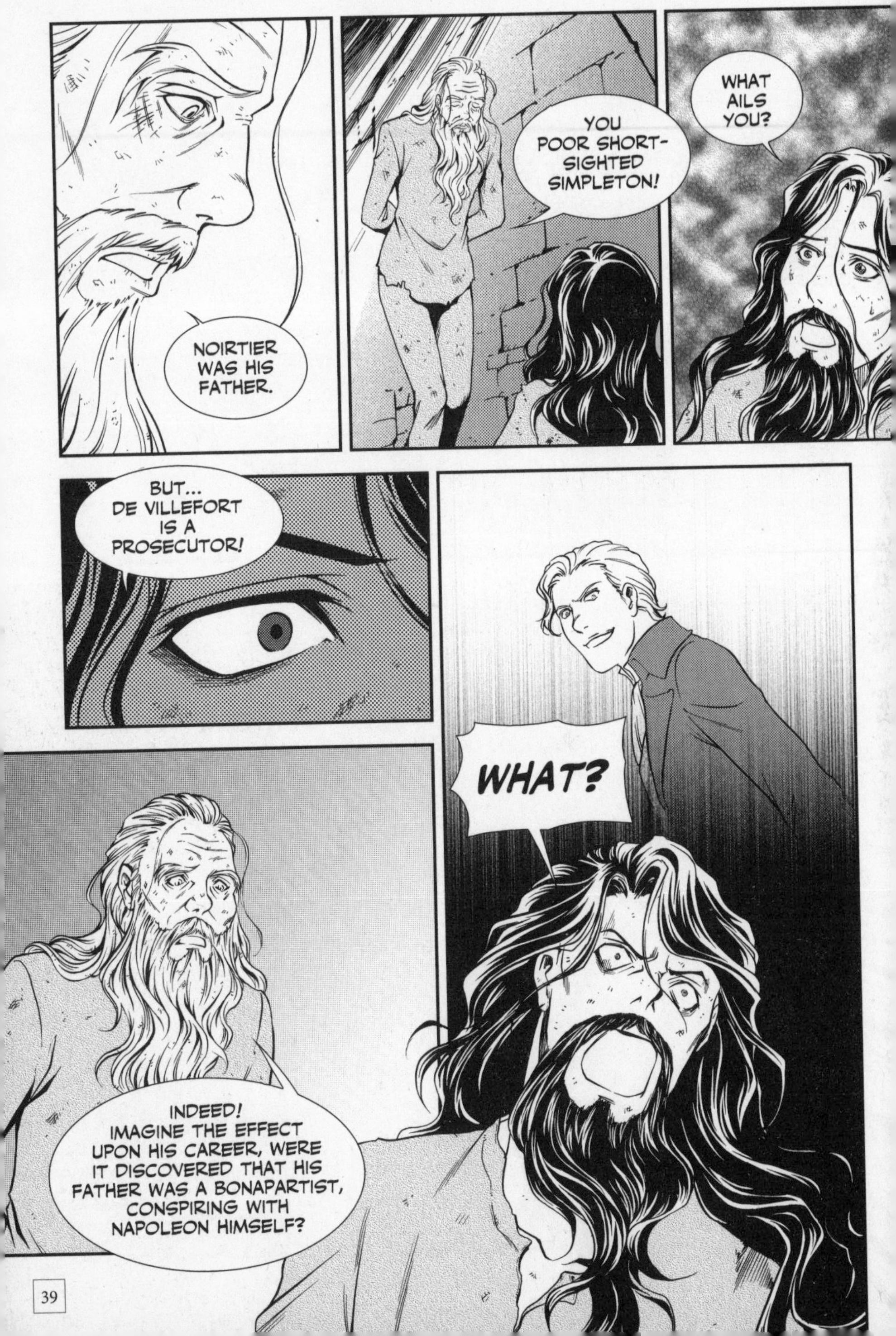
WHAT AILS YOU?
YOU POOR SHORT-SIGHTED SIMPLETON!
NOIRTIER WAS HIS FATHER.
WHAT?
BUT... DE VILLEFORT IS A PROSECUTOR!
INDEED! IMAGINE THE EFFECT UPON HIS CAREER, WERE IT DISCOVERED THAT HIS FATHER WAS A BONAPARTIST, CONSPIRING WITH NAPOLEON HIMSELF?

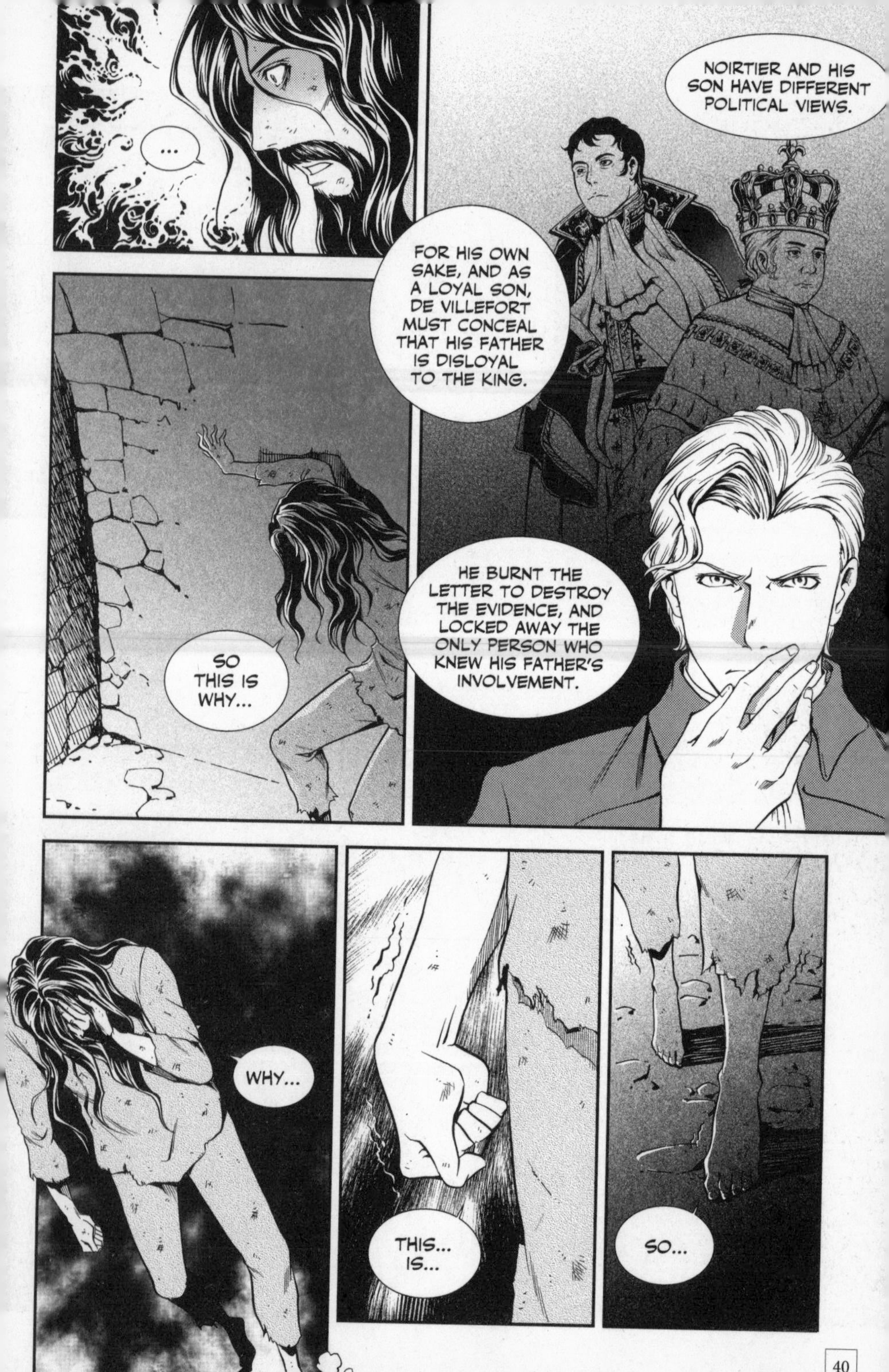
NOIRTIER AND HIS SON HAVE DIFFERENT POLITICAL VIEWS.
FOR HIS OWN SAKE, AND AS A LOYAL SON, DE VILLEFORT MUST CONCEAL THAT HIS FATHER IS DISLOYAL TO THE KING.
HE BURNT THE LETTER TO DESTROY THE EVIDENCE, AND LOCKED AWAY THE ONLY PERSON WHO KNEW HIS FATHER'S INVOLVEMENT.
...
SO THIS IS WHY...
SO...
THIS... IS...
WHY...

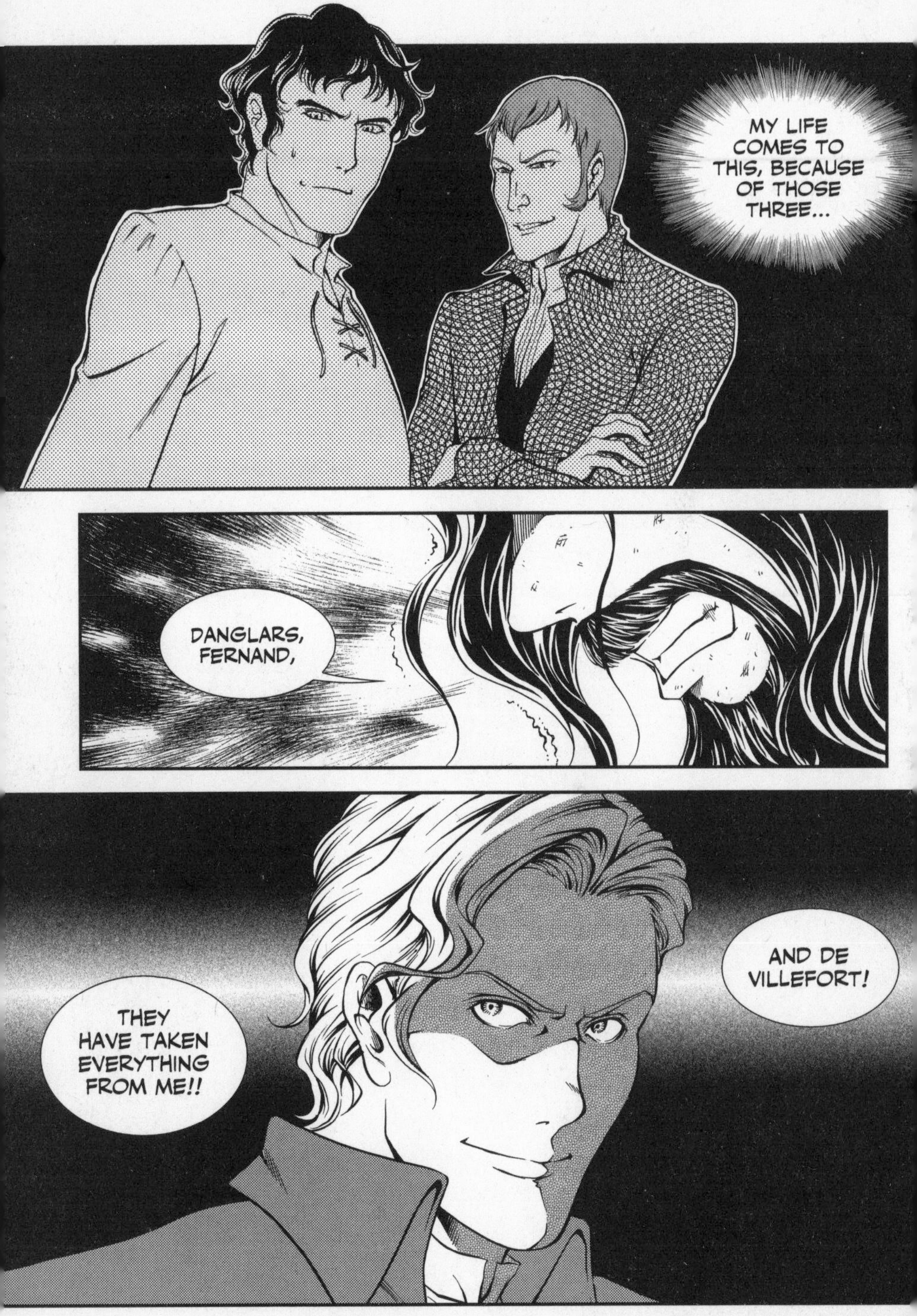
MY LIFE COMES TO THIS, BECAUSE OF THOSE THREE...
DANGLARS, FERNAND,
AND DE VILLEFORT!
THEY HAVE TAKEN EVERYTHING FROM ME!!

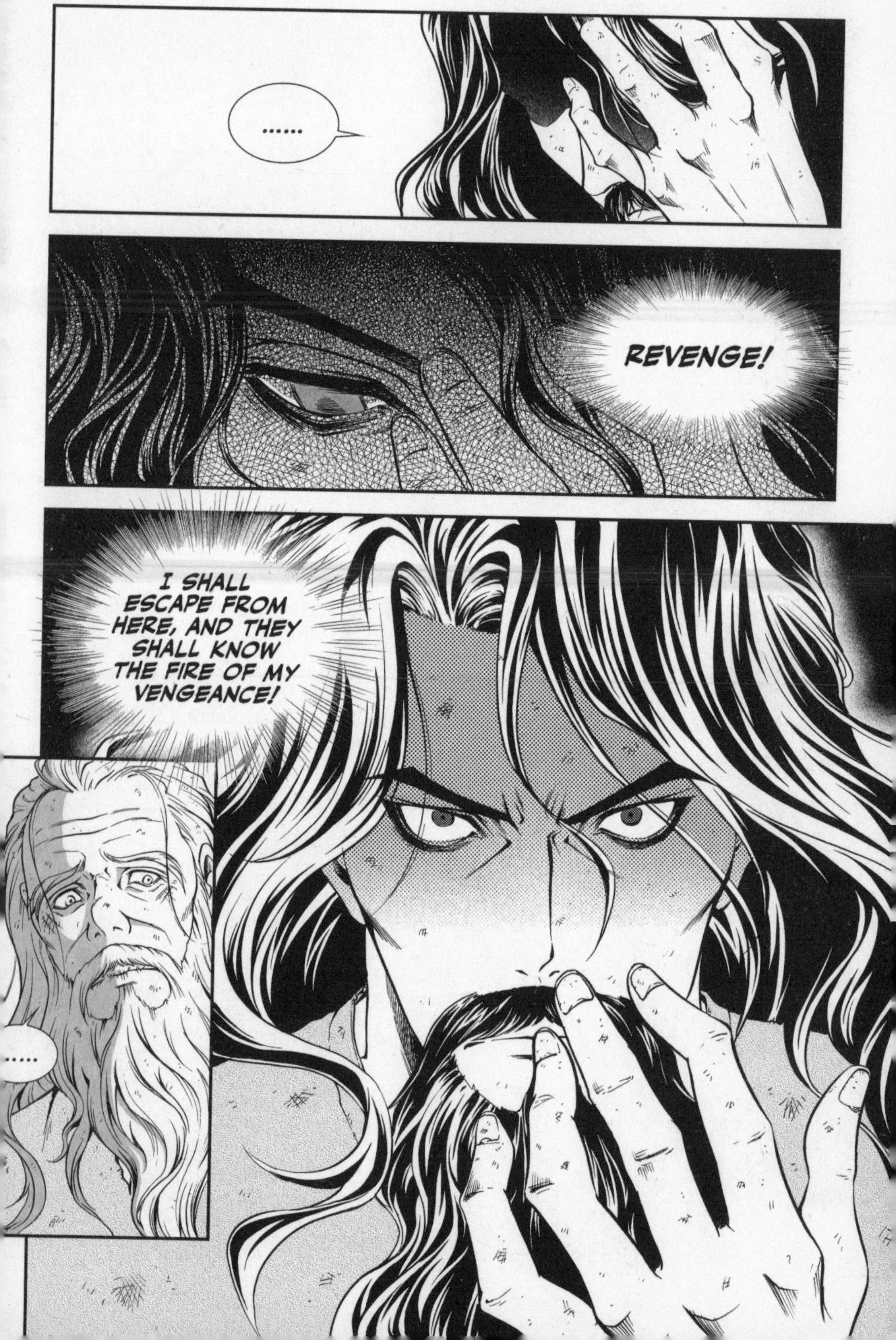
......
REVENGE!
I SHALL ESCAPE FROM HERE, AND THEY SHALL KNOW THE FIRE OF MY VENGEANCE!
......

CHAPTER 3 - REVENGE

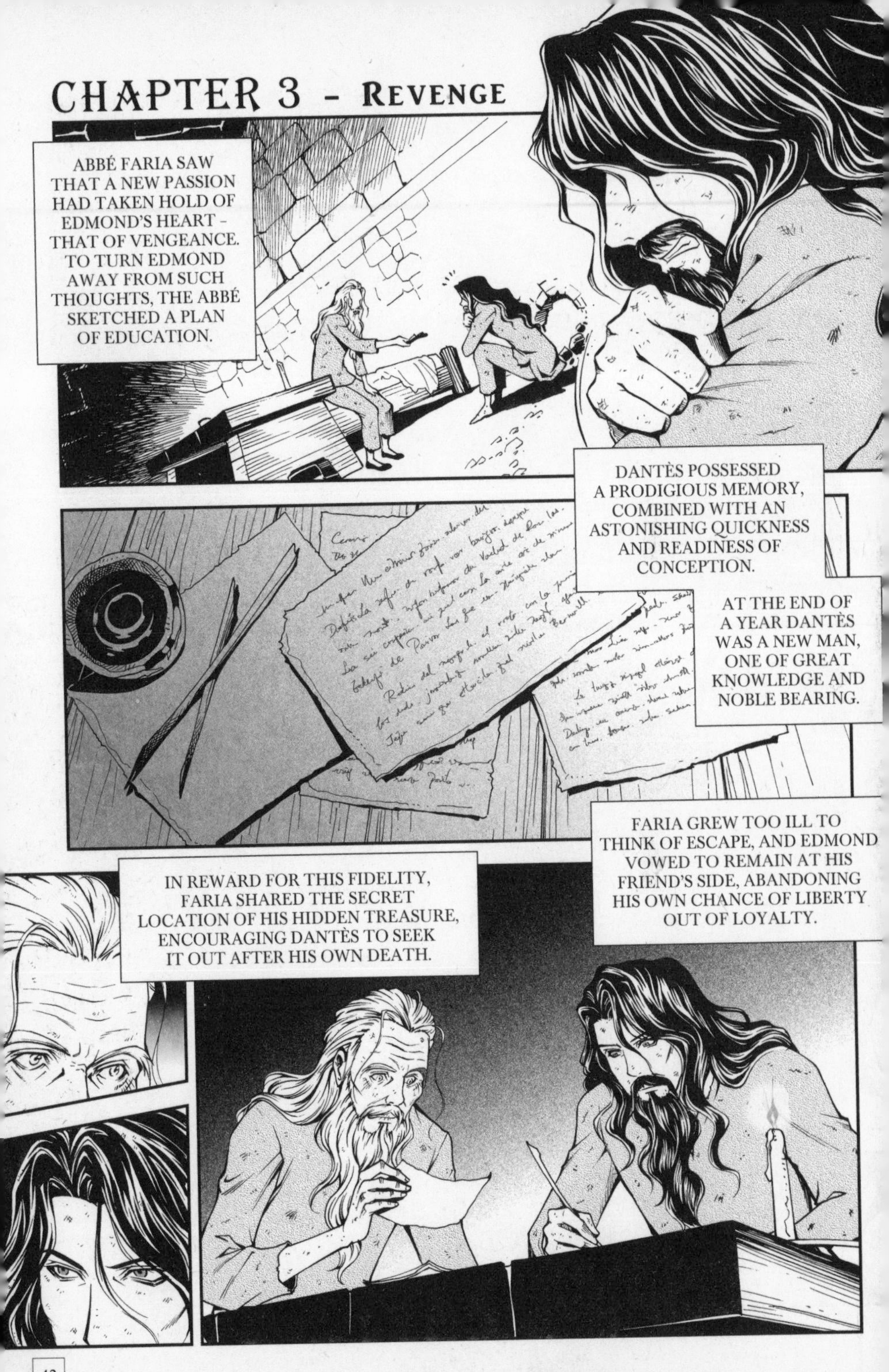

ABBÉ FARIA SAW THAT A NEW PASSION HAD TAKEN HOLD OF EDMOND'S HEART – THAT OF VENGEANCE. TO TURN EDMOND AWAY FROM SUCH THOUGHTS, THE ABBÉ SKETCHED A PLAN OF EDUCATION.
DANTÈS POSSESSED A PRODIGIOUS MEMORY, COMBINED WITH AN ASTONISHING QUICKNESS AND READINESS OF CONCEPTION.
AT THE END OF A YEAR DANTÈS WAS A NEW MAN, ONE OF GREAT KNOWLEDGE AND NOBLE BEARING.
FARIA GREW TOO ILL TO THINK OF ESCAPE, AND EDMOND VOWED TO REMAIN AT HIS FRIEND'S SIDE, ABANDONING HIS OWN CHANCE OF LIBERTY OUT OF LOYALTY.
IN REWARD FOR THIS FIDELITY, FARIA SHARED THE SECRET LOCATION OF HIS HIDDEN TREASURE, ENCOURAGING DANTÈS TO SEEK IT OUT AFTER HIS OWN DEATH.

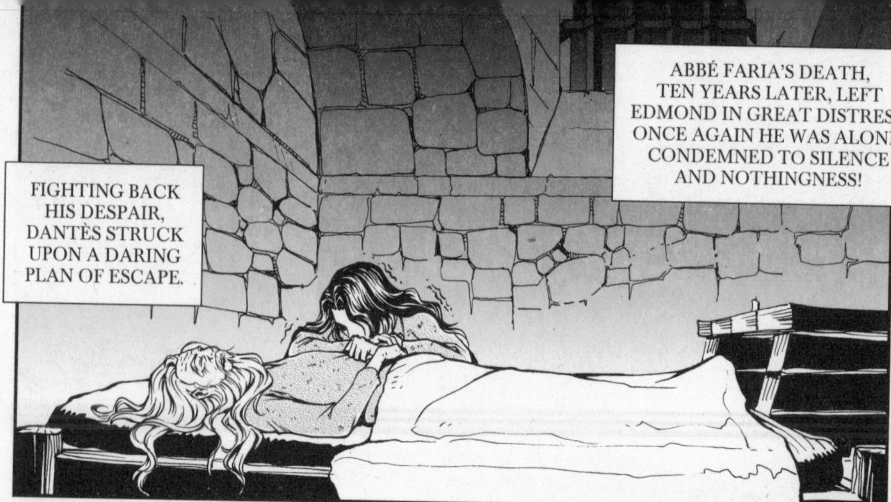
ABBÉ FARIA'S DEATH, TEN YEARS LATER, LEFT EDMOND IN GREAT DISTRESS. ONCE AGAIN HE WAS ALONE, CONDEMNED TO SILENCE AND NOTHINGNESS!
FIGHTING BACK HIS DESPAIR, DANTÈS STRUCK UPON A DARING PLAN OF ESCAPE.
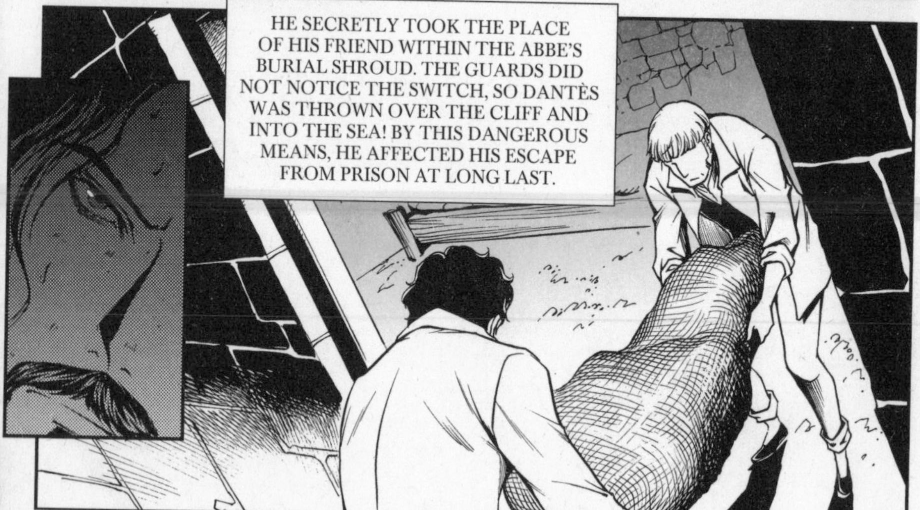
HE SECRETLY TOOK THE PLACE OF HIS FRIEND WITHIN THE ABBE'S BURIAL SHROUD. THE GUARDS DID NOT NOTICE THE SWITCH, SO DANTÈS WAS THROWN OVER THE CLIFF AND INTO THE SEA! BY THIS DANGEROUS MEANS, HE AFFECTED HIS ESCAPE FROM PRISON AT LONG LAST.
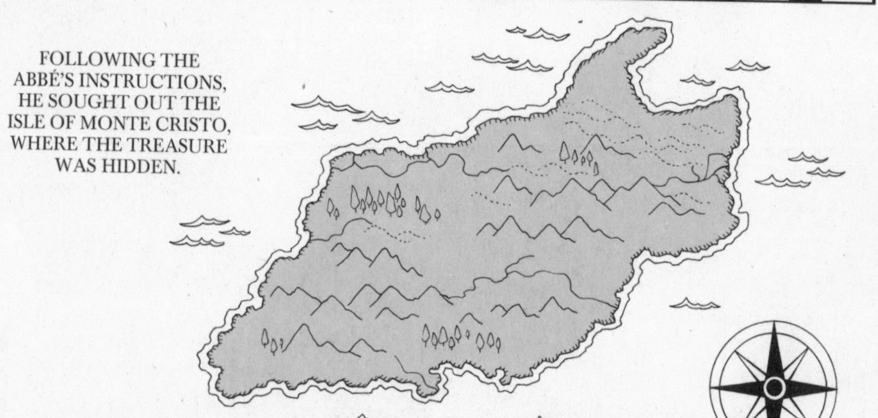
FOLLOWING THE ABBÉ'S INSTRUCTIONS, HE SOUGHT OUT THE ISLE OF MONTE CRISTO, WHERE THE TREASURE WAS HIDDEN.

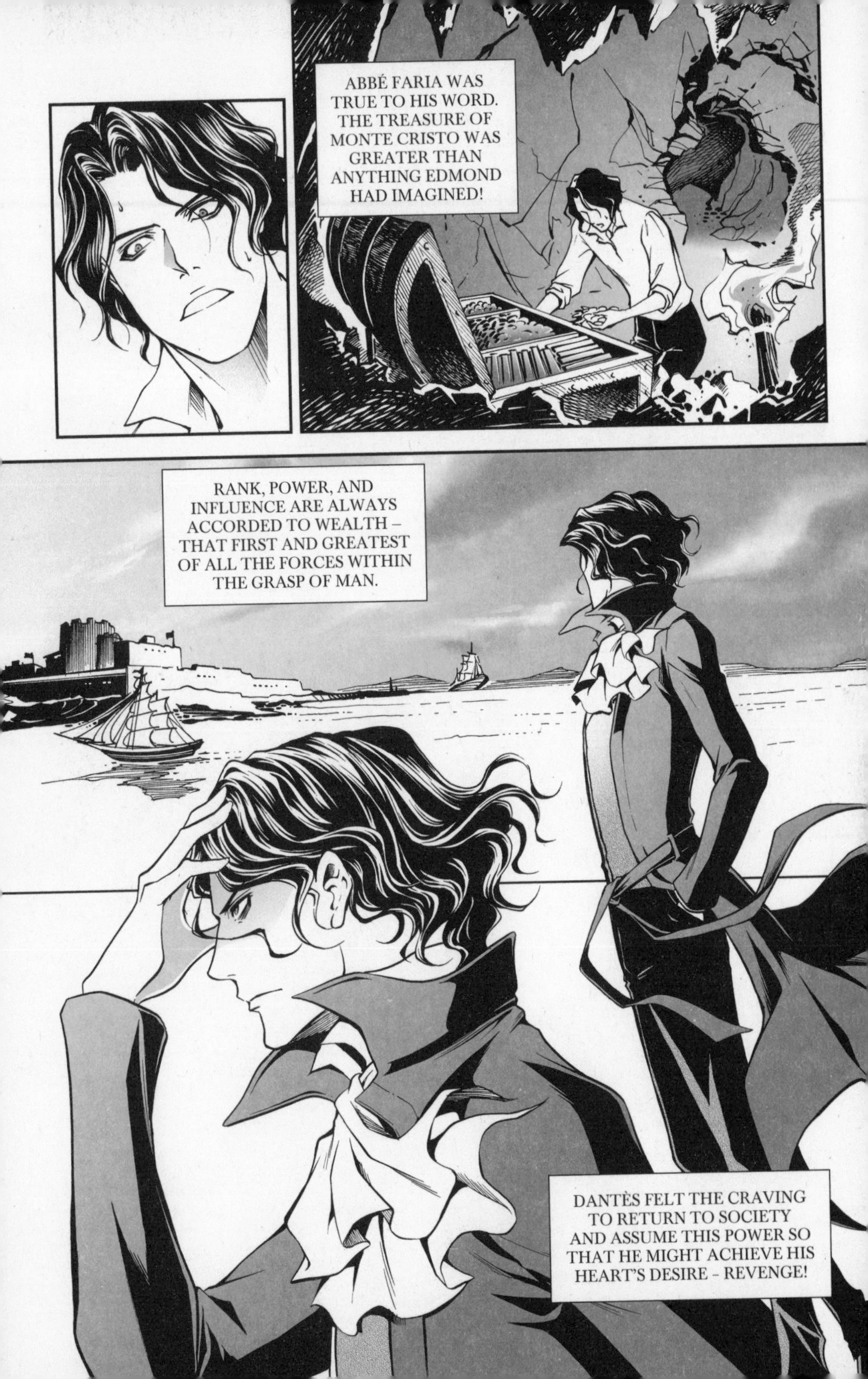
ABBÉ FARIA WAS TRUE TO HIS WORD. THE TREASURE OF MONTE CRISTO WAS GREATER THAN ANYTHING EDMOND HAD IMAGINED!
RANK, POWER, AND INFLUENCE ARE ALWAYS ACCORDED TO WEALTH – THAT FIRST AND GREATEST OF ALL THE FORCES WITHIN THE GRASP OF MAN.
DANTÈS FELT THE CRAVING TO RETURN TO SOCIETY AND ASSUME THIS POWER SO THAT HE MIGHT ACHIEVE HIS HEART'S DESIRE – REVENGE!

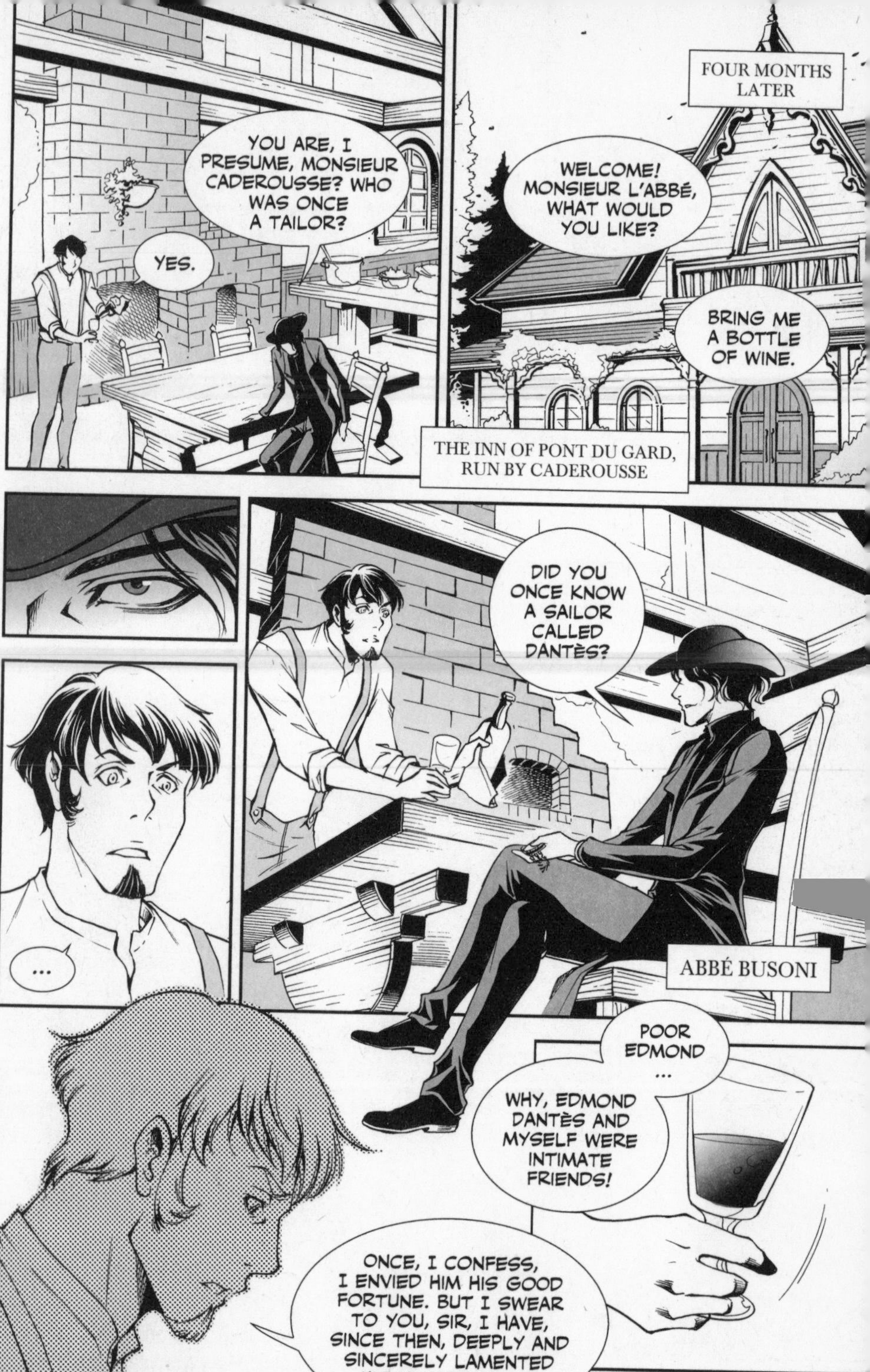
FOUR MONTHS LATER
WELCOME! MONSIEUR L'ABBÉ, WHAT WOULD YOU LIKE?
BRING ME A BOTTLE OF WINE.
THE INN OF PONT DU GARD, RUN BY CADEROUSSE
YOU ARE, I PRESUME, MONSIEUR CADEROUSSE? WHO WAS ONCE A TAILOR?
YES.
DID YOU ONCE KNOW A SAILOR CALLED DANTÈS?
ABBÉ BUSONI
...
POOR EDMOND ...
WHY, EDMOND DANTÈS AND MYSELF WERE INTIMATE FRIENDS!
ONCE, I CONFESS, I ENVIED HIM HIS GOOD FORTUNE. BUT I SWEAR TO YOU, SIR, I HAVE, SINCE THEN, DEEPLY AND SINCERELY LAMENTED HIS UNHAPPY FATE.

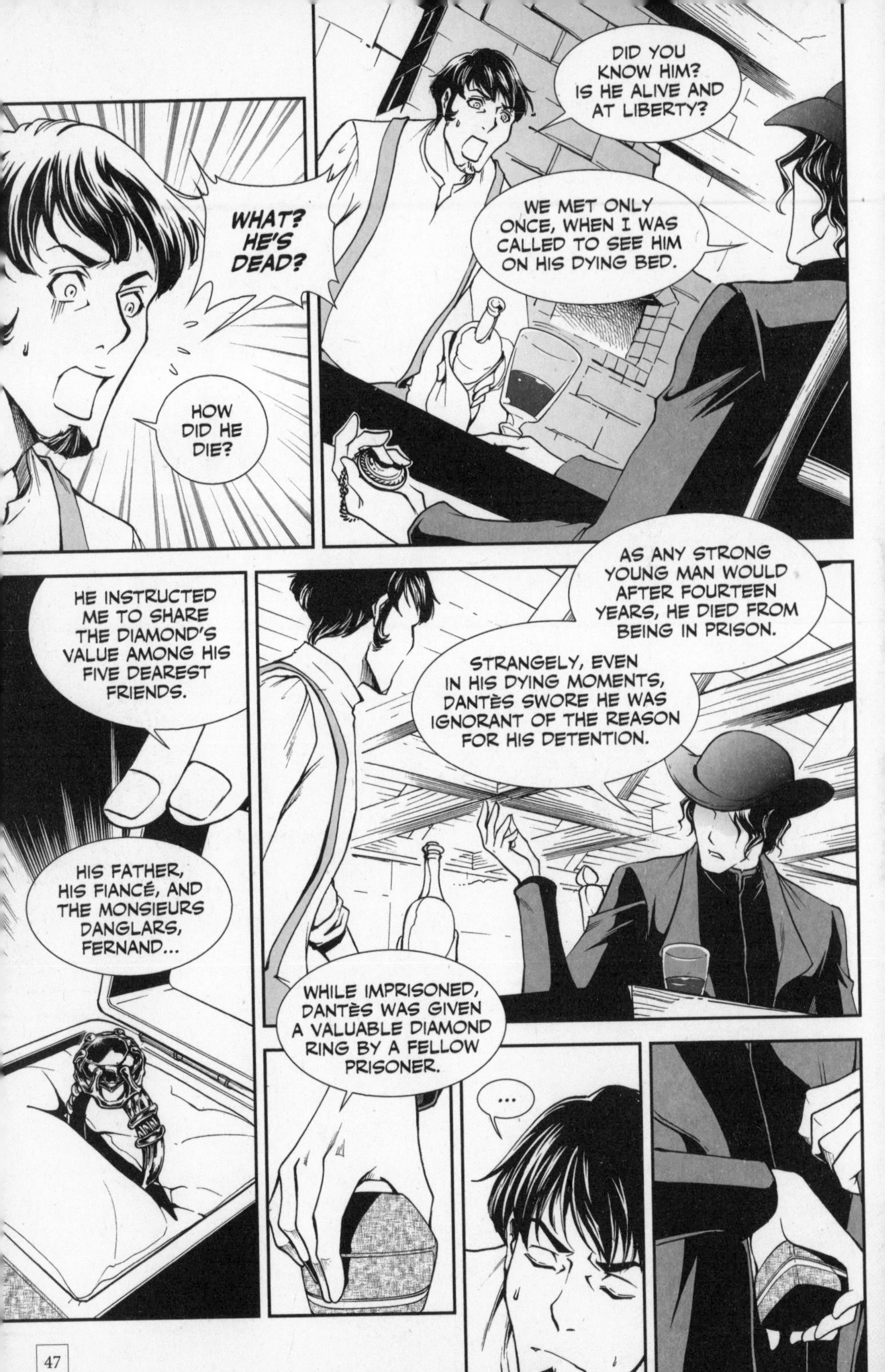
DID YOU KNOW HIM? IS HE ALIVE AND AT LIBERTY?
WE MET ONLY ONCE, WHEN I WAS CALLED TO SEE HIM ON HIS DYING BED.
WHAT? HE'S DEAD?
HOW DID HE DIE?
AS ANY STRONG YOUNG MAN WOULD AFTER FOURTEEN YEARS, HE DIED FROM BEING IN PRISON.
STRANGELY, EVEN IN HIS DYING MOMENTS, DANTÈS SWORE HE WAS IGNORANT OF THE REASON FOR HIS DETENTION.
WHILE IMPRISONED, DANTÈS WAS GIVEN A VALUABLE DIAMOND RING BY A FELLOW PRISONER.
HE INSTRUCTED ME TO SHARE THE DIAMOND'S VALUE AMONG HIS FIVE DEAREST FRIENDS.
HIS FATHER, HIS FIANCÉ, AND THE MONSIEURS DANGLARS, FERNAND...
...

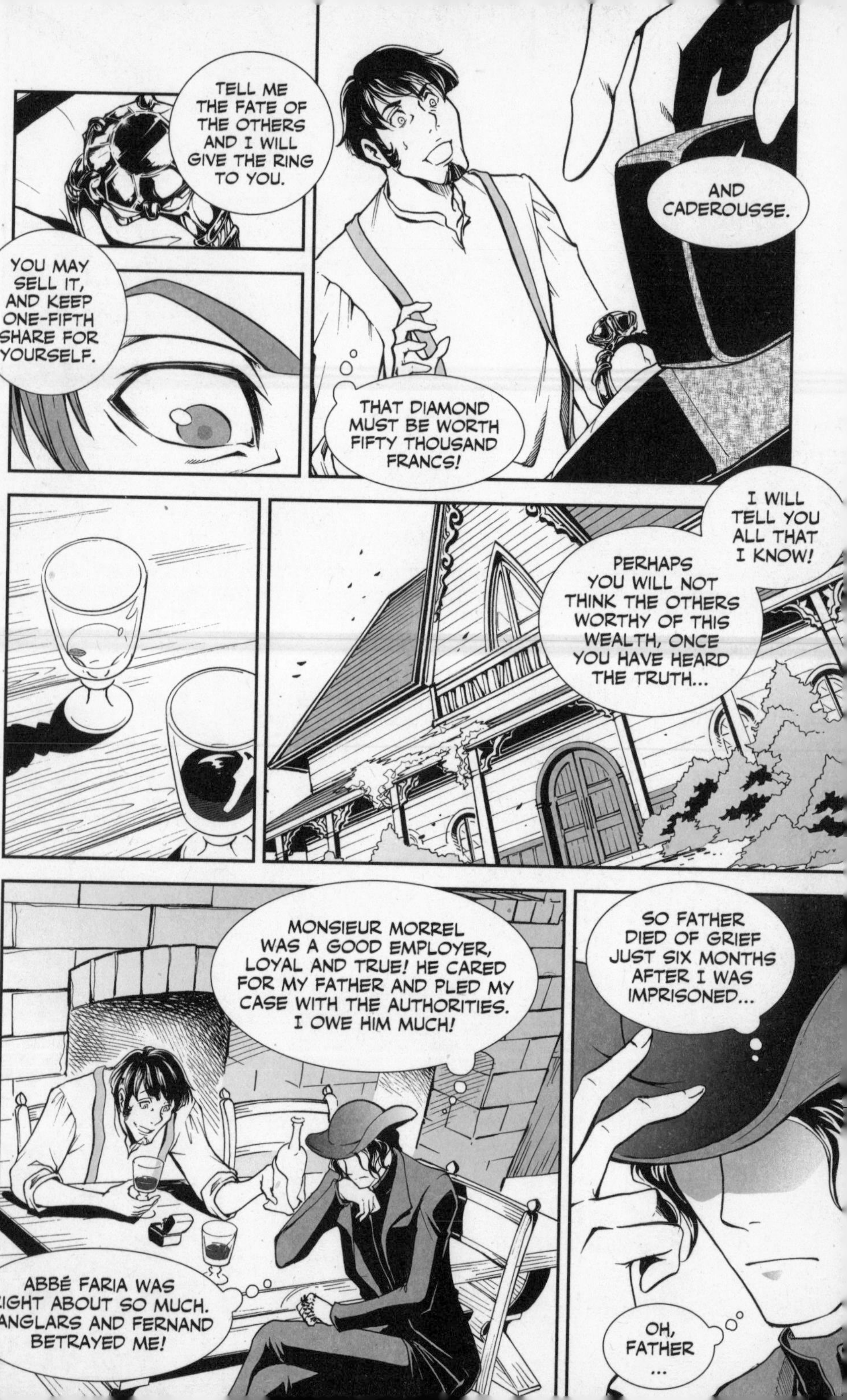
AND CADEROUSSE.
TELL ME THE FATE OF THE OTHERS AND I WILL GIVE THE RING TO YOU.
THAT DIAMOND MUST BE WORTH FIFTY THOUSAND FRANCS!
YOU MAY SELL IT, AND KEEP ONE-FIFTH SHARE FOR YOURSELF.
I WILL TELL YOU ALL THAT I KNOW!
PERHAPS YOU WILL NOT THINK THE OTHERS WORTHY OF THIS WEALTH, ONCE YOU HAVE HEARD THE TRUTH...
SO FATHER DIED OF GRIEF JUST SIX MONTHS AFTER I WAS IMPRISONED...
OH, FATHER ...
MONSIEUR MORREL WAS A GOOD EMPLOYER, LOYAL AND TRUE! HE CARED FOR MY FATHER AND PLED MY CASE WITH THE AUTHORITIES. I OWE HIM MUCH!
ABBÉ FARIA WAS RIGHT ABOUT SO MUCH. DANGLARS AND FERNAND BETRAYED ME!

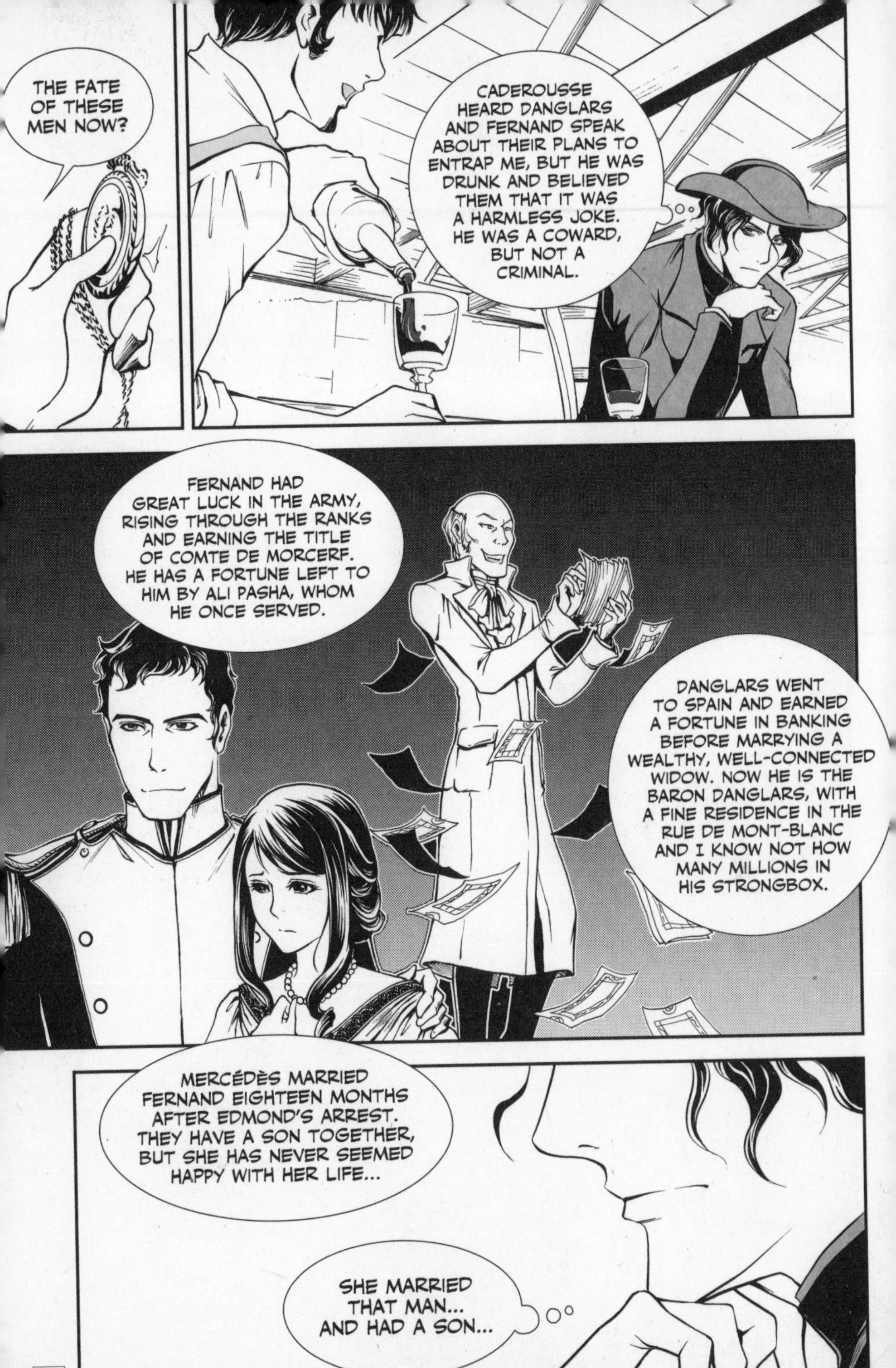
THE FATE OF THESE MEN NOW?
CADEROUSSE HEARD DANGLARS AND FERNAND SPEAK ABOUT THEIR PLANS TO ENTRAP ME, BUT HE WAS DRUNK AND BELIEVED THEM THAT IT WAS A HARMLESS JOKE. HE WAS A COWARD, BUT NOT A CRIMINAL.
FERNAND HAD GREAT LUCK IN THE ARMY, RISING THROUGH THE RANKS AND EARNING THE TITLE OF COMTE DE MORCERF. HE HAS A FORTUNE LEFT TO HIM BY ALI PASHA, WHOM HE ONCE SERVED.
DANGLARS WENT TO SPAIN AND EARNED A FORTUNE IN BANKING BEFORE MARRYING A WEALTHY, WELL-CONNECTED WIDOW. NOW HE IS THE BARON DANGLARS, WITH A FINE RESIDENCE IN THE RUE DE MONT-BLANC AND I KNOW NOT HOW MANY MILLIONS IN HIS STRONGBOX.
MERCÉDÈS MARRIED FERNAND EIGHTEEN MONTHS AFTER EDMOND'S ARREST. THEY HAVE A SON TOGETHER, BUT SHE HAS NEVER SEEMED HAPPY WITH HER LIFE...
SHE MARRIED THAT MAN... AND HAD A SON...

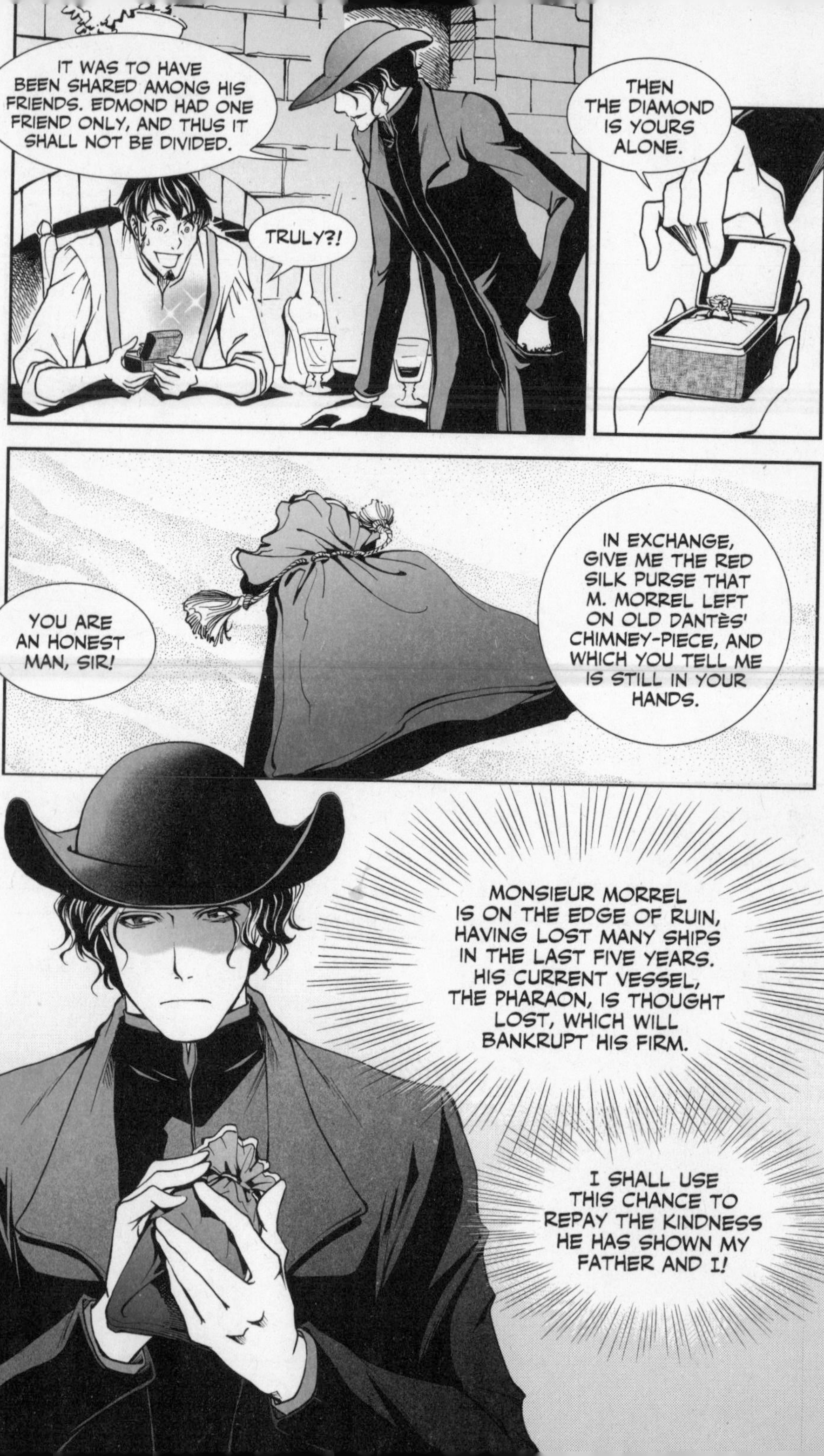
THEN THE DIAMOND IS YOURS ALONE.
IT WAS TO HAVE BEEN SHARED AMONG HIS FRIENDS. EDMOND HAD ONE FRIEND ONLY, AND THUS IT SHALL NOT BE DIVIDED.
TRULY?!
IN EXCHANGE, GIVE ME THE RED SILK PURSE THAT M. MORREL LEFT ON OLD DANTÈS' CHIMNEY-PIECE, AND WHICH YOU TELL ME IS STILL IN YOUR HANDS.
YOU ARE AN HONEST MAN, SIR!
MONSIEUR MORREL IS ON THE EDGE OF RUIN, HAVING LOST MANY SHIPS IN THE LAST FIVE YEARS. HIS CURRENT VESSEL, THE PHARAON, IS THOUGHT LOST, WHICH WILL BANKRUPT HIS FIRM.
I SHALL USE THIS CHANCE TO REPAY THE KINDNESS HE HAS SHOWN MY FATHER AND I!

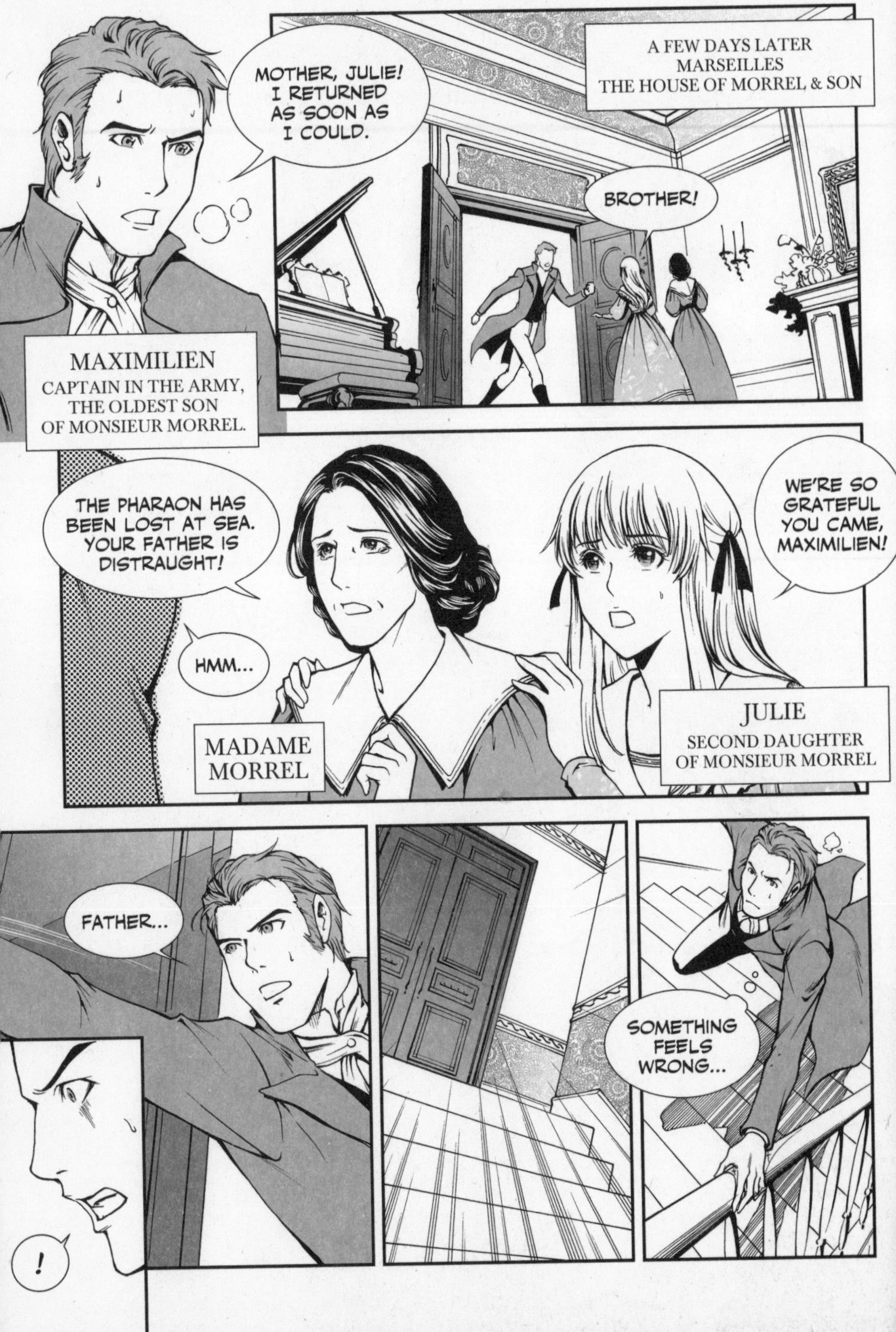
A FEW DAYS LATER
MARSEILLES
THE HOUSE OF MORREL & SON
BROTHER!
MOTHER, JULIE! I RETURNED AS SOON AS I COULD.
MAXIMILIEN
CAPTAIN IN THE ARMY, THE OLDEST SON OF MONSIEUR MORREL.
WE'RE SO GRATEFUL YOU CAME, MAXIMILIEN!
THE PHARAON HAS BEEN LOST AT SEA. YOUR FATHER IS DISTRAUGHT!
JULIE
SECOND DAUGHTER OF MONSIEUR MORREL
HMM...
MADAME MORREL
SOMETHING FEELS WRONG...
FATHER...
!

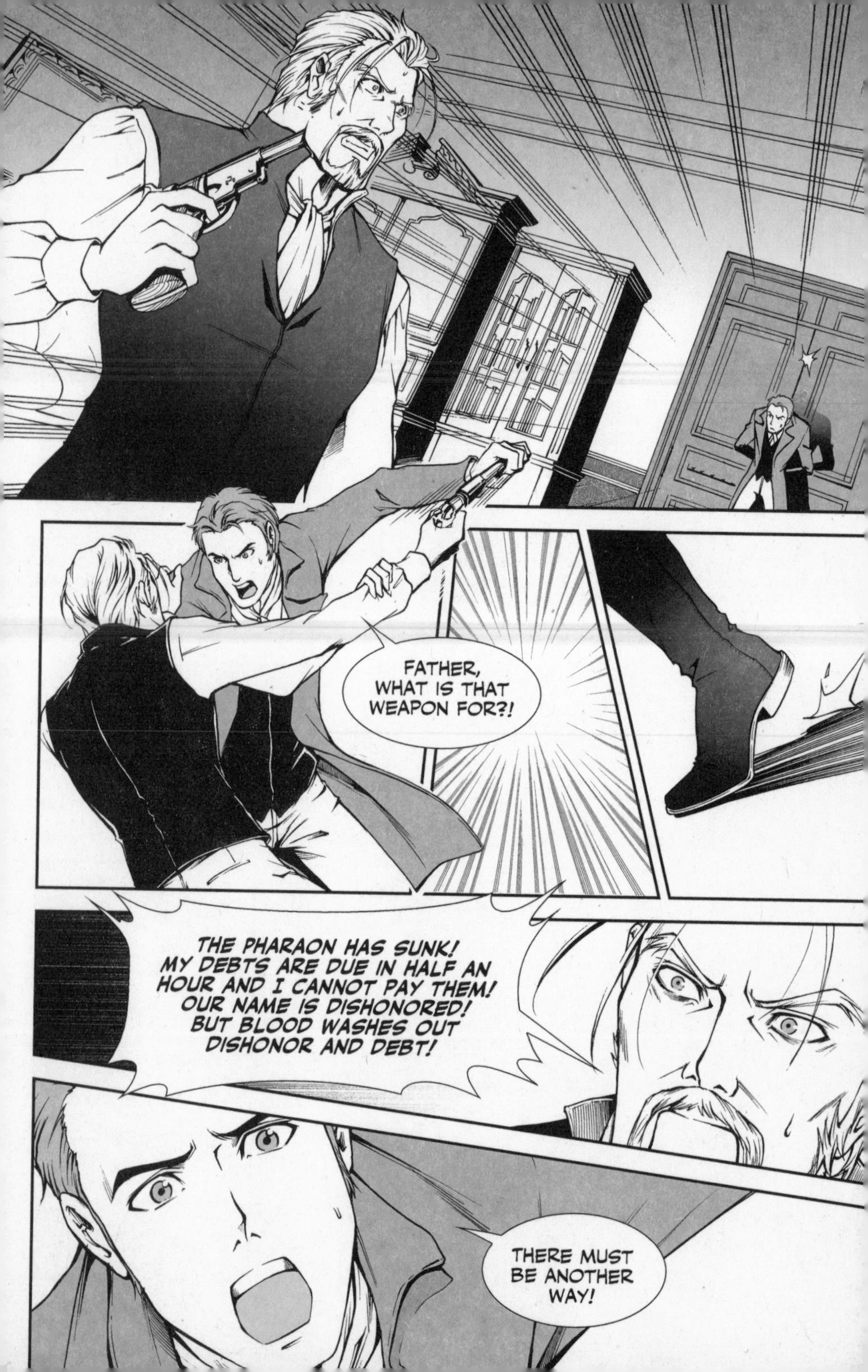
FATHER, WHAT IS THAT WEAPON FOR?!
THE PHARAON HAS SUNK! MY DEBTS ARE DUE IN HALF AN HOUR AND I CANNOT PAY THEM! OUR NAME IS DISHONORED! BUT BLOOD WASHES OUT DISHONOR AND DEBT!
THERE MUST BE ANOTHER WAY!

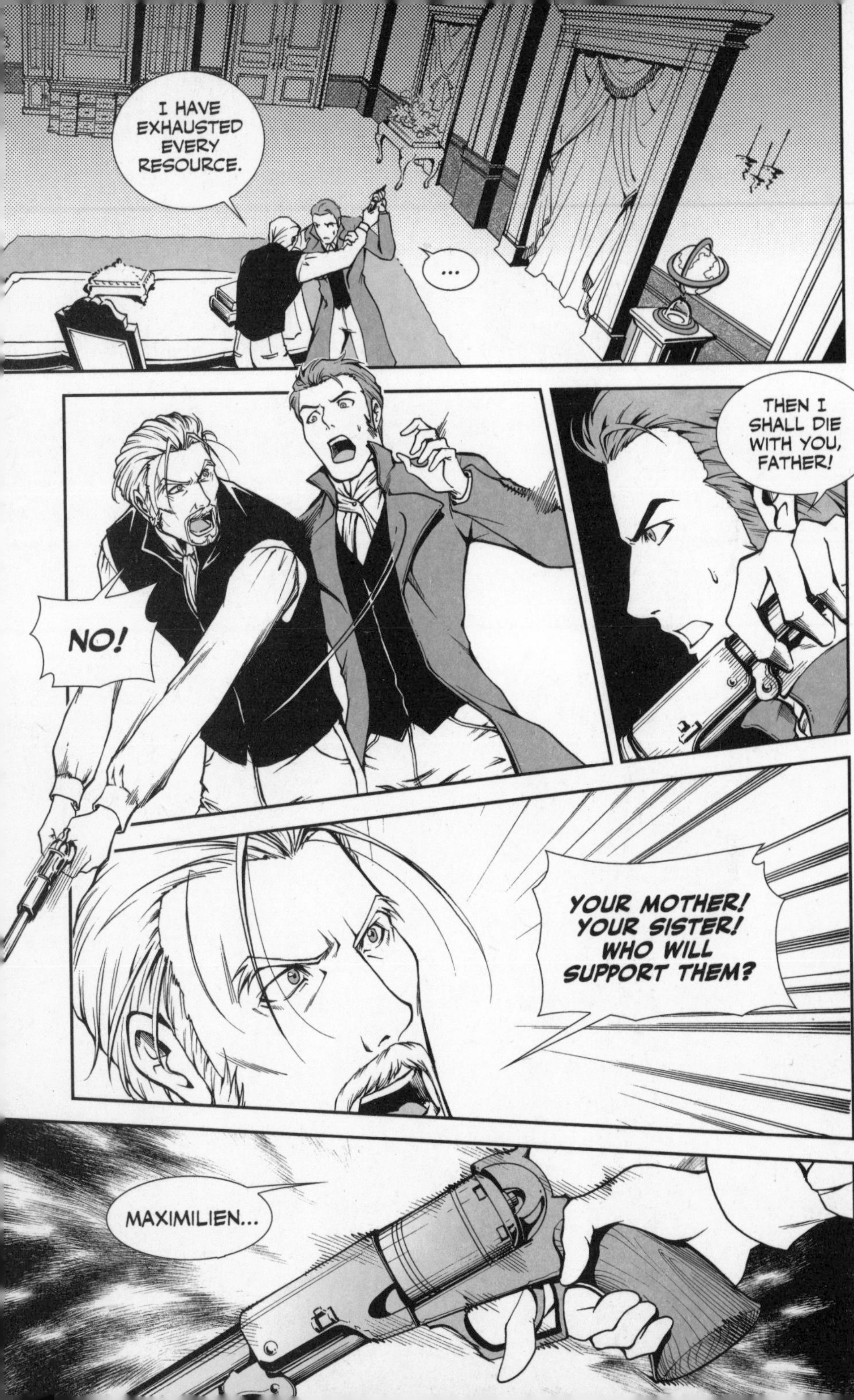
I HAVE EXHAUSTED EVERY RESOURCE.
...
THEN I SHALL DIE WITH YOU, FATHER!
NO!
YOUR MOTHER! YOUR SISTER! WHO WILL SUPPORT THEM?
MAXIMILIEN...

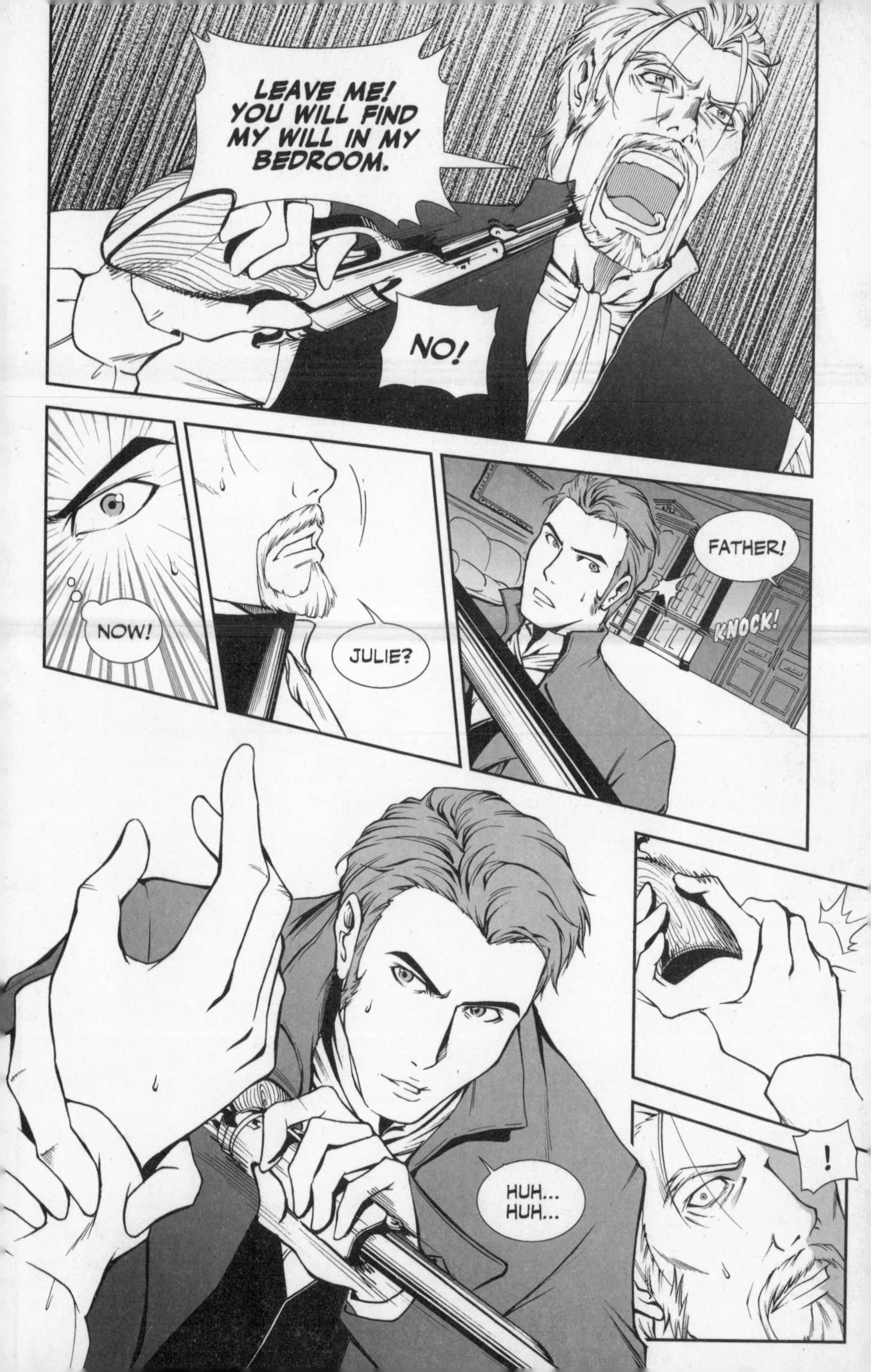
LEAVE ME! YOU WILL FIND MY WILL IN MY BEDROOM.
NO!
FATHER!
KNOCK!
JULIE?
NOW!
!
HUH... HUH...

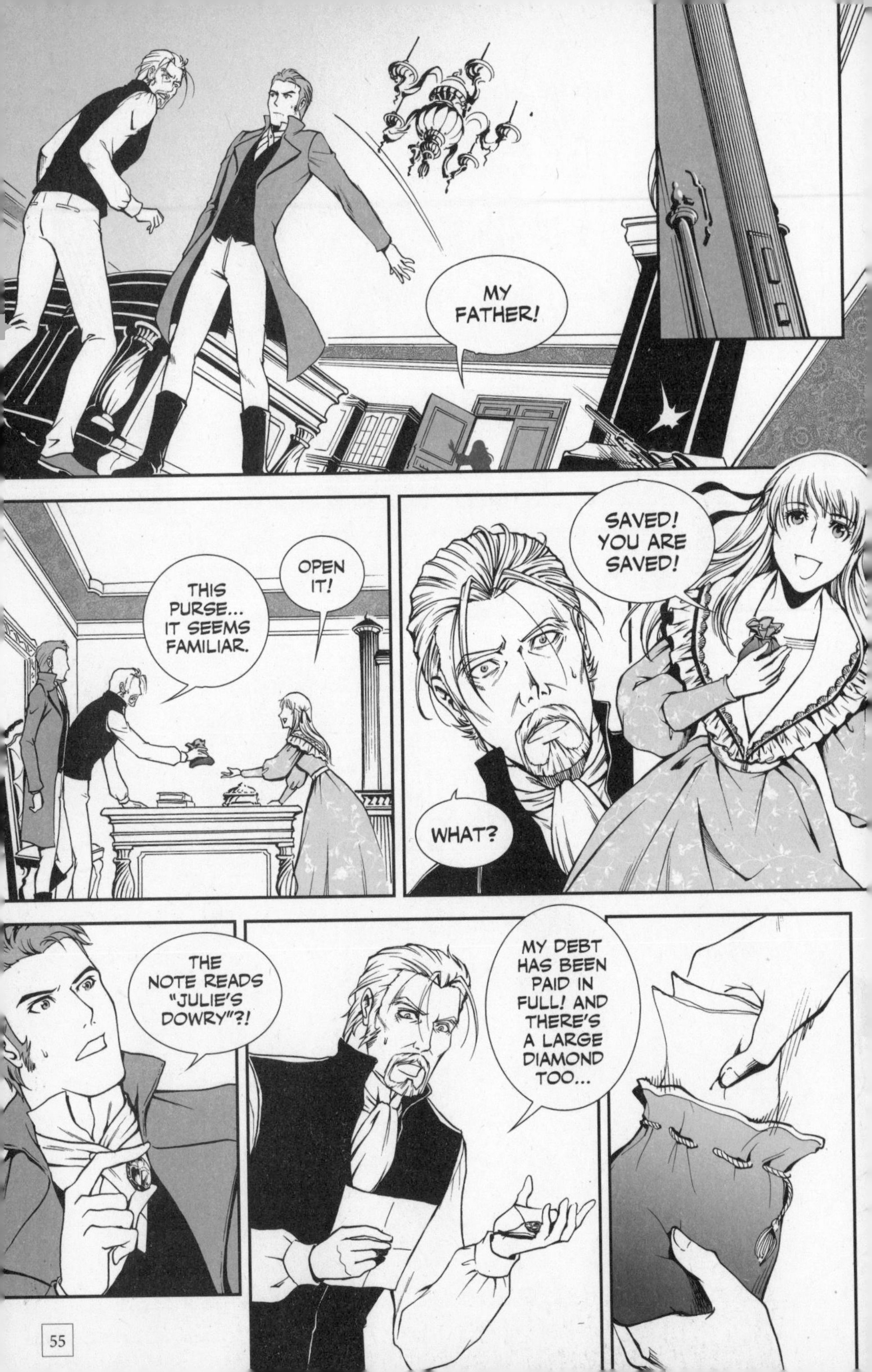
MY FATHER!
SAVED! YOU ARE SAVED!
WHAT?
OPEN IT!
THIS PURSE... IT SEEMS FAMILIAR.
MY DEBT HAS BEEN PAID IN FULL! AND THERE'S A LARGE DIAMOND TOO...
THE NOTE READS "JULIE'S DOWRY"?!

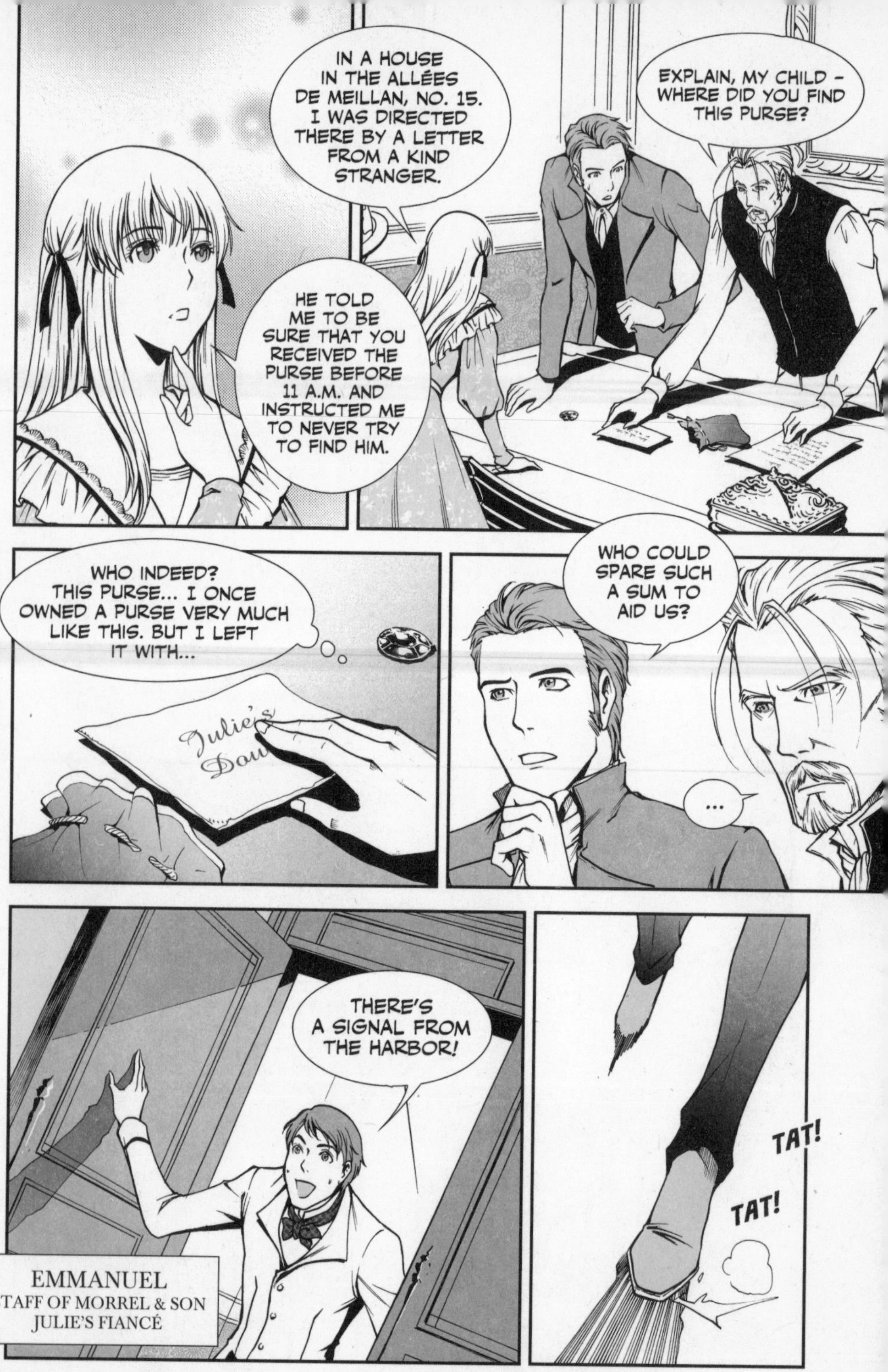
EXPLAIN, MY CHILD - WHERE DID YOU FIND THIS PURSE?
IN A HOUSE IN THE ALLÉES DE MEILLAN, NO. 15. I WAS DIRECTED THERE BY A LETTER FROM A KIND STRANGER.
HE TOLD ME TO BE SURE THAT YOU RECEIVED THE PURSE BEFORE 11 A.M. AND INSTRUCTED ME TO NEVER TRY TO FIND HIM.
WHO COULD SPARE SUCH A SUM TO AID US?
...
WHO INDEED? THIS PURSE... I ONCE OWNED A PURSE VERY MUCH LIKE THIS. BUT I LEFT IT WITH...
Julie's
TAT!
TAT!
THERE'S A SIGNAL FROM THE HARBOR!
EMMANUEL
STAFF OF MORREL & SON
JULIE'S FIANCÉ

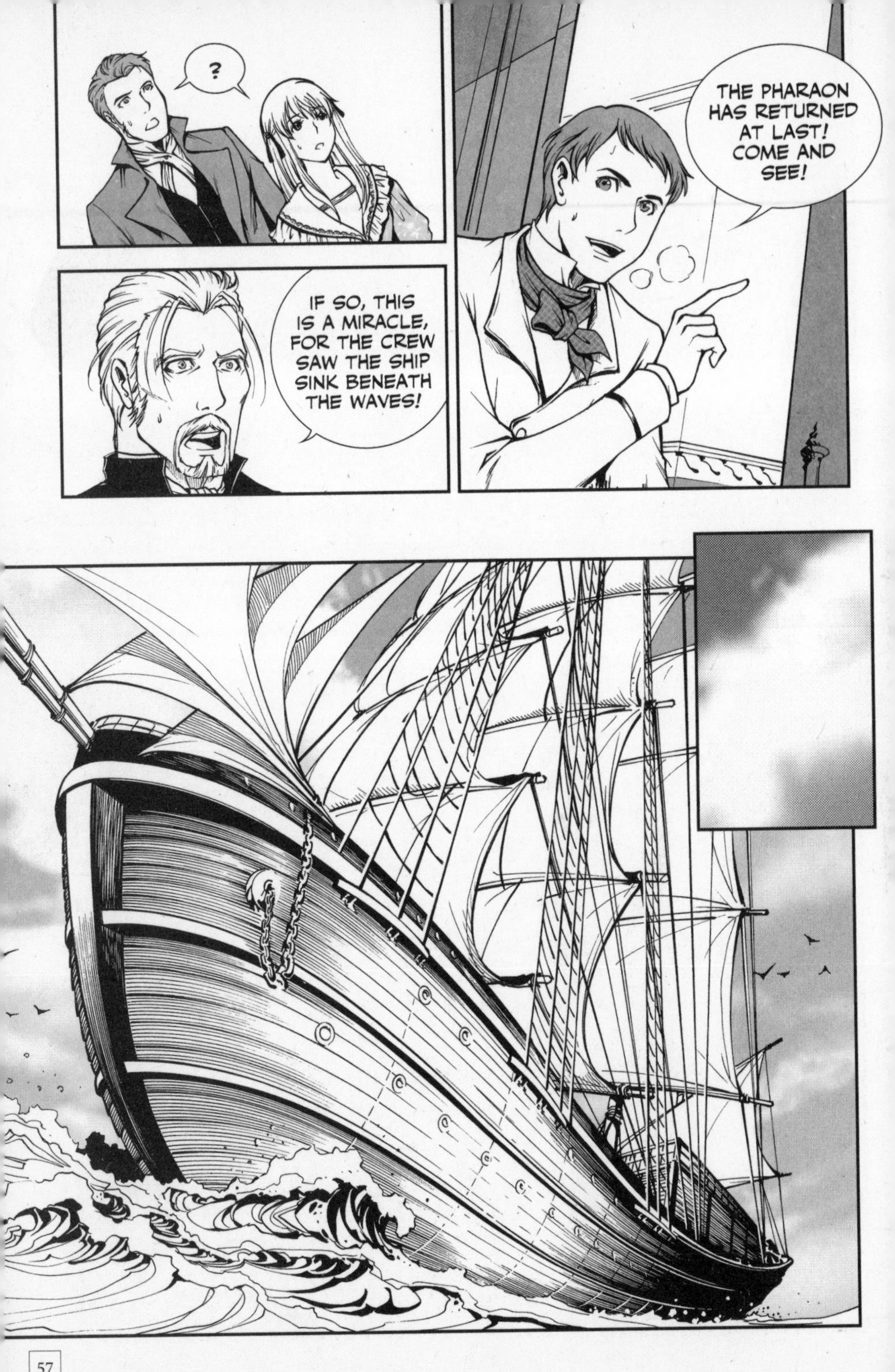
THE PHARAON HAS RETURNED AT LAST! COME AND SEE!
?
IF SO, THIS IS A MIRACLE, FOR THE CREW SAW THE SHIP SINK BENEATH THE WAVES!

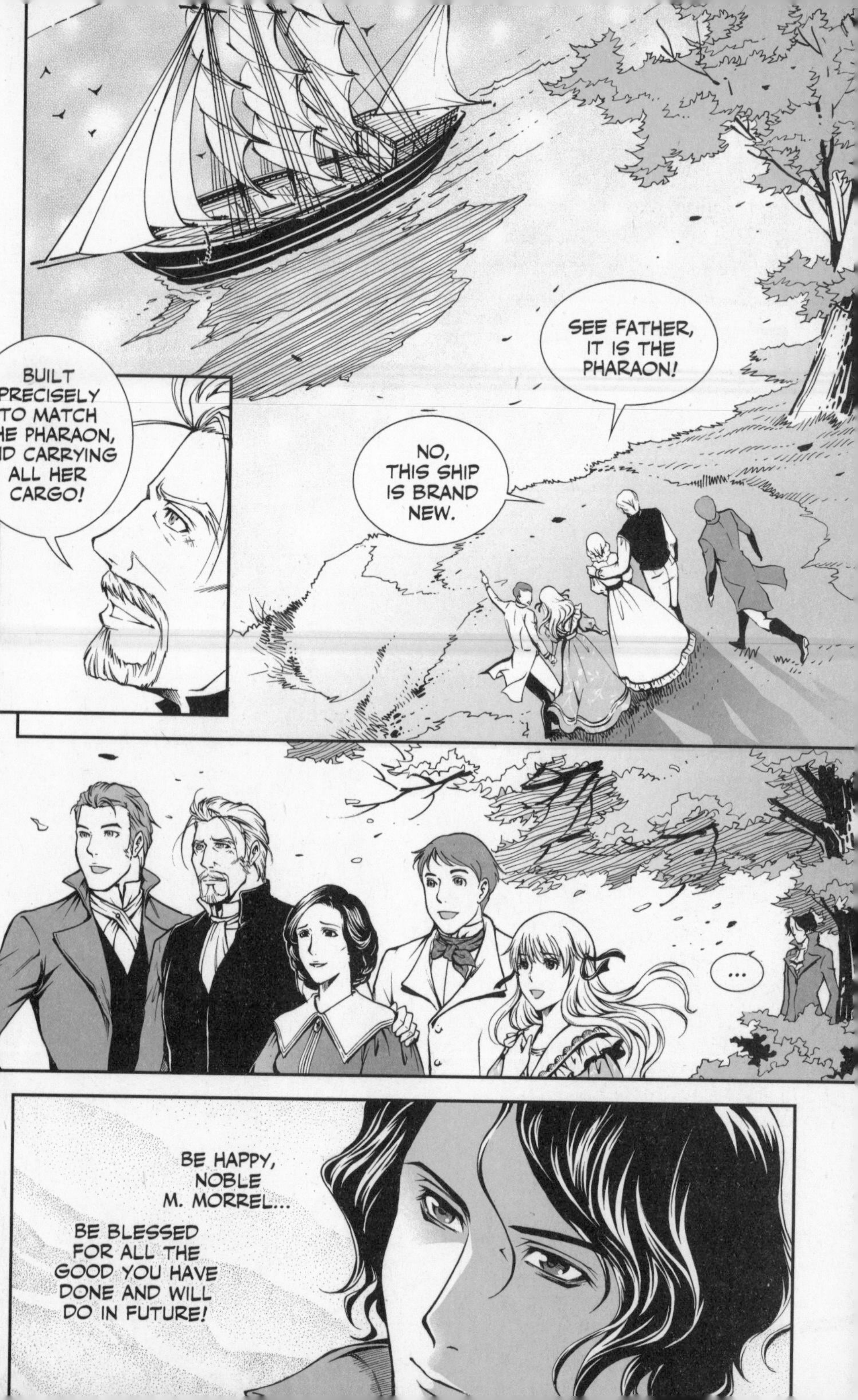
SEE FATHER, IT IS THE PHARAON!
NO, THIS SHIP IS BRAND NEW.
BUILT PRECISELY TO MATCH THE PHARAON, AND CARRYING ALL HER CARGO!
...
BE HAPPY, NOBLE M. MORREL...
BE BLESSED FOR ALL THE GOOD YOU HAVE DONE AND WILL DO IN FUTURE!

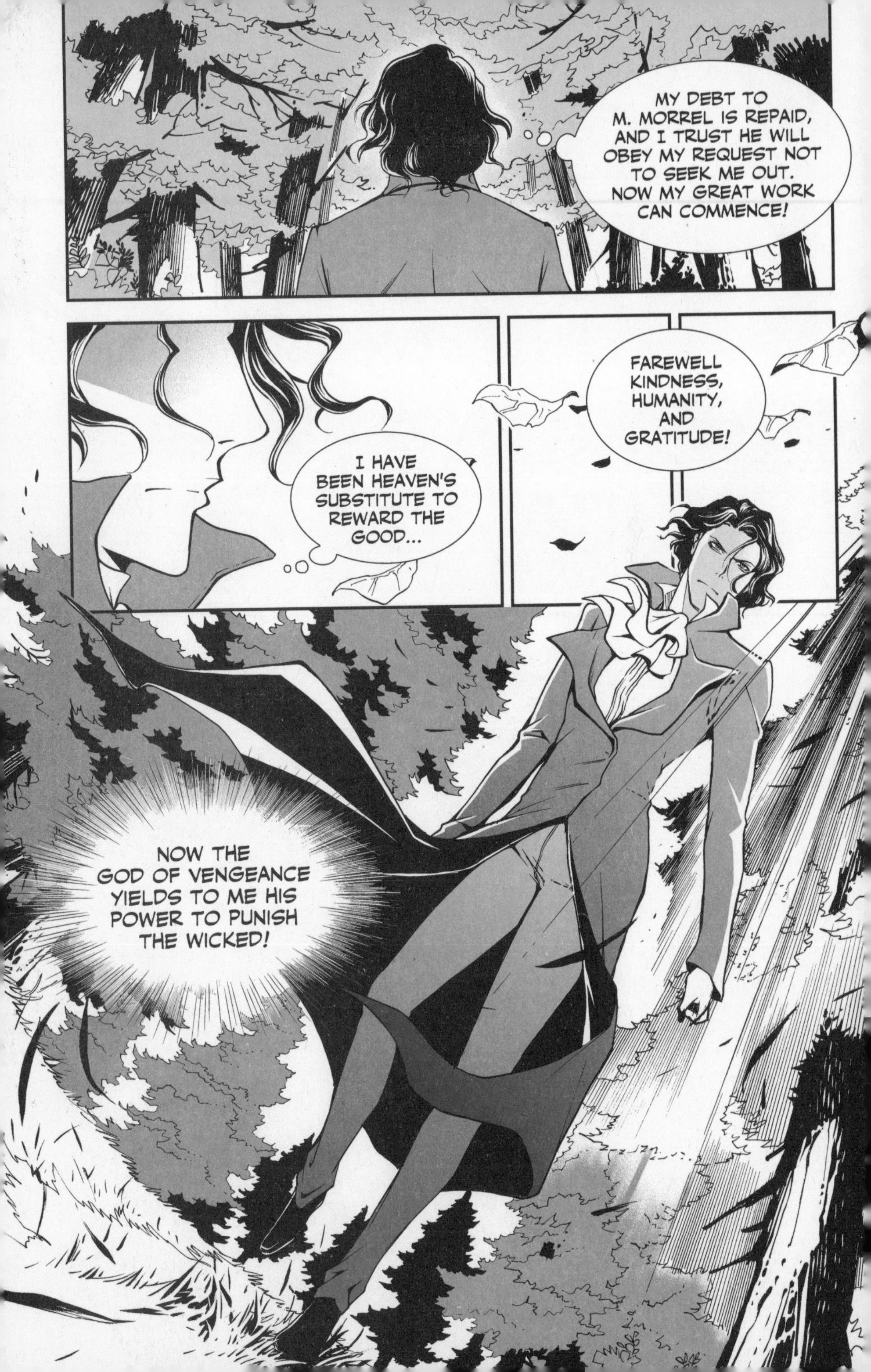
MY DEBT TO M. MORREL IS REPAID, AND I TRUST HE WILL OBEY MY REQUEST NOT TO SEEK ME OUT. NOW MY GREAT WORK CAN COMMENCE!
FAREWELL KINDNESS, HUMANITY, AND GRATITUDE!
I HAVE BEEN HEAVEN'S SUBSTITUTE TO REWARD THE GOOD...
NOW THE GOD OF VENGEANCE YIELDS TO ME HIS POWER TO PUNISH THE WICKED!

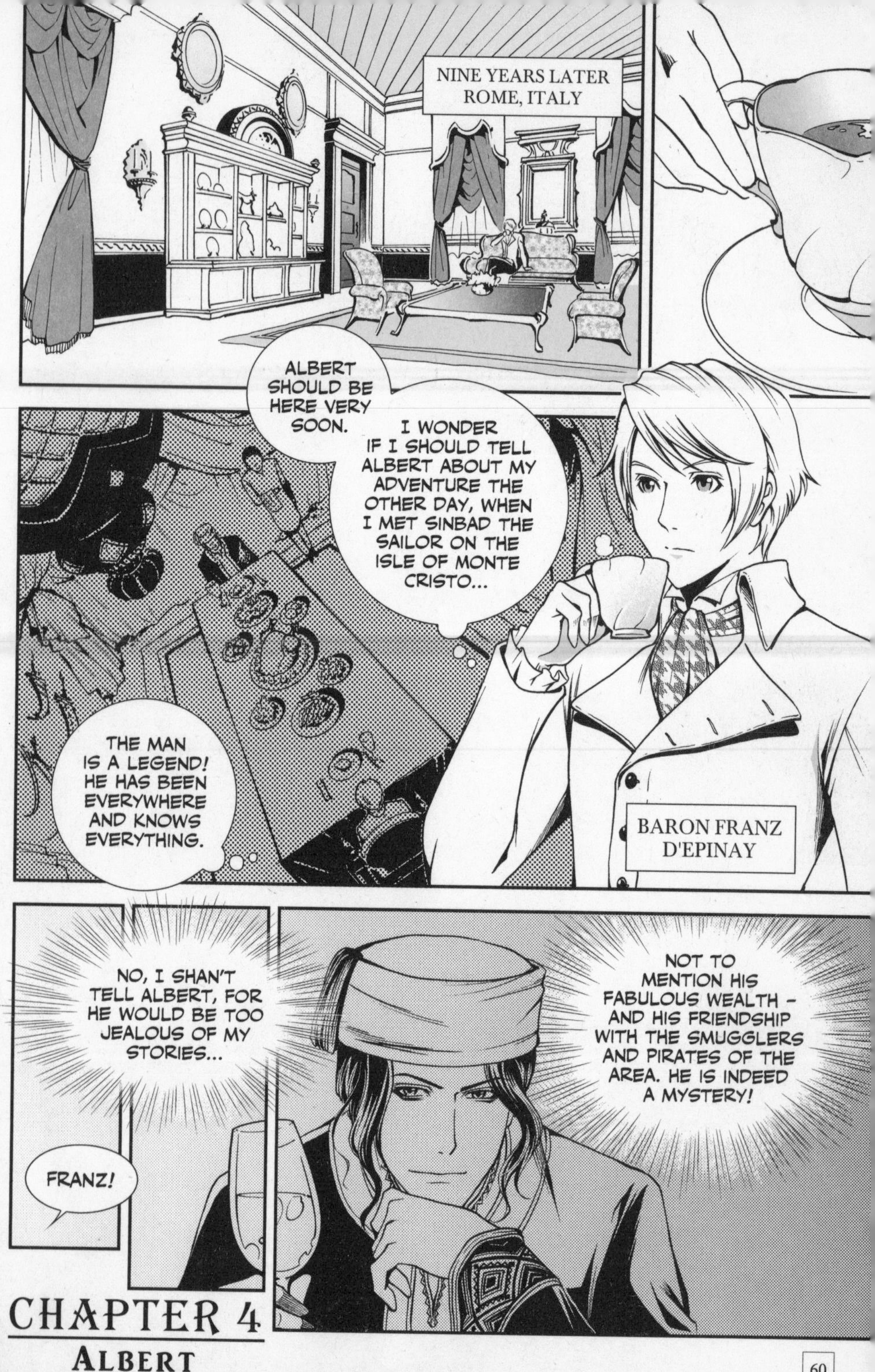
NINE YEARS LATER
ROME, ITALY
ALBERT SHOULD BE HERE VERY SOON.
I WONDER IF I SHOULD TELL ALBERT ABOUT MY ADVENTURE THE OTHER DAY, WHEN I MET SINBAD THE SAILOR ON THE ISLE OF MONTE CRISTO...
BARON FRANZ D'EPINAY
THE MAN IS A LEGEND! HE HAS BEEN EVERYWHERE AND KNOWS EVERYTHING.
NOT TO MENTION HIS FABULOUS WEALTH – AND HIS FRIENDSHIP WITH THE SMUGGLERS AND PIRATES OF THE AREA. HE IS INDEED A MYSTERY!
NO, I SHAN'T TELL ALBERT, FOR HE WOULD BE TOO JEALOUS OF MY STORIES...
FRANZ!

CHAPTER 4
ALBERT

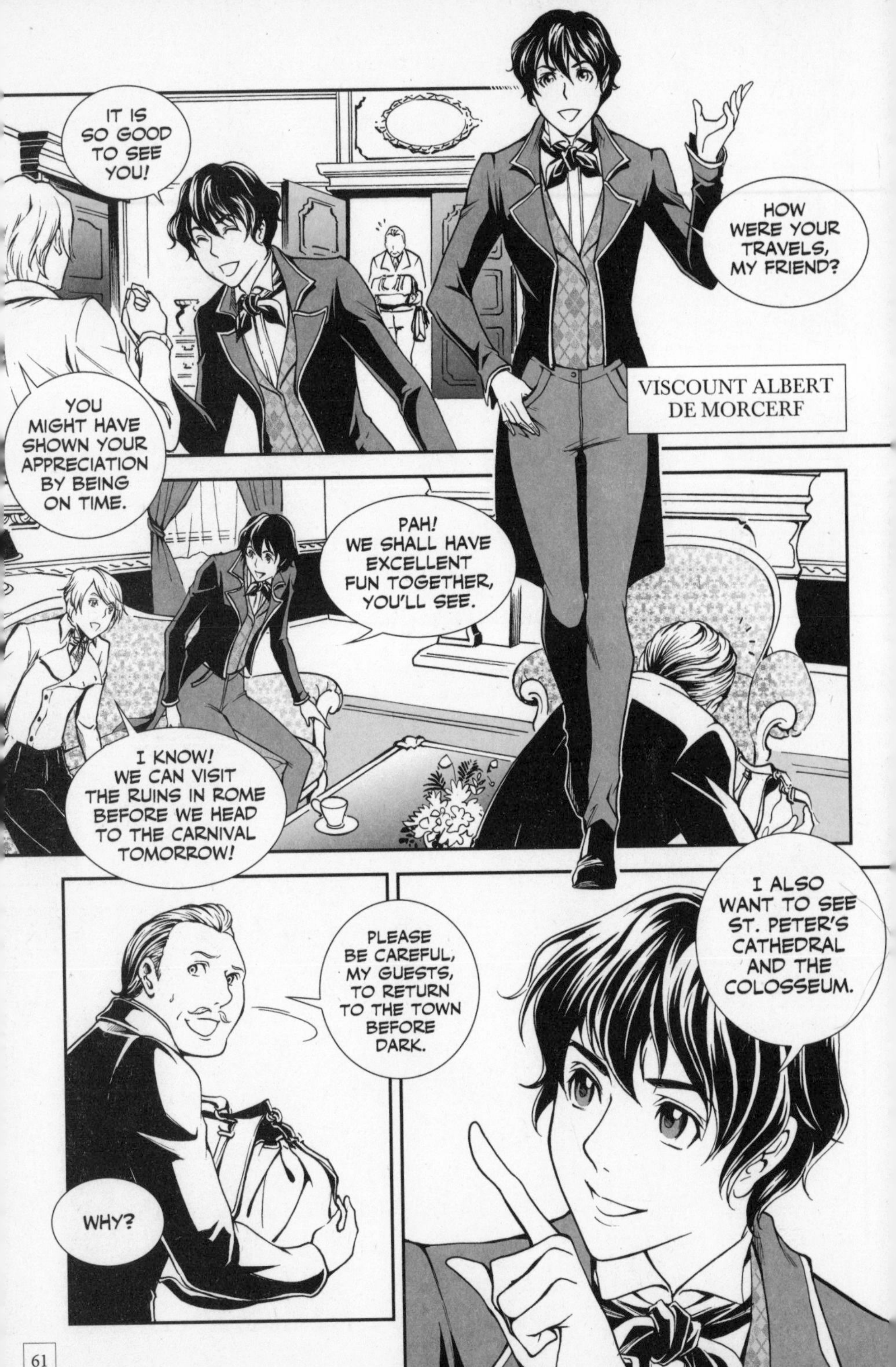
HOW WERE YOUR TRAVELS, MY FRIEND?
VISCOUNT ALBERT DE MORCERF
IT IS SO GOOD TO SEE YOU!
YOU MIGHT HAVE SHOWN YOUR APPRECIATION BY BEING ON TIME.
PAH! WE SHALL HAVE EXCELLENT FUN TOGETHER, YOU'LL SEE.
I KNOW! WE CAN VISIT THE RUINS IN ROME BEFORE WE HEAD TO THE CARNIVAL TOMORROW!
I ALSO WANT TO SEE ST. PETER'S CATHEDRAL AND THE COLOSSEUM.
PLEASE BE CAREFUL, MY GUESTS, TO RETURN TO THE TOWN BEFORE DARK.
WHY?

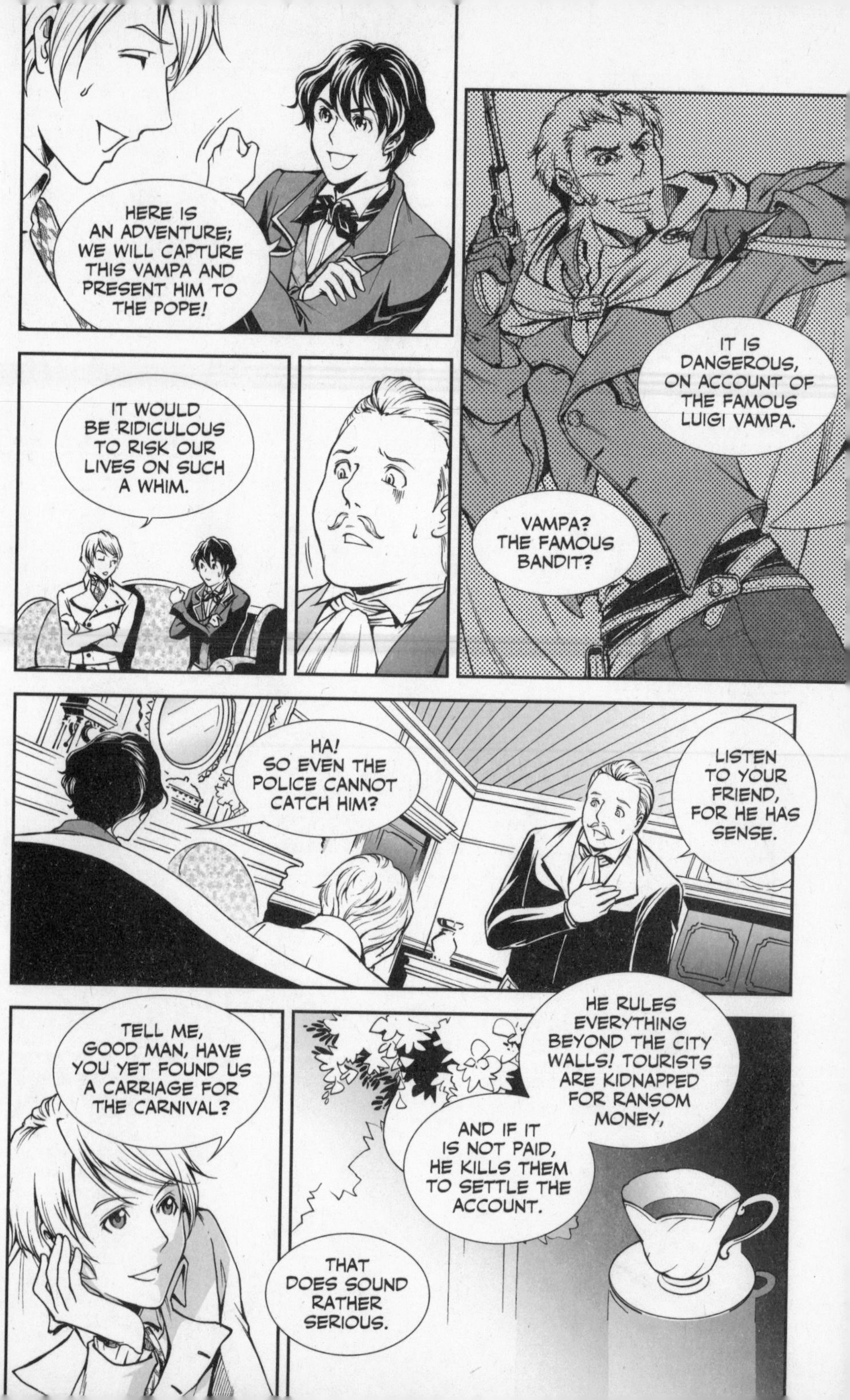
IT IS DANGEROUS, ON ACCOUNT OF THE FAMOUS LUIGI VAMPA.
VAMPA? THE FAMOUS BANDIT?
HERE IS AN ADVENTURE; WE WILL CAPTURE THIS VAMPA AND PRESENT HIM TO THE POPE!
IT WOULD BE RIDICULOUS TO RISK OUR LIVES ON SUCH A WHIM.
LISTEN TO YOUR FRIEND, FOR HE HAS SENSE.
HA! SO EVEN THE POLICE CANNOT CATCH HIM?
HE RULES EVERYTHING BEYOND THE CITY WALLS! TOURISTS ARE KIDNAPPED FOR RANSOM MONEY,
AND IF IT IS NOT PAID, HE KILLS THEM TO SETTLE THE ACCOUNT.
THAT DOES SOUND RATHER SERIOUS.
TELL ME, GOOD MAN, HAVE YOU YET FOUND US A CARRIAGE FOR THE CARNIVAL?

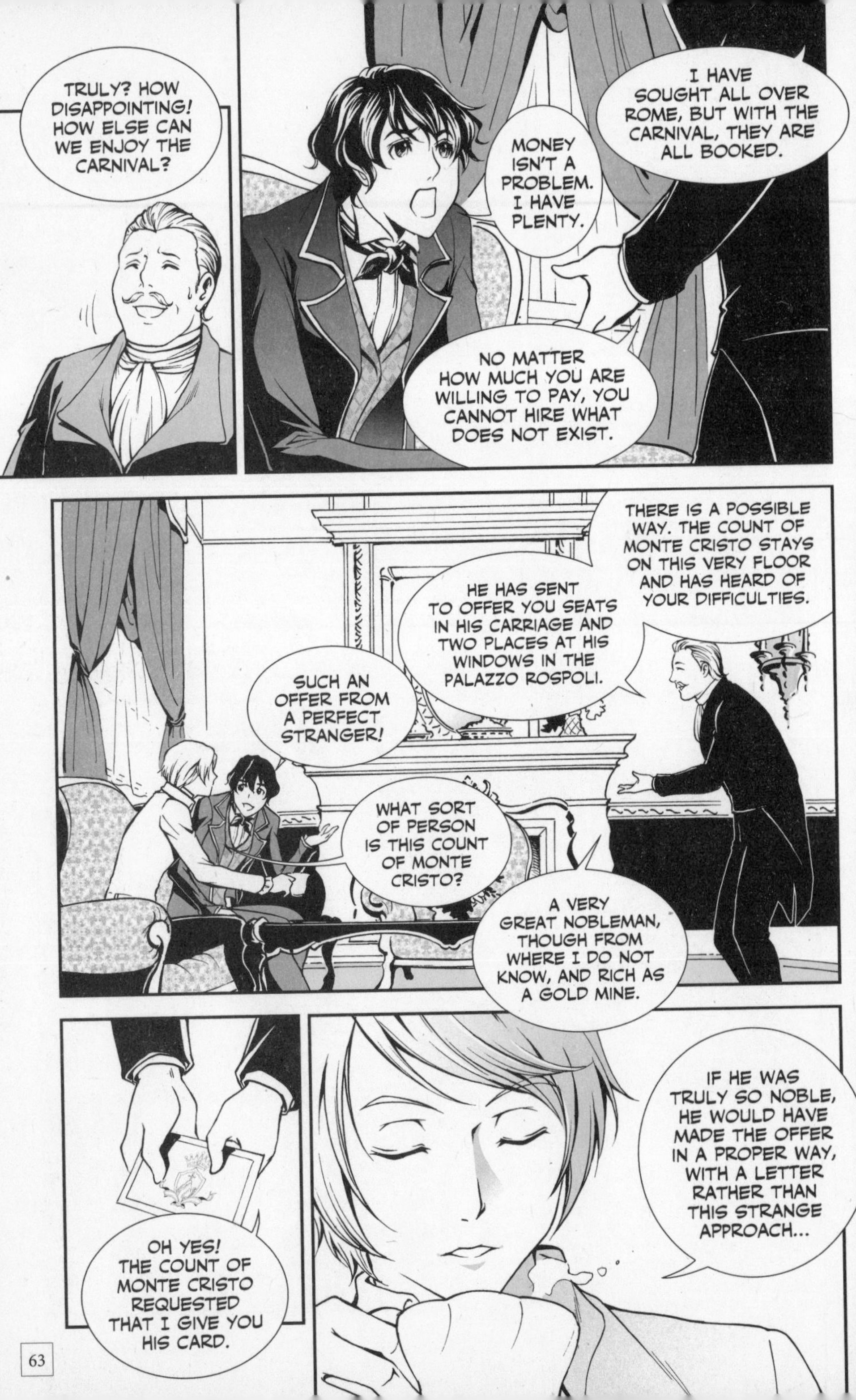
I HAVE SOUGHT ALL OVER ROME, BUT WITH THE CARNIVAL, THEY ARE ALL BOOKED.
MONEY ISN'T A PROBLEM. I HAVE PLENTY.
NO MATTER HOW MUCH YOU ARE WILLING TO PAY, YOU CANNOT HIRE WHAT DOES NOT EXIST.
TRULY? HOW DISAPPOINTING! HOW ELSE CAN WE ENJOY THE CARNIVAL?
THERE IS A POSSIBLE WAY. THE COUNT OF MONTE CRISTO STAYS ON THIS VERY FLOOR AND HAS HEARD OF YOUR DIFFICULTIES.
HE HAS SENT TO OFFER YOU SEATS IN HIS CARRIAGE AND TWO PLACES AT HIS WINDOWS IN THE PALAZZO ROSPOLI.
SUCH AN OFFER FROM A PERFECT STRANGER!
WHAT SORT OF PERSON IS THIS COUNT OF MONTE CRISTO?
A VERY GREAT NOBLEMAN, THOUGH FROM WHERE I DO NOT KNOW, AND RICH AS A GOLD MINE.
IF HE WAS TRULY SO NOBLE, HE WOULD HAVE MADE THE OFFER IN A PROPER WAY, WITH A LETTER RATHER THAN THIS STRANGE APPROACH...
OH YES! THE COUNT OF MONTE CRISTO REQUESTED THAT I GIVE YOU HIS CARD.

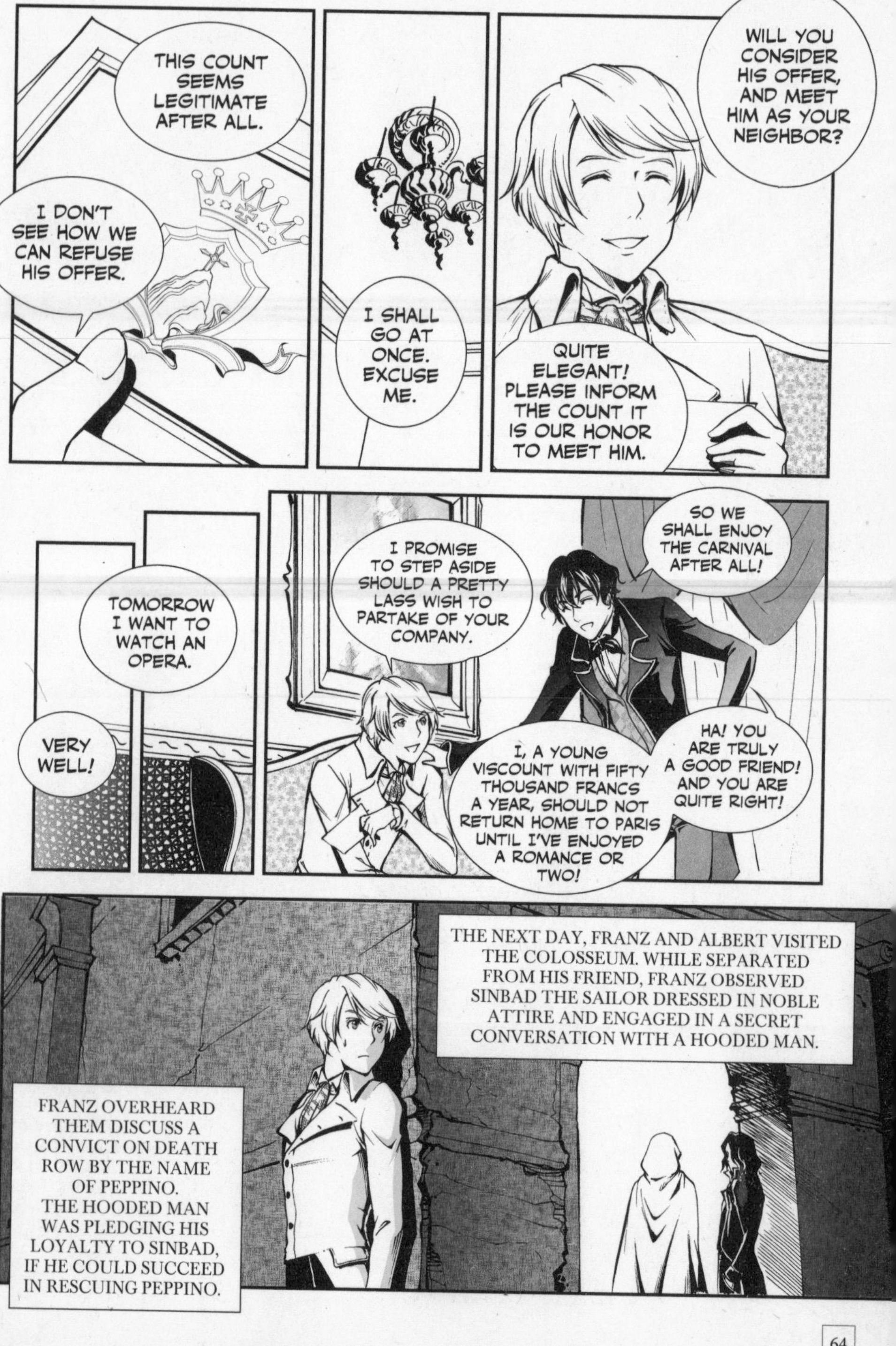
WILL YOU CONSIDER HIS OFFER, AND MEET HIM AS YOUR NEIGHBOR?
QUITE ELEGANT! PLEASE INFORM THE COUNT IT IS OUR HONOR TO MEET HIM.
I SHALL GO AT ONCE. EXCUSE ME.
THIS COUNT SEEMS LEGITIMATE AFTER ALL.
I DON'T SEE HOW WE CAN REFUSE HIS OFFER.
SO WE SHALL ENJOY THE CARNIVAL AFTER ALL!
I PROMISE TO STEP ASIDE SHOULD A PRETTY LASS WISH TO PARTAKE OF YOUR COMPANY.
HA! YOU ARE TRULY A GOOD FRIEND! AND YOU ARE QUITE RIGHT!
I, A YOUNG VISCOUNT WITH FIFTY THOUSAND FRANCS A YEAR, SHOULD NOT RETURN HOME TO PARIS UNTIL I'VE ENJOYED A ROMANCE OR TWO!
TOMORROW I WANT TO WATCH AN OPERA.
VERY WELL!
THE NEXT DAY, FRANZ AND ALBERT VISITED THE COLOSSEUM. WHILE SEPARATED FROM HIS FRIEND, FRANZ OBSERVED SINBAD THE SAILOR DRESSED IN NOBLE ATTIRE AND ENGAGED IN A SECRET CONVERSATION WITH A HOODED MAN.
FRANZ OVERHEARD THEM DISCUSS A CONVICT ON DEATH ROW BY THE NAME OF PEPPINO. THE HOODED MAN WAS PLEDGING HIS LOYALTY TO SINBAD, IF HE COULD SUCCEED IN RESCUING PEPPINO.

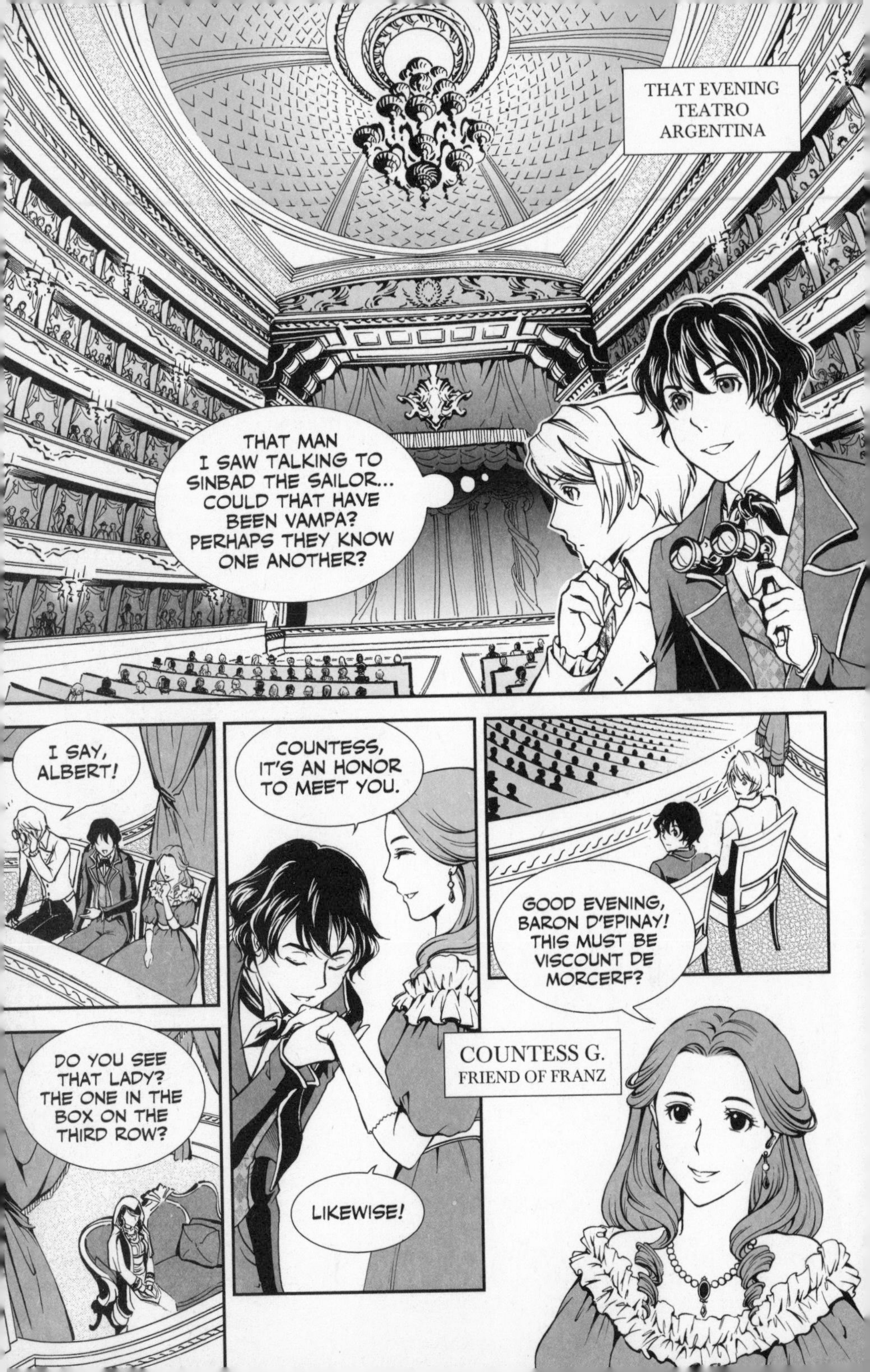
THAT EVENING
TEATRO
ARGENTINA
THAT MAN I SAW TALKING TO SINBAD THE SAILOR... COULD THAT HAVE BEEN VAMPA? PERHAPS THEY KNOW ONE ANOTHER?
GOOD EVENING, BARON D'EPINAY! THIS MUST BE VISCOUNT DE MORCERF?
COUNTESS G.
FRIEND OF FRANZ
COUNTESS, IT'S AN HONOR TO MEET YOU.
LIKEWISE!
I SAY, ALBERT!
DO YOU SEE THAT LADY? THE ONE IN THE BOX ON THE THIRD ROW?

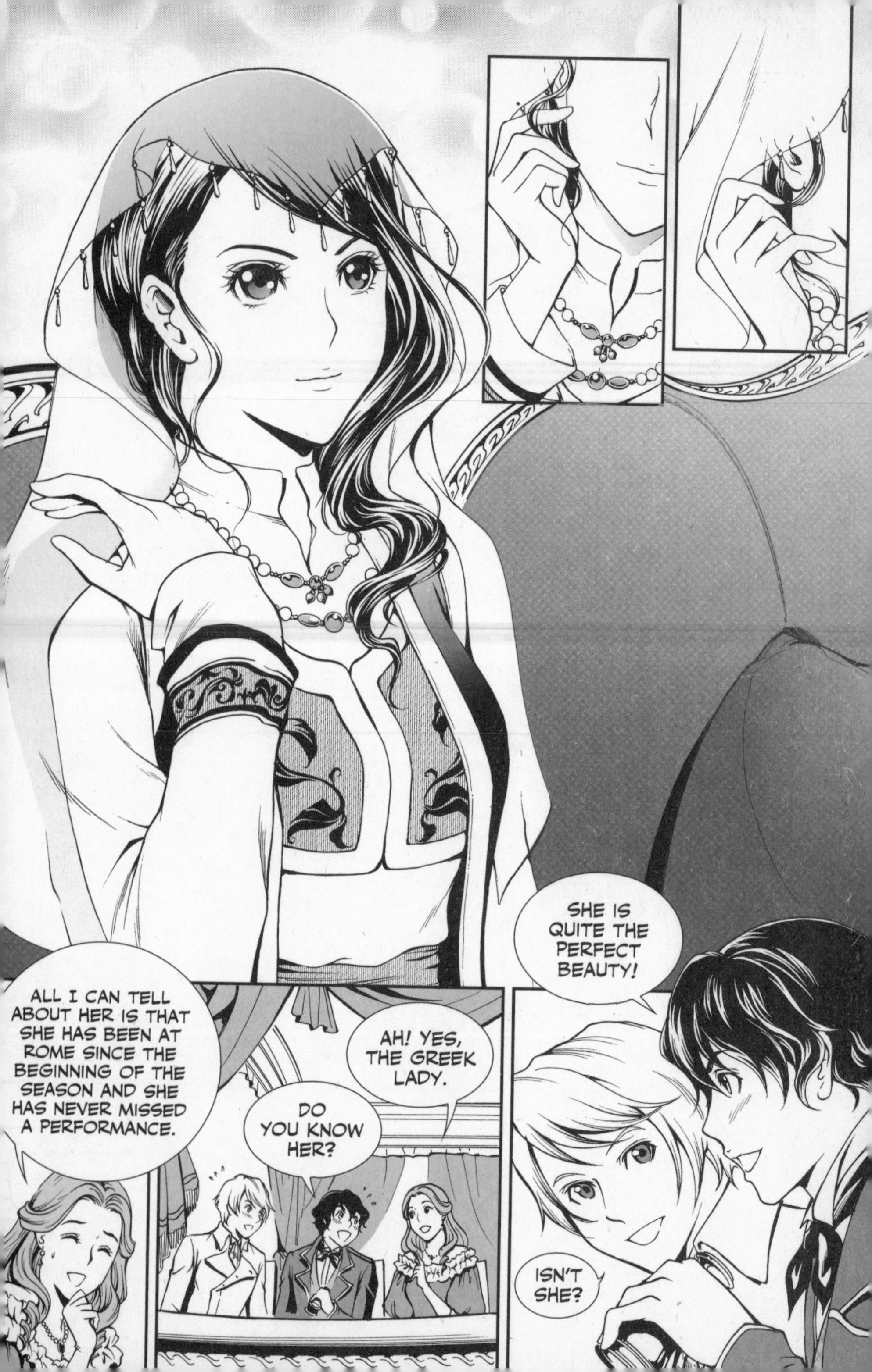
SHE IS QUITE THE PERFECT BEAUTY!
ISN'T SHE?
AH! YES, THE GREEK LADY.
DO YOU KNOW HER?
ALL I CAN TELL ABOUT HER IS THAT SHE HAS BEEN AT ROME SINCE THE BEGINNING OF THE SEASON AND SHE HAS NEVER MISSED A PERFORMANCE.

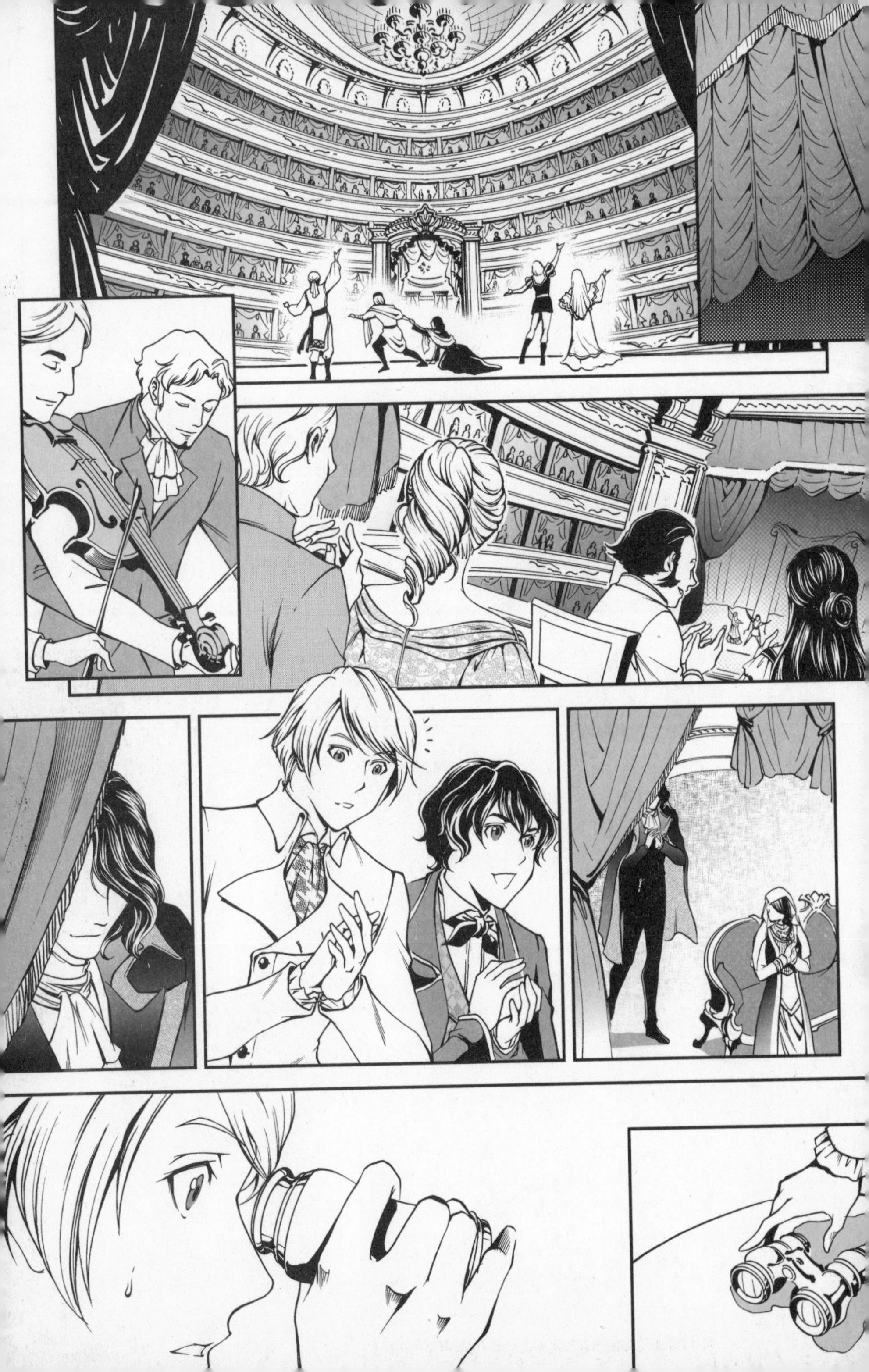

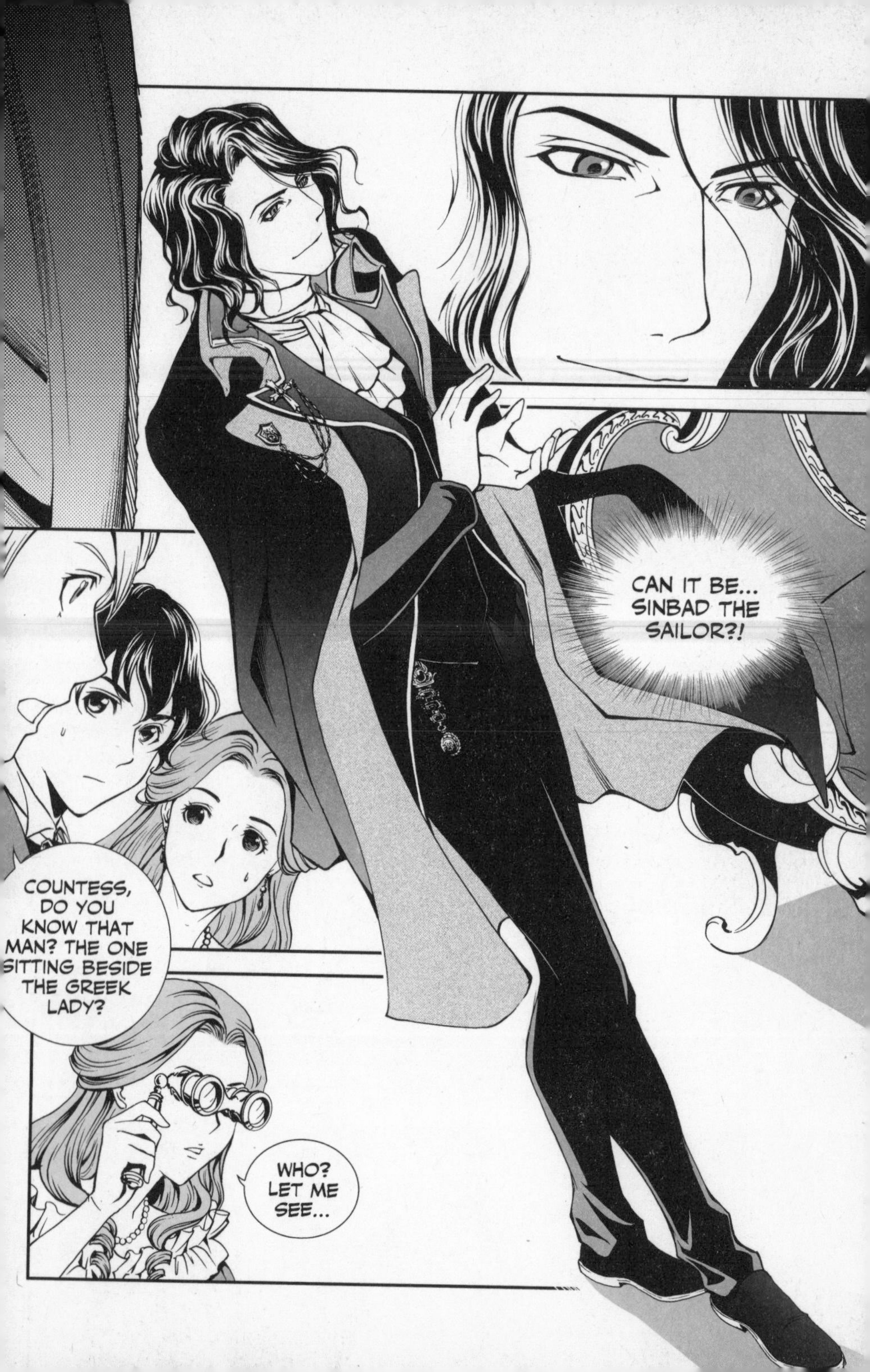
CAN IT BE... SINBAD THE SAILOR?!
COUNTESS, DO YOU KNOW THAT MAN? THE ONE SITTING BESIDE THE GREEK LADY?
WHO? LET ME SEE...

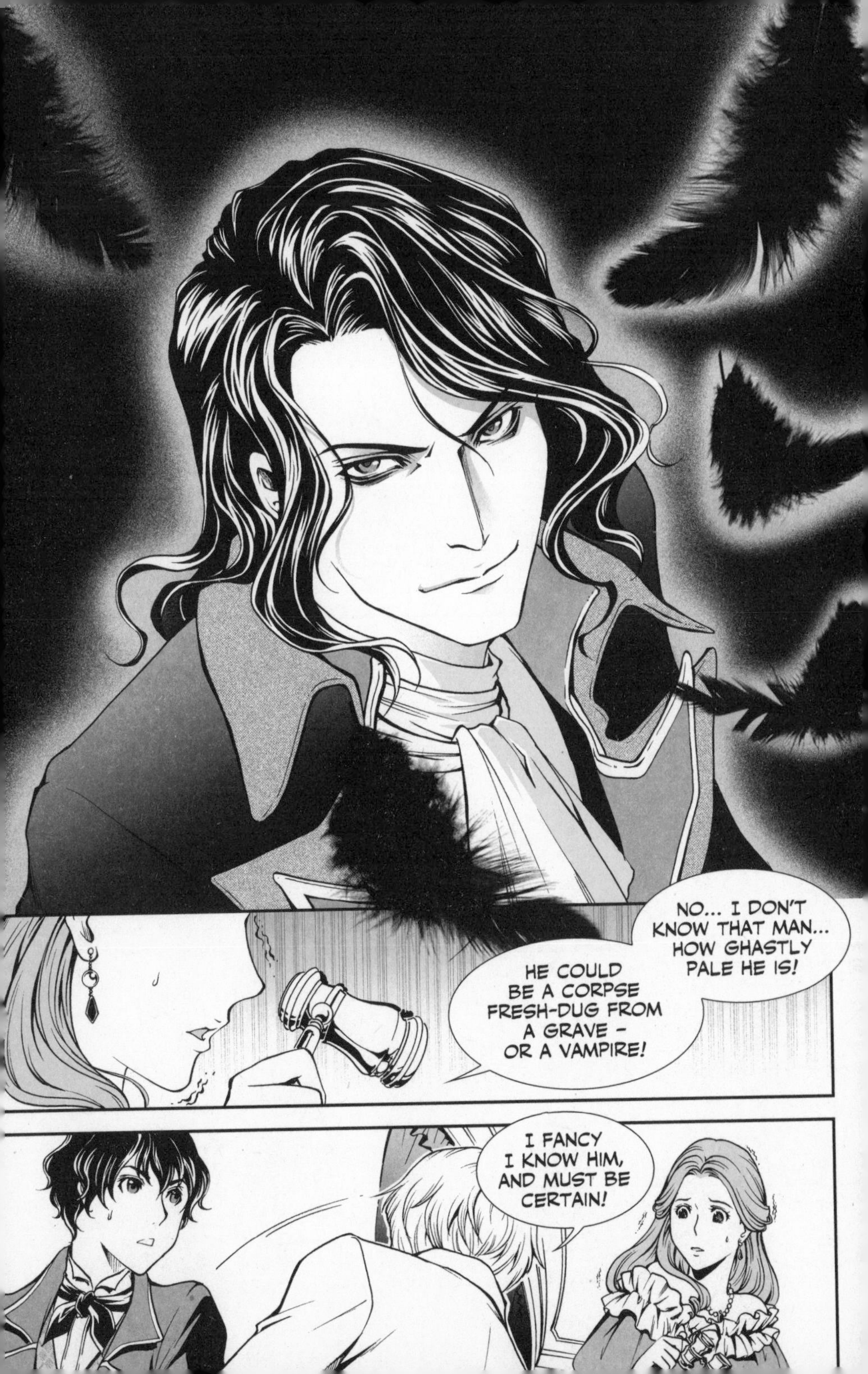
NO... I DON'T KNOW THAT MAN... HOW GHASTLY PALE HE IS!
HE COULD BE A CORPSE FRESH-DUG FROM A GRAVE - OR A VAMPIRE!
I FANCY I KNOW HIM, AND MUST BE CERTAIN!

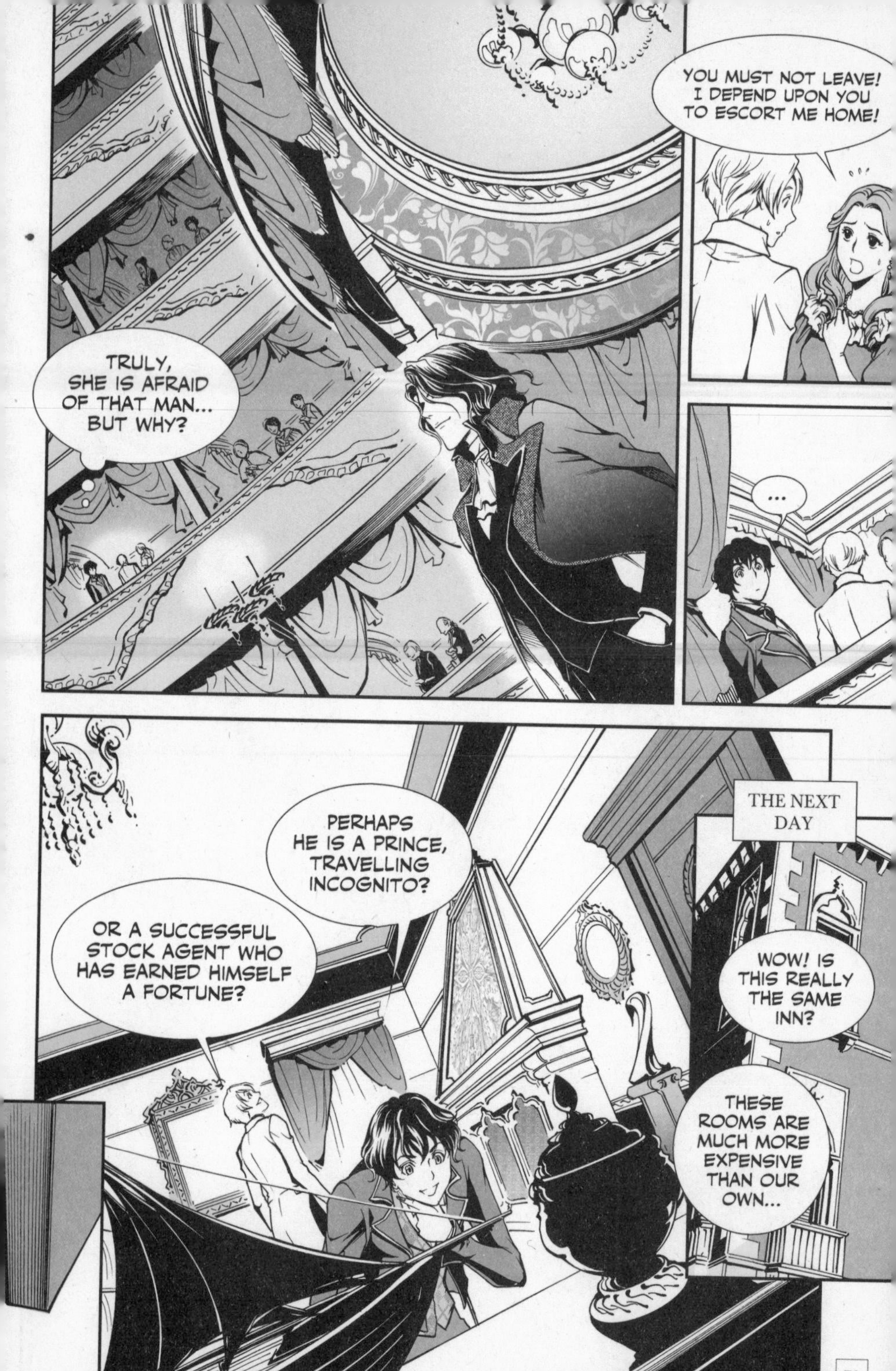
YOU MUST NOT LEAVE! I DEPEND UPON YOU TO ESCORT ME HOME!
...
TRULY, SHE IS AFRAID OF THAT MAN... BUT WHY?
THE NEXT DAY
WOW! IS THIS REALLY THE SAME INN?
THESE ROOMS ARE MUCH MORE EXPENSIVE THAN OUR OWN...
PERHAPS HE IS A PRINCE, TRAVELLING INCOGNITO?
OR A SUCCESSFUL STOCK AGENT WHO HAS EARNED HIMSELF A FORTUNE?

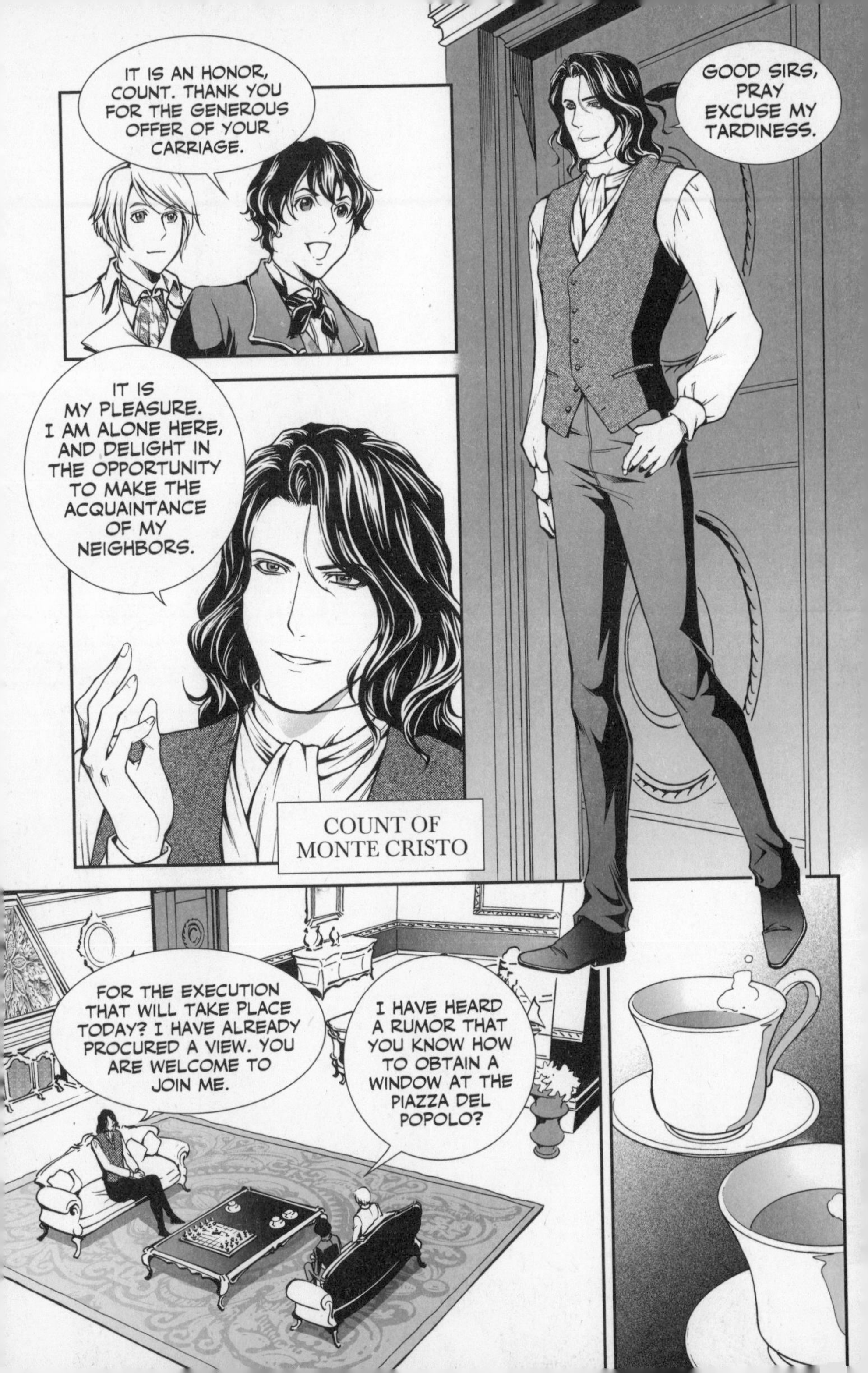
GOOD SIRS, PRAY EXCUSE MY TARDINESS.
IT IS AN HONOR, COUNT. THANK YOU FOR THE GENEROUS OFFER OF YOUR CARRIAGE.
IT IS MY PLEASURE. I AM ALONE HERE, AND DELIGHT IN THE OPPORTUNITY TO MAKE THE ACQUAINTANCE OF MY NEIGHBORS.
COUNT OF MONTE CRISTO
I HAVE HEARD A RUMOR THAT YOU KNOW HOW TO OBTAIN A WINDOW AT THE PIAZZA DEL POPOLO?
FOR THE EXECUTION THAT WILL TAKE PLACE TODAY? I HAVE ALREADY PROCURED A VIEW. YOU ARE WELCOME TO JOIN ME.

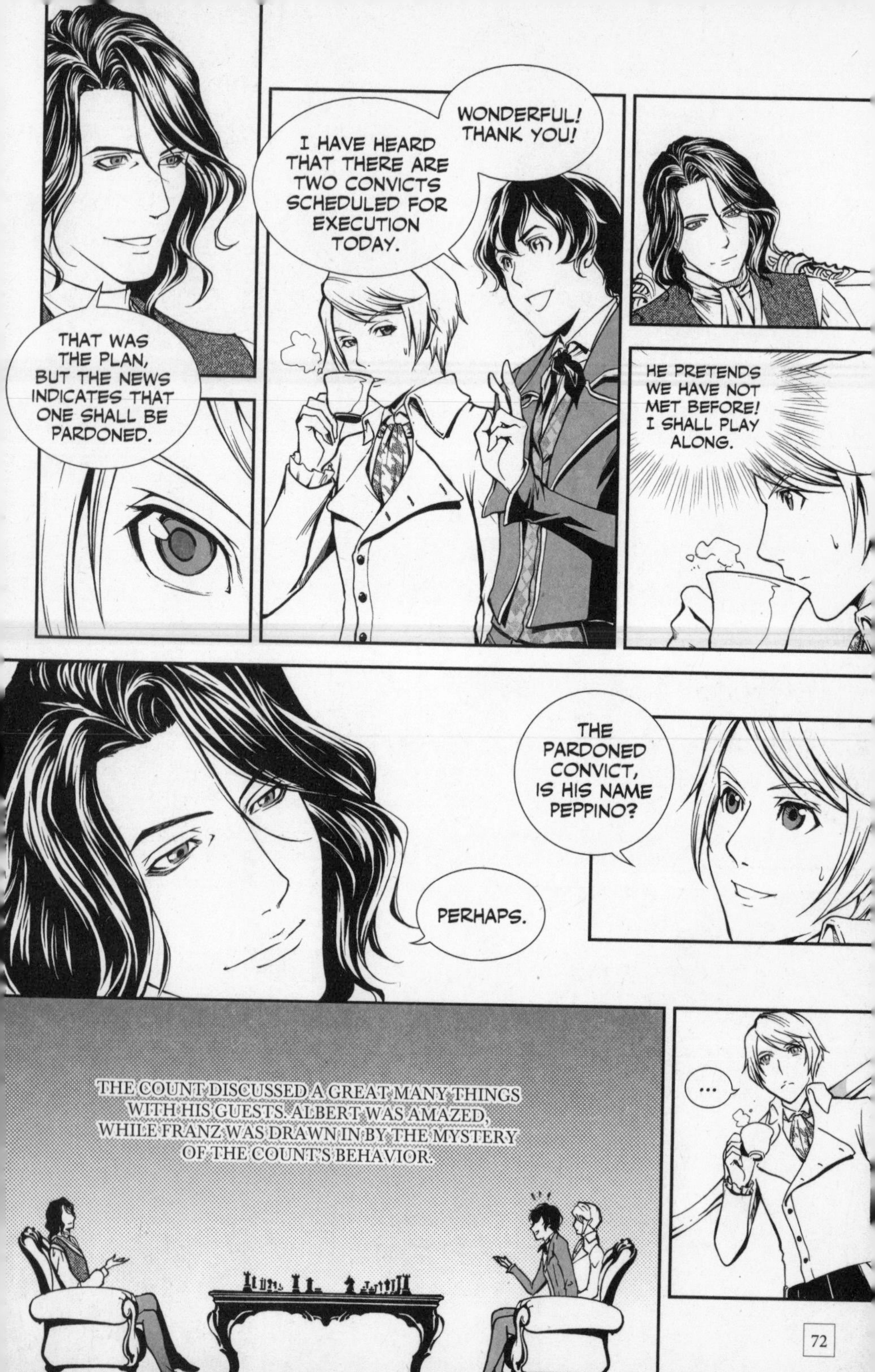
HE PRETENDS WE HAVE NOT MET BEFORE! I SHALL PLAY ALONG.
WONDERFUL! THANK YOU!
I HAVE HEARD THAT THERE ARE TWO CONVICTS SCHEDULED FOR EXECUTION TODAY.
THAT WAS THE PLAN, BUT THE NEWS INDICATES THAT ONE SHALL BE PARDONED.
THE PARDONED CONVICT, IS HIS NAME PEPPINO?
PERHAPS.
...
THE COUNT DISCUSSED A GREAT MANY THINGS WITH HIS GUESTS. ALBERT WAS AMAZED, WHILE FRANZ WAS DRAWN IN BY THE MYSTERY OF THE COUNT'S BEHAVIOR.

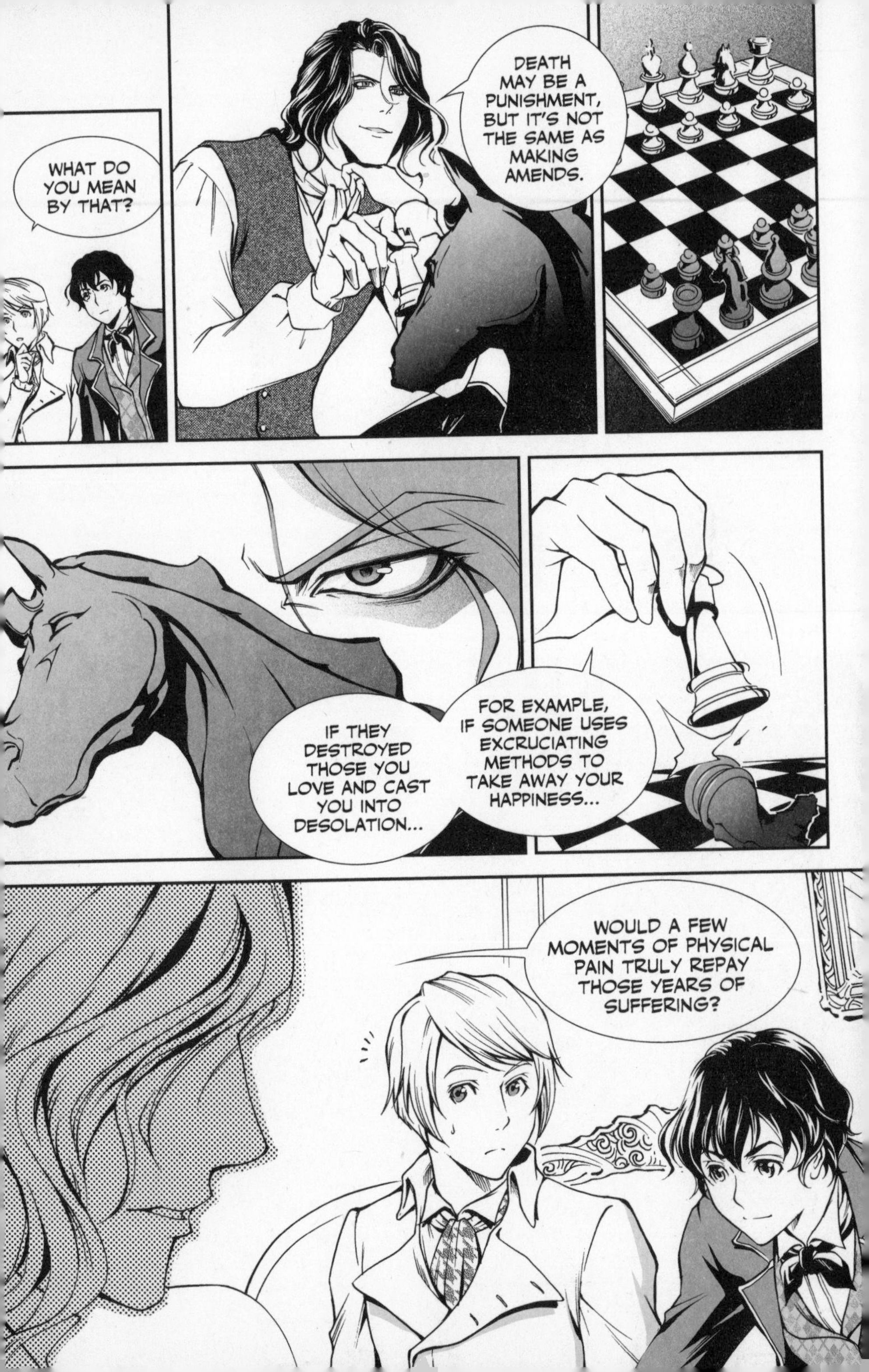
DEATH MAY BE A PUNISHMENT, BUT IT'S NOT THE SAME AS MAKING AMENDS.
WHAT DO YOU MEAN BY THAT?
FOR EXAMPLE, IF SOMEONE USES EXCRUCIATING METHODS TO TAKE AWAY YOUR HAPPINESS...
IF THEY DESTROYED THOSE YOU LOVE AND CAST YOU INTO DESOLATION...
WOULD A FEW MOMENTS OF PHYSICAL PAIN TRULY REPAY THOSE YEARS OF SUFFERING?

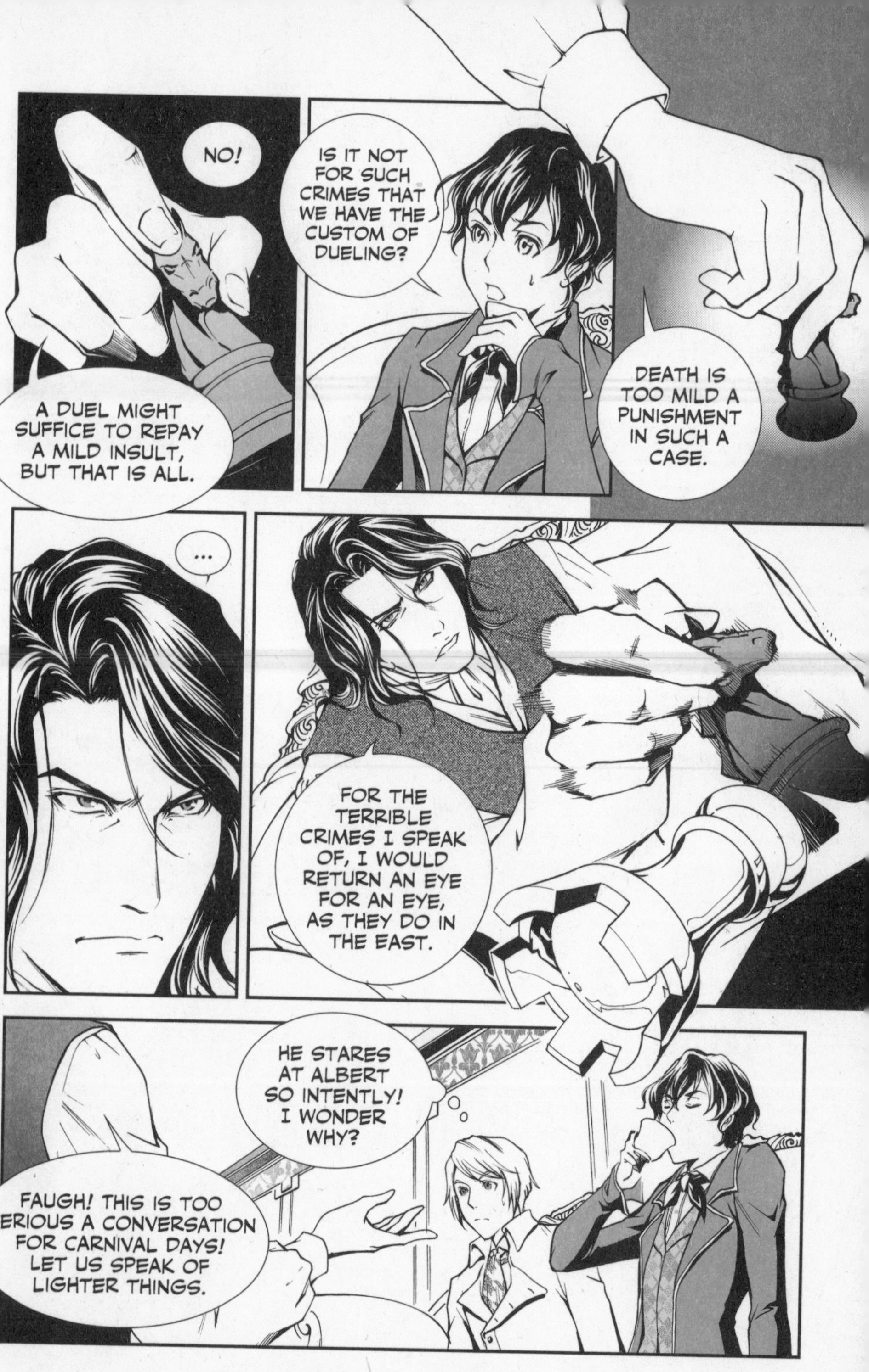
IS IT NOT FOR SUCH CRIMES THAT WE HAVE THE CUSTOM OF DUELING?
NO!
A DUEL MIGHT SUFFICE TO REPAY A MILD INSULT, BUT THAT IS ALL.
DEATH IS TOO MILD A PUNISHMENT IN SUCH A CASE.
FOR THE TERRIBLE CRIMES I SPEAK OF, I WOULD RETURN AN EYE FOR AN EYE, AS THEY DO IN THE EAST.
...
HE STARES AT ALBERT SO INTENTLY! I WONDER WHY?
FAUGH! THIS IS TOO SERIOUS A CONVERSATION FOR CARNIVAL DAYS! LET US SPEAK OF LIGHTER THINGS.

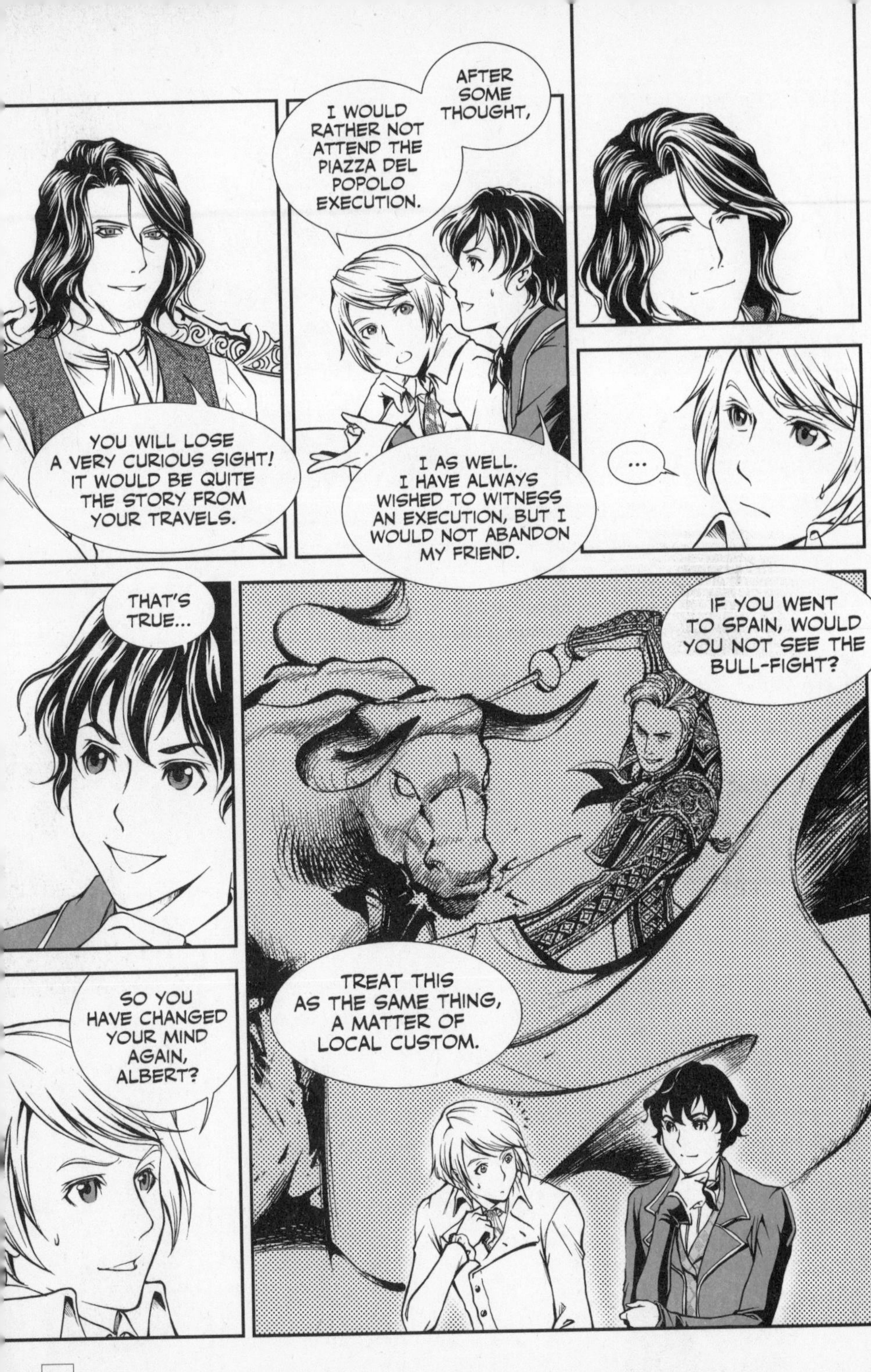
...
AFTER SOME THOUGHT,
I WOULD RATHER NOT ATTEND THE PIAZZA DEL POPOLO EXECUTION.
I AS WELL. I HAVE ALWAYS WISHED TO WITNESS AN EXECUTION, BUT I WOULD NOT ABANDON MY FRIEND.
YOU WILL LOSE A VERY CURIOUS SIGHT! IT WOULD BE QUITE THE STORY FROM YOUR TRAVELS.
IF YOU WENT TO SPAIN, WOULD YOU NOT SEE THE BULL-FIGHT?
TREAT THIS AS THE SAME THING, A MATTER OF LOCAL CUSTOM.
THAT'S TRUE...
SO YOU HAVE CHANGED YOUR MIND AGAIN, ALBERT?

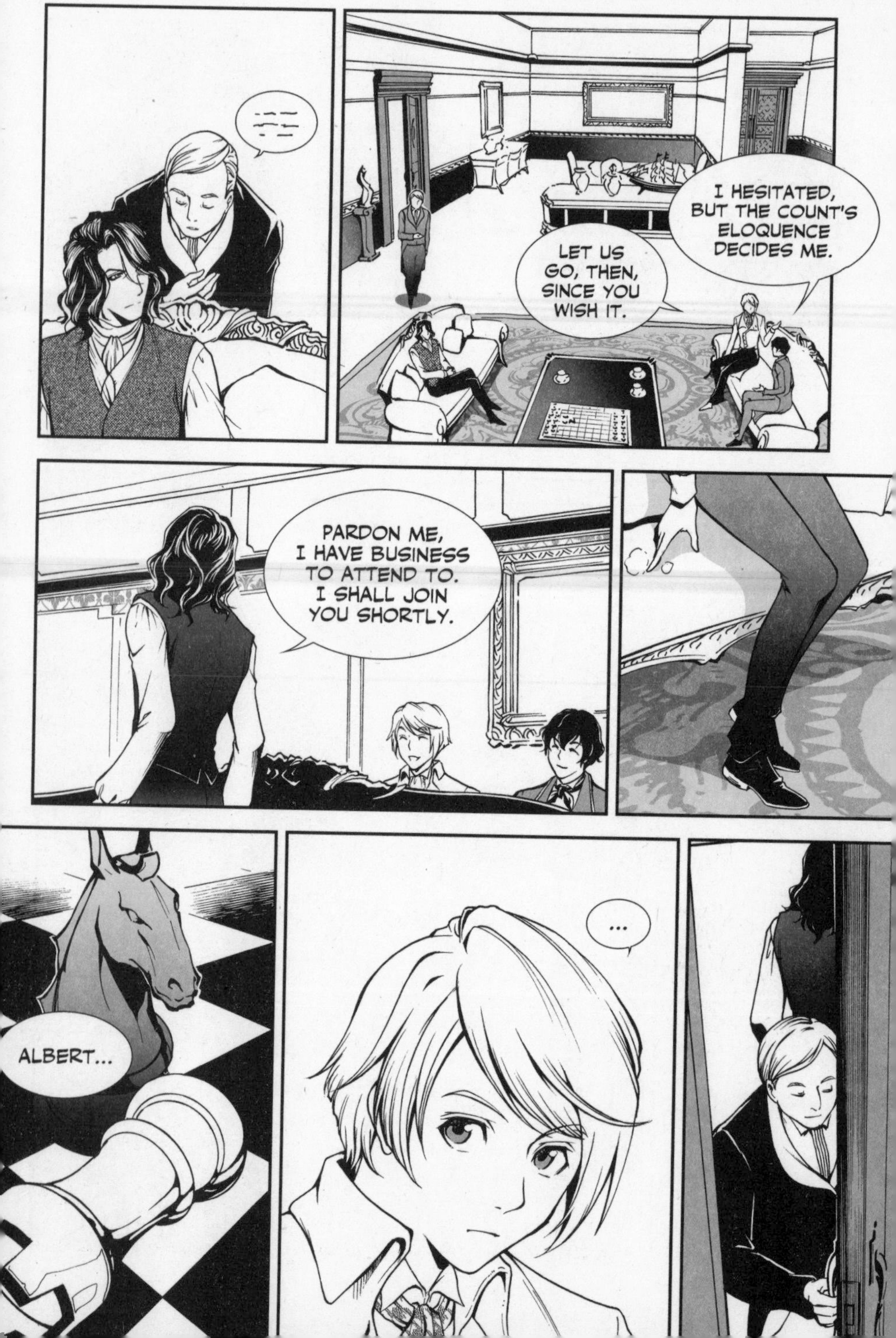
I HESITATED, BUT THE COUNT'S ELOQUENCE DECIDES ME.
LET US GO, THEN, SINCE YOU WISH IT.
PARDON ME, I HAVE BUSINESS TO ATTEND TO. I SHALL JOIN YOU SHORTLY.
...
ALBERT...

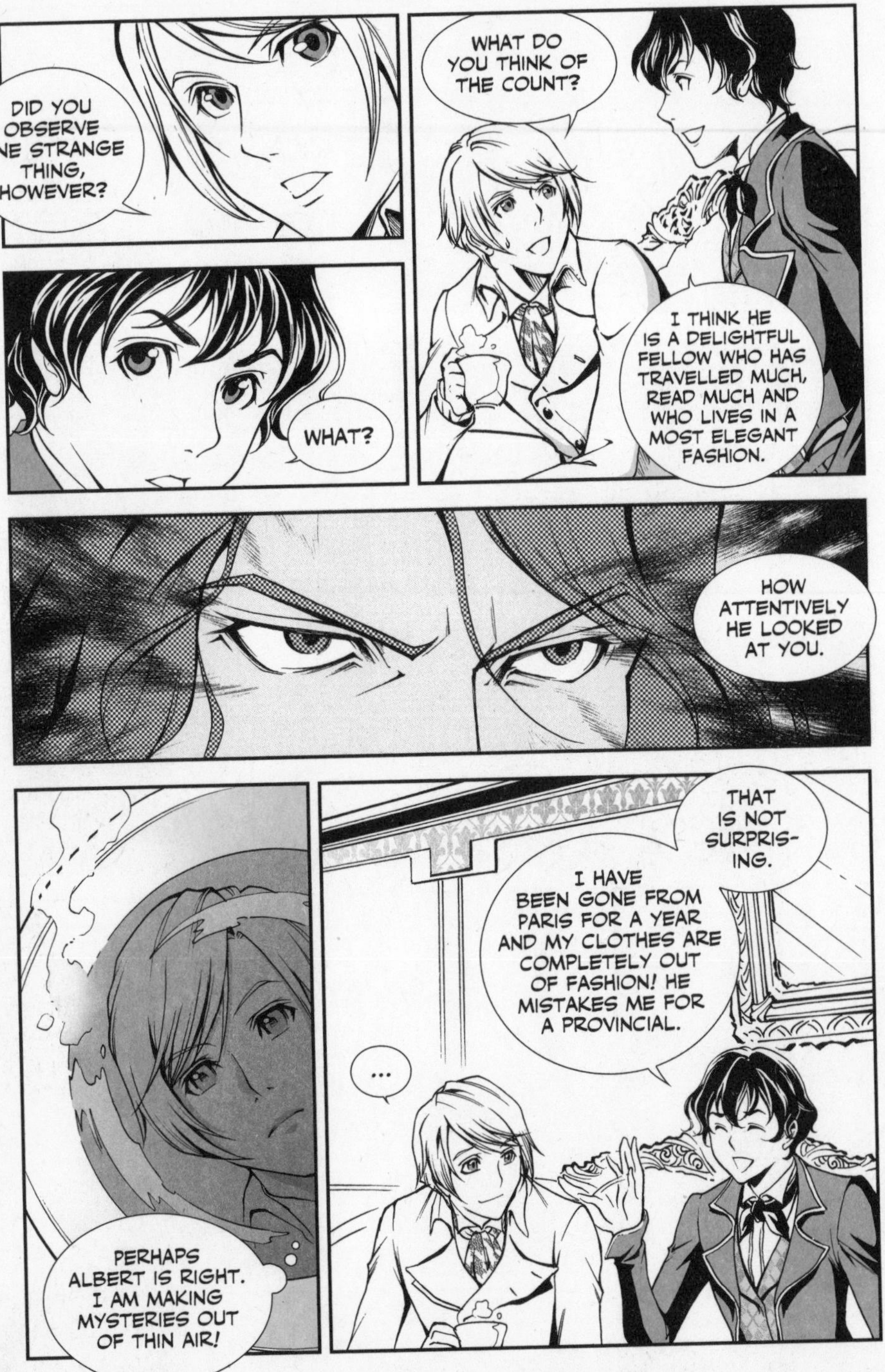
WHAT DO YOU THINK OF THE COUNT?
I THINK HE IS A DELIGHTFUL FELLOW WHO HAS TRAVELLED MUCH, READ MUCH AND WHO LIVES IN A MOST ELEGANT FASHION.
DID YOU OBSERVE ONE STRANGE THING, HOWEVER?
WHAT?
HOW ATTENTIVELY HE LOOKED AT YOU.
THAT IS NOT SURPRIS-ING.
I HAVE BEEN GONE FROM PARIS FOR A YEAR AND MY CLOTHES ARE COMPLETELY OUT OF FASHION! HE MISTAKES ME FOR A PROVINCIAL.
...
PERHAPS ALBERT IS RIGHT. I AM MAKING MYSTERIES OUT OF THIN AIR!

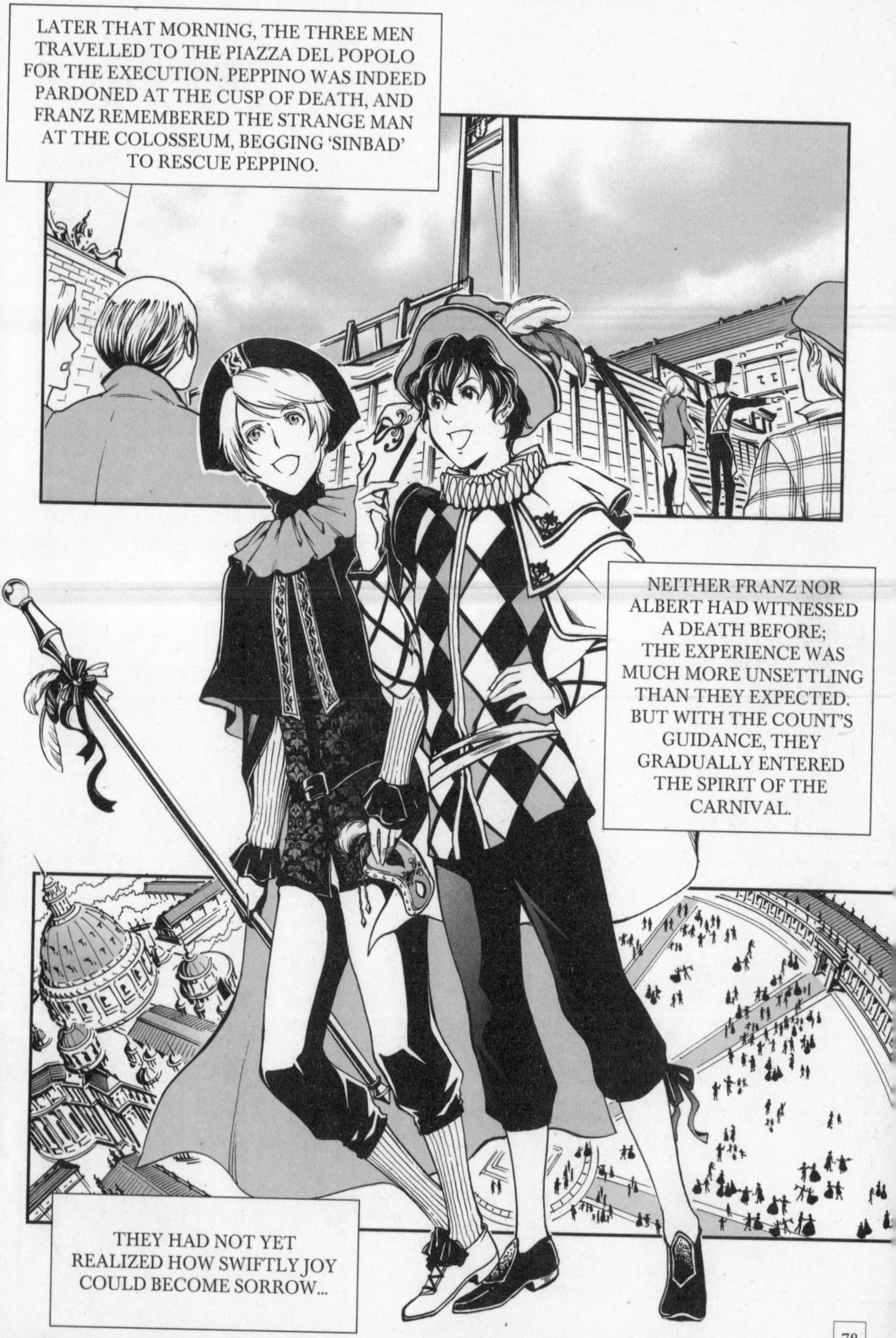
LATER THAT MORNING, THE THREE MEN TRAVELLED TO THE PIAZZA DEL POPOLO FOR THE EXECUTION. PEPPINO WAS INDEED PARDONED AT THE CUSP OF DEATH, AND FRANZ REMEMBERED THE STRANGE MAN AT THE COLOSSEUM, BEGGING 'SINBAD' TO RESCUE PEPPINO.
NEITHER FRANZ NOR ALBERT HAD WITNESSED A DEATH BEFORE; THE EXPERIENCE WAS MUCH MORE UNSETTLING THAN THEY EXPECTED. BUT WITH THE COUNT'S GUIDANCE, THEY GRADUALLY ENTERED THE SPIRIT OF THE CARNIVAL.
THEY HAD NOT YET REALIZED HOW SWIFTLY JOY COULD BECOME SORROW...

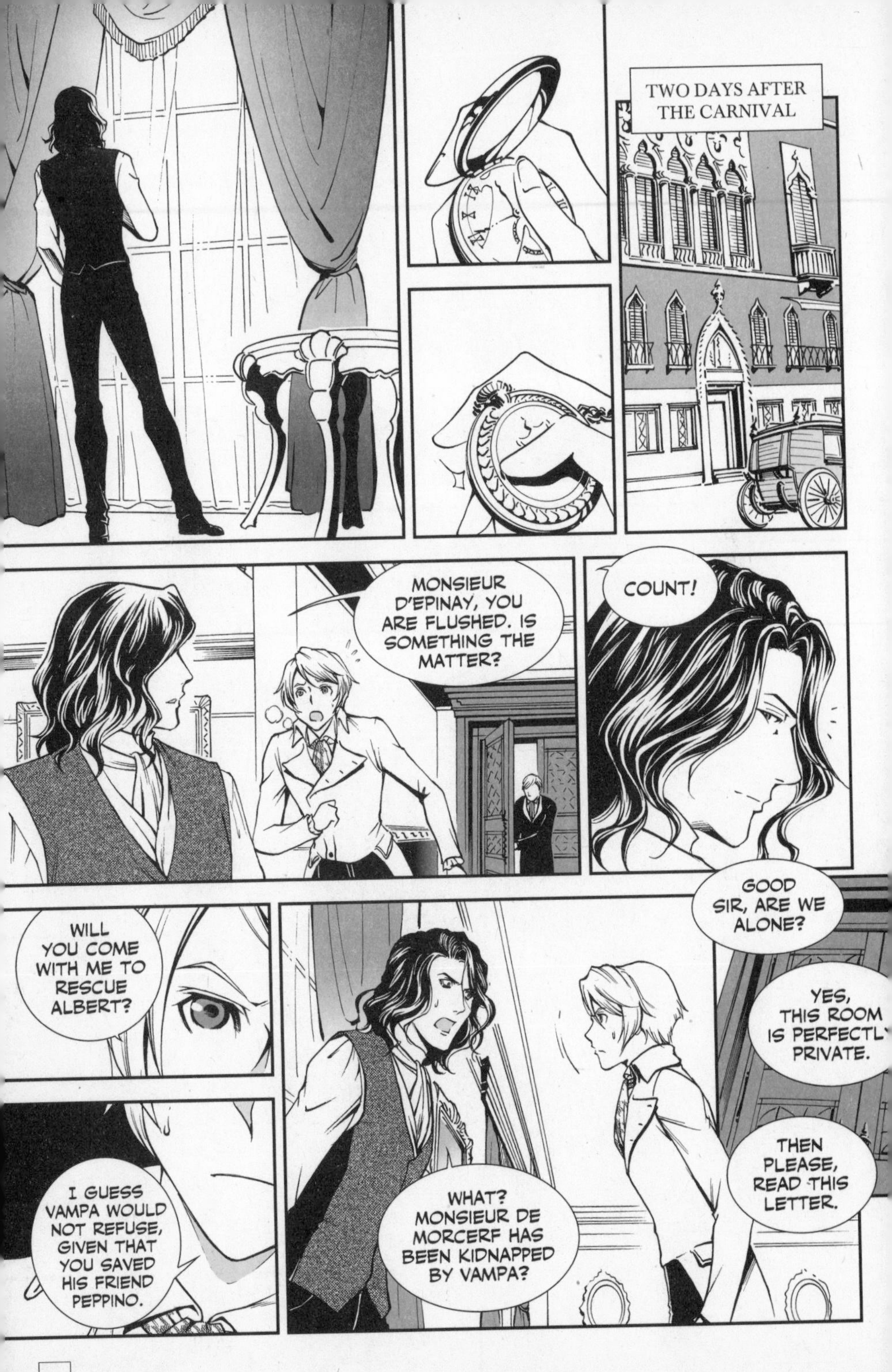
TWO DAYS AFTER THE CARNIVAL
COUNT!
MONSIEUR D'EPINAY, YOU ARE FLUSHED. IS SOMETHING THE MATTER?
GOOD SIR, ARE WE ALONE?
YES, THIS ROOM IS PERFECTL PRIVATE.
THEN PLEASE, READ THIS LETTER.
WHAT? MONSIEUR DE MORCERF HAS BEEN KIDNAPPED BY VAMPA?
WILL YOU COME WITH ME TO RESCUE ALBERT?
I GUESS VAMPA WOULD NOT REFUSE, GIVEN THAT YOU SAVED HIS FRIEND PEPPINO.

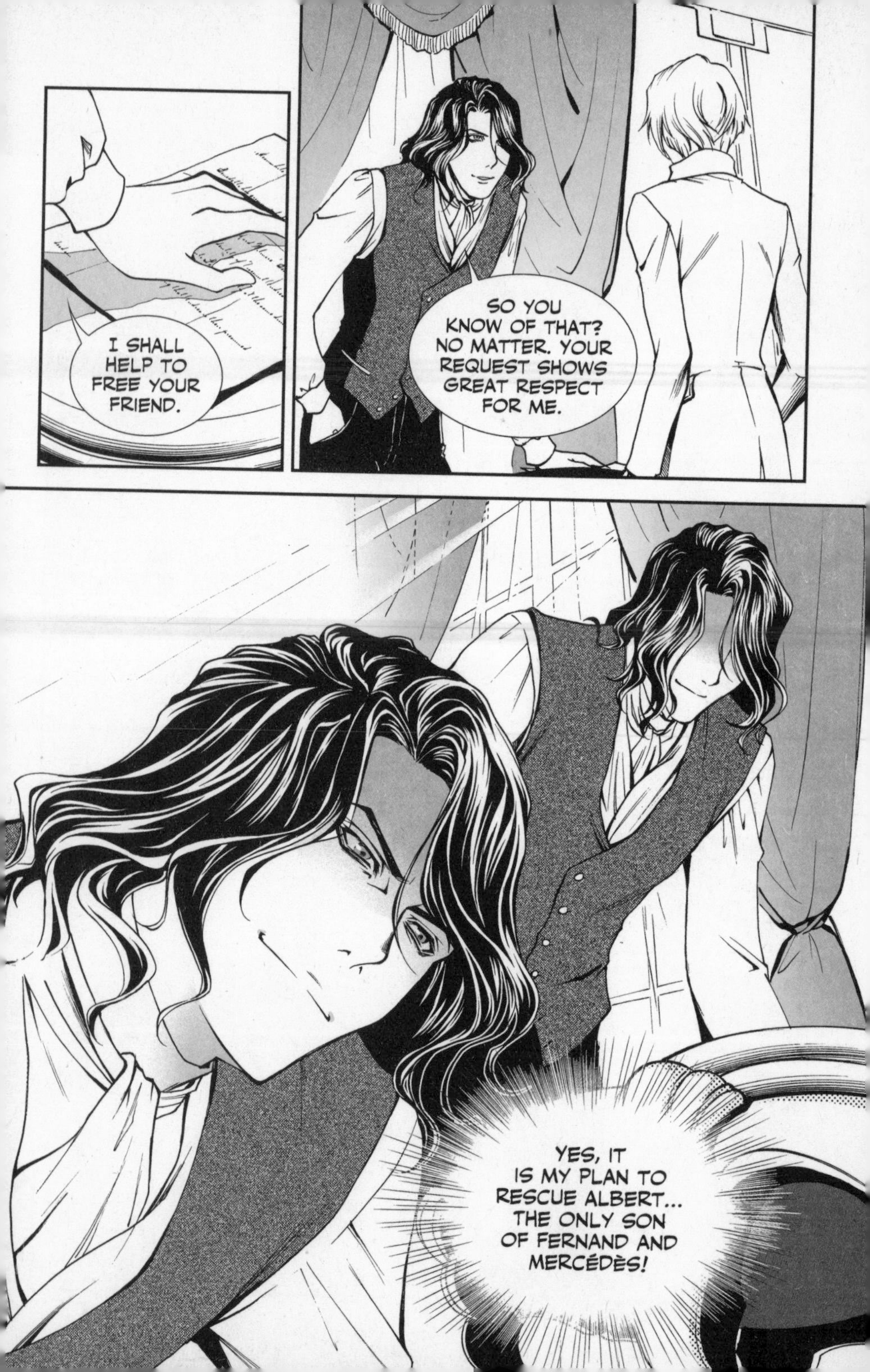
SO YOU KNOW OF THAT? NO MATTER. YOUR REQUEST SHOWS GREAT RESPECT FOR ME.
I SHALL HELP TO FREE YOUR FRIEND.
YES, IT IS MY PLAN TO RESCUE ALBERT...
THE ONLY SON OF FERNAND AND MERCÉDÈS!

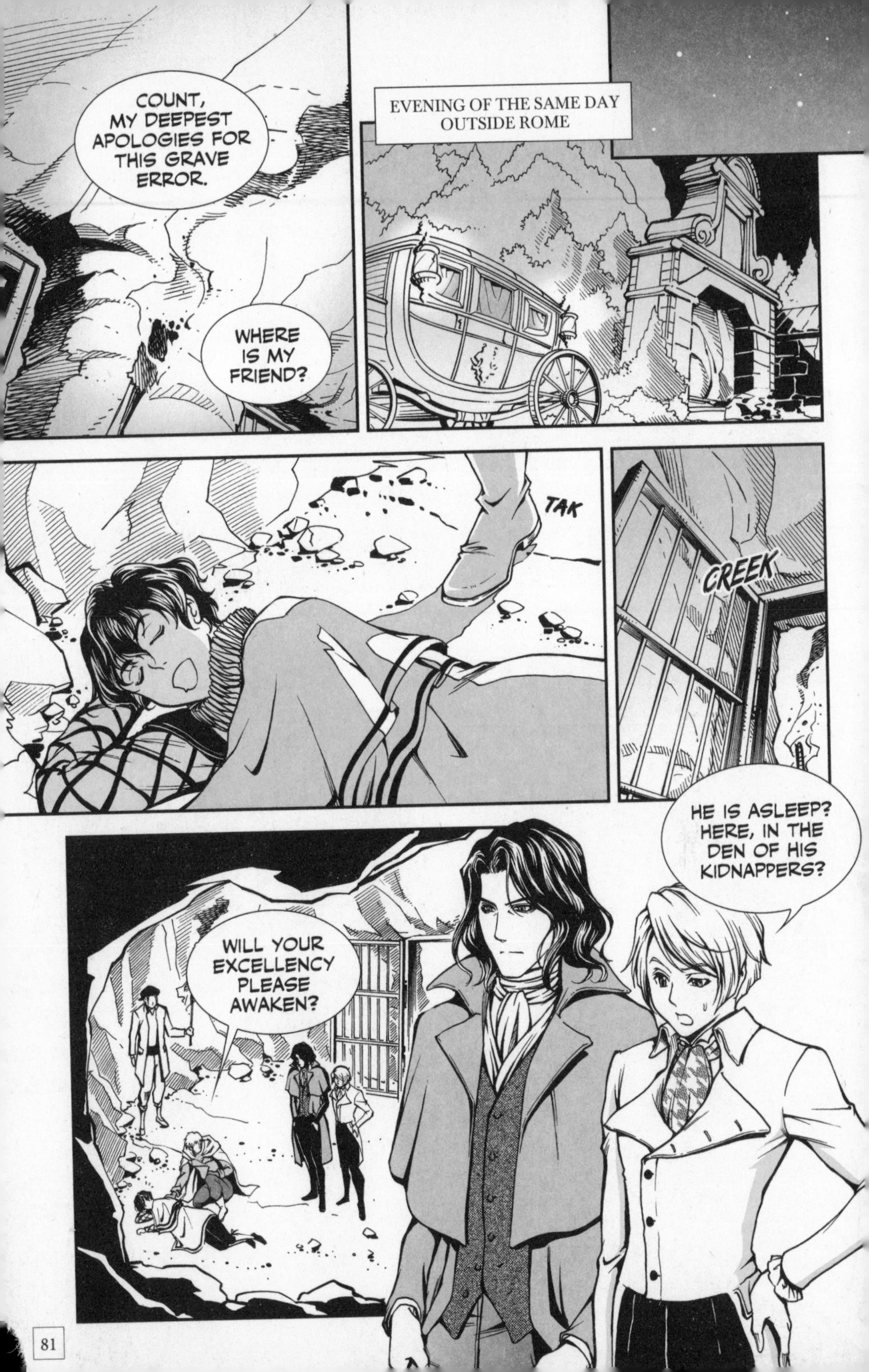
EVENING OF THE SAME DAY
OUTSIDE ROME
COUNT, MY DEEPEST APOLOGIES FOR THIS GRAVE ERROR.
WHERE IS MY FRIEND?
CREEK
TAK
HE IS ASLEEP? HERE, IN THE DEN OF HIS KIDNAPPERS?
WILL YOUR EXCELLENCY PLEASE AWAKEN?

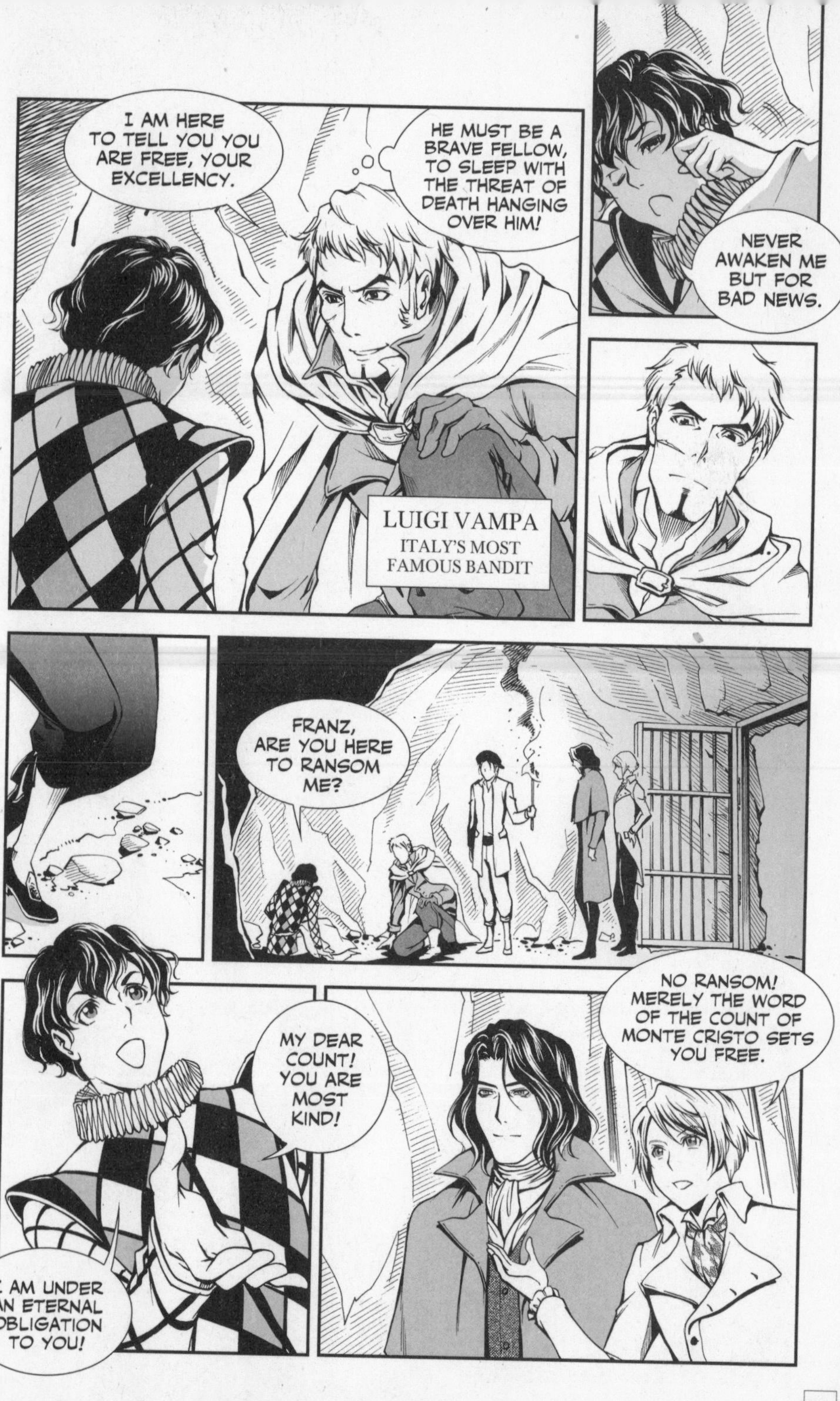
NEVER AWAKEN ME BUT FOR BAD NEWS.
HE MUST BE A BRAVE FELLOW, TO SLEEP WITH THE THREAT OF DEATH HANGING OVER HIM!
I AM HERE TO TELL YOU YOU ARE FREE, YOUR EXCELLENCY.
LUIGI VAMPA
ITALY'S MOST FAMOUS BANDIT
FRANZ, ARE YOU HERE TO RANSOM ME?
NO RANSOM! MERELY THE WORD OF THE COUNT OF MONTE CRISTO SETS YOU FREE.
MY DEAR COUNT! YOU ARE MOST KIND!
I AM UNDER AN ETERNAL OBLIGATION TO YOU!

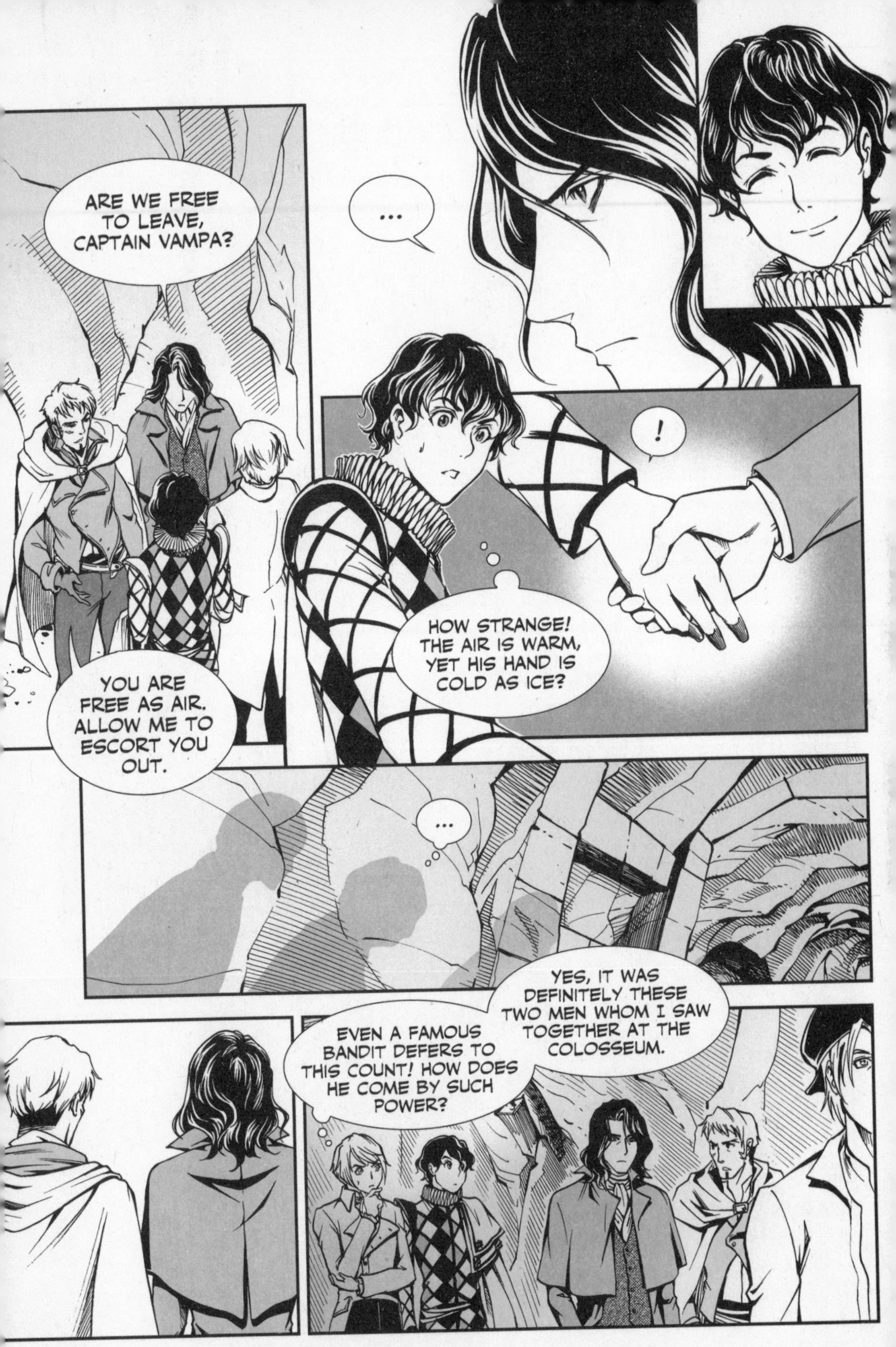
...
!
HOW STRANGE! THE AIR IS WARM, YET HIS HAND IS COLD AS ICE?
ARE WE FREE TO LEAVE, CAPTAIN VAMPA?
YOU ARE FREE AS AIR. ALLOW ME TO ESCORT YOU OUT.
...
YES, IT WAS DEFINITELY THESE TWO MEN WHOM I SAW TOGETHER AT THE COLOSSEUM.
EVEN A FAMOUS BANDIT DEFERS TO THIS COUNT! HOW DOES HE COME BY SUCH POWER?

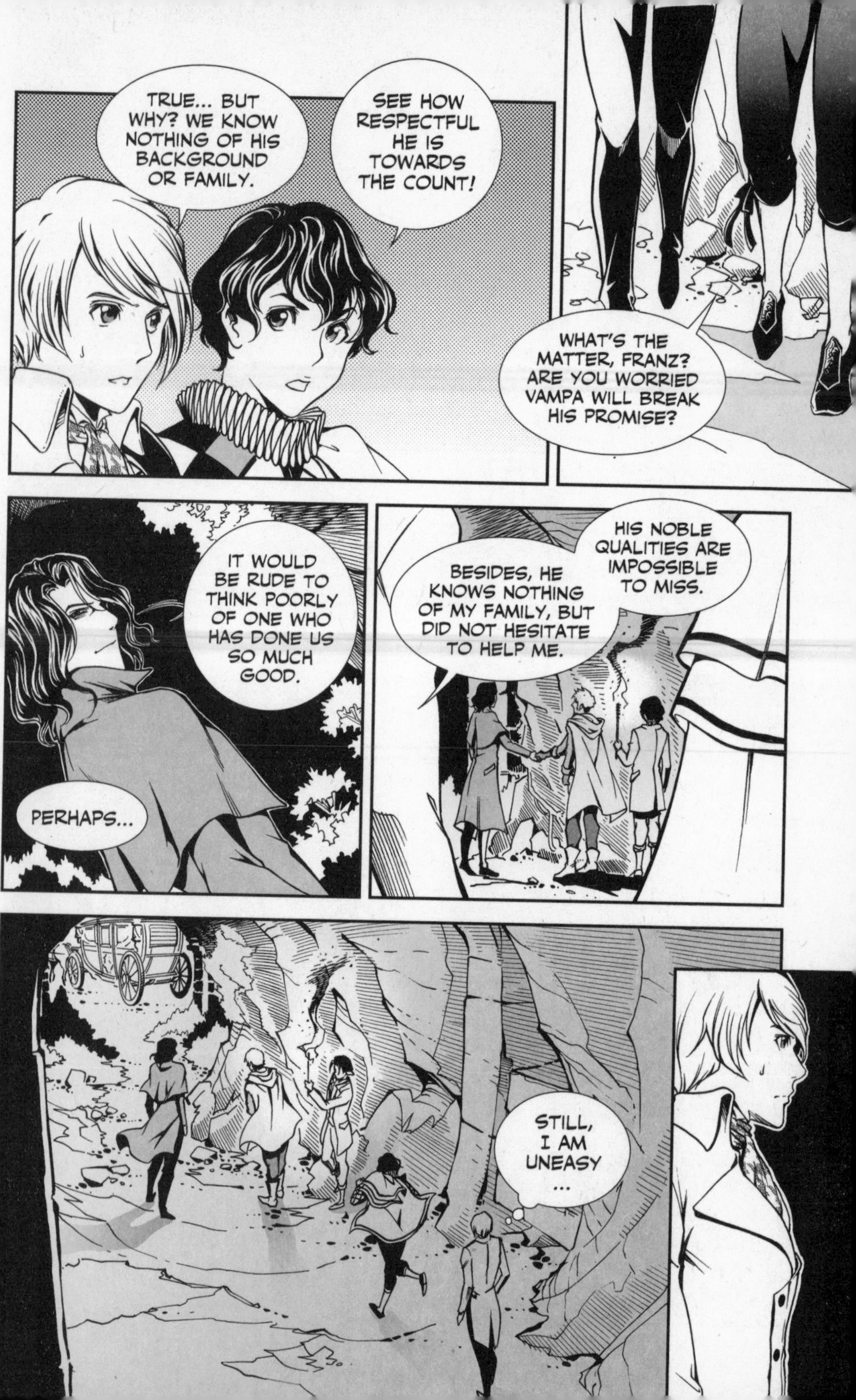
WHAT'S THE MATTER, FRANZ? ARE YOU WORRIED VAMPA WILL BREAK HIS PROMISE?
SEE HOW RESPECTFUL HE IS TOWARDS THE COUNT!
TRUE... BUT WHY? WE KNOW NOTHING OF HIS BACKGROUND OR FAMILY.
HIS NOBLE QUALITIES ARE IMPOSSIBLE TO MISS.
BESIDES, HE KNOWS NOTHING OF MY FAMILY, BUT DID NOT HESITATE TO HELP ME.
IT WOULD BE RUDE TO THINK POORLY OF ONE WHO HAS DONE US SO MUCH GOOD.
PERHAPS...
STILL, I AM UNEASY ...

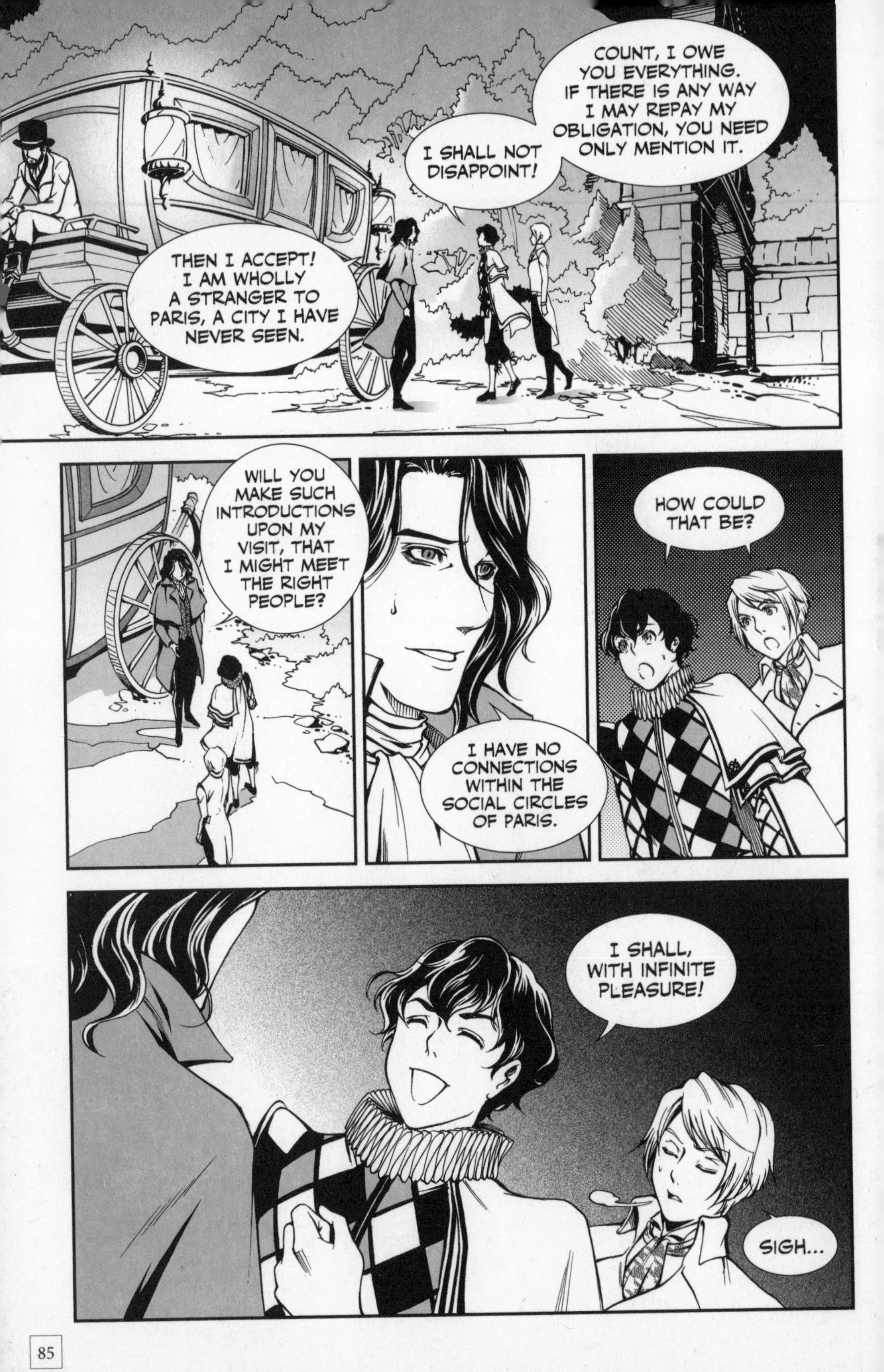
COUNT, I OWE YOU EVERYTHING. IF THERE IS ANY WAY I MAY REPAY MY OBLIGATION, YOU NEED ONLY MENTION IT.
I SHALL NOT DISAPPOINT!
THEN I ACCEPT! I AM WHOLLY A STRANGER TO PARIS, A CITY I HAVE NEVER SEEN.
HOW COULD THAT BE?
I HAVE NO CONNECTIONS WITHIN THE SOCIAL CIRCLES OF PARIS.
WILL YOU MAKE SUCH INTRODUCTIONS UPON MY VISIT, THAT I MIGHT MEET THE RIGHT PEOPLE?
I SHALL, WITH INFINITE PLEASURE!
SIGH...

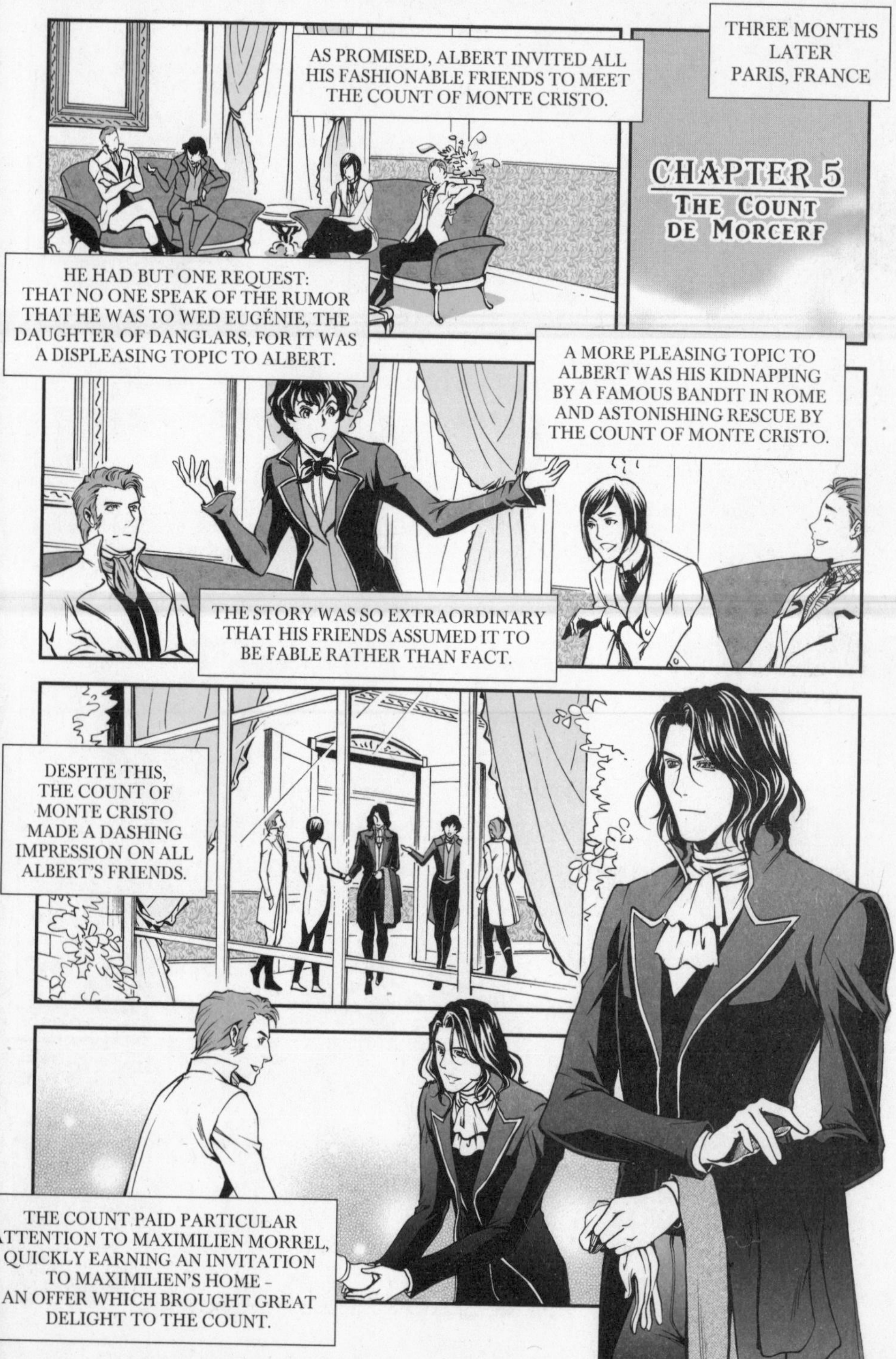
THREE MONTHS LATER PARIS, FRANCE
CHAPTER 5
THE COUNT DE MORCERF
AS PROMISED, ALBERT INVITED ALL HIS FASHIONABLE FRIENDS TO MEET THE COUNT OF MONTE CRISTO.
HE HAD BUT ONE REQUEST: THAT NO ONE SPEAK OF THE RUMOR THAT HE WAS TO WED EUGÉNIE, THE DAUGHTER OF DANGLARS, FOR IT WAS A DISPLEASING TOPIC TO ALBERT.
A MORE PLEASING TOPIC TO ALBERT WAS HIS KIDNAPPING BY A FAMOUS BANDIT IN ROME AND ASTONISHING RESCUE BY THE COUNT OF MONTE CRISTO.
THE STORY WAS SO EXTRAORDINARY THAT HIS FRIENDS ASSUMED IT TO BE FABLE RATHER THAN FACT.
DESPITE THIS, THE COUNT OF MONTE CRISTO MADE A DASHING IMPRESSION ON ALL ALBERT'S FRIENDS.
THE COUNT PAID PARTICULAR TTENTION TO MAXIMILIEN MORREL, QUICKLY EARNING AN INVITATION TO MAXIMILIEN'S HOME – AN OFFER WHICH BROUGHT GREAT DELIGHT TO THE COUNT.

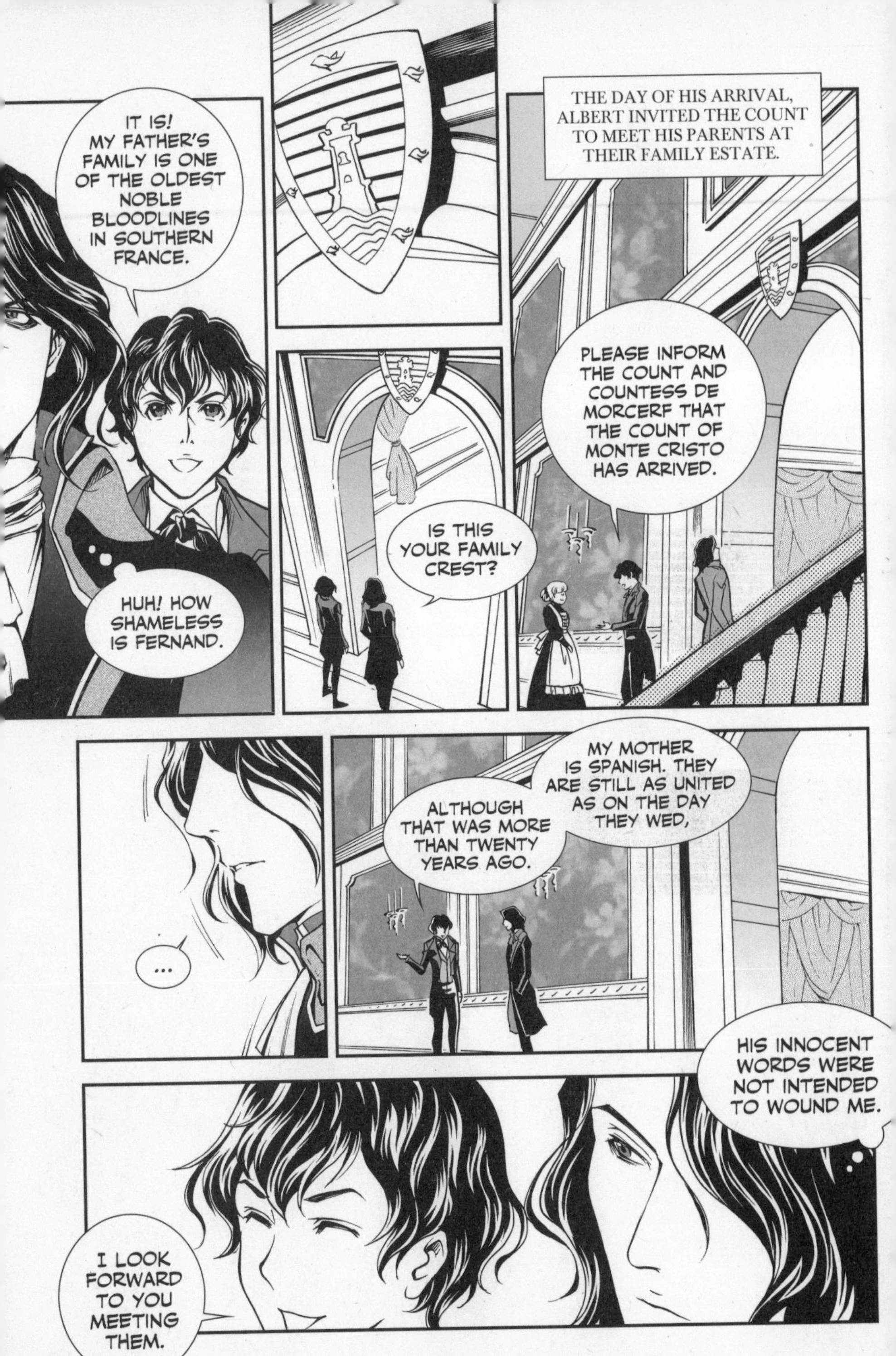
THE DAY OF HIS ARRIVAL, ALBERT INVITED THE COUNT TO MEET HIS PARENTS AT THEIR FAMILY ESTATE.
PLEASE INFORM THE COUNT AND COUNTESS DE MORCERF THAT THE COUNT OF MONTE CRISTO HAS ARRIVED.
IS THIS YOUR FAMILY CREST?
IT IS! MY FATHER'S FAMILY IS ONE OF THE OLDEST NOBLE BLOODLINES IN SOUTHERN FRANCE.
HUH! HOW SHAMELESS IS FERNAND.
MY MOTHER IS SPANISH. THEY ARE STILL AS UNITED AS ON THE DAY THEY WED,
ALTHOUGH THAT WAS MORE THAN TWENTY YEARS AGO.
...
HIS INNOCENT WORDS WERE NOT INTENDED TO WOUND ME.
I LOOK FORWARD TO YOU MEETING THEM.

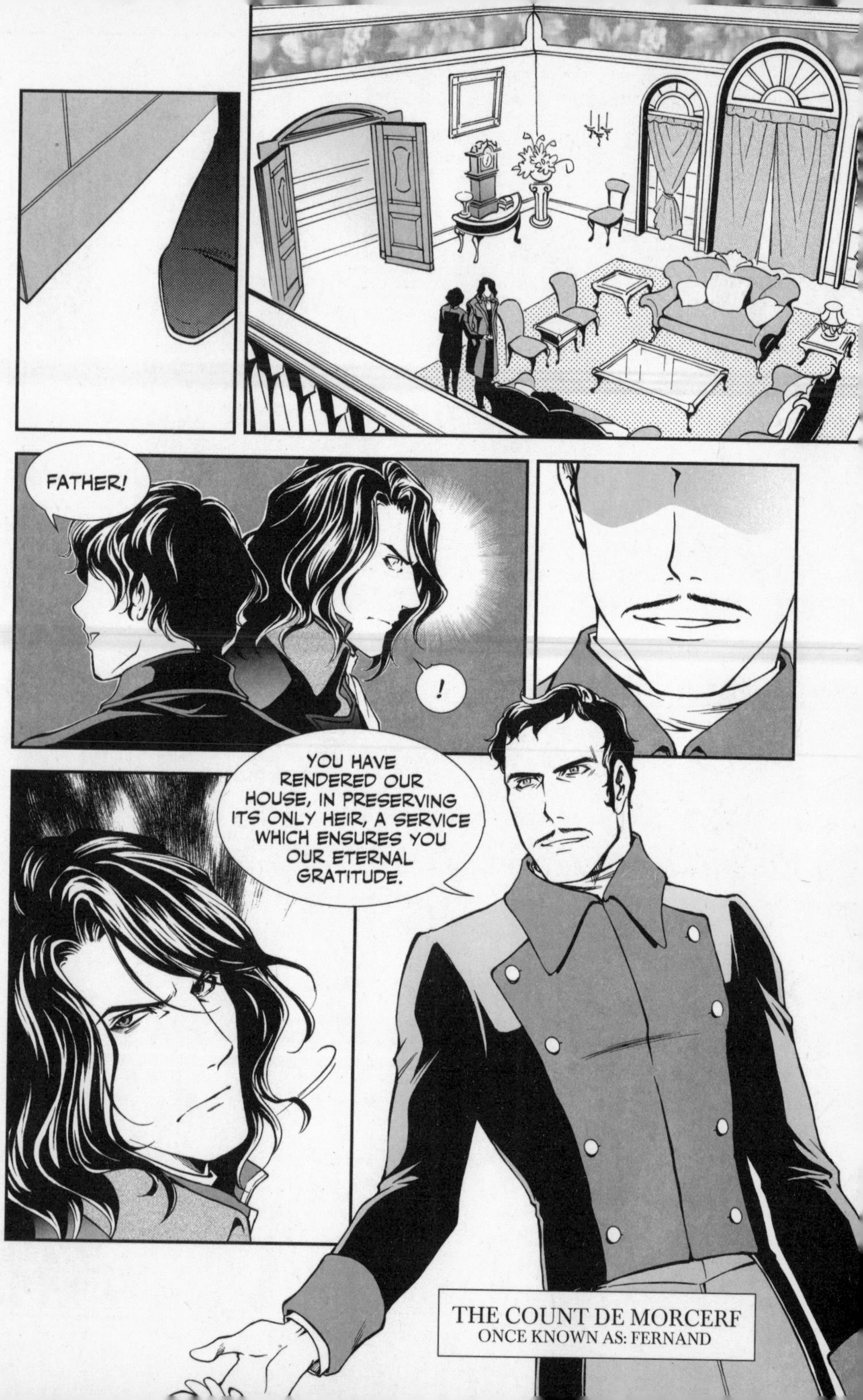
FATHER!
!
YOU HAVE RENDERED OUR HOUSE, IN PRESERVING ITS ONLY HEIR, A SERVICE WHICH ENSURES YOU OUR ETERNAL GRATITUDE.
THE COUNT DE MORCERF
ONCE KNOWN AS: FERNAND

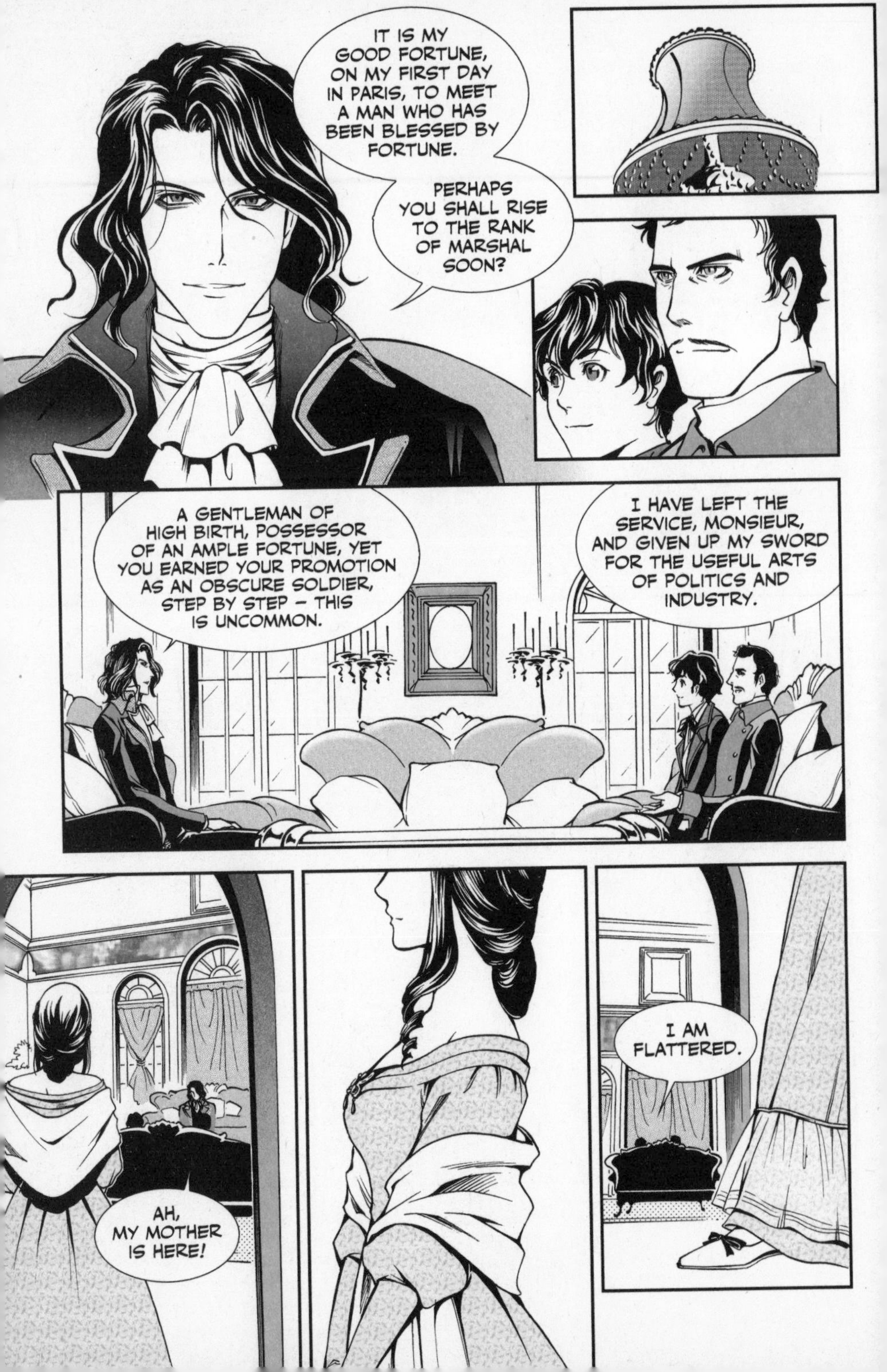
IT IS MY GOOD FORTUNE, ON MY FIRST DAY IN PARIS, TO MEET A MAN WHO HAS BEEN BLESSED BY FORTUNE.
PERHAPS YOU SHALL RISE TO THE RANK OF MARSHAL SOON?
I HAVE LEFT THE SERVICE, MONSIEUR, AND GIVEN UP MY SWORD FOR THE USEFUL ARTS OF POLITICS AND INDUSTRY.
A GENTLEMAN OF HIGH BIRTH, POSSESSOR OF AN AMPLE FORTUNE, YET YOU EARNED YOUR PROMOTION AS AN OBSCURE SOLDIER, STEP BY STEP – THIS IS UNCOMMON.
I AM FLATTERED.
AH, MY MOTHER IS HERE!

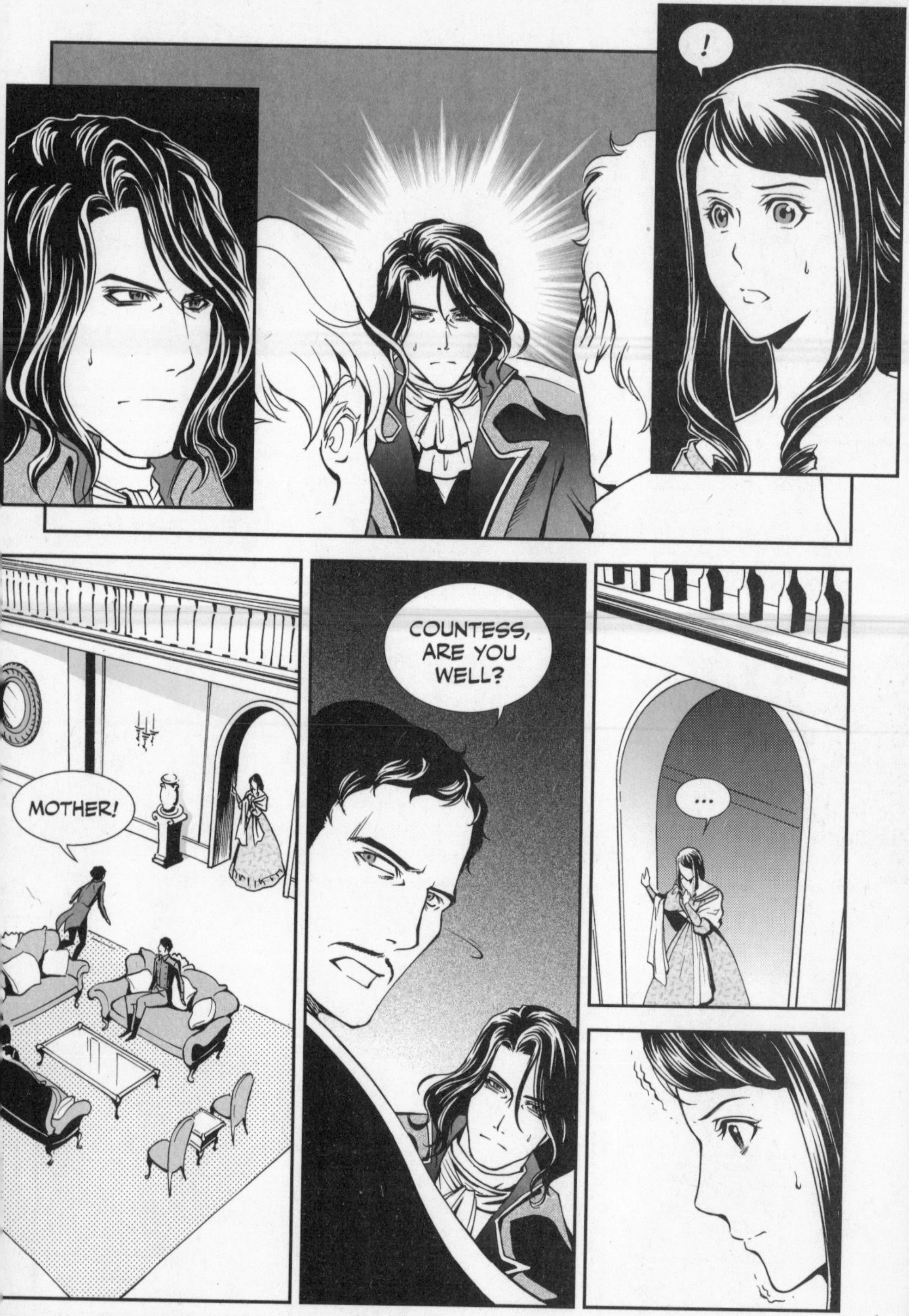
!
...
COUNTESS, ARE YOU WELL?
MOTHER!

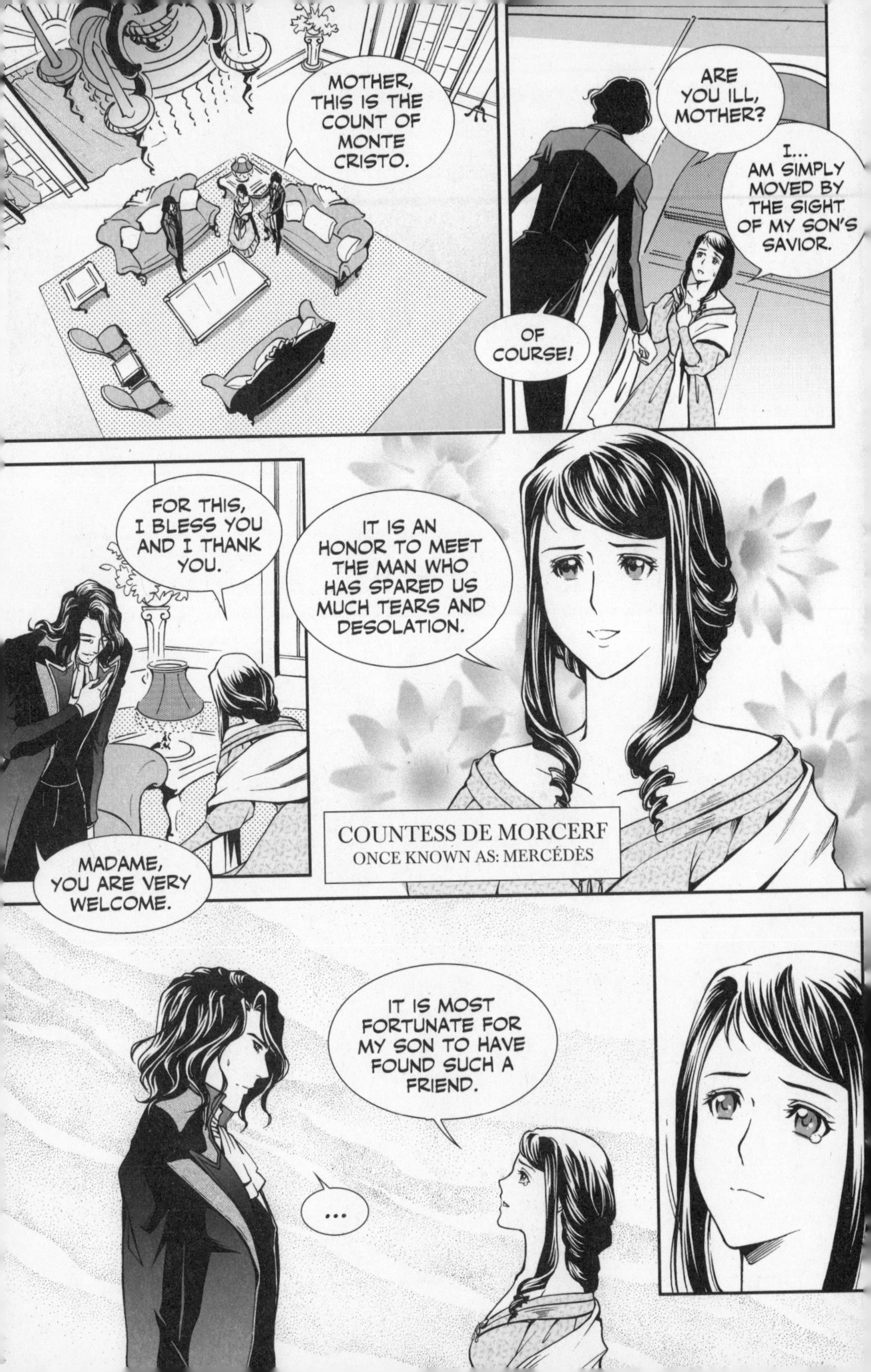
ARE YOU ILL, MOTHER?
I... AM SIMPLY MOVED BY THE SIGHT OF MY SON'S SAVIOR.
OF COURSE!
MOTHER, THIS IS THE COUNT OF MONTE CRISTO.
IT IS AN HONOR TO MEET THE MAN WHO HAS SPARED US MUCH TEARS AND DESOLATION.
COUNTESS DE MORCERF
ONCE KNOWN AS: MERCÉDÈS
FOR THIS, I BLESS YOU AND I THANK YOU.
MADAME, YOU ARE VERY WELCOME.
IT IS MOST FORTUNATE FOR MY SON TO HAVE FOUND SUCH A FRIEND.
...

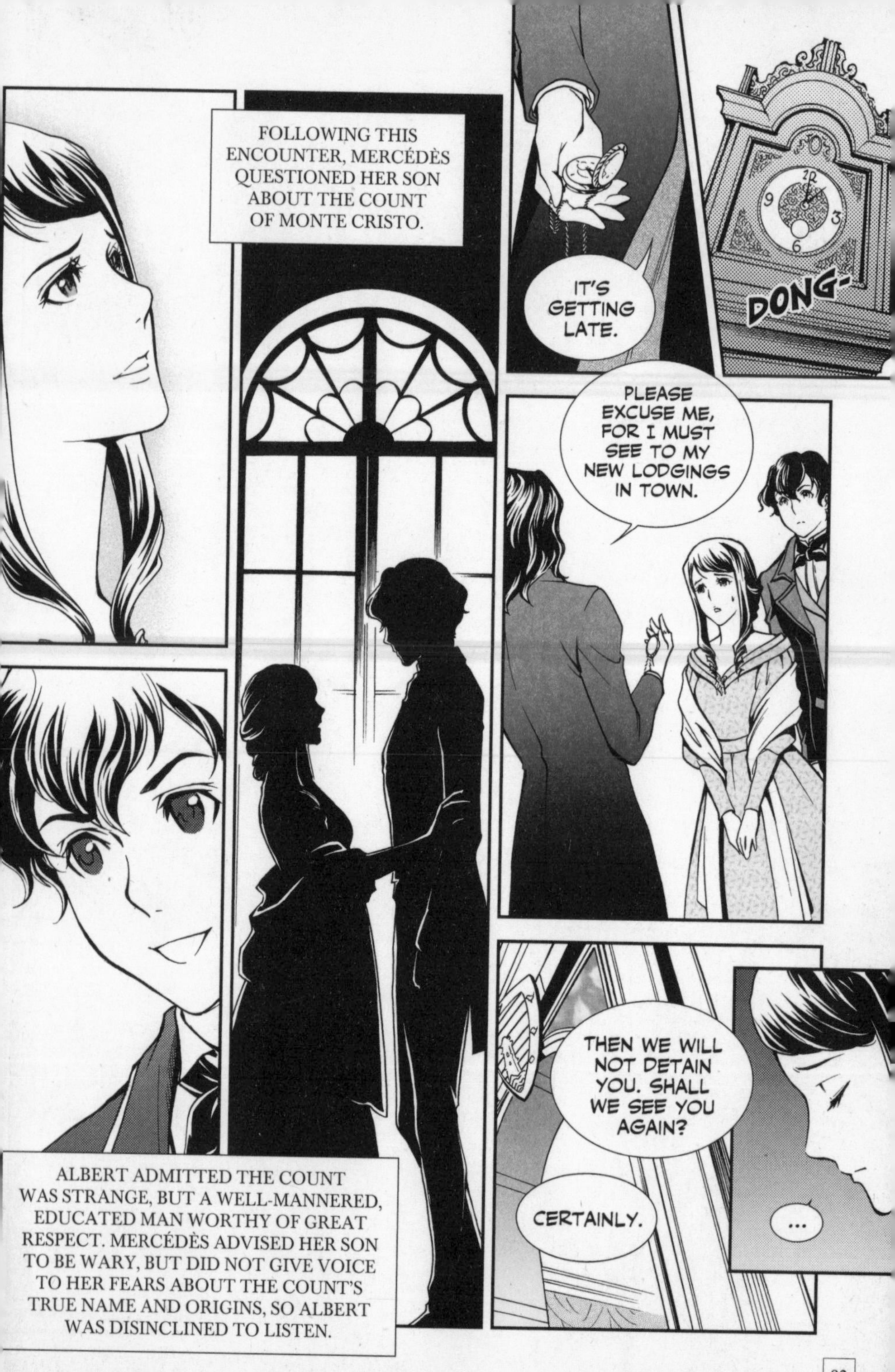
DONG-
IT'S GETTING LATE.
PLEASE EXCUSE ME, FOR I MUST SEE TO MY NEW LODGINGS IN TOWN.
...
THEN WE WILL NOT DETAIN YOU. SHALL WE SEE YOU AGAIN?
CERTAINLY.
FOLLOWING THIS ENCOUNTER, MERCÉDÈS QUESTIONED HER SON ABOUT THE COUNT OF MONTE CRISTO.
ALBERT ADMITTED THE COUNT WAS STRANGE, BUT A WELL-MANNERED, EDUCATED MAN WORTHY OF GREAT RESPECT. MERCÉDÈS ADVISED HER SON TO BE WARY, BUT DID NOT GIVE VOICE TO HER FEARS ABOUT THE COUNT'S TRUE NAME AND ORIGINS, SO ALBERT WAS DISINCLINED TO LISTEN.

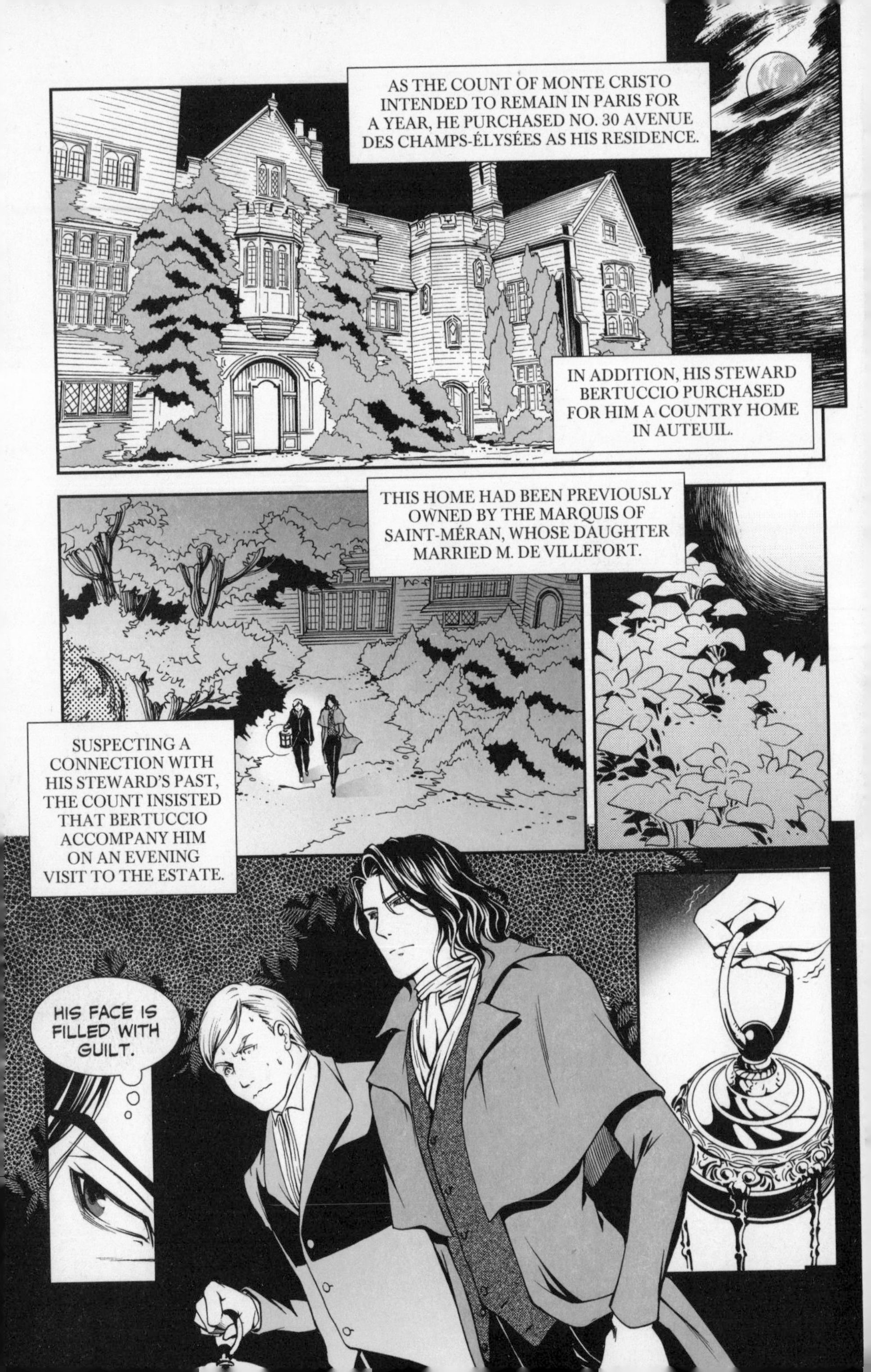
AS THE COUNT OF MONTE CRISTO INTENDED TO REMAIN IN PARIS FOR A YEAR, HE PURCHASED NO. 30 AVENUE DES CHAMPS-ÉLYSÉES AS HIS RESIDENCE.
IN ADDITION, HIS STEWARD BERTUCCIO PURCHASED FOR HIM A COUNTRY HOME IN AUTEUIL.
THIS HOME HAD BEEN PREVIOUSLY OWNED BY THE MARQUIS OF SAINT-MÉRAN, WHOSE DAUGHTER MARRIED M. DE VILLEFORT.
SUSPECTING A CONNECTION WITH HIS STEWARD'S PAST, THE COUNT INSISTED THAT BERTUCCIO ACCOMPANY HIM ON AN EVENING VISIT TO THE ESTATE.
HIS FACE IS FILLED WITH GUILT.

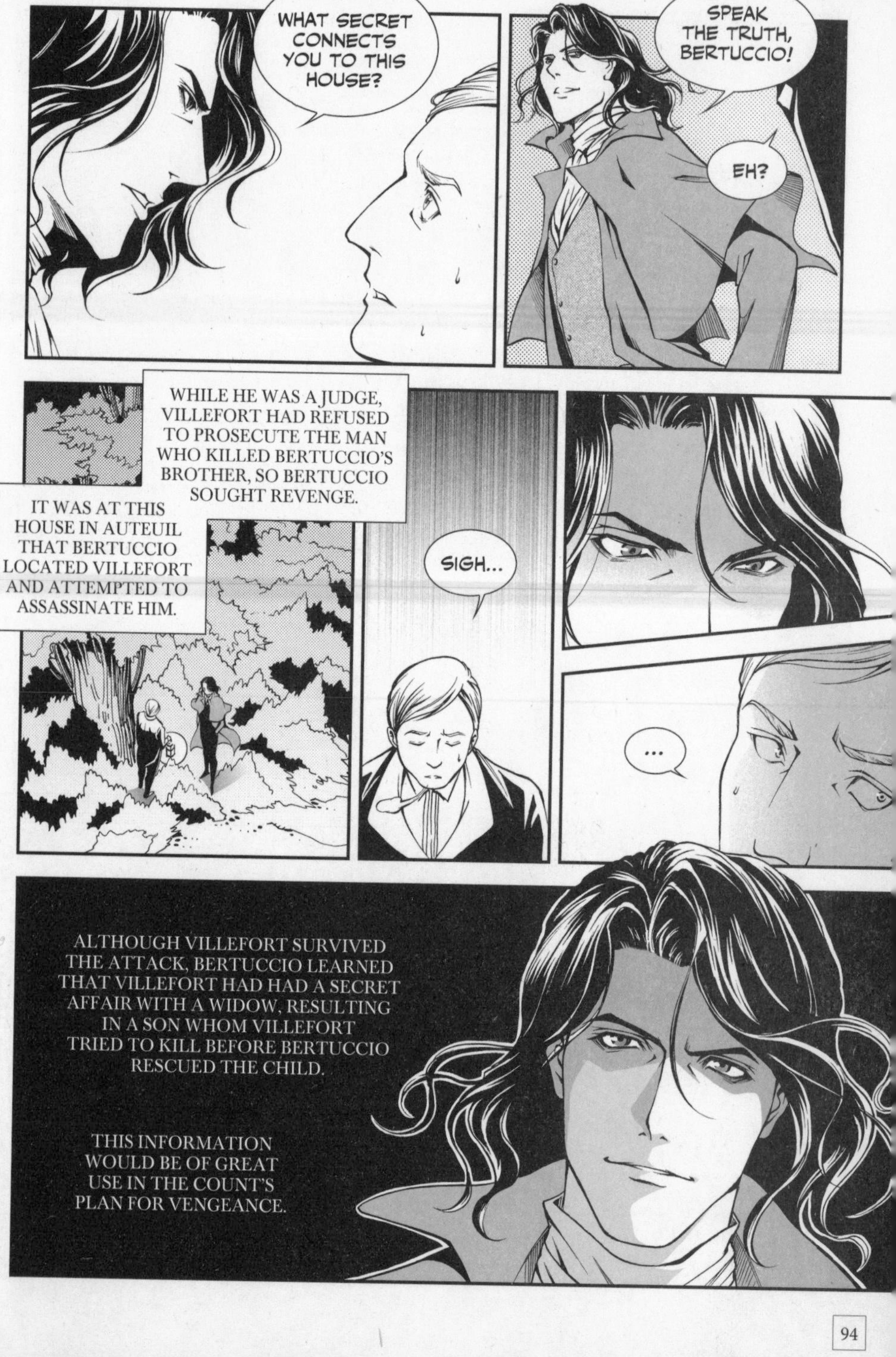
SPEAK THE TRUTH, BERTUCCIO!
EH?
WHAT SECRET CONNECTS YOU TO THIS HOUSE?
...
SIGH...
WHILE HE WAS A JUDGE, VILLEFORT HAD REFUSED TO PROSECUTE THE MAN WHO KILLED BERTUCCIO'S BROTHER, SO BERTUCCIO SOUGHT REVENGE.
IT WAS AT THIS HOUSE IN AUTEUIL THAT BERTUCCIO LOCATED VILLEFORT AND ATTEMPTED TO ASSASSINATE HIM.
ALTHOUGH VILLEFORT SURVIVED THE ATTACK, BERTUCCIO LEARNED THAT VILLEFORT HAD HAD A SECRET AFFAIR WITH A WIDOW, RESULTING IN A SON WHOM VILLEFORT TRIED TO KILL BEFORE BERTUCCIO RESCUED THE CHILD.
THIS INFORMATION WOULD BE OF GREAT USE IN THE COUNT'S PLAN FOR VENGEANCE.

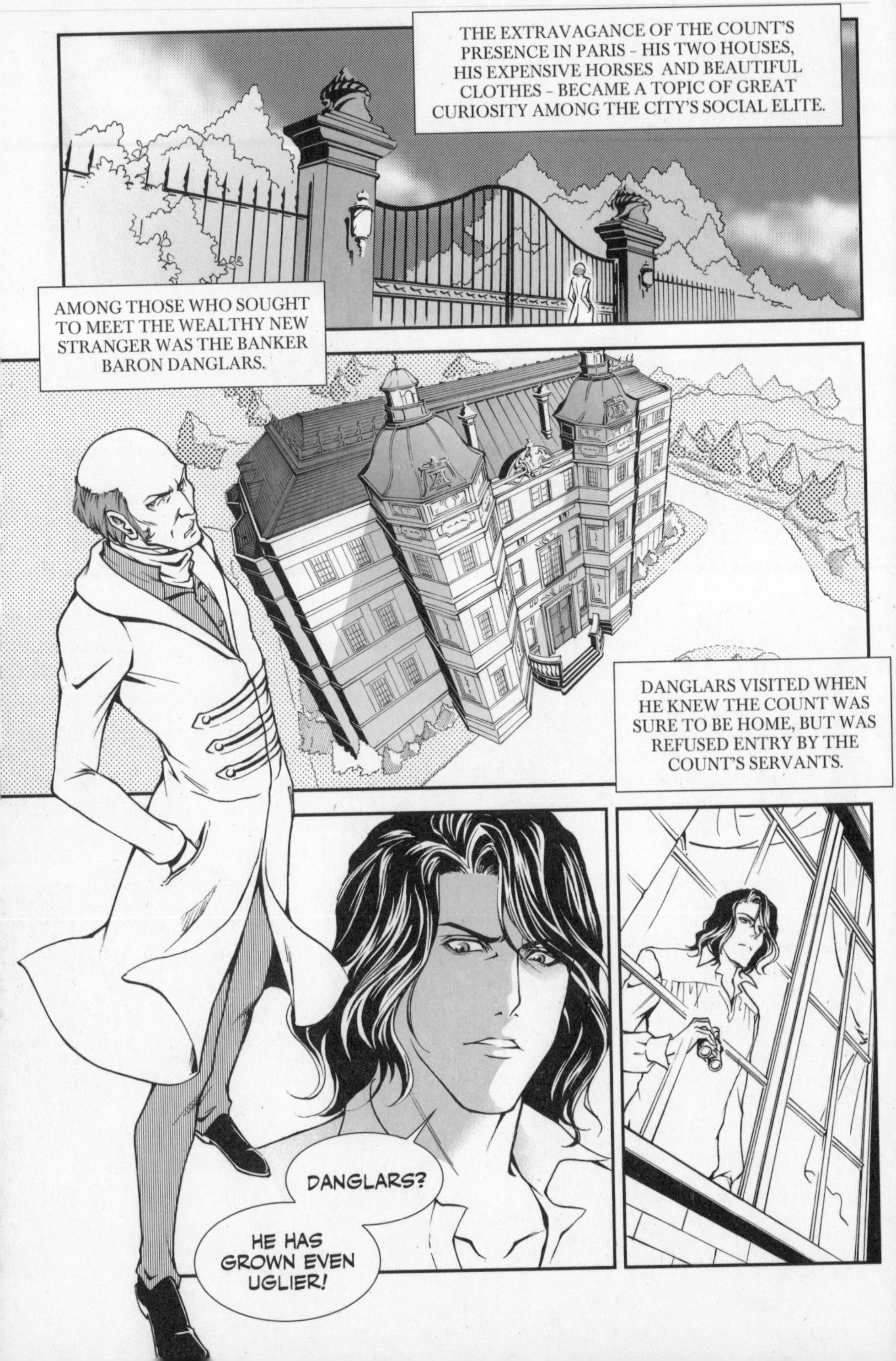
THE EXTRAVAGANCE OF THE COUNT'S PRESENCE IN PARIS – HIS TWO HOUSES, HIS EXPENSIVE HORSES AND BEAUTIFUL CLOTHES – BECAME A TOPIC OF GREAT CURIOSITY AMONG THE CITY'S SOCIAL ELITE.
AMONG THOSE WHO SOUGHT TO MEET THE WEALTHY NEW STRANGER WAS THE BANKER BARON DANGLARS.
DANGLARS VISITED WHEN HE KNEW THE COUNT WAS SURE TO BE HOME, BUT WAS REFUSED ENTRY BY THE COUNT'S SERVANTS.
DANGLARS?
HE HAS GROWN EVEN UGLIER!

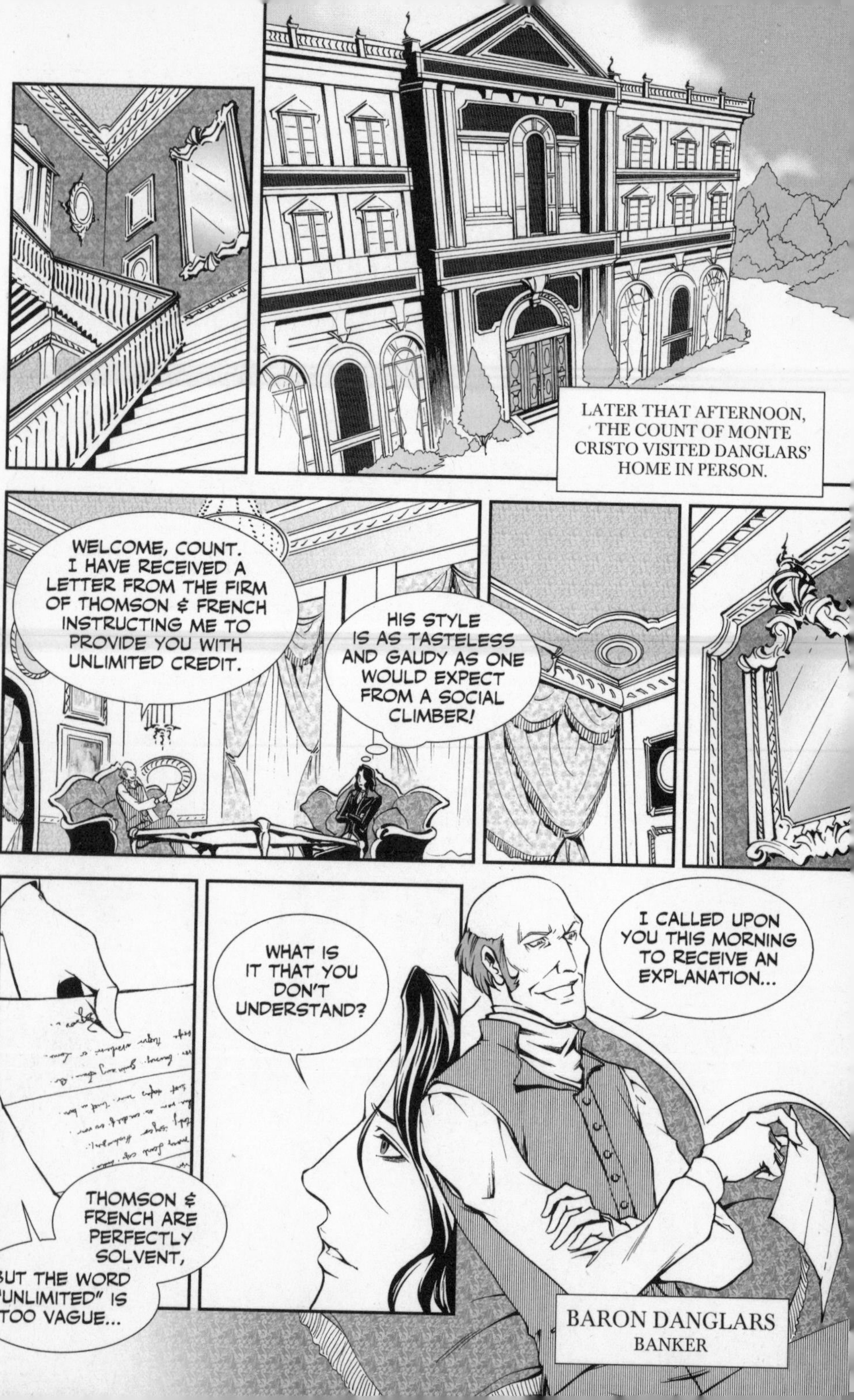
LATER THAT AFTERNOON, THE COUNT OF MONTE CRISTO VISITED DANGLARS' HOME IN PERSON.
WELCOME, COUNT. I HAVE RECEIVED A LETTER FROM THE FIRM OF THOMSON & FRENCH INSTRUCTING ME TO PROVIDE YOU WITH UNLIMITED CREDIT.
HIS STYLE IS AS TASTELESS AND GAUDY AS ONE WOULD EXPECT FROM A SOCIAL CLIMBER!
I CALLED UPON YOU THIS MORNING TO RECEIVE AN EXPLANATION...
WHAT IS IT THAT YOU DON'T UNDERSTAND?
BARON DANGLARS
BANKER
THOMSON & FRENCH ARE PERFECTLY SOLVENT,
BUT THE WORD "UNLIMITED" IS TOO VAGUE...

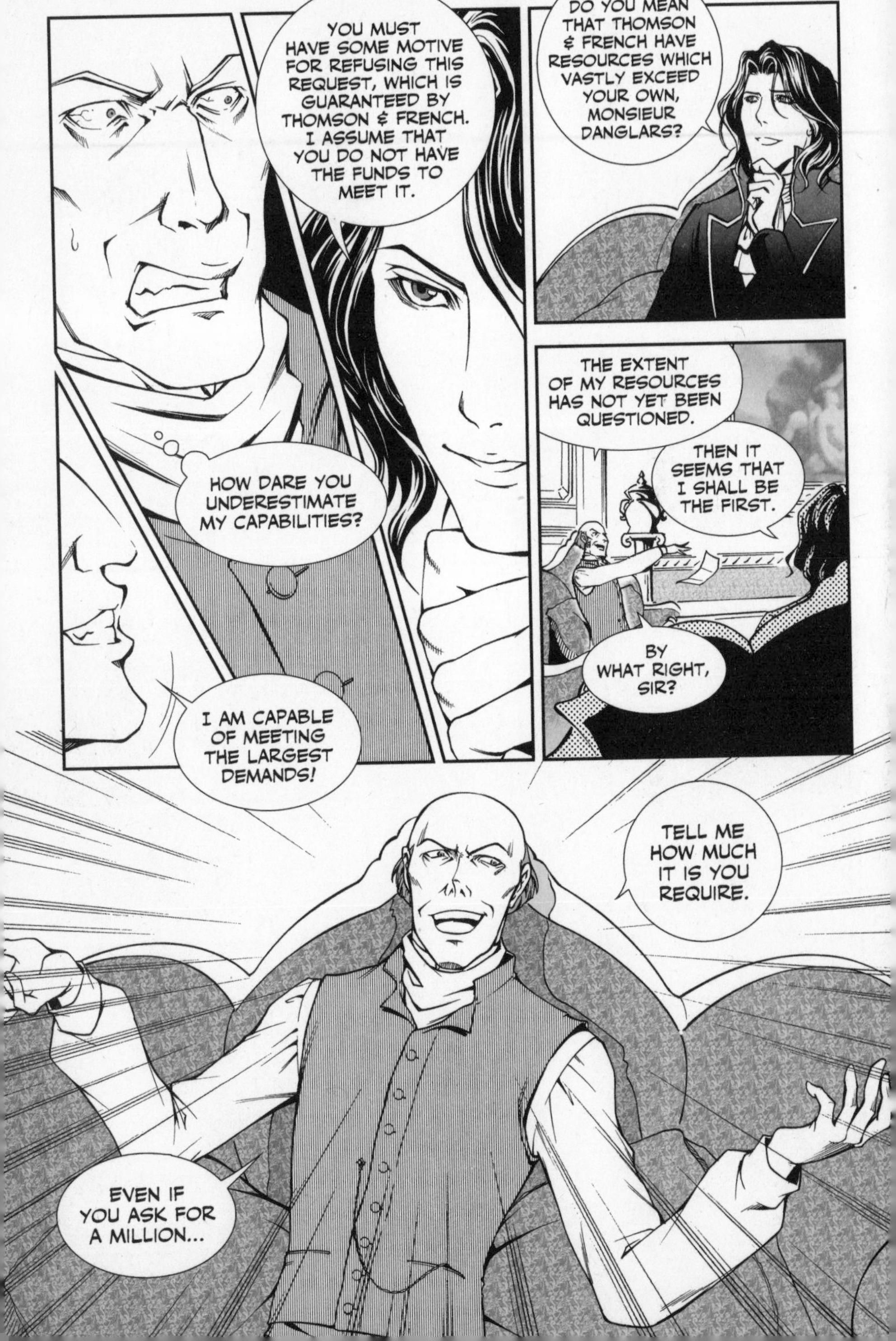
DO YOU MEAN THAT THOMSON & FRENCH HAVE RESOURCES WHICH VASTLY EXCEED YOUR OWN, MONSIEUR DANGLARS?
THE EXTENT OF MY RESOURCES HAS NOT YET BEEN QUESTIONED.
THEN IT SEEMS THAT I SHALL BE THE FIRST.
BY WHAT RIGHT, SIR?
YOU MUST HAVE SOME MOTIVE FOR REFUSING THIS REQUEST, WHICH IS GUARANTEED BY THOMSON & FRENCH. I ASSUME THAT YOU DO NOT HAVE THE FUNDS TO MEET IT.
HOW DARE YOU UNDERESTIMATE MY CAPABILITIES?
I AM CAPABLE OF MEETING THE LARGEST DEMANDS!
TELL ME HOW MUCH IT IS YOU REQUIRE.
EVEN IF YOU ASK FOR A MILLION...

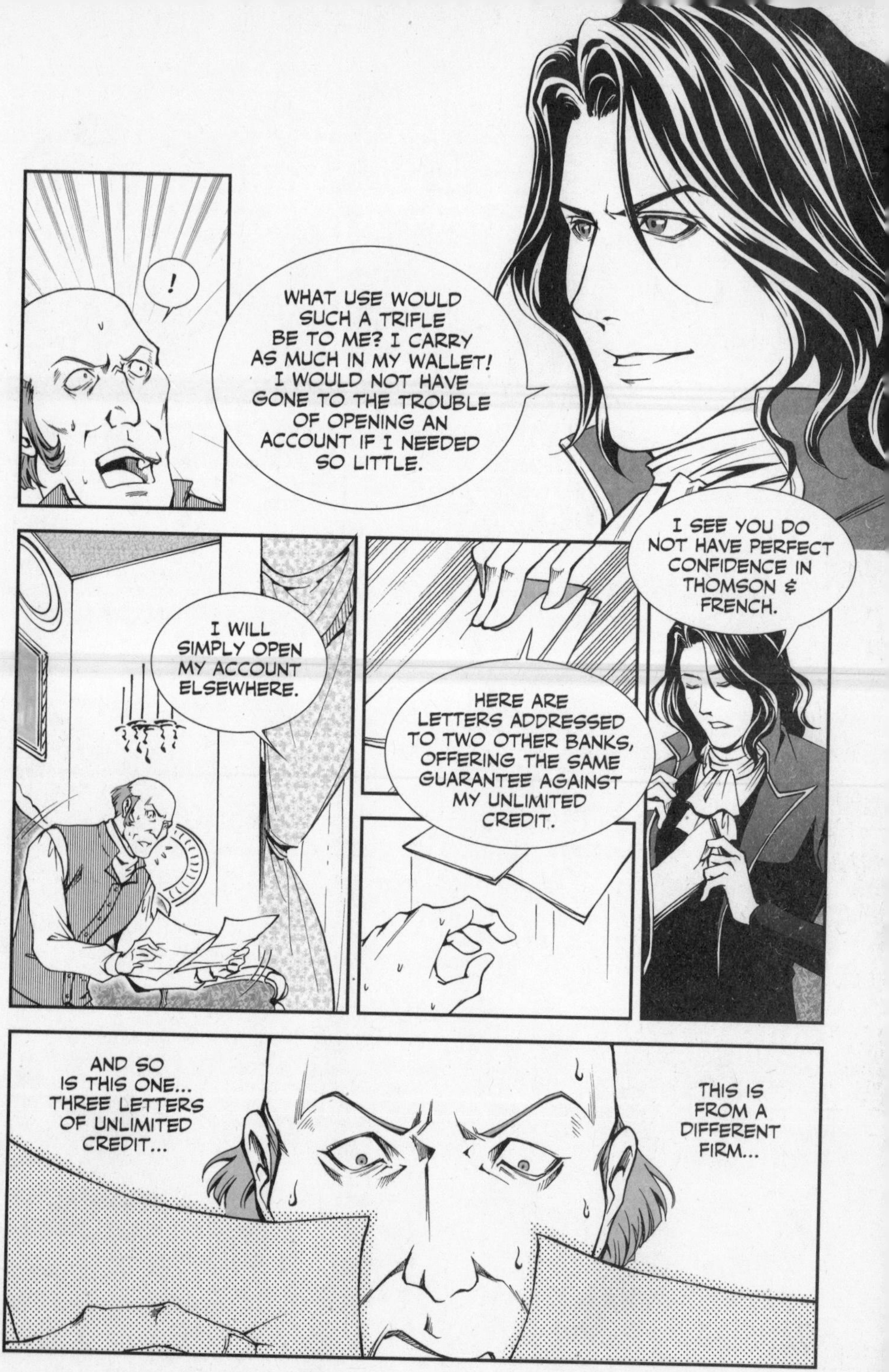
WHAT USE WOULD SUCH A TRIFLE BE TO ME? I CARRY AS MUCH IN MY WALLET! I WOULD NOT HAVE GONE TO THE TROUBLE OF OPENING AN ACCOUNT IF I NEEDED SO LITTLE.
!
I SEE YOU DO NOT HAVE PERFECT CONFIDENCE IN THOMSON & FRENCH.
HERE ARE LETTERS ADDRESSED TO TWO OTHER BANKS, OFFERING THE SAME GUARANTEE AGAINST MY UNLIMITED CREDIT.
I WILL SIMPLY OPEN MY ACCOUNT ELSEWHERE.
THIS IS FROM A DIFFERENT FIRM...
AND SO IS THIS ONE... THREE LETTERS OF UNLIMITED CREDIT...

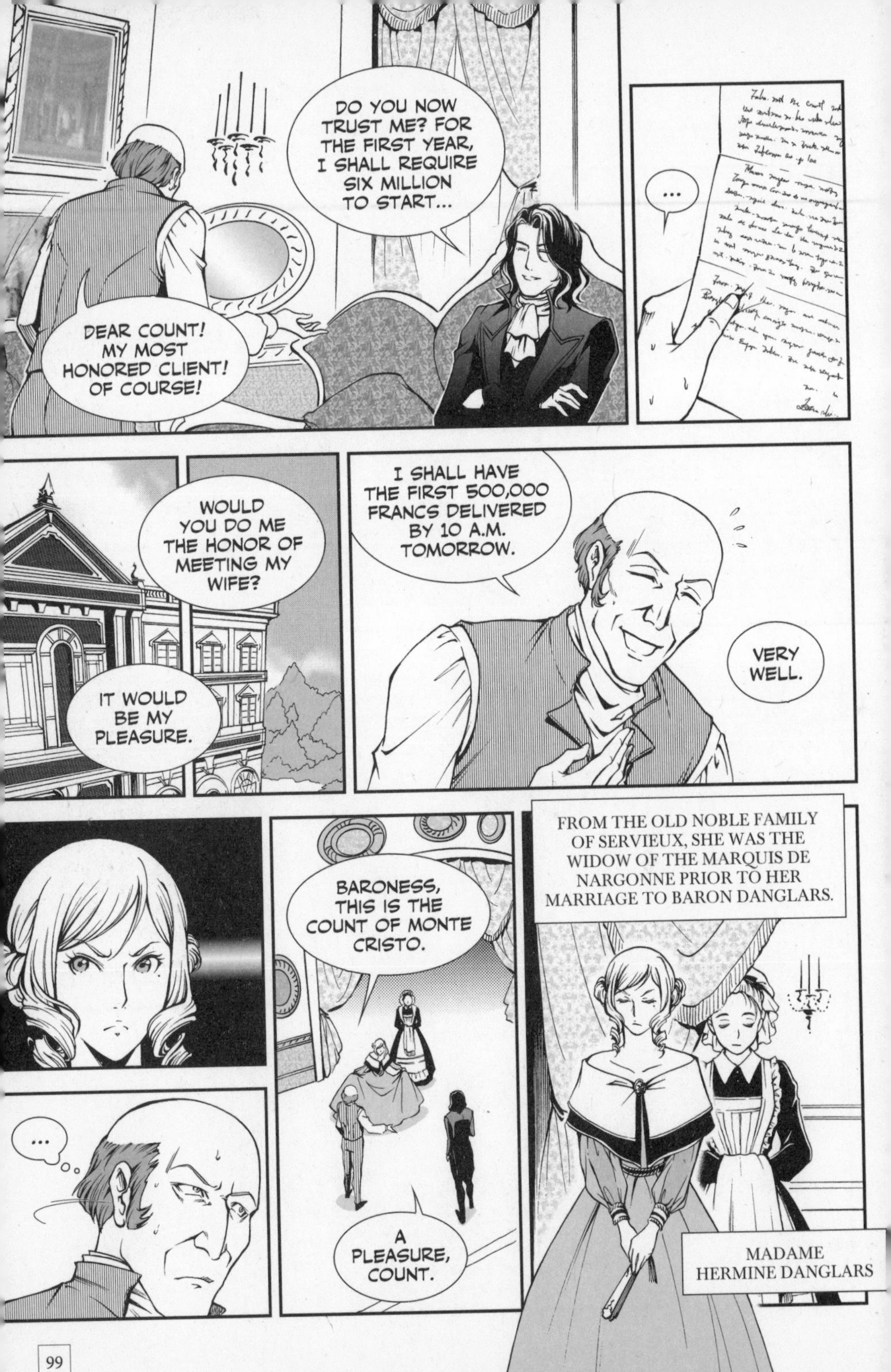
...
DO YOU NOW TRUST ME? FOR THE FIRST YEAR, I SHALL REQUIRE SIX MILLION TO START...
DEAR COUNT! MY MOST HONORED CLIENT! OF COURSE!
I SHALL HAVE THE FIRST 500,000 FRANCS DELIVERED BY 10 A.M. TOMORROW.
VERY WELL.
WOULD YOU DO ME THE HONOR OF MEETING MY WIFE?
IT WOULD BE MY PLEASURE.
FROM THE OLD NOBLE FAMILY OF SERVIEUX, SHE WAS THE WIDOW OF THE MARQUIS DE NARGONNE PRIOR TO HER MARRIAGE TO BARON DANGLARS.
MADAME HERMINE DANGLARS
BARONESS, THIS IS THE COUNT OF MONTE CRISTO.
A PLEASURE, COUNT.
...

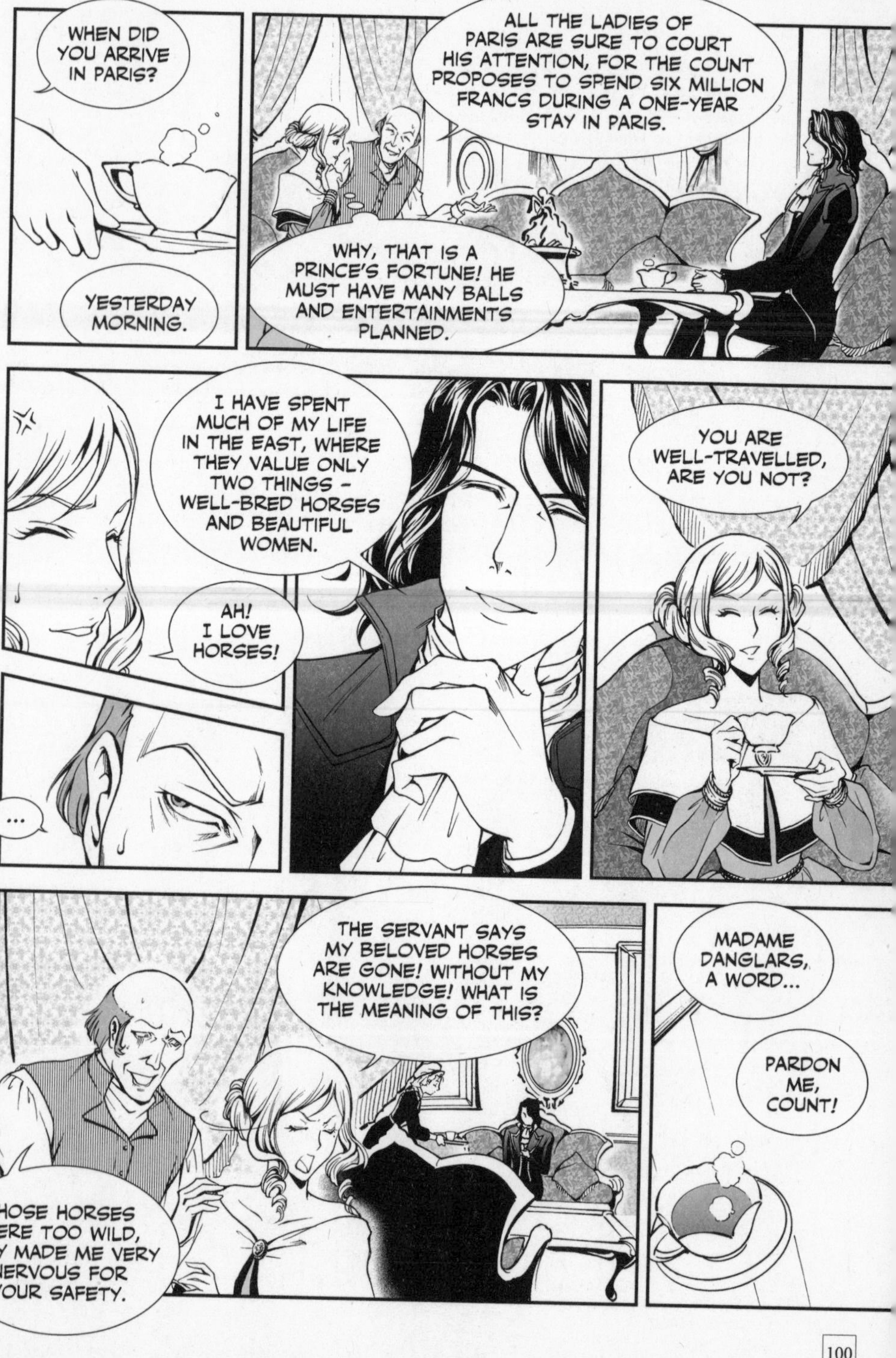
ALL THE LADIES OF PARIS ARE SURE TO COURT HIS ATTENTION, FOR THE COUNT PROPOSES TO SPEND SIX MILLION FRANCS DURING A ONE-YEAR STAY IN PARIS.
WHY, THAT IS A PRINCE'S FORTUNE! HE MUST HAVE MANY BALLS AND ENTERTAINMENTS PLANNED.
WHEN DID YOU ARRIVE IN PARIS?
YESTERDAY MORNING.
YOU ARE WELL-TRAVELLED, ARE YOU NOT?
I HAVE SPENT MUCH OF MY LIFE IN THE EAST, WHERE THEY VALUE ONLY TWO THINGS - WELL-BRED HORSES AND BEAUTIFUL WOMEN.
AH! I LOVE HORSES!
...
MADAME DANGLARS, A WORD...
PARDON ME, COUNT!
THE SERVANT SAYS MY BELOVED HORSES ARE GONE! WITHOUT MY KNOWLEDGE! WHAT IS THE MEANING OF THIS?
THOSE HORSES WERE TOO WILD, THEY MADE ME VERY NERVOUS FOR YOUR SAFETY.

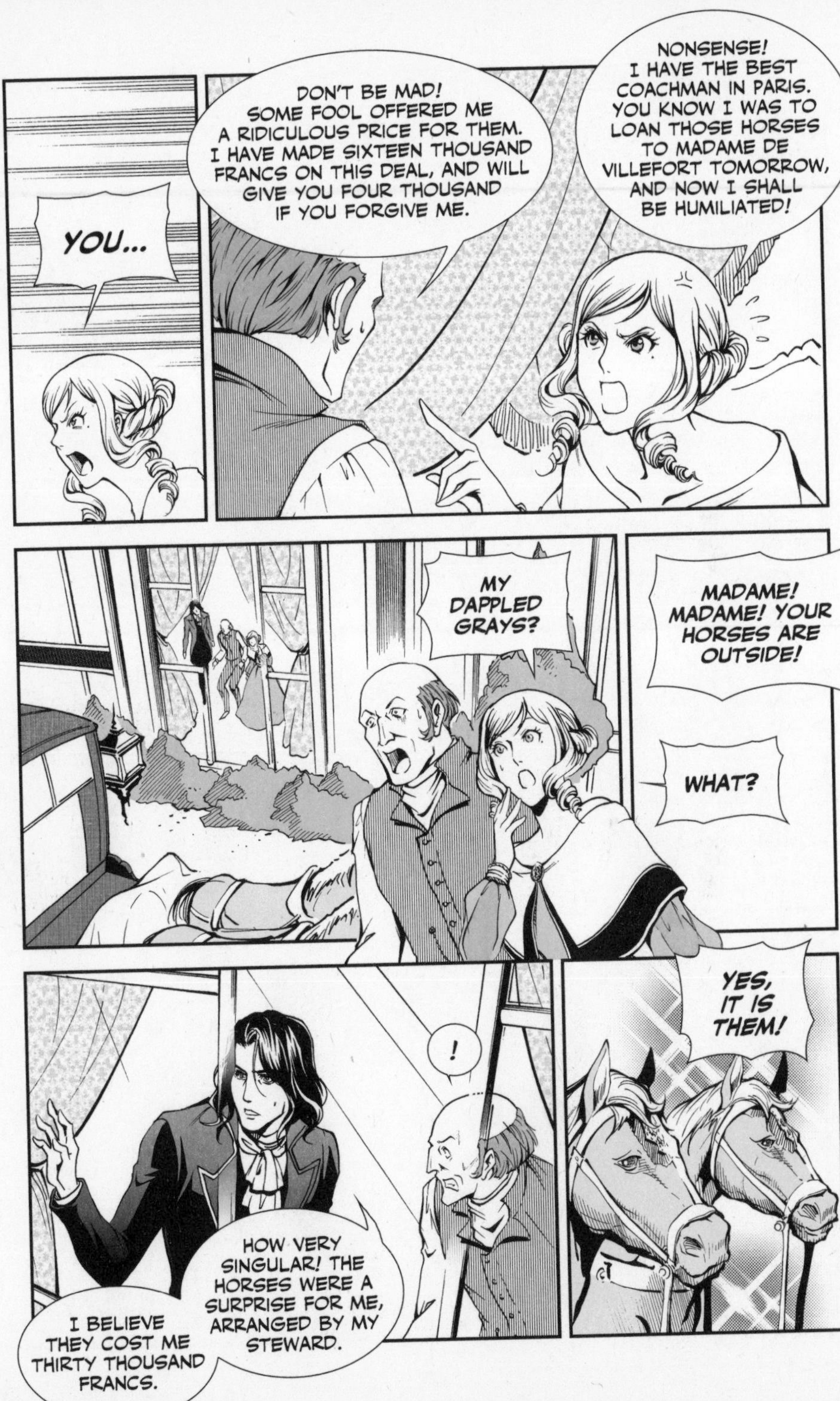
NONSENSE! I HAVE THE BEST COACHMAN IN PARIS. YOU KNOW I WAS TO LOAN THOSE HORSES TO MADAME DE VILLEFORT TOMORROW, AND NOW I SHALL BE HUMILIATED!
DON'T BE MAD! SOME FOOL OFFERED ME A RIDICULOUS PRICE FOR THEM. I HAVE MADE SIXTEEN THOUSAND FRANCS ON THIS DEAL, AND WILL GIVE YOU FOUR THOUSAND IF YOU FORGIVE ME.
YOU...
MADAME! MADAME! YOUR HORSES ARE OUTSIDE!
WHAT?
MY DAPPLED GRAYS?
YES, IT IS THEM!
!
HOW VERY SINGULAR! THE HORSES WERE A SURPRISE FOR ME, ARRANGED BY MY STEWARD.
I BELIEVE THEY COST ME THIRTY THOUSAND FRANCS.

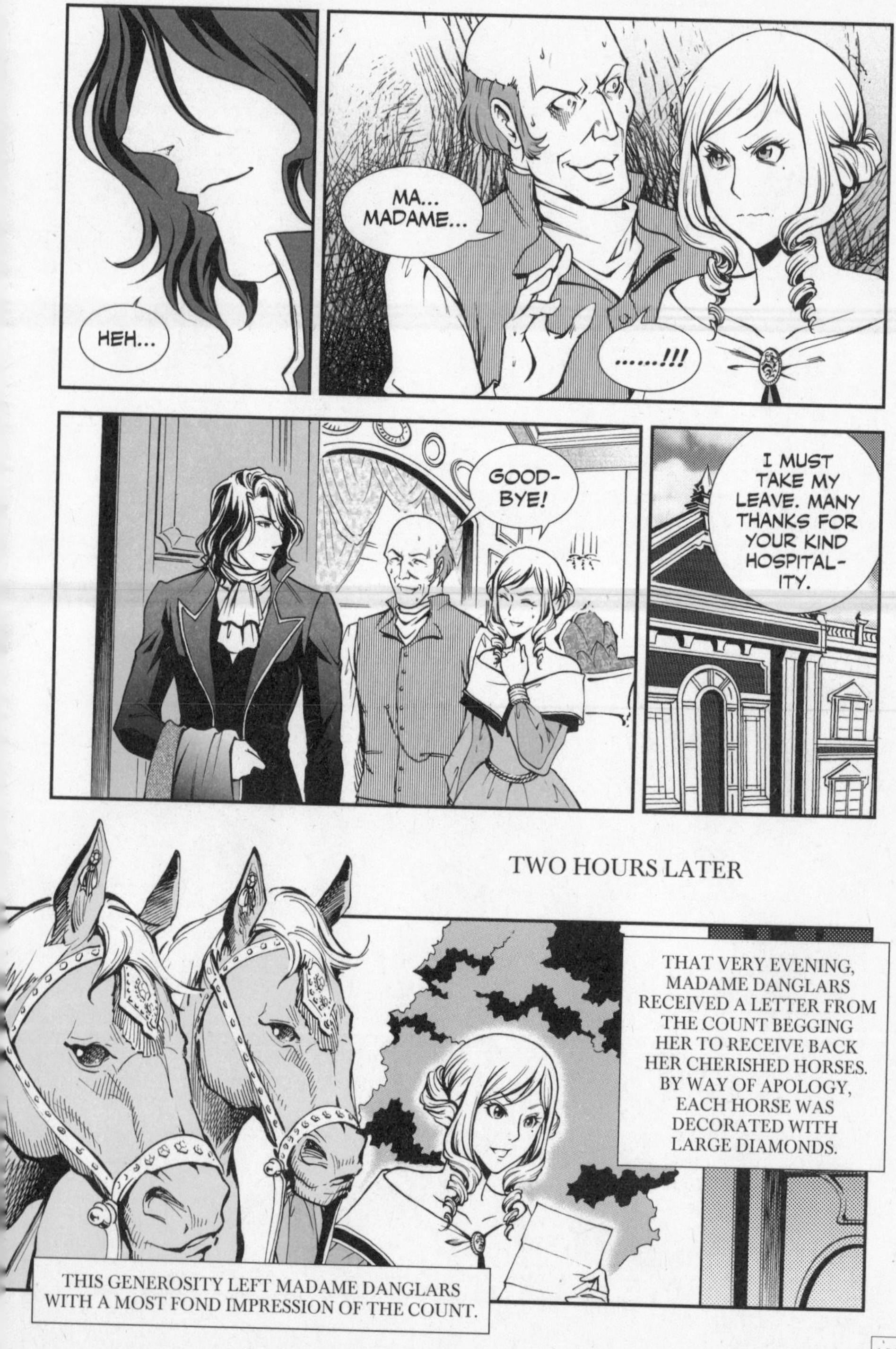
MA... MADAME...
......!!!
HEH...
I MUST TAKE MY LEAVE. MANY THANKS FOR YOUR KIND HOSPITAL-ITY.
GOOD-BYE!
TWO HOURS LATER
THAT VERY EVENING, MADAME DANGLARS RECEIVED A LETTER FROM THE COUNT BEGGING HER TO RECEIVE BACK HER CHERISHED HORSES. BY WAY OF APOLOGY, EACH HORSE WAS DECORATED WITH LARGE DIAMONDS.
THIS GENEROSITY LEFT MADAME DANGLARS WITH A MOST FOND IMPRESSION OF THE COUNT.

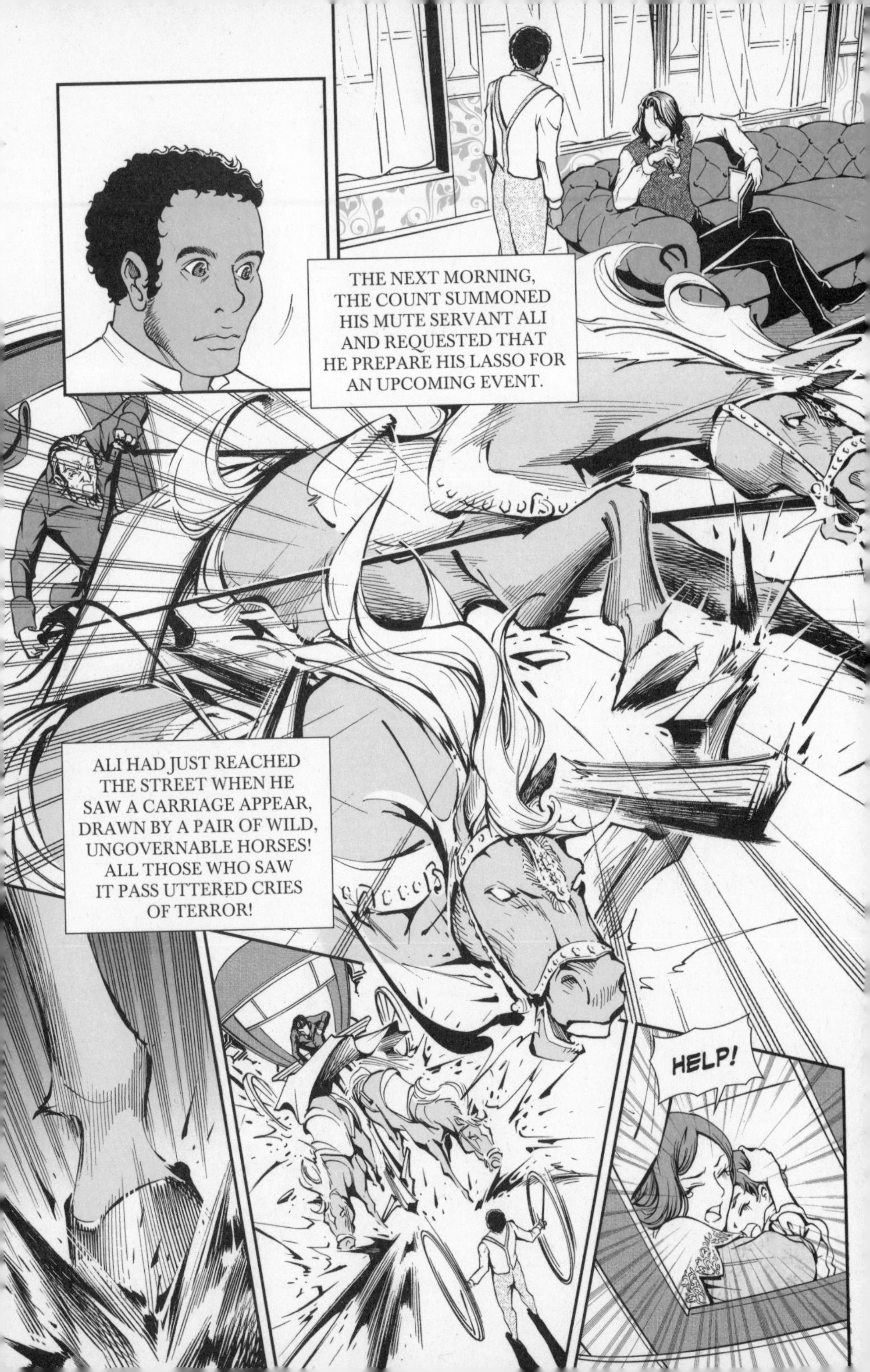
THE NEXT MORNING, THE COUNT SUMMONED HIS MUTE SERVANT ALI AND REQUESTED THAT HE PREPARE HIS LASSO FOR AN UPCOMING EVENT.
ALI HAD JUST REACHED THE STREET WHEN HE SAW A CARRIAGE APPEAR, DRAWN BY A PAIR OF WILD, UNGOVERNABLE HORSES! ALL THOSE WHO SAW IT PASS UTTERED CRIES OF TERROR!
HELP!

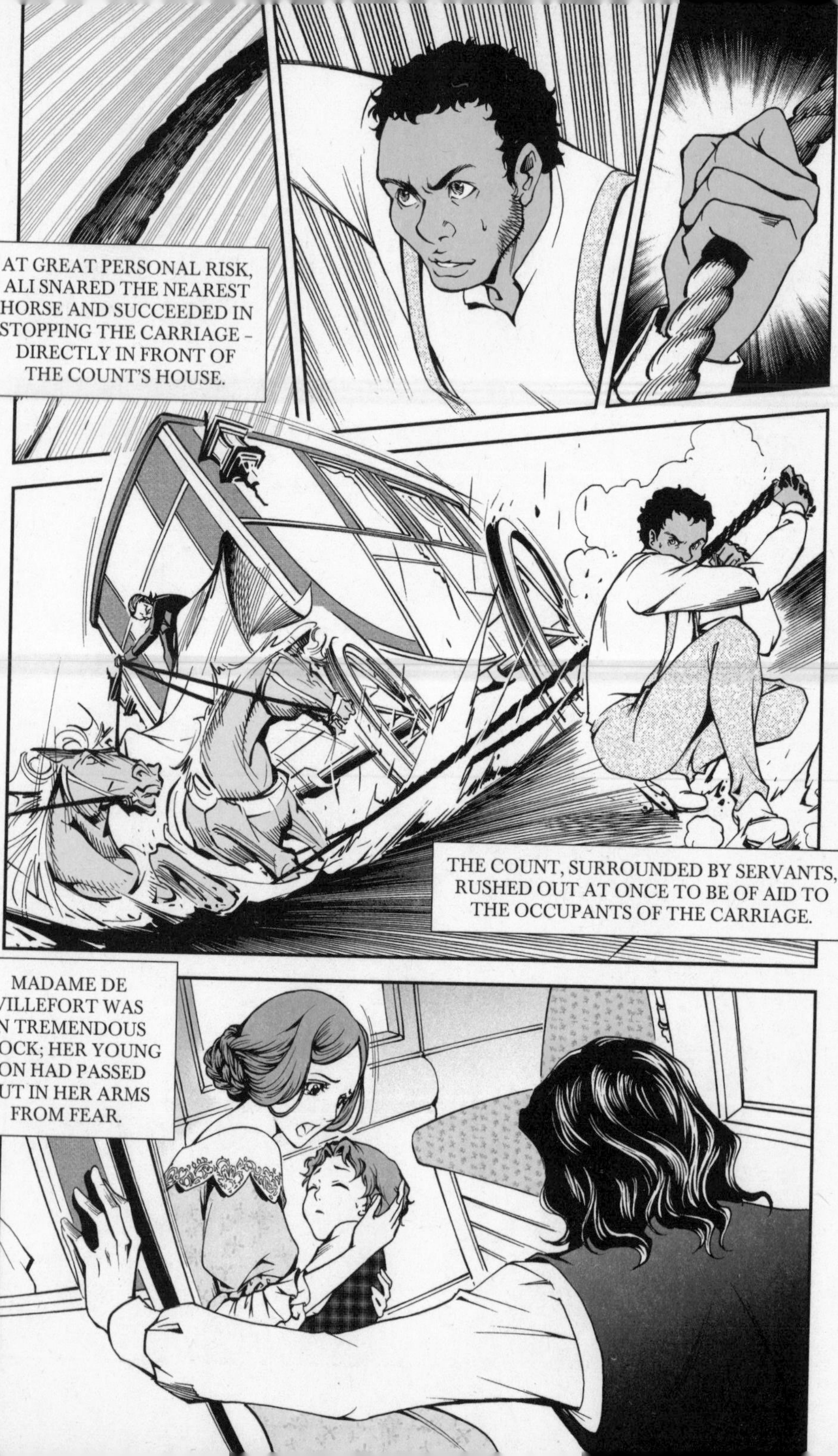
AT GREAT PERSONAL RISK, ALI SNARED THE NEAREST HORSE AND SUCCEEDED IN STOPPING THE CARRIAGE – DIRECTLY IN FRONT OF THE COUNT'S HOUSE.
THE COUNT, SURROUNDED BY SERVANTS, RUSHED OUT AT ONCE TO BE OF AID TO THE OCCUPANTS OF THE CARRIAGE.
MADAME DE VILLEFORT WAS IN TREMENDOUS SHOCK; HER YOUNG SON HAD PASSED OUT IN HER ARMS FROM FEAR.

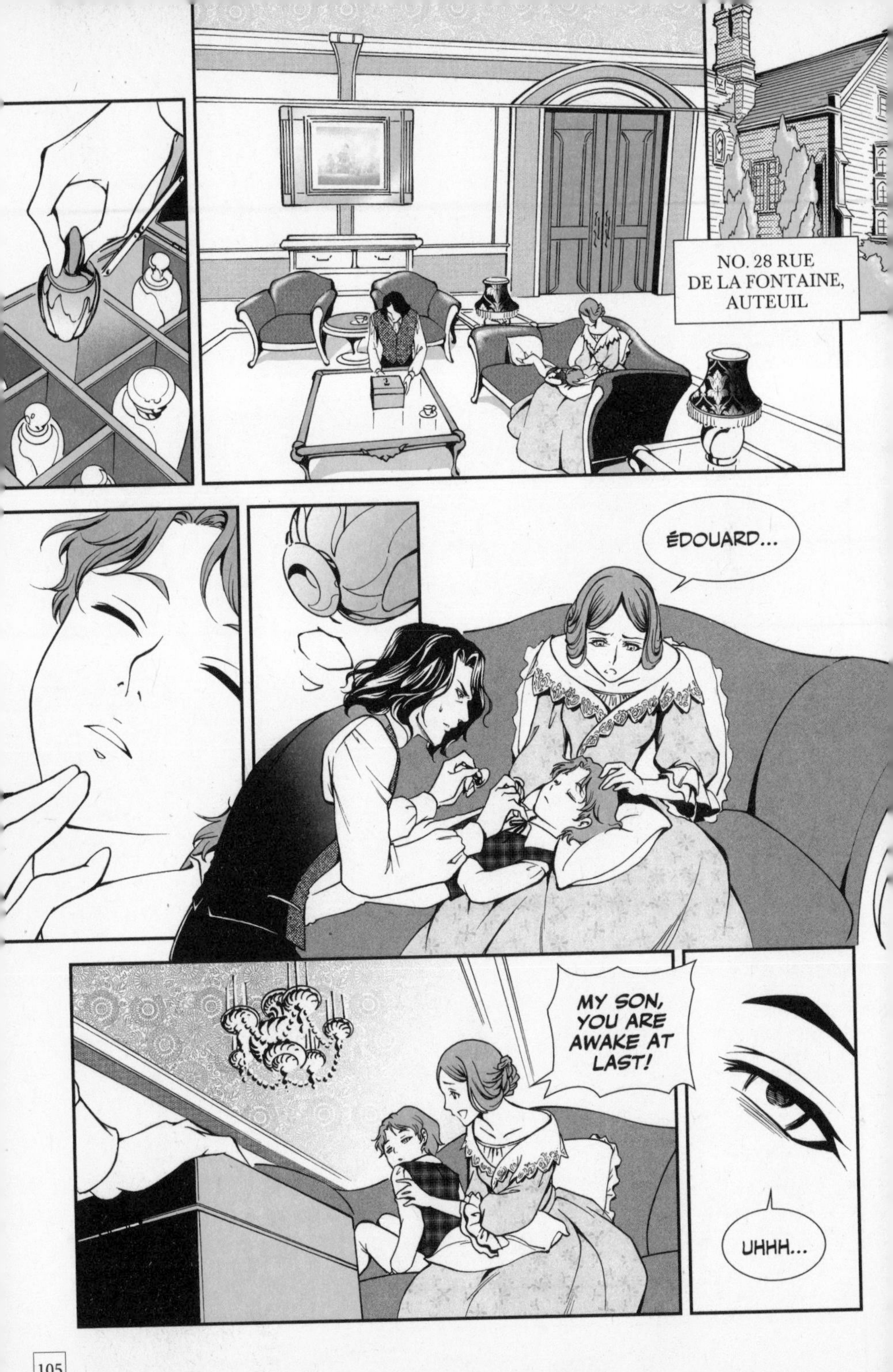
NO. 28 RUE DE LA FONTAINE, AUTEUIL
ÉDOUARD...
UHHH...
MY SON, YOU ARE AWAKE AT LAST!

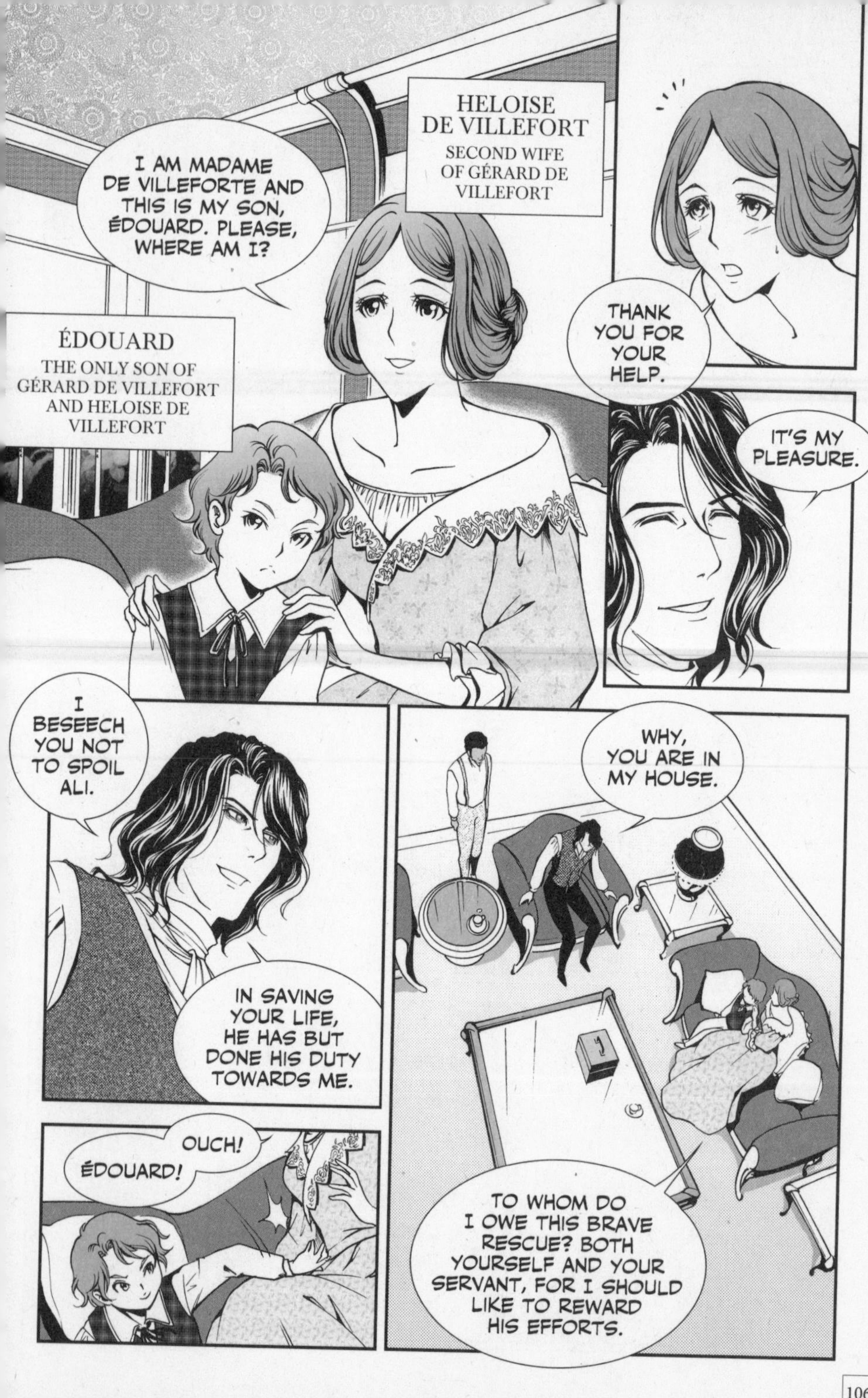
THANK YOU FOR YOUR HELP.
IT'S MY PLEASURE.
HELOISE DE VILLEFORT
SECOND WIFE OF GÉRARD DE VILLEFORT
I AM MADAME DE VILLEFORTE AND THIS IS MY SON, ÉDOUARD. PLEASE, WHERE AM I?
ÉDOUARD
THE ONLY SON OF GÉRARD DE VILLEFORT AND HELOISE DE VILLEFORT
WHY, YOU ARE IN MY HOUSE.
TO WHOM DO I OWE THIS BRAVE RESCUE? BOTH YOURSELF AND YOUR SERVANT, FOR I SHOULD LIKE TO REWARD HIS EFFORTS.
I BESEECH YOU NOT TO SPOIL ALI.
IN SAVING YOUR LIFE, HE HAS BUT DONE HIS DUTY TOWARDS ME.
OUCH!
ÉDOUARD!

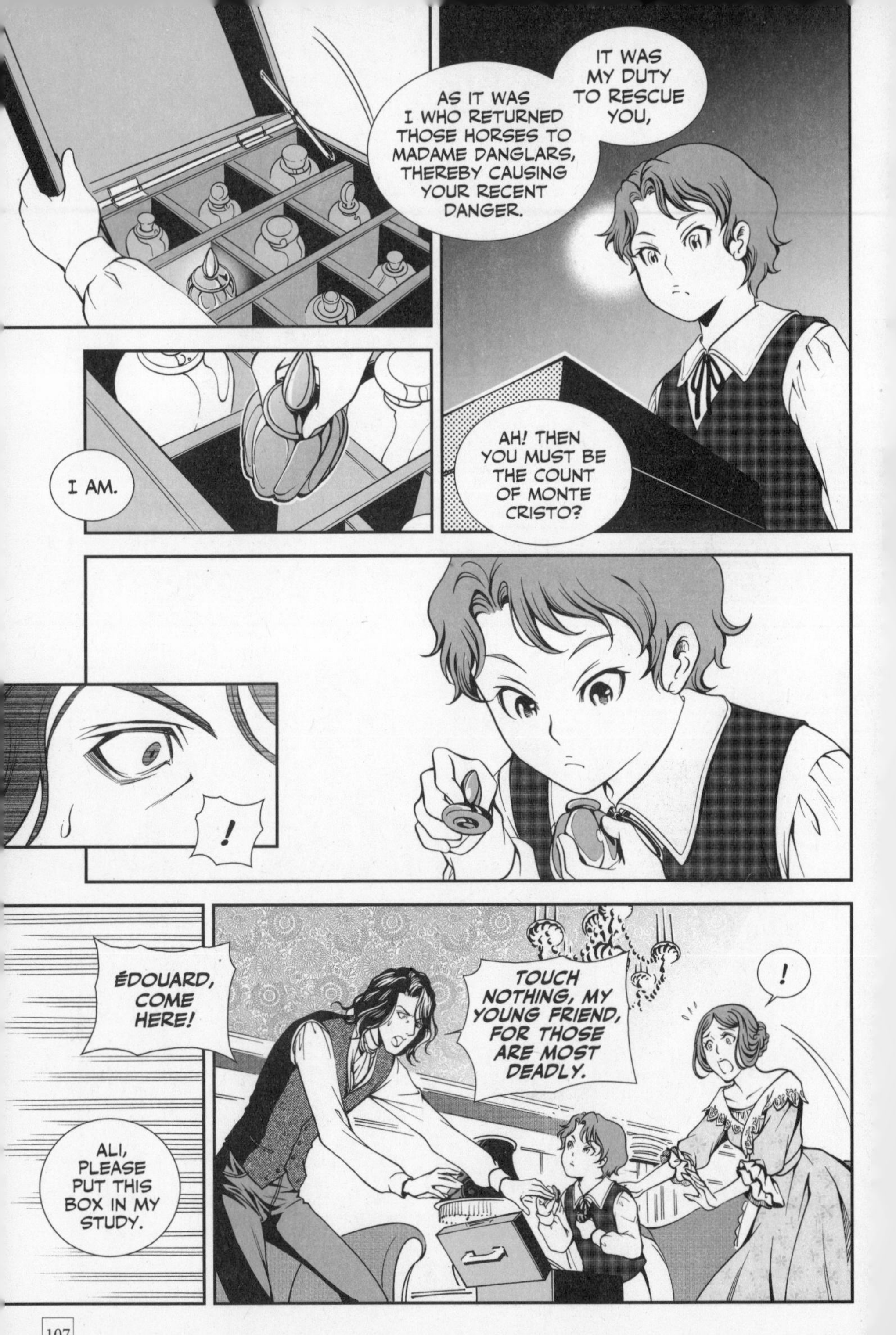
IT WAS MY DUTY TO RESCUE YOU,
AS IT WAS I WHO RETURNED THOSE HORSES TO MADAME DANGLARS, THEREBY CAUSING YOUR RECENT DANGER.
AH! THEN YOU MUST BE THE COUNT OF MONTE CRISTO?
I AM.
!
!
TOUCH NOTHING, MY YOUNG FRIEND, FOR THOSE ARE MOST DEADLY.
ÉDOUARD, COME HERE!
ALI, PLEASE PUT THIS BOX IN MY STUDY.

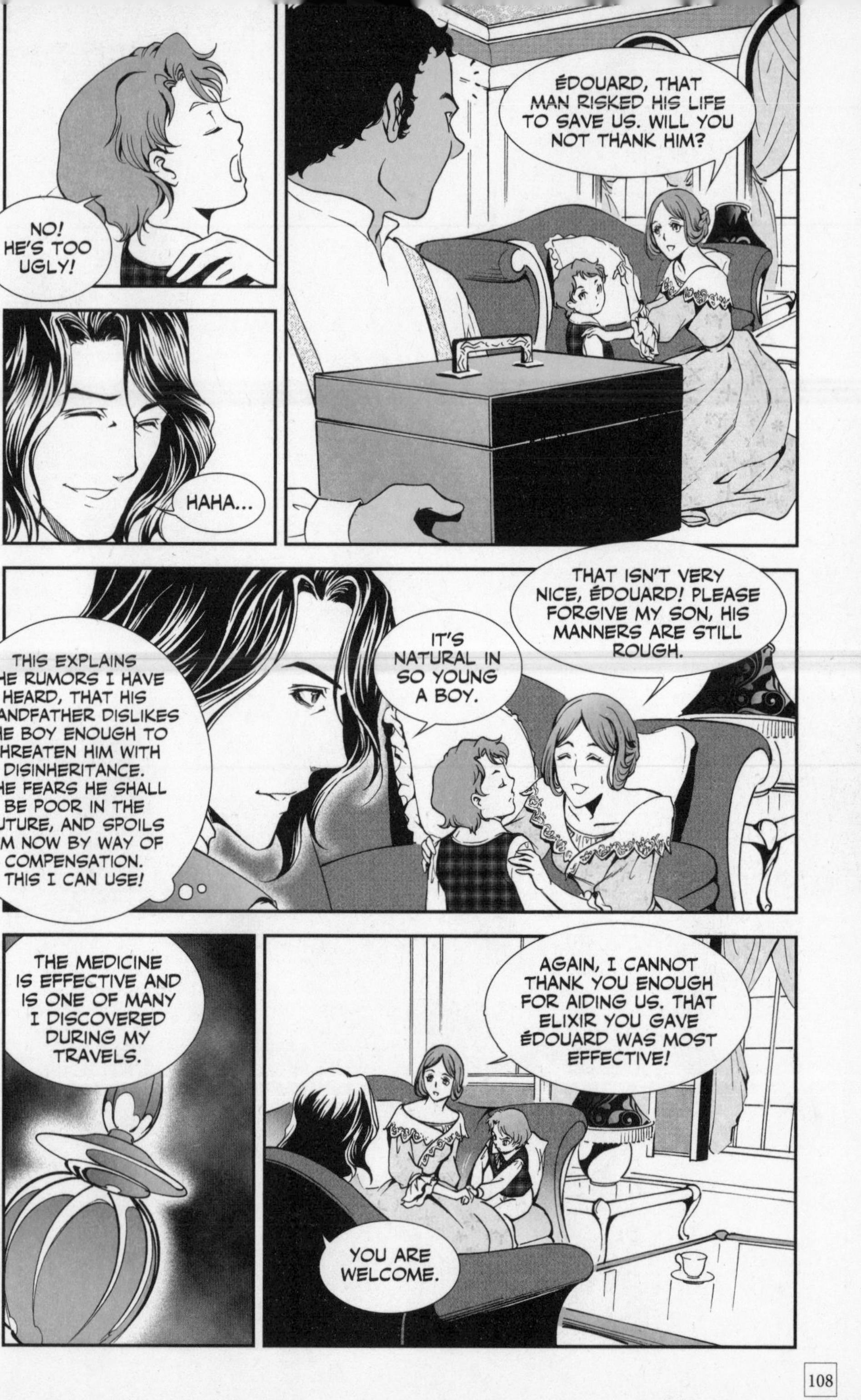
ÉDOUARD, THAT MAN RISKED HIS LIFE TO SAVE US. WILL YOU NOT THANK HIM?
NO! HE'S TOO UGLY!
HAHA...
THAT ISN'T VERY NICE, ÉDOUARD! PLEASE FORGIVE MY SON, HIS MANNERS ARE STILL ROUGH.
IT'S NATURAL IN SO YOUNG A BOY.
THIS EXPLAINS THE RUMORS I HAVE HEARD, THAT HIS GRANDFATHER DISLIKES THE BOY ENOUGH TO THREATEN HIM WITH DISINHERITANCE. SHE FEARS HE SHALL BE POOR IN THE FUTURE, AND SPOILS HIM NOW BY WAY OF COMPENSATION. THIS I CAN USE!
AGAIN, I CANNOT THANK YOU ENOUGH FOR AIDING US. THAT ELIXIR YOU GAVE ÉDOUARD WAS MOST EFFECTIVE!
YOU ARE WELCOME.
THE MEDICINE IS EFFECTIVE AND IS ONE OF MANY I DISCOVERED DURING MY TRAVELS.

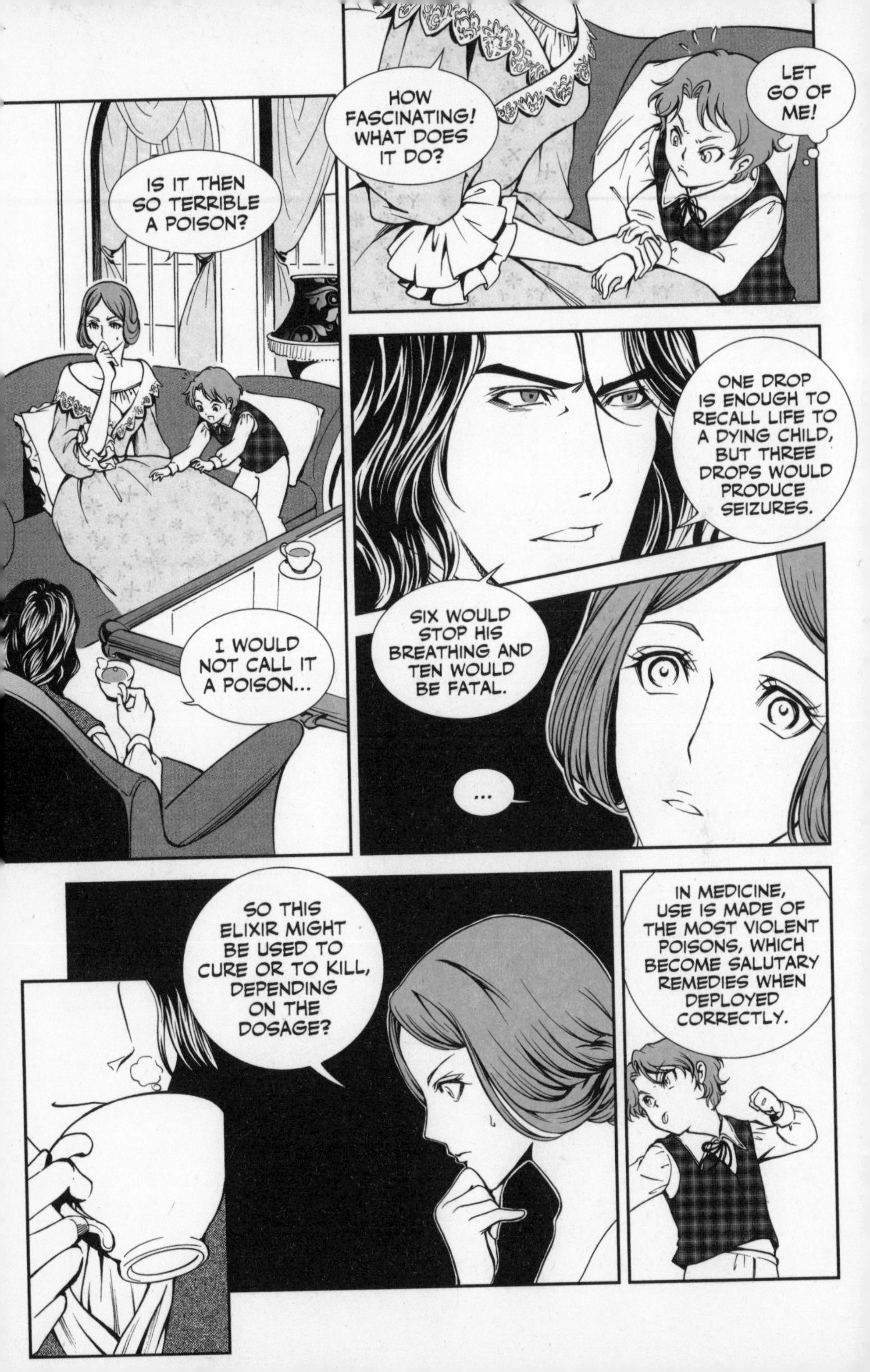
LET GO OF ME!
HOW FASCINATING! WHAT DOES IT DO?
ONE DROP IS ENOUGH TO RECALL LIFE TO A DYING CHILD, BUT THREE DROPS WOULD PRODUCE SEIZURES.
SIX WOULD STOP HIS BREATHING AND TEN WOULD BE FATAL.
...
IS IT THEN SO TERRIBLE A POISON?
I WOULD NOT CALL IT A POISON...
IN MEDICINE, USE IS MADE OF THE MOST VIOLENT POISONS, WHICH BECOME SALUTARY REMEDIES WHEN DEPLOYED CORRECTLY.
SO THIS ELIXIR MIGHT BE USED TO CURE OR TO KILL, DEPENDING ON THE DOSAGE?

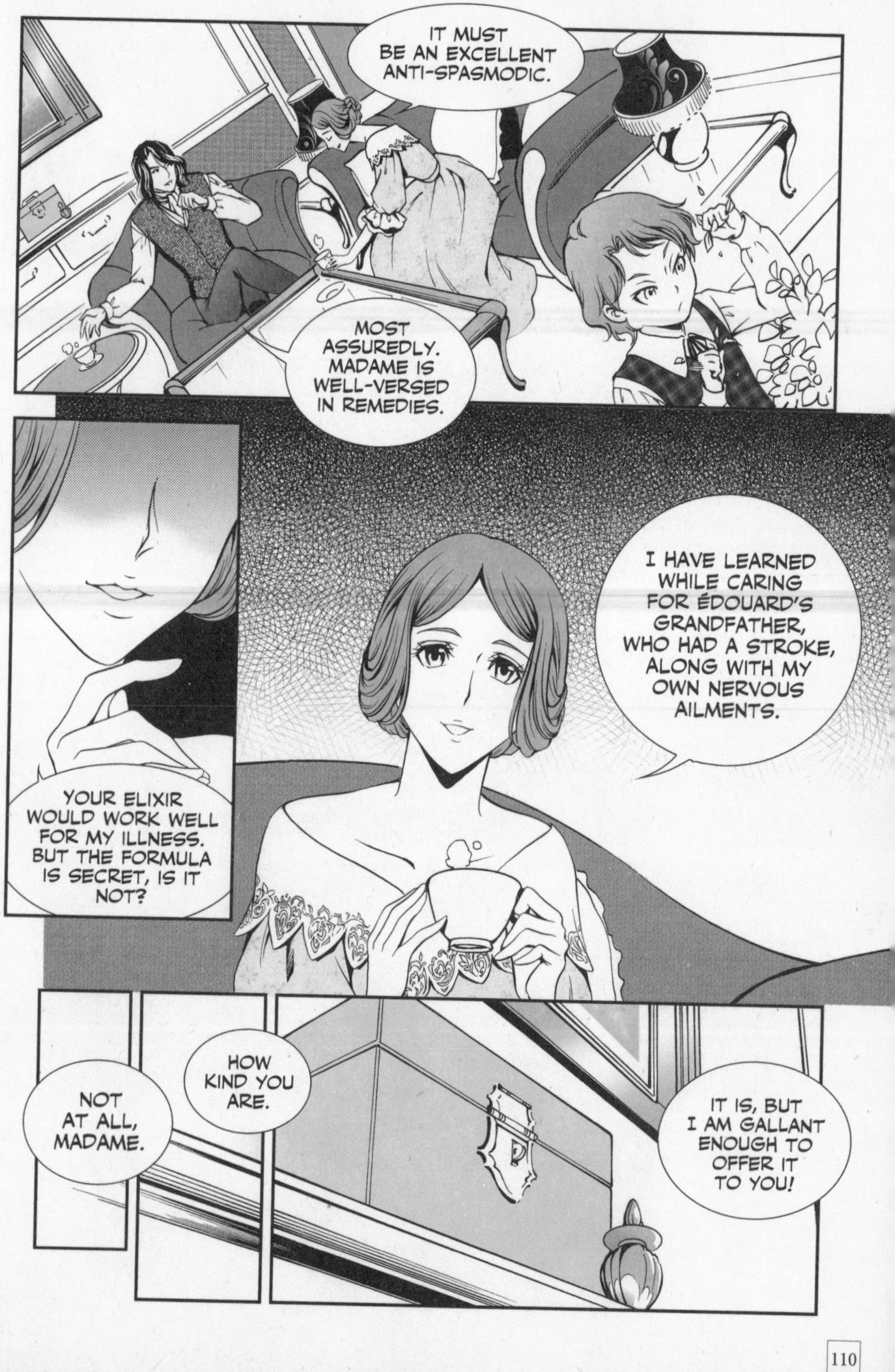
IT MUST BE AN EXCELLENT ANTI-SPASMODIC.
MOST ASSUREDLY. MADAME IS WELL-VERSED IN REMEDIES.
I HAVE LEARNED WHILE CARING FOR ÉDOUARD'S GRANDFATHER, WHO HAD A STROKE, ALONG WITH MY OWN NERVOUS AILMENTS.
YOUR ELIXIR WOULD WORK WELL FOR MY ILLNESS. BUT THE FORMULA IS SECRET, IS IT NOT?
IT IS, BUT I AM GALLANT ENOUGH TO OFFER IT TO YOU!
HOW KIND YOU ARE.
NOT AT ALL, MADAME.

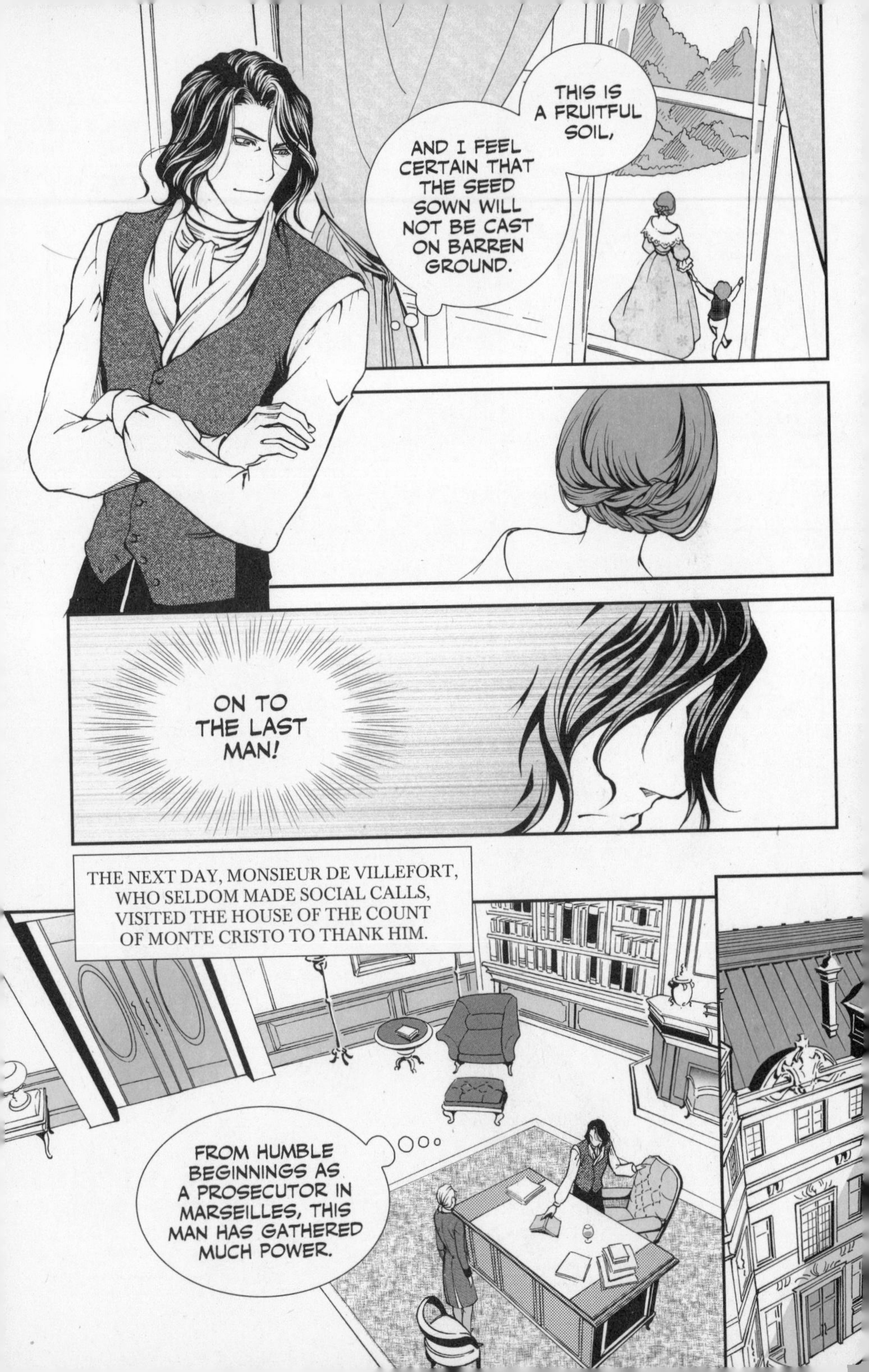
THIS IS A FRUITFUL SOIL,
AND I FEEL CERTAIN THAT THE SEED SOWN WILL NOT BE CAST ON BARREN GROUND.
ON TO THE LAST MAN!
THE NEXT DAY, MONSIEUR DE VILLEFORT, WHO SELDOM MADE SOCIAL CALLS, VISITED THE HOUSE OF THE COUNT OF MONTE CRISTO TO THANK HIM.
FROM HUMBLE BEGINNINGS AS A PROSECUTOR IN MARSEILLES, THIS MAN HAS GATHERED MUCH POWER.

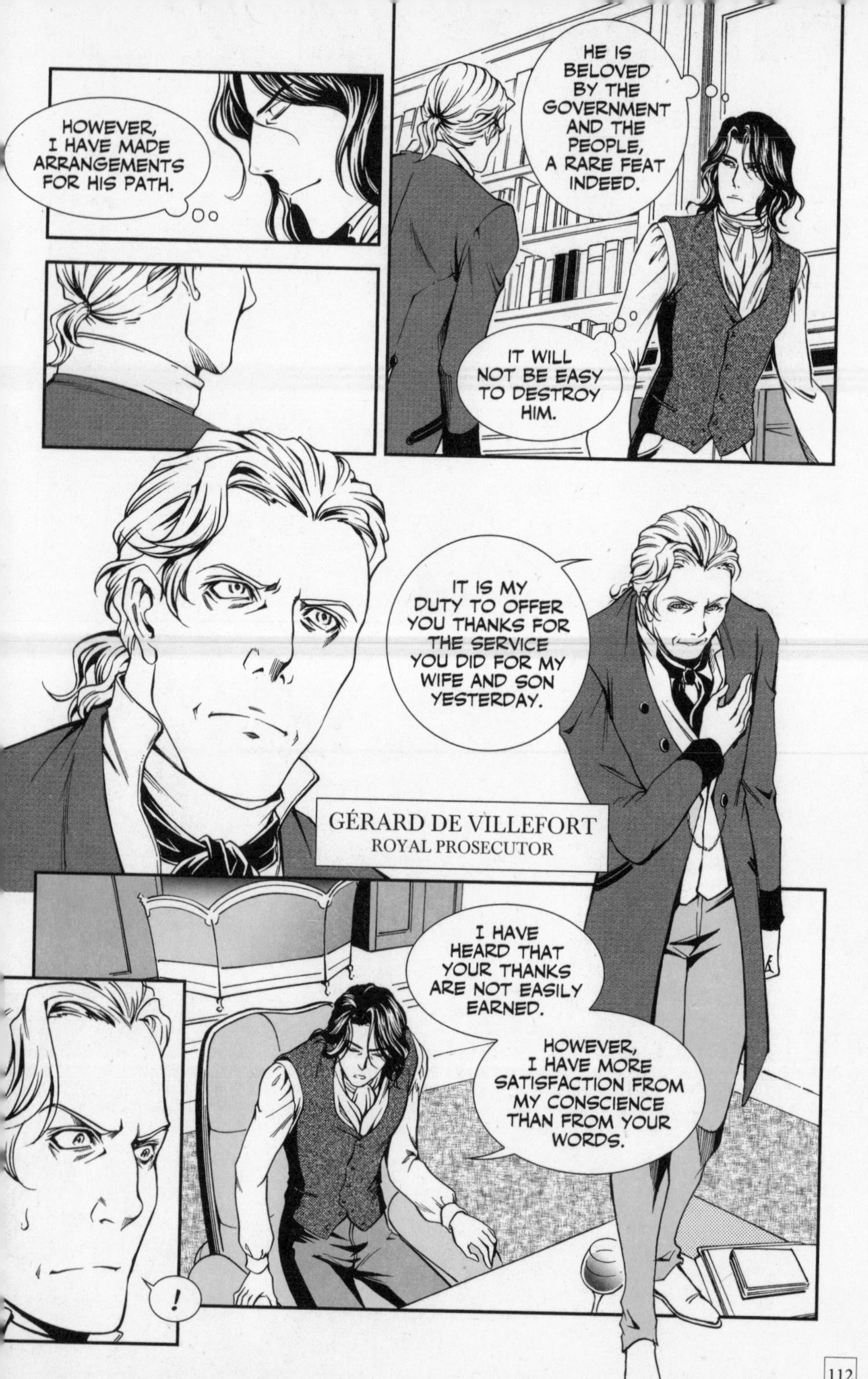
HE IS BELOVED BY THE GOVERNMENT AND THE PEOPLE, A RARE FEAT INDEED.
IT WILL NOT BE EASY TO DESTROY HIM.
HOWEVER, I HAVE MADE ARRANGEMENTS FOR HIS PATH.
IT IS MY DUTY TO OFFER YOU THANKS FOR THE SERVICE YOU DID FOR MY WIFE AND SON YESTERDAY.
GÉRARD DE VILLEFORT
ROYAL PROSECUTOR
I HAVE HEARD THAT YOUR THANKS ARE NOT EASILY EARNED.
HOWEVER, I HAVE MORE SATISFACTION FROM MY CONSCIENCE THAN FROM YOUR WORDS.
!

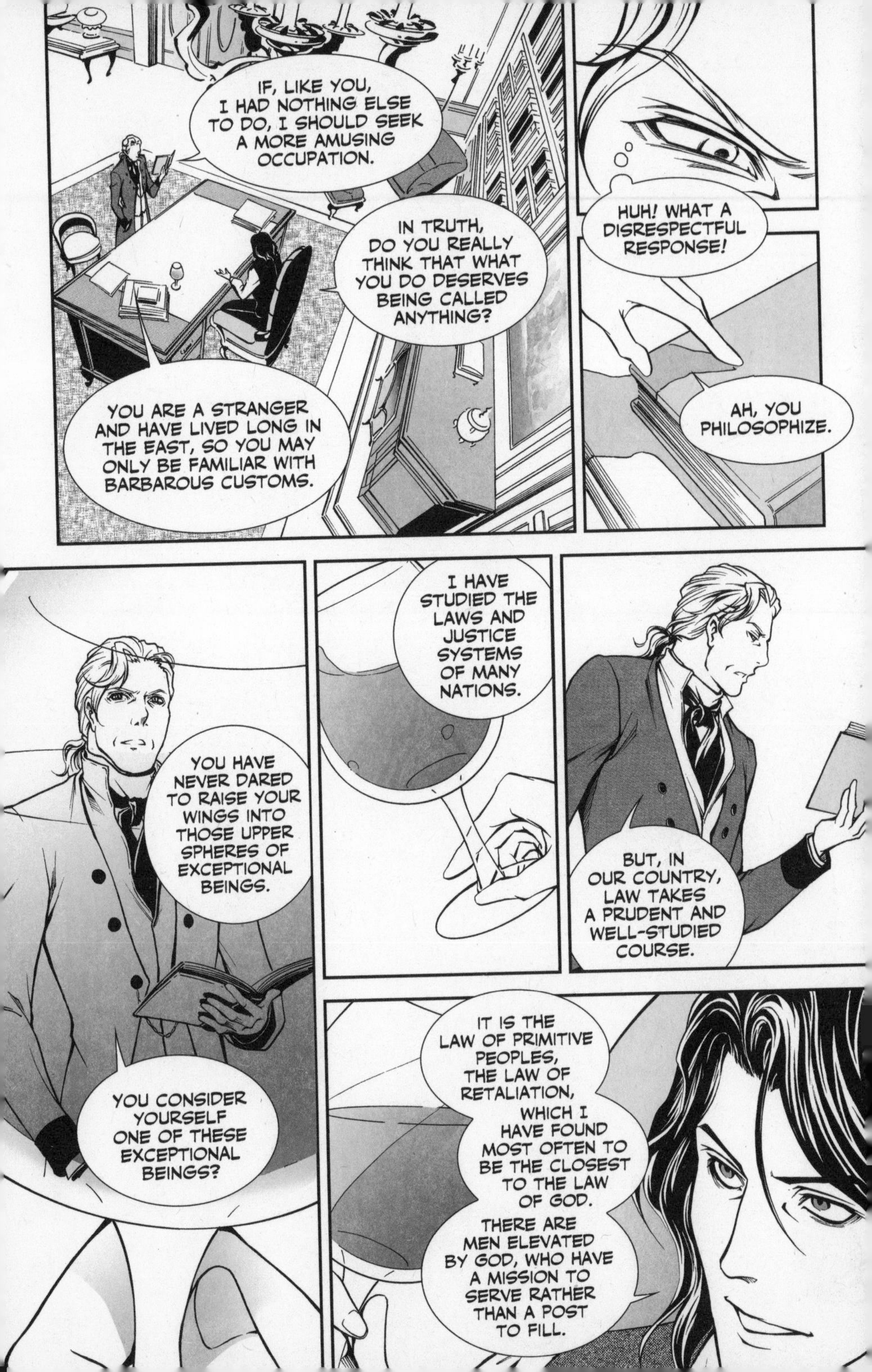

HUH! WHAT A DISRESPECTFUL RESPONSE!
AH, YOU PHILOSOPHIZE.
IF, LIKE YOU, I HAD NOTHING ELSE TO DO, I SHOULD SEEK A MORE AMUSING OCCUPATION.
IN TRUTH, DO YOU REALLY THINK THAT WHAT YOU DO DESERVES BEING CALLED ANYTHING?
YOU ARE A STRANGER AND HAVE LIVED LONG IN THE EAST, SO YOU MAY ONLY BE FAMILIAR WITH BARBAROUS CUSTOMS.
BUT, IN OUR COUNTRY, LAW TAKES A PRUDENT AND WELL-STUDIED COURSE.
I HAVE STUDIED THE LAWS AND JUSTICE SYSTEMS OF MANY NATIONS.
IT IS THE LAW OF PRIMITIVE PEOPLES, THE LAW OF RETALIATION,
WHICH I HAVE FOUND MOST OFTEN TO BE THE CLOSEST TO THE LAW OF GOD.
THERE ARE MEN ELEVATED BY GOD, WHO HAVE A MISSION TO SERVE RATHER THAN A POST TO FILL.
YOU HAVE NEVER DARED TO RAISE YOUR WINGS INTO THOSE UPPER SPHERES OF EXCEPTIONAL BEINGS.
YOU CONSIDER YOURSELF ONE OF THESE EXCEPTIONAL BEINGS?

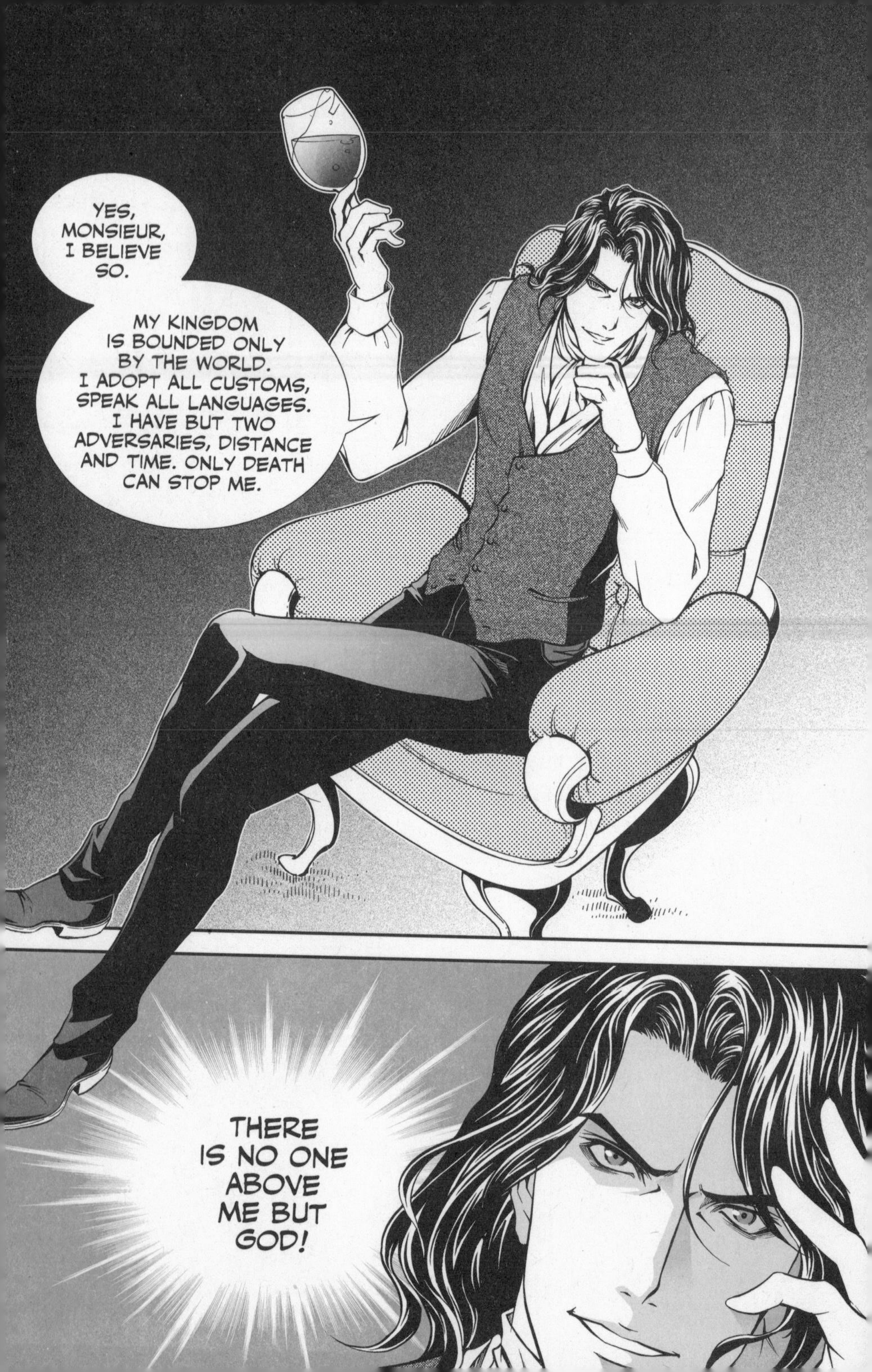
YES, MONSIEUR, I BELIEVE SO.
MY KINGDOM IS BOUNDED ONLY BY THE WORLD. I ADOPT ALL CUSTOMS, SPEAK ALL LANGUAGES. I HAVE BUT TWO ADVERSARIES, DISTANCE AND TIME. ONLY DEATH CAN STOP ME.
THERE IS NO ONE ABOVE ME BUT GOD!

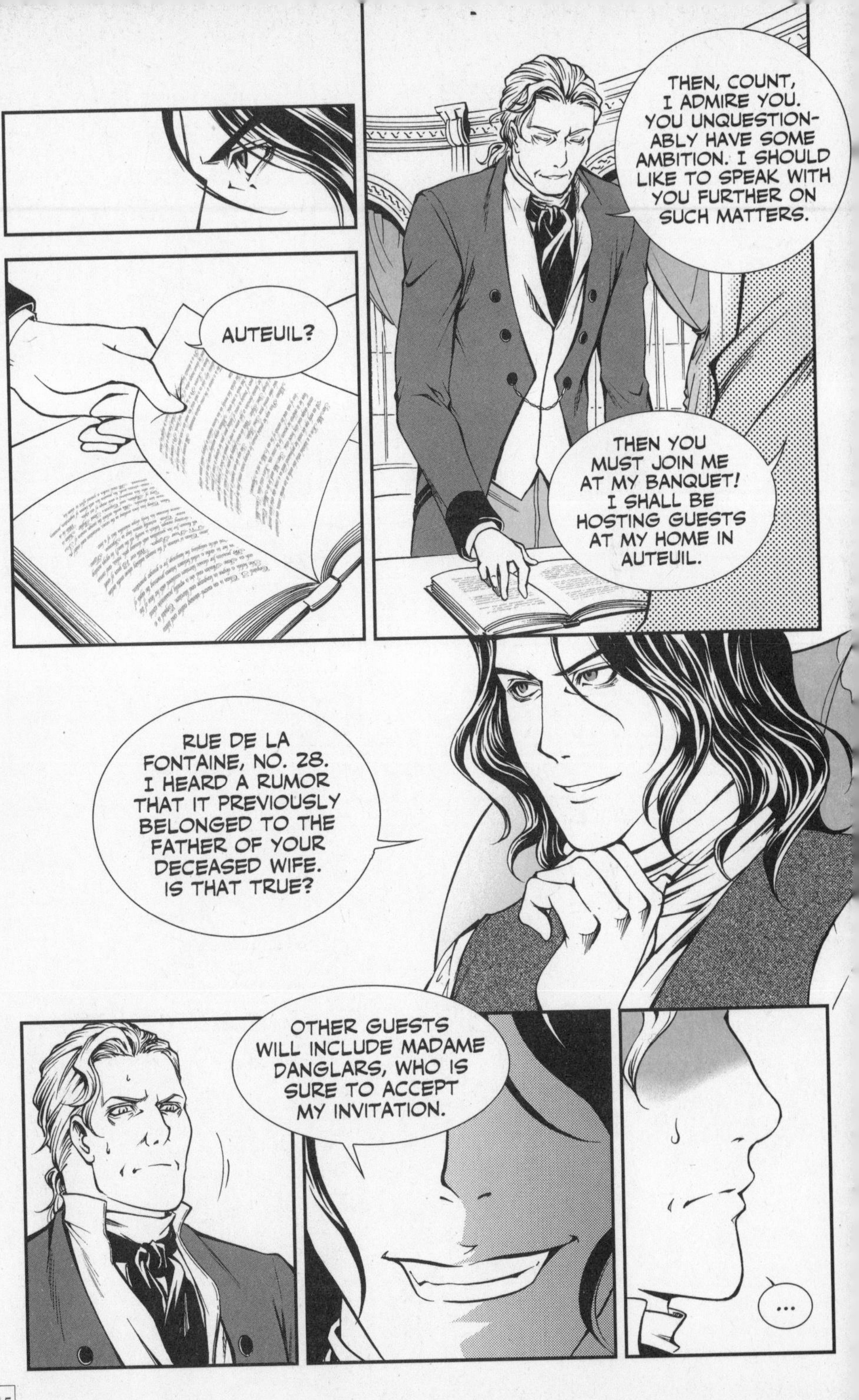
THEN, COUNT, I ADMIRE YOU. YOU UNQUESTION-ABLY HAVE SOME AMBITION. I SHOULD LIKE TO SPEAK WITH YOU FURTHER ON SUCH MATTERS.
THEN YOU MUST JOIN ME AT MY BANQUET! I SHALL BE HOSTING GUESTS AT MY HOME IN AUTEUIL.
AUTEUIL?
RUE DE LA FONTAINE, NO. 28. I HEARD A RUMOR THAT IT PREVIOUSLY BELONGED TO THE FATHER OF YOUR DECEASED WIFE. IS THAT TRUE?
...
OTHER GUESTS WILL INCLUDE MADAME DANGLARS, WHO IS SURE TO ACCEPT MY INVITATION.

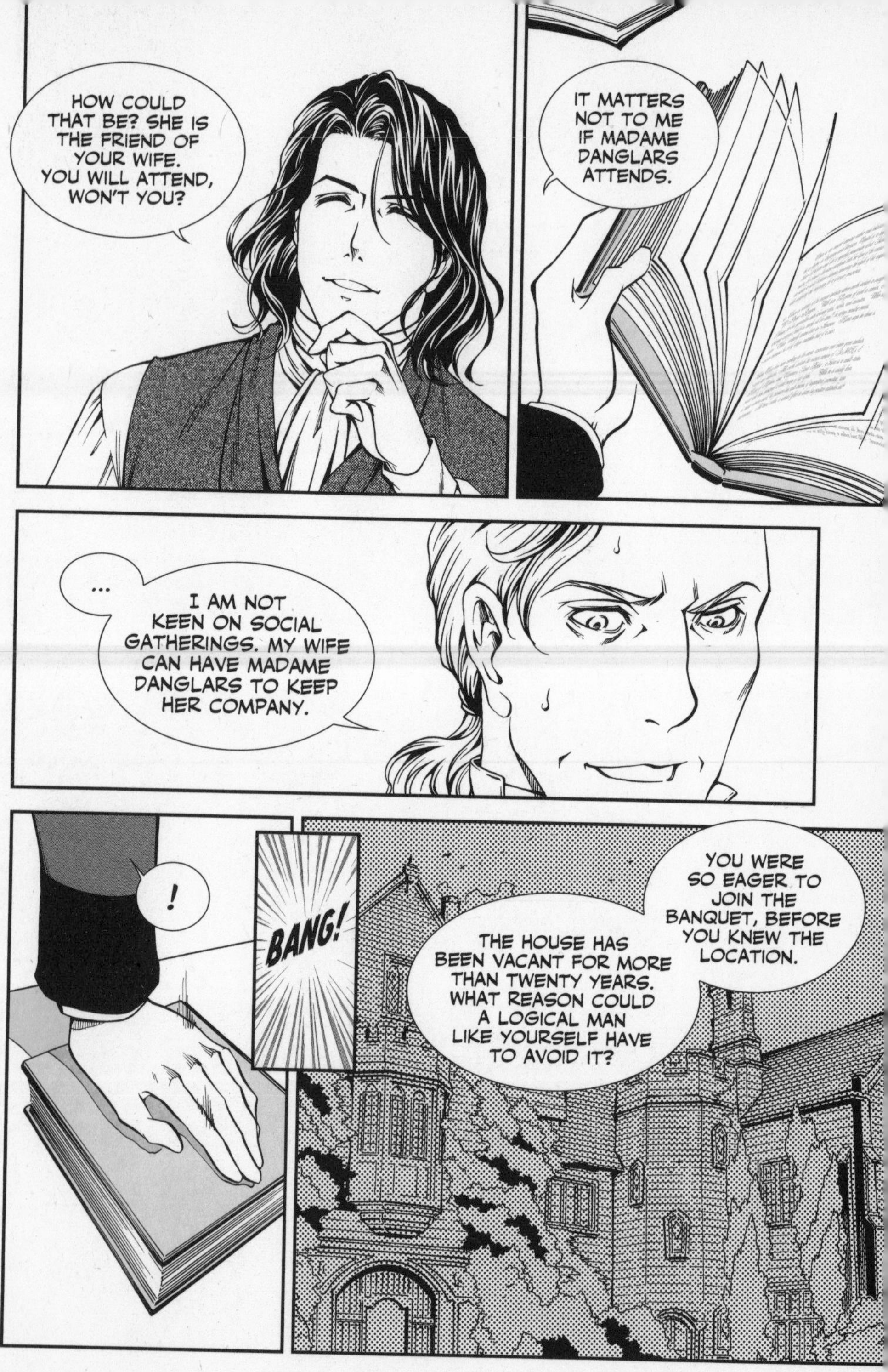
IT MATTERS NOT TO ME IF MADAME DANGLARS ATTENDS.
HOW COULD THAT BE? SHE IS THE FRIEND OF YOUR WIFE. YOU WILL ATTEND, WON'T YOU?
...
I AM NOT KEEN ON SOCIAL GATHERINGS. MY WIFE CAN HAVE MADAME DANGLARS TO KEEP HER COMPANY.
YOU WERE SO EAGER TO JOIN THE BANQUET, BEFORE YOU KNEW THE LOCATION.
THE HOUSE HAS BEEN VACANT FOR MORE THAN TWENTY YEARS. WHAT REASON COULD A LOGICAL MAN LIKE YOURSELF HAVE TO AVOID IT?
BANG!
!

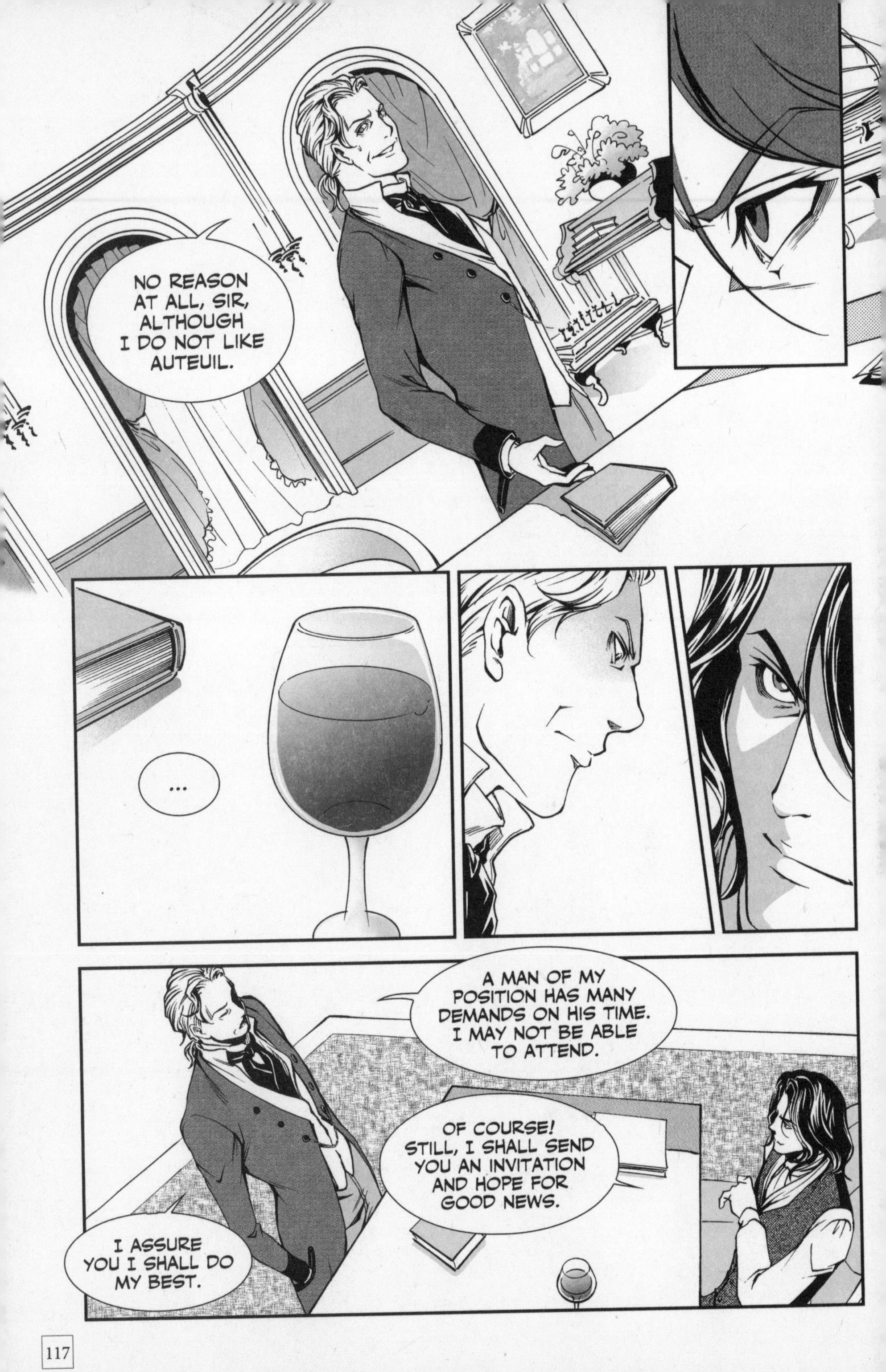
NO REASON AT ALL, SIR, ALTHOUGH I DO NOT LIKE AUTEUIL.
...
A MAN OF MY POSITION HAS MANY DEMANDS ON HIS TIME. I MAY NOT BE ABLE TO ATTEND.
OF COURSE! STILL, I SHALL SEND YOU AN INVITATION AND HOPE FOR GOOD NEWS.
I ASSURE YOU I SHALL DO MY BEST.

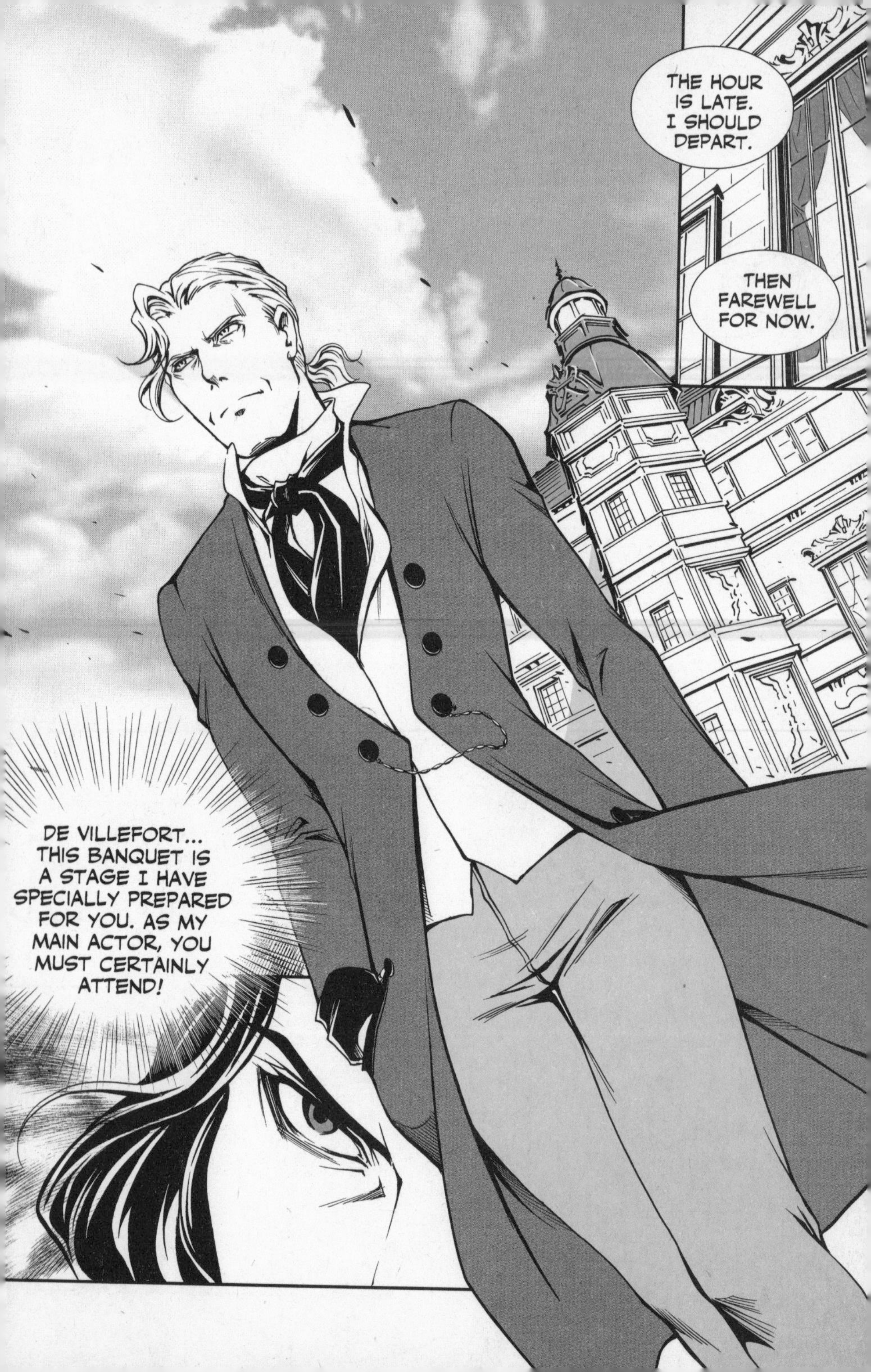
THE HOUR IS LATE. I SHOULD DEPART.
THEN FAREWELL FOR NOW.
DE VILLEFORT... THIS BANQUET IS A STAGE I HAVE SPECIALLY PREPARED FOR YOU. AS MY MAIN ACTOR, YOU MUST CERTAINLY ATTEND!

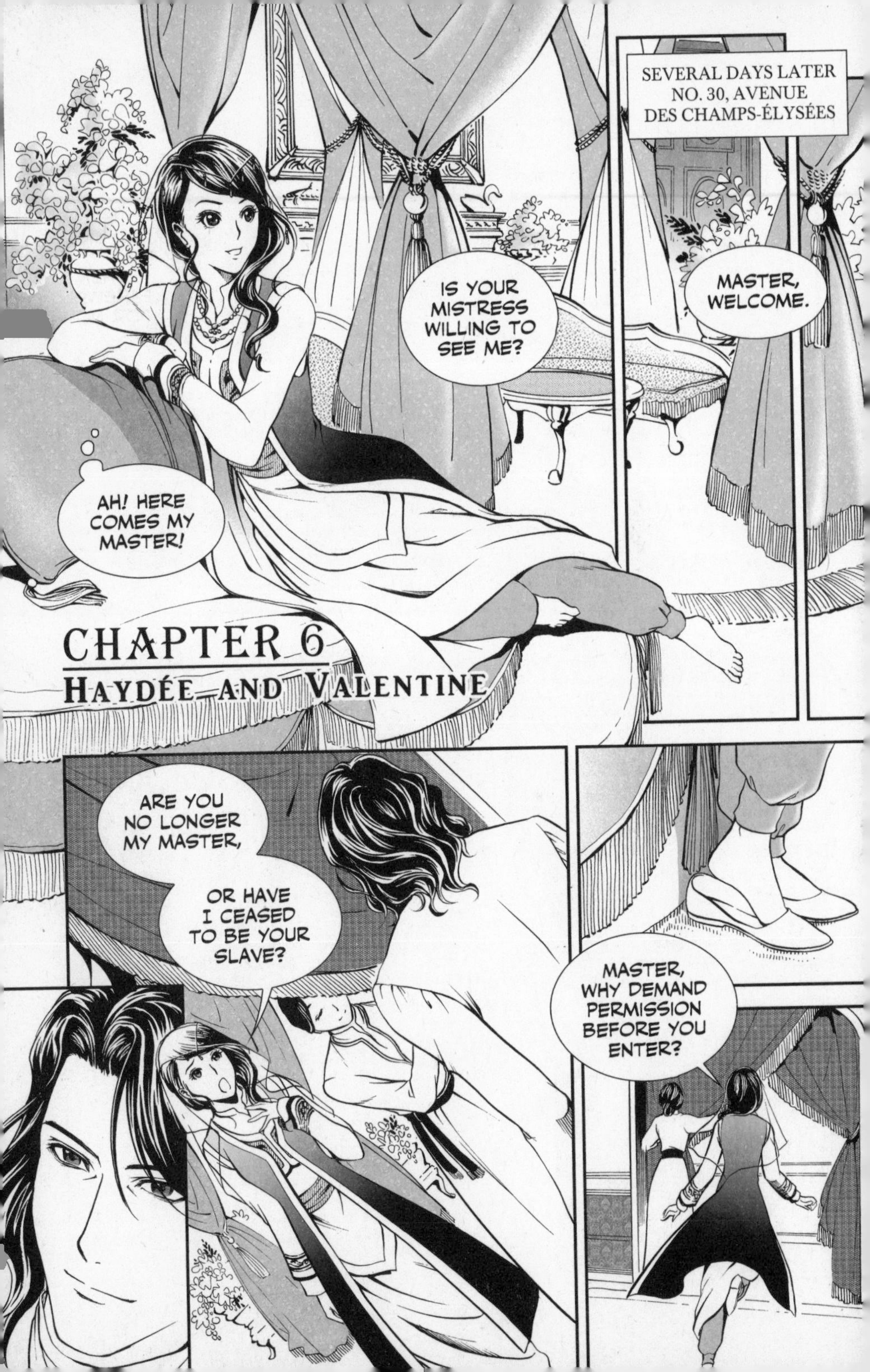
SEVERAL DAYS LATER
NO. 30, AVENUE
DES CHAMPS-ÉLYSÉES
MASTER, WELCOME.
IS YOUR MISTRESS WILLING TO SEE ME?
AH! HERE COMES MY MASTER!
CHAPTER 6
HAYDÉE AND VALENTINE
MASTER, WHY DEMAND PERMISSION BEFORE YOU ENTER?
ARE YOU NO LONGER MY MASTER,
OR HAVE I CEASED TO BE YOUR SLAVE?

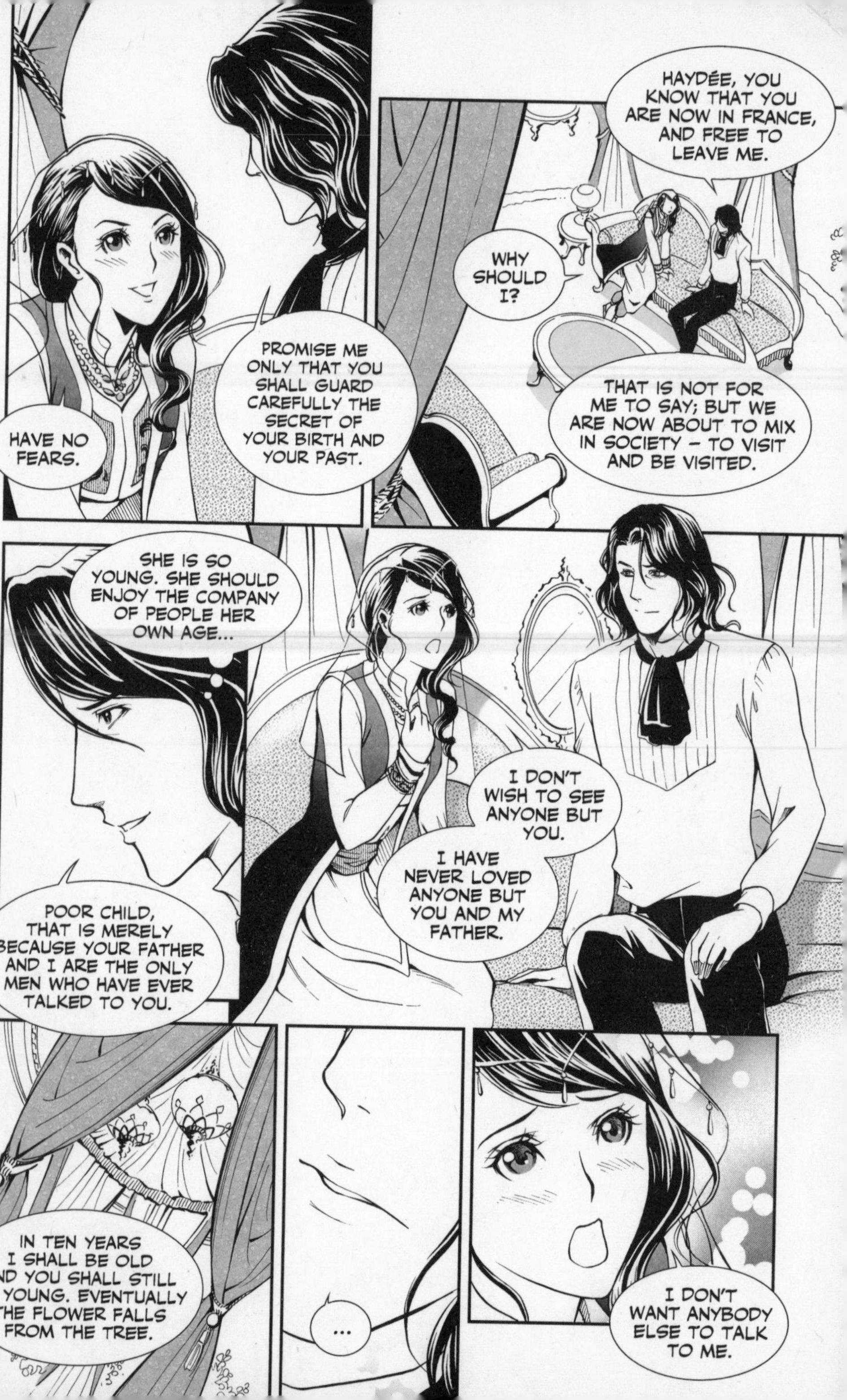
HAYDÉE, YOU KNOW THAT YOU ARE NOW IN FRANCE, AND FREE TO LEAVE ME.
WHY SHOULD I?
THAT IS NOT FOR ME TO SAY; BUT WE ARE NOW ABOUT TO MIX IN SOCIETY – TO VISIT AND BE VISITED.
PROMISE ME ONLY THAT YOU SHALL GUARD CAREFULLY THE SECRET OF YOUR BIRTH AND YOUR PAST.
HAVE NO FEARS.
I DON'T WISH TO SEE ANYONE BUT YOU.
I HAVE NEVER LOVED ANYONE BUT YOU AND MY FATHER.
SHE IS SO YOUNG. SHE SHOULD ENJOY THE COMPANY OF PEOPLE HER OWN AGE...
POOR CHILD, THAT IS MERELY BECAUSE YOUR FATHER AND I ARE THE ONLY MEN WHO HAVE EVER TALKED TO YOU.
I DON'T WANT ANYBODY ELSE TO TALK TO ME.
...
IN TEN YEARS I SHALL BE OLD AND YOU SHALL STILL BE YOUNG. EVENTUALLY THE FLOWER FALLS FROM THE TREE.

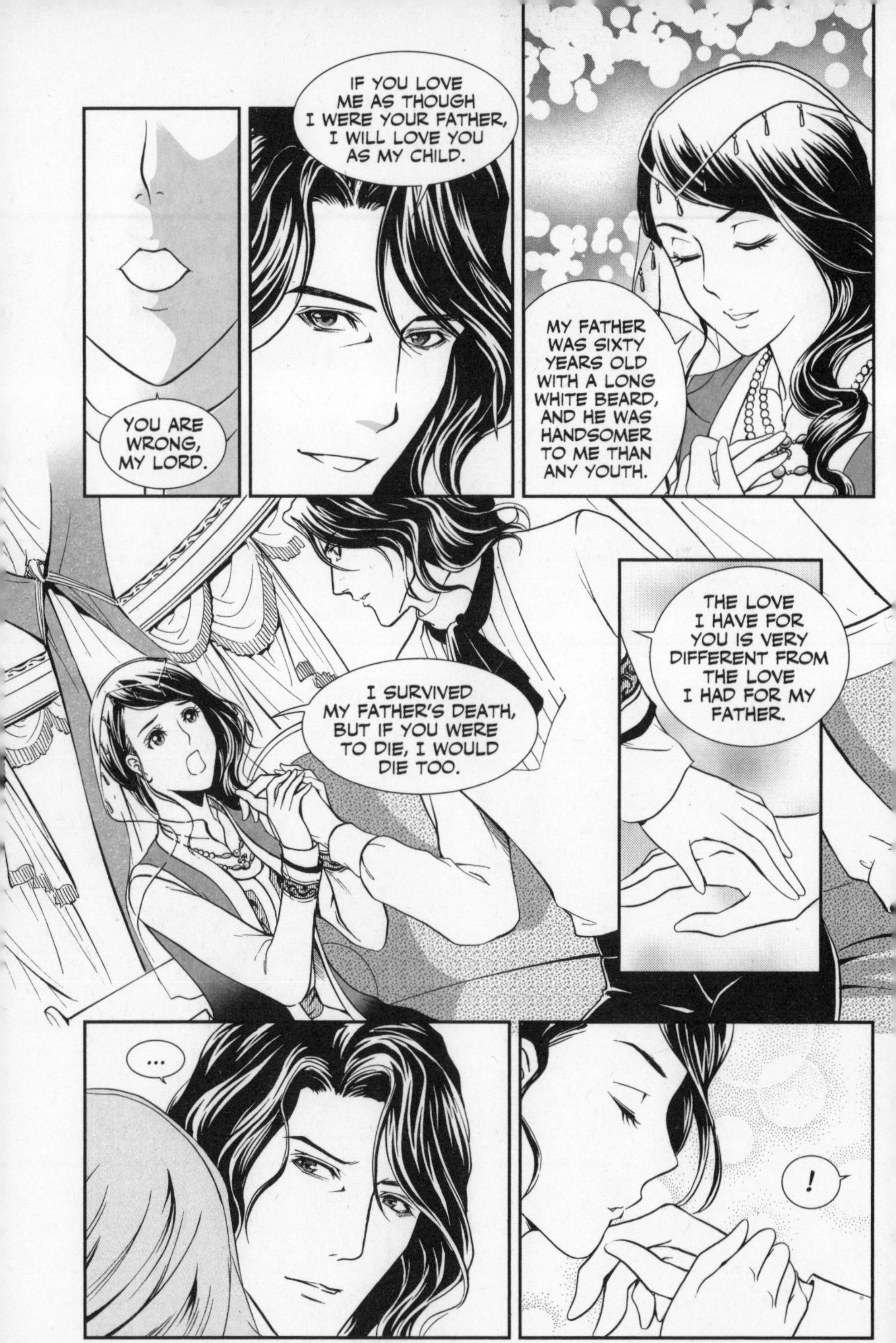
MY FATHER WAS SIXTY YEARS OLD WITH A LONG WHITE BEARD, AND HE WAS HANDSOMER TO ME THAN ANY YOUTH.
IF YOU LOVE ME AS THOUGH I WERE YOUR FATHER, I WILL LOVE YOU AS MY CHILD.
YOU ARE WRONG, MY LORD.
THE LOVE I HAVE FOR YOU IS VERY DIFFERENT FROM THE LOVE I HAD FOR MY FATHER.
I SURVIVED MY FATHER'S DEATH, BUT IF YOU WERE TO DIE, I WOULD DIE TOO.
!
...

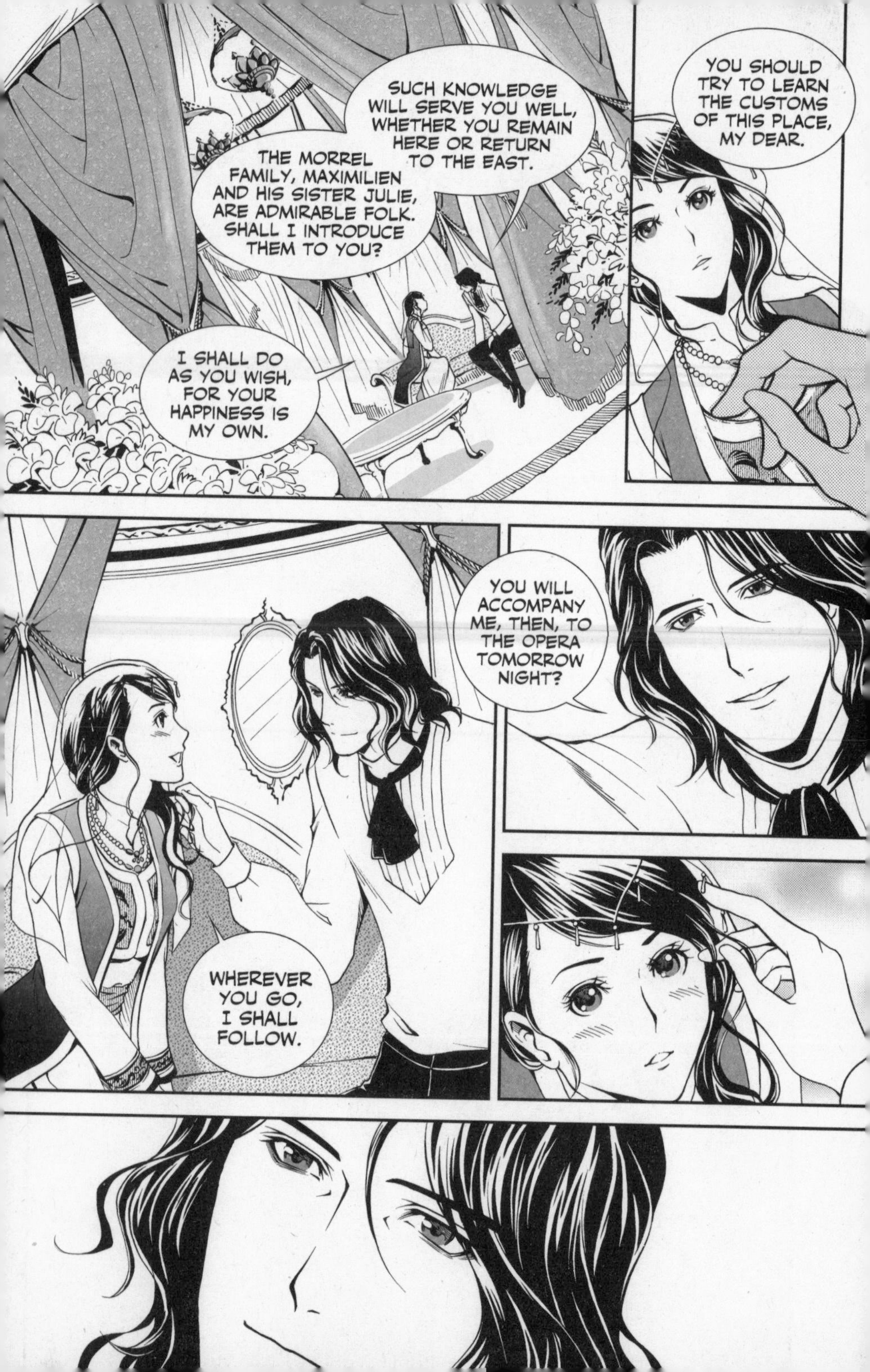
YOU SHOULD TRY TO LEARN THE CUSTOMS OF THIS PLACE, MY DEAR.
SUCH KNOWLEDGE WILL SERVE YOU WELL, WHETHER YOU REMAIN HERE OR RETURN TO THE EAST.
THE MORREL FAMILY, MAXIMILIEN AND HIS SISTER JULIE, ARE ADMIRABLE FOLK. SHALL I INTRODUCE THEM TO YOU?
I SHALL DO AS YOU WISH, FOR YOUR HAPPINESS IS MY OWN.
YOU WILL ACCOMPANY ME, THEN, TO THE OPERA TOMORROW NIGHT?
WHEREVER YOU GO, I SHALL FOLLOW.

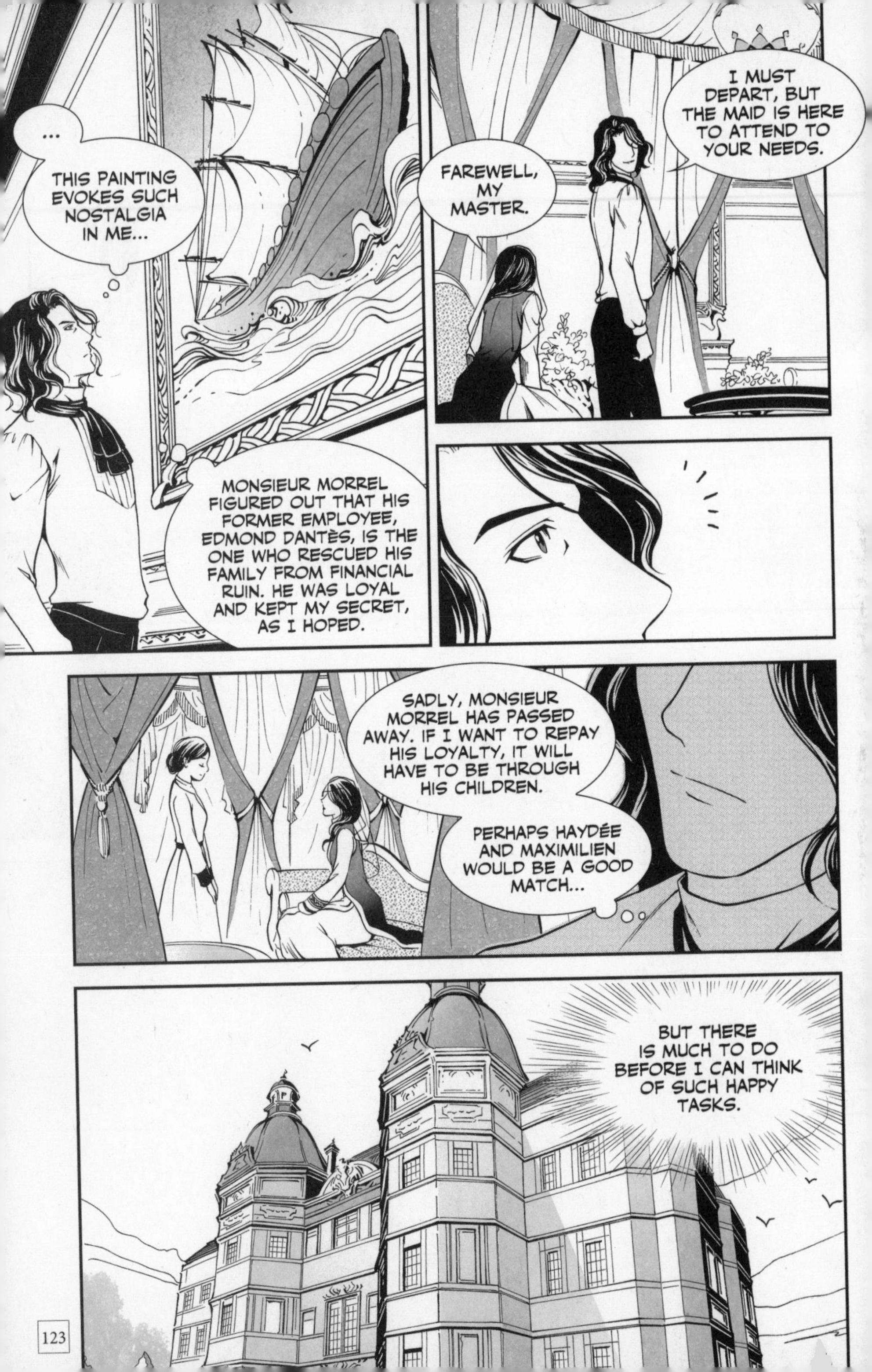
I MUST DEPART, BUT THE MAID IS HERE TO ATTEND TO YOUR NEEDS.
FAREWELL, MY MASTER.
...
THIS PAINTING EVOKES SUCH NOSTALGIA IN ME...
MONSIEUR MORREL FIGURED OUT THAT HIS FORMER EMPLOYEE, EDMOND DANTÈS, IS THE ONE WHO RESCUED HIS FAMILY FROM FINANCIAL RUIN. HE WAS LOYAL AND KEPT MY SECRET, AS I HOPED.
SADLY, MONSIEUR MORREL HAS PASSED AWAY. IF I WANT TO REPAY HIS LOYALTY, IT WILL HAVE TO BE THROUGH HIS CHILDREN.
PERHAPS HAYDÉE AND MAXIMILIEN WOULD BE A GOOD MATCH...
BUT THERE IS MUCH TO DO BEFORE I CAN THINK OF SUCH HAPPY TASKS.

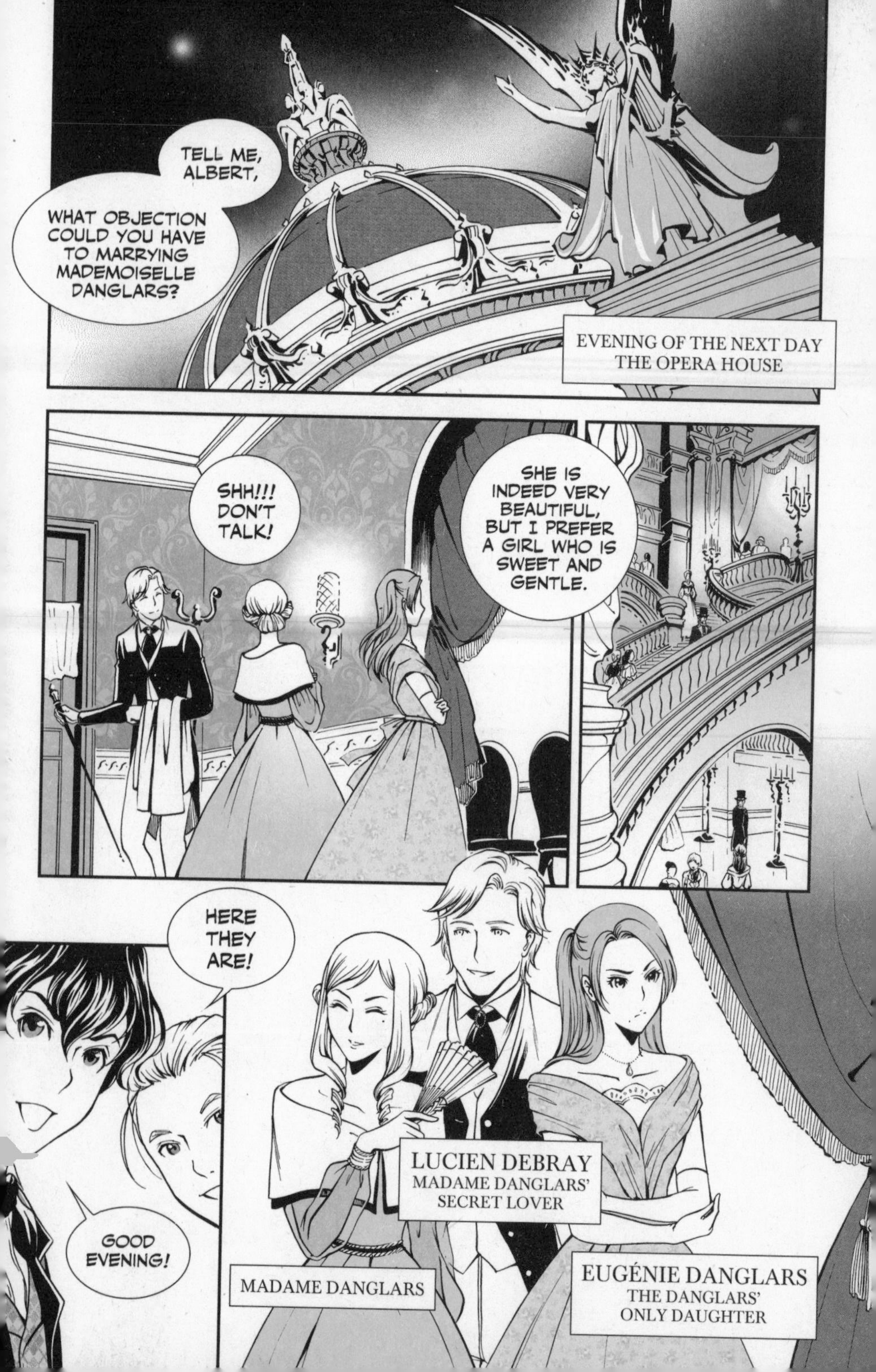
TELL ME, ALBERT,
WHAT OBJECTION COULD YOU HAVE TO MARRYING MADEMOISELLE DANGLARS?
EVENING OF THE NEXT DAY
THE OPERA HOUSE
SHE IS INDEED VERY BEAUTIFUL, BUT I PREFER A GIRL WHO IS SWEET AND GENTLE.
SHH!!! DON'T TALK!
LUCIEN DEBRAY
MADAME DANGLARS' SECRET LOVER
EUGÉNIE DANGLARS
THE DANGLARS' ONLY DAUGHTER
MADAME DANGLARS
HERE THEY ARE!
GOOD EVENING!

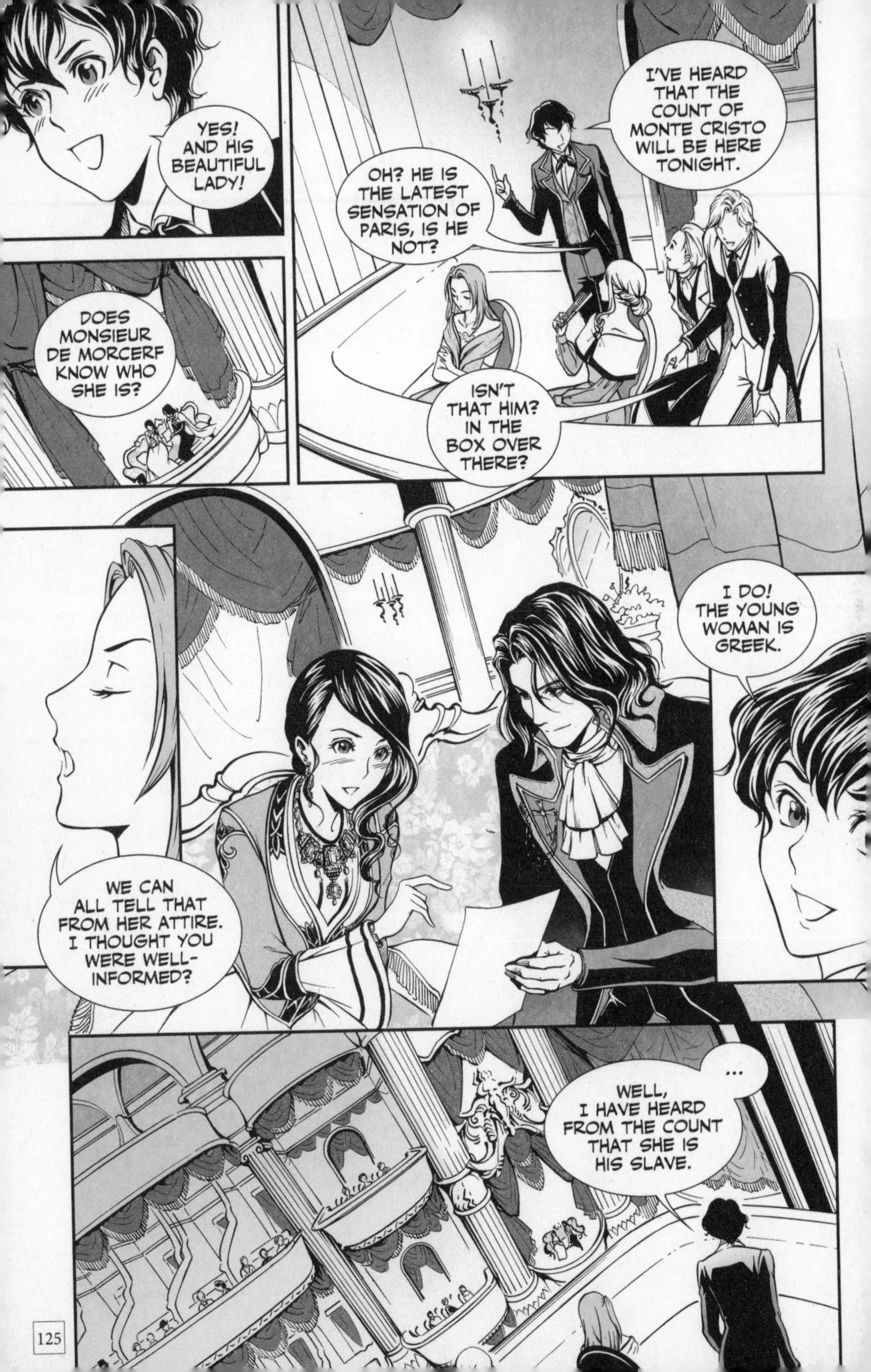
I'VE HEARD THAT THE COUNT OF MONTE CRISTO WILL BE HERE TONIGHT.
OH? HE IS THE LATEST SENSATION OF PARIS, IS HE NOT?
ISN'T THAT HIM? IN THE BOX OVER THERE?
YES! AND HIS BEAUTIFUL LADY!
DOES MONSIEUR DE MORCERF KNOW WHO SHE IS?
I DO! THE YOUNG WOMAN IS GREEK.
WE CAN ALL TELL THAT FROM HER ATTIRE. I THOUGHT YOU WERE WELL-INFORMED?
...
WELL, I HAVE HEARD FROM THE COUNT THAT SHE IS HIS SLAVE.

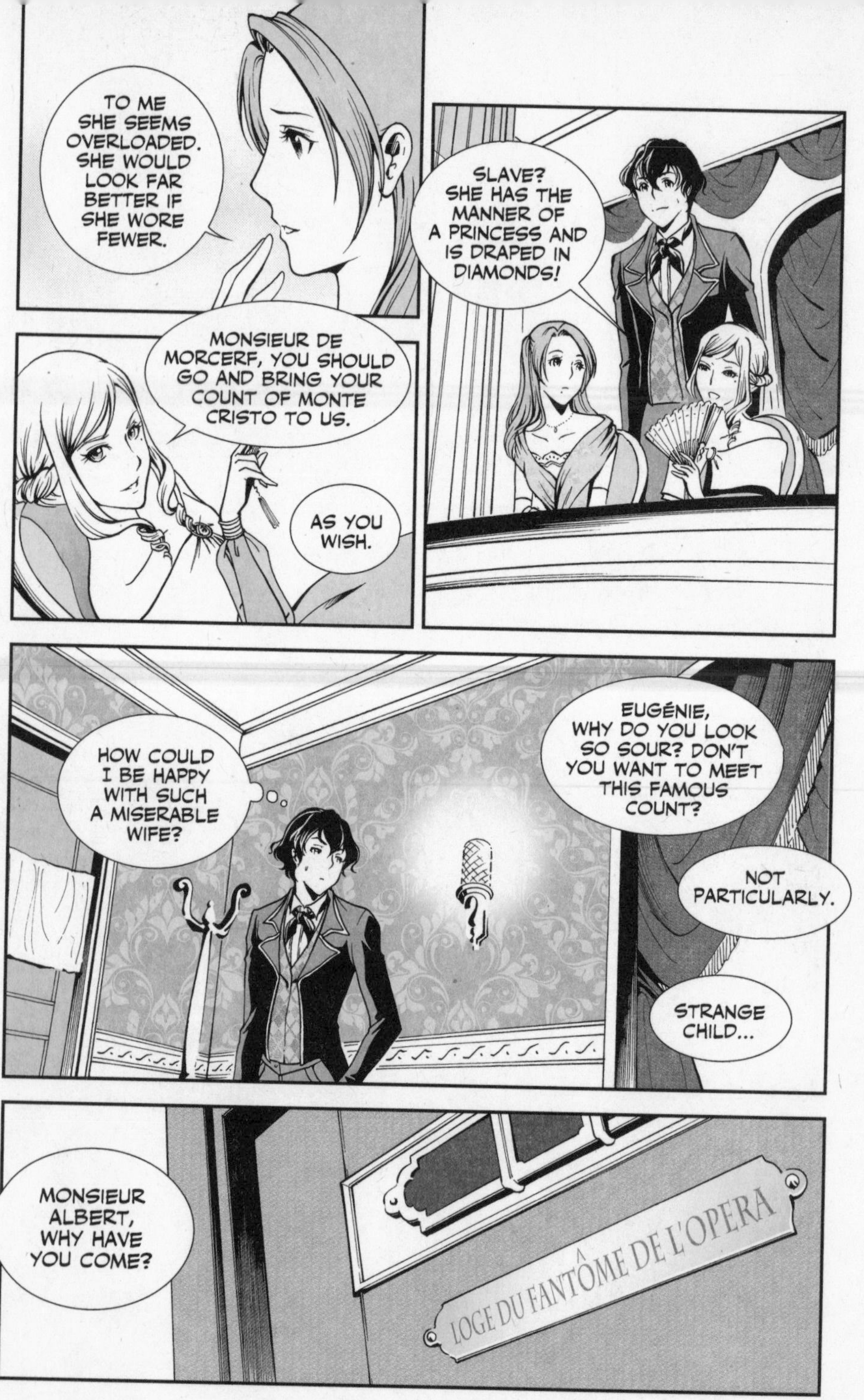
SLAVE? SHE HAS THE MANNER OF A PRINCESS AND IS DRAPED IN DIAMONDS!
TO ME SHE SEEMS OVERLOADED. SHE WOULD LOOK FAR BETTER IF SHE WORE FEWER.
MONSIEUR DE MORCERF, YOU SHOULD GO AND BRING YOUR COUNT OF MONTE CRISTO TO US.
AS YOU WISH.
EUGÉNIE, WHY DO YOU LOOK SO SOUR? DON'T YOU WANT TO MEET THIS FAMOUS COUNT?
HOW COULD I BE HAPPY WITH SUCH A MISERABLE WIFE?
NOT PARTICULARLY.
STRANGE CHILD...
LOGE DU FANTÔME DE L'OPERA
MONSIEUR ALBERT, WHY HAVE YOU COME?

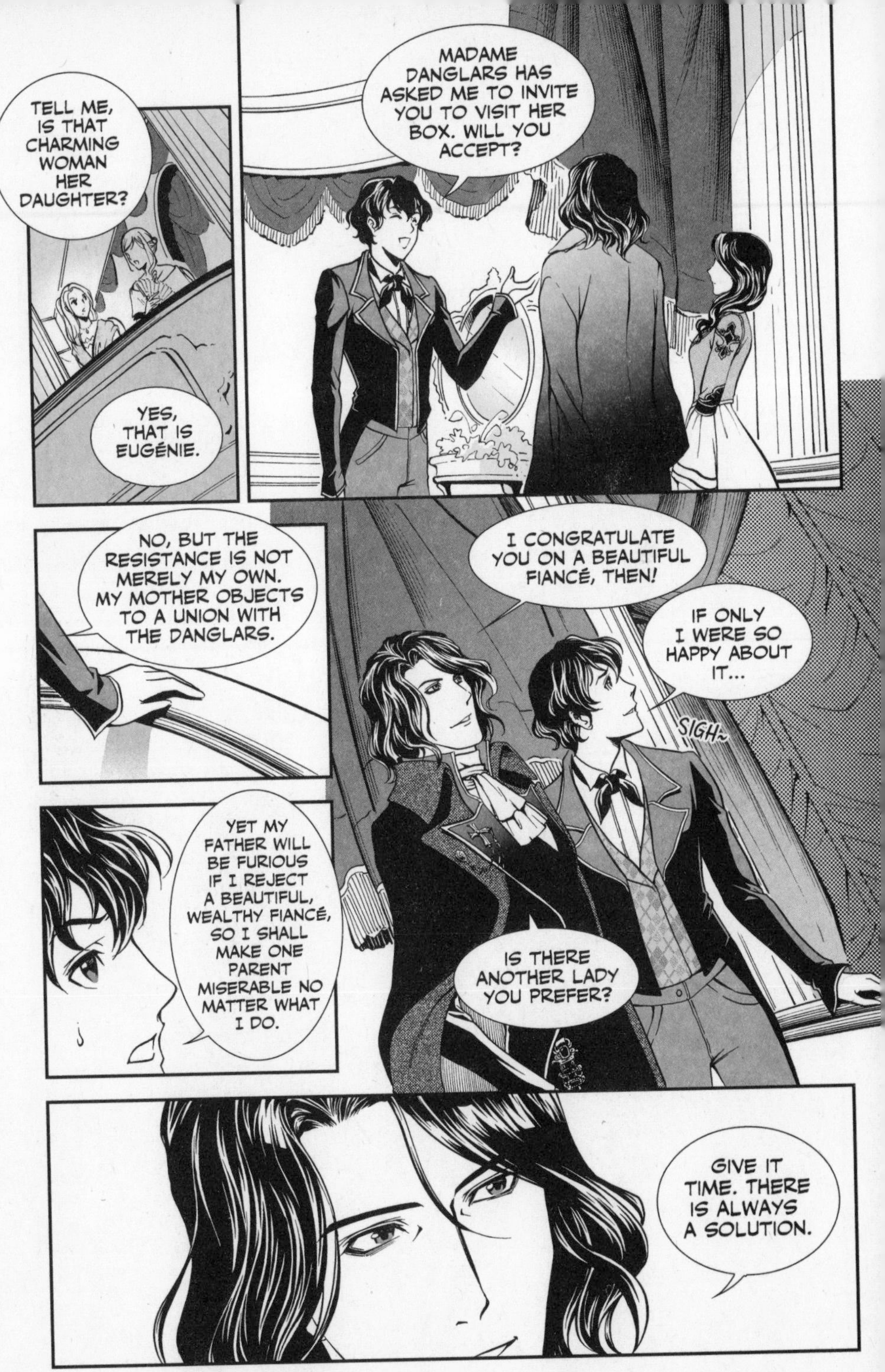
MADAME DANGLARS HAS ASKED ME TO INVITE YOU TO VISIT HER BOX. WILL YOU ACCEPT?
TELL ME, IS THAT CHARMING WOMAN HER DAUGHTER?
YES, THAT IS EUGÉNIE.
I CONGRATULATE YOU ON A BEAUTIFUL FIANCÉ, THEN!
IF ONLY I WERE SO HAPPY ABOUT IT...
SIGH~
IS THERE ANOTHER LADY YOU PREFER?
NO, BUT THE RESISTANCE IS NOT MERELY MY OWN. MY MOTHER OBJECTS TO A UNION WITH THE DANGLARS.
YET MY FATHER WILL BE FURIOUS IF I REJECT A BEAUTIFUL, WEALTHY FIANCÉ, SO I SHALL MAKE ONE PARENT MISERABLE NO MATTER WHAT I DO.
GIVE IT TIME. THERE IS ALWAYS A SOLUTION.

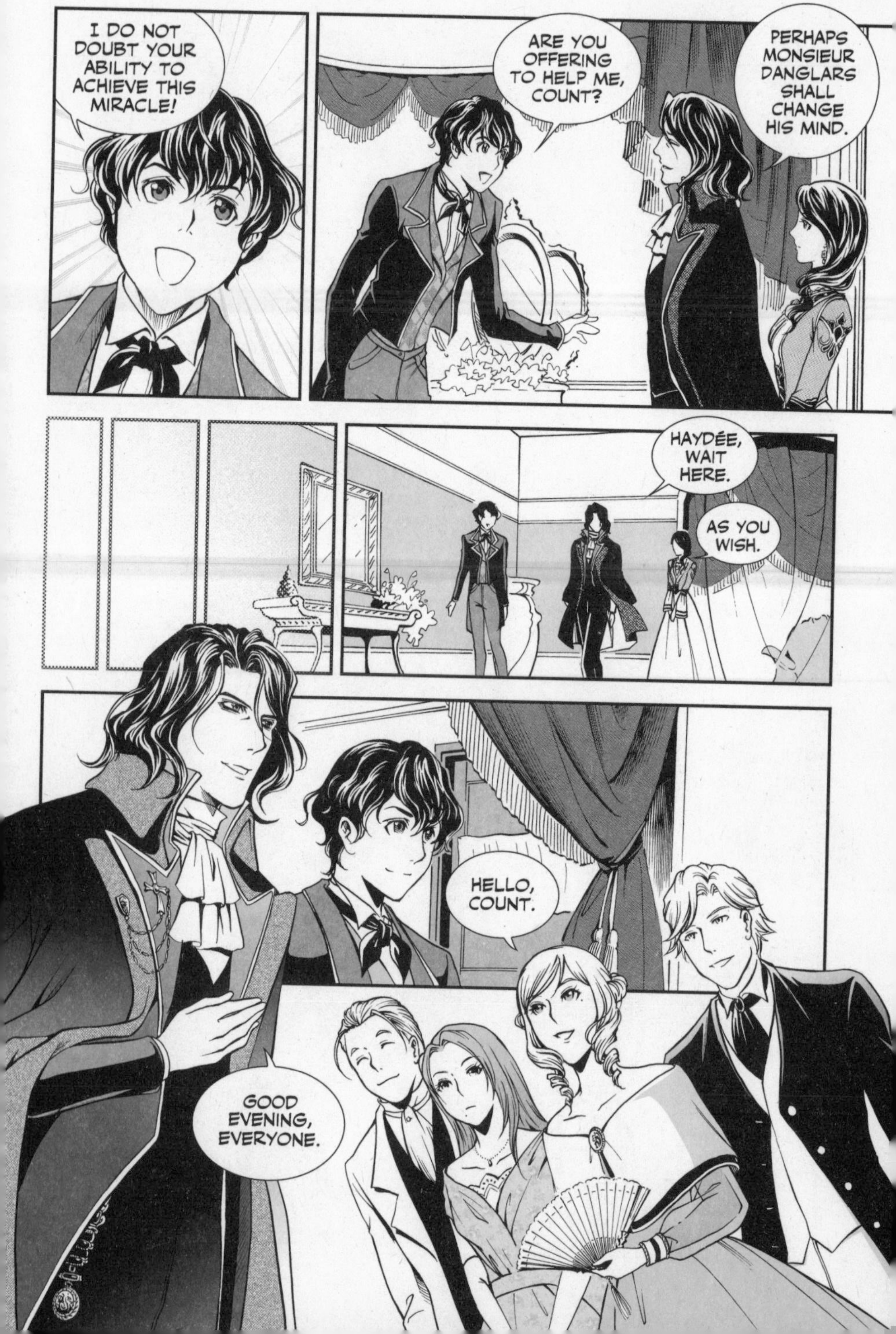
PERHAPS MONSIEUR DANGLARS SHALL CHANGE HIS MIND.
ARE YOU OFFERING TO HELP ME, COUNT?
I DO NOT DOUBT YOUR ABILITY TO ACHIEVE THIS MIRACLE!
HAYDÉE, WAIT HERE.
AS YOU WISH.
HELLO, COUNT.
GOOD EVENING, EVERYONE.

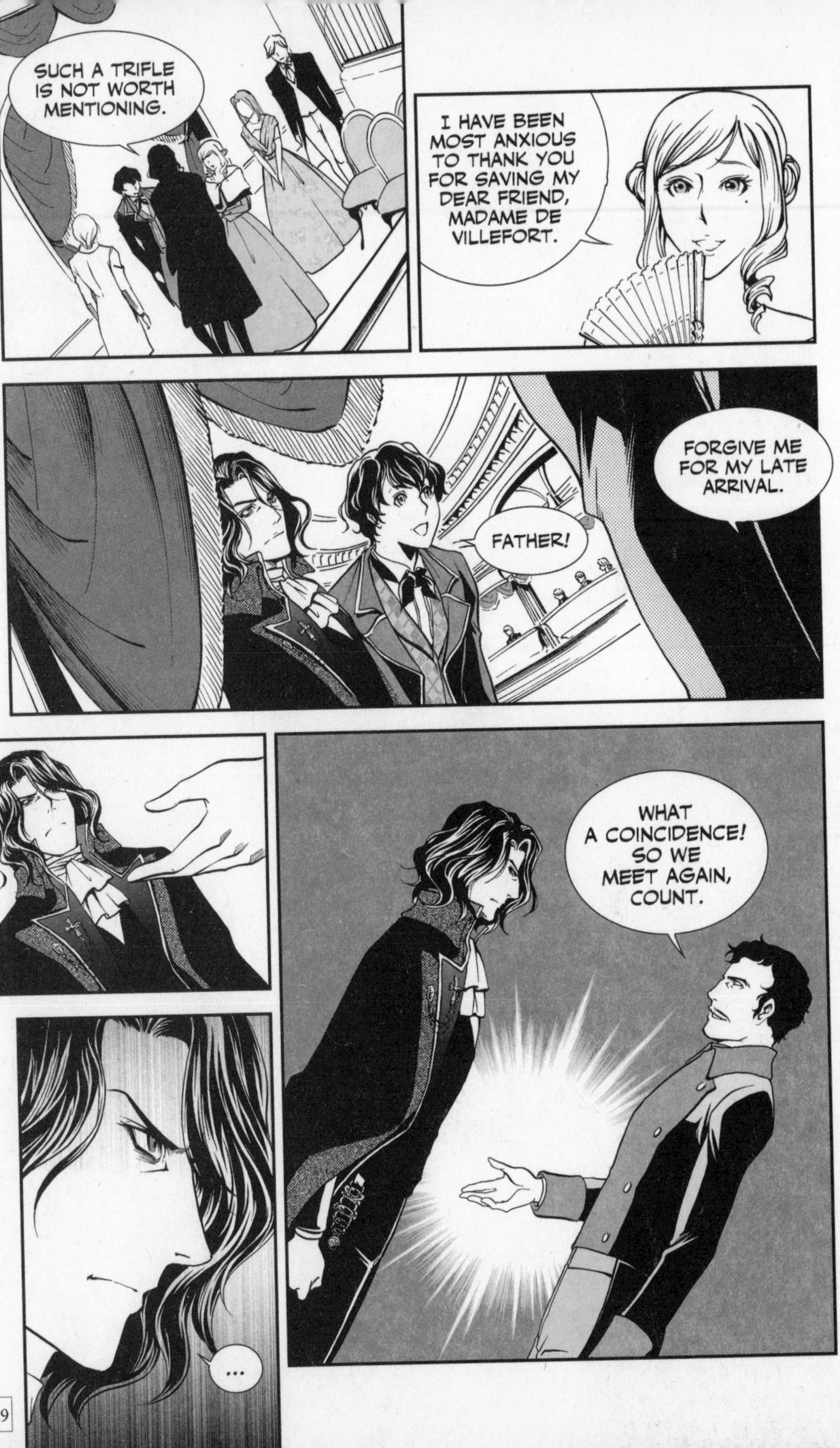
I HAVE BEEN MOST ANXIOUS TO THANK YOU FOR SAVING MY DEAR FRIEND, MADAME DE VILLEFORT.
SUCH A TRIFLE IS NOT WORTH MENTIONING.
FORGIVE ME FOR MY LATE ARRIVAL.
FATHER!
WHAT A COINCIDENCE! SO WE MEET AGAIN, COUNT.
...

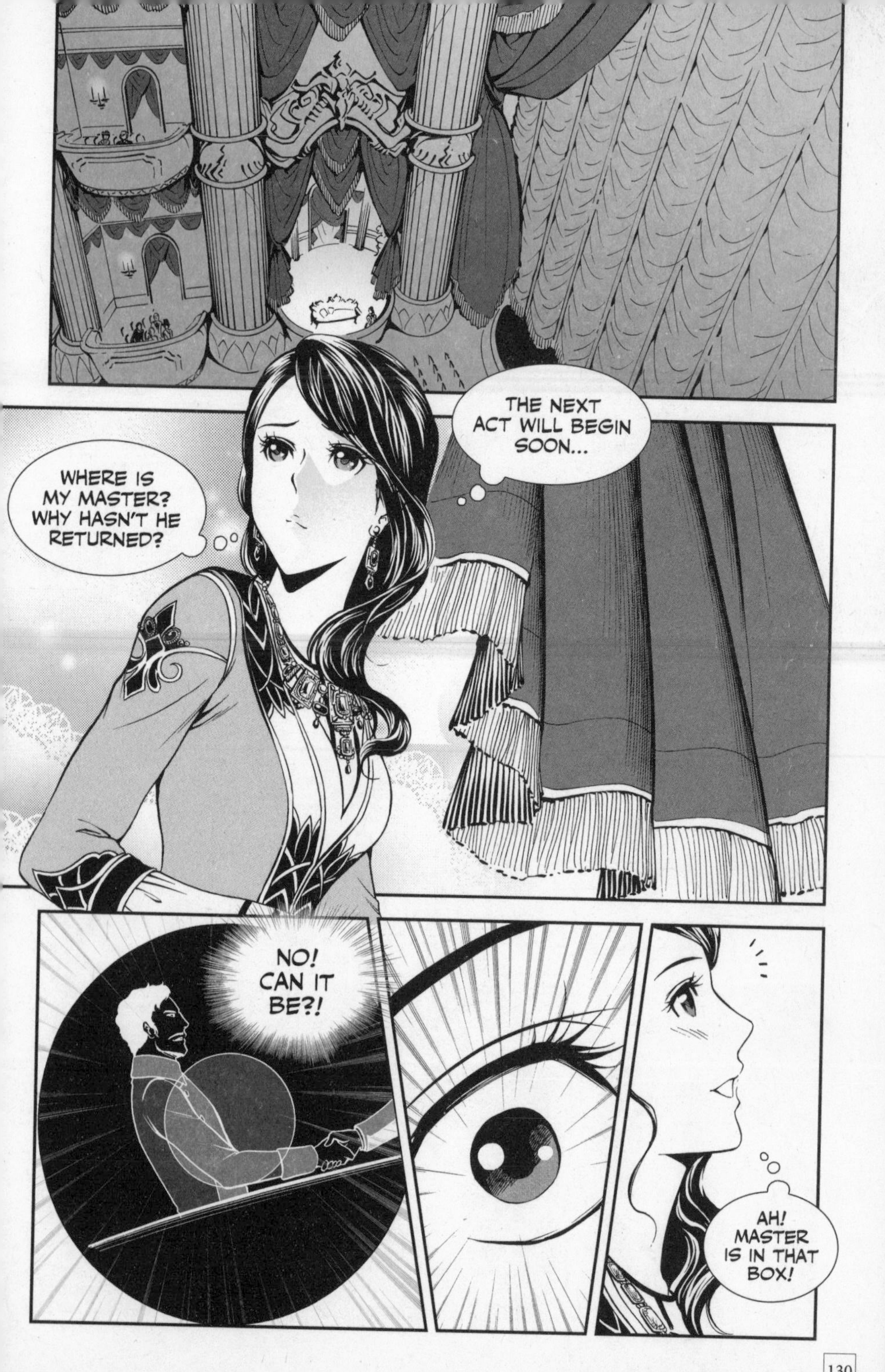
THE NEXT ACT WILL BEGIN SOON...
WHERE IS MY MASTER? WHY HASN'T HE RETURNED?
AH! MASTER IS IN THAT BOX!
NO! CAN IT BE?!

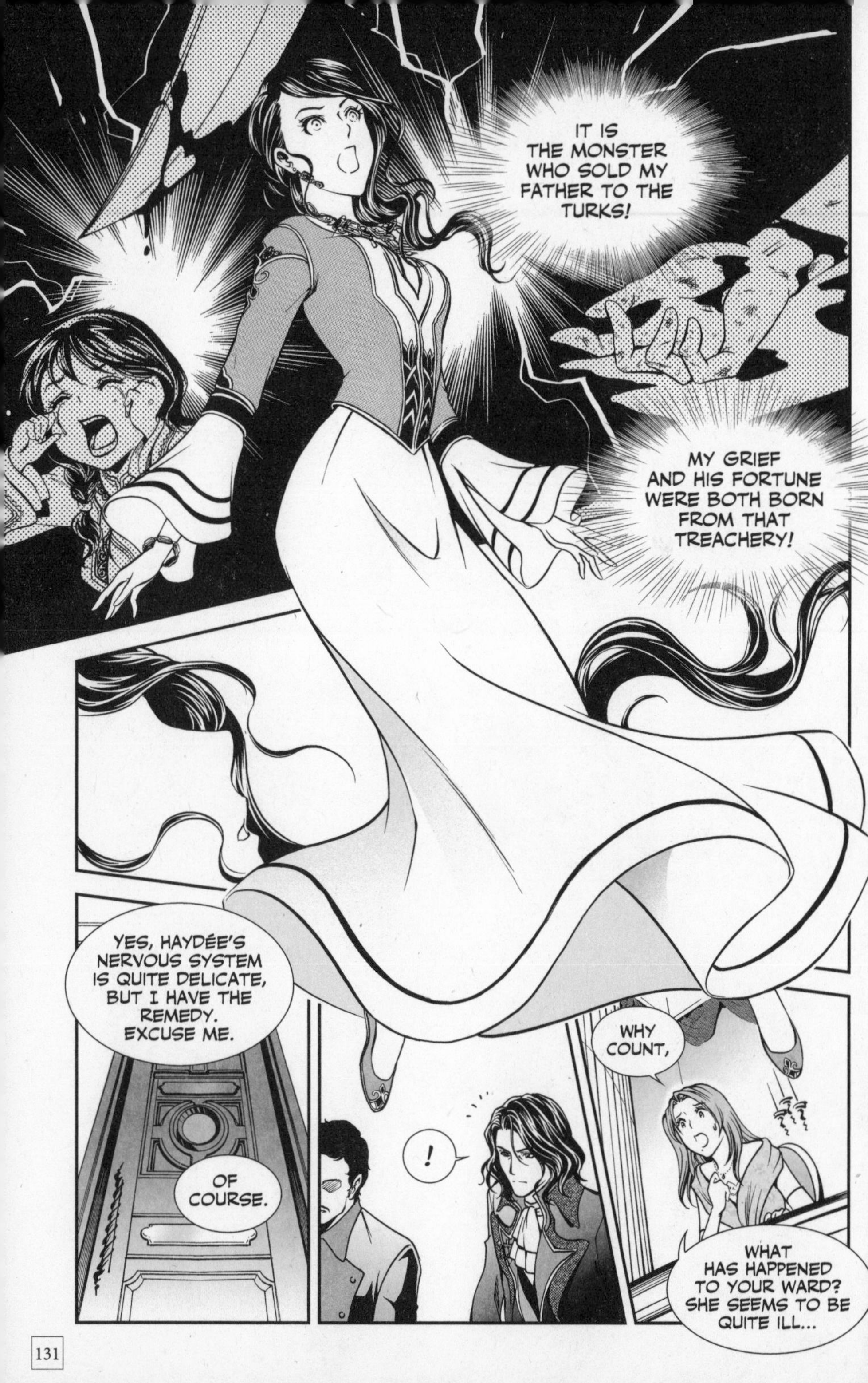
IT IS THE MONSTER WHO SOLD MY FATHER TO THE TURKS!
MY GRIEF AND HIS FORTUNE WERE BOTH BORN FROM THAT TREACHERY!
WHY COUNT,
WHAT HAS HAPPENED TO YOUR WARD? SHE SEEMS TO BE QUITE ILL...
!
YES, HAYDÉE'S NERVOUS SYSTEM IS QUITE DELICATE, BUT I HAVE THE REMEDY. EXCUSE ME.
OF COURSE.

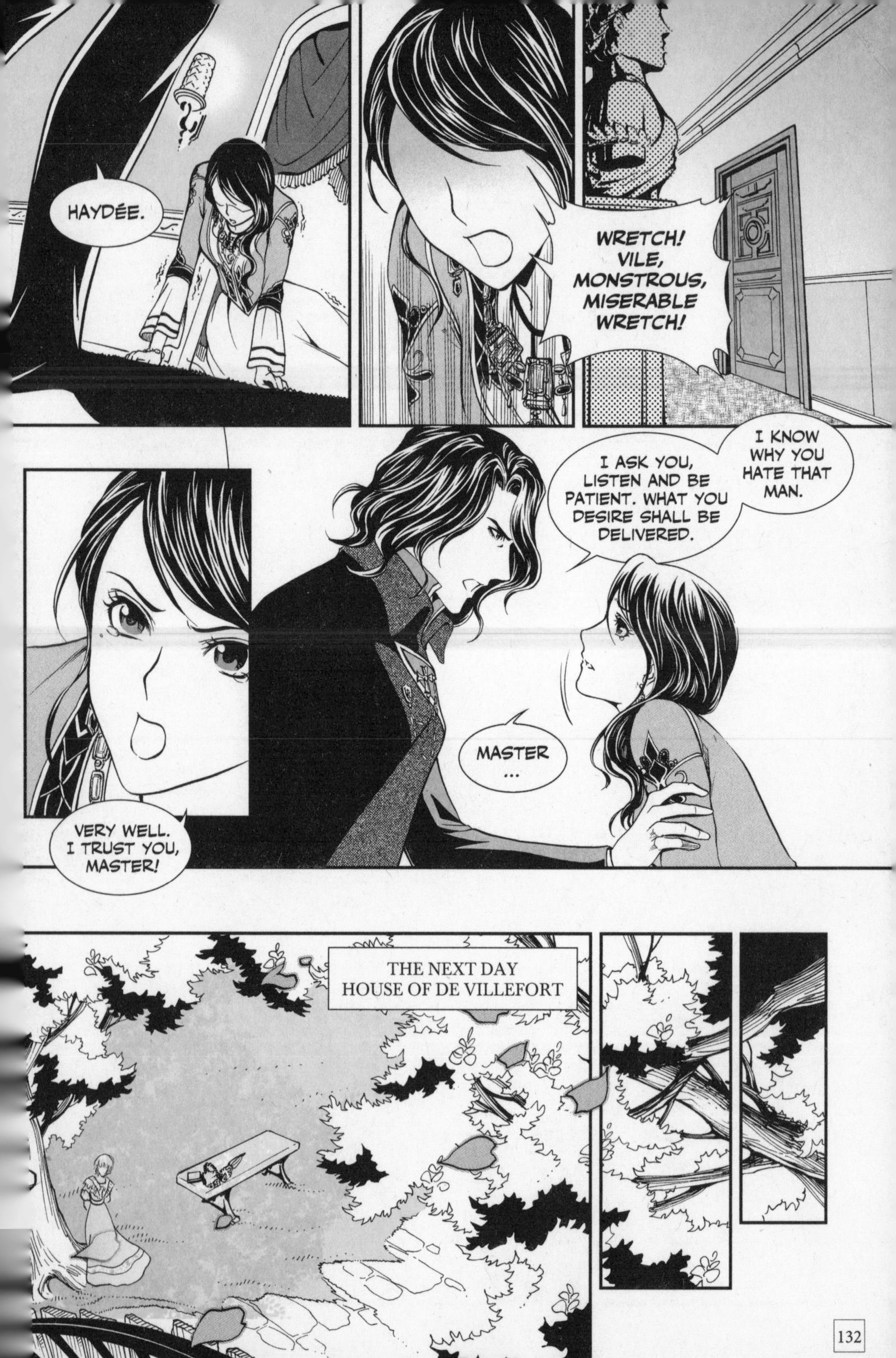
WRETCH! VILE, MONSTROUS, MISERABLE WRETCH!
HAYDÉE.
I KNOW WHY YOU HATE THAT MAN.
I ASK YOU, LISTEN AND BE PATIENT. WHAT YOU DESIRE SHALL BE DELIVERED.
MASTER ...
VERY WELL. I TRUST YOU, MASTER!
THE NEXT DAY
HOUSE OF DE VILLEFORT

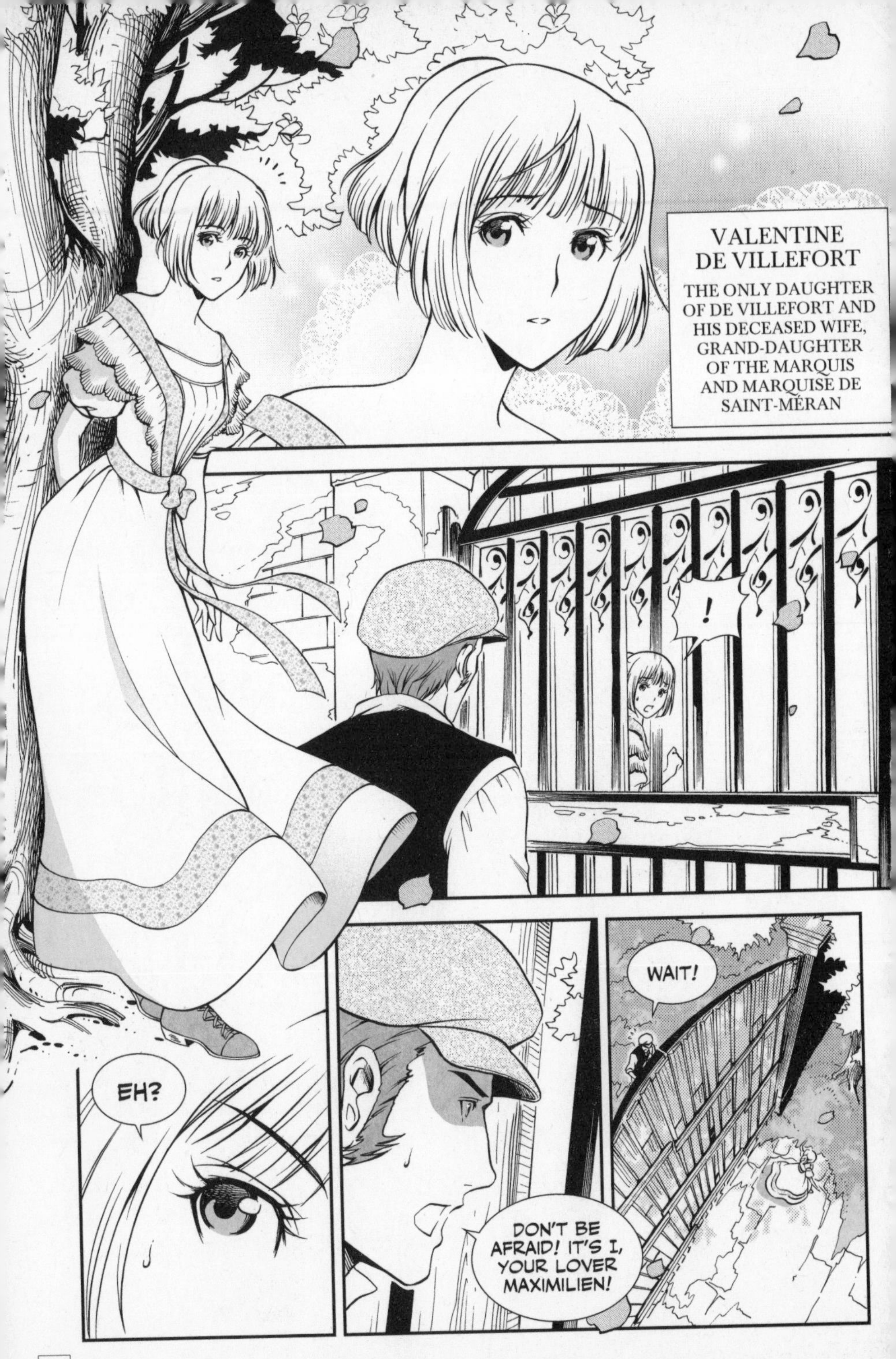
VALENTINE DE VILLEFORT
THE ONLY DAUGHTER OF DE VILLEFORT AND HIS DECEASED WIFE, GRAND-DAUGHTER OF THE MARQUIS AND MARQUISE DE SAINT-MÉRAN
!
WAIT!
DON'T BE AFRAID! IT'S I, YOUR LOVER MAXIMILIEN!
EH?

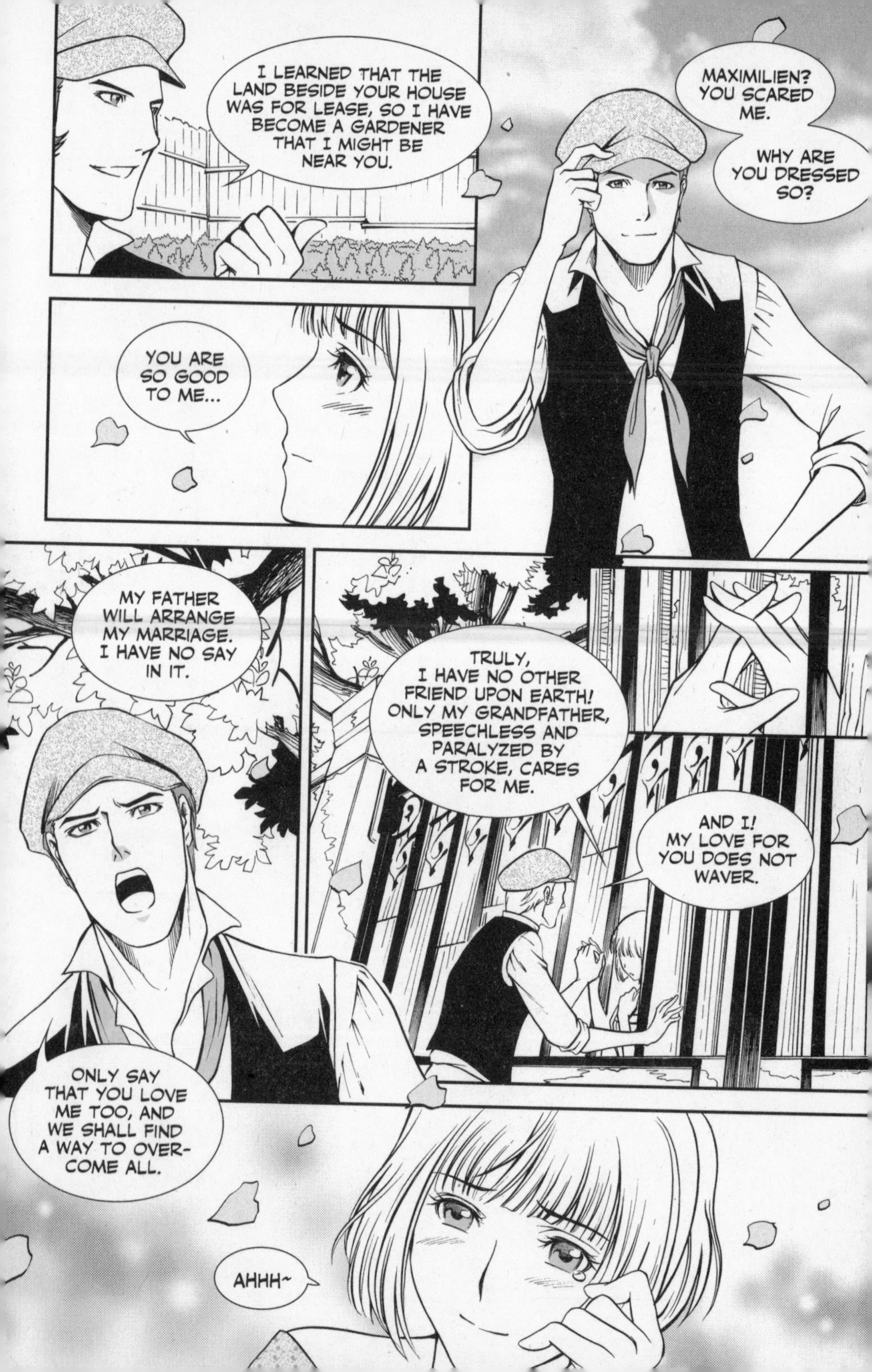
MAXIMILIEN? YOU SCARED ME.
WHY ARE YOU DRESSED SO?
I LEARNED THAT THE LAND BESIDE YOUR HOUSE WAS FOR LEASE, SO I HAVE BECOME A GARDENER THAT I MIGHT BE NEAR YOU.
YOU ARE SO GOOD TO ME...
TRULY, I HAVE NO OTHER FRIEND UPON EARTH! ONLY MY GRANDFATHER, SPEECHLESS AND PARALYZED BY A STROKE, CARES FOR ME.
AND I! MY LOVE FOR YOU DOES NOT WAVER.
MY FATHER WILL ARRANGE MY MARRIAGE. I HAVE NO SAY IN IT.
ONLY SAY THAT YOU LOVE ME TOO, AND WE SHALL FIND A WAY TO OVER-COME ALL.
AHHH~

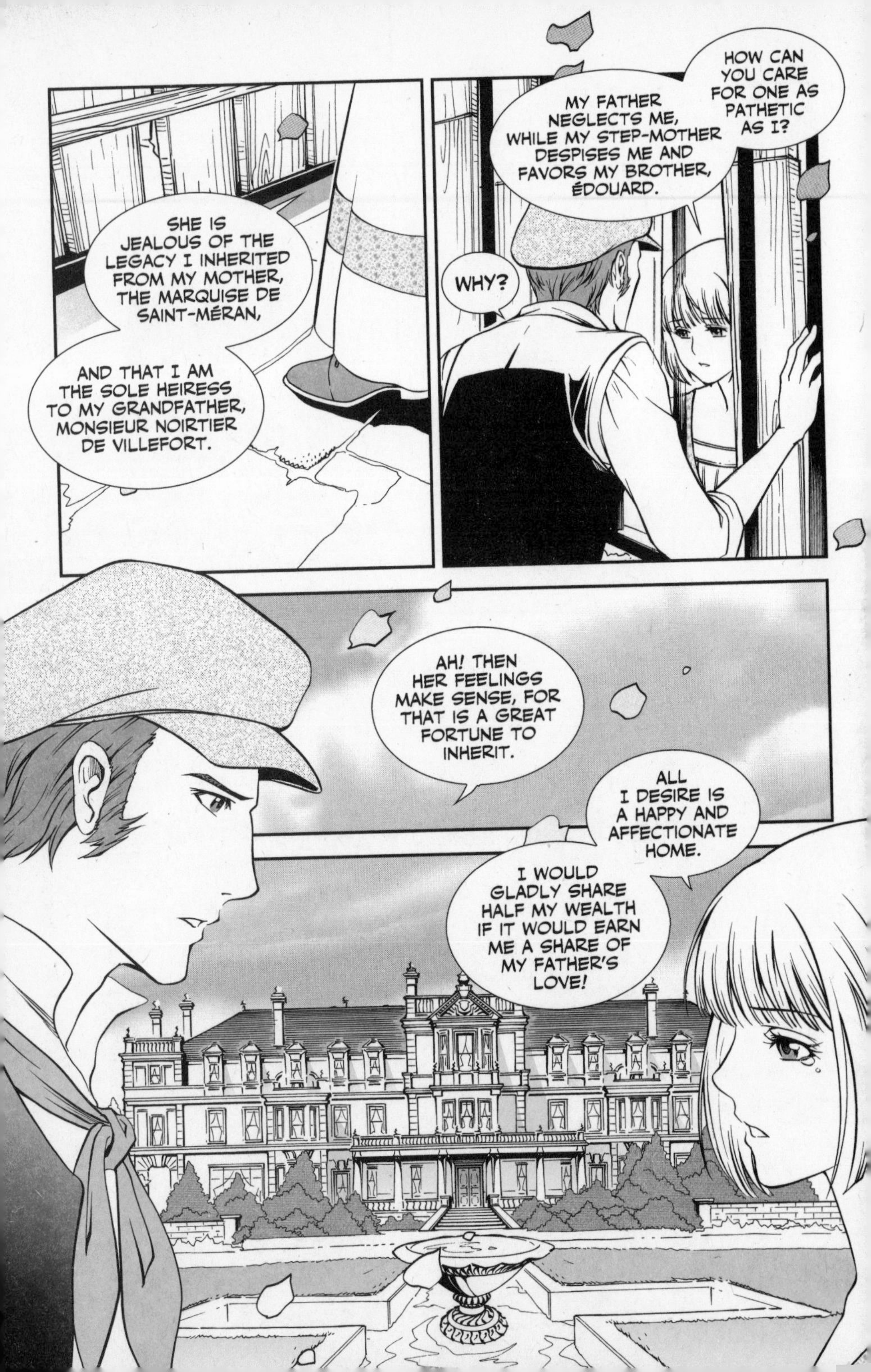
HOW CAN YOU CARE FOR ONE AS PATHETIC AS I?
MY FATHER NEGLECTS ME, WHILE MY STEP-MOTHER DESPISES ME AND FAVORS MY BROTHER, ÉDOUARD.
WHY?
SHE IS JEALOUS OF THE LEGACY I INHERITED FROM MY MOTHER, THE MARQUISE DE SAINT-MÉRAN,
AND THAT I AM THE SOLE HEIRESS TO MY GRANDFATHER, MONSIEUR NOIRTIER DE VILLEFORT.
AH! THEN HER FEELINGS MAKE SENSE, FOR THAT IS A GREAT FORTUNE TO INHERIT.
ALL I DESIRE IS A HAPPY AND AFFECTIONATE HOME.
I WOULD GLADLY SHARE HALF MY WEALTH IF IT WOULD EARN ME A SHARE OF MY FATHER'S LOVE!

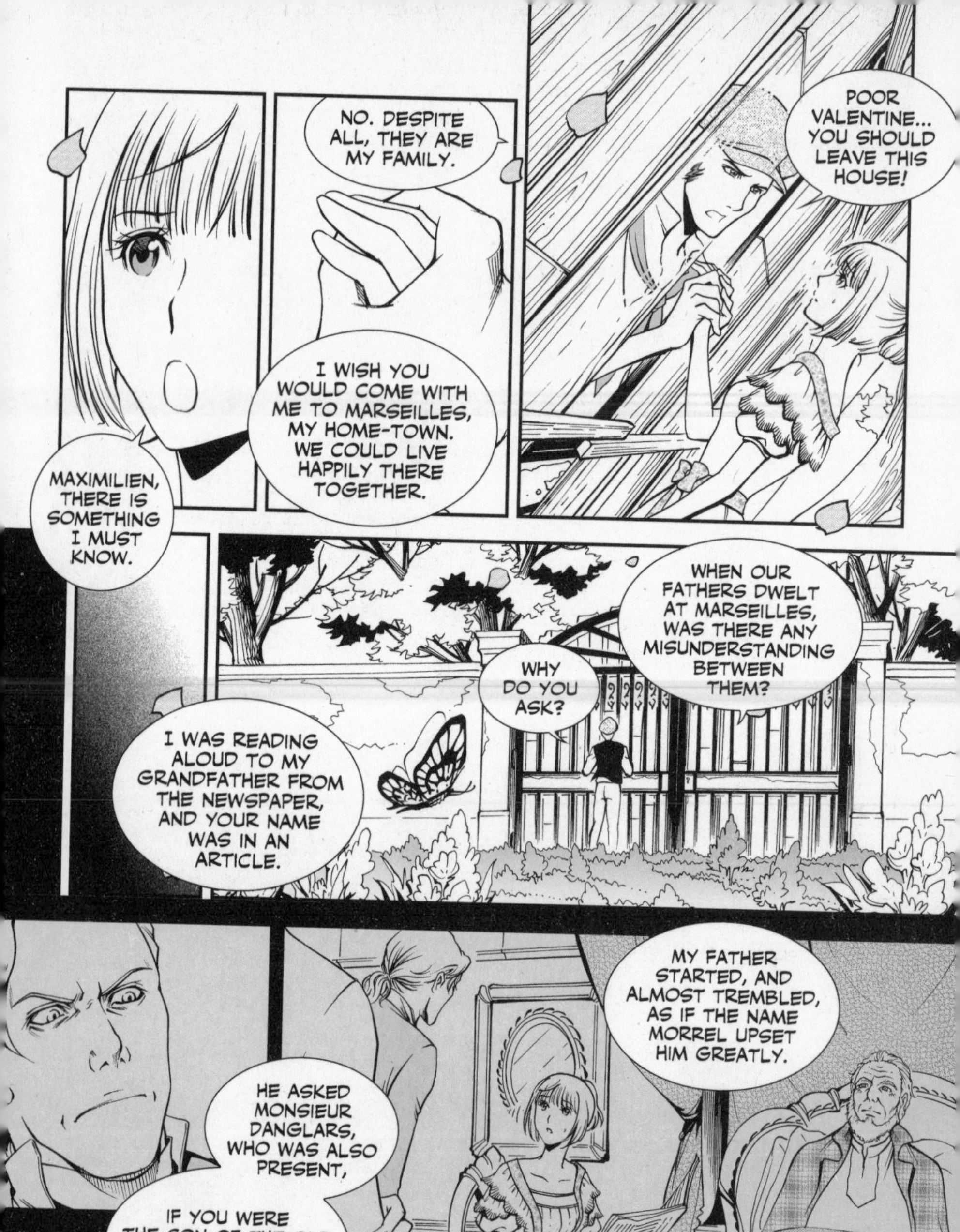
POOR VALENTINE... YOU SHOULD LEAVE THIS HOUSE!
NO. DESPITE ALL, THEY ARE MY FAMILY.
I WISH YOU WOULD COME WITH ME TO MARSEILLES, MY HOME-TOWN. WE COULD LIVE HAPPILY THERE TOGETHER.
MAXIMILIEN, THERE IS SOMETHING I MUST KNOW.
WHEN OUR FATHERS DWELT AT MARSEILLES, WAS THERE ANY MISUNDERSTANDING BETWEEN THEM?
WHY DO YOU ASK?
I WAS READING ALOUD TO MY GRANDFATHER FROM THE NEWSPAPER, AND YOUR NAME WAS IN AN ARTICLE.
MY FATHER STARTED, AND ALMOST TREMBLED, AS IF THE NAME MORREL UPSET HIM GREATLY.
HE ASKED MONSIEUR DANGLARS, WHO WAS ALSO PRESENT,
IF YOU WERE THE SON OF THE OLD SHIPOWNER FROM MARSEILLES.

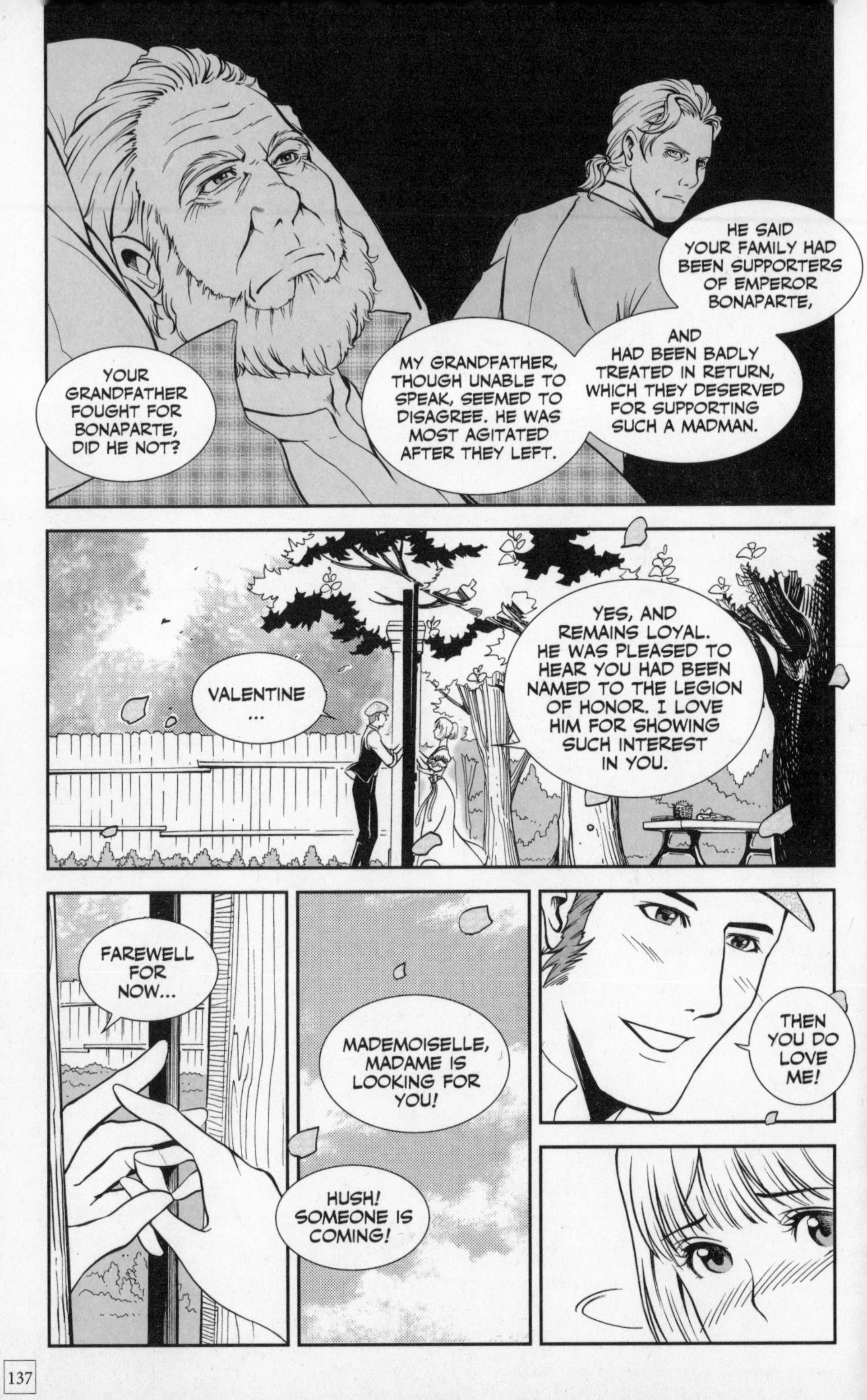
HE SAID YOUR FAMILY HAD BEEN SUPPORTERS OF EMPEROR BONAPARTE,
AND HAD BEEN BADLY TREATED IN RETURN, WHICH THEY DESERVED FOR SUPPORTING SUCH A MADMAN.
MY GRANDFATHER, THOUGH UNABLE TO SPEAK, SEEMED TO DISAGREE. HE WAS MOST AGITATED AFTER THEY LEFT.
YOUR GRANDFATHER FOUGHT FOR BONAPARTE, DID HE NOT?
YES, AND REMAINS LOYAL. HE WAS PLEASED TO HEAR YOU HAD BEEN NAMED TO THE LEGION OF HONOR. I LOVE HIM FOR SHOWING SUCH INTEREST IN YOU.
VALENTINE ...
THEN YOU DO LOVE ME!
MADEMOISELLE, MADAME IS LOOKING FOR YOU!
HUSH! SOMEONE IS COMING!
FAREWELL FOR NOW...

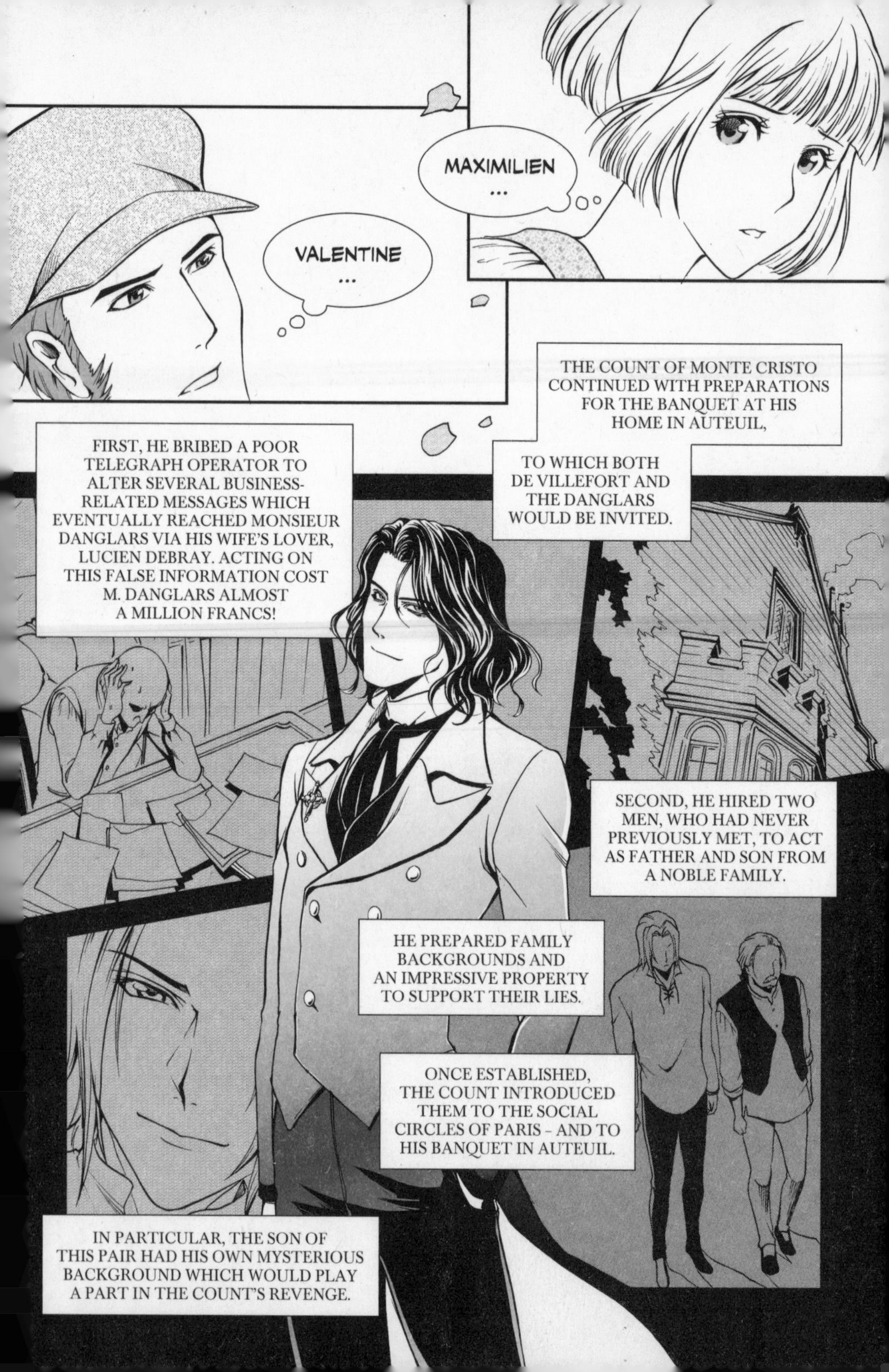
MAXIMILIEN ...
VALENTINE ...
THE COUNT OF MONTE CRISTO CONTINUED WITH PREPARATIONS FOR THE BANQUET AT HIS HOME IN AUTEUIL,
TO WHICH BOTH DE VILLEFORT AND THE DANGLARS WOULD BE INVITED.
FIRST, HE BRIBED A POOR TELEGRAPH OPERATOR TO ALTER SEVERAL BUSINESS-RELATED MESSAGES WHICH EVENTUALLY REACHED MONSIEUR DANGLARS VIA HIS WIFE'S LOVER, LUCIEN DEBRAY. ACTING ON THIS FALSE INFORMATION COST M. DANGLARS ALMOST A MILLION FRANCS!
SECOND, HE HIRED TWO MEN, WHO HAD NEVER PREVIOUSLY MET, TO ACT AS FATHER AND SON FROM A NOBLE FAMILY.
HE PREPARED FAMILY BACKGROUNDS AND AN IMPRESSIVE PROPERTY TO SUPPORT THEIR LIES.
ONCE ESTABLISHED, THE COUNT INTRODUCED THEM TO THE SOCIAL CIRCLES OF PARIS - AND TO HIS BANQUET IN AUTEUIL.
IN PARTICULAR, THE SON OF THIS PAIR HAD HIS OWN MYSTERIOUS BACKGROUND WHICH WOULD PLAY A PART IN THE COUNT'S REVENGE.

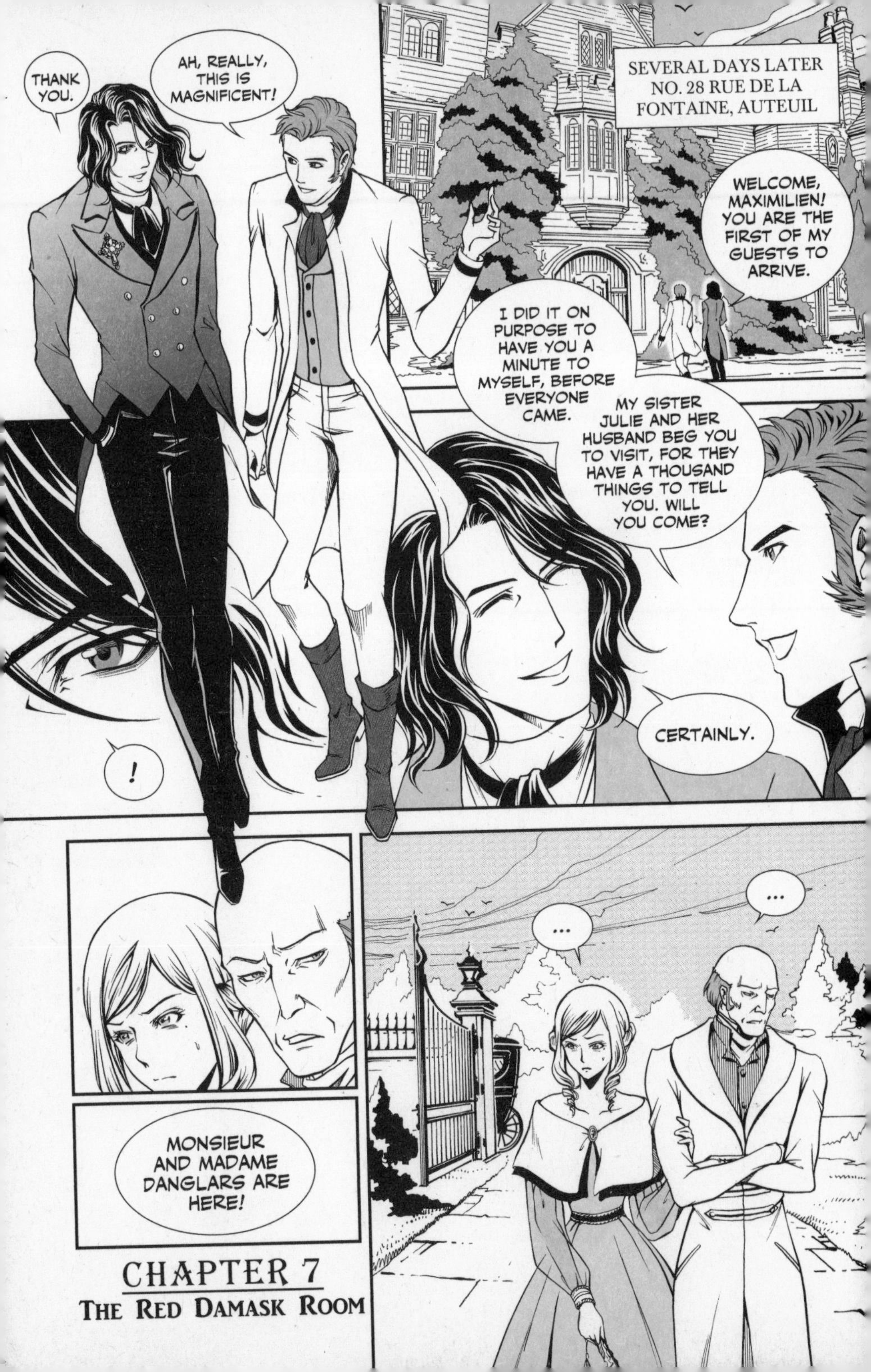
SEVERAL DAYS LATER NO. 28 RUE DE LA FONTAINE, AUTEUIL
WELCOME, MAXIMILIEN! YOU ARE THE FIRST OF MY GUESTS TO ARRIVE.
I DID IT ON PURPOSE TO HAVE YOU A MINUTE TO MYSELF, BEFORE EVERYONE CAME.
AH, REALLY, THIS IS MAGNIFICENT!
THANK YOU.
MY SISTER JULIE AND HER HUSBAND BEG YOU TO VISIT, FOR THEY HAVE A THOUSAND THINGS TO TELL YOU. WILL YOU COME?
CERTAINLY.
!
...
...
MONSIEUR AND MADAME DANGLARS ARE HERE!

CHAPTER 7

THE RED DAMASK ROOM

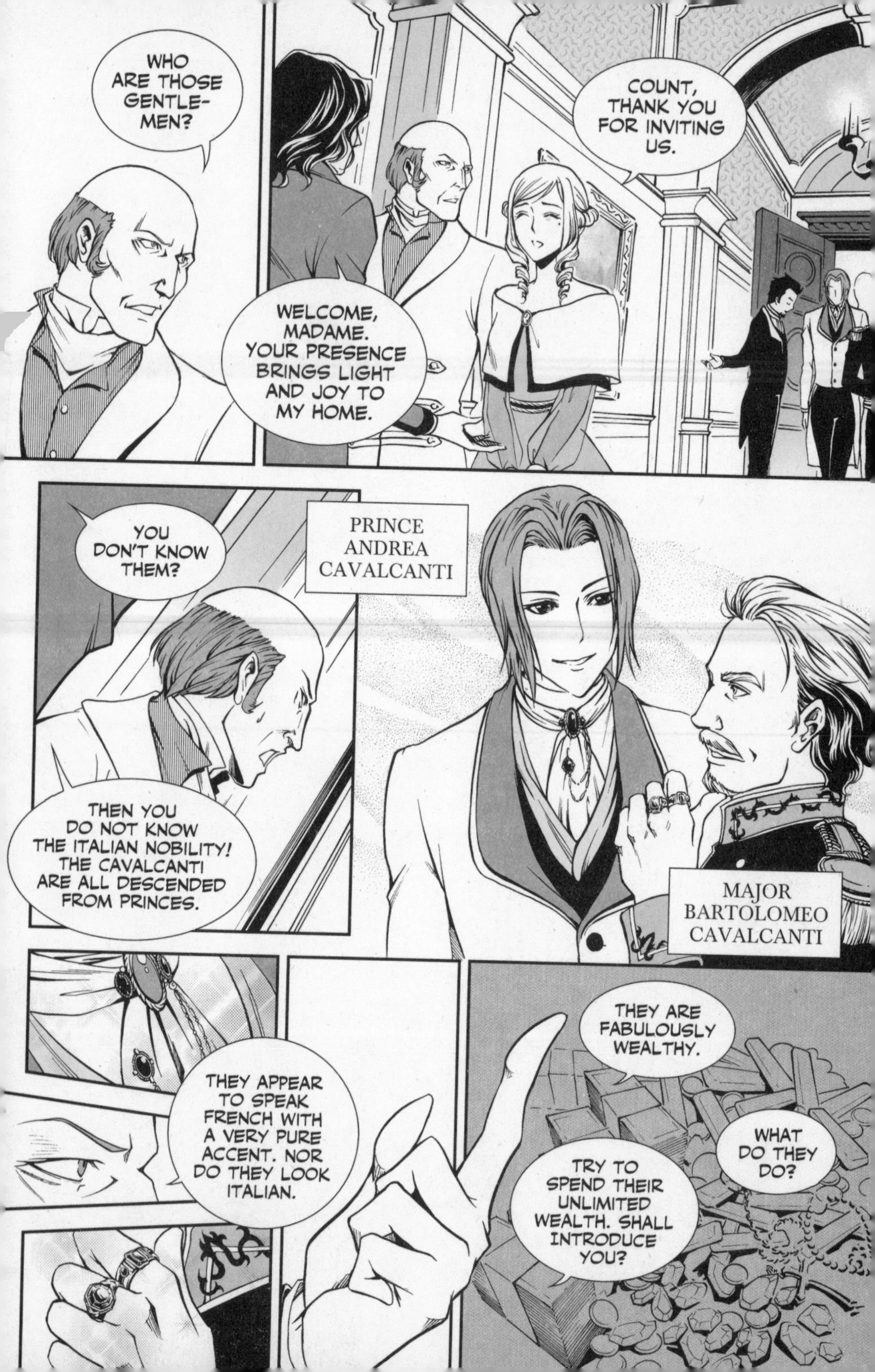
COUNT, THANK YOU FOR INVITING US.
WELCOME, MADAME. YOUR PRESENCE BRINGS LIGHT AND JOY TO MY HOME.
WHO ARE THOSE GENTLE-MEN?
PRINCE ANDREA CAVALCANTI
MAJOR BARTOLOMEO CAVALCANTI
YOU DON'T KNOW THEM?
THEN YOU DO NOT KNOW THE ITALIAN NOBILITY! THE CAVALCANTI ARE ALL DESCENDED FROM PRINCES.
THEY ARE FABULOUSLY WEALTHY.
WHAT DO THEY DO?
TRY TO SPEND THEIR UNLIMITED WEALTH. SHALL INTRODUCE YOU?
THEY APPEAR TO SPEAK FRENCH WITH A VERY PURE ACCENT. NOR DO THEY LOOK ITALIAN.

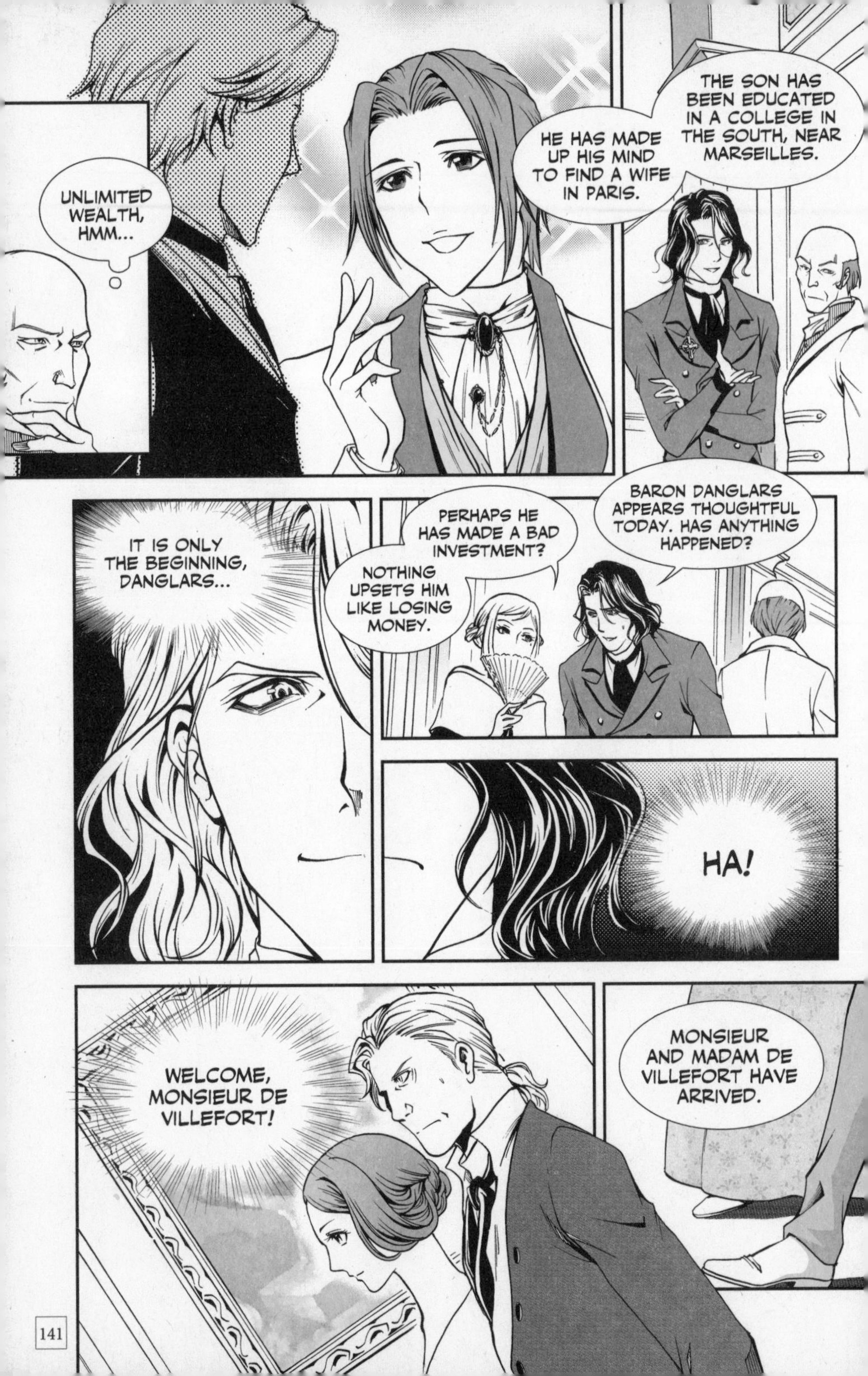
THE SON HAS BEEN EDUCATED IN A COLLEGE IN THE SOUTH, NEAR MARSEILLES.
HE HAS MADE UP HIS MIND TO FIND A WIFE IN PARIS.
UNLIMITED WEALTH, HMM...
BARON DANGLARS APPEARS THOUGHTFUL TODAY. HAS ANYTHING HAPPENED?
PERHAPS HE HAS MADE A BAD INVESTMENT?
NOTHING UPSETS HIM LIKE LOSING MONEY.
HA!
IT IS ONLY THE BEGINNING, DANGLARS...
MONSIEUR AND MADAM DE VILLEFORT HAVE ARRIVED.
WELCOME, MONSIEUR DE VILLEFORT!

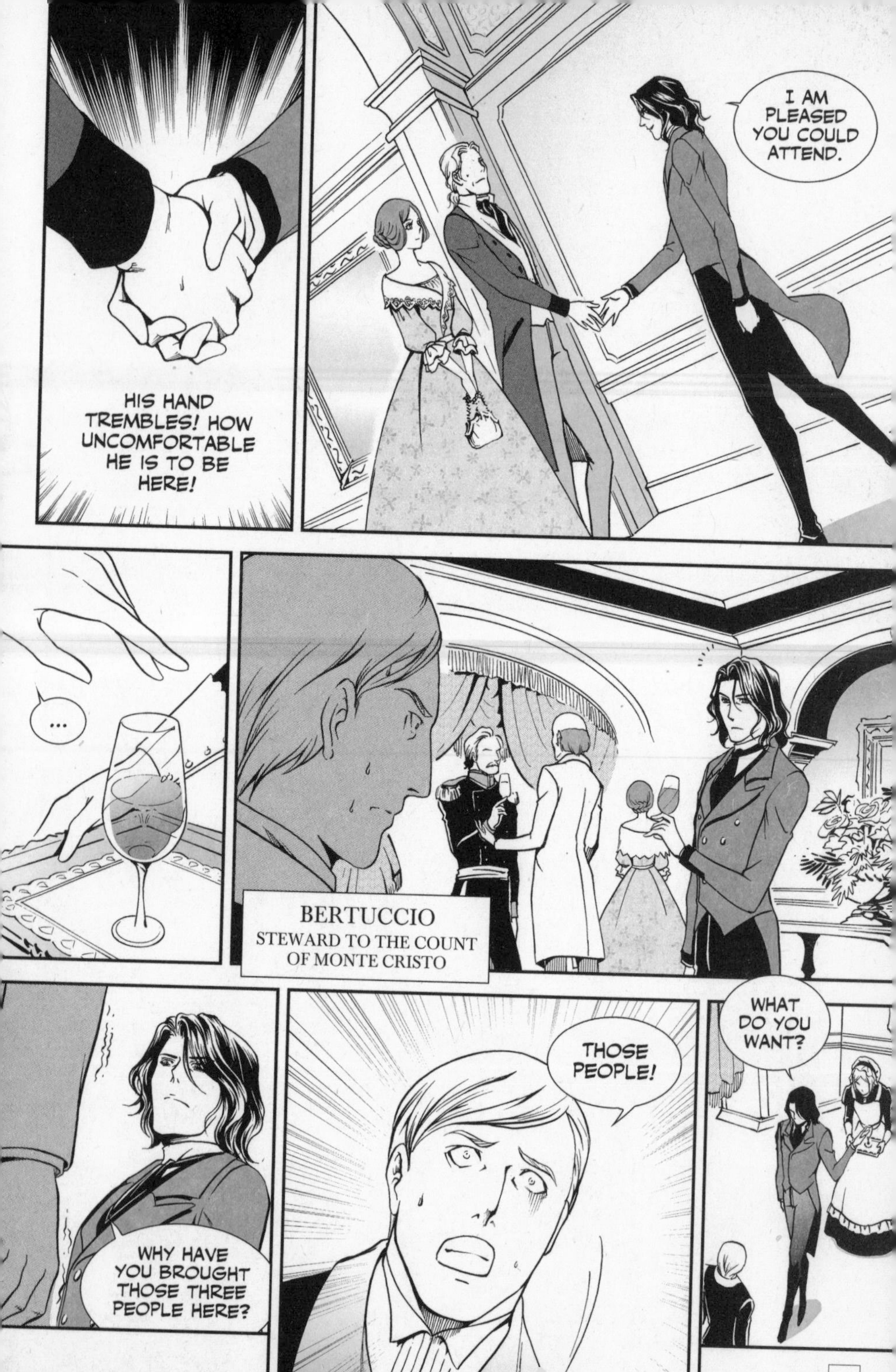
I AM PLEASED YOU COULD ATTEND.
HIS HAND TREMBLES! HOW UNCOMFORTABLE HE IS TO BE HERE!
BERTUCCIO
STEWARD TO THE COUNT OF MONTE CRISTO
...
WHAT DO YOU WANT?
THOSE PEOPLE!
WHY HAVE YOU BROUGHT THOSE THREE PEOPLE HERE?

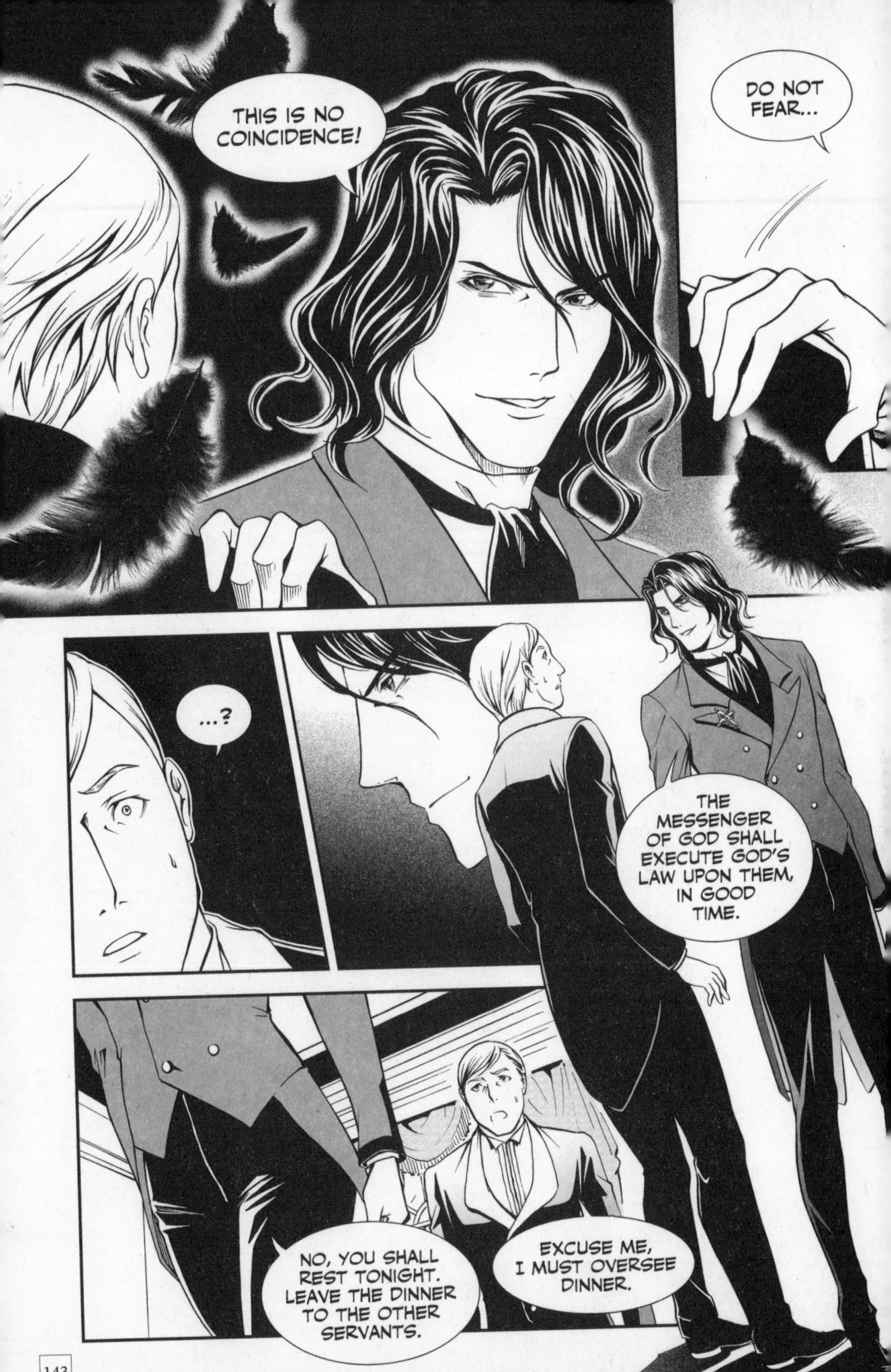
DO NOT FEAR...
THIS IS NO COINCIDENCE!
THE MESSENGER OF GOD SHALL EXECUTE GOD'S LAW UPON THEM, IN GOOD TIME.
...?
EXCUSE ME, I MUST OVERSEE DINNER.
NO, YOU SHALL REST TONIGHT. LEAVE THE DINNER TO THE OTHER SERVANTS.

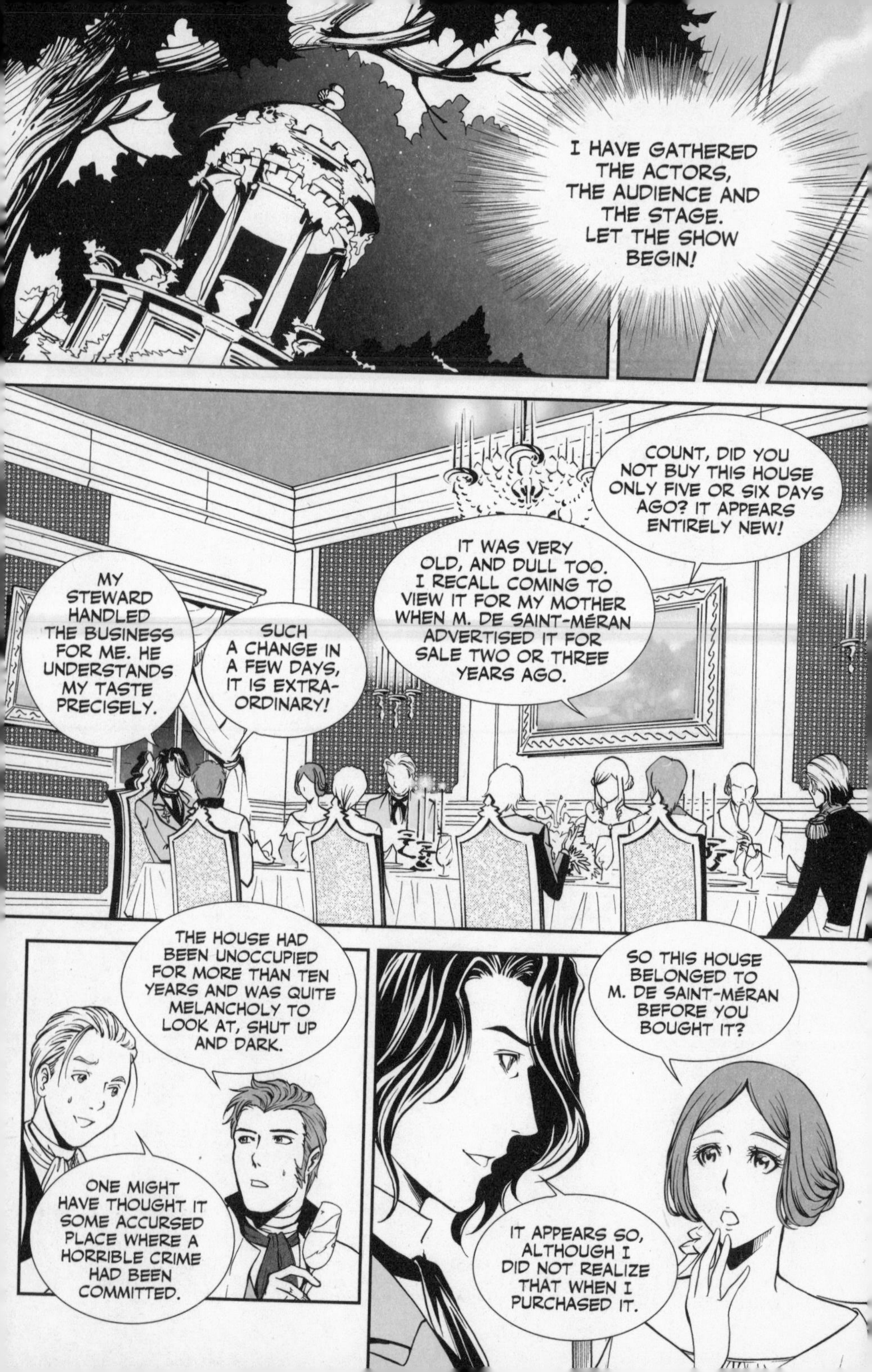
I HAVE GATHERED THE ACTORS, THE AUDIENCE AND THE STAGE. LET THE SHOW BEGIN!
COUNT, DID YOU NOT BUY THIS HOUSE ONLY FIVE OR SIX DAYS AGO? IT APPEARS ENTIRELY NEW!
IT WAS VERY OLD, AND DULL TOO. I RECALL COMING TO VIEW IT FOR MY MOTHER WHEN M. DE SAINT-MÉRAN ADVERTISED IT FOR SALE TWO OR THREE YEARS AGO.
SUCH A CHANGE IN A FEW DAYS, IT IS EXTRA-ORDINARY!
MY STEWARD HANDLED THE BUSINESS FOR ME. HE UNDERSTANDS MY TASTE PRECISELY.
SO THIS HOUSE BELONGED TO M. DE SAINT-MÉRAN BEFORE YOU BOUGHT IT?
IT APPEARS SO, ALTHOUGH I DID NOT REALIZE THAT WHEN I PURCHASED IT.
THE HOUSE HAD BEEN UNOCCUPIED FOR MORE THAN TEN YEARS AND WAS QUITE MELANCHOLY TO LOOK AT, SHUT UP AND DARK.
ONE MIGHT HAVE THOUGHT IT SOME ACCURSED PLACE WHERE A HORRIBLE CRIME HAD BEEN COMMITTED.

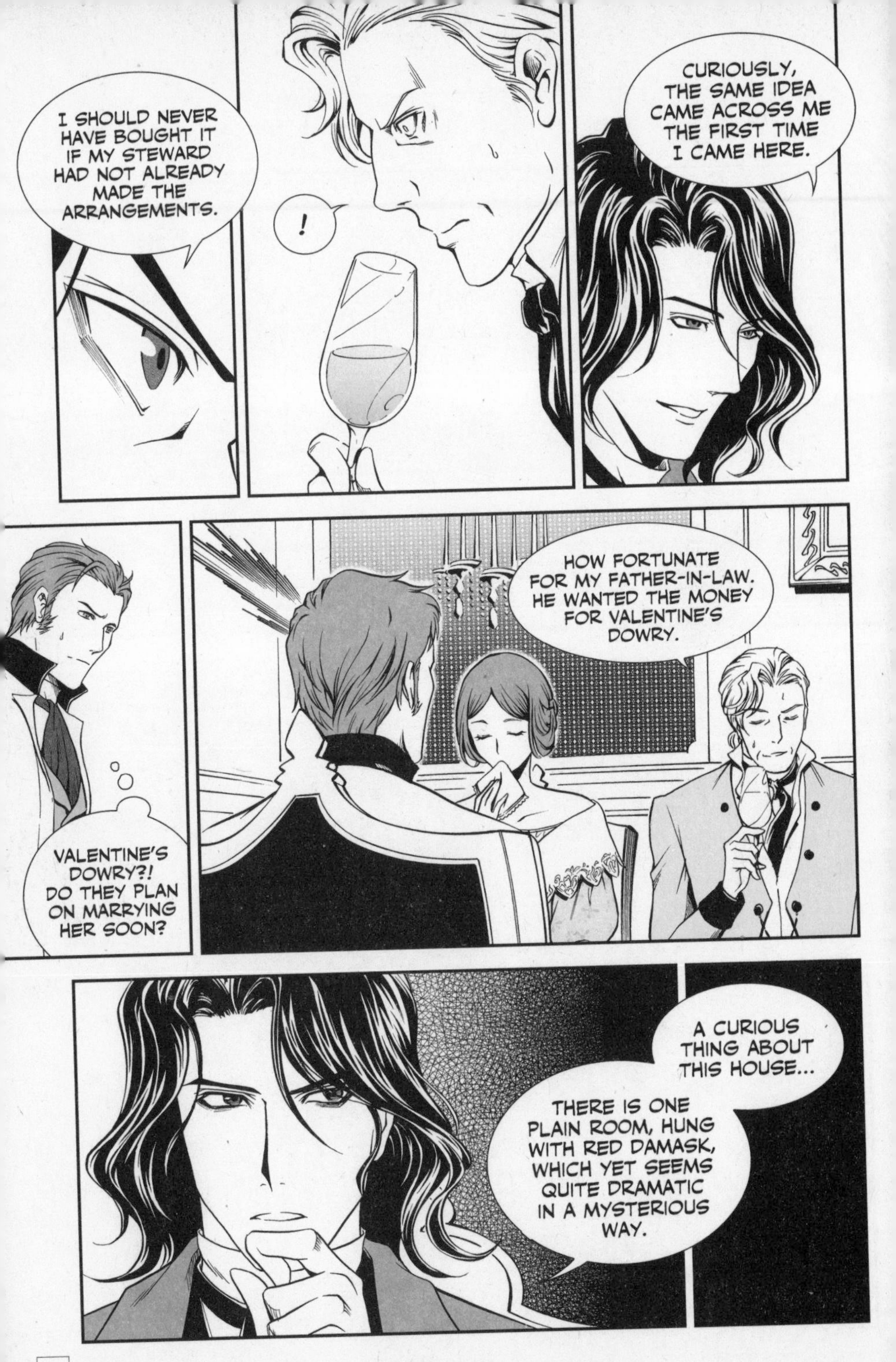
CURIOUSLY, THE SAME IDEA CAME ACROSS ME THE FIRST TIME I CAME HERE.
!
I SHOULD NEVER HAVE BOUGHT IT IF MY STEWARD HAD NOT ALREADY MADE THE ARRANGEMENTS.
HOW FORTUNATE FOR MY FATHER-IN-LAW. HE WANTED THE MONEY FOR VALENTINE'S DOWRY.
VALENTINE'S DOWRY?! DO THEY PLAN ON MARRYING HER SOON?
A CURIOUS THING ABOUT THIS HOUSE...
THERE IS ONE PLAIN ROOM, HUNG WITH RED DAMASK, WHICH YET SEEMS QUITE DRAMATIC IN A MYSTERIOUS WAY.

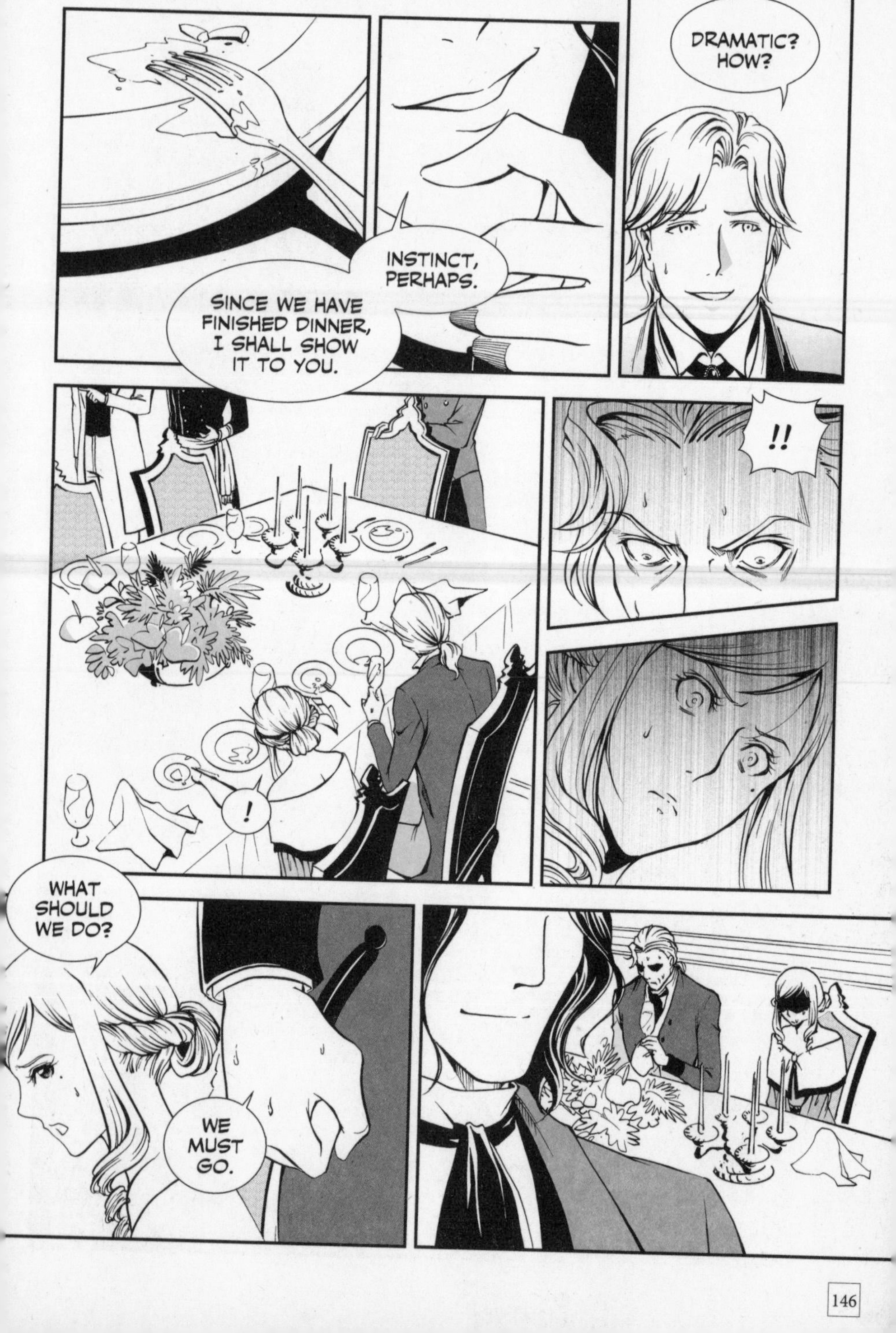
DRAMATIC? HOW?
INSTINCT, PERHAPS.
SINCE WE HAVE FINISHED DINNER, I SHALL SHOW IT TO YOU.
!!
!
WHAT SHOULD WE DO?
WE MUST GO.

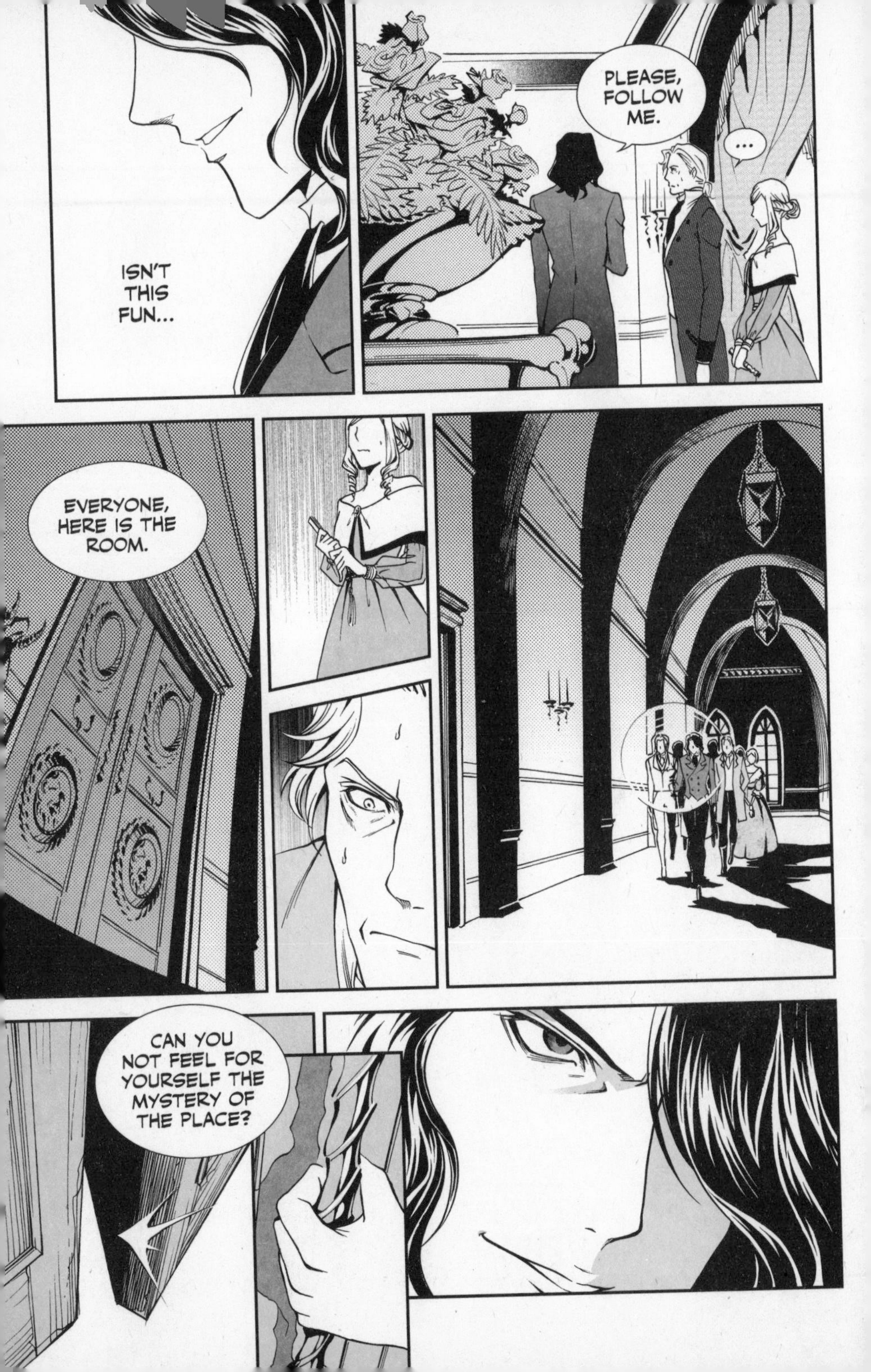
PLEASE, FOLLOW ME.
...
ISN'T THIS FUN...
EVERYONE, HERE IS THE ROOM.
CAN YOU NOT FEEL FOR YOURSELF THE MYSTERY OF THE PLACE?

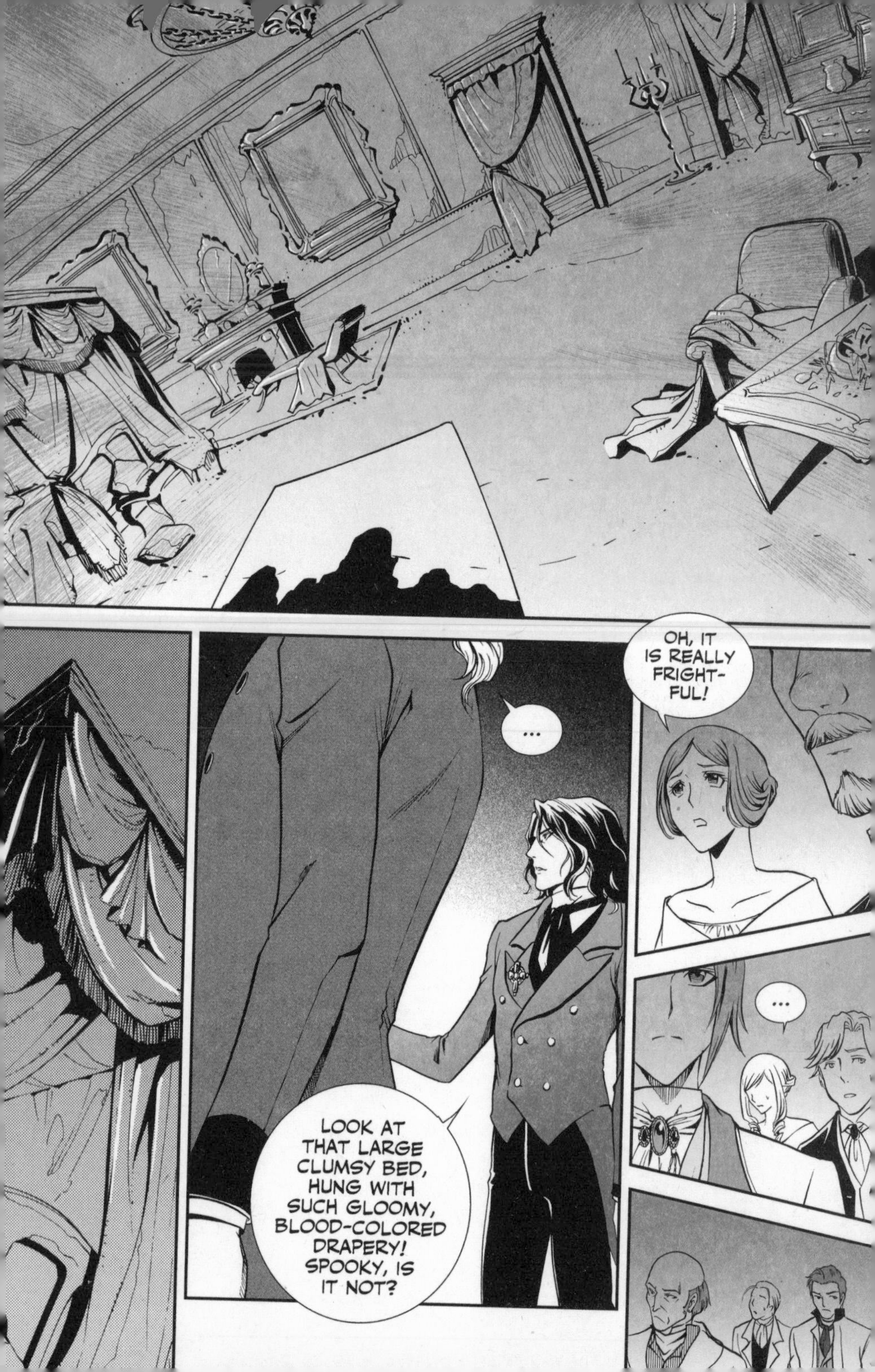
OH, IT IS REALLY FRIGHT-FUL!
...
...
LOOK AT THAT LARGE CLUMSY BED, HUNG WITH SUCH GLOOMY, BLOOD-COLORED DRAPERY! SPOOKY, IS IT NOT?

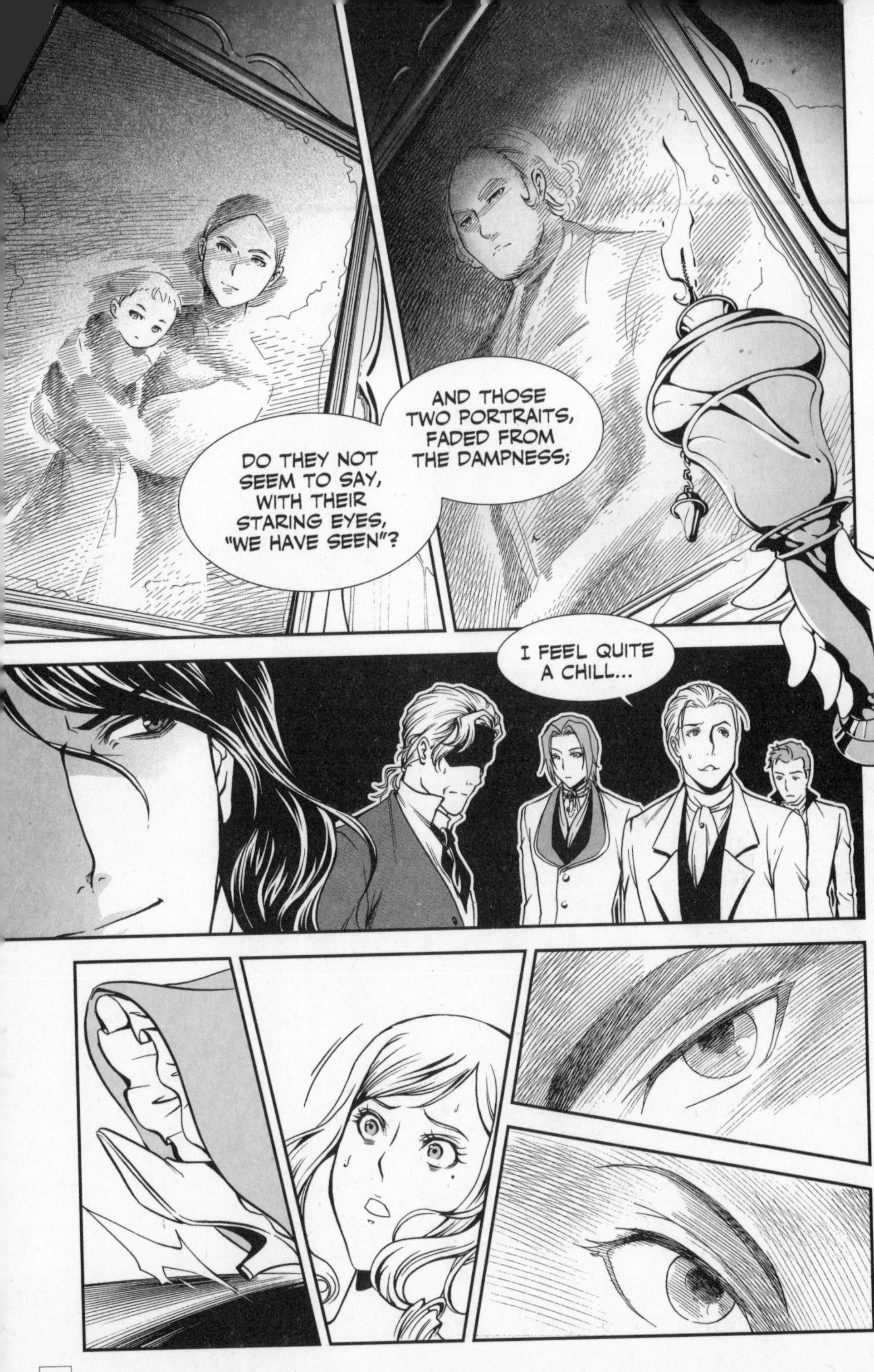
AND THOSE TWO PORTRAITS, FADED FROM THE DAMPNESS;
DO THEY NOT SEEM TO SAY, WITH THEIR STARING EYES, "WE HAVE SEEN"?
I FEEL QUITE A CHILL...

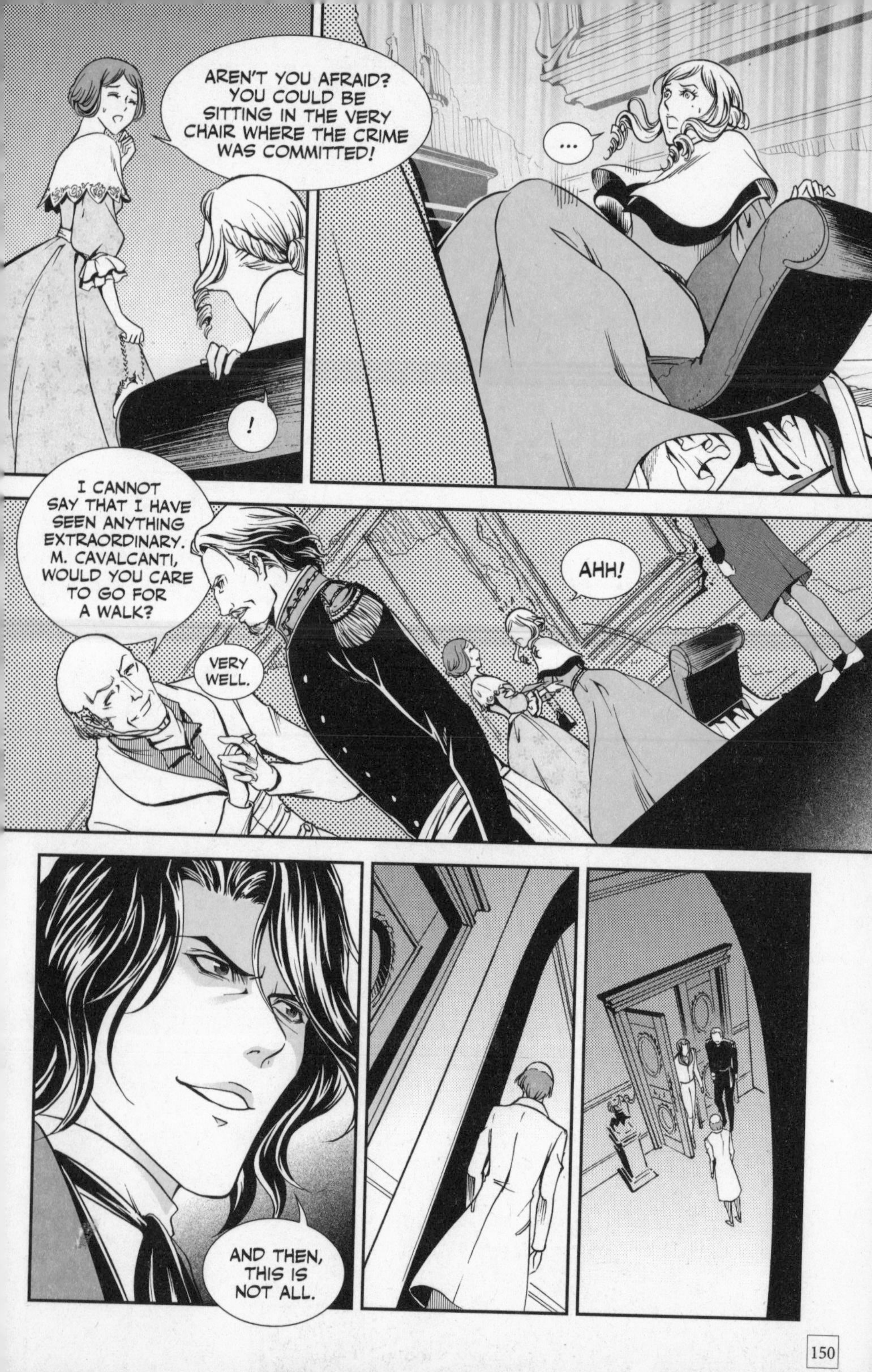
...
AREN'T YOU AFRAID? YOU COULD BE SITTING IN THE VERY CHAIR WHERE THE CRIME WAS COMMITTED!
!
AHH!
I CANNOT SAY THAT I HAVE SEEN ANYTHING EXTRAORDINARY. M. CAVALCANTI, WOULD YOU CARE TO GO FOR A WALK?
VERY WELL.
AND THEN, THIS IS NOT ALL.

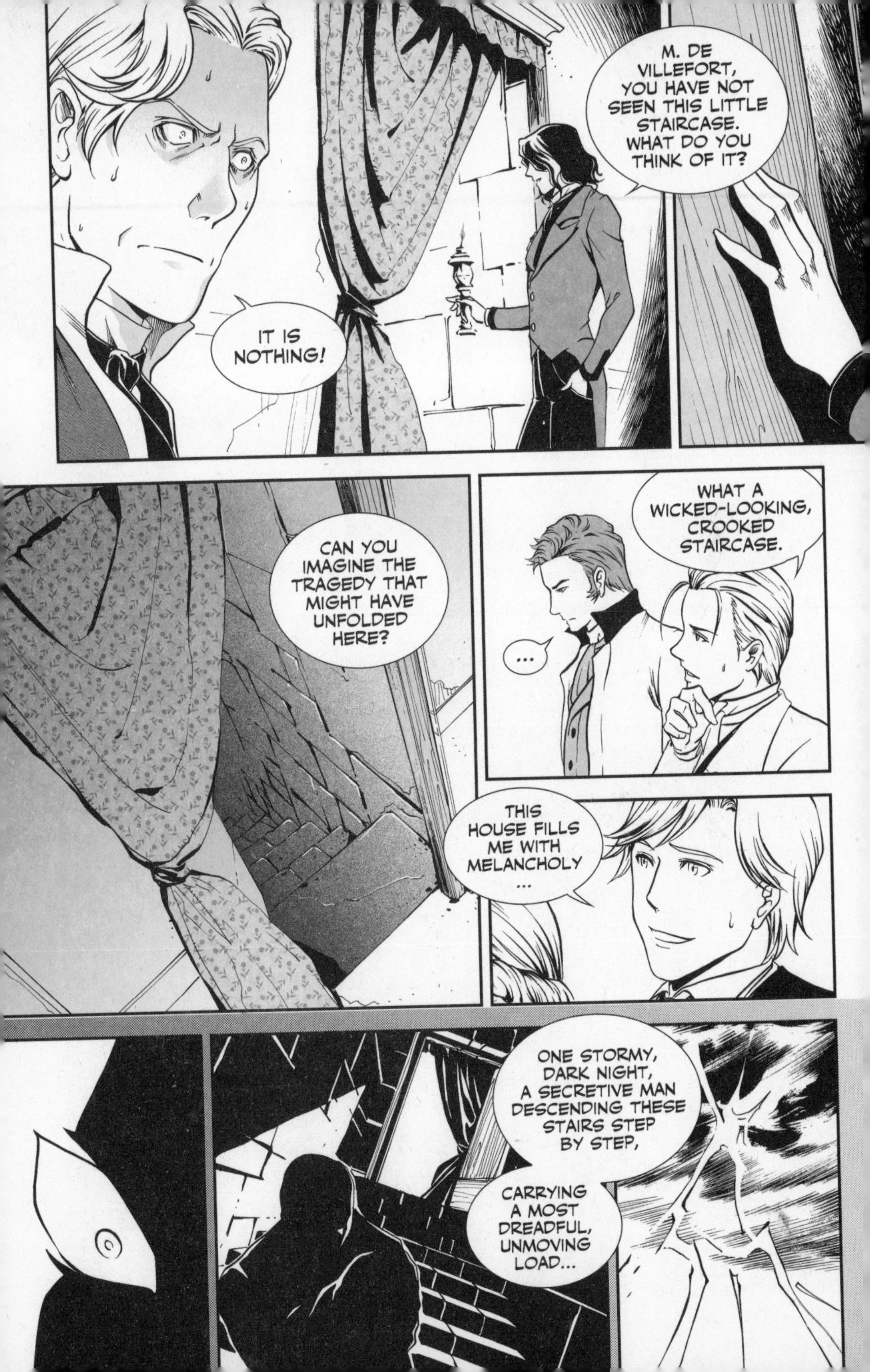
M. DE VILLEFORT, YOU HAVE NOT SEEN THIS LITTLE STAIRCASE. WHAT DO YOU THINK OF IT?
IT IS NOTHING!
WHAT A WICKED-LOOKING, CROOKED STAIRCASE.
...
THIS HOUSE FILLS ME WITH MELANCHOLY ...
CAN YOU IMAGINE THE TRAGEDY THAT MIGHT HAVE UNFOLDED HERE?
ONE STORMY, DARK NIGHT, A SECRETIVE MAN DESCENDING THESE STAIRS STEP BY STEP,
CARRYING A MOST DREADFUL, UNMOVING LOAD...

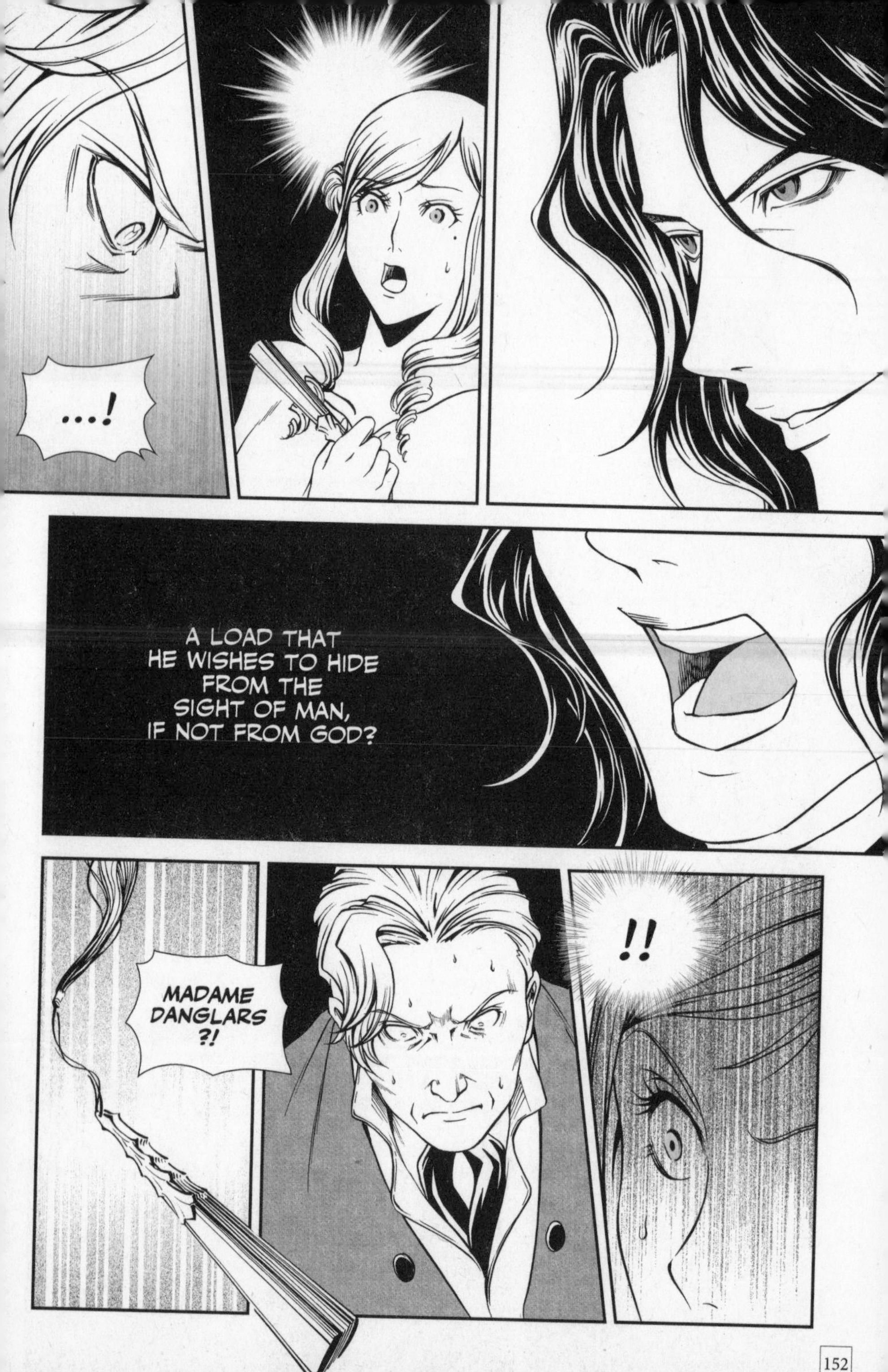
...!
A LOAD THAT HE WISHES TO HIDE FROM THE SIGHT OF MAN, IF NOT FROM GOD?
!!
MADAME DANGLARS ?!

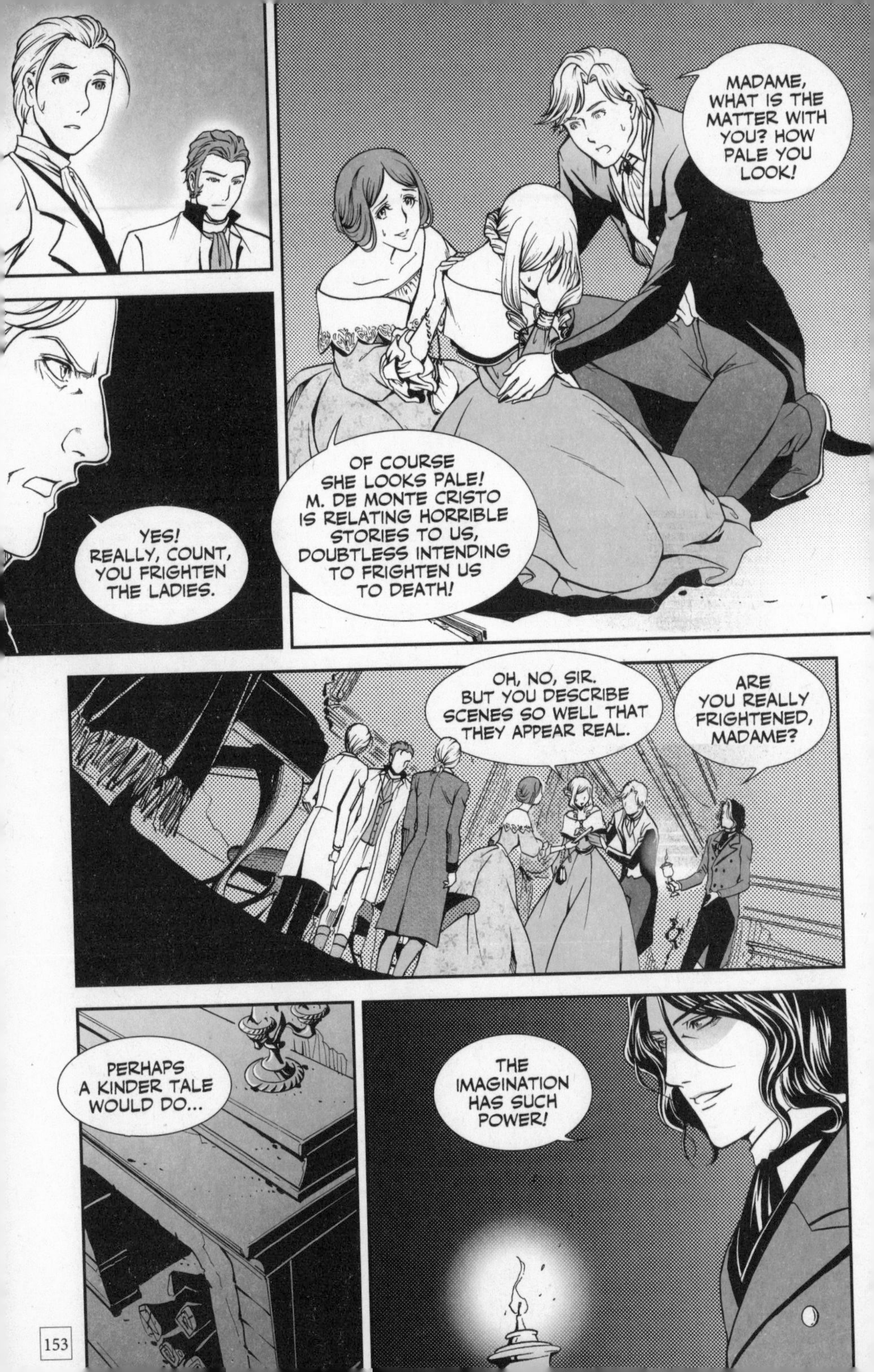

MADAME, WHAT IS THE MATTER WITH YOU? HOW PALE YOU LOOK!
OF COURSE SHE LOOKS PALE! M. DE MONTE CRISTO IS RELATING HORRIBLE STORIES TO US, DOUBTLESS INTENDING TO FRIGHTEN US TO DEATH!
YES! REALLY, COUNT, YOU FRIGHTEN THE LADIES.
ARE YOU REALLY FRIGHTENED, MADAME?
OH, NO, SIR. BUT YOU DESCRIBE SCENES SO WELL THAT THEY APPEAR REAL.
THE IMAGINATION HAS SUCH POWER!
PERHAPS A KINDER TALE WOULD DO...

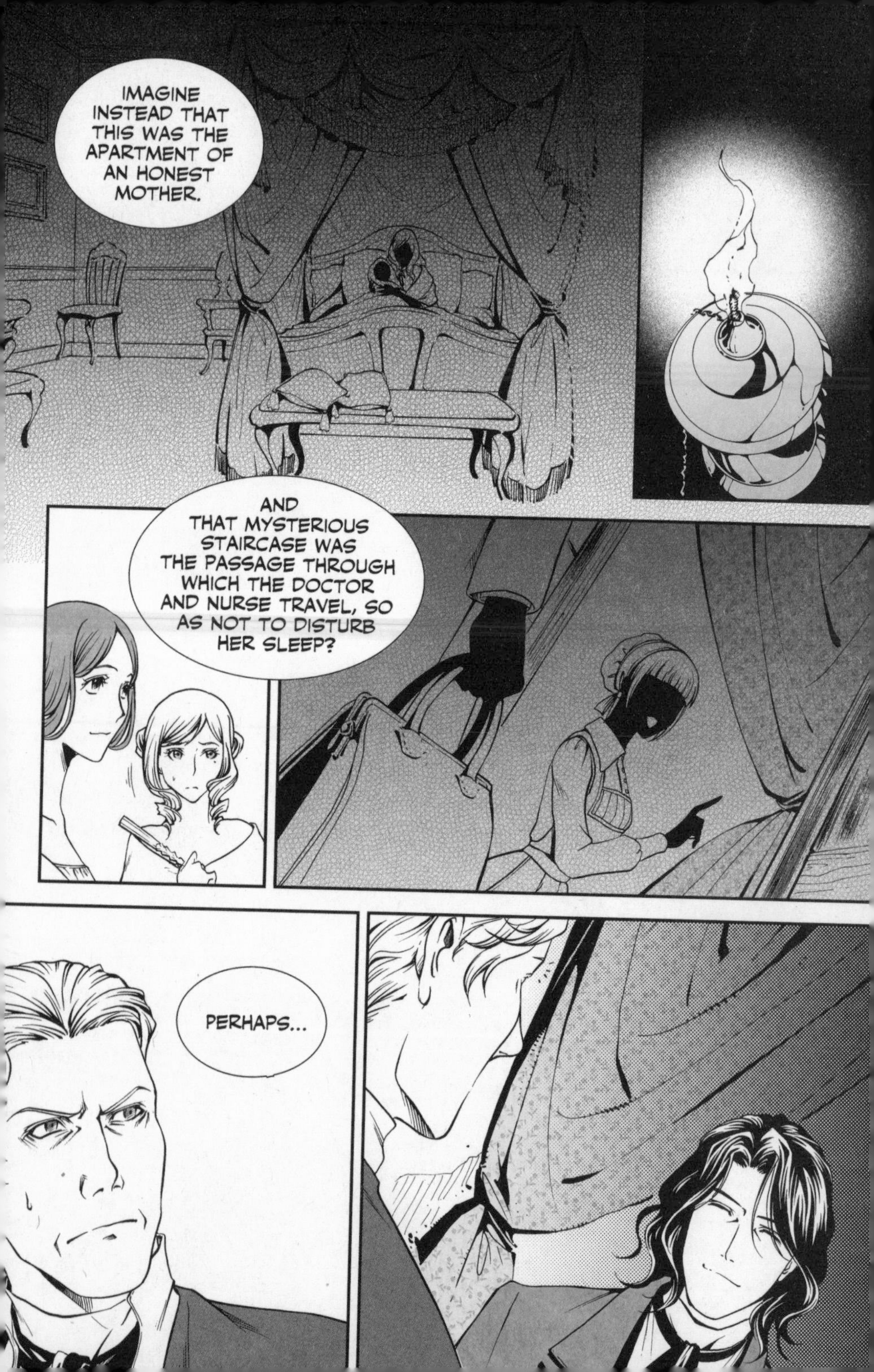
IMAGINE INSTEAD THAT THIS WAS THE APARTMENT OF AN HONEST MOTHER.
AND THAT MYSTERIOUS STAIRCASE WAS THE PASSAGE THROUGH WHICH THE DOCTOR AND NURSE TRAVEL, SO AS NOT TO DISTURB HER SLEEP?
PERHAPS...

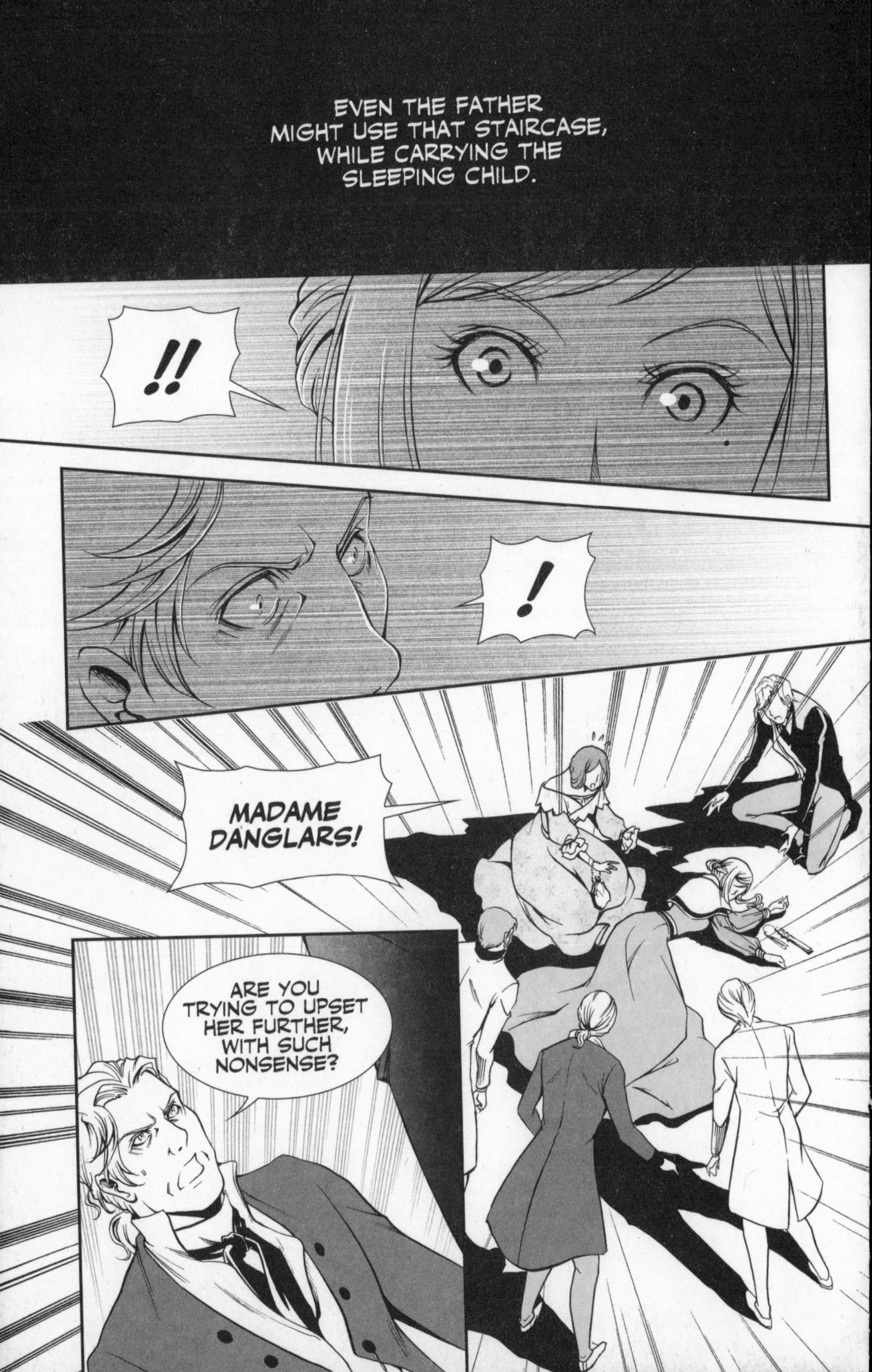
EVEN THE FATHER MIGHT USE THAT STAIRCASE, WHILE CARRYING THE SLEEPING CHILD.
!!
!
MADAME DANGLARS!
ARE YOU TRYING TO UPSET HER FURTHER, WITH SUCH NONSENSE?

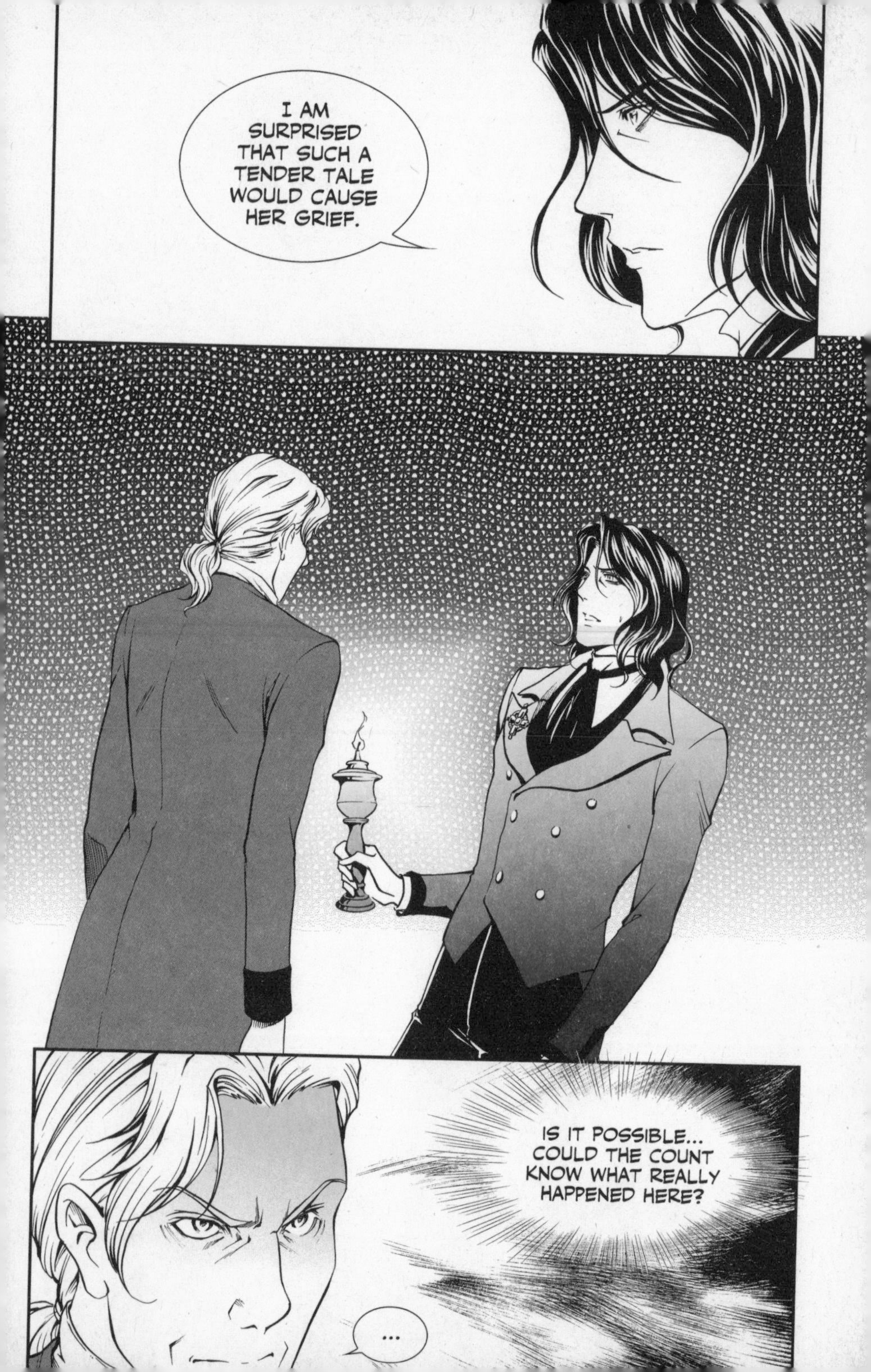
I AM SURPRISED THAT SUCH A TENDER TALE WOULD CAUSE HER GRIEF.
IS IT POSSIBLE... COULD THE COUNT KNOW WHAT REALLY HAPPENED HERE?
...

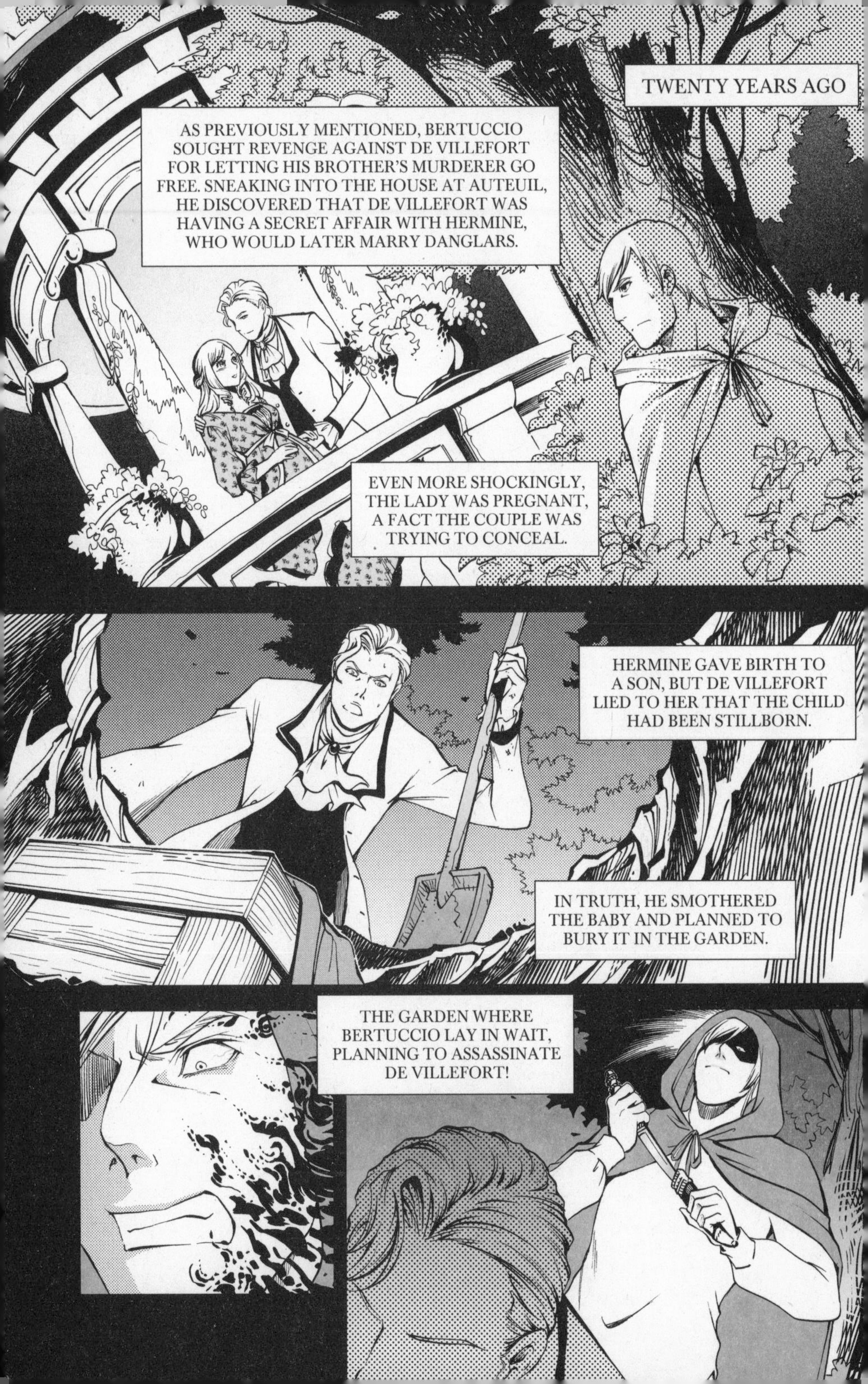
TWENTY YEARS AGO
AS PREVIOUSLY MENTIONED, BERTUCCIO SOUGHT REVENGE AGAINST DE VILLEFORT FOR LETTING HIS BROTHER'S MURDERER GO FREE. SNEAKING INTO THE HOUSE AT AUTEUIL, HE DISCOVERED THAT DE VILLEFORT WAS HAVING A SECRET AFFAIR WITH HERMINE, WHO WOULD LATER MARRY DANGLARS.
EVEN MORE SHOCKINGLY, THE LADY WAS PREGNANT, A FACT THE COUPLE WAS TRYING TO CONCEAL.
HERMINE GAVE BIRTH TO A SON, BUT DE VILLEFORT LIED TO HER THAT THE CHILD HAD BEEN STILLBORN.
IN TRUTH, HE SMOTHERED THE BABY AND PLANNED TO BURY IT IN THE GARDEN.
THE GARDEN WHERE BERTUCCIO LAY IN WAIT, PLANNING TO ASSASSINATE DE VILLEFORT!

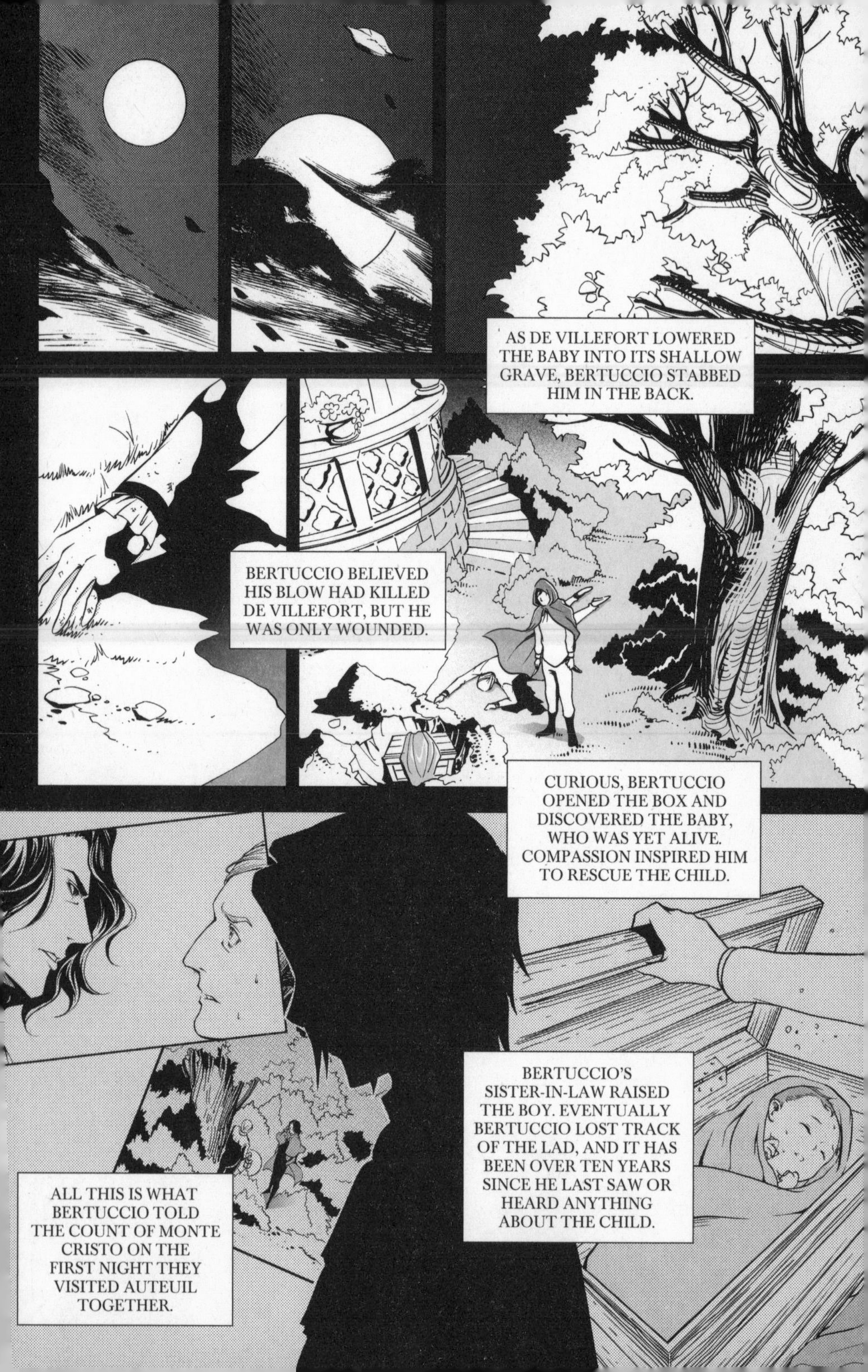
AS DE VILLEFORT LOWERED THE BABY INTO ITS SHALLOW GRAVE, BERTUCCIO STABBED HIM IN THE BACK.
BERTUCCIO BELIEVED HIS BLOW HAD KILLED DE VILLEFORT, BUT HE WAS ONLY WOUNDED.
CURIOUS, BERTUCCIO OPENED THE BOX AND DISCOVERED THE BABY, WHO WAS YET ALIVE. COMPASSION INSPIRED HIM TO RESCUE THE CHILD.
BERTUCCIO'S SISTER-IN-LAW RAISED THE BOY. EVENTUALLY BERTUCCIO LOST TRACK OF THE LAD, AND IT HAS BEEN OVER TEN YEARS SINCE HE LAST SAW OR HEARD ANYTHING ABOUT THE CHILD.
ALL THIS IS WHAT BERTUCCIO TOLD THE COUNT OF MONTE CRISTO ON THE FIRST NIGHT THEY VISITED AUTEUIL TOGETHER.

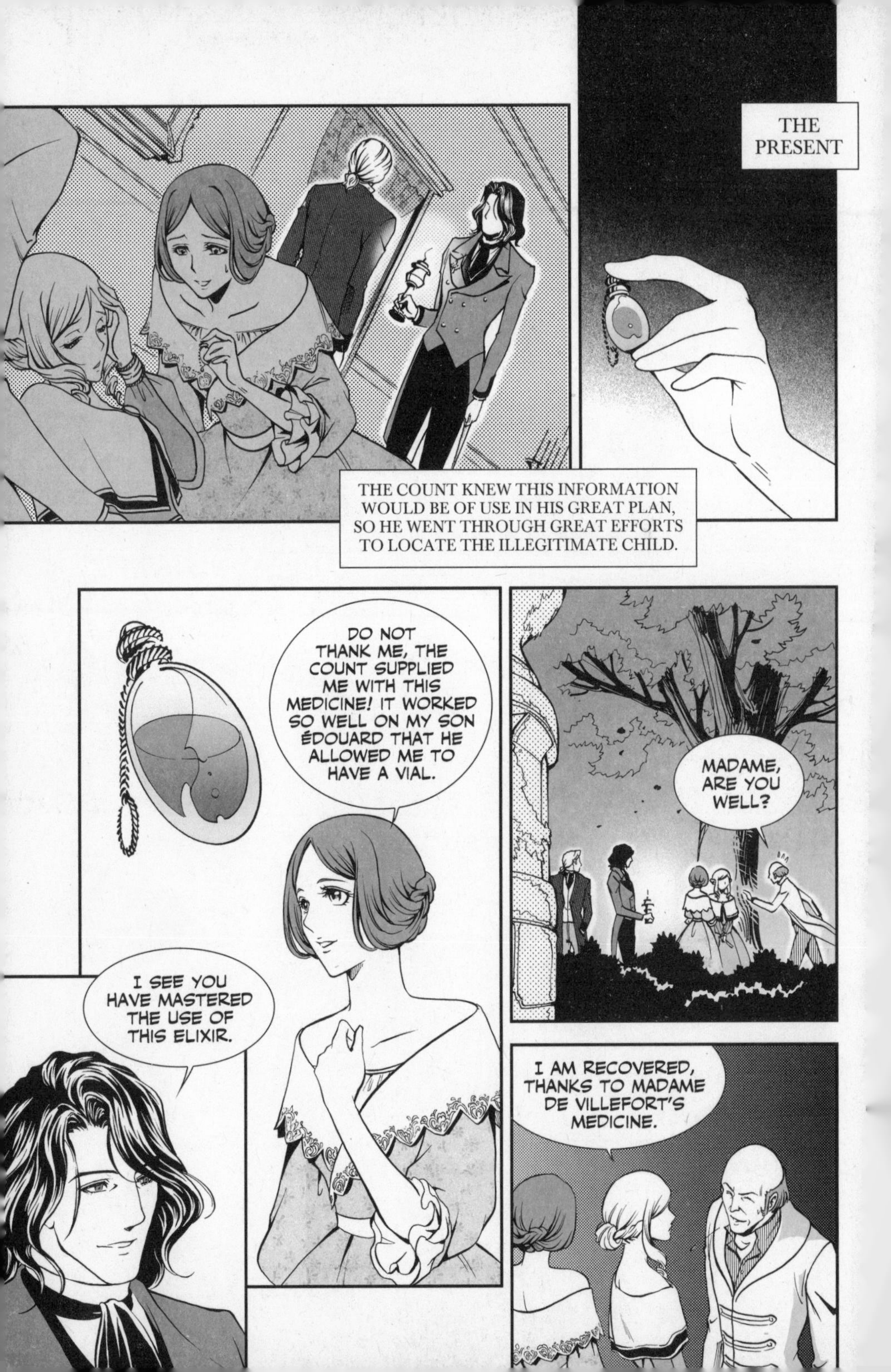
THE PRESENT
THE COUNT KNEW THIS INFORMATION WOULD BE OF USE IN HIS GREAT PLAN, SO HE WENT THROUGH GREAT EFFORTS TO LOCATE THE ILLEGITIMATE CHILD.
MADAME, ARE YOU WELL?
I AM RECOVERED, THANKS TO MADAME DE VILLEFORT'S MEDICINE.
DO NOT THANK ME, THE COUNT SUPPLIED ME WITH THIS MEDICINE! IT WORKED SO WELL ON MY SON ÉDOUARD THAT HE ALLOWED ME TO HAVE A VIAL.
I SEE YOU HAVE MASTERED THE USE OF THIS ELIXIR.

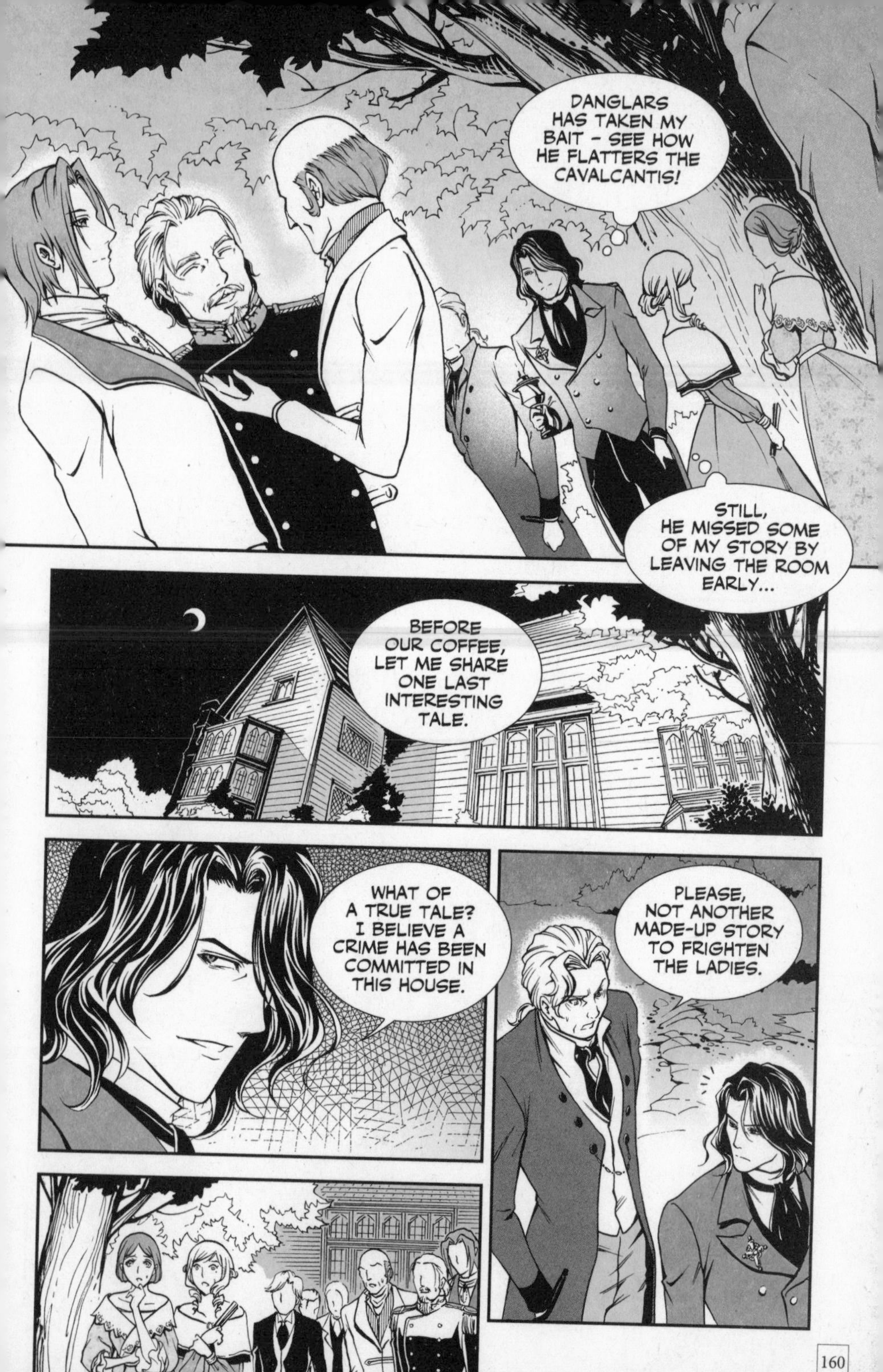
DANGLARS HAS TAKEN MY BAIT - SEE HOW HE FLATTERS THE CAVALCANTIS!
STILL, HE MISSED SOME OF MY STORY BY LEAVING THE ROOM EARLY...
BEFORE OUR COFFEE, LET ME SHARE ONE LAST INTERESTING TALE.
PLEASE, NOT ANOTHER MADE-UP STORY TO FRIGHTEN THE LADIES.
WHAT OF A TRUE TALE? I BELIEVE A CRIME HAS BEEN COMMITTED IN THIS HOUSE.

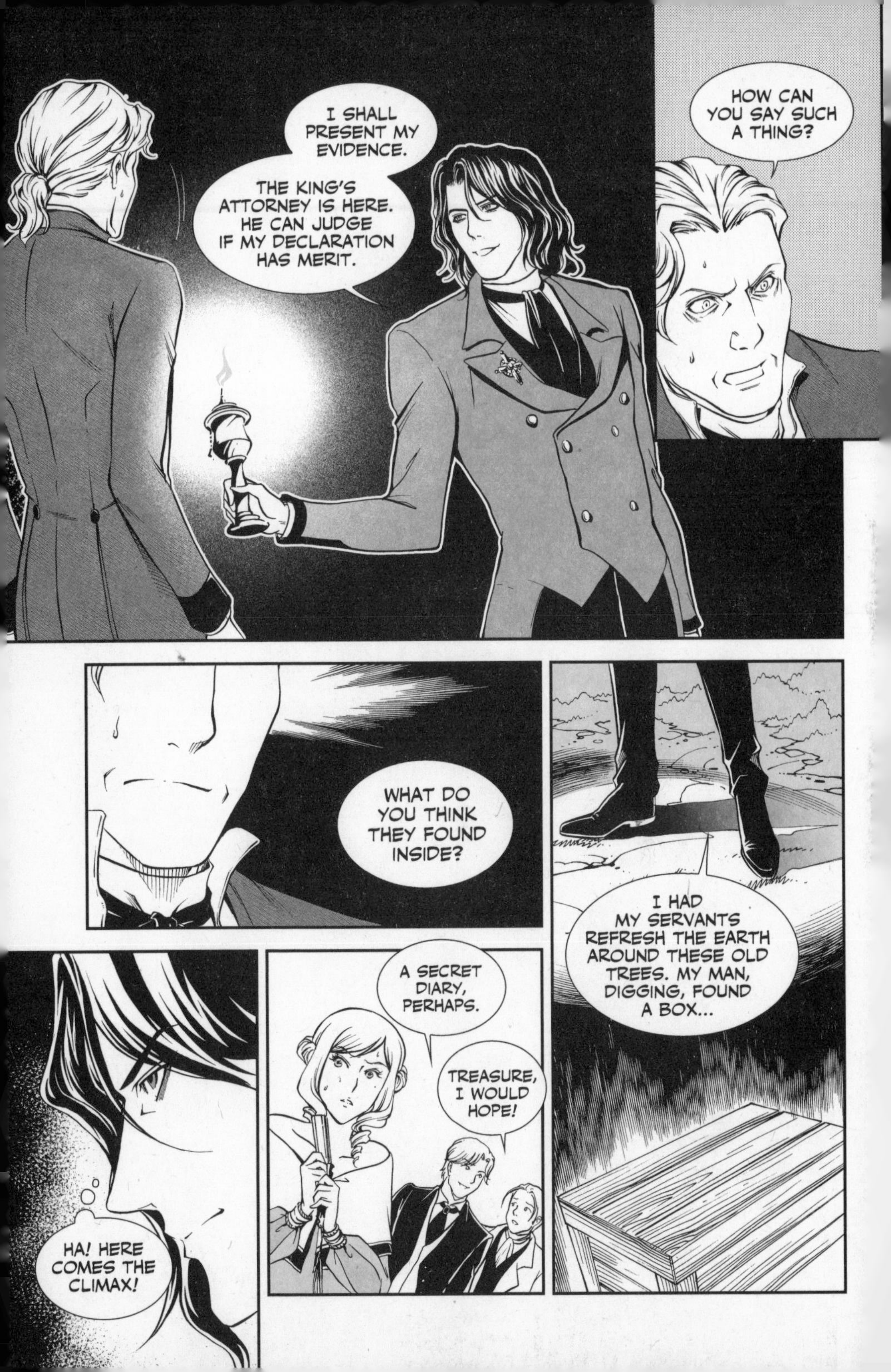
HOW CAN YOU SAY SUCH A THING?
I SHALL PRESENT MY EVIDENCE.
THE KING'S ATTORNEY IS HERE. HE CAN JUDGE IF MY DECLARATION HAS MERIT.
I HAD MY SERVANTS REFRESH THE EARTH AROUND THESE OLD TREES. MY MAN, DIGGING, FOUND A BOX...
WHAT DO YOU THINK THEY FOUND INSIDE?
A SECRET DIARY, PERHAPS.
TREASURE, I WOULD HOPE!
HA! HERE COMES THE CLIMAX!

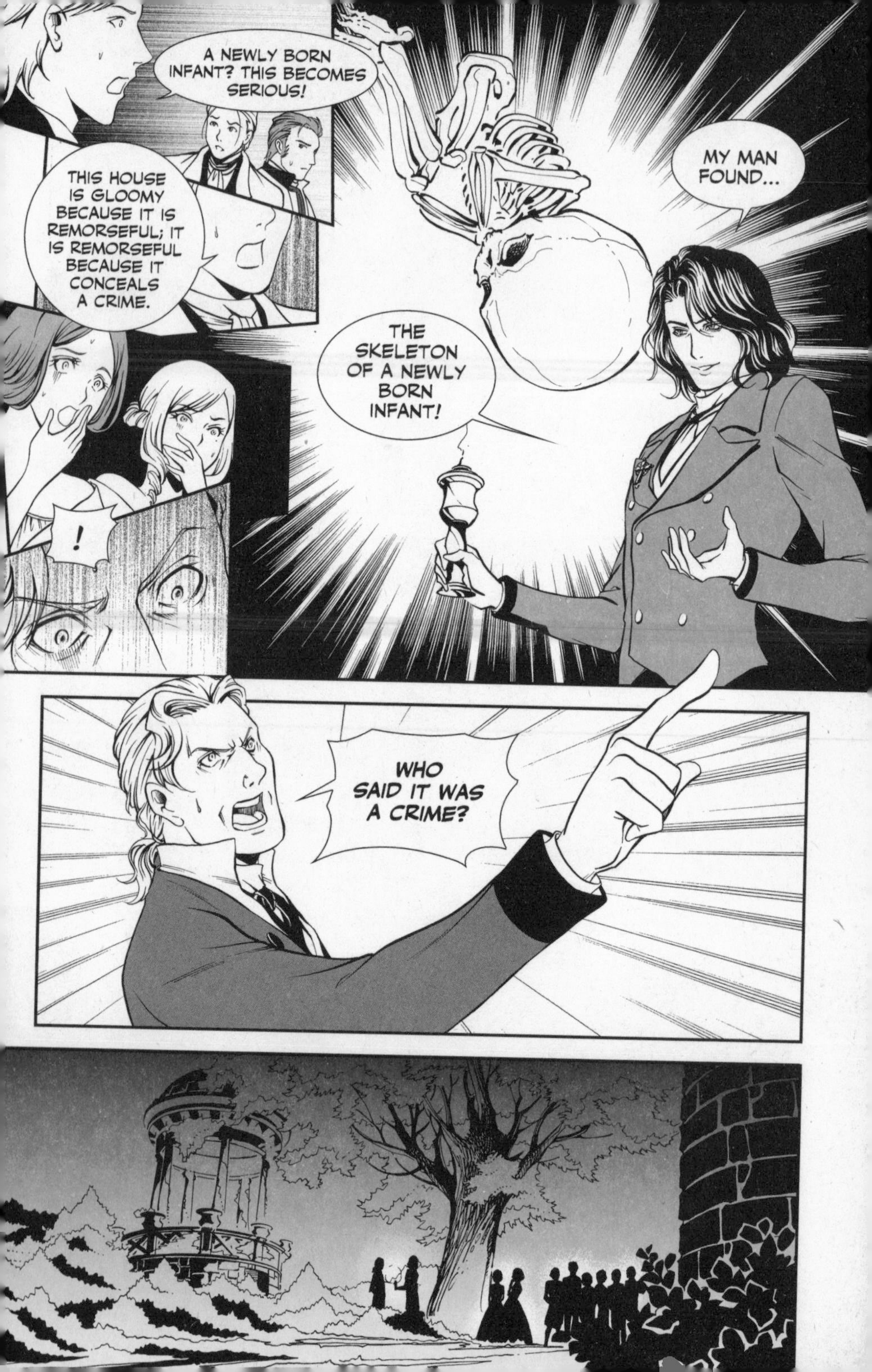
MY MAN FOUND...
THE SKELETON OF A NEWLY BORN INFANT!
A NEWLY BORN INFANT? THIS BECOMES SERIOUS!
THIS HOUSE IS GLOOMY BECAUSE IT IS REMORSEFUL; IT IS REMORSEFUL BECAUSE IT CONCEALS A CRIME.
!
WHO SAID IT WAS A CRIME?

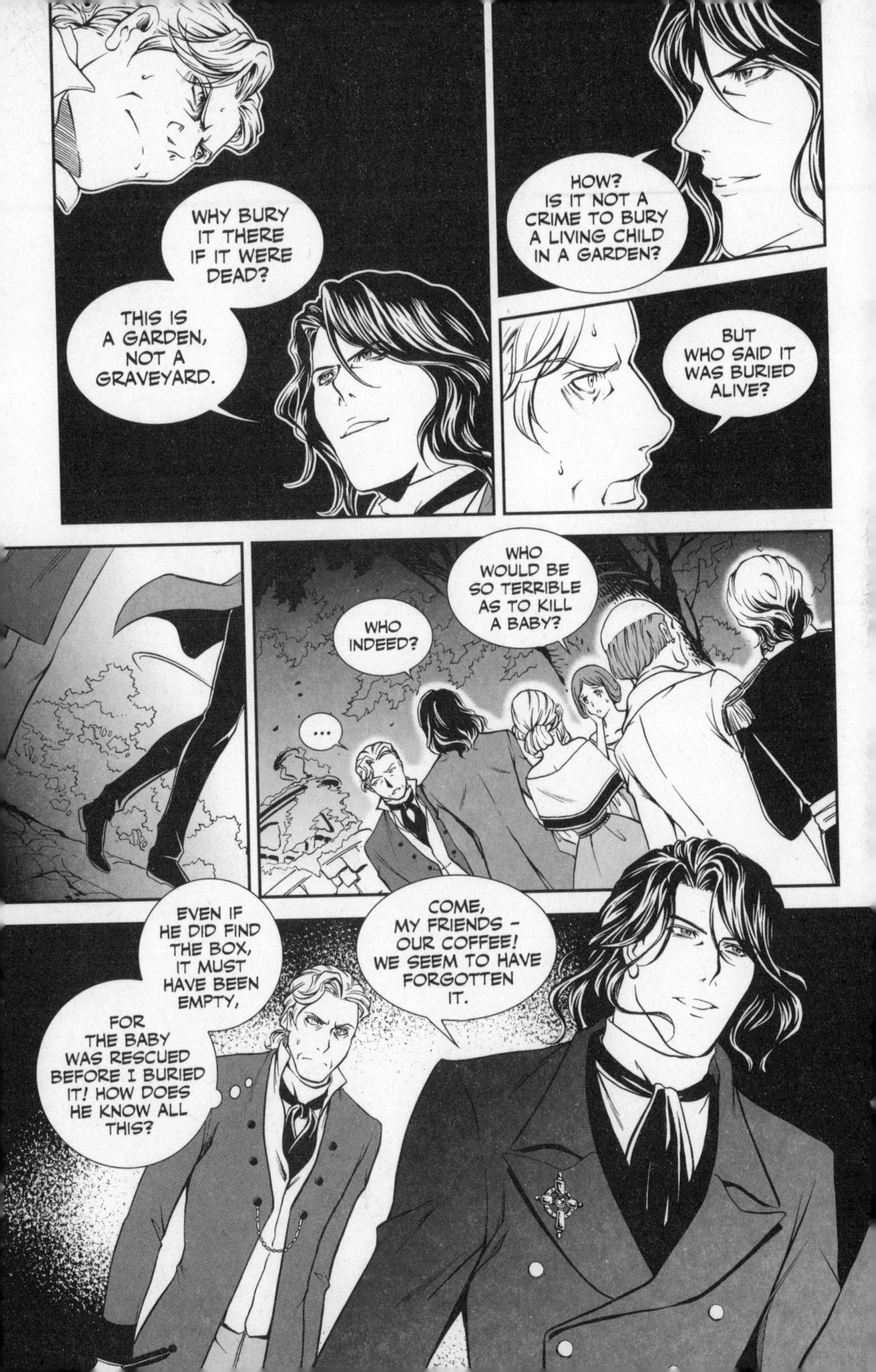
HOW? IS IT NOT A CRIME TO BURY A LIVING CHILD IN A GARDEN?
BUT WHO SAID IT WAS BURIED ALIVE?
WHY BURY IT THERE IF IT WERE DEAD?
THIS IS A GARDEN, NOT A GRAVEYARD.
WHO WOULD BE SO TERRIBLE AS TO KILL A BABY?
WHO INDEED?
...
COME, MY FRIENDS - OUR COFFEE! WE SEEM TO HAVE FORGOTTEN IT.
EVEN IF HE DID FIND THE BOX, IT MUST HAVE BEEN EMPTY,
FOR THE BABY WAS RESCUED BEFORE I BURIED IT! HOW DOES HE KNOW ALL THIS?

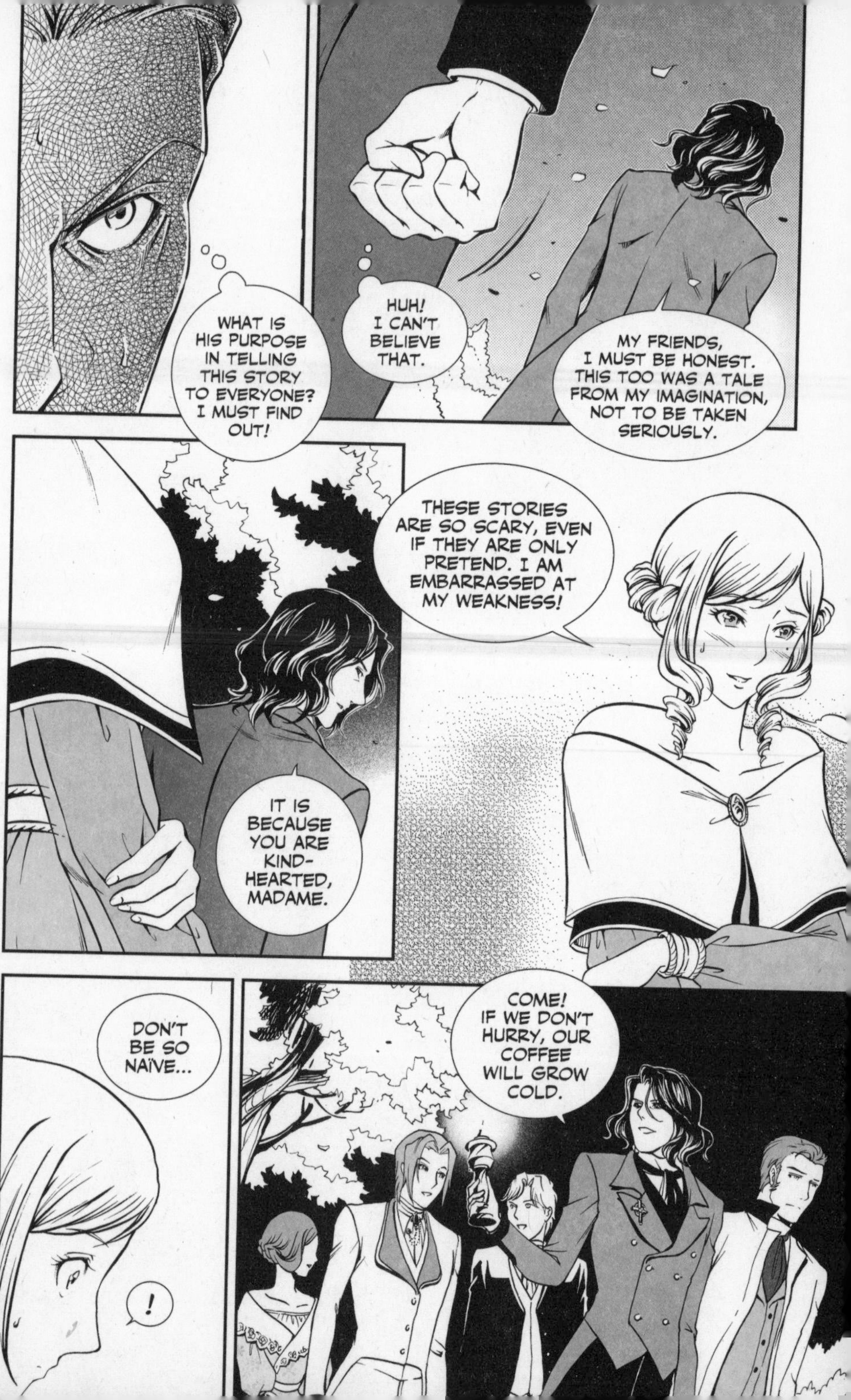
MY FRIENDS, I MUST BE HONEST. THIS TOO WAS A TALE FROM MY IMAGINATION, NOT TO BE TAKEN SERIOUSLY.
HUH! I CAN'T BELIEVE THAT.
WHAT IS HIS PURPOSE IN TELLING THIS STORY TO EVERYONE? I MUST FIND OUT!
THESE STORIES ARE SO SCARY, EVEN IF THEY ARE ONLY PRETEND. I AM EMBARRASSED AT MY WEAKNESS!
IT IS BECAUSE YOU ARE KIND-HEARTED, MADAME.
COME! IF WE DON'T HURRY, OUR COFFEE WILL GROW COLD.
DON'T BE SO NAÏVE...
!

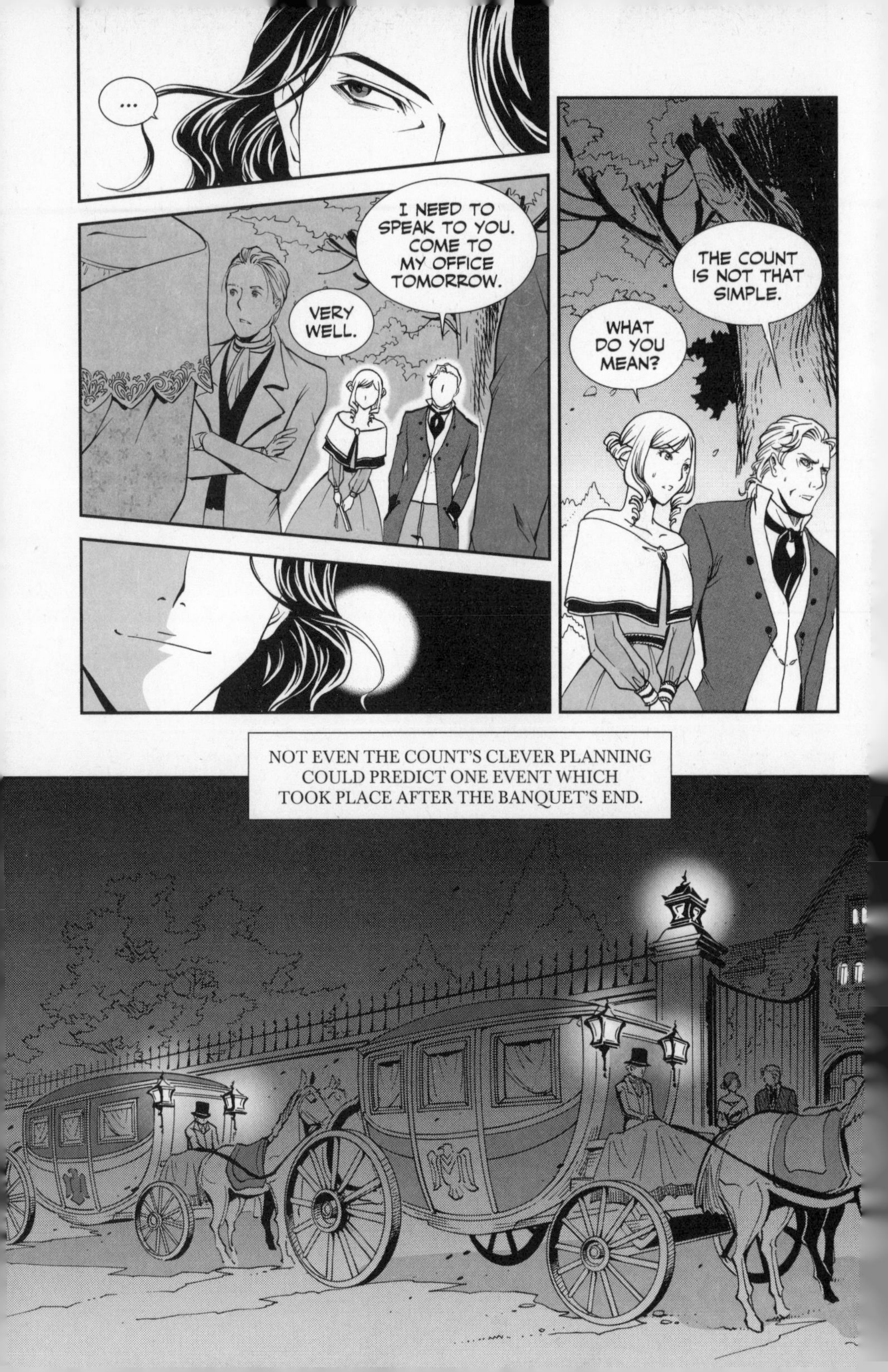
THE COUNT IS NOT THAT SIMPLE.
WHAT DO YOU MEAN?
...
I NEED TO SPEAK TO YOU. COME TO MY OFFICE TOMORROW.
VERY WELL.
NOT EVEN THE COUNT'S CLEVER PLANNING COULD PREDICT ONE EVENT WHICH TOOK PLACE AFTER THE BANQUET'S END.

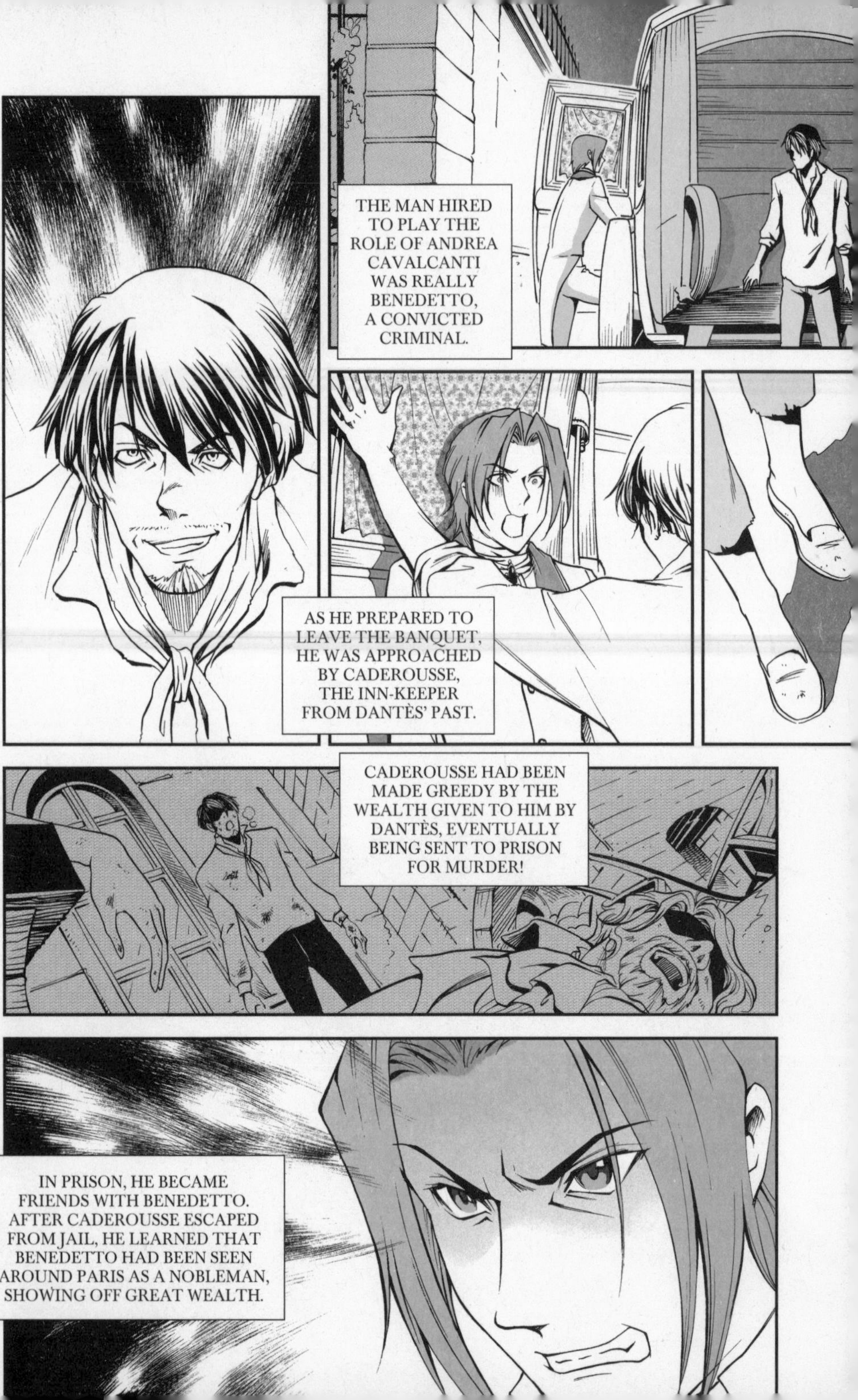
THE MAN HIRED TO PLAY THE ROLE OF ANDREA CAVALCANTI WAS REALLY BENEDETTO, A CONVICTED CRIMINAL.
AS HE PREPARED TO LEAVE THE BANQUET, HE WAS APPROACHED BY CADEROUSSE, THE INN-KEEPER FROM DANTÈS' PAST.
CADEROUSSE HAD BEEN MADE GREEDY BY THE WEALTH GIVEN TO HIM BY DANTÈS, EVENTUALLY BEING SENT TO PRISON FOR MURDER!
IN PRISON, HE BECAME FRIENDS WITH BENEDETTO. AFTER CADEROUSSE ESCAPED FROM JAIL, HE LEARNED THAT BENEDETTO HAD BEEN SEEN AROUND PARIS AS A NOBLEMAN, SHOWING OFF GREAT WEALTH.

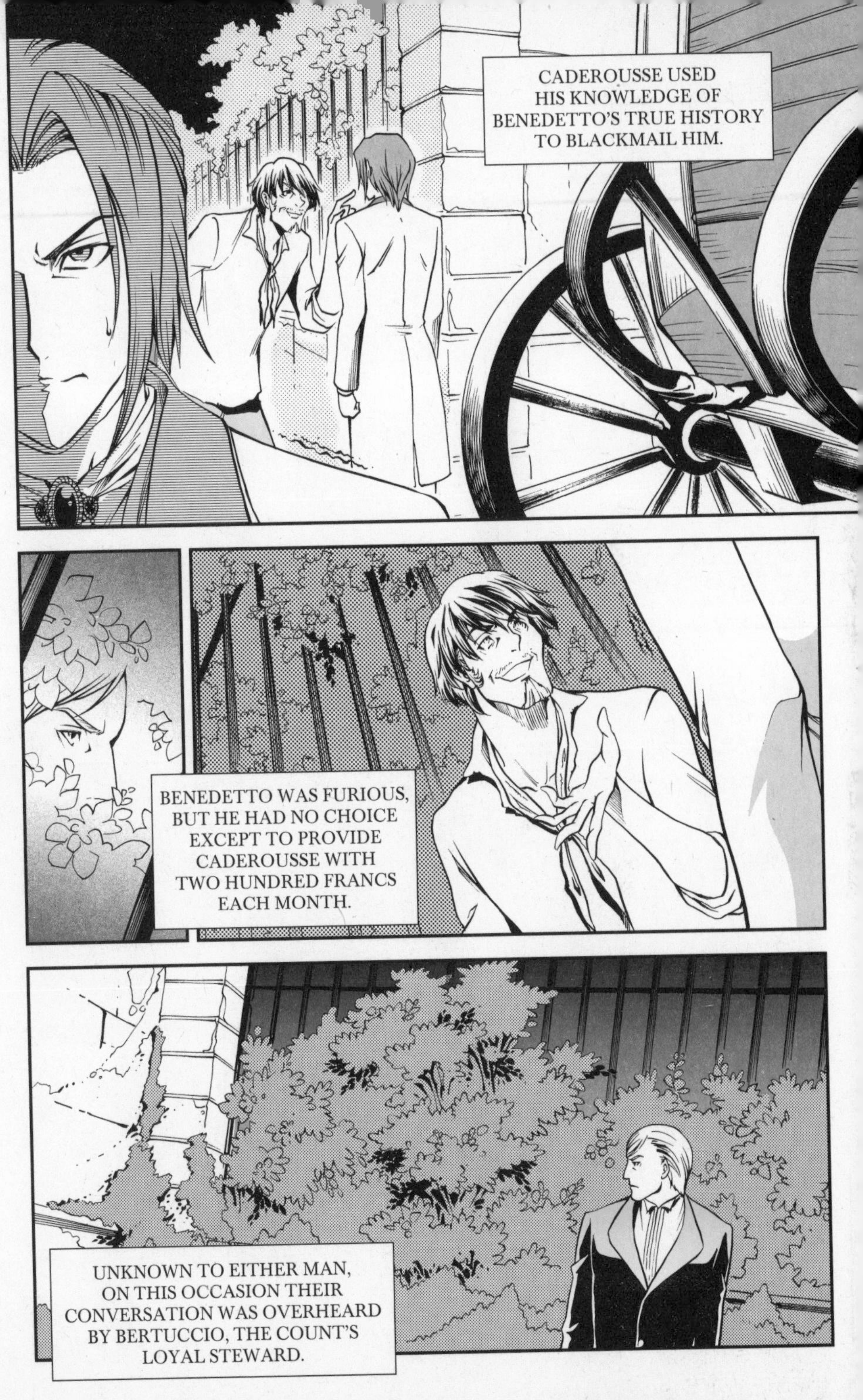
CADEROUSSE USED HIS KNOWLEDGE OF BENEDETTO'S TRUE HISTORY TO BLACKMAIL HIM.
BENEDETTO WAS FURIOUS, BUT HE HAD NO CHOICE EXCEPT TO PROVIDE CADEROUSSE WITH TWO HUNDRED FRANCS EACH MONTH.
UNKNOWN TO EITHER MAN, ON THIS OCCASION THEIR CONVERSATION WAS OVERHEARD BY BERTUCCIO, THE COUNT'S LOYAL STEWARD.

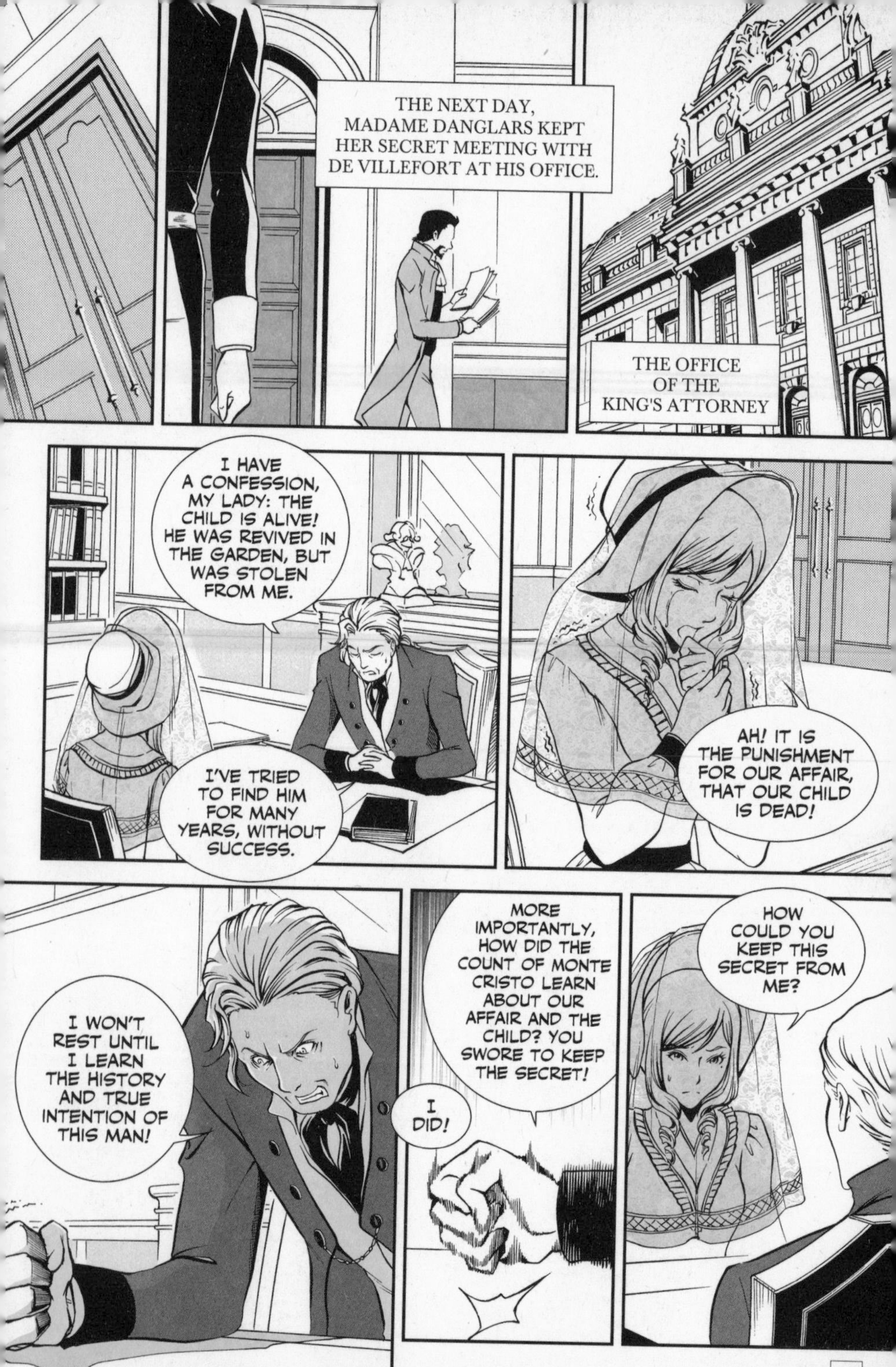
THE OFFICE OF THE KING'S ATTORNEY
THE NEXT DAY, MADAME DANGLARS KEPT HER SECRET MEETING WITH DE VILLEFORT AT HIS OFFICE.
AH! IT IS THE PUNISHMENT FOR OUR AFFAIR, THAT OUR CHILD IS DEAD!
I HAVE A CONFESSION, MY LADY: THE CHILD IS ALIVE! HE WAS REVIVED IN THE GARDEN, BUT WAS STOLEN FROM ME.
I'VE TRIED TO FIND HIM FOR MANY YEARS, WITHOUT SUCCESS.
HOW COULD YOU KEEP THIS SECRET FROM ME?
MORE IMPORTANTLY, HOW DID THE COUNT OF MONTE CRISTO LEARN ABOUT OUR AFFAIR AND THE CHILD? YOU SWORE TO KEEP THE SECRET!
I DID!
I WON'T REST UNTIL I LEARN THE HISTORY AND TRUE INTENTION OF THIS MAN!

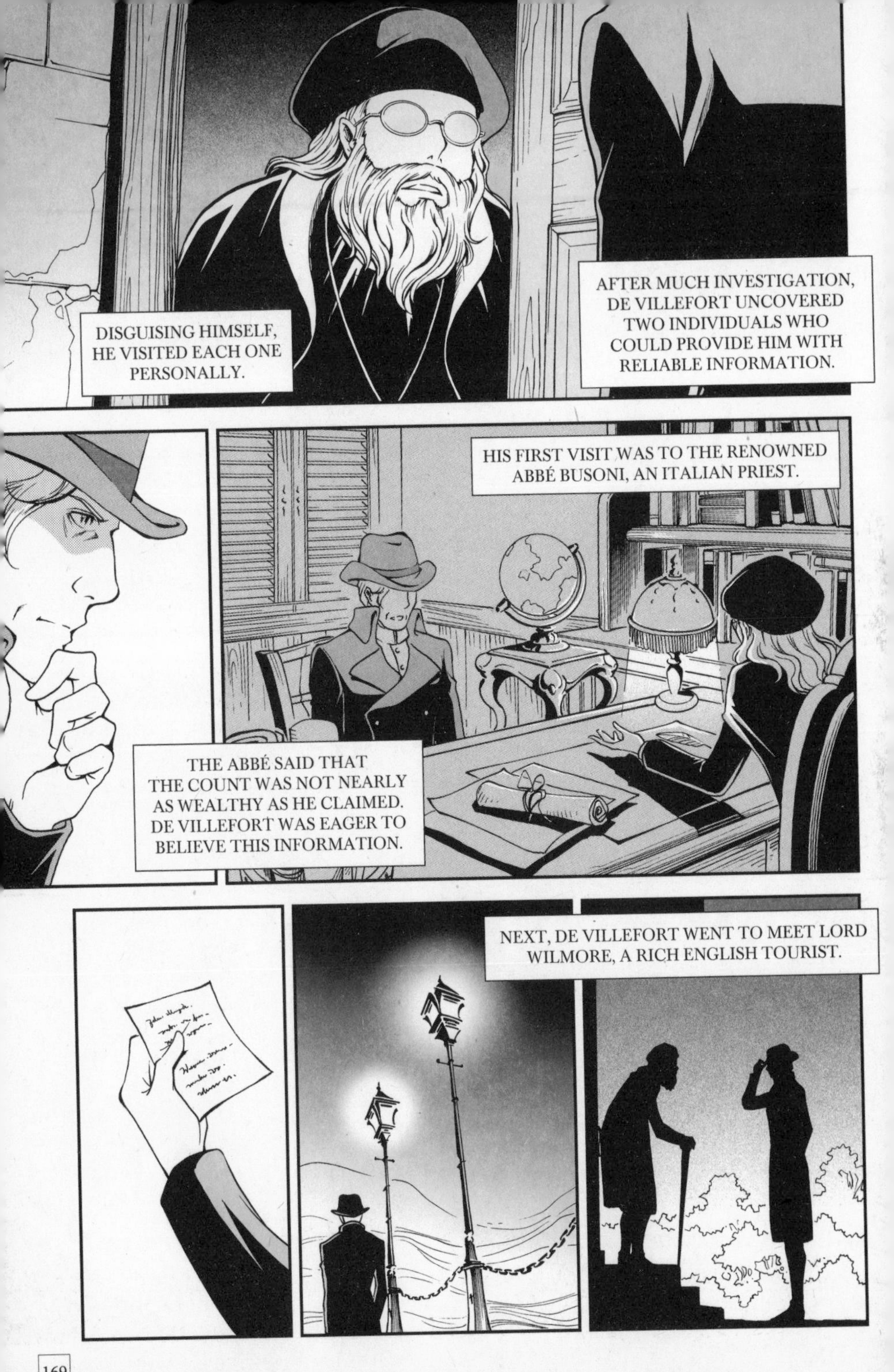
AFTER MUCH INVESTIGATION, DE VILLEFORT UNCOVERED TWO INDIVIDUALS WHO COULD PROVIDE HIM WITH RELIABLE INFORMATION.
DISGUISING HIMSELF, HE VISITED EACH ONE PERSONALLY.
HIS FIRST VISIT WAS TO THE RENOWNED ABBÉ BUSONI, AN ITALIAN PRIEST.
THE ABBÉ SAID THAT THE COUNT WAS NOT NEARLY AS WEALTHY AS HE CLAIMED. DE VILLEFORT WAS EAGER TO BELIEVE THIS INFORMATION.
NEXT, DE VILLEFORT WENT TO MEET LORD WILMORE, A RICH ENGLISH TOURIST.

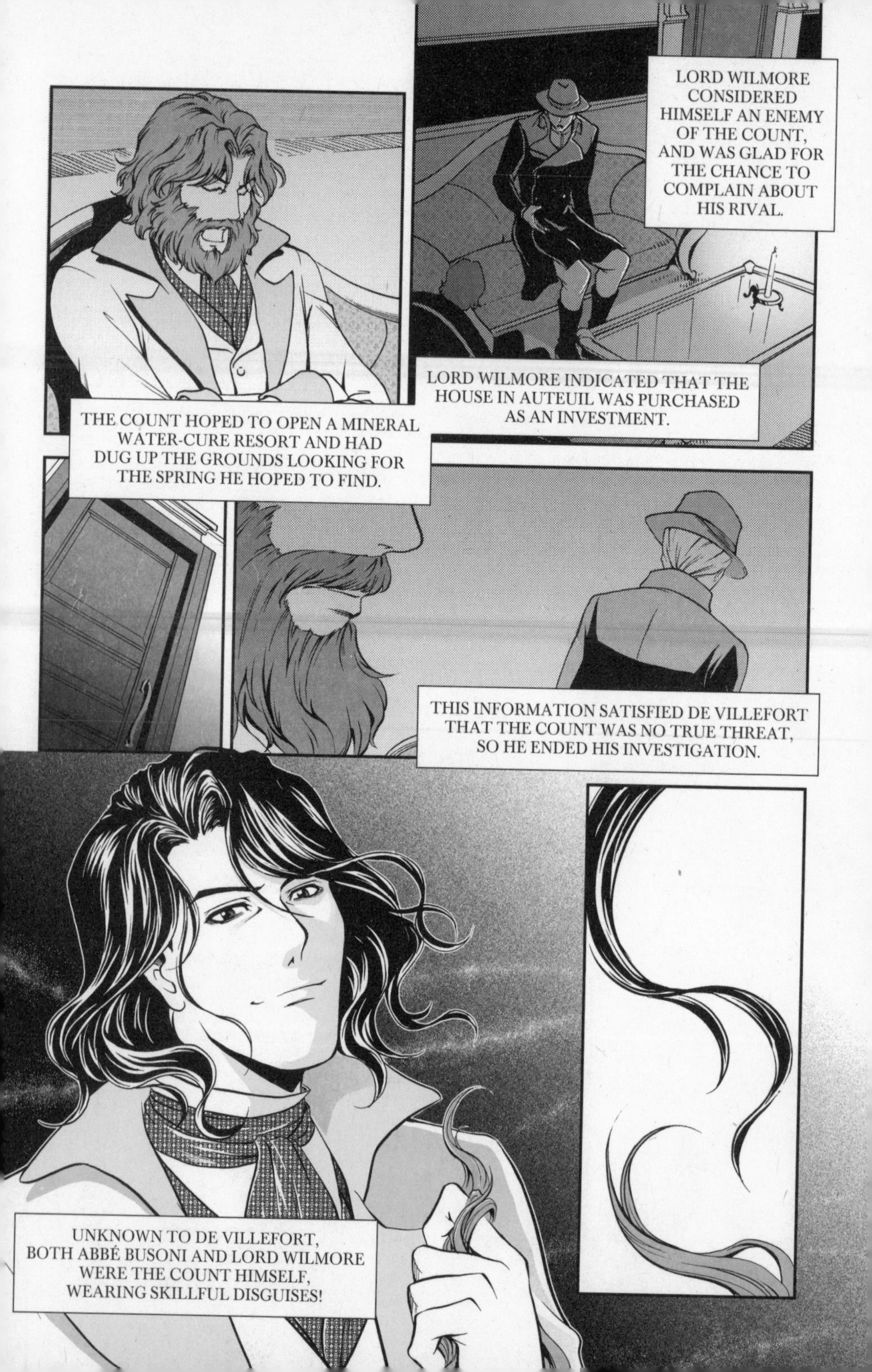
LORD WILMORE CONSIDERED HIMSELF AN ENEMY OF THE COUNT, AND WAS GLAD FOR THE CHANCE TO COMPLAIN ABOUT HIS RIVAL.
LORD WILMORE INDICATED THAT THE HOUSE IN AUTEUIL WAS PURCHASED AS AN INVESTMENT.
THE COUNT HOPED TO OPEN A MINERAL WATER-CURE RESORT AND HAD DUG UP THE GROUNDS LOOKING FOR THE SPRING HE HOPED TO FIND.
THIS INFORMATION SATISFIED DE VILLEFORT THAT THE COUNT WAS NO TRUE THREAT, SO HE ENDED HIS INVESTIGATION.
UNKNOWN TO DE VILLEFORT, BOTH ABBÉ BUSONI AND LORD WILMORE WERE THE COUNT HIMSELF, WEARING SKILLFUL DISGUISES!

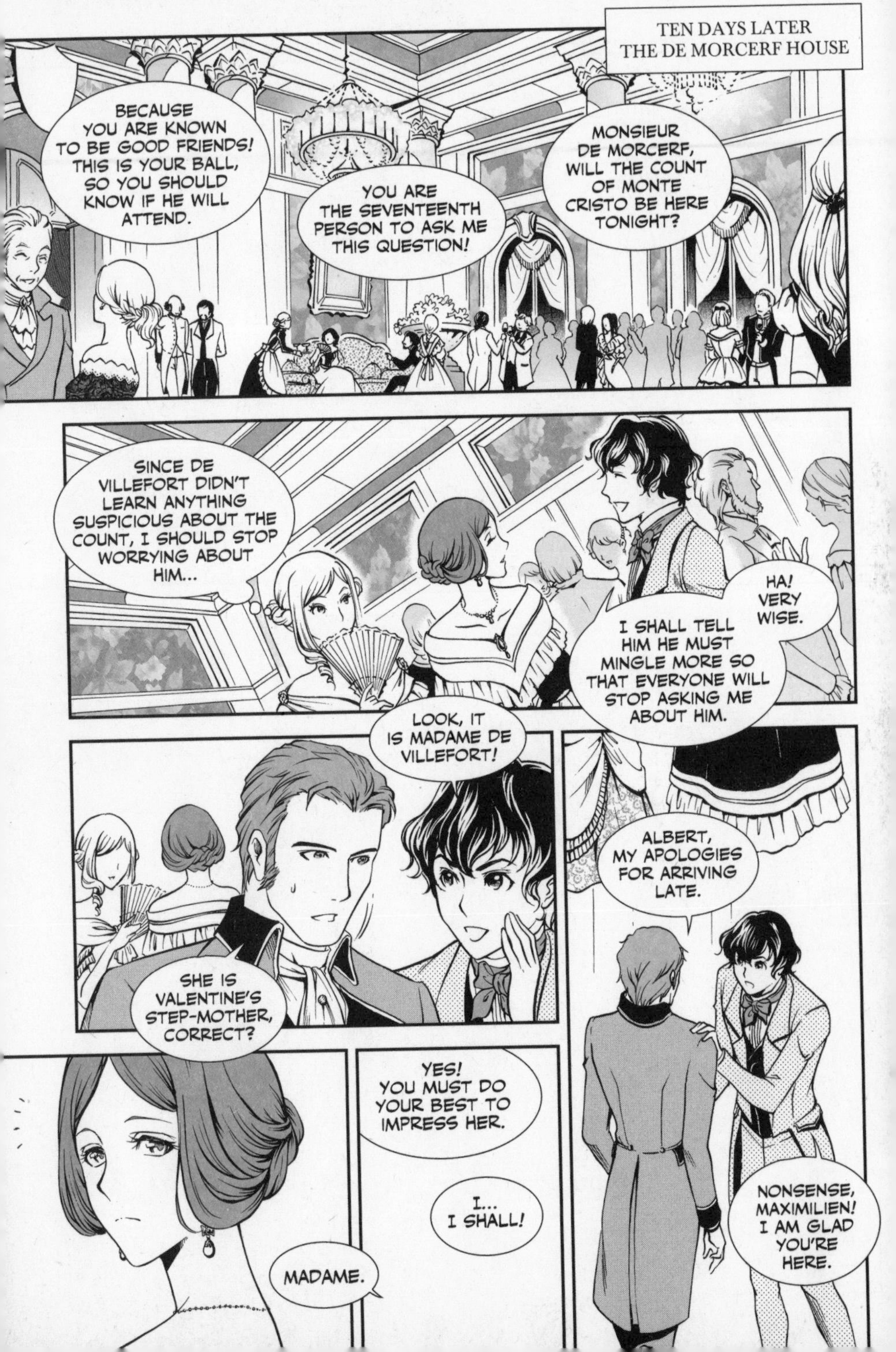
TEN DAYS LATER
THE DE MORCERF HOUSE
MONSIEUR DE MORCERF, WILL THE COUNT OF MONTE CRISTO BE HERE TONIGHT?
YOU ARE THE SEVENTEENTH PERSON TO ASK ME THIS QUESTION!
BECAUSE YOU ARE KNOWN TO BE GOOD FRIENDS! THIS IS YOUR BALL, SO YOU SHOULD KNOW IF HE WILL ATTEND.
HA! VERY WISE.
I SHALL TELL HIM HE MUST MINGLE MORE SO THAT EVERYONE WILL STOP ASKING ME ABOUT HIM.
SINCE DE VILLEFORT DIDN'T LEARN ANYTHING SUSPICIOUS ABOUT THE COUNT, I SHOULD STOP WORRYING ABOUT HIM...
ALBERT, MY APOLOGIES FOR ARRIVING LATE.
NONSENSE, MAXIMILIEN! I AM GLAD YOU'RE HERE.
LOOK, IT IS MADAME DE VILLEFORT!
SHE IS VALENTINE'S STEP-MOTHER, CORRECT?
YES! YOU MUST DO YOUR BEST TO IMPRESS HER.
I... I SHALL!
MADAME.

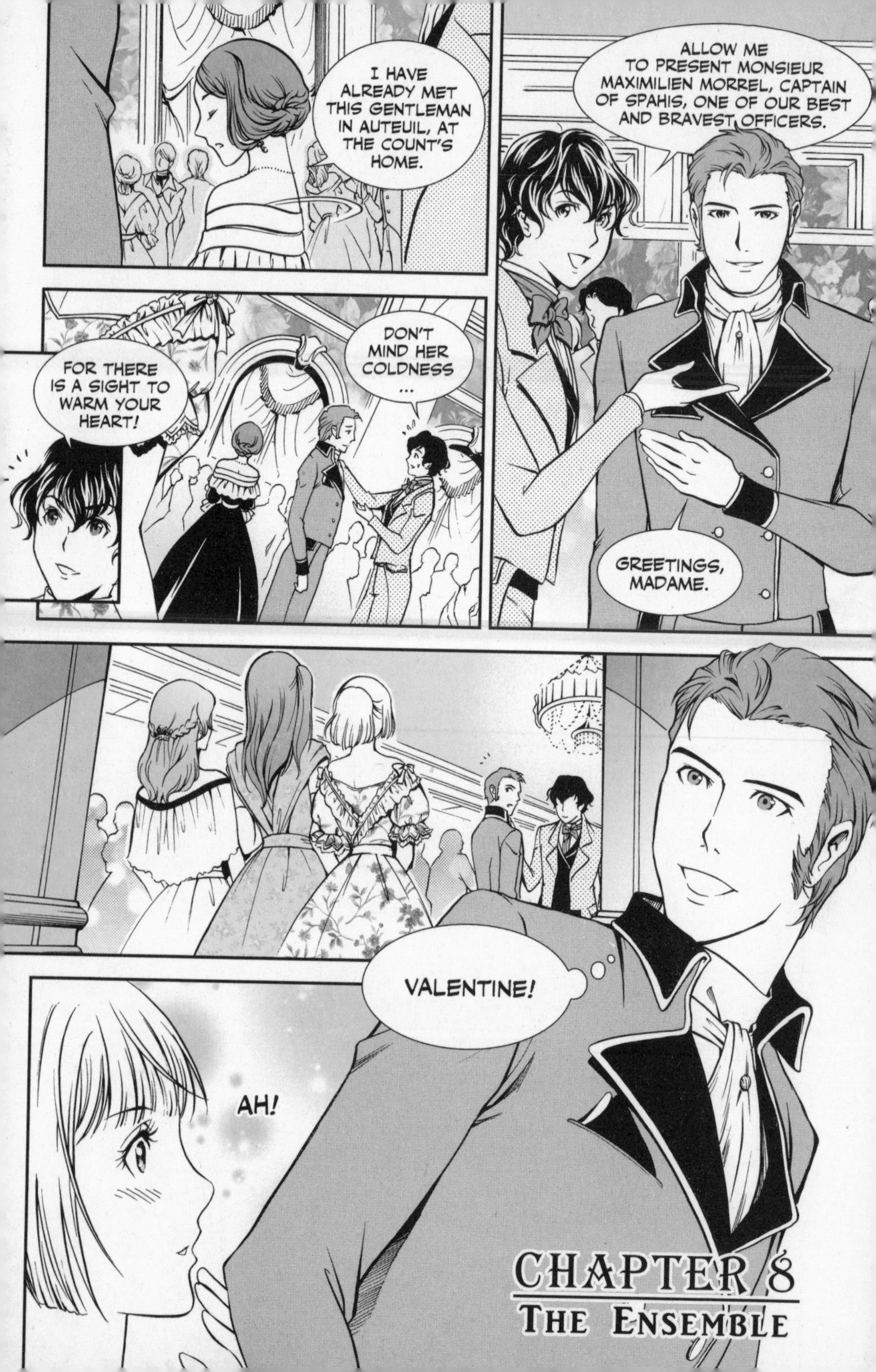
ALLOW ME TO PRESENT MONSIEUR MAXIMILIEN MORREL, CAPTAIN OF SPAHIS, ONE OF OUR BEST AND BRAVEST OFFICERS.
GREETINGS, MADAME.
I HAVE ALREADY MET THIS GENTLEMAN IN AUTEUIL, AT THE COUNT'S HOME.
DON'T MIND HER COLDNESS ...
FOR THERE IS A SIGHT TO WARM YOUR HEART!
VALENTINE!
AH!
CHAPTER 8
THE ENSEMBLE

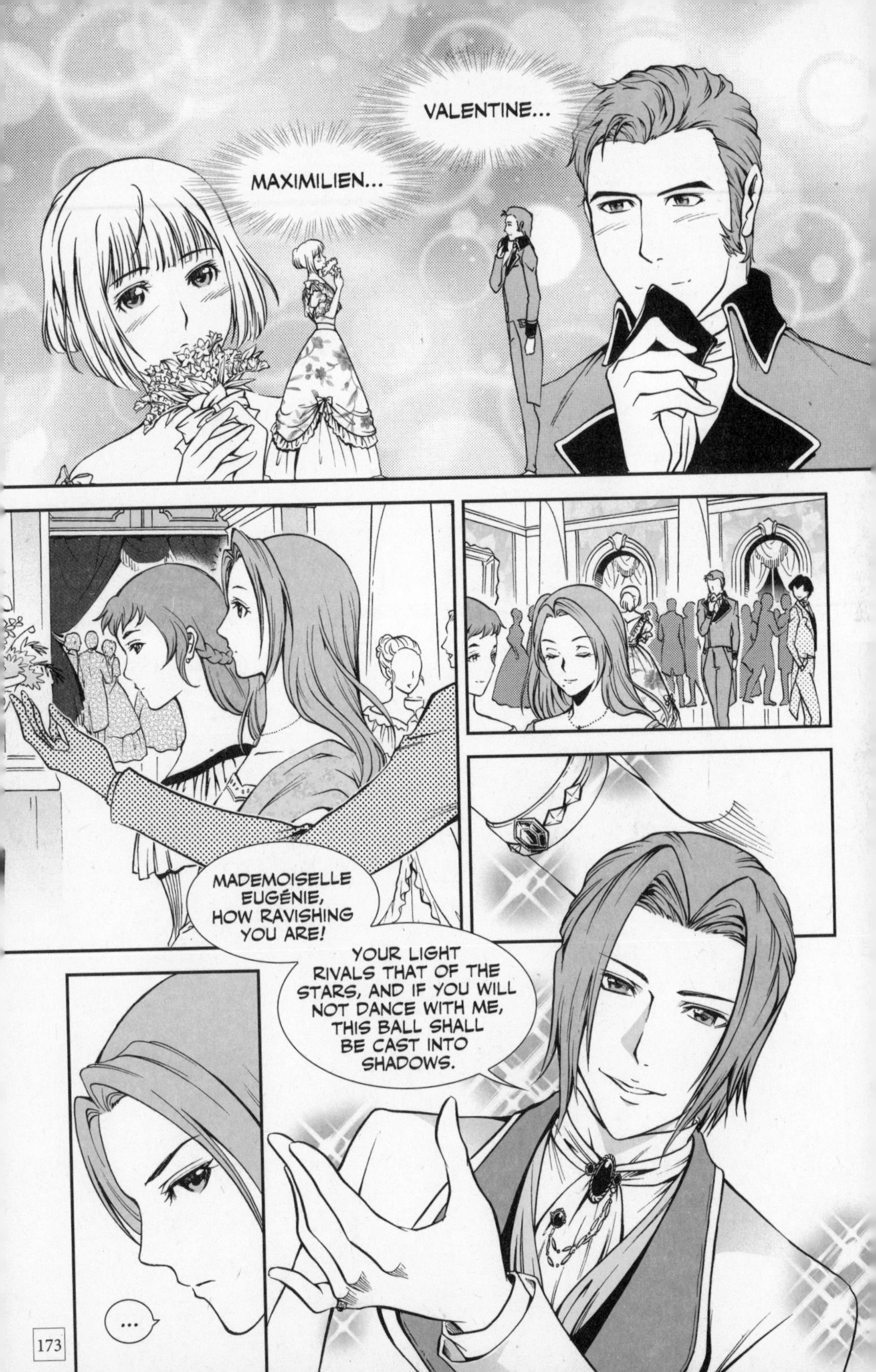
VALENTINE...
MAXIMILIEN...
MADEMOISELLE EUGÉNIE, HOW RAVISHING YOU ARE!
YOUR LIGHT RIVALS THAT OF THE STARS, AND IF YOU WILL NOT DANCE WITH ME, THIS BALL SHALL BE CAST INTO SHADOWS.
...

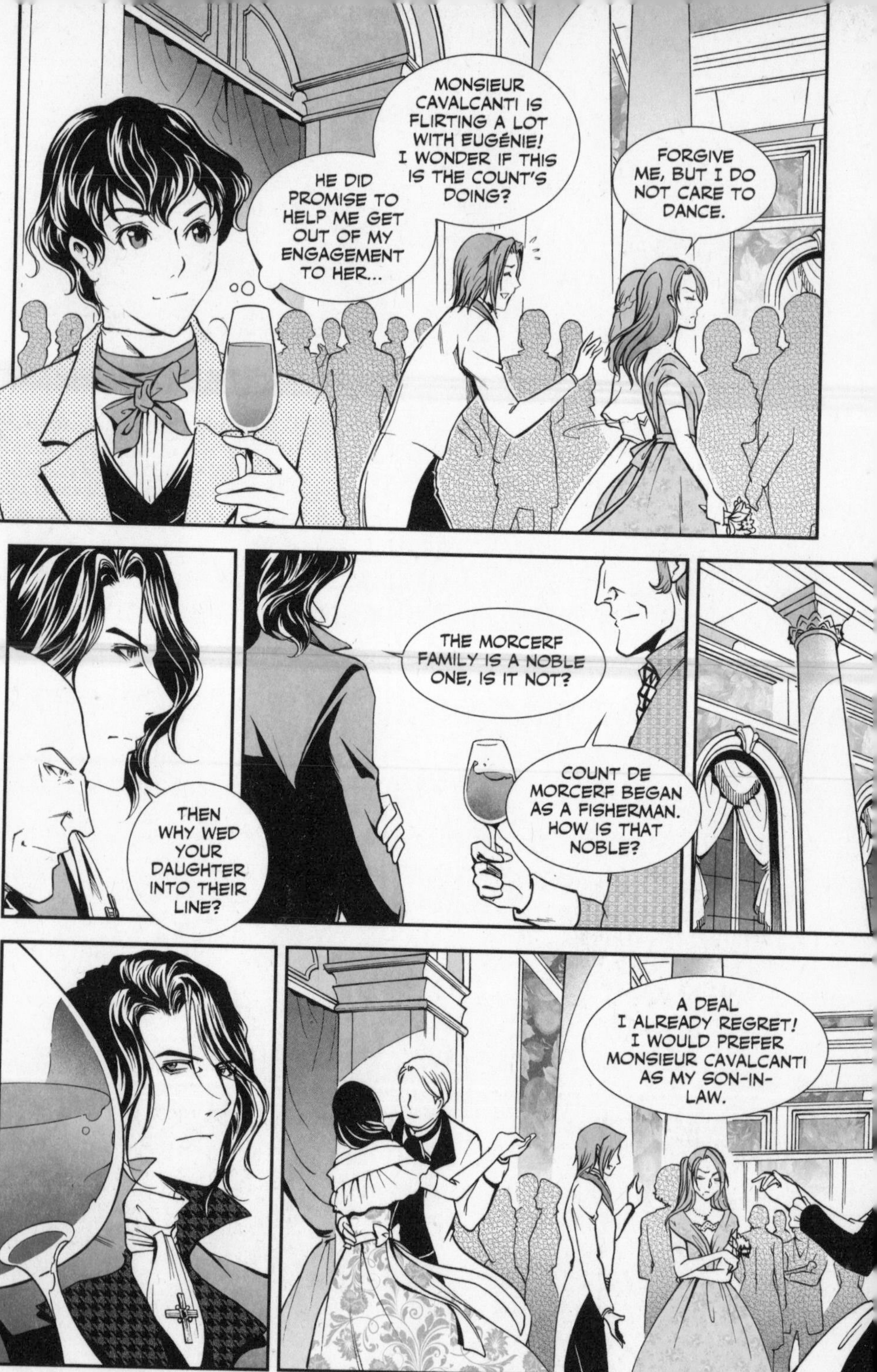
MONSIEUR CAVALCANTI IS FLIRTING A LOT WITH EUGÉNIE! I WONDER IF THIS IS THE COUNT'S DOING?
FORGIVE ME, BUT I DO NOT CARE TO DANCE.
HE DID PROMISE TO HELP ME GET OUT OF MY ENGAGEMENT TO HER...
THE MORCERF FAMILY IS A NOBLE ONE, IS IT NOT?
COUNT DE MORCERF BEGAN AS A FISHERMAN. HOW IS THAT NOBLE?
THEN WHY WED YOUR DAUGHTER INTO THEIR LINE?
A DEAL I ALREADY REGRET! I WOULD PREFER MONSIEUR CAVALCANTI AS MY SON-IN-LAW.

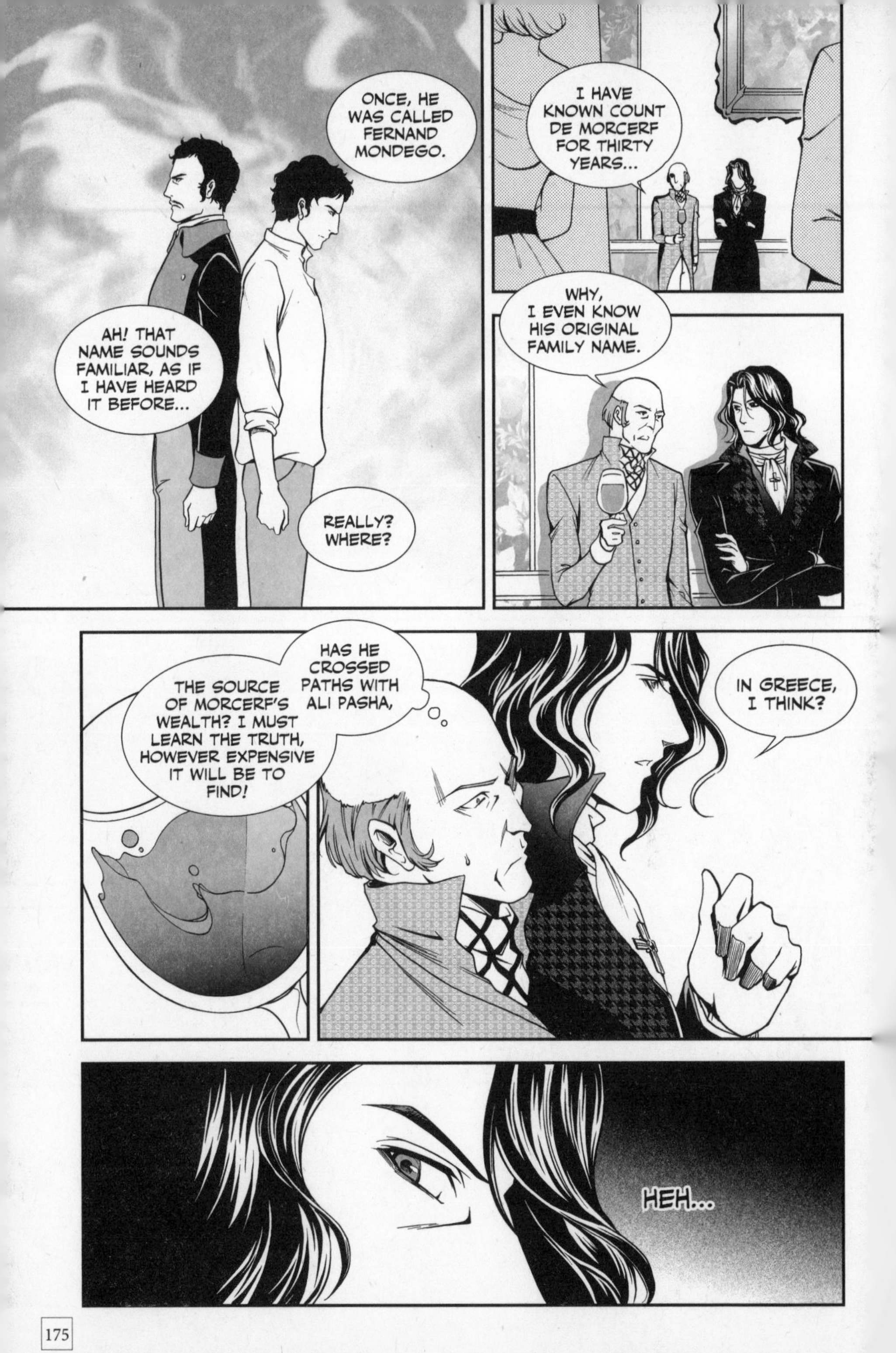
I HAVE KNOWN COUNT DE MORCERF FOR THIRTY YEARS...
WHY, I EVEN KNOW HIS ORIGINAL FAMILY NAME.
ONCE, HE WAS CALLED FERNAND MONDEGO.
AH! THAT NAME SOUNDS FAMILIAR, AS IF I HAVE HEARD IT BEFORE...
REALLY? WHERE?
IN GREECE, I THINK?
HAS HE CROSSED PATHS WITH ALI PASHA, THE SOURCE OF MORCERF'S WEALTH? I MUST LEARN THE TRUTH, HOWEVER EXPENSIVE IT WILL BE TO FIND!
HEH...

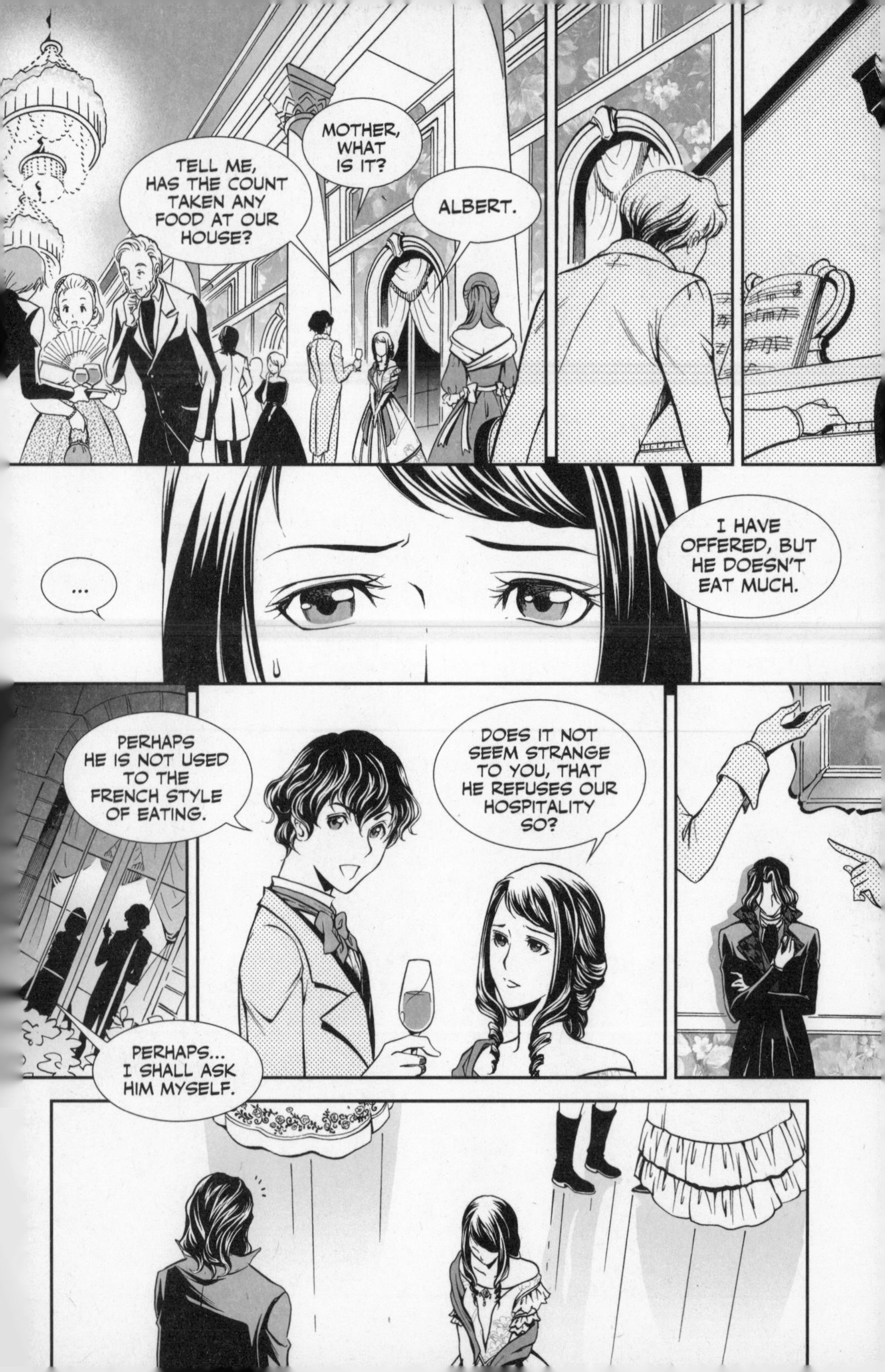
ALBERT.
MOTHER, WHAT IS IT?
TELL ME, HAS THE COUNT TAKEN ANY FOOD AT OUR HOUSE?
I HAVE OFFERED, BUT HE DOESN'T EAT MUCH.
...
DOES IT NOT SEEM STRANGE TO YOU, THAT HE REFUSES OUR HOSPITALITY SO?
PERHAPS HE IS NOT USED TO THE FRENCH STYLE OF EATING.
PERHAPS... I SHALL ASK HIM MYSELF.

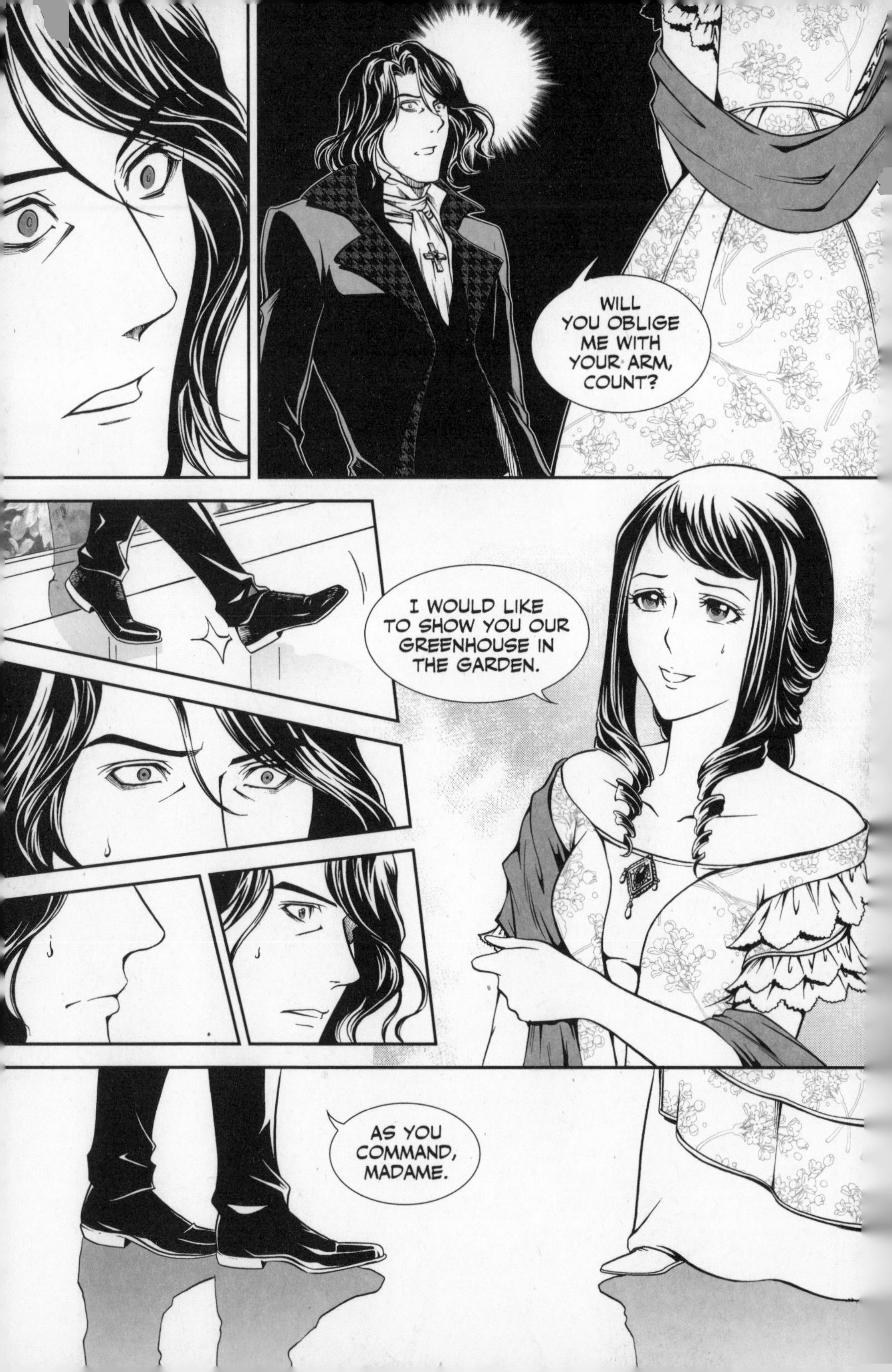
WILL YOU OBLIGE ME WITH YOUR ARM, COUNT?
I WOULD LIKE TO SHOW YOU OUR GREENHOUSE IN THE GARDEN.
AS YOU COMMAND, MADAME.

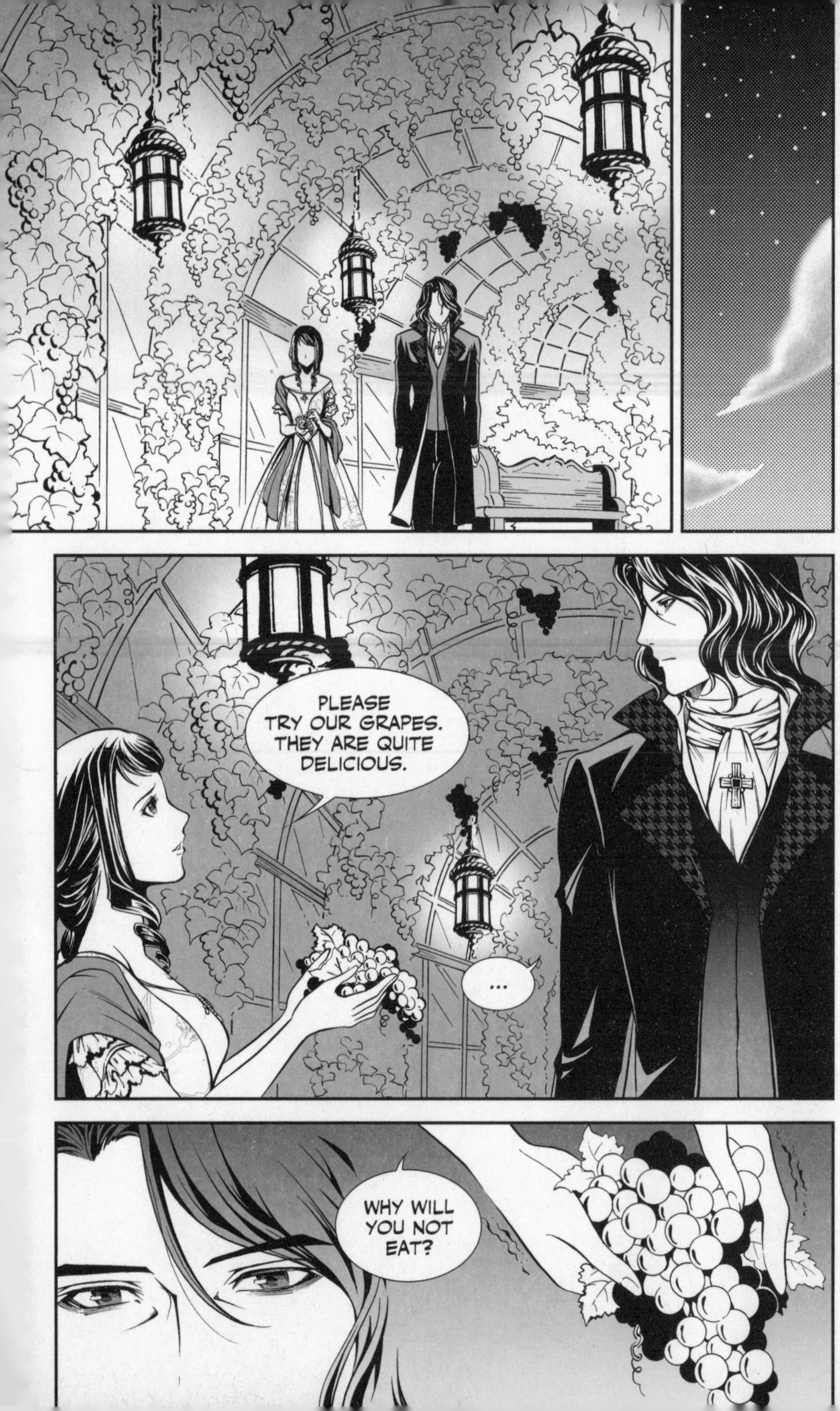
PLEASE TRY OUR GRAPES. THEY ARE QUITE DELICIOUS.
...
WHY WILL YOU NOT EAT?

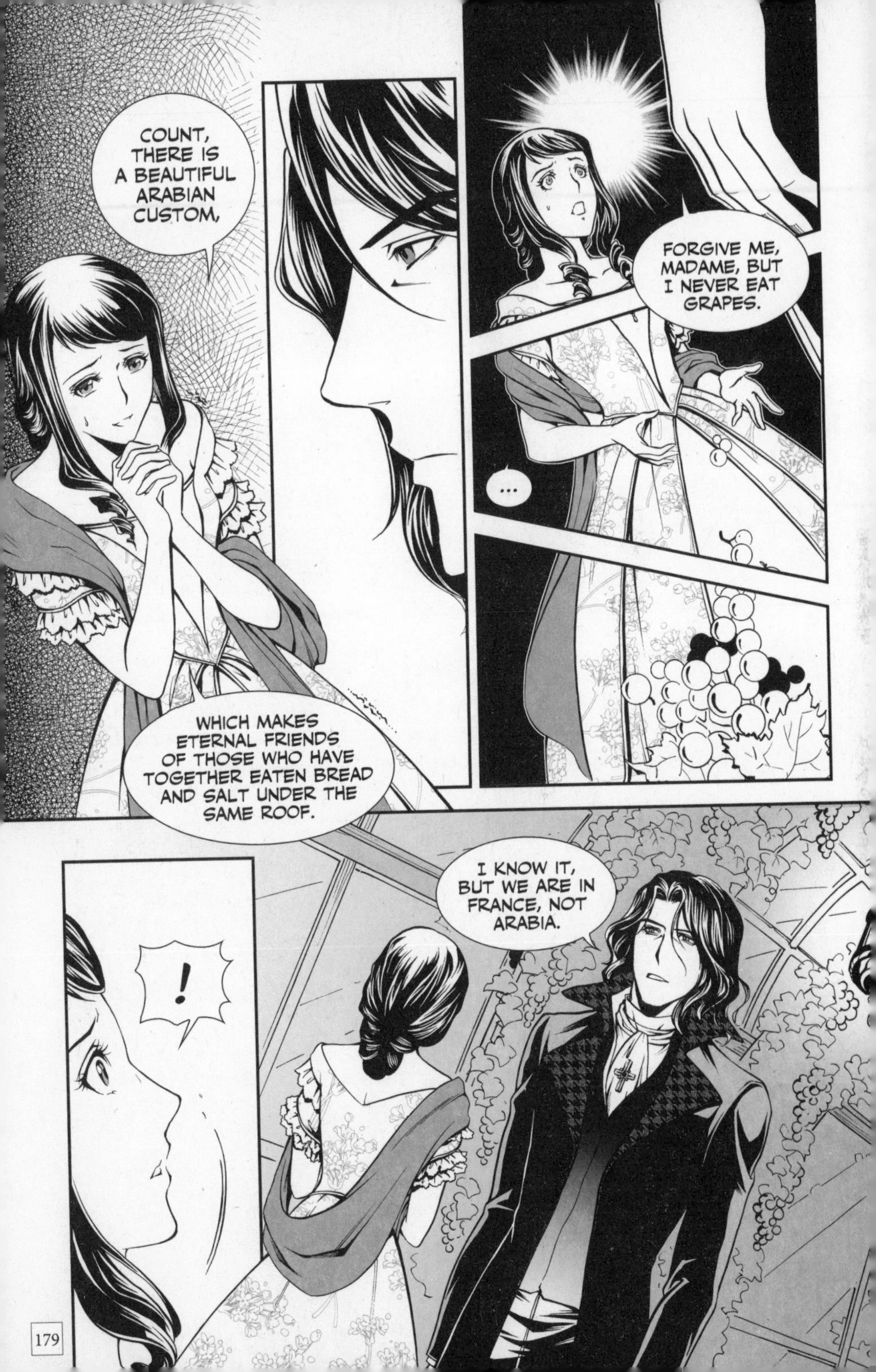
FORGIVE ME, MADAME, BUT I NEVER EAT GRAPES.
...
COUNT, THERE IS A BEAUTIFUL ARABIAN CUSTOM,
WHICH MAKES ETERNAL FRIENDS OF THOSE WHO HAVE TOGETHER EATEN BREAD AND SALT UNDER THE SAME ROOF.
I KNOW IT, BUT WE ARE IN FRANCE, NOT ARABIA.
!

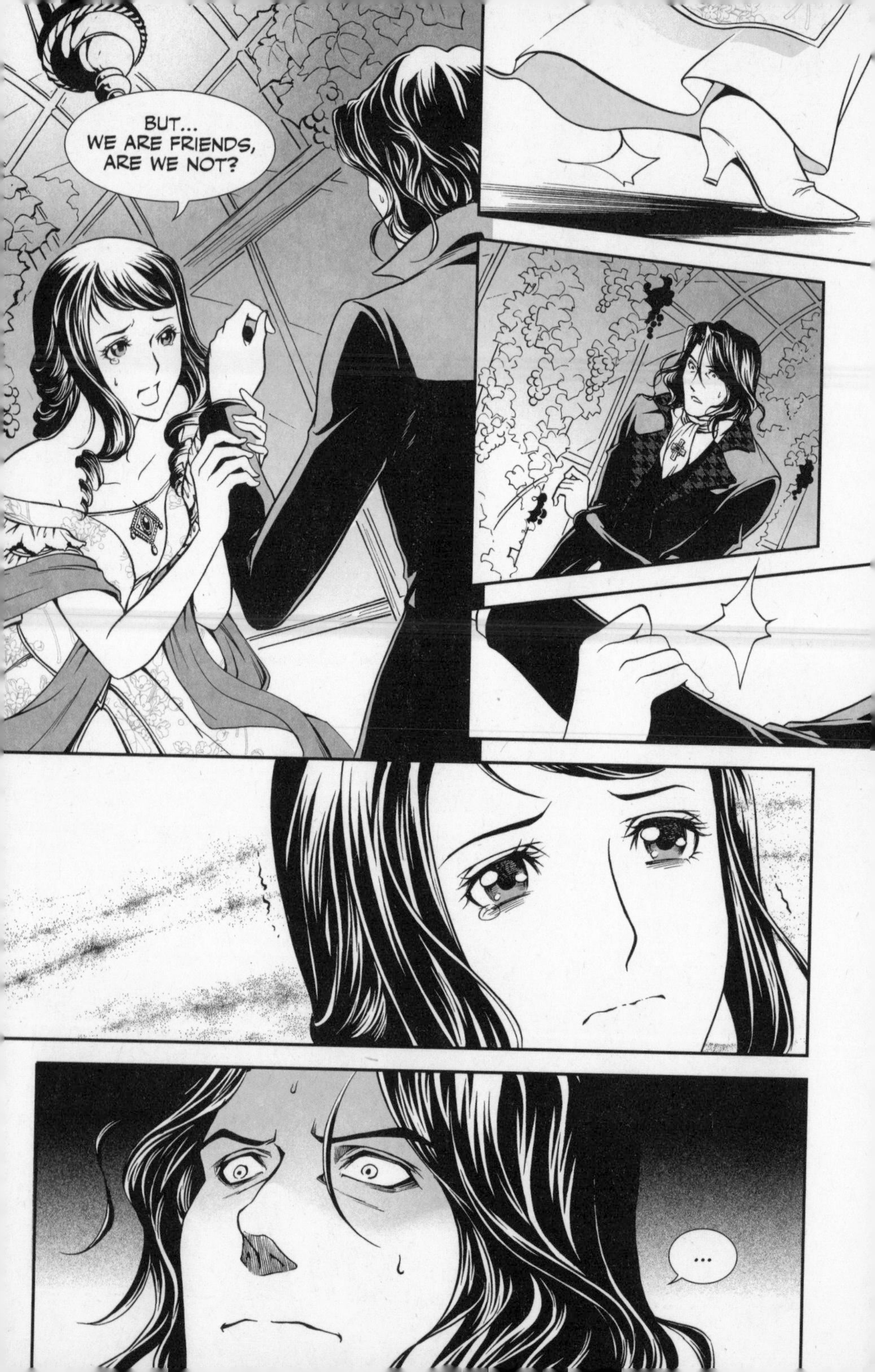
BUT... WE ARE FRIENDS, ARE WE NOT?
...

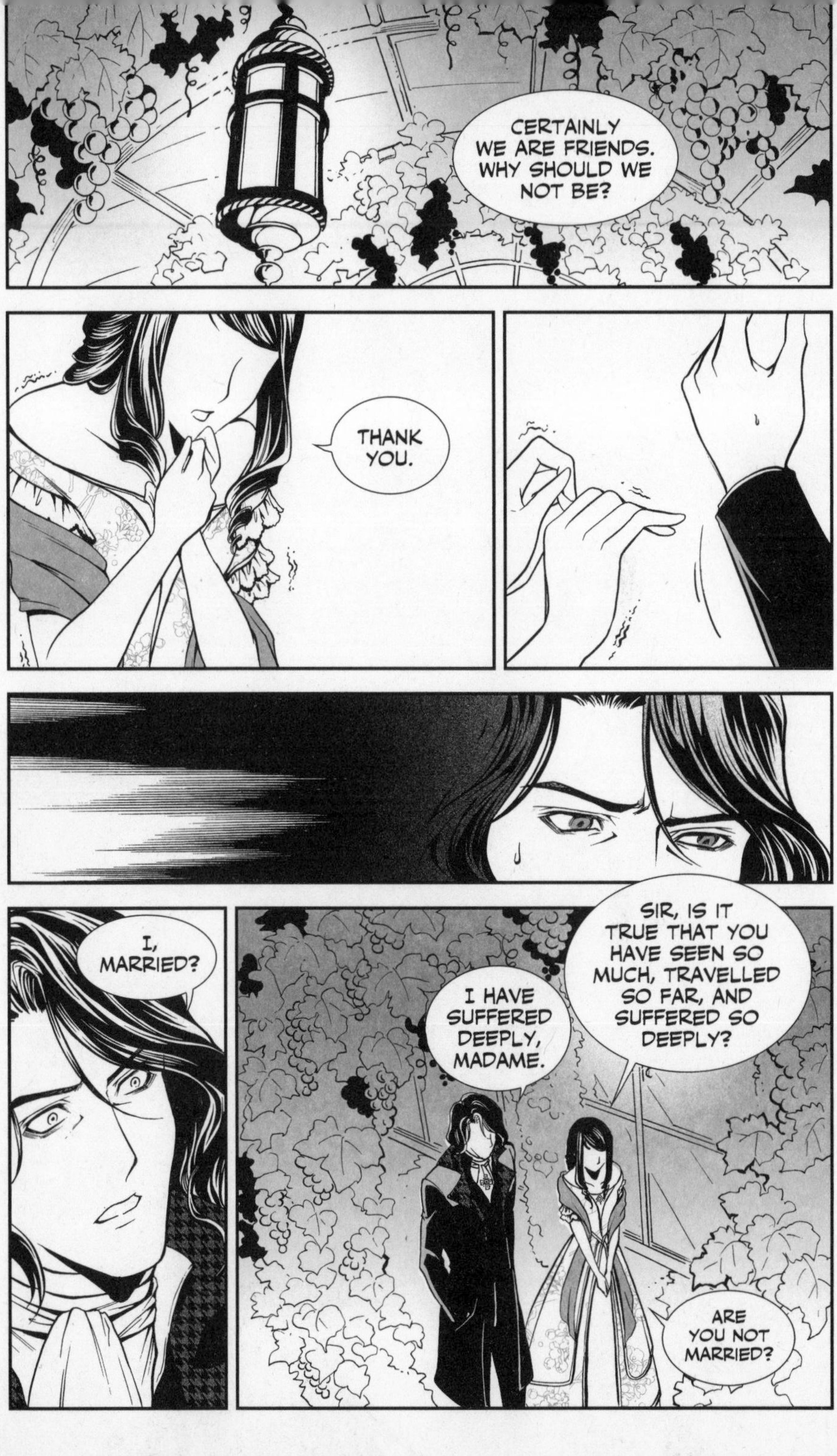
CERTAINLY WE ARE FRIENDS. WHY SHOULD WE NOT BE?
THANK YOU.
SIR, IS IT TRUE THAT YOU HAVE SEEN SO MUCH, TRAVELLED SO FAR, AND SUFFERED SO DEEPLY?
I HAVE SUFFERED DEEPLY, MADAME.
ARE YOU NOT MARRIED?
I, MARRIED?

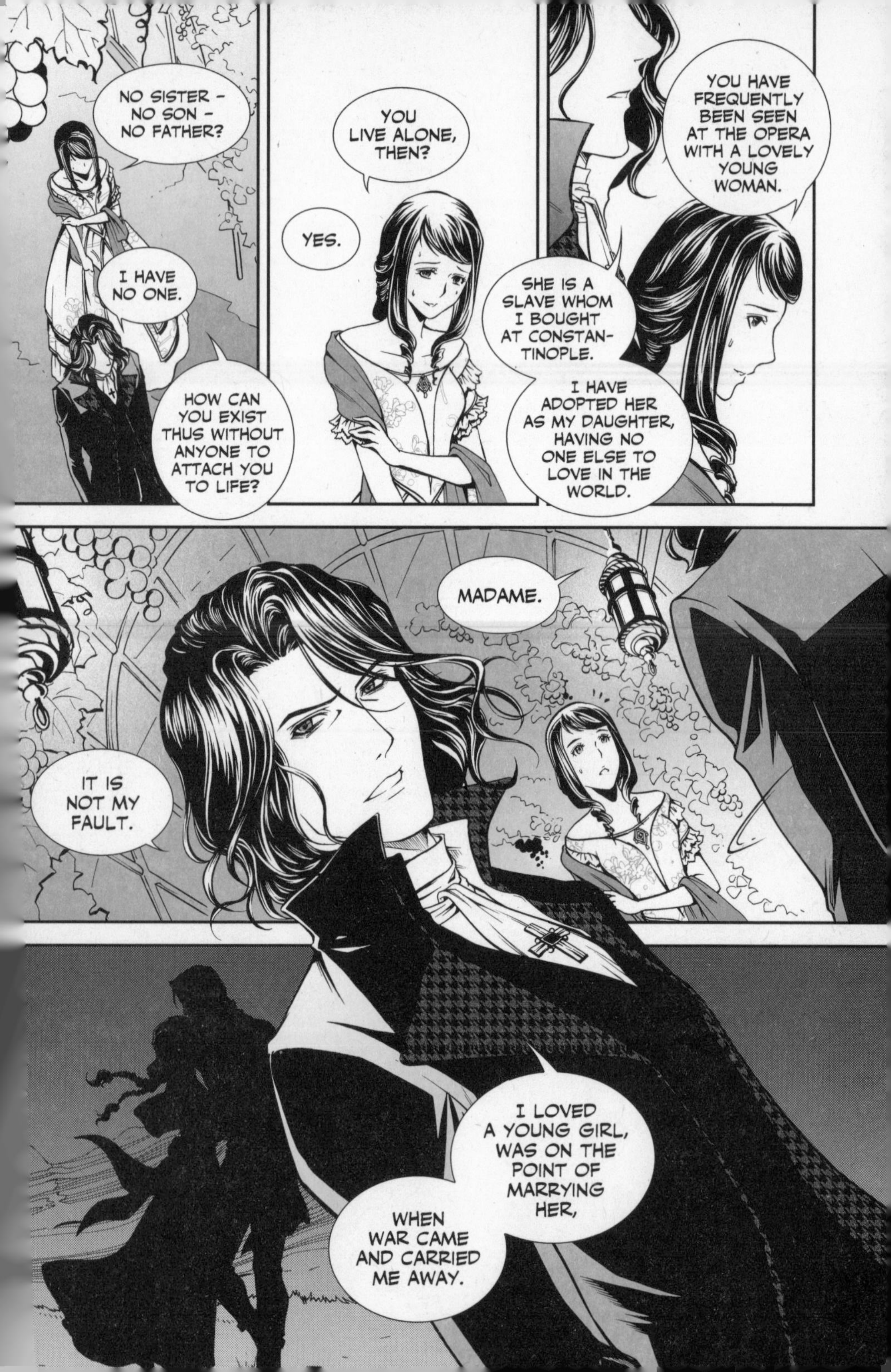
NO SISTER - NO SON - NO FATHER?
I HAVE NO ONE.
HOW CAN YOU EXIST THUS WITHOUT ANYONE TO ATTACH YOU TO LIFE?
YOU LIVE ALONE, THEN?
YES.
YOU HAVE FREQUENTLY BEEN SEEN AT THE OPERA WITH A LOVELY YOUNG WOMAN.
SHE IS A SLAVE WHOM I BOUGHT AT CONSTANTINOPLE.
I HAVE ADOPTED HER AS MY DAUGHTER, HAVING NO ONE ELSE TO LOVE IN THE WORLD.
IT IS NOT MY FAULT.
MADAME.
I LOVED A YOUNG GIRL, WAS ON THE POINT OF MARRYING HER,
WHEN WAR CAME AND CARRIED ME AWAY.

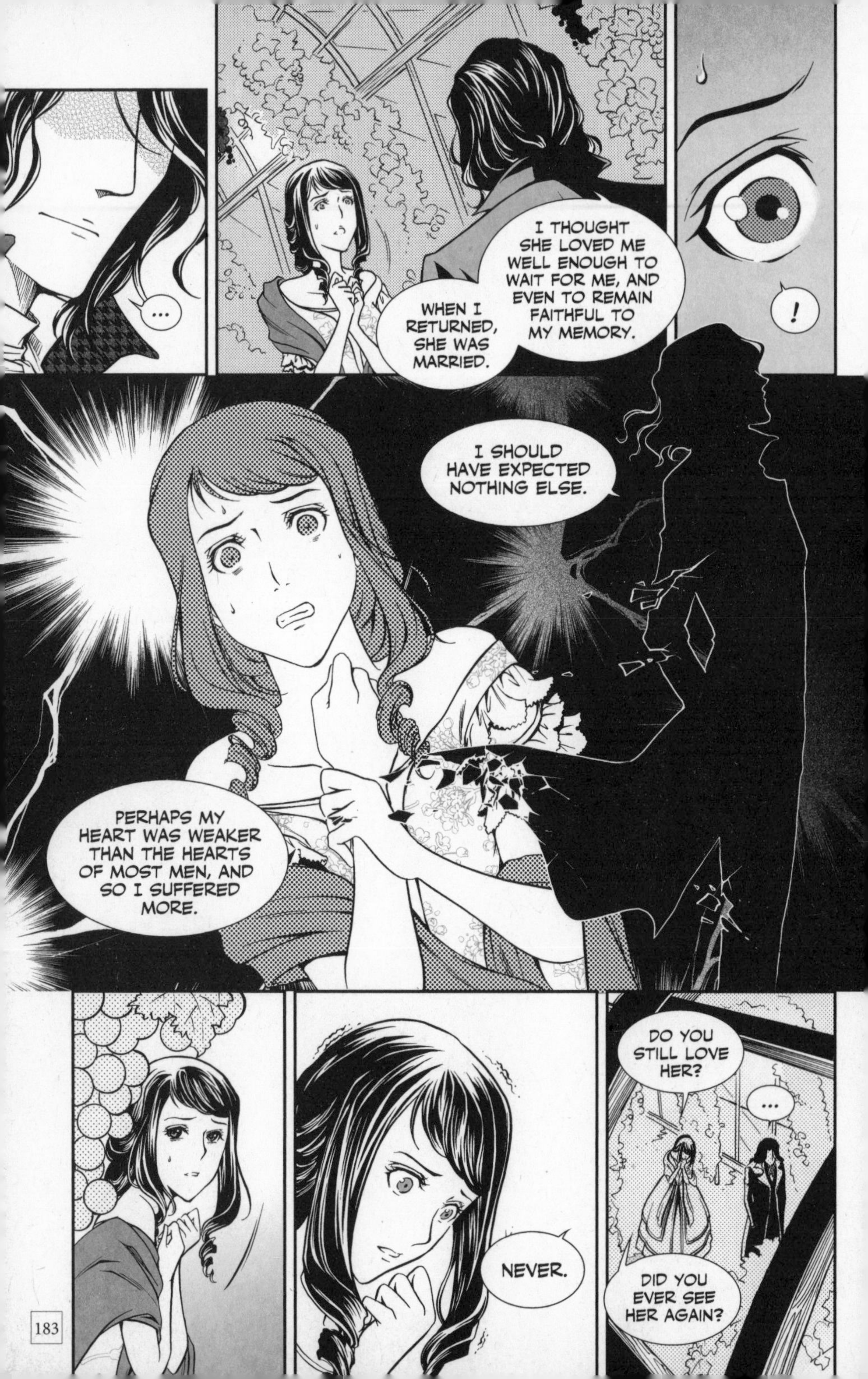
!
I THOUGHT SHE LOVED ME WELL ENOUGH TO WAIT FOR ME, AND EVEN TO REMAIN FAITHFUL TO MY MEMORY.
WHEN I RETURNED, SHE WAS MARRIED.
...
I SHOULD HAVE EXPECTED NOTHING ELSE.
PERHAPS MY HEART WAS WEAKER THAN THE HEARTS OF MOST MEN, AND SO I SUFFERED MORE.
DO YOU STILL LOVE HER?
...
DID YOU EVER SEE HER AGAIN?
NEVER.

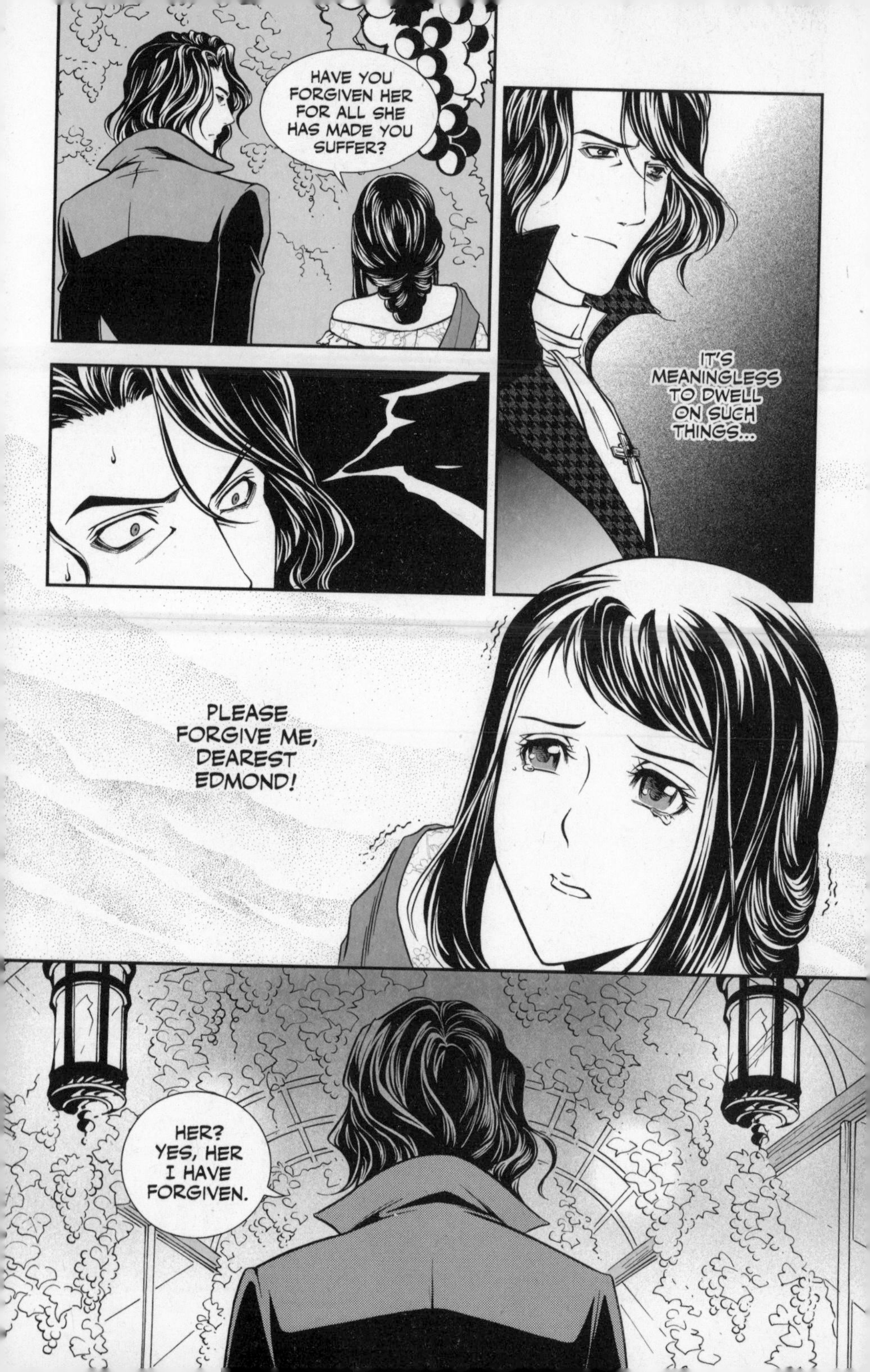
IT'S MEANINGLESS TO DWELL ON SUCH THINGS...
HAVE YOU FORGIVEN HER FOR ALL SHE HAS MADE YOU SUFFER?
PLEASE FORGIVE ME, DEAREST EDMOND!
HER? YES, HER I HAVE FORGIVEN.

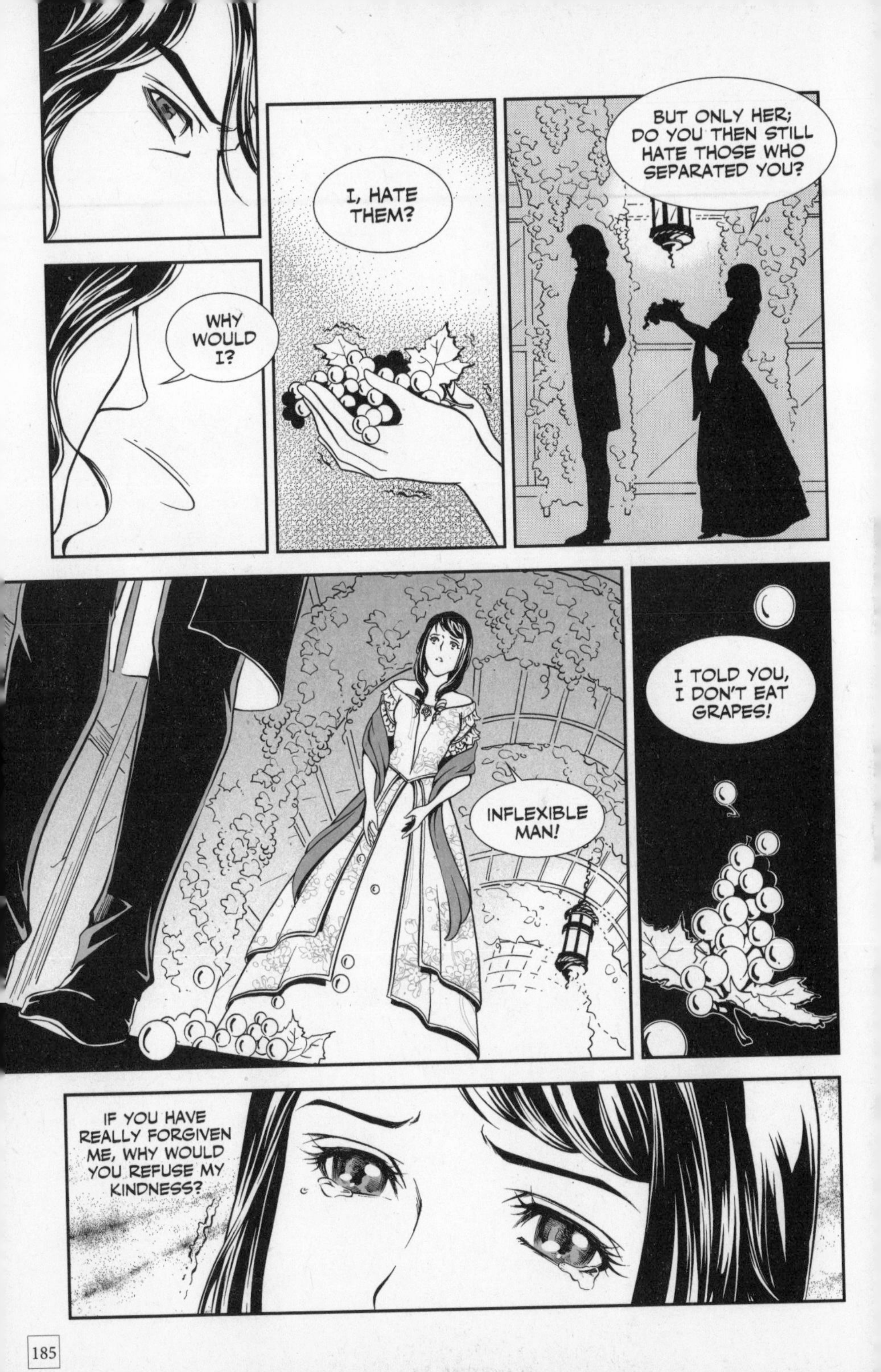
BUT ONLY HER; DO YOU THEN STILL HATE THOSE WHO SEPARATED YOU?
I, HATE THEM?
WHY WOULD I?
I TOLD YOU, I DON'T EAT GRAPES!
INFLEXIBLE MAN!
IF YOU HAVE REALLY FORGIVEN ME, WHY WOULD YOU REFUSE MY KINDNESS?

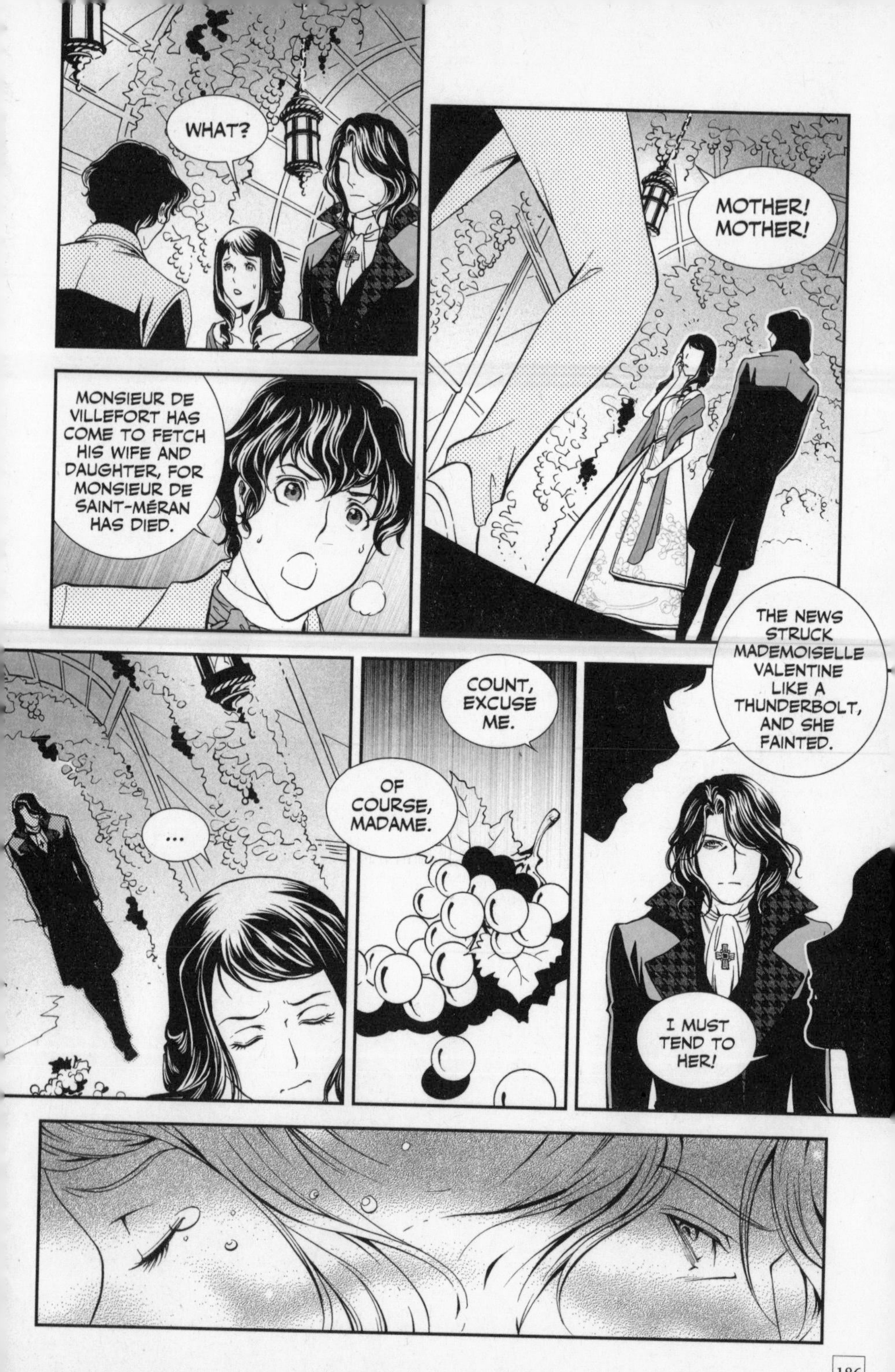
MOTHER! MOTHER!
WHAT?
MONSIEUR DE VILLEFORT HAS COME TO FETCH HIS WIFE AND DAUGHTER, FOR MONSIEUR DE SAINT-MÉRAN HAS DIED.
THE NEWS STRUCK MADEMOISELLE VALENTINE LIKE A THUNDERBOLT, AND SHE FAINTED.
I MUST TEND TO HER!
COUNT, EXCUSE ME.
OF COURSE, MADAME.
...

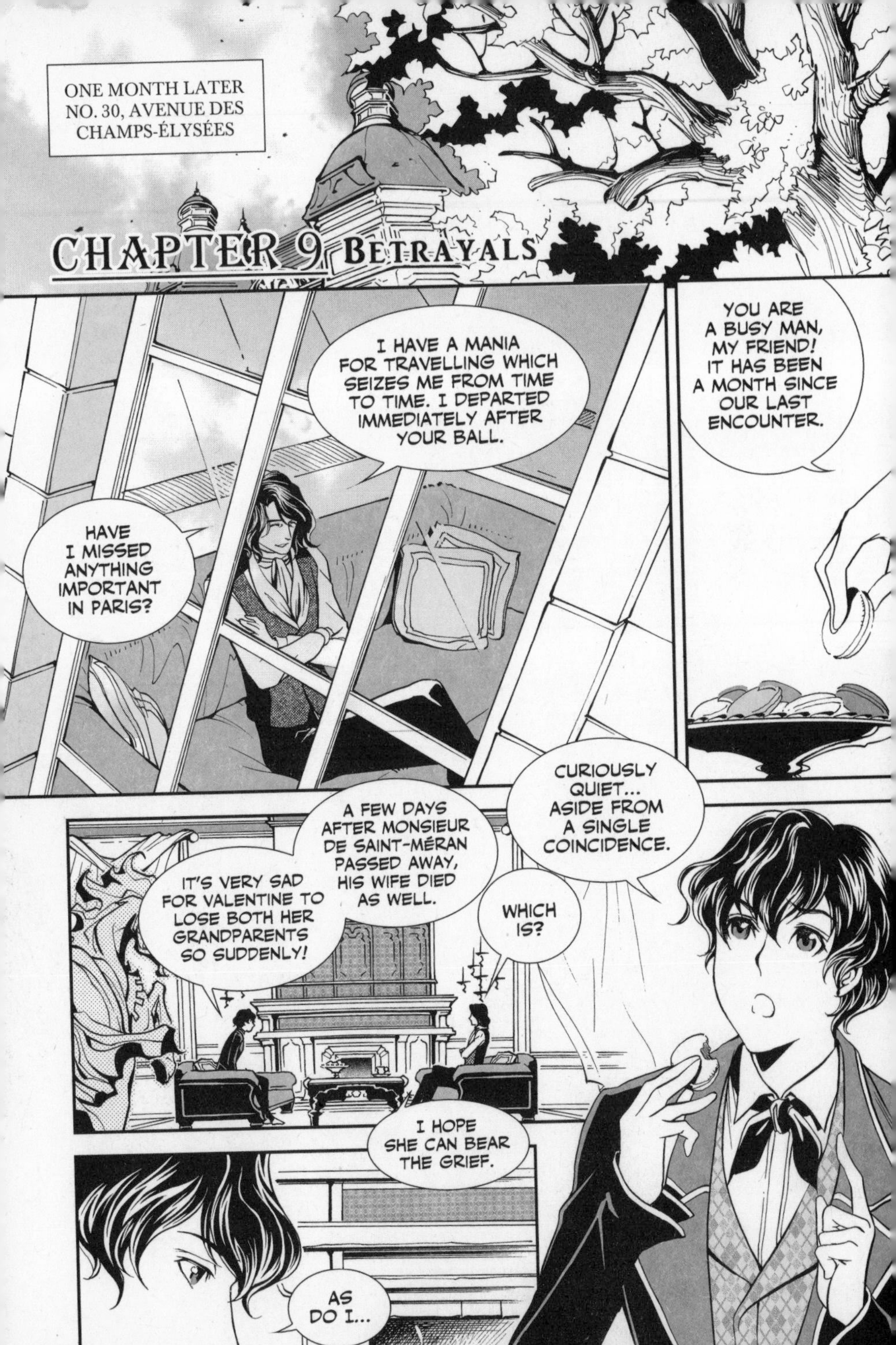
ONE MONTH LATER
NO. 30, AVENUE DES CHAMPS-ÉLYSÉES
CHAPTER 9 BETRAYALS
YOU ARE A BUSY MAN, MY FRIEND! IT HAS BEEN A MONTH SINCE OUR LAST ENCOUNTER.
I HAVE A MANIA FOR TRAVELLING WHICH SEIZES ME FROM TIME TO TIME. I DEPARTED IMMEDIATELY AFTER YOUR BALL.
HAVE I MISSED ANYTHING IMPORTANT IN PARIS?
CURIOUSLY QUIET... ASIDE FROM A SINGLE COINCIDENCE.
WHICH IS?
A FEW DAYS AFTER MONSIEUR DE SAINT-MÉRAN PASSED AWAY, HIS WIFE DIED AS WELL.
IT'S VERY SAD FOR VALENTINE TO LOSE BOTH HER GRANDPARENTS SO SUDDENLY!
I HOPE SHE CAN BEAR THE GRIEF.
AS DO I...

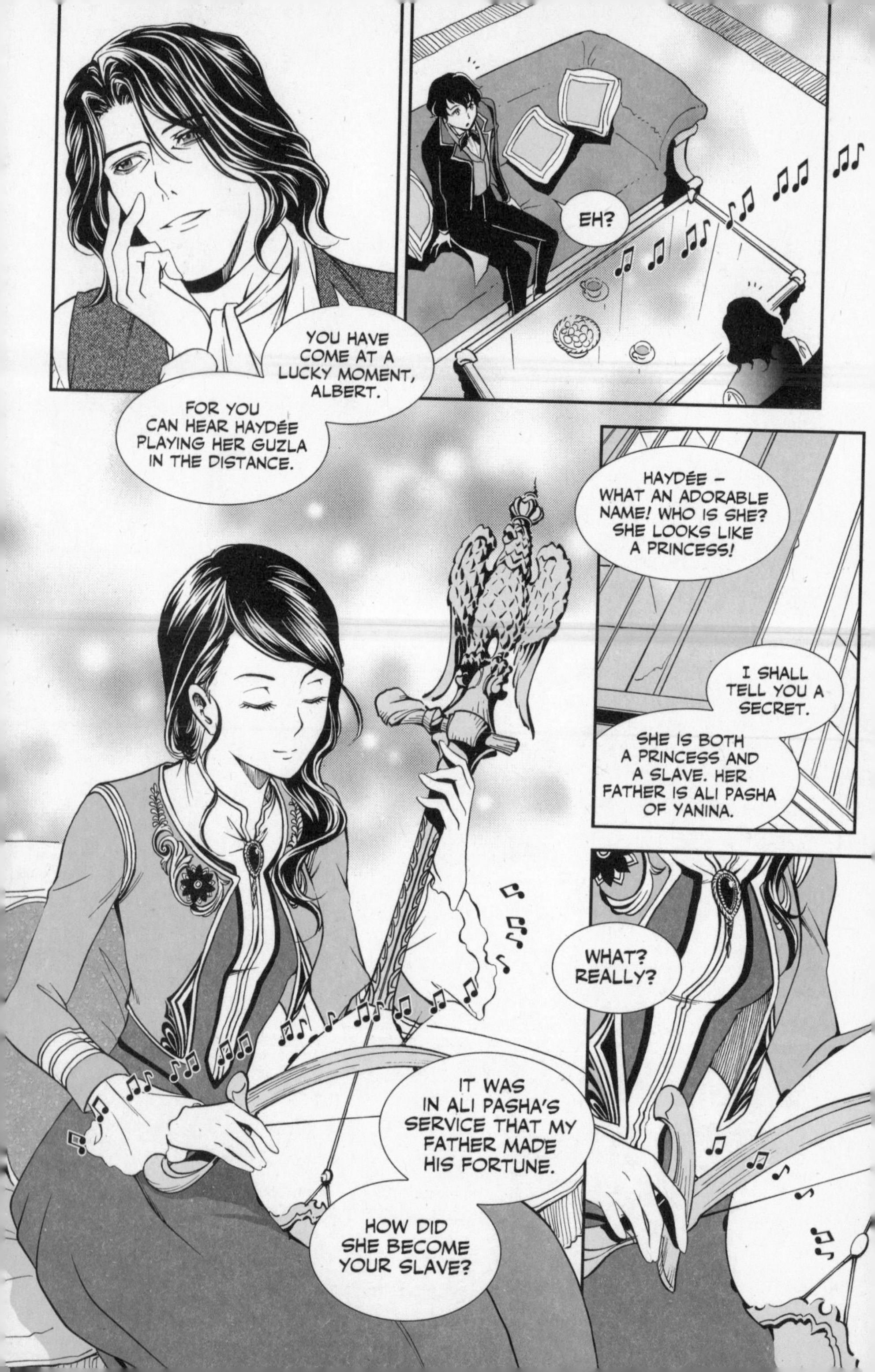
EH?
YOU HAVE COME AT A LUCKY MOMENT, ALBERT.
FOR YOU CAN HEAR HAYDÉE PLAYING HER GUZLA IN THE DISTANCE.
HAYDÉE – WHAT AN ADORABLE NAME! WHO IS SHE? SHE LOOKS LIKE A PRINCESS!
I SHALL TELL YOU A SECRET.
SHE IS BOTH A PRINCESS AND A SLAVE. HER FATHER IS ALI PASHA OF YANINA.
WHAT? REALLY?
IT WAS IN ALI PASHA'S SERVICE THAT MY FATHER MADE HIS FORTUNE.
HOW DID SHE BECOME YOUR SLAVE?

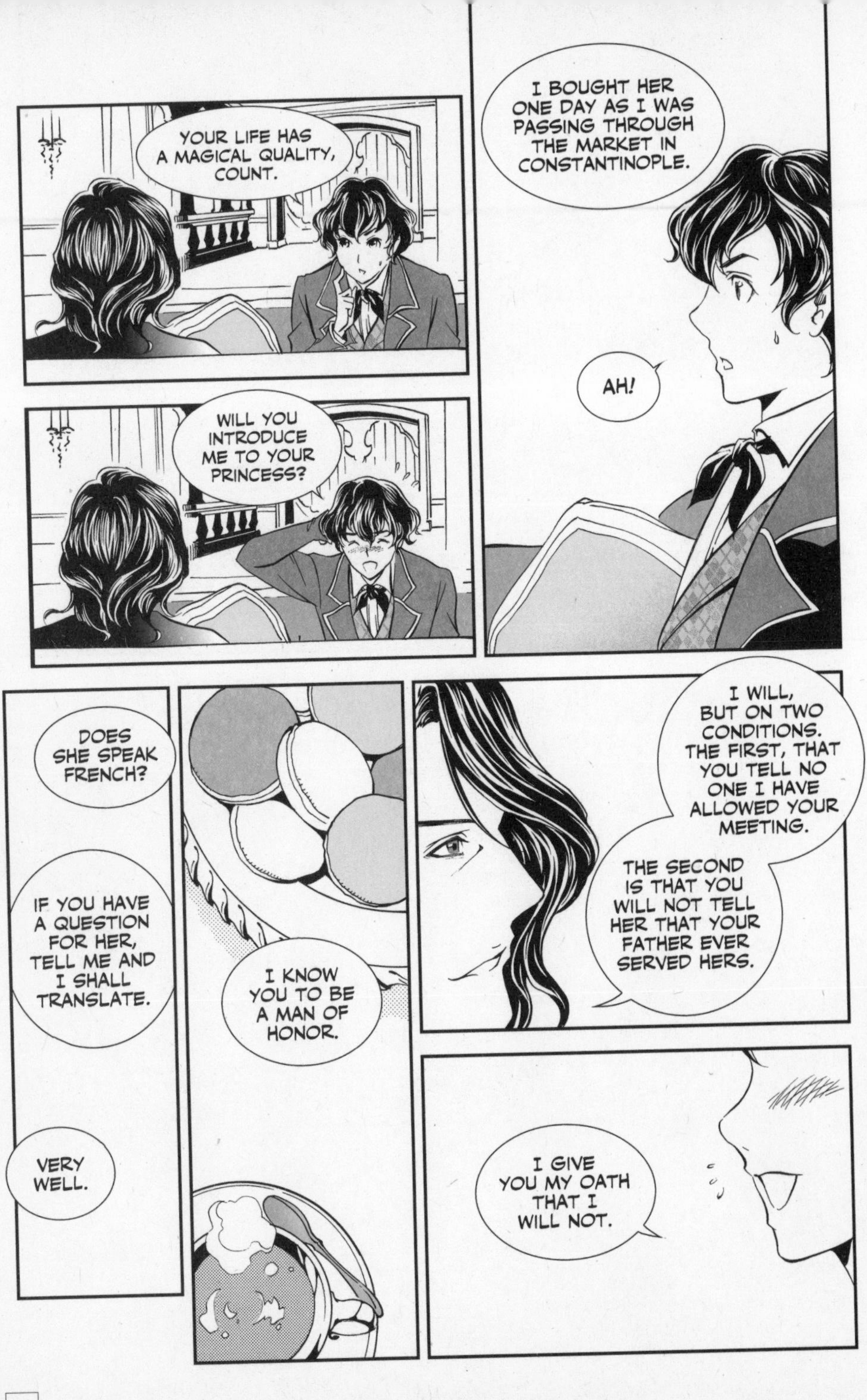

I BOUGHT HER ONE DAY AS I WAS PASSING THROUGH THE MARKET IN CONSTANTINOPLE.
AH!
YOUR LIFE HAS A MAGICAL QUALITY, COUNT.
WILL YOU INTRODUCE ME TO YOUR PRINCESS?
I WILL, BUT ON TWO CONDITIONS. THE FIRST, THAT YOU TELL NO ONE I HAVE ALLOWED YOUR MEETING.
THE SECOND IS THAT YOU WILL NOT TELL HER THAT YOUR FATHER EVER SERVED HERS.
I GIVE YOU MY OATH THAT I WILL NOT.
I KNOW YOU TO BE A MAN OF HONOR.
DOES SHE SPEAK FRENCH?
IF YOU HAVE A QUESTION FOR HER, TELL ME AND I SHALL TRANSLATE.
VERY WELL.

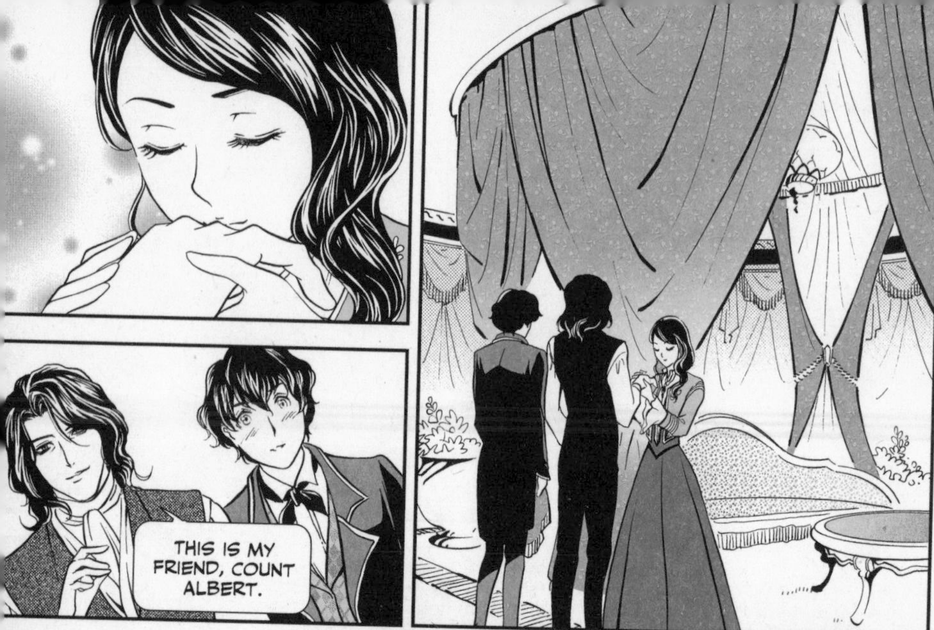
THIS IS MY FRIEND, COUNT ALBERT.

NOTE FOR READERS : SQUARE BALLOONS MEANS THE CHARACTERS ARE SPEAKING IN GREEK.

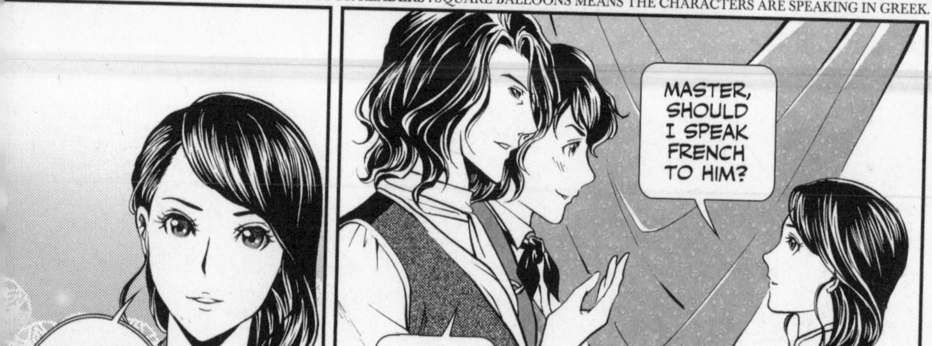
MASTER, SHOULD I SPEAK FRENCH TO HIM?
NO, SPEAK ITALIAN.
SIR, YOU ARE MOST WELCOME AS THE FRIEND OF MY LORD AND MASTER.

NOTE FOR READERS : DOUBLE-LINED BALLOONS MEANS THE CHARACTERS ARE SPEAKING IN ITALIAN.

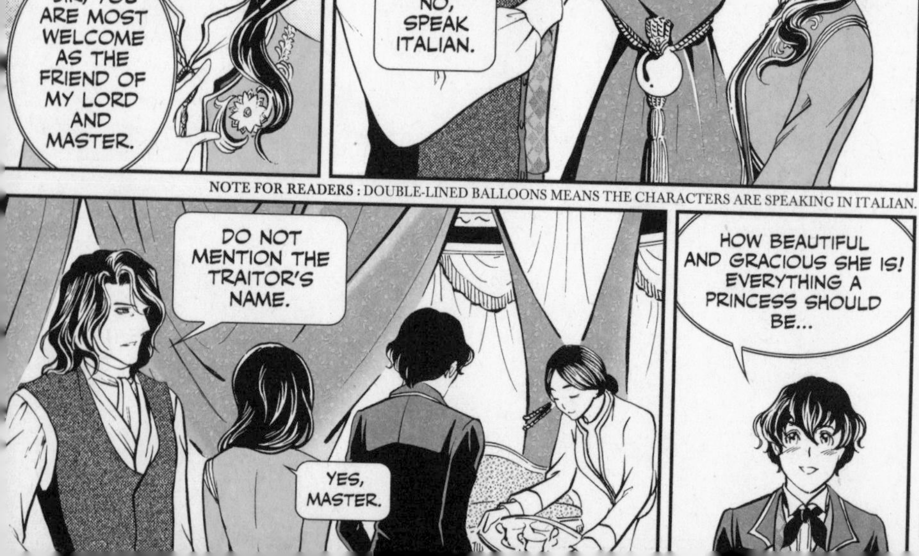
HOW BEAUTIFUL AND GRACIOUS SHE IS! EVERYTHING A PRINCESS SHOULD BE...
DO NOT MENTION THE TRAITOR'S NAME.
YES, MASTER.

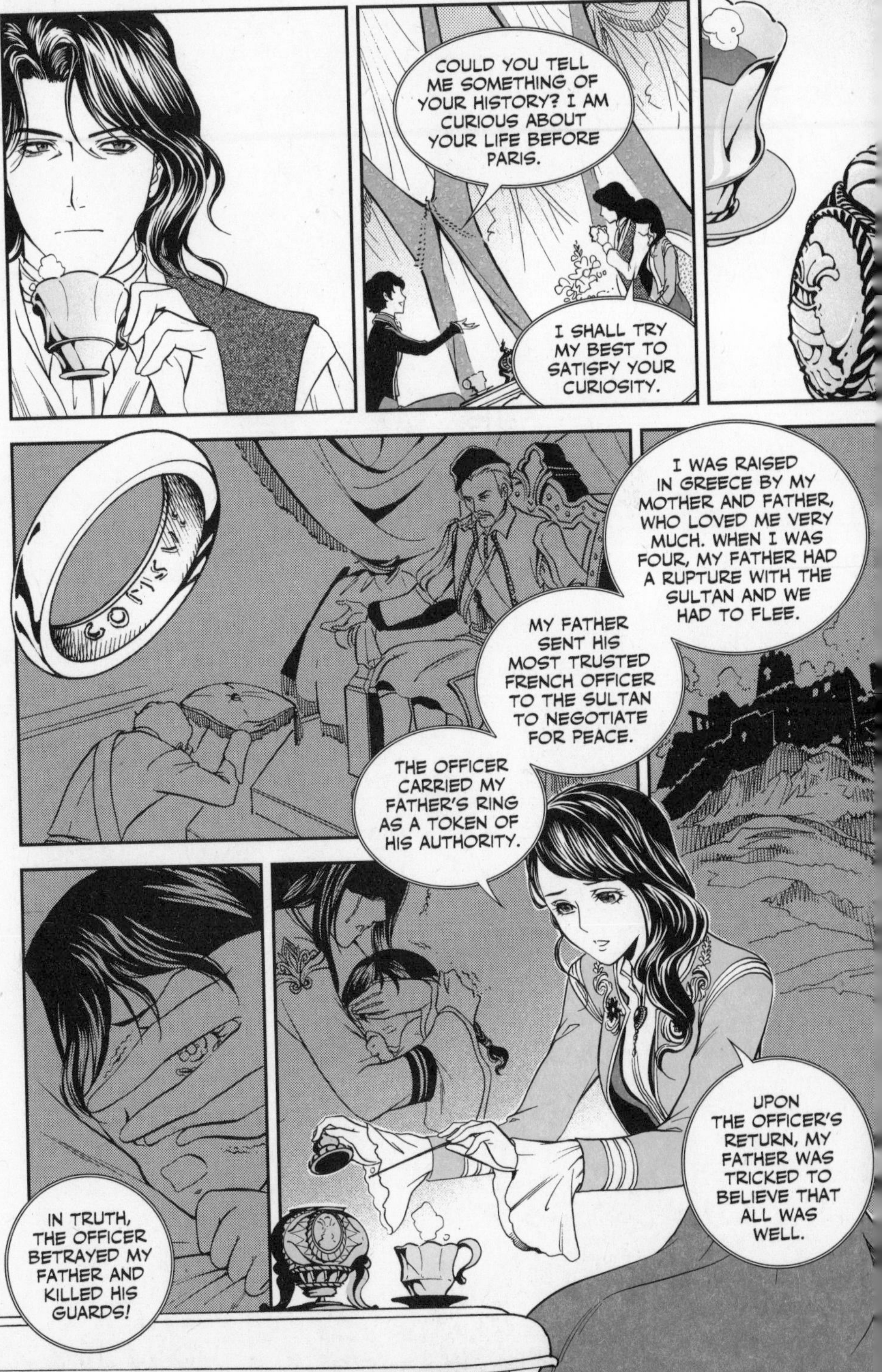
COULD YOU TELL ME SOMETHING OF YOUR HISTORY? I AM CURIOUS ABOUT YOUR LIFE BEFORE PARIS.
I SHALL TRY MY BEST TO SATISFY YOUR CURIOSITY.
I WAS RAISED IN GREECE BY MY MOTHER AND FATHER, WHO LOVED ME VERY MUCH. WHEN I WAS FOUR, MY FATHER HAD A RUPTURE WITH THE SULTAN AND WE HAD TO FLEE.
MY FATHER SENT HIS MOST TRUSTED FRENCH OFFICER TO THE SULTAN TO NEGOTIATE FOR PEACE.
THE OFFICER CARRIED MY FATHER'S RING AS A TOKEN OF HIS AUTHORITY.
UPON THE OFFICER'S RETURN, MY FATHER WAS TRICKED TO BELIEVE THAT ALL WAS WELL.
IN TRUTH, THE OFFICER BETRAYED MY FATHER AND KILLED HIS GUARDS!

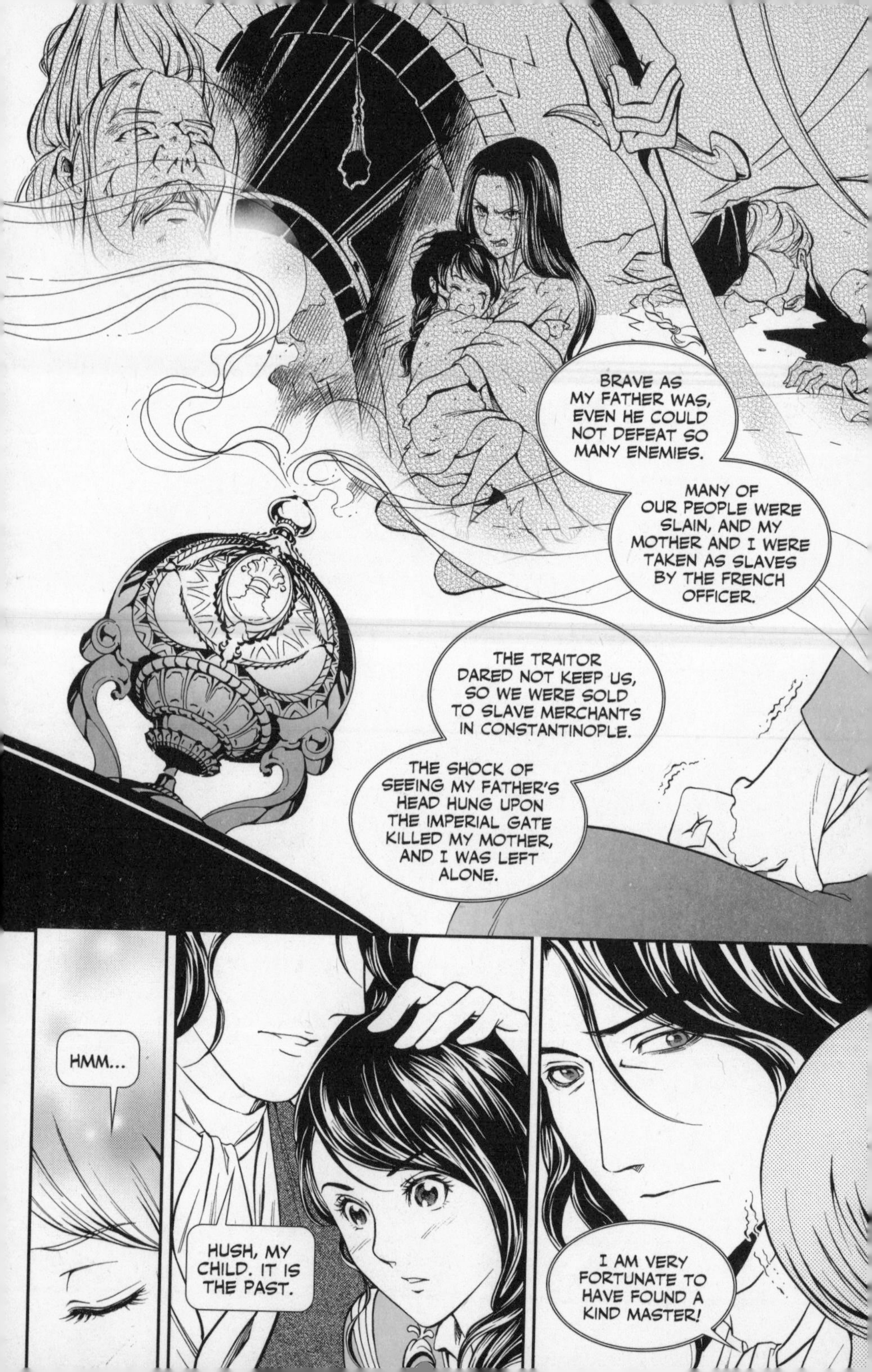
BRAVE AS MY FATHER WAS, EVEN HE COULD NOT DEFEAT SO MANY ENEMIES.
MANY OF OUR PEOPLE WERE SLAIN, AND MY MOTHER AND I WERE TAKEN AS SLAVES BY THE FRENCH OFFICER.
THE TRAITOR DARED NOT KEEP US, SO WE WERE SOLD TO SLAVE MERCHANTS IN CONSTANTINOPLE.
THE SHOCK OF SEEING MY FATHER'S HEAD HUNG UPON THE IMPERIAL GATE KILLED MY MOTHER, AND I WAS LEFT ALONE.
I AM VERY FORTUNATE TO HAVE FOUND A KIND MASTER!
HUSH, MY CHILD. IT IS THE PAST.
HMM...

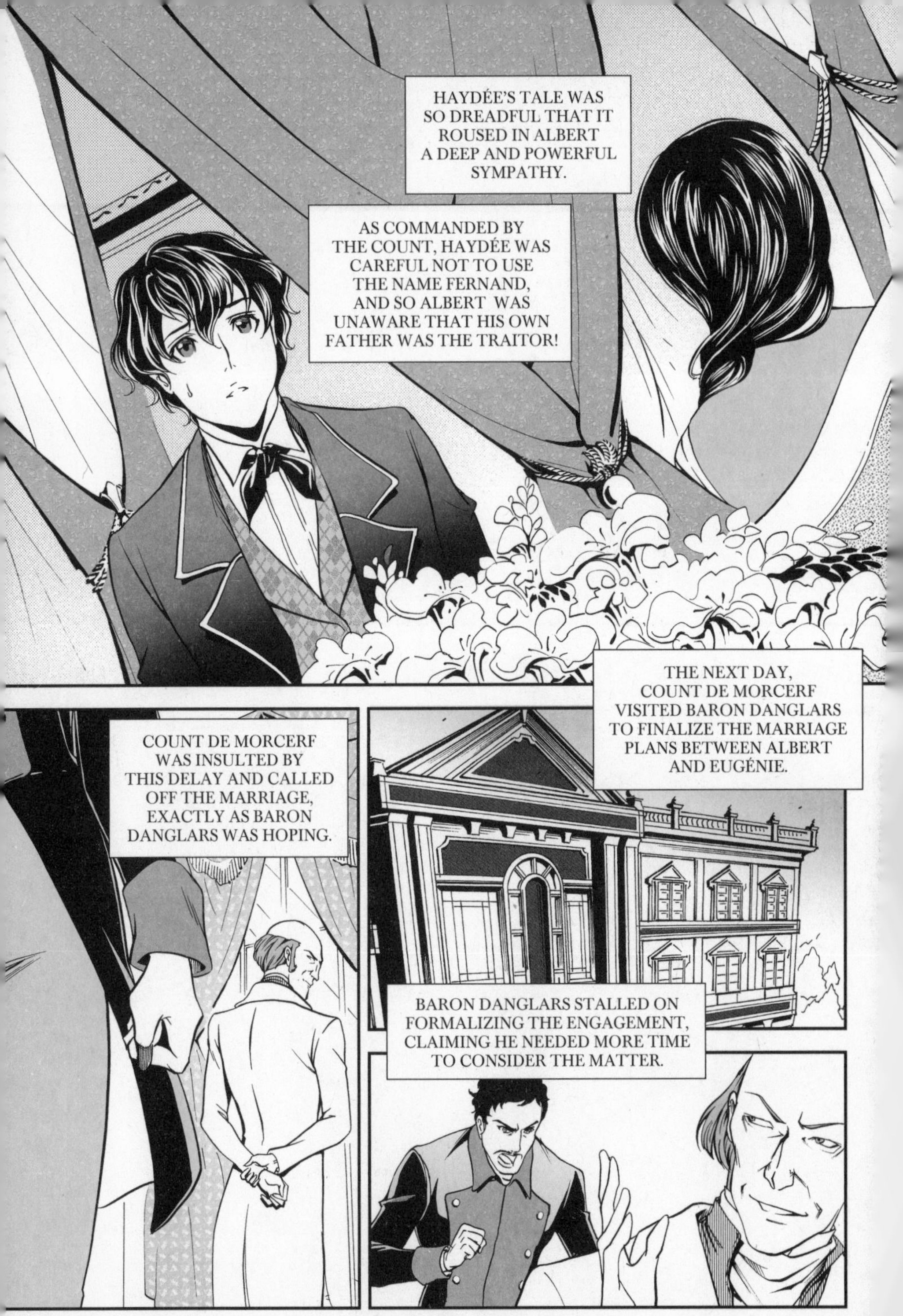
HAYDÉE'S TALE WAS SO DREADFUL THAT IT ROUSED IN ALBERT A DEEP AND POWERFUL SYMPATHY.
AS COMMANDED BY THE COUNT, HAYDÉE WAS CAREFUL NOT TO USE THE NAME FERNAND, AND SO ALBERT WAS UNAWARE THAT HIS OWN FATHER WAS THE TRAITOR!
THE NEXT DAY, COUNT DE MORCERF VISITED BARON DANGLARS TO FINALIZE THE MARRIAGE PLANS BETWEEN ALBERT AND EUGÉNIE.
BARON DANGLARS STALLED ON FORMALIZING THE ENGAGEMENT, CLAIMING HE NEEDED MORE TIME TO CONSIDER THE MATTER.
COUNT DE MORCERF WAS INSULTED BY THIS DELAY AND CALLED OFF THE MARRIAGE, EXACTLY AS BARON DANGLARS WAS HOPING.

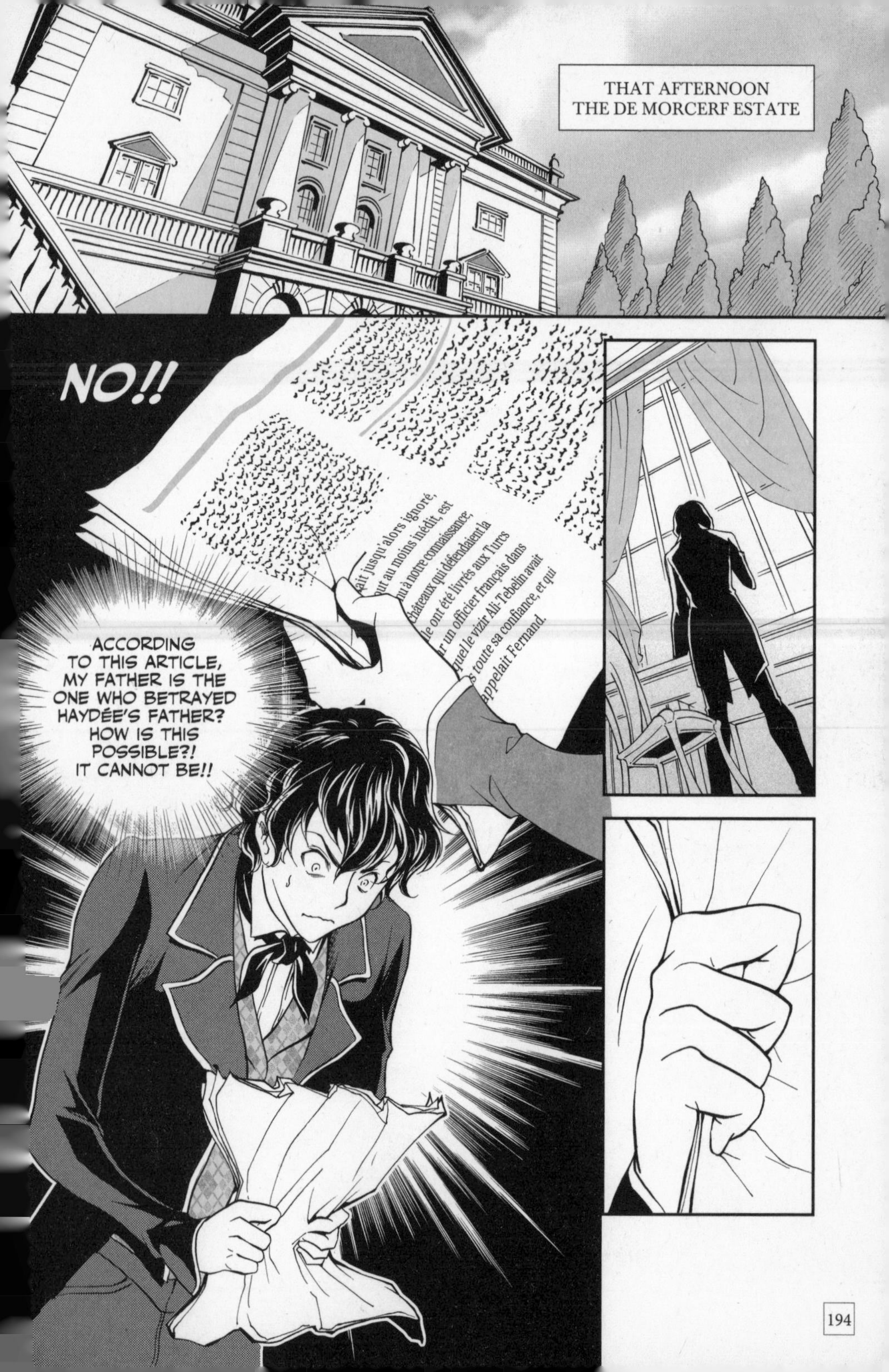
THAT AFTERNOON
THE DE MORCERF ESTATE
NO!!
ait jusqu'alors ignoré,
out au moins inédit, est
nu à notre connaissance,
châteaux qui défendaient la
le ont été livrés aux Turcs
r un officier français dans
quel le vizir Ali-Tebelin avait
s toute sa confiance, et qui
appelait Fernand.
ACCORDING TO THIS ARTICLE, MY FATHER IS THE ONE WHO BETRAYED HAYDÉE'S FATHER? HOW IS THIS POSSIBLE?! IT CANNOT BE!!

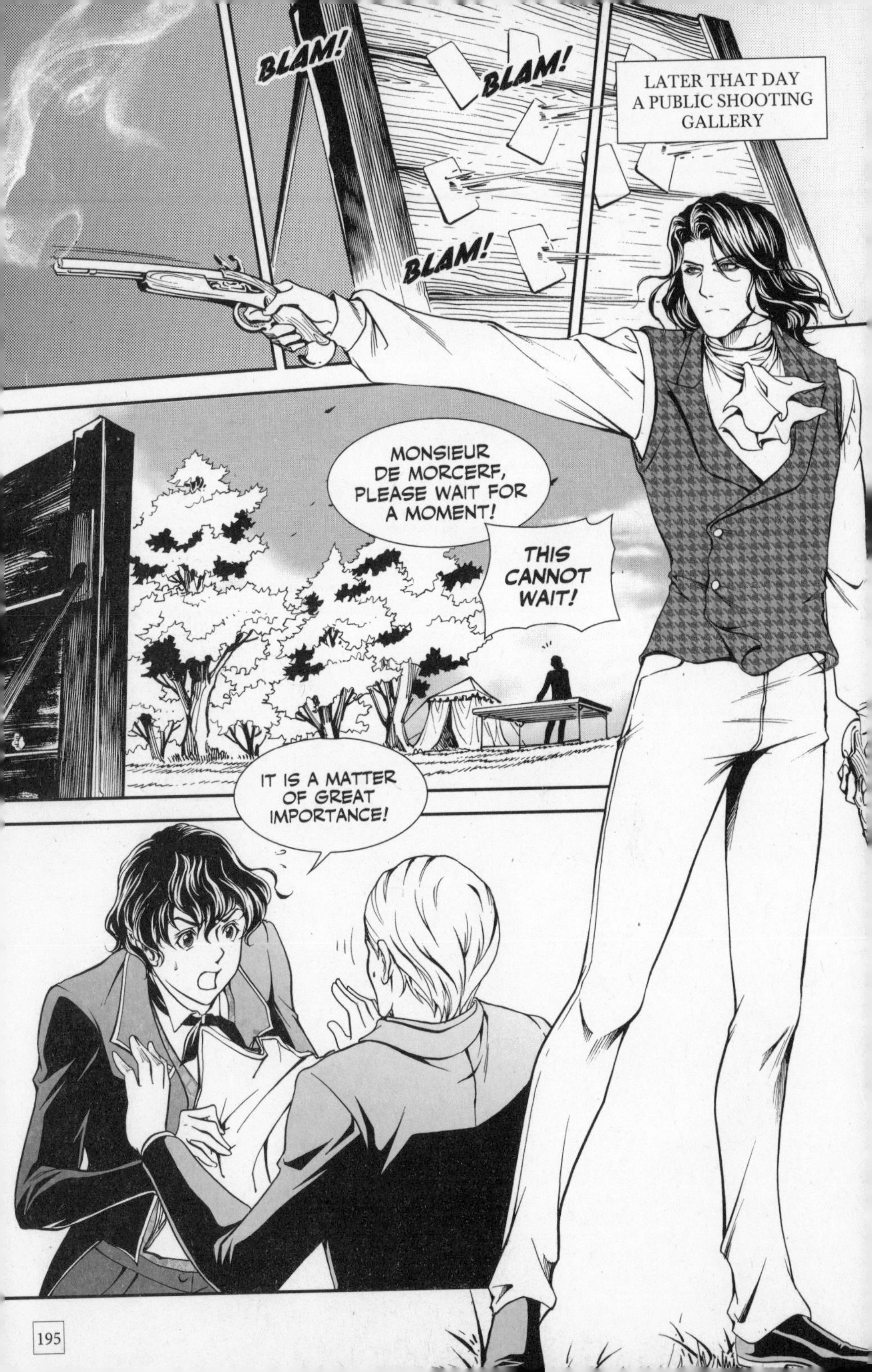
LATER THAT DAY
A PUBLIC SHOOTING
GALLERY
BLAM!
BLAM!
BLAM!
MONSIEUR DE MORCERF, PLEASE WAIT FOR A MOMENT!
THIS CANNOT WAIT!
IT IS A MATTER OF GREAT IMPORTANCE!

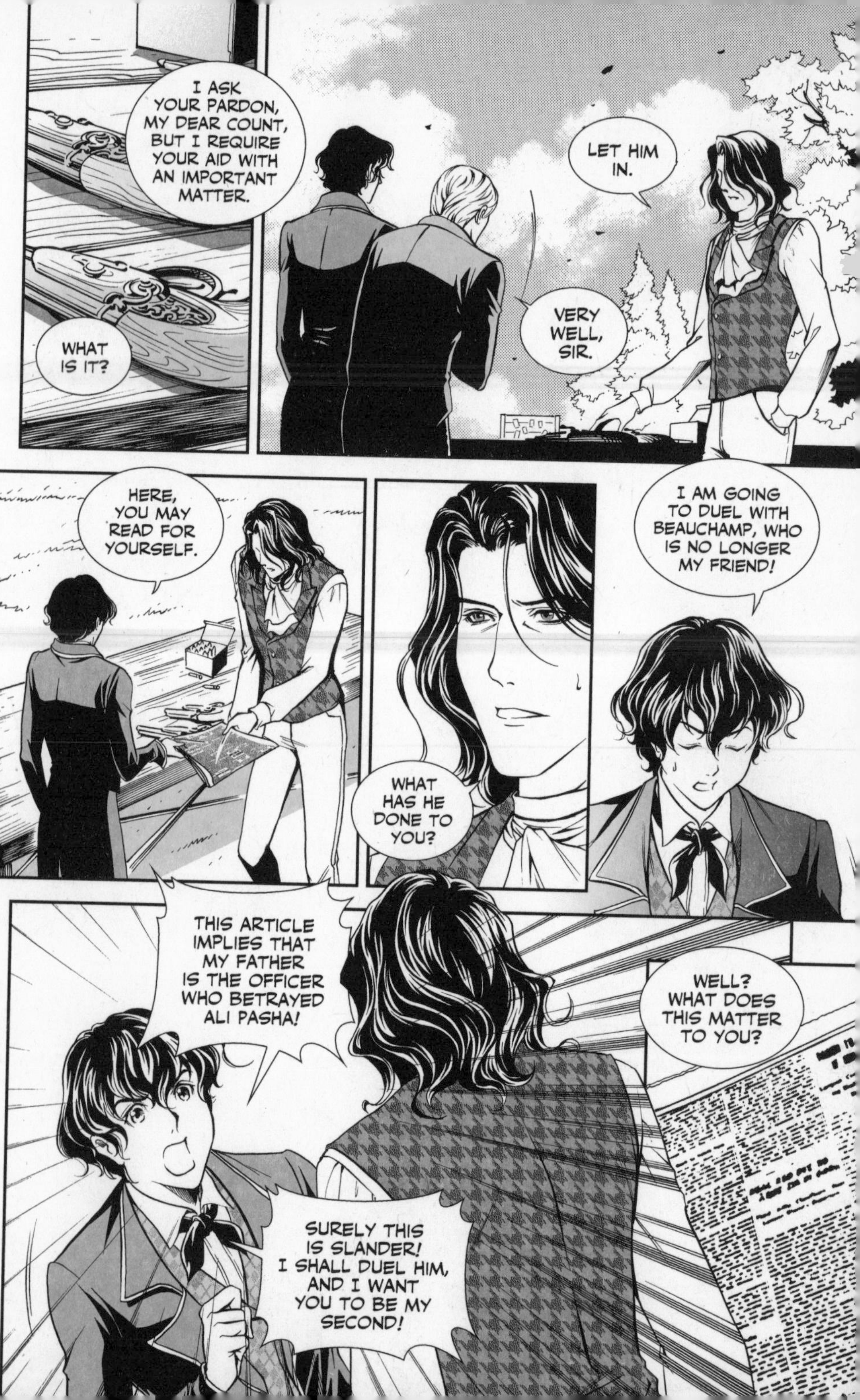
LET HIM IN.
VERY WELL, SIR.
I ASK YOUR PARDON, MY DEAR COUNT, BUT I REQUIRE YOUR AID WITH AN IMPORTANT MATTER.
WHAT IS IT?
I AM GOING TO DUEL WITH BEAUCHAMP, WHO IS NO LONGER MY FRIEND!
WHAT HAS HE DONE TO YOU?
HERE, YOU MAY READ FOR YOURSELF.
WELL? WHAT DOES THIS MATTER TO YOU?
THIS ARTICLE IMPLIES THAT MY FATHER IS THE OFFICER WHO BETRAYED ALI PASHA!
SURELY THIS IS SLANDER! I SHALL DUEL HIM, AND I WANT YOU TO BE MY SECOND!

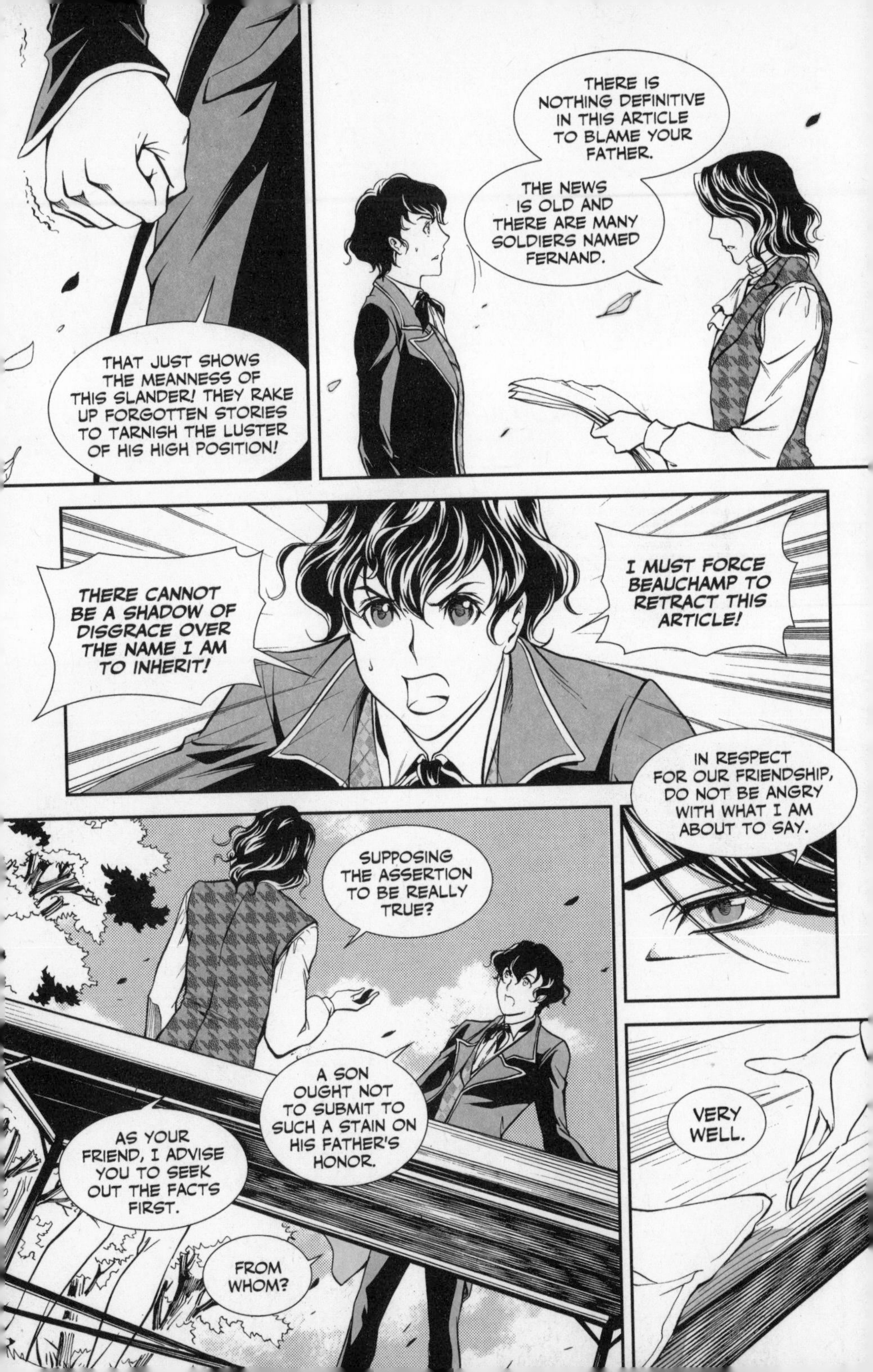
THERE IS NOTHING DEFINITIVE IN THIS ARTICLE TO BLAME YOUR FATHER.
THE NEWS IS OLD AND THERE ARE MANY SOLDIERS NAMED FERNAND.
THAT JUST SHOWS THE MEANNESS OF THIS SLANDER! THEY RAKE UP FORGOTTEN STORIES TO TARNISH THE LUSTER OF HIS HIGH POSITION!
I MUST FORCE BEAUCHAMP TO RETRACT THIS ARTICLE!
THERE CANNOT BE A SHADOW OF DISGRACE OVER THE NAME I AM TO INHERIT!
IN RESPECT FOR OUR FRIENDSHIP, DO NOT BE ANGRY WITH WHAT I AM ABOUT TO SAY.
VERY WELL.
SUPPOSING THE ASSERTION TO BE REALLY TRUE?
A SON OUGHT NOT TO SUBMIT TO SUCH A STAIN ON HIS FATHER'S HONOR.
AS YOUR FRIEND, I ADVISE YOU TO SEEK OUT THE FACTS FIRST.
FROM WHOM?

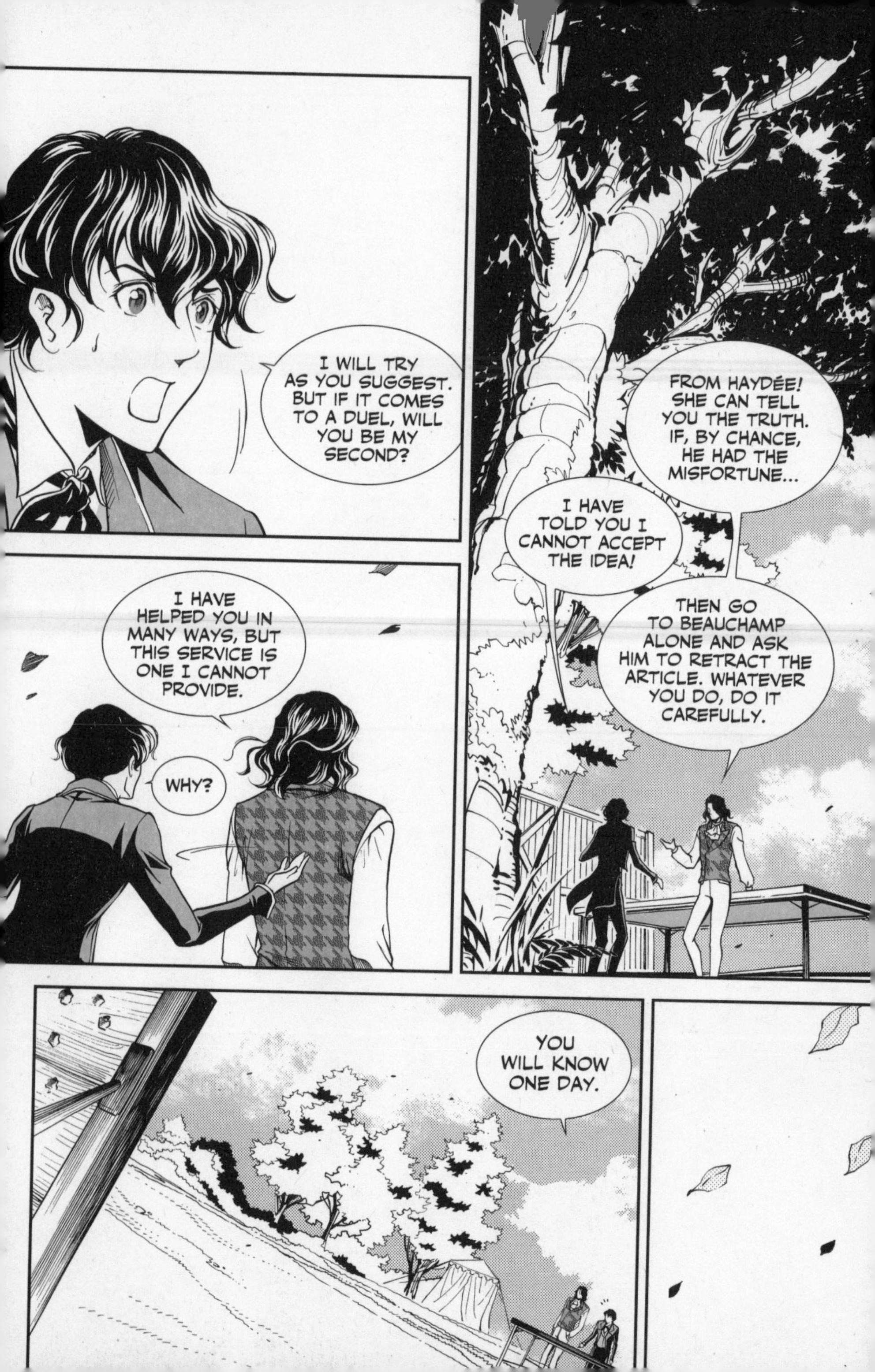
FROM HAYDÉE! SHE CAN TELL YOU THE TRUTH. IF, BY CHANCE, HE HAD THE MISFORTUNE...
I HAVE TOLD YOU I CANNOT ACCEPT THE IDEA!
THEN GO TO BEAUCHAMP ALONE AND ASK HIM TO RETRACT THE ARTICLE. WHATEVER YOU DO, DO IT CAREFULLY.
I WILL TRY AS YOU SUGGEST. BUT IF IT COMES TO A DUEL, WILL YOU BE MY SECOND?
I HAVE HELPED YOU IN MANY WAYS, BUT THIS SERVICE IS ONE I CANNOT PROVIDE.
WHY?
YOU WILL KNOW ONE DAY.

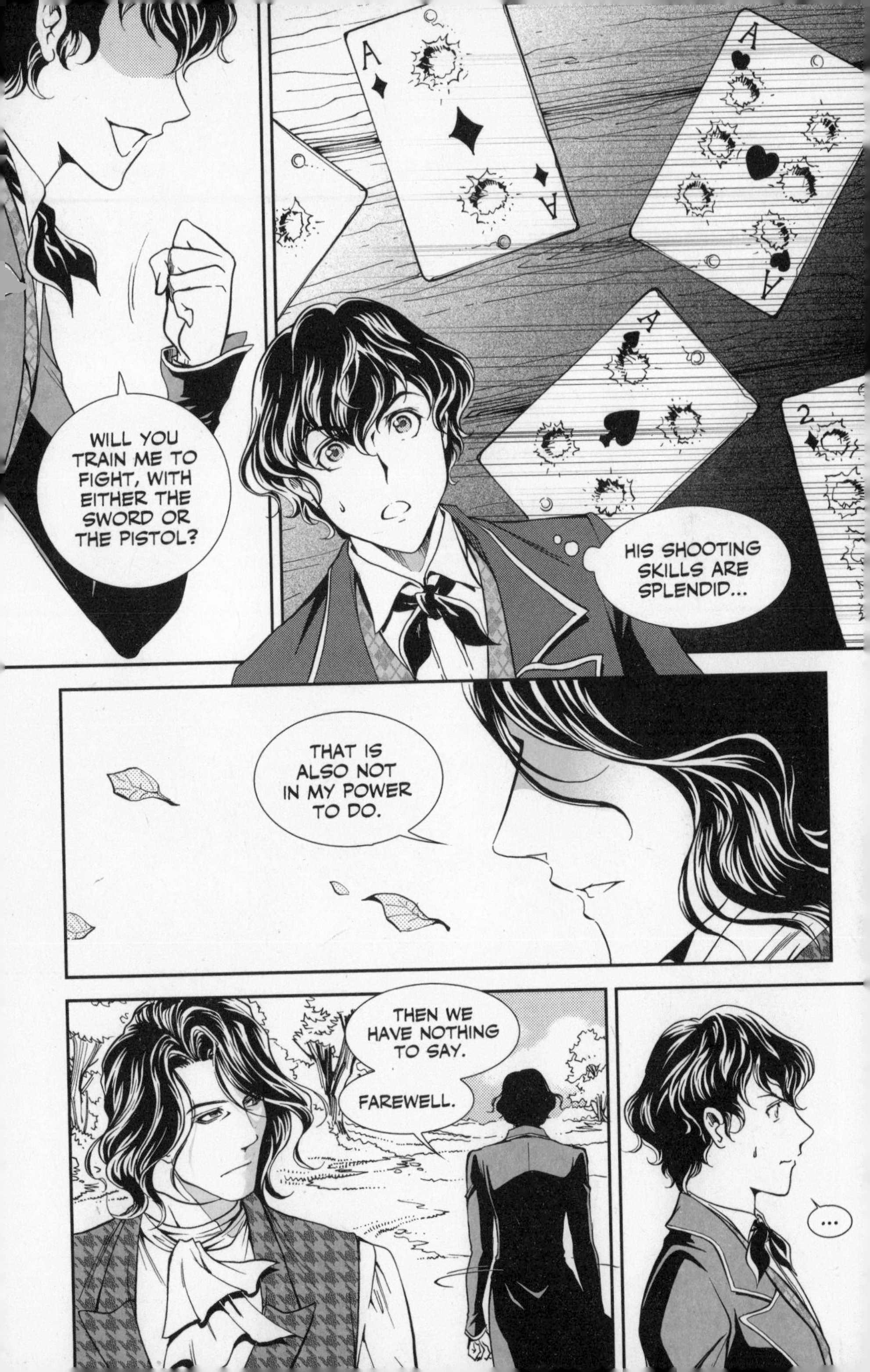
HIS SHOOTING SKILLS ARE SPLENDID...
WILL YOU TRAIN ME TO FIGHT, WITH EITHER THE SWORD OR THE PISTOL?
THAT IS ALSO NOT IN MY POWER TO DO.
...
THEN WE HAVE NOTHING TO SAY.
FAREWELL.

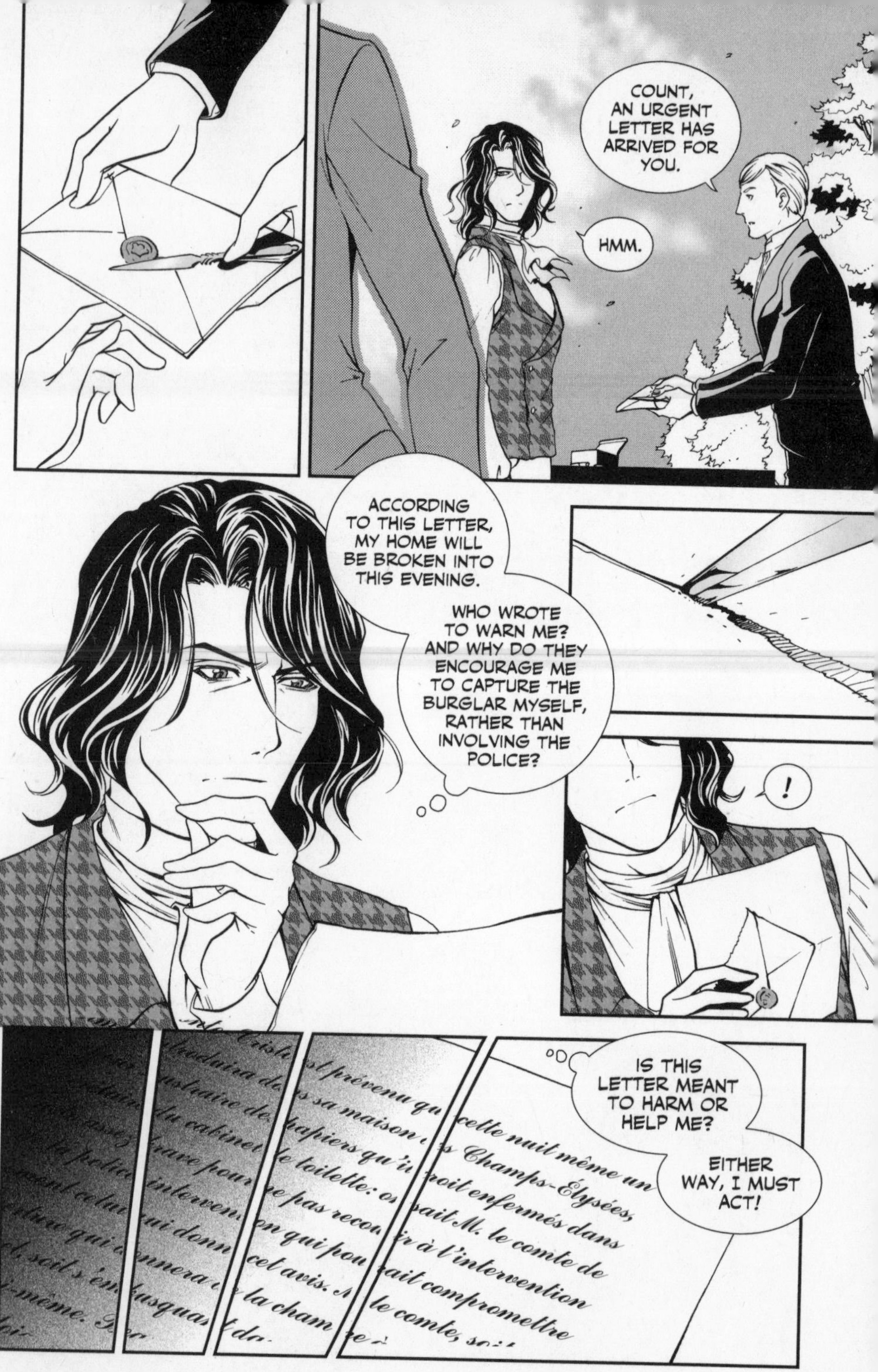
COUNT, AN URGENT LETTER HAS ARRIVED FOR YOU.
HMM.
!
ACCORDING TO THIS LETTER, MY HOME WILL BE BROKEN INTO THIS EVENING.
WHO WROTE TO WARN ME? AND WHY DO THEY ENCOURAGE ME TO CAPTURE THE BURGLAR MYSELF, RATHER THAN INVOLVING THE POLICE?
IS THIS LETTER MEANT TO HARM OR HELP ME?
EITHER WAY, I MUST ACT!

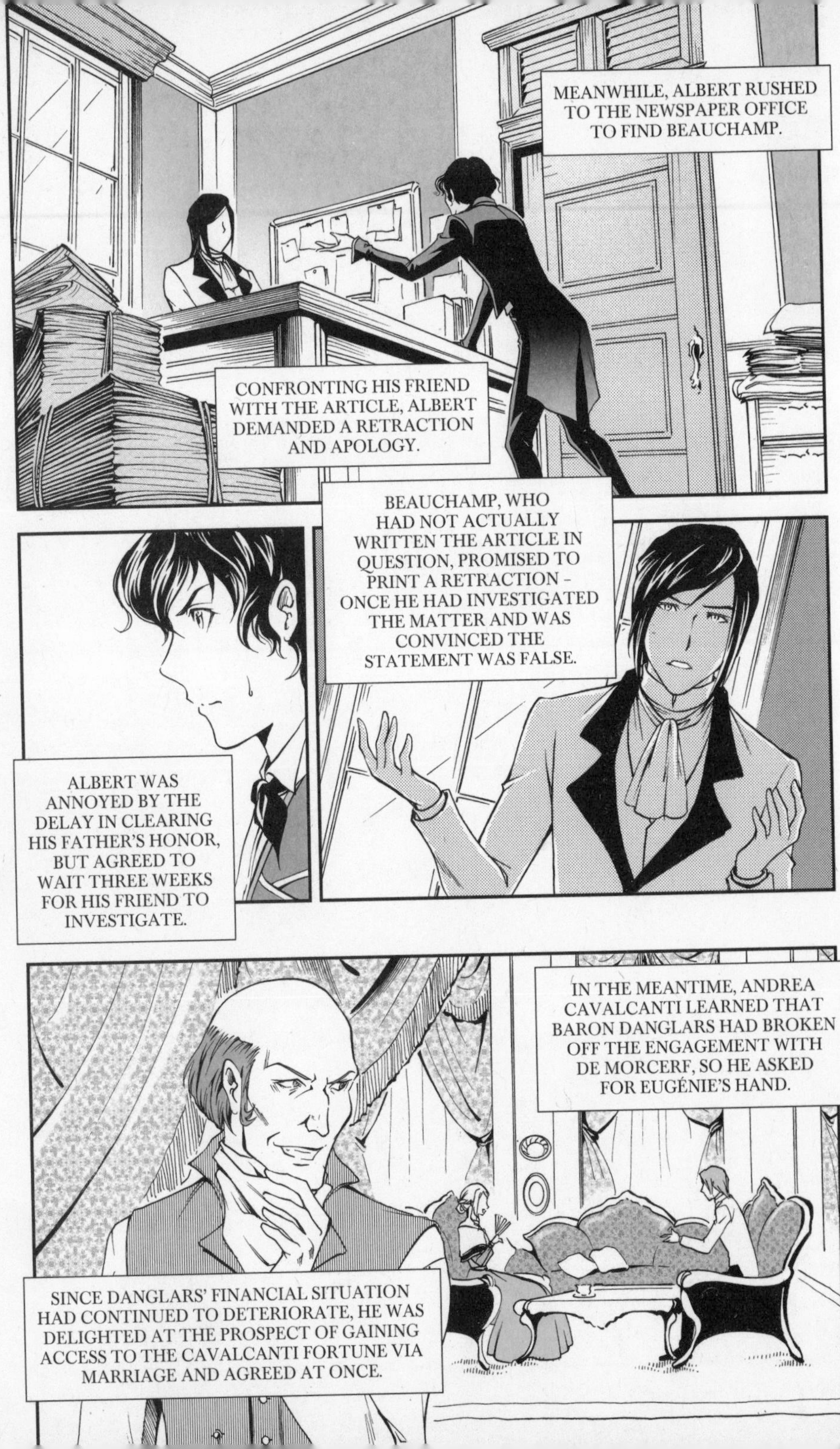
MEANWHILE, ALBERT RUSHED TO THE NEWSPAPER OFFICE TO FIND BEAUCHAMP.
CONFRONTING HIS FRIEND WITH THE ARTICLE, ALBERT DEMANDED A RETRACTION AND APOLOGY.
BEAUCHAMP, WHO HAD NOT ACTUALLY WRITTEN THE ARTICLE IN QUESTION, PROMISED TO PRINT A RETRACTION – ONCE HE HAD INVESTIGATED THE MATTER AND WAS CONVINCED THE STATEMENT WAS FALSE.
ALBERT WAS ANNOYED BY THE DELAY IN CLEARING HIS FATHER'S HONOR, BUT AGREED TO WAIT THREE WEEKS FOR HIS FRIEND TO INVESTIGATE.
IN THE MEANTIME, ANDREA CAVALCANTI LEARNED THAT BARON DANGLARS HAD BROKEN OFF THE ENGAGEMENT WITH DE MORCERF, SO HE ASKED FOR EUGÉNIE'S HAND.
SINCE DANGLARS' FINANCIAL SITUATION HAD CONTINUED TO DETERIORATE, HE WAS DELIGHTED AT THE PROSPECT OF GAINING ACCESS TO THE CAVALCANTI FORTUNE VIA MARRIAGE AND AGREED AT ONCE.

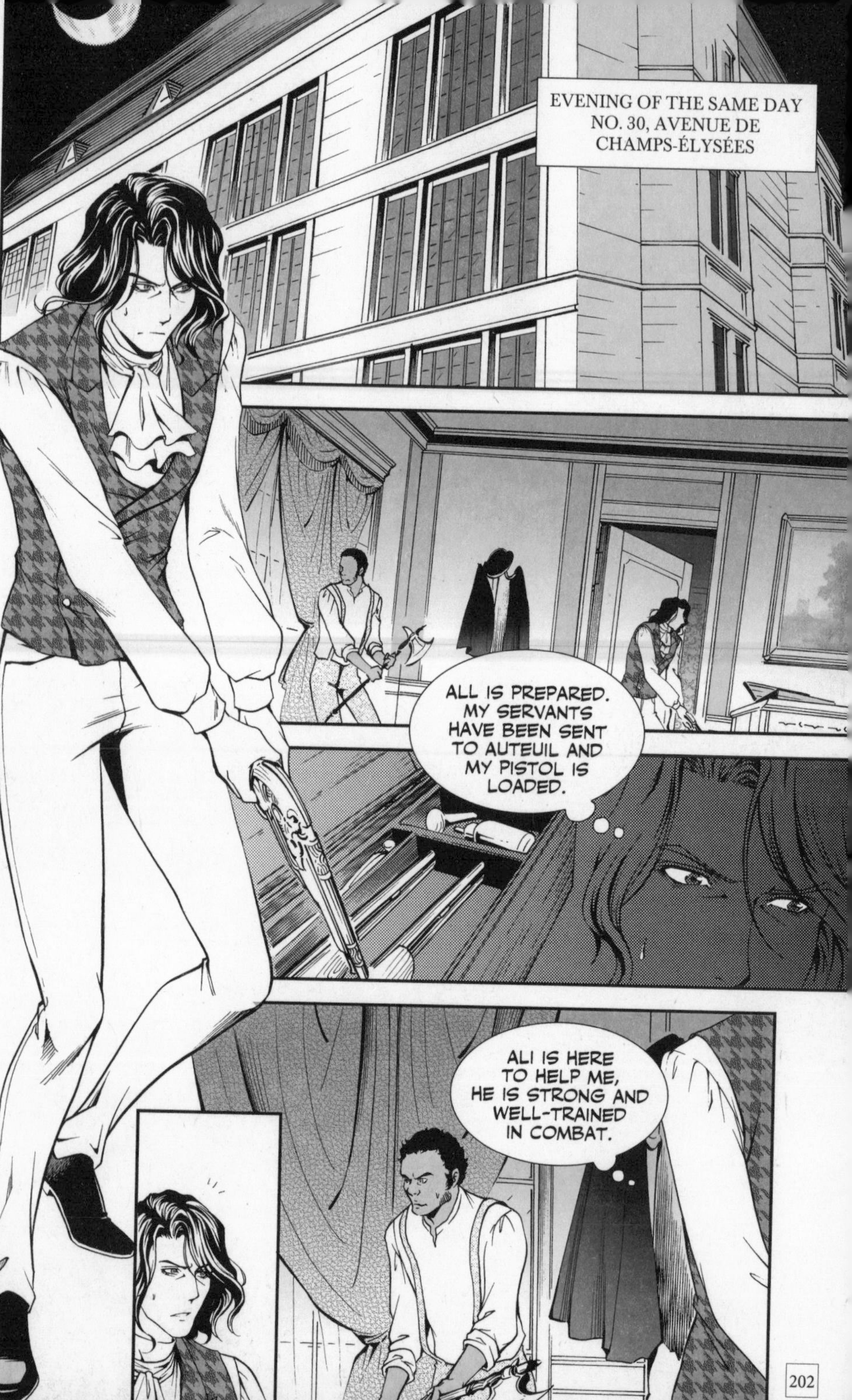
EVENING OF THE SAME DAY NO. 30, AVENUE DE CHAMPS-ÉLYSÉES
ALL IS PREPARED. MY SERVANTS HAVE BEEN SENT TO AUTEUIL AND MY PISTOL IS LOADED.
ALI IS HERE TO HELP ME, HE IS STRONG AND WELL-TRAINED IN COMBAT.

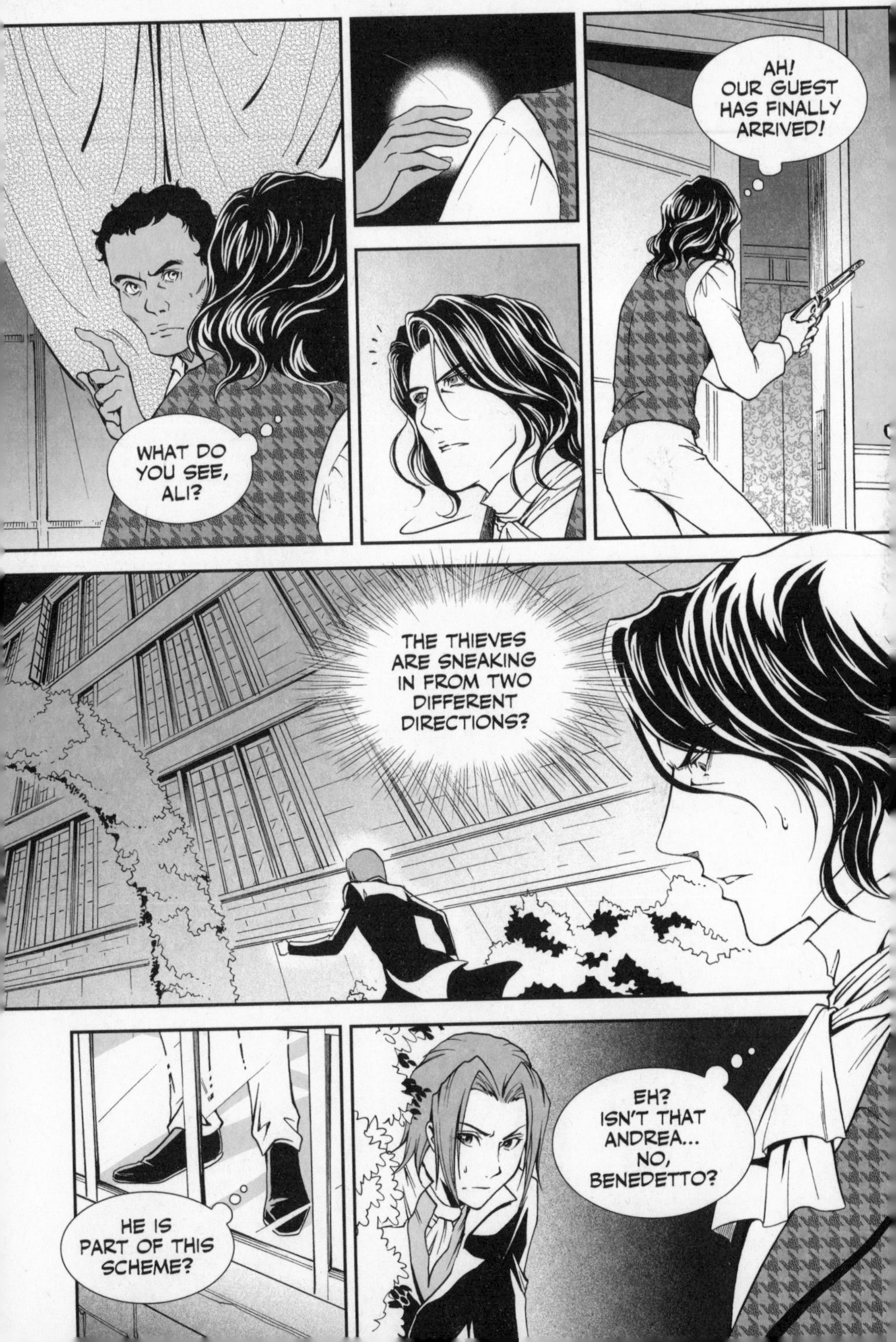
AH! OUR GUEST HAS FINALLY ARRIVED!
WHAT DO YOU SEE, ALI?
THE THIEVES ARE SNEAKING IN FROM TWO DIFFERENT DIRECTIONS?
EH? ISN'T THAT ANDREA... NO, BENEDETTO?
HE IS PART OF THIS SCHEME?

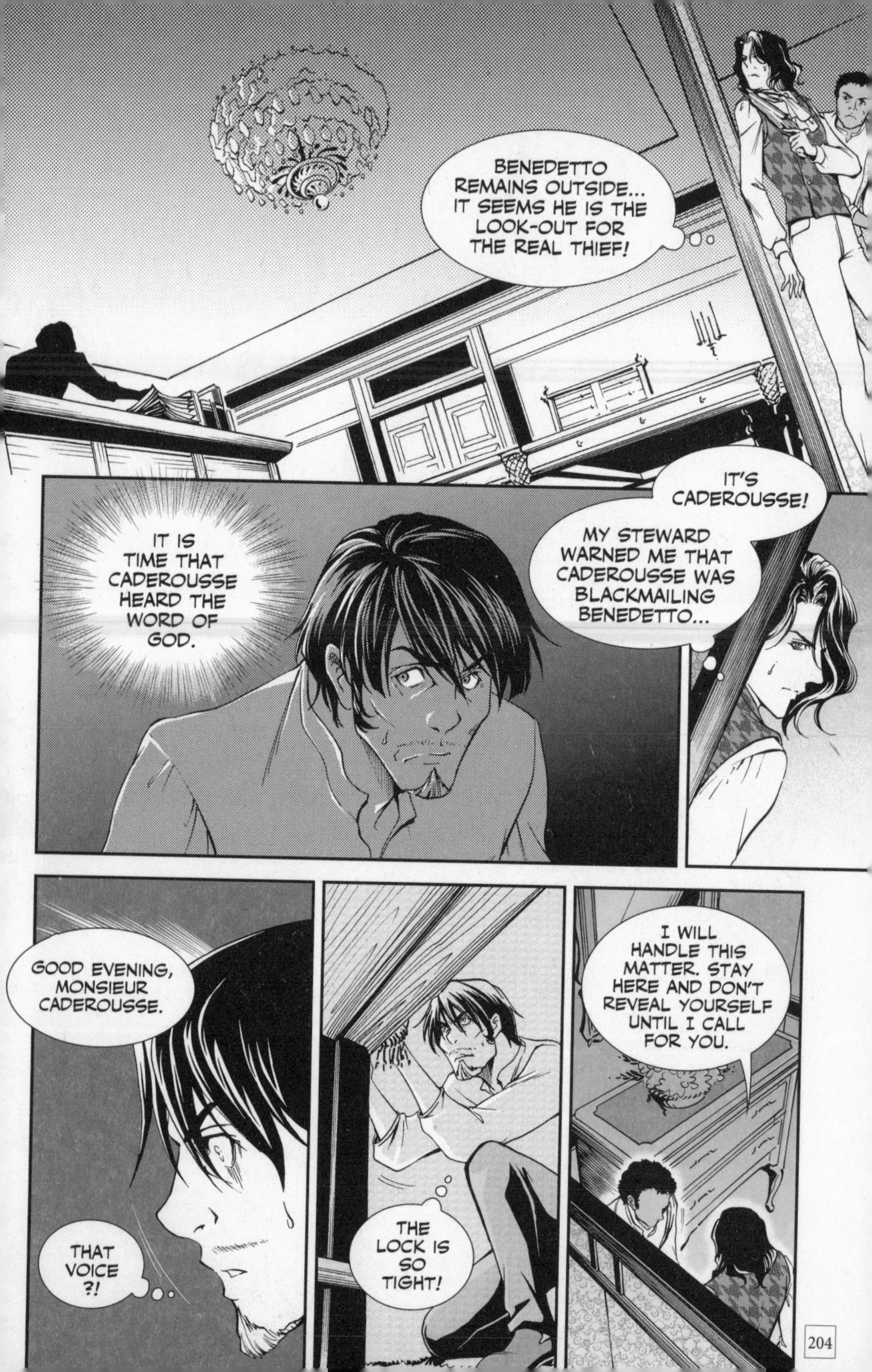
BENEDETTO REMAINS OUTSIDE... IT SEEMS HE IS THE LOOK-OUT FOR THE REAL THIEF!
IT'S CADEROUSSE!
MY STEWARD WARNED ME THAT CADEROUSSE WAS BLACKMAILING BENEDETTO...
IT IS TIME THAT CADEROUSSE HEARD THE WORD OF GOD.
I WILL HANDLE THIS MATTER. STAY HERE AND DON'T REVEAL YOURSELF UNTIL I CALL FOR YOU.
THE LOCK IS SO TIGHT!
GOOD EVENING, MONSIEUR CADEROUSSE.
THAT VOICE ?!

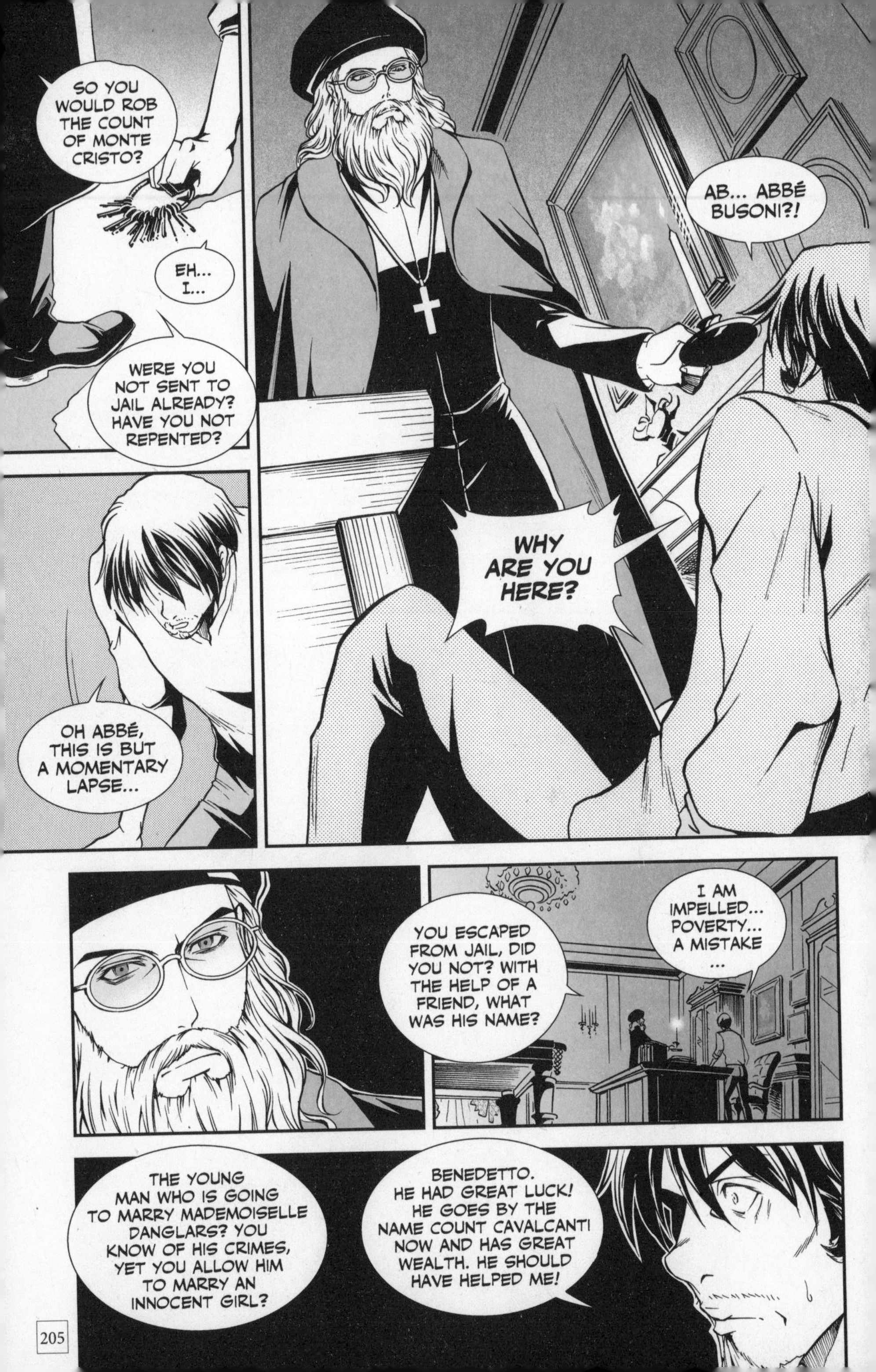
AB... ABBÉ BUSONI?!
WHY ARE YOU HERE?
SO YOU WOULD ROB THE COUNT OF MONTE CRISTO?
EH... I...
WERE YOU NOT SENT TO JAIL ALREADY? HAVE YOU NOT REPENTED?
OH ABBÉ, THIS IS BUT A MOMENTARY LAPSE...
I AM IMPELLED... POVERTY... A MISTAKE ...
YOU ESCAPED FROM JAIL, DID YOU NOT? WITH THE HELP OF A FRIEND, WHAT WAS HIS NAME?
BENEDETTO. HE HAD GREAT LUCK! HE GOES BY THE NAME COUNT CAVALCANTI NOW AND HAS GREAT WEALTH. HE SHOULD HAVE HELPED ME!
THE YOUNG MAN WHO IS GOING TO MARRY MADEMOISELLE DANGLARS? YOU KNOW OF HIS CRIMES, YET YOU ALLOW HIM TO MARRY AN INNOCENT GIRL?

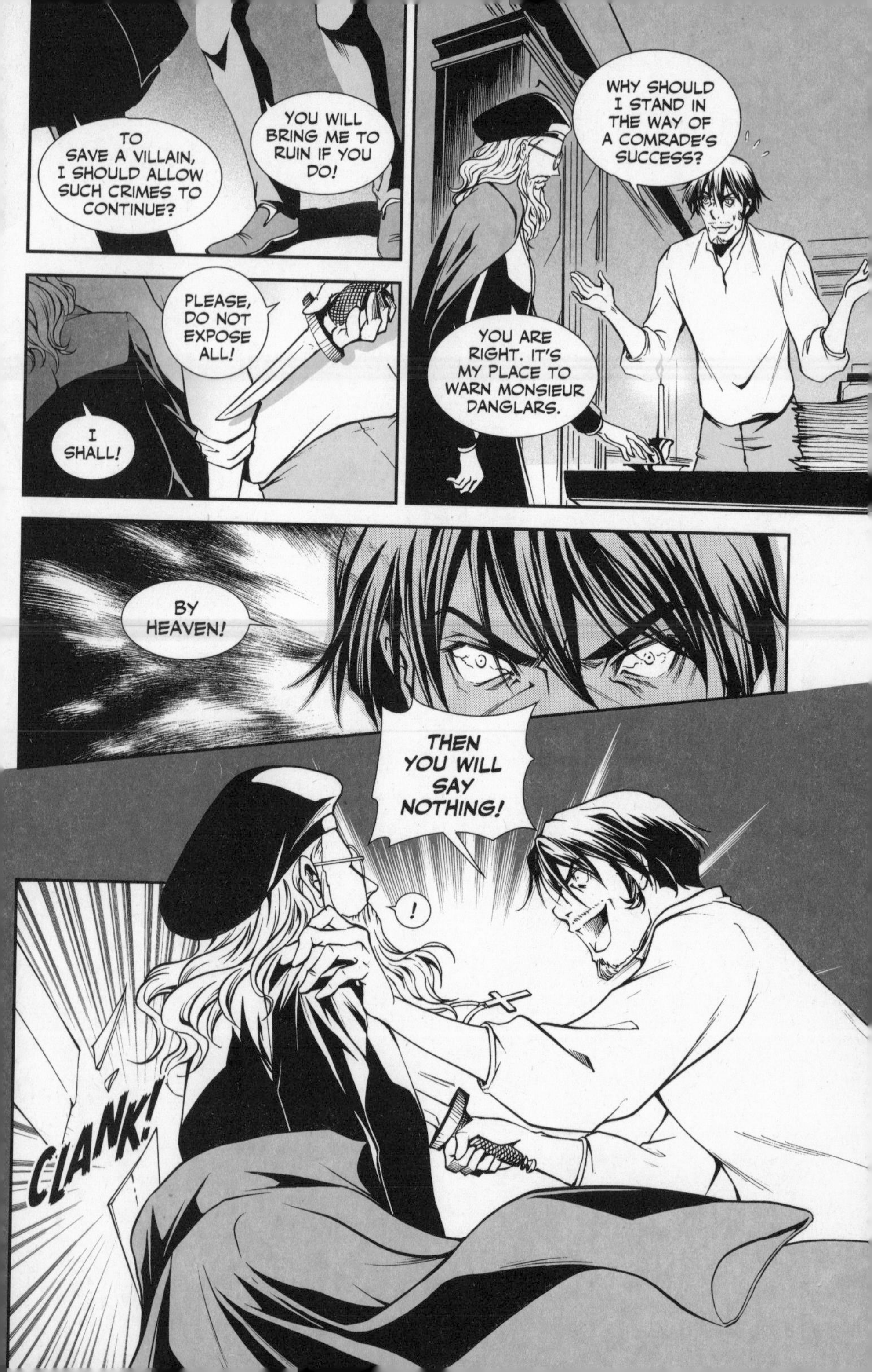
WHY SHOULD I STAND IN THE WAY OF A COMRADE'S SUCCESS?
YOU ARE RIGHT. IT'S MY PLACE TO WARN MONSIEUR DANGLARS.
YOU WILL BRING ME TO RUIN IF YOU DO!
TO SAVE A VILLAIN, I SHOULD ALLOW SUCH CRIMES TO CONTINUE?
PLEASE, DO NOT EXPOSE ALL!
I SHALL!
BY HEAVEN!
THEN YOU WILL SAY NOTHING!
!
CLANK!

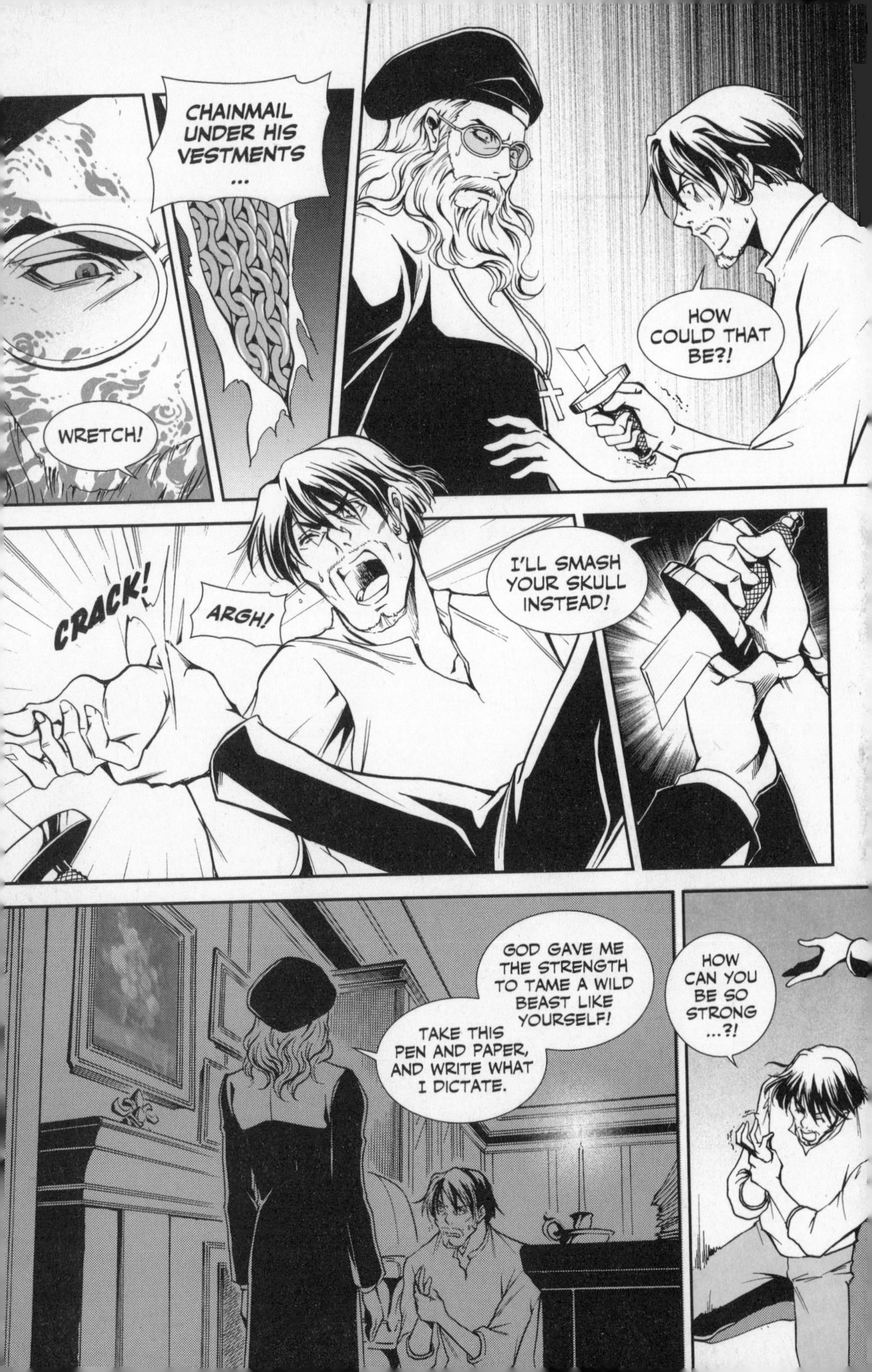
HOW COULD THAT BE?!
CHAINMAIL UNDER HIS VESTMENTS ...
WRETCH!
I'LL SMASH YOUR SKULL INSTEAD!
ARGH!
CRACK!
HOW CAN YOU BE SO STRONG ...?!
GOD GAVE ME THE STRENGTH TO TAME A WILD BEAST LIKE YOURSELF!
TAKE THIS PEN AND PAPER, AND WRITE WHAT I DICTATE.

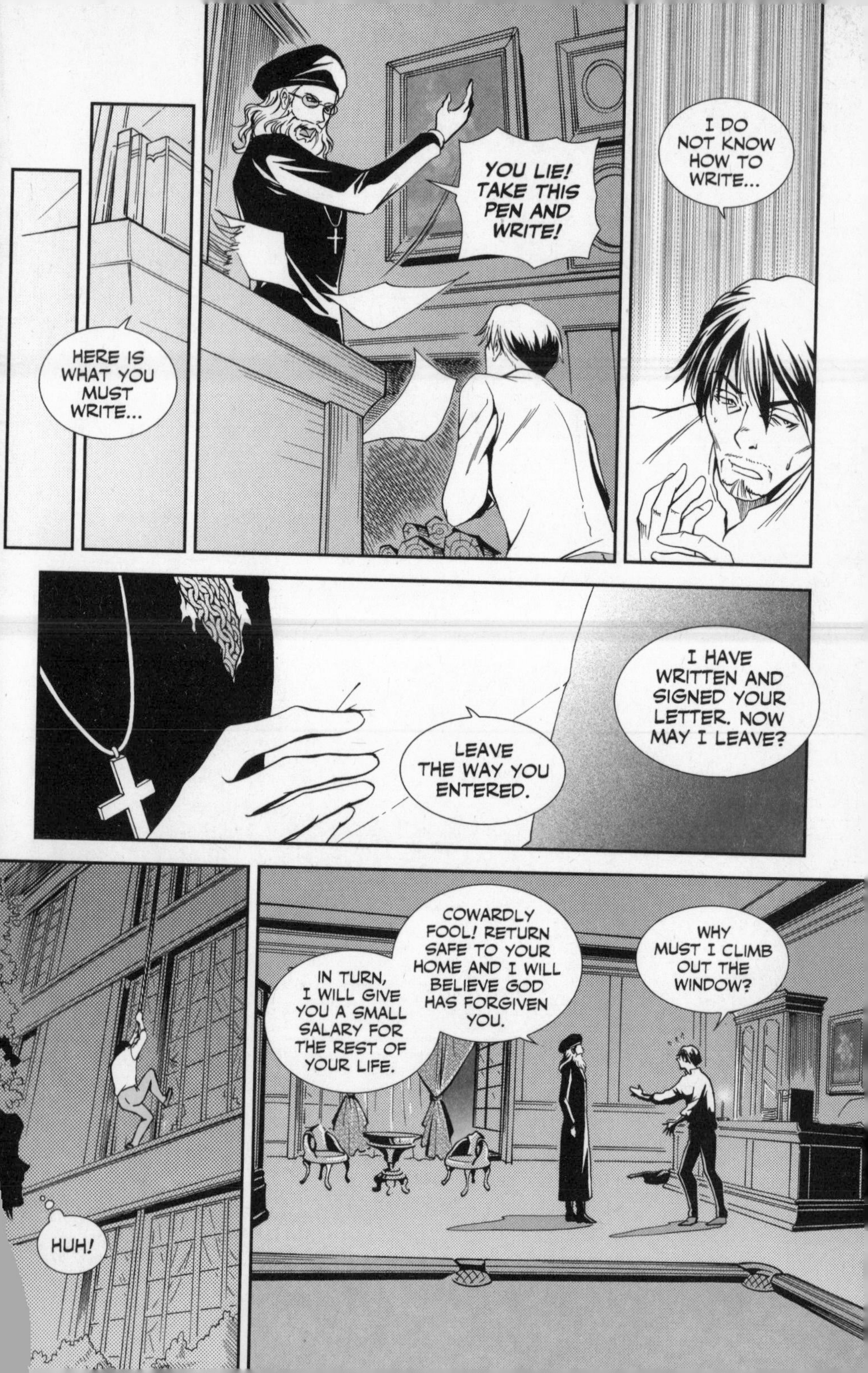
I DO NOT KNOW HOW TO WRITE...
YOU LIE! TAKE THIS PEN AND WRITE!
HERE IS WHAT YOU MUST WRITE...
I HAVE WRITTEN AND SIGNED YOUR LETTER. NOW MAY I LEAVE?
LEAVE THE WAY YOU ENTERED.
WHY MUST I CLIMB OUT THE WINDOW?
COWARDLY FOOL! RETURN SAFE TO YOUR HOME AND I WILL BELIEVE GOD HAS FORGIVEN YOU.
IN TURN, I WILL GIVE YOU A SMALL SALARY FOR THE REST OF YOUR LIFE.
HUH!

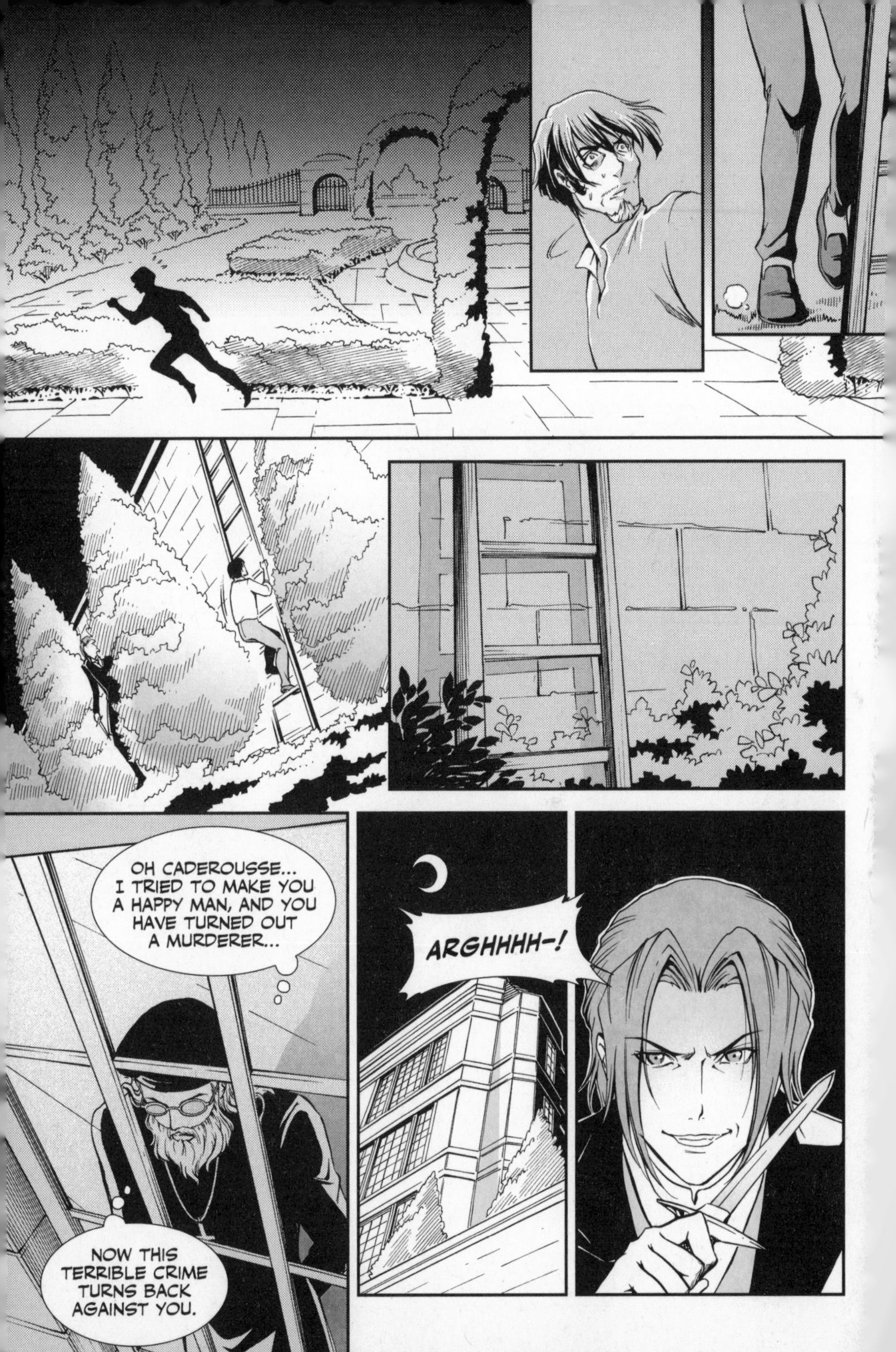
ARGHHHH-!
OH CADEROUSSE... I TRIED TO MAKE YOU A HAPPY MAN, AND YOU HAVE TURNED OUT A MURDERER...
NOW THIS TERRIBLE CRIME TURNS BACK AGAINST YOU.

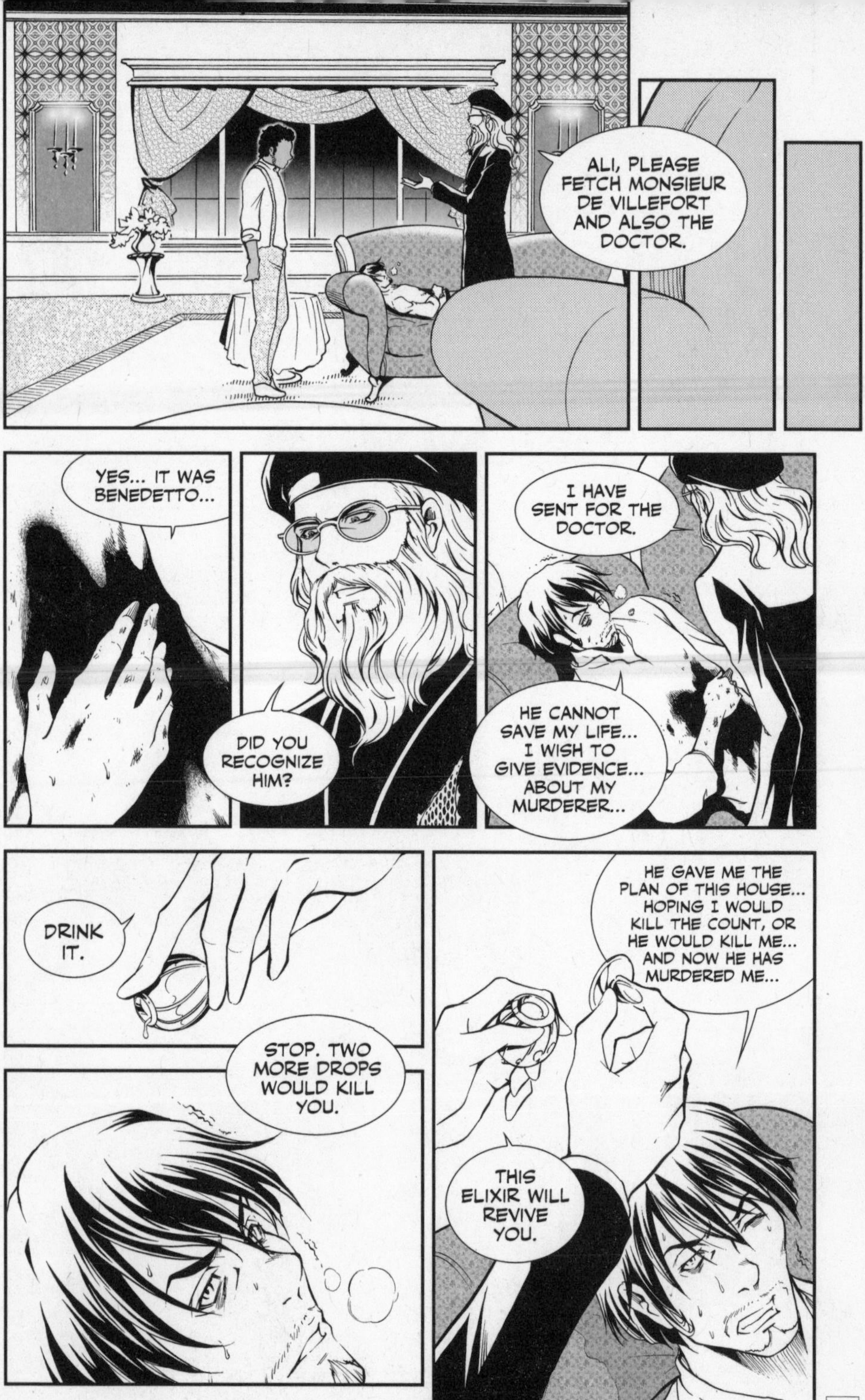
ALI, PLEASE FETCH MONSIEUR DE VILLEFORT AND ALSO THE DOCTOR.
I HAVE SENT FOR THE DOCTOR.
HE CANNOT SAVE MY LIFE... I WISH TO GIVE EVIDENCE... ABOUT MY MURDERER...
DID YOU RECOGNIZE HIM?
YES... IT WAS BENEDETTO...
HE GAVE ME THE PLAN OF THIS HOUSE... HOPING I WOULD KILL THE COUNT, OR HE WOULD KILL ME... AND NOW HE HAS MURDERED ME...
THIS ELIXIR WILL REVIVE YOU.
DRINK IT.
STOP. TWO MORE DROPS WOULD KILL YOU.

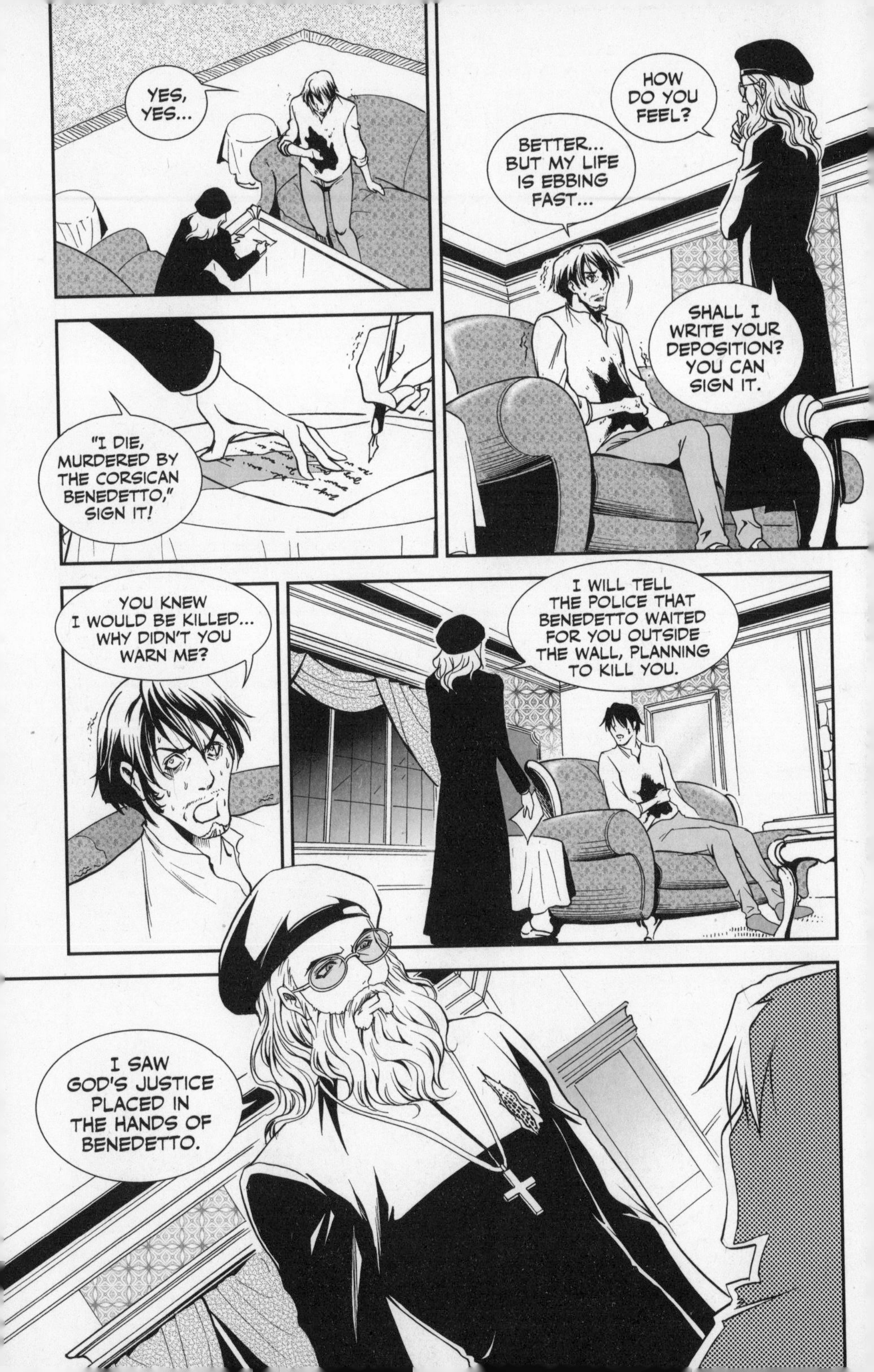
HOW DO YOU FEEL?
BETTER... BUT MY LIFE IS EBBING FAST...
SHALL I WRITE YOUR DEPOSITION? YOU CAN SIGN IT.
YES, YES...
"I DIE, MURDERED BY THE CORSICAN BENEDETTO," SIGN IT!
I WILL TELL THE POLICE THAT BENEDETTO WAITED FOR YOU OUTSIDE THE WALL, PLANNING TO KILL YOU.
YOU KNEW I WOULD BE KILLED... WHY DIDN'T YOU WARN ME?
I SAW GOD'S JUSTICE PLACED IN THE HANDS OF BENEDETTO.

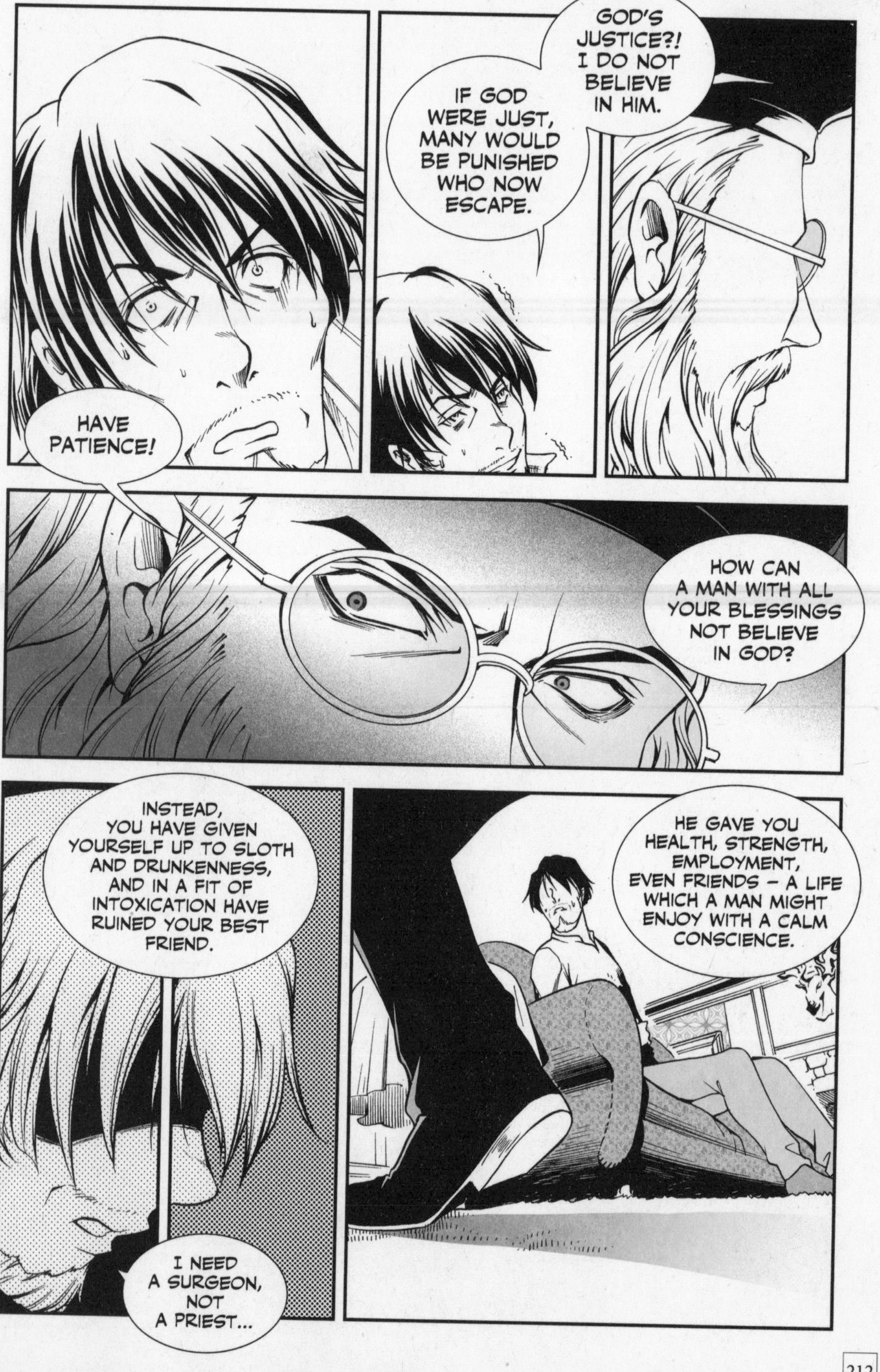
GOD'S JUSTICE?! I DO NOT BELIEVE IN HIM.
IF GOD WERE JUST, MANY WOULD BE PUNISHED WHO NOW ESCAPE.
HAVE PATIENCE!
HOW CAN A MAN WITH ALL YOUR BLESSINGS NOT BELIEVE IN GOD?
HE GAVE YOU HEALTH, STRENGTH, EMPLOYMENT, EVEN FRIENDS – A LIFE WHICH A MAN MIGHT ENJOY WITH A CALM CONSCIENCE.
INSTEAD, YOU HAVE GIVEN YOURSELF UP TO SLOTH AND DRUNKENNESS, AND IN A FIT OF INTOXICATION HAVE RUINED YOUR BEST FRIEND.
I NEED A SURGEON, NOT A PRIEST...

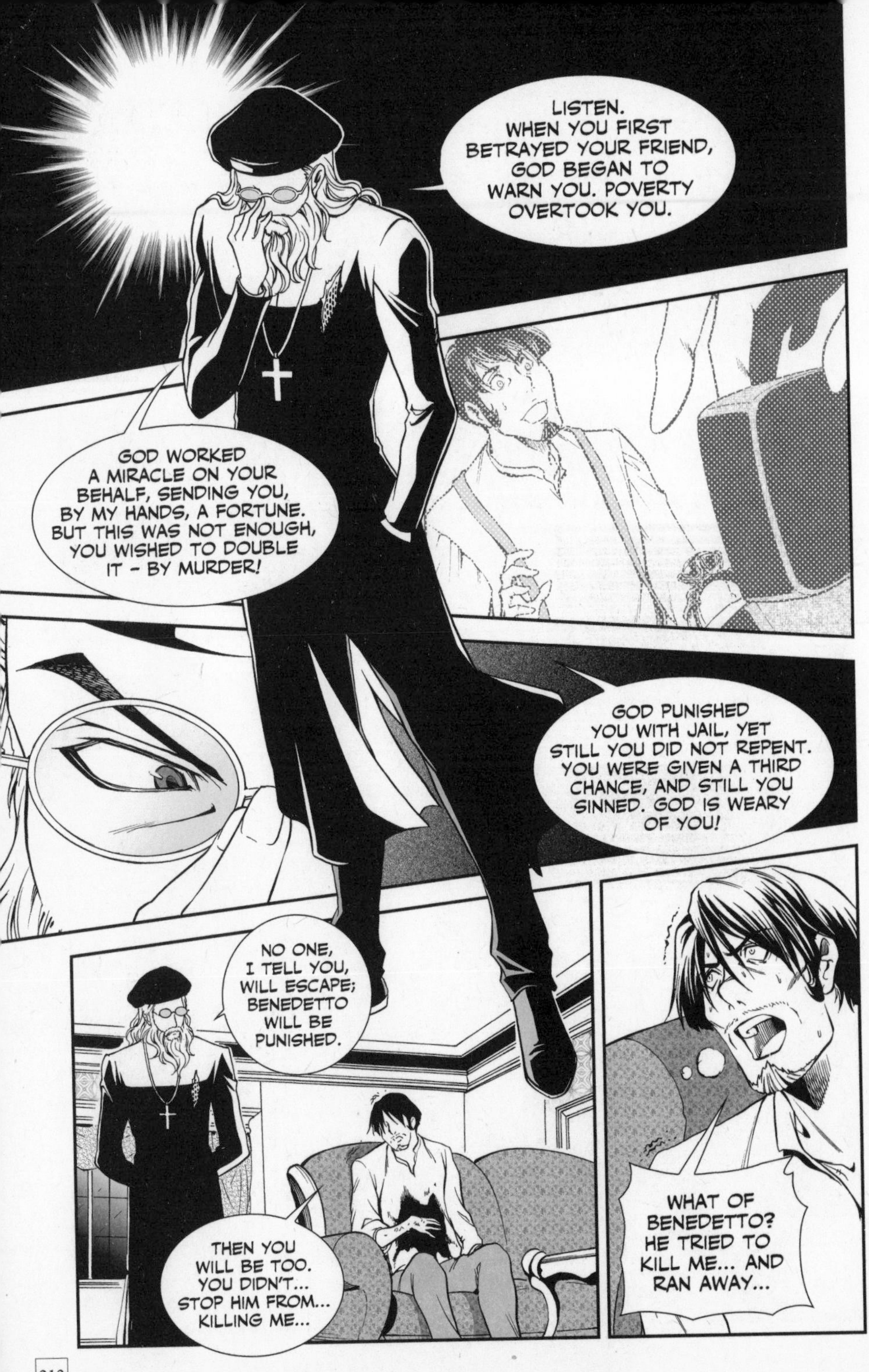
LISTEN. WHEN YOU FIRST BETRAYED YOUR FRIEND, GOD BEGAN TO WARN YOU. POVERTY OVERTOOK YOU.
GOD WORKED A MIRACLE ON YOUR BEHALF, SENDING YOU, BY MY HANDS, A FORTUNE. BUT THIS WAS NOT ENOUGH, YOU WISHED TO DOUBLE IT - BY MURDER!
GOD PUNISHED YOU WITH JAIL, YET STILL YOU DID NOT REPENT. YOU WERE GIVEN A THIRD CHANCE, AND STILL YOU SINNED. GOD IS WEARY OF YOU!
WHAT OF BENEDETTO? HE TRIED TO KILL ME... AND RAN AWAY...
NO ONE, I TELL YOU, WILL ESCAPE; BENEDETTO WILL BE PUNISHED.
THEN YOU WILL BE TOO. YOU DIDN'T... STOP HIM FROM... KILLING ME...

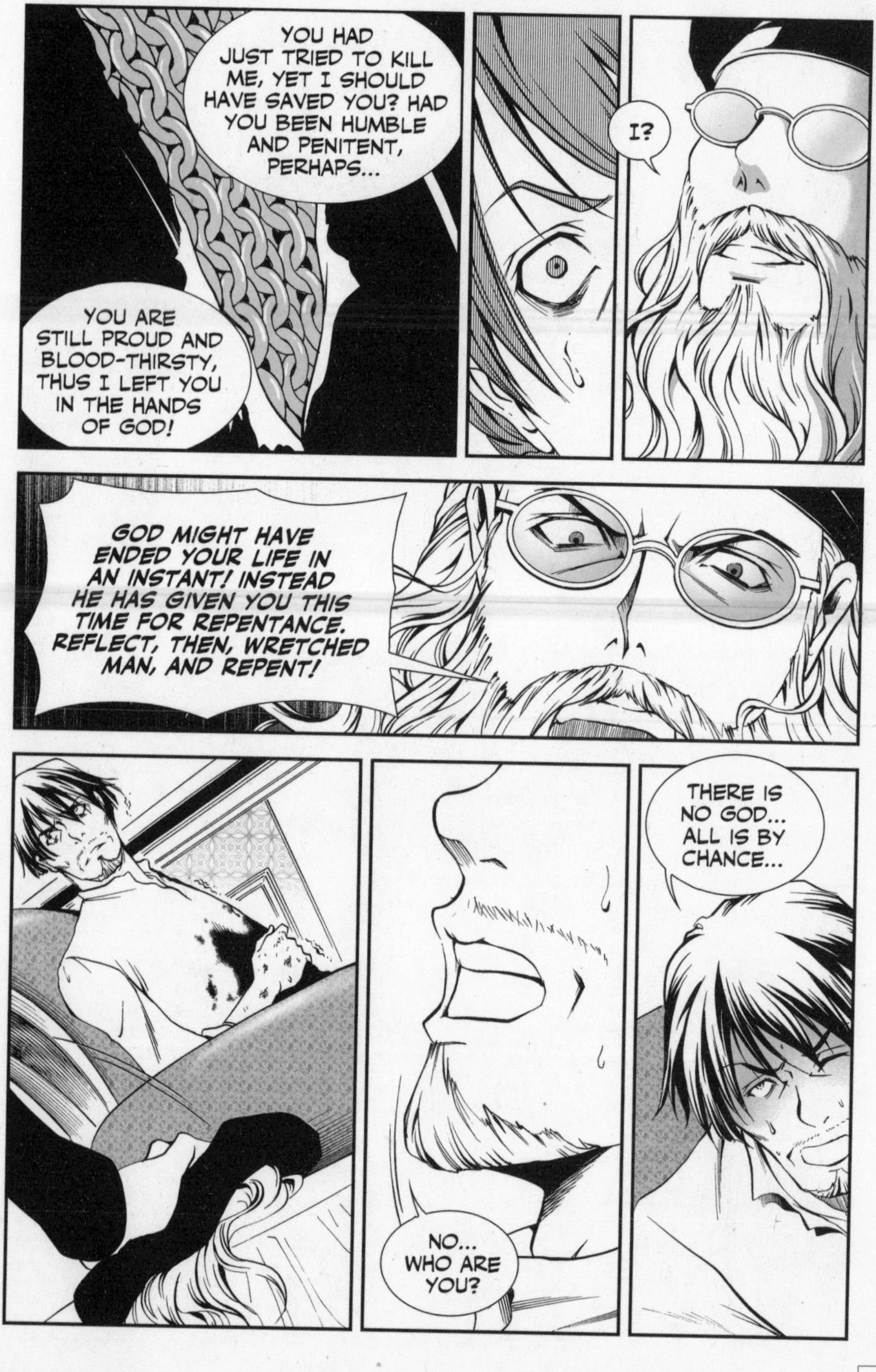
I?
YOU HAD JUST TRIED TO KILL ME, YET I SHOULD HAVE SAVED YOU? HAD YOU BEEN HUMBLE AND PENITENT, PERHAPS...
YOU ARE STILL PROUD AND BLOOD-THIRSTY, THUS I LEFT YOU IN THE HANDS OF GOD!
GOD MIGHT HAVE ENDED YOUR LIFE IN AN INSTANT! INSTEAD HE HAS GIVEN YOU THIS TIME FOR REPENTANCE. REFLECT, THEN, WRETCHED MAN, AND REPENT!
THERE IS NO GOD... ALL IS BY CHANCE...
NO... WHO ARE YOU?

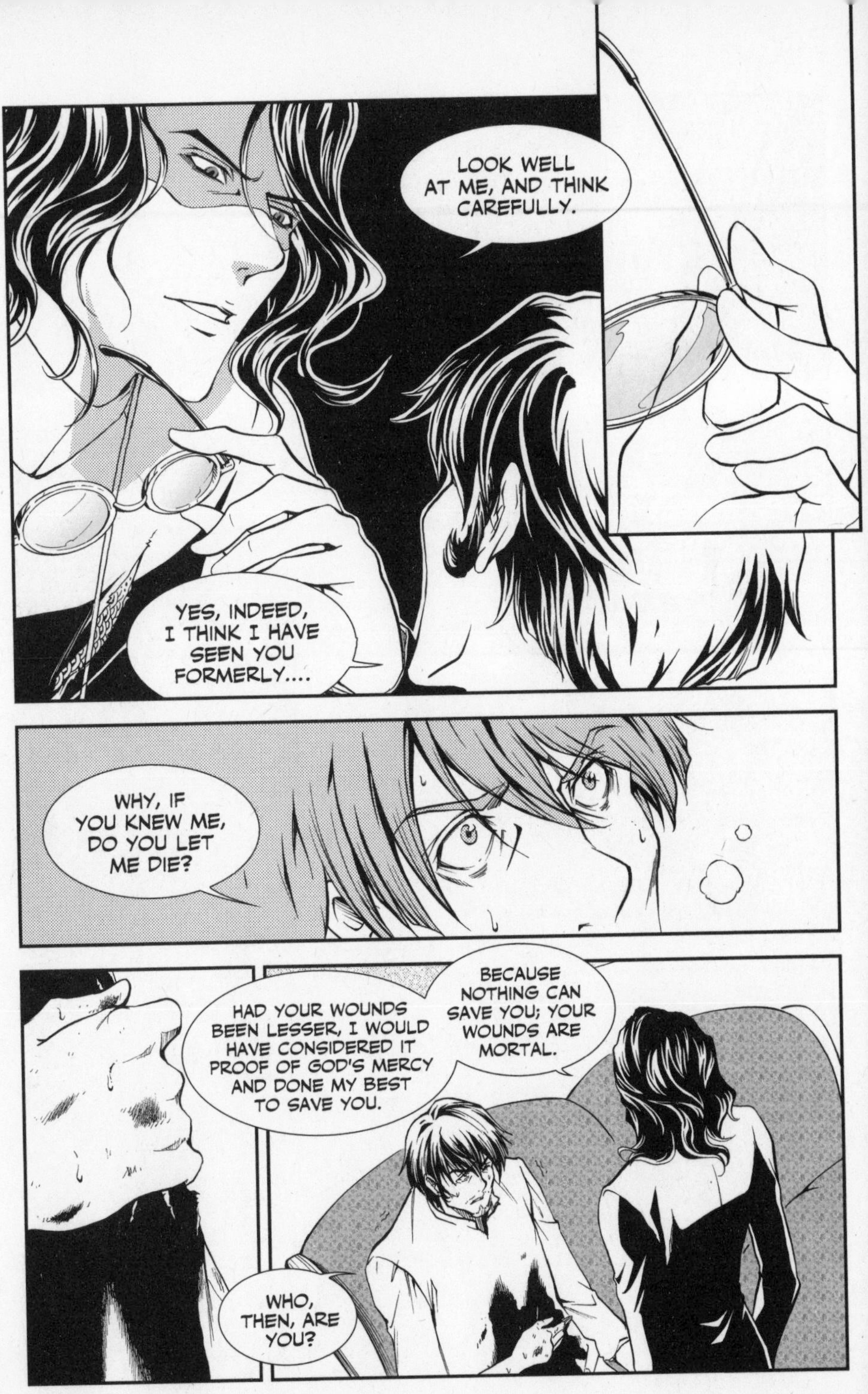
LOOK WELL AT ME, AND THINK CAREFULLY.
YES, INDEED, I THINK I HAVE SEEN YOU FORMERLY....
WHY, IF YOU KNEW ME, DO YOU LET ME DIE?
BECAUSE NOTHING CAN SAVE YOU; YOUR WOUNDS ARE MORTAL.
HAD YOUR WOUNDS BEEN LESSER, I WOULD HAVE CONSIDERED IT PROOF OF GOD'S MERCY AND DONE MY BEST TO SAVE YOU.
WHO, THEN, ARE YOU?

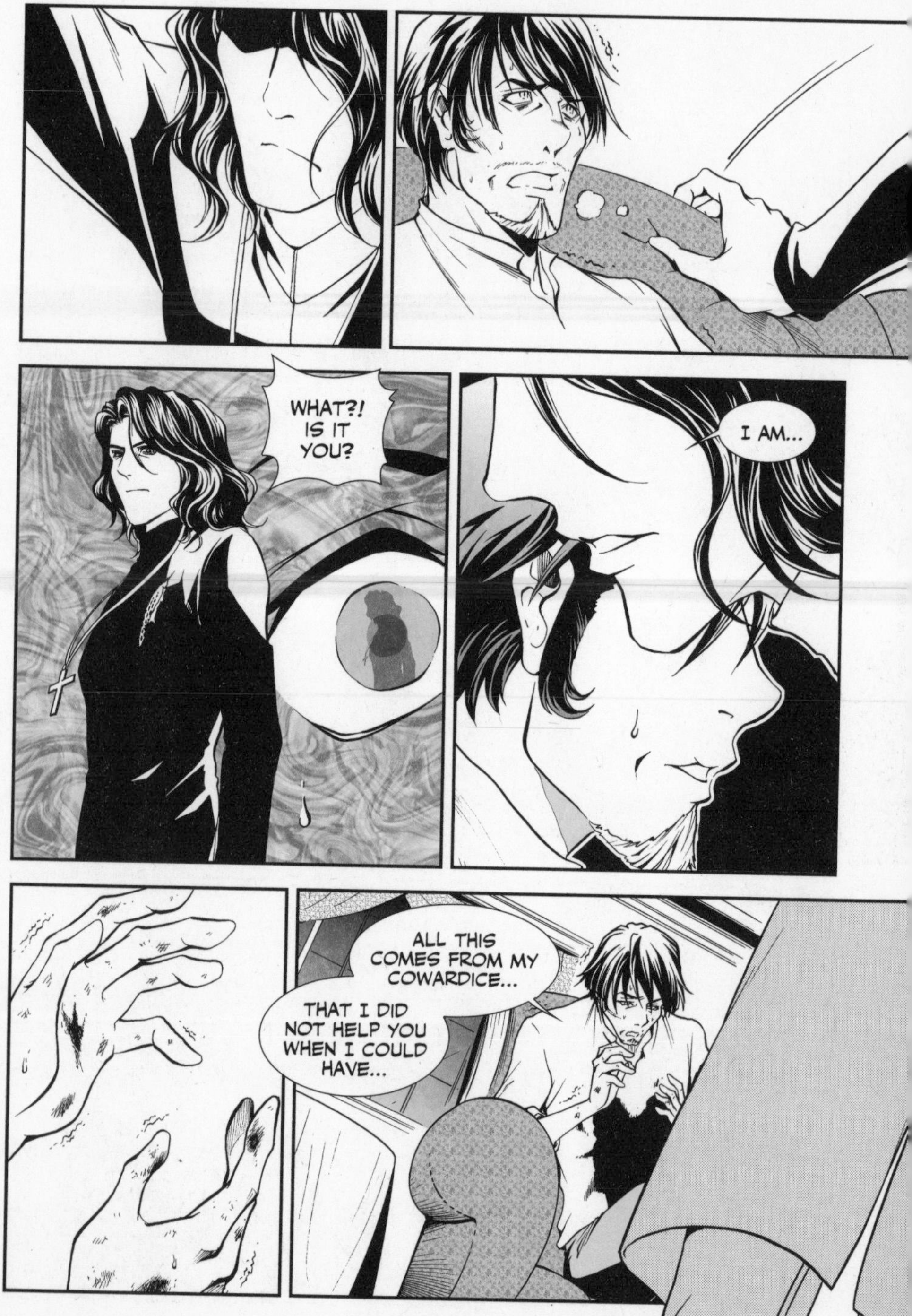
I AM...
WHAT?! IS IT YOU?
ALL THIS COMES FROM MY COWARDICE...
THAT I DID NOT HELP YOU WHEN I COULD HAVE...

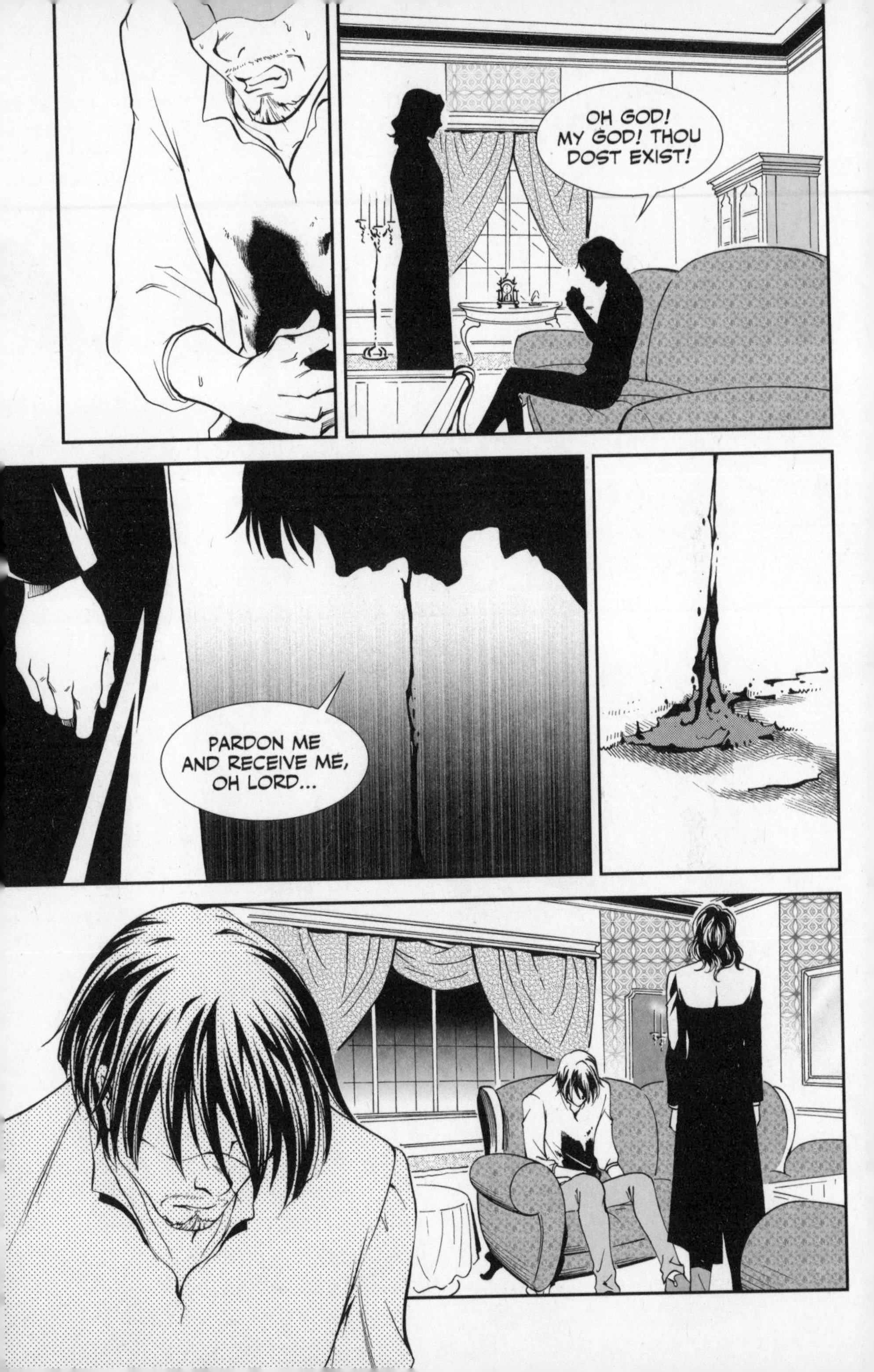
OH GOD! MY GOD! THOU DOST EXIST!
PARDON ME AND RECEIVE ME, OH LORD...

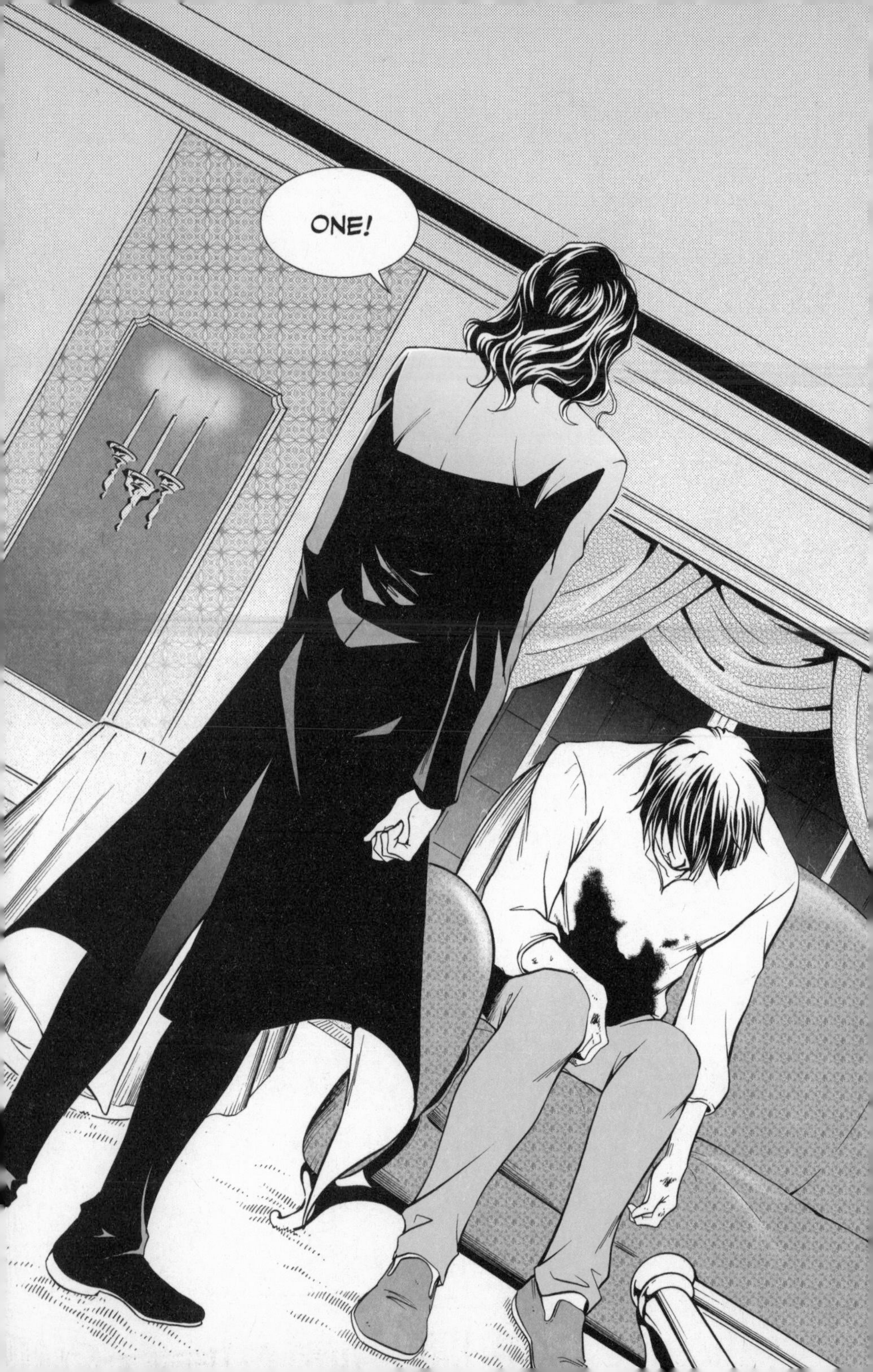
ONE!

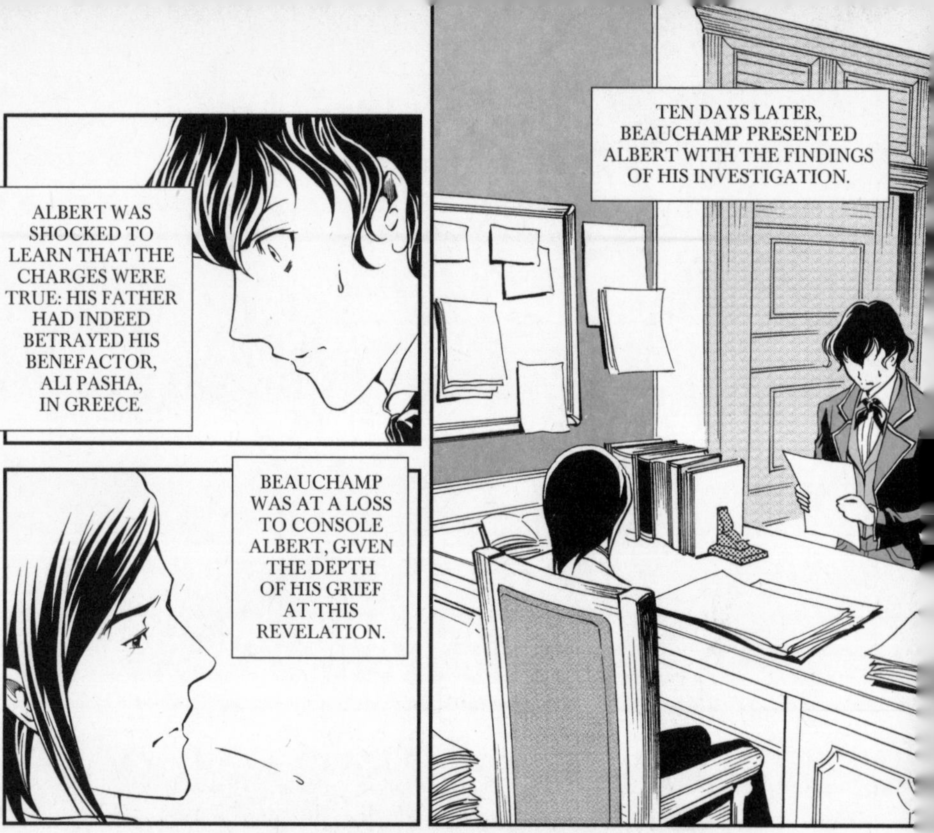
TEN DAYS LATER, BEAUCHAMP PRESENTED ALBERT WITH THE FINDINGS OF HIS INVESTIGATION.
ALBERT WAS SHOCKED TO LEARN THAT THE CHARGES WERE TRUE: HIS FATHER HAD INDEED BETRAYED HIS BENEFACTOR, ALI PASHA, IN GREECE.
BEAUCHAMP WAS AT A LOSS TO CONSOLE ALBERT, GIVEN THE DEPTH OF HIS GRIEF AT THIS REVELATION.

FURTHER, BEAUCHAMP'S INVESTIGATIONS WERE REPORTED IN A DIFFERENT NEWSPAPER, CREATING A LARGE SCANDAL. SINCE COUNT DE MORCERF WAS A GOVERNMENT EMPLOYEE, A TRIAL WAS IMMEDIATELY SCHEDULED.

CHAPTER 10 Father and Son

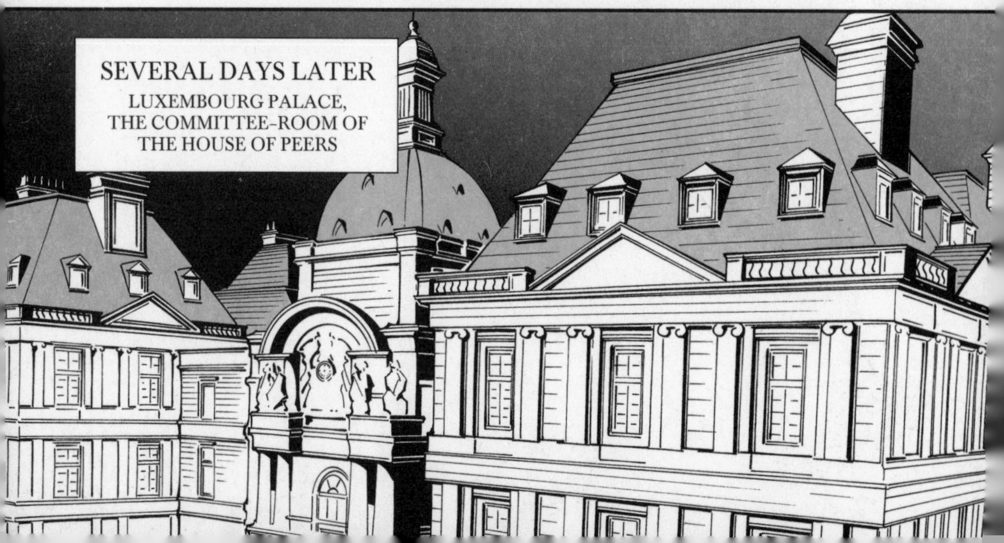
SEVERAL DAYS LATER
LUXEMBOURG PALACE, THE COMMITTEE-ROOM OF THE HOUSE OF PEERS

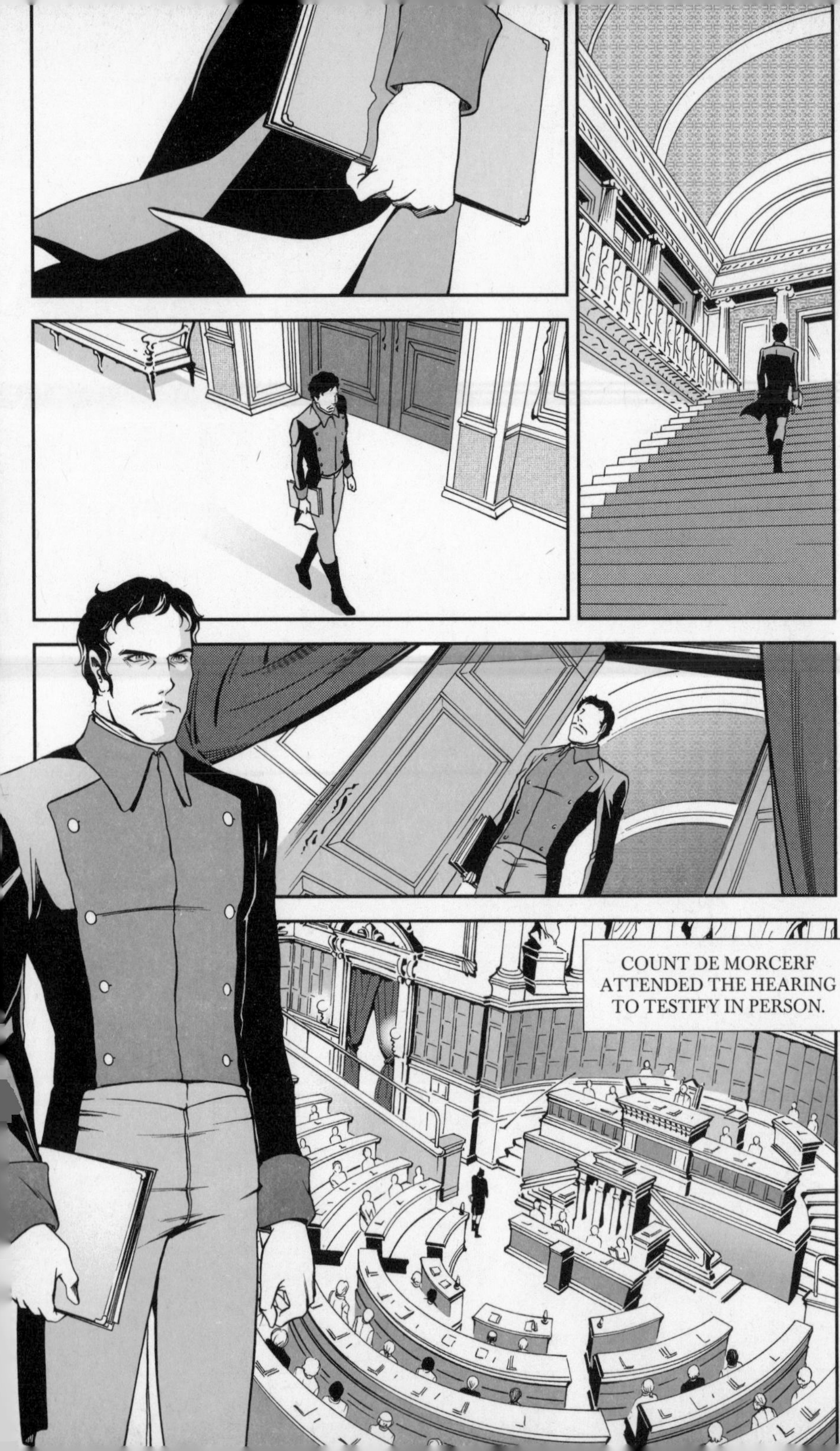
COUNT DE MORCERF ATTENDED THE HEARING TO TESTIFY IN PERSON.

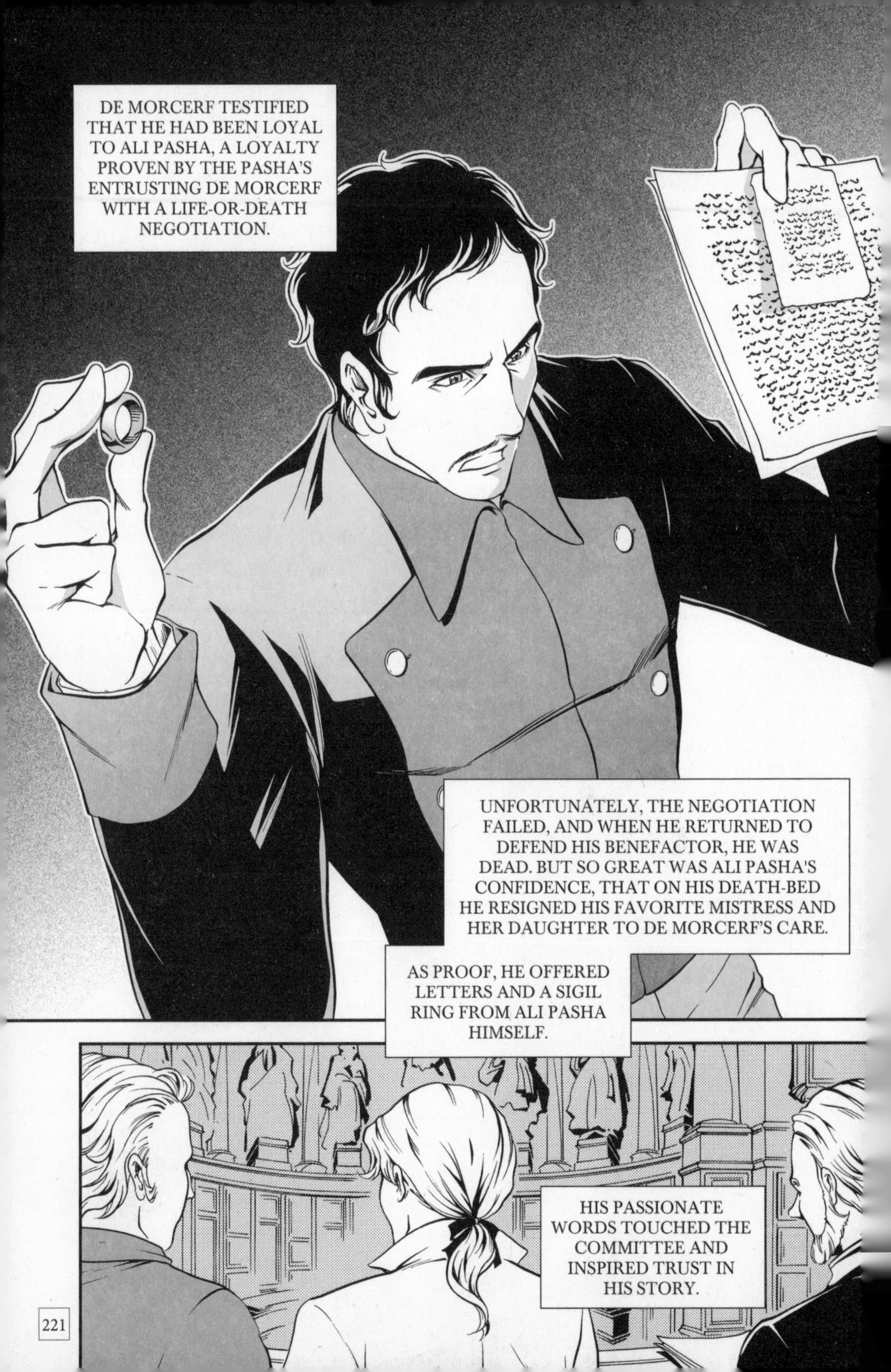
DE MORCERF TESTIFIED THAT HE HAD BEEN LOYAL TO ALI PASHA, A LOYALTY PROVEN BY THE PASHA'S ENTRUSTING DE MORCERF WITH A LIFE-OR-DEATH NEGOTIATION.
UNFORTUNATELY, THE NEGOTIATION FAILED, AND WHEN HE RETURNED TO DEFEND HIS BENEFACTOR, HE WAS DEAD. BUT SO GREAT WAS ALI PASHA'S CONFIDENCE, THAT ON HIS DEATH-BED HE RESIGNED HIS FAVORITE MISTRESS AND HER DAUGHTER TO DE MORCERF'S CARE.
AS PROOF, HE OFFERED LETTERS AND A SIGIL RING FROM ALI PASHA HIMSELF.
HIS PASSIONATE WORDS TOUCHED THE COMMITTEE AND INSPIRED TRUST IN HIS STORY.

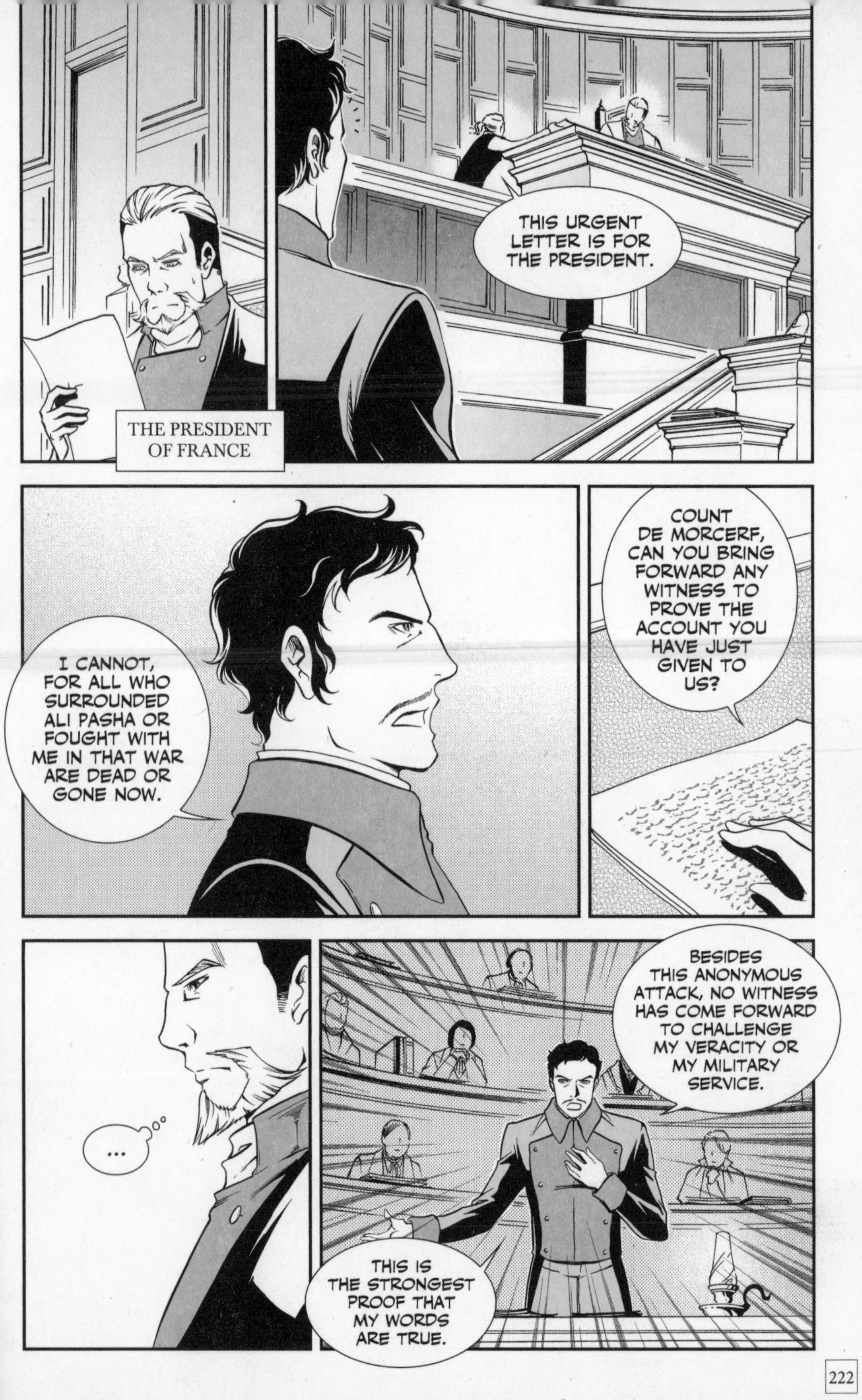
THIS URGENT LETTER IS FOR THE PRESIDENT.
THE PRESIDENT OF FRANCE
COUNT DE MORCERF, CAN YOU BRING FORWARD ANY WITNESS TO PROVE THE ACCOUNT YOU HAVE JUST GIVEN TO US?
I CANNOT, FOR ALL WHO SURROUNDED ALI PASHA OR FOUGHT WITH ME IN THAT WAR ARE DEAD OR GONE NOW.
BESIDES THIS ANONYMOUS ATTACK, NO WITNESS HAS COME FORWARD TO CHALLENGE MY VERACITY OR MY MILITARY SERVICE.
THIS IS THE STRONGEST PROOF THAT MY WORDS ARE TRUE.
...

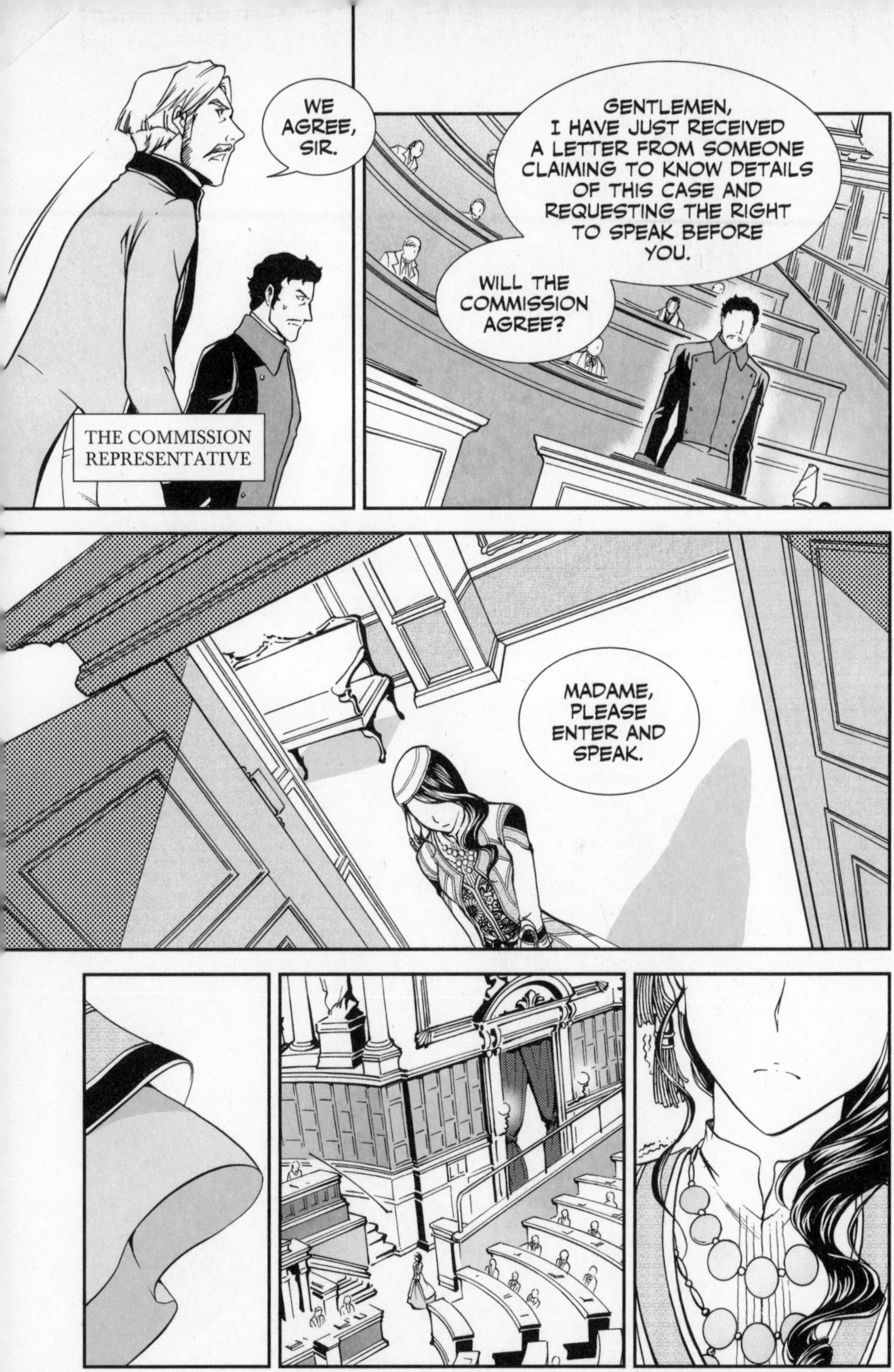
GENTLEMEN, I HAVE JUST RECEIVED A LETTER FROM SOMEONE CLAIMING TO KNOW DETAILS OF THIS CASE AND REQUESTING THE RIGHT TO SPEAK BEFORE YOU.
WILL THE COMMISSION AGREE?
WE AGREE, SIR.
THE COMMISSION REPRESENTATIVE
MADAME, PLEASE ENTER AND SPEAK.

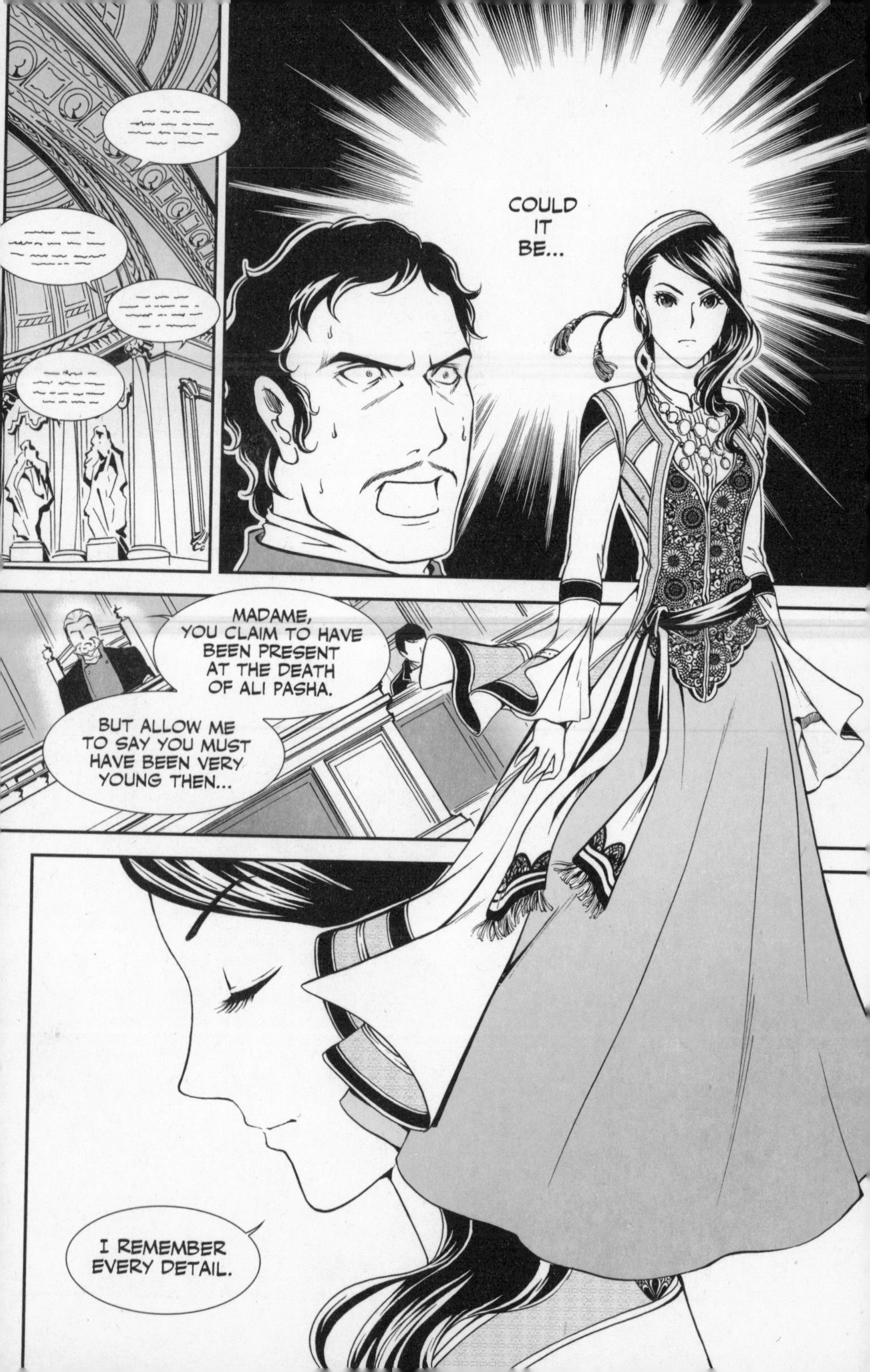
COULD IT BE...
MADAME, YOU CLAIM TO HAVE BEEN PRESENT AT THE DEATH OF ALI PASHA.
BUT ALLOW ME TO SAY YOU MUST HAVE BEEN VERY YOUNG THEN...
I REMEMBER EVERY DETAIL.

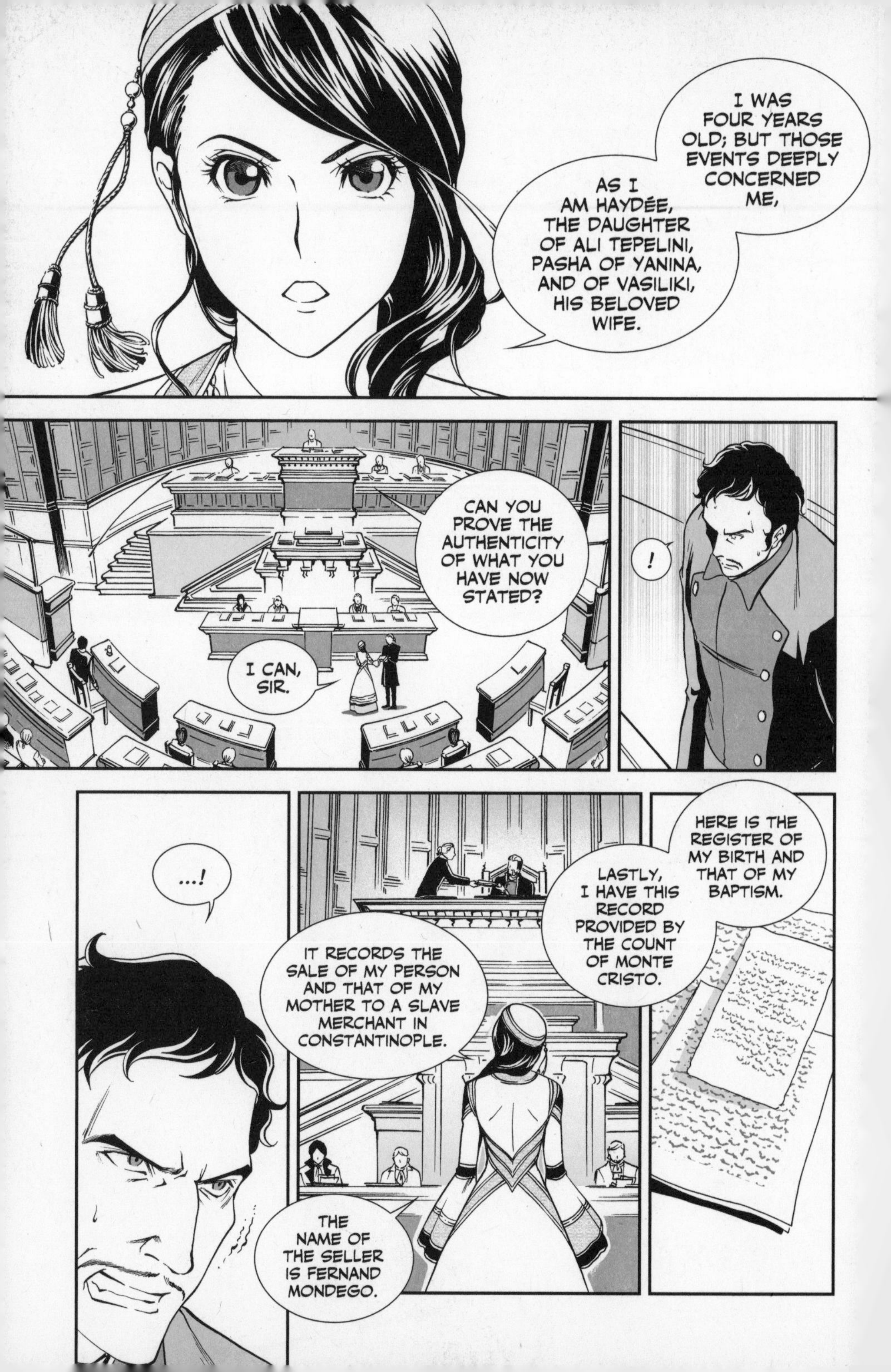
I WAS FOUR YEARS OLD; BUT THOSE EVENTS DEEPLY CONCERNED ME,
AS I AM HAYDÉE, THE DAUGHTER OF ALI TEPELINI, PASHA OF YANINA, AND OF VASILIKI, HIS BELOVED WIFE.
!
CAN YOU PROVE THE AUTHENTICITY OF WHAT YOU HAVE NOW STATED?
I CAN, SIR.
HERE IS THE REGISTER OF MY BIRTH AND THAT OF MY BAPTISM.
LASTLY, I HAVE THIS RECORD PROVIDED BY THE COUNT OF MONTE CRISTO.
IT RECORDS THE SALE OF MY PERSON AND THAT OF MY MOTHER TO A SLAVE MERCHANT IN CONSTANTINOPLE.
THE NAME OF THE SELLER IS FERNAND MONDEGO.
...!

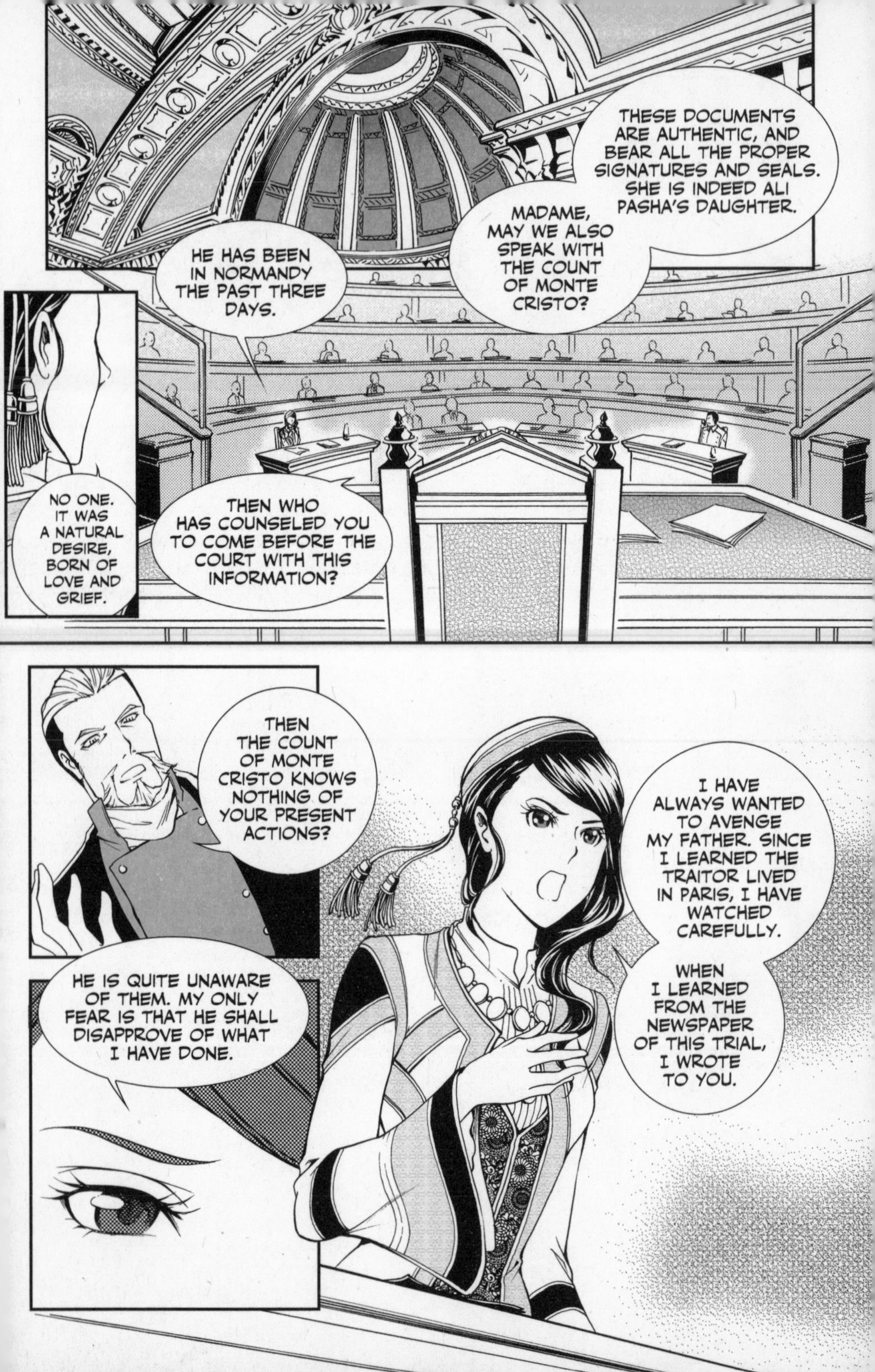
THESE DOCUMENTS ARE AUTHENTIC, AND BEAR ALL THE PROPER SIGNATURES AND SEALS. SHE IS INDEED ALI PASHA'S DAUGHTER.
MADAME, MAY WE ALSO SPEAK WITH THE COUNT OF MONTE CRISTO?
HE HAS BEEN IN NORMANDY THE PAST THREE DAYS.
THEN WHO HAS COUNSELED YOU TO COME BEFORE THE COURT WITH THIS INFORMATION?
NO ONE. IT WAS A NATURAL DESIRE, BORN OF LOVE AND GRIEF.
I HAVE ALWAYS WANTED TO AVENGE MY FATHER. SINCE I LEARNED THE TRAITOR LIVED IN PARIS, I HAVE WATCHED CAREFULLY.
WHEN I LEARNED FROM THE NEWSPAPER OF THIS TRIAL, I WROTE TO YOU.
THEN THE COUNT OF MONTE CRISTO KNOWS NOTHING OF YOUR PRESENT ACTIONS?
HE IS QUITE UNAWARE OF THEM. MY ONLY FEAR IS THAT HE SHALL DISAPPROVE OF WHAT I HAVE DONE.

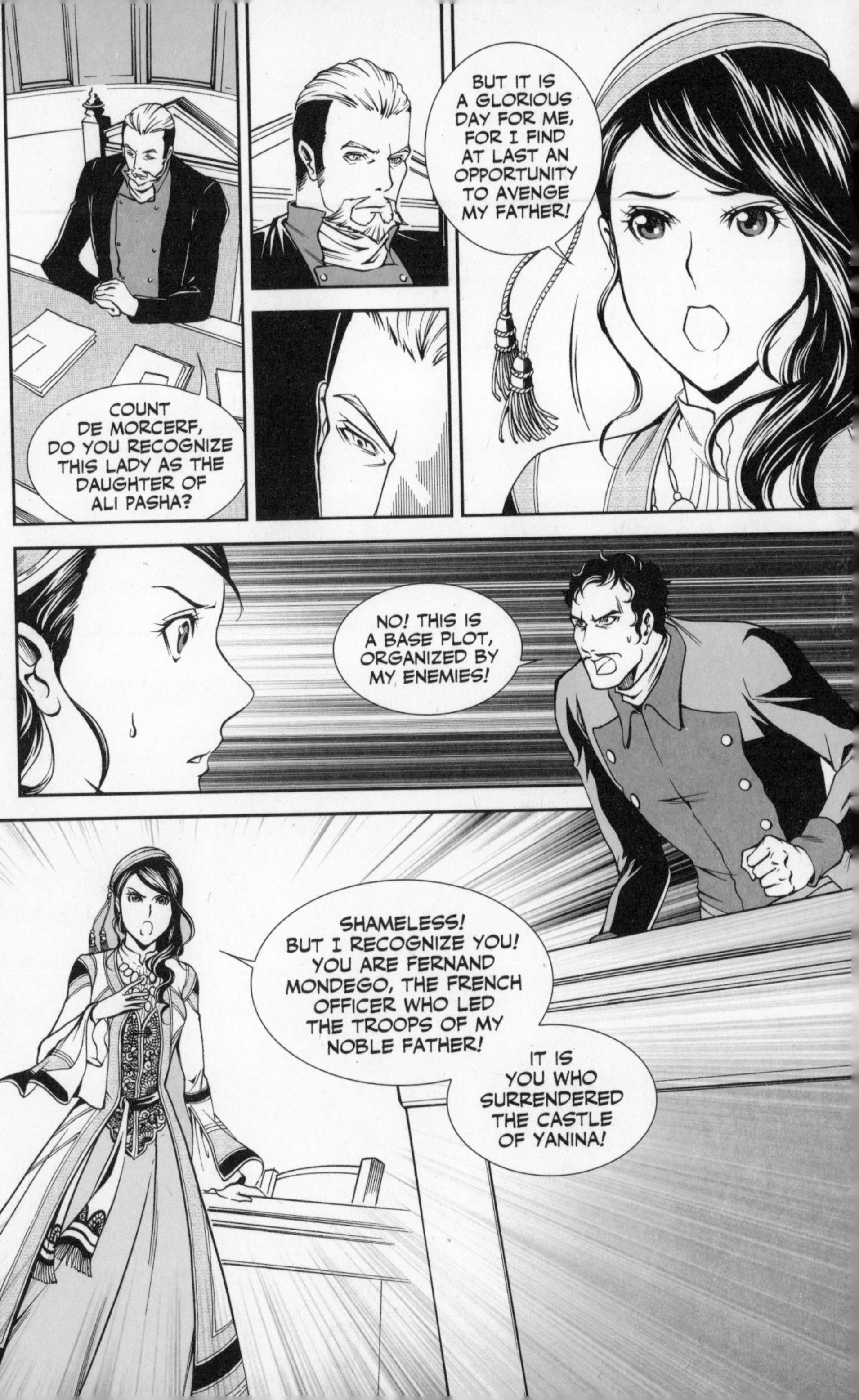
BUT IT IS A GLORIOUS DAY FOR ME, FOR I FIND AT LAST AN OPPORTUNITY TO AVENGE MY FATHER!
COUNT DE MORCERF, DO YOU RECOGNIZE THIS LADY AS THE DAUGHTER OF ALI PASHA?
NO! THIS IS A BASE PLOT, ORGANIZED BY MY ENEMIES!
SHAMELESS! BUT I RECOGNIZE YOU! YOU ARE FERNAND MONDEGO, THE FRENCH OFFICER WHO LED THE TROOPS OF MY NOBLE FATHER!
IT IS YOU WHO SURRENDERED THE CASTLE OF YANINA!

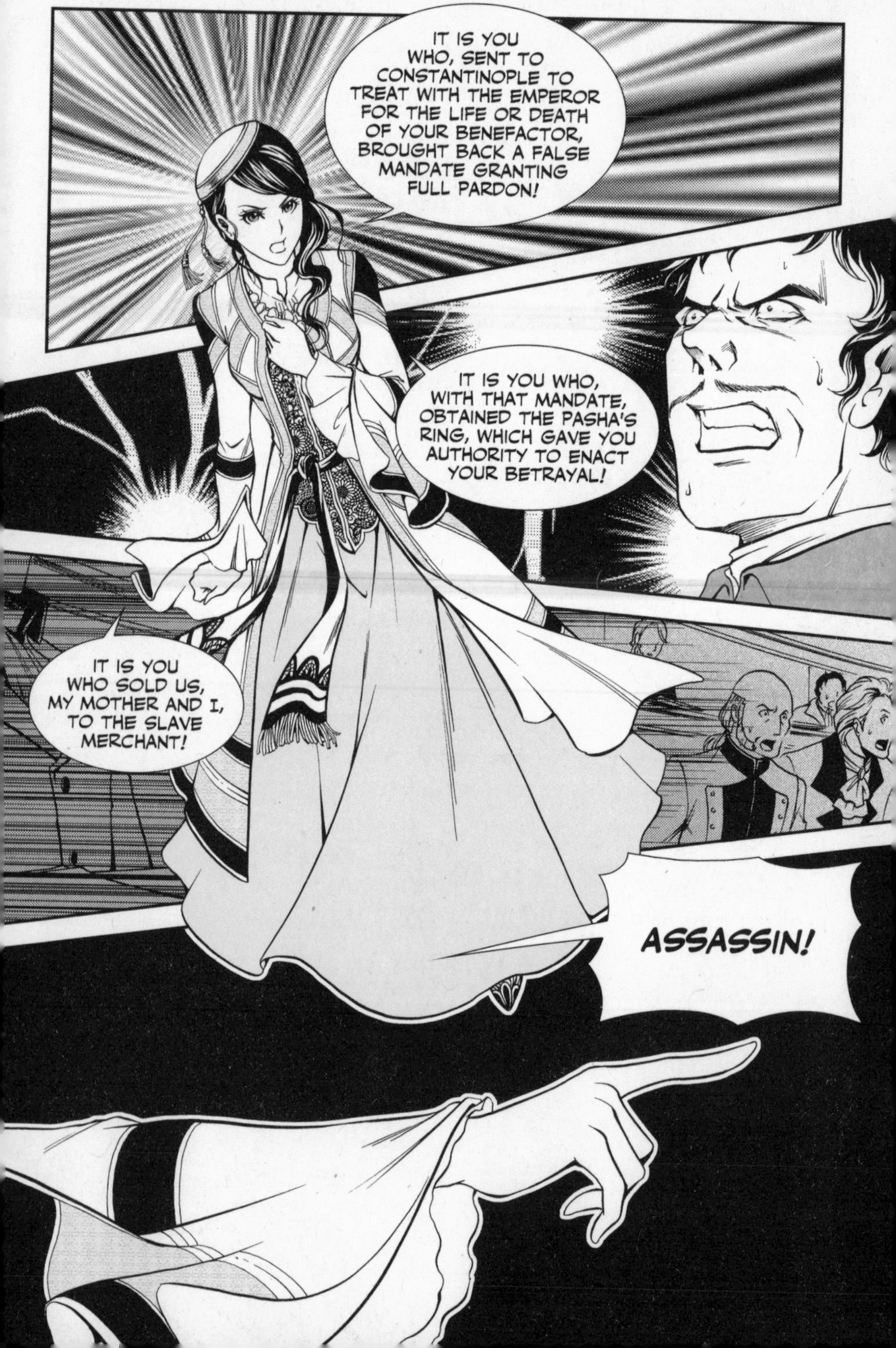
IT IS YOU WHO, SENT TO CONSTANTINOPLE TO TREAT WITH THE EMPEROR FOR THE LIFE OR DEATH OF YOUR BENEFACTOR, BROUGHT BACK A FALSE MANDATE GRANTING FULL PARDON!
IT IS YOU WHO, WITH THAT MANDATE, OBTAINED THE PASHA'S RING, WHICH GAVE YOU AUTHORITY TO ENACT YOUR BETRAYAL!
IT IS YOU WHO SOLD US, MY MOTHER AND I, TO THE SLAVE MERCHANT!
ASSASSIN!

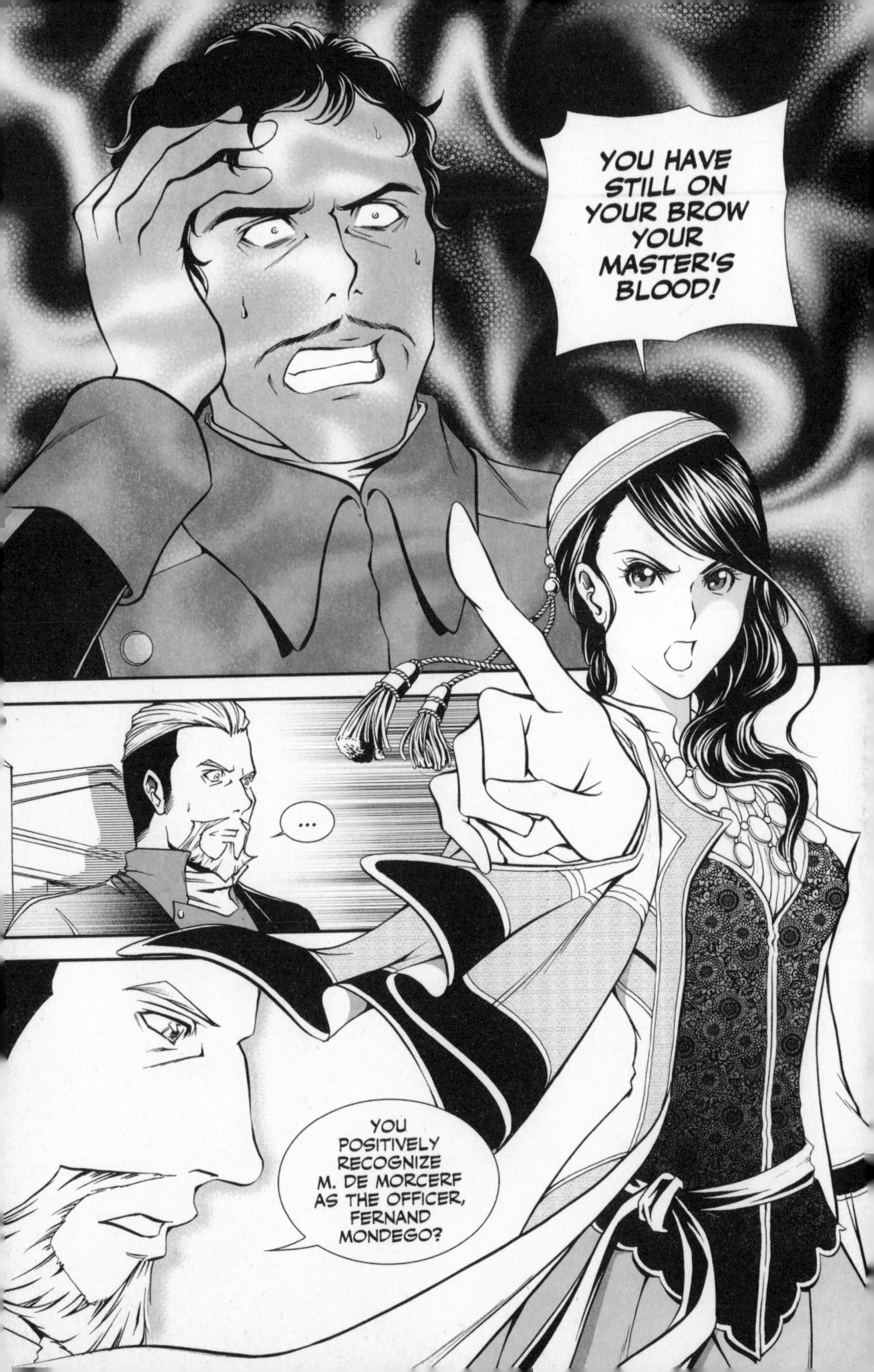
YOU HAVE STILL ON YOUR BROW YOUR MASTER'S BLOOD!
...
YOU POSITIVELY RECOGNIZE M. DE MORCERF AS THE OFFICER, FERNAND MONDEGO?

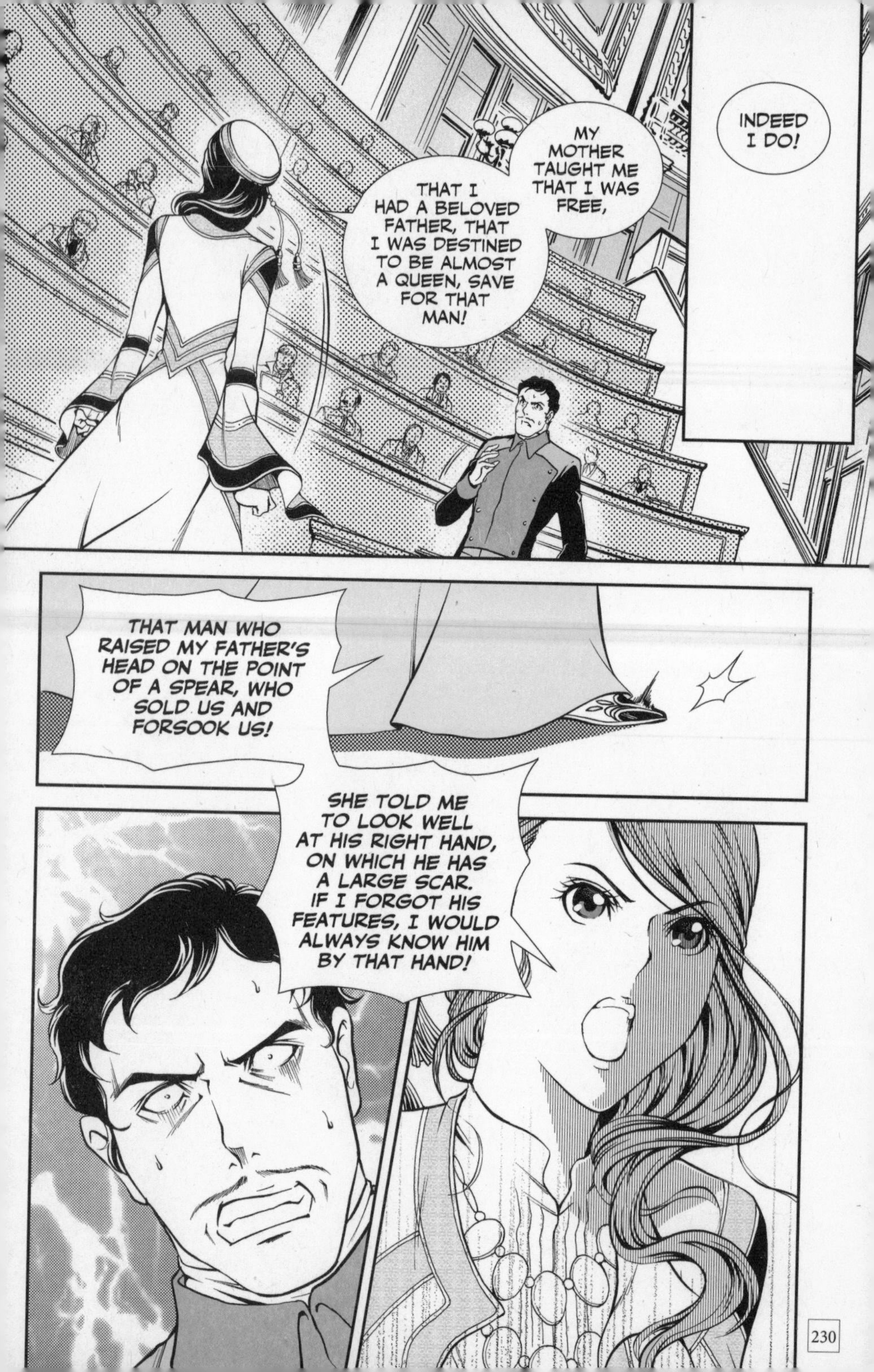
INDEED I DO!
MY MOTHER TAUGHT ME THAT I WAS FREE,
THAT I HAD A BELOVED FATHER, THAT I WAS DESTINED TO BE ALMOST A QUEEN, SAVE FOR THAT MAN!
THAT MAN WHO RAISED MY FATHER'S HEAD ON THE POINT OF A SPEAR, WHO SOLD US AND FORSOOK US!
SHE TOLD ME TO LOOK WELL AT HIS RIGHT HAND, ON WHICH HE HAS A LARGE SCAR. IF I FORGOT HIS FEATURES, I WOULD ALWAYS KNOW HIM BY THAT HAND!

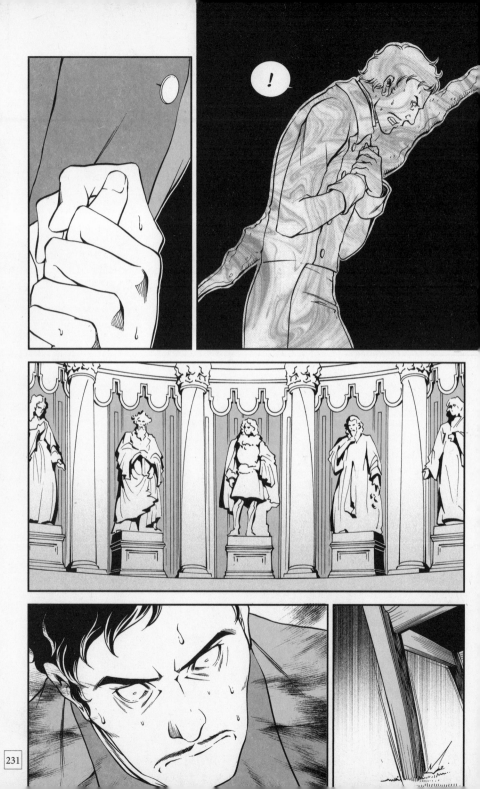

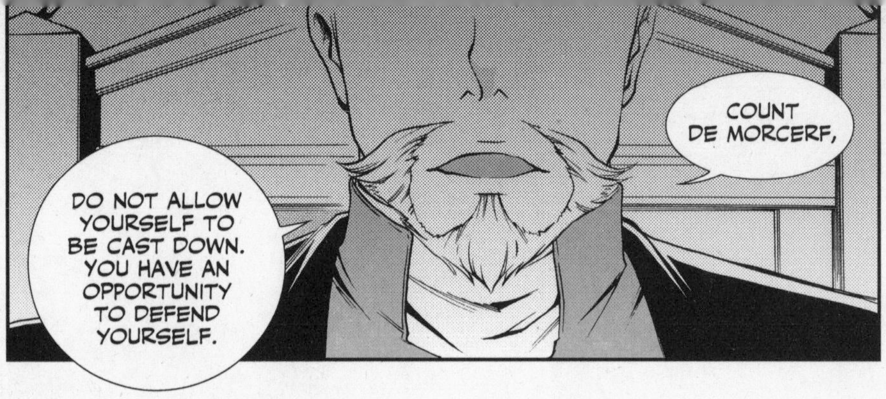
COUNT DE MORCERF,
DO NOT ALLOW YOURSELF TO BE CAST DOWN. YOU HAVE AN OPPORTUNITY TO DEFEND YOURSELF.

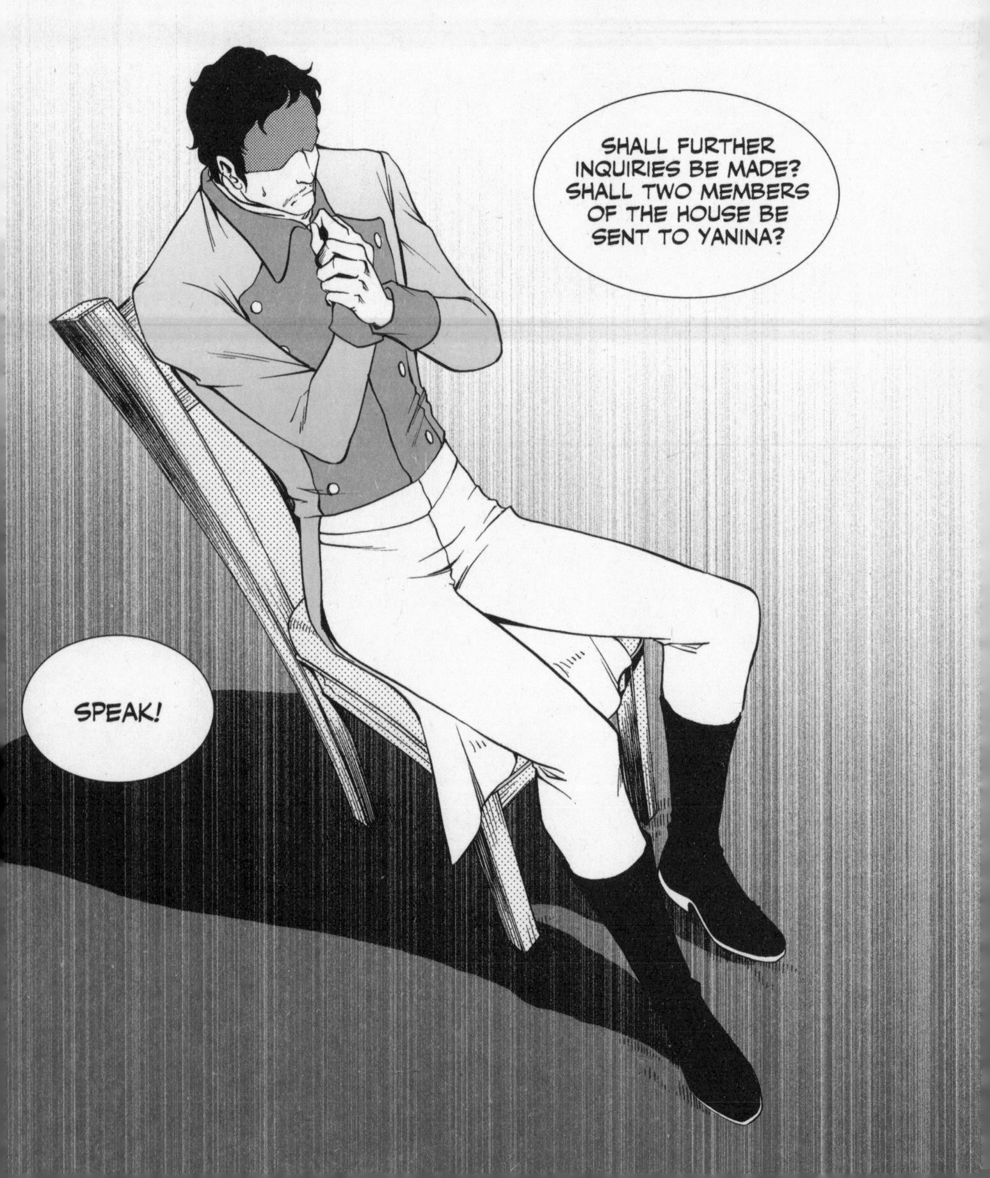
SHALL FURTHER INQUIRIES BE MADE? SHALL TWO MEMBERS OF THE HOUSE BE SENT TO YANINA?
SPEAK!

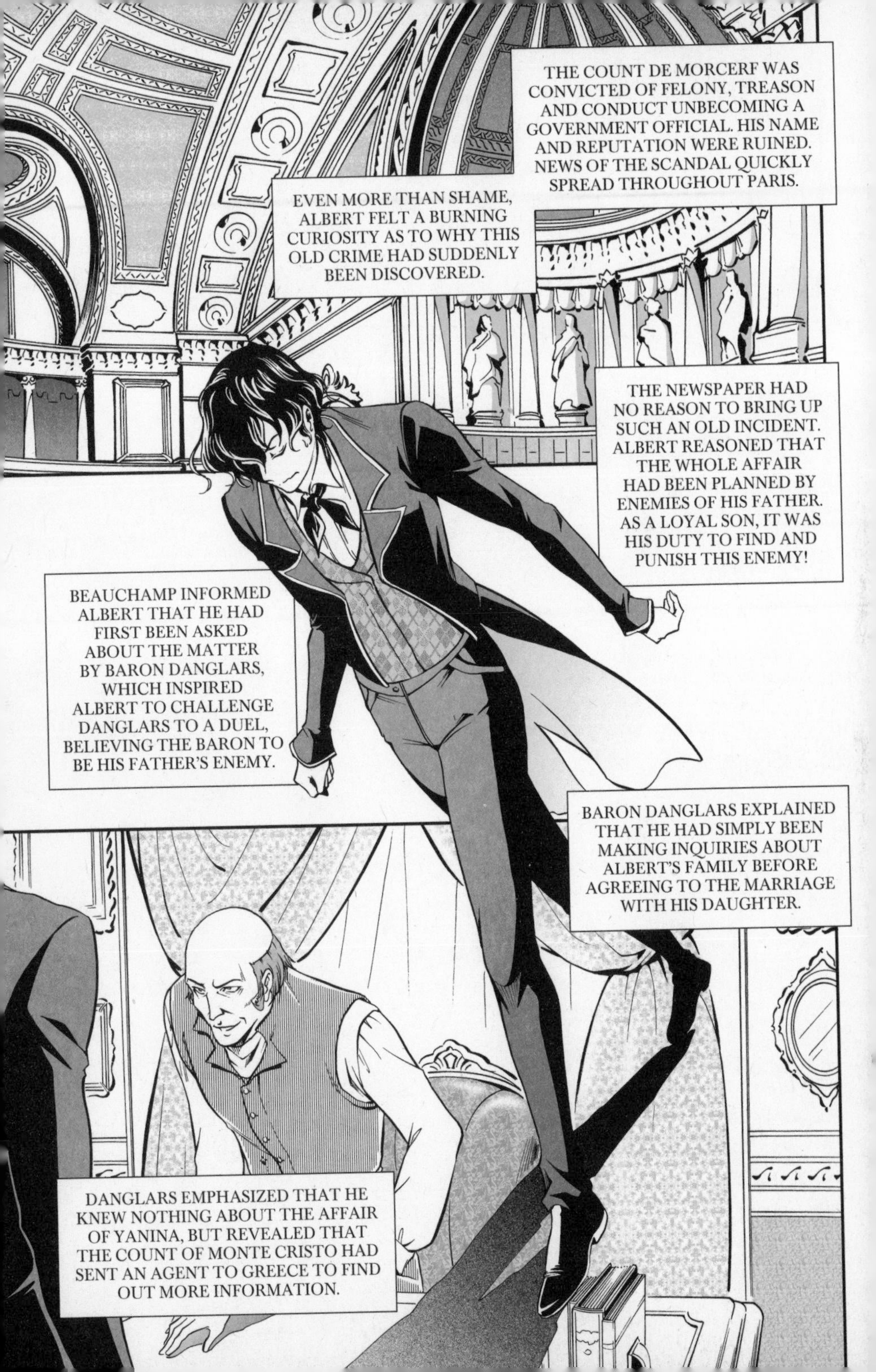
THE COUNT DE MORCERF WAS CONVICTED OF FELONY, TREASON AND CONDUCT UNBECOMING A GOVERNMENT OFFICIAL. HIS NAME AND REPUTATION WERE RUINED. NEWS OF THE SCANDAL QUICKLY SPREAD THROUGHOUT PARIS.
EVEN MORE THAN SHAME, ALBERT FELT A BURNING CURIOSITY AS TO WHY THIS OLD CRIME HAD SUDDENLY BEEN DISCOVERED.
THE NEWSPAPER HAD NO REASON TO BRING UP SUCH AN OLD INCIDENT. ALBERT REASONED THAT THE WHOLE AFFAIR HAD BEEN PLANNED BY ENEMIES OF HIS FATHER. AS A LOYAL SON, IT WAS HIS DUTY TO FIND AND PUNISH THIS ENEMY!
BEAUCHAMP INFORMED ALBERT THAT HE HAD FIRST BEEN ASKED ABOUT THE MATTER BY BARON DANGLARS, WHICH INSPIRED ALBERT TO CHALLENGE DANGLARS TO A DUEL, BELIEVING THE BARON TO BE HIS FATHER'S ENEMY.
BARON DANGLARS EXPLAINED THAT HE HAD SIMPLY BEEN MAKING INQUIRIES ABOUT ALBERT'S FAMILY BEFORE AGREEING TO THE MARRIAGE WITH HIS DAUGHTER.
DANGLARS EMPHASIZED THAT HE KNEW NOTHING ABOUT THE AFFAIR OF YANINA, BUT REVEALED THAT THE COUNT OF MONTE CRISTO HAD SENT AN AGENT TO GREECE TO FIND OUT MORE INFORMATION.

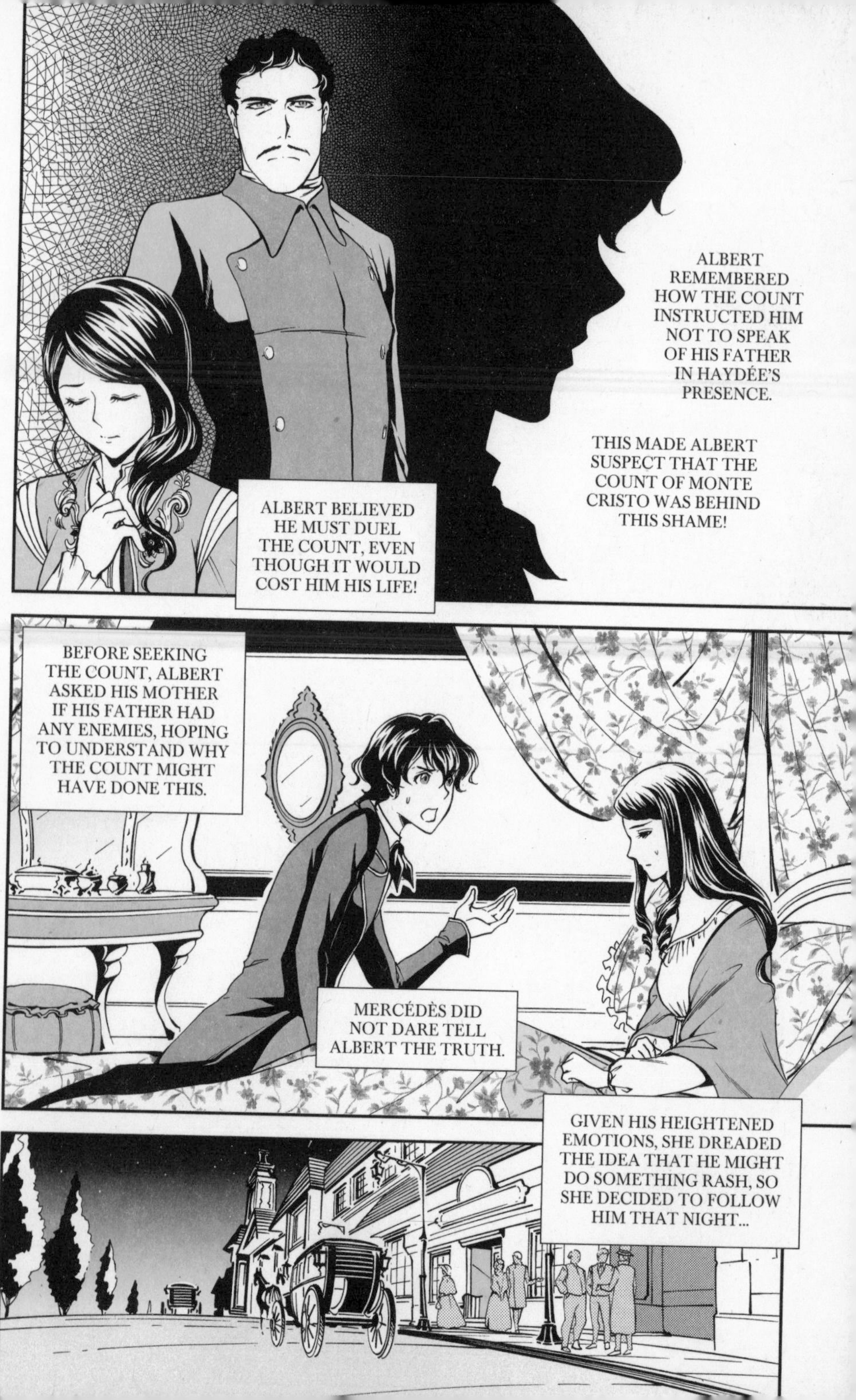
ALBERT REMEMBERED HOW THE COUNT INSTRUCTED HIM NOT TO SPEAK OF HIS FATHER IN HAYDÉE'S PRESENCE.
THIS MADE ALBERT SUSPECT THAT THE COUNT OF MONTE CRISTO WAS BEHIND THIS SHAME!
ALBERT BELIEVED HE MUST DUEL THE COUNT, EVEN THOUGH IT WOULD COST HIM HIS LIFE!
BEFORE SEEKING THE COUNT, ALBERT ASKED HIS MOTHER IF HIS FATHER HAD ANY ENEMIES, HOPING TO UNDERSTAND WHY THE COUNT MIGHT HAVE DONE THIS.
MERCÉDÈS DID NOT DARE TELL ALBERT THE TRUTH.
GIVEN HIS HEIGHTENED EMOTIONS, SHE DREADED THE IDEA THAT HE MIGHT DO SOMETHING RASH, SO SHE DECIDED TO FOLLOW HIM THAT NIGHT...

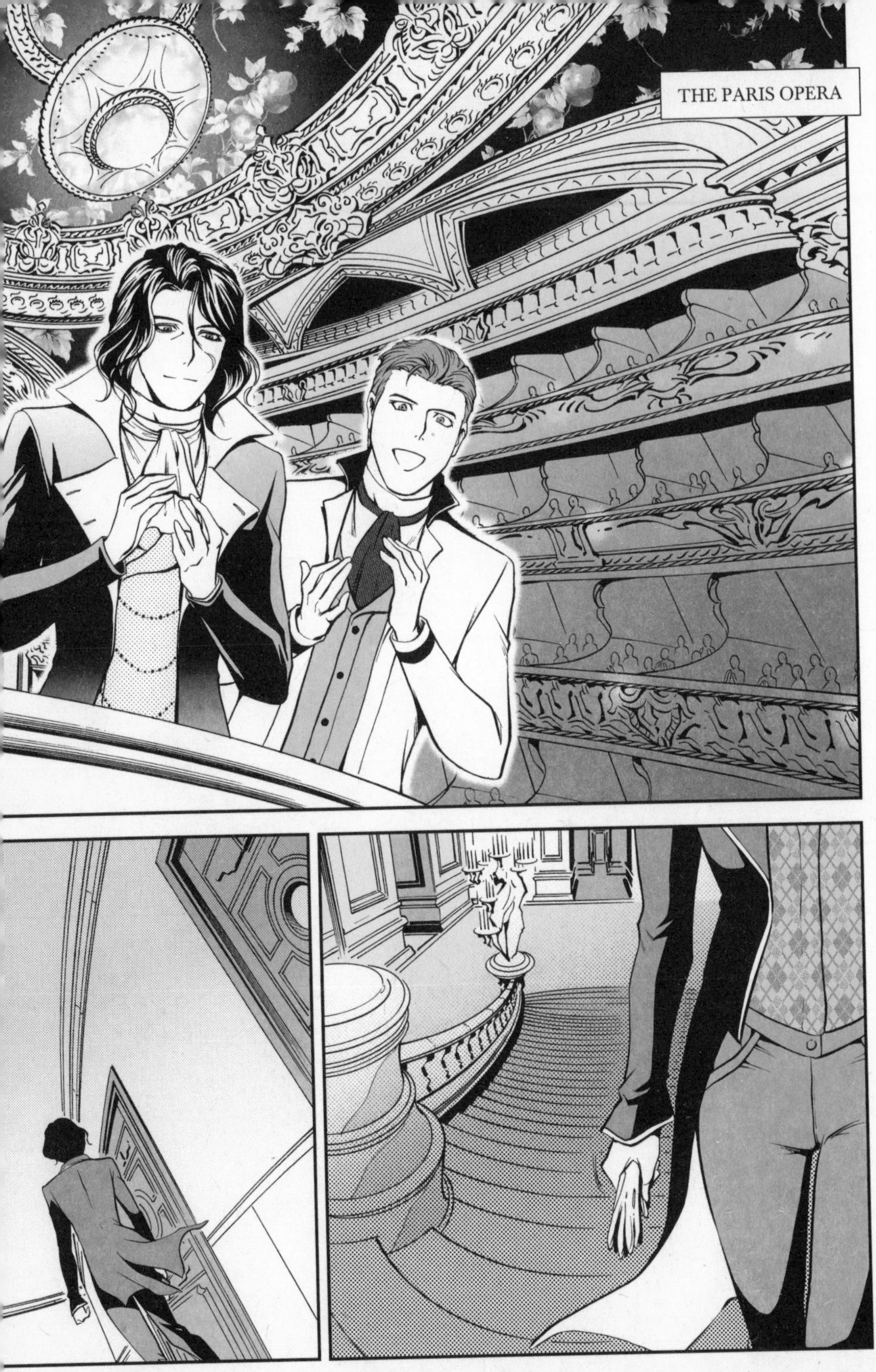
THE PARIS OPERA

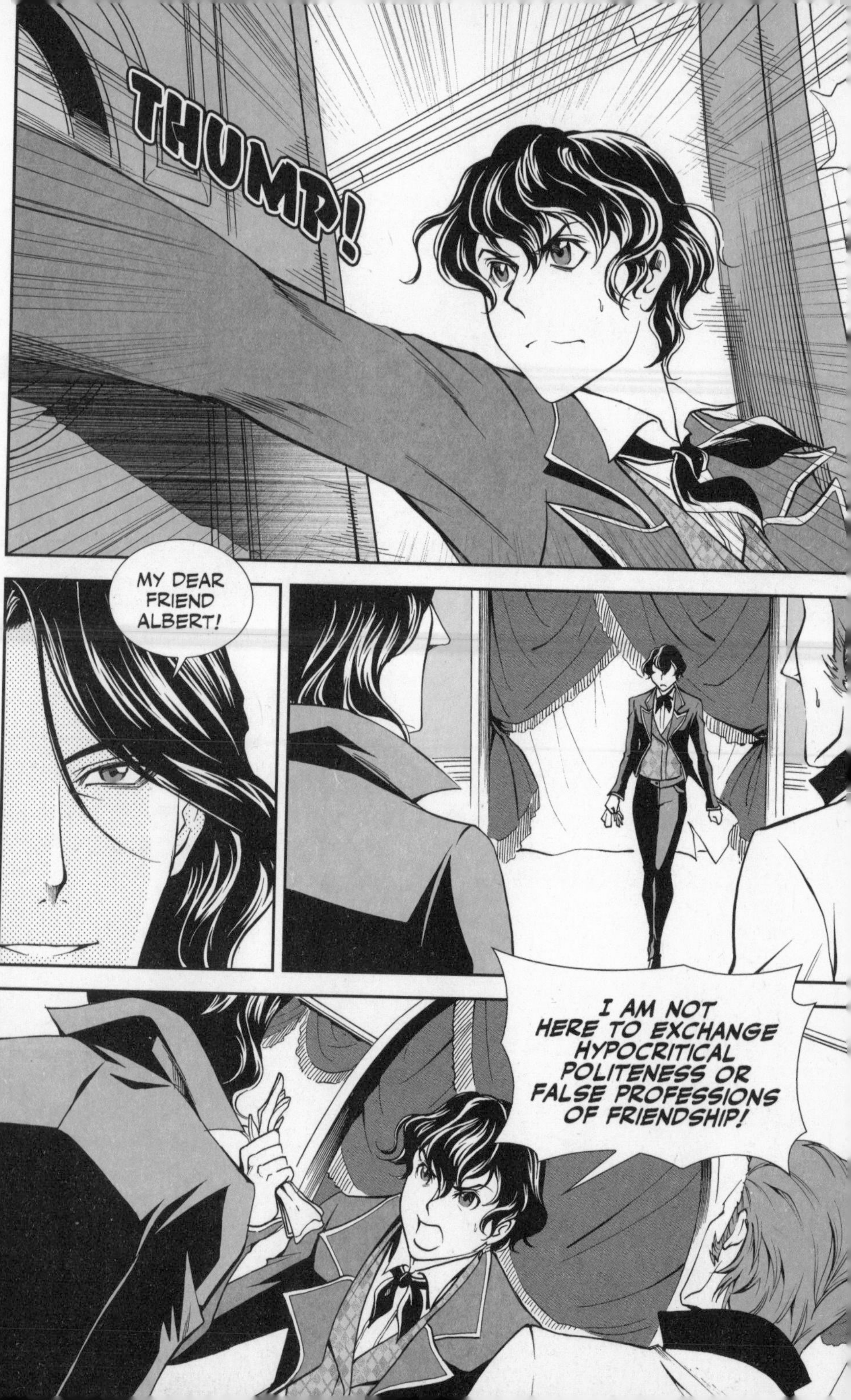
THUMP!
MY DEAR FRIEND ALBERT!
I AM NOT HERE TO EXCHANGE HYPOCRITICAL POLITENESS OR FALSE PROFESSIONS OF FRIENDSHIP!

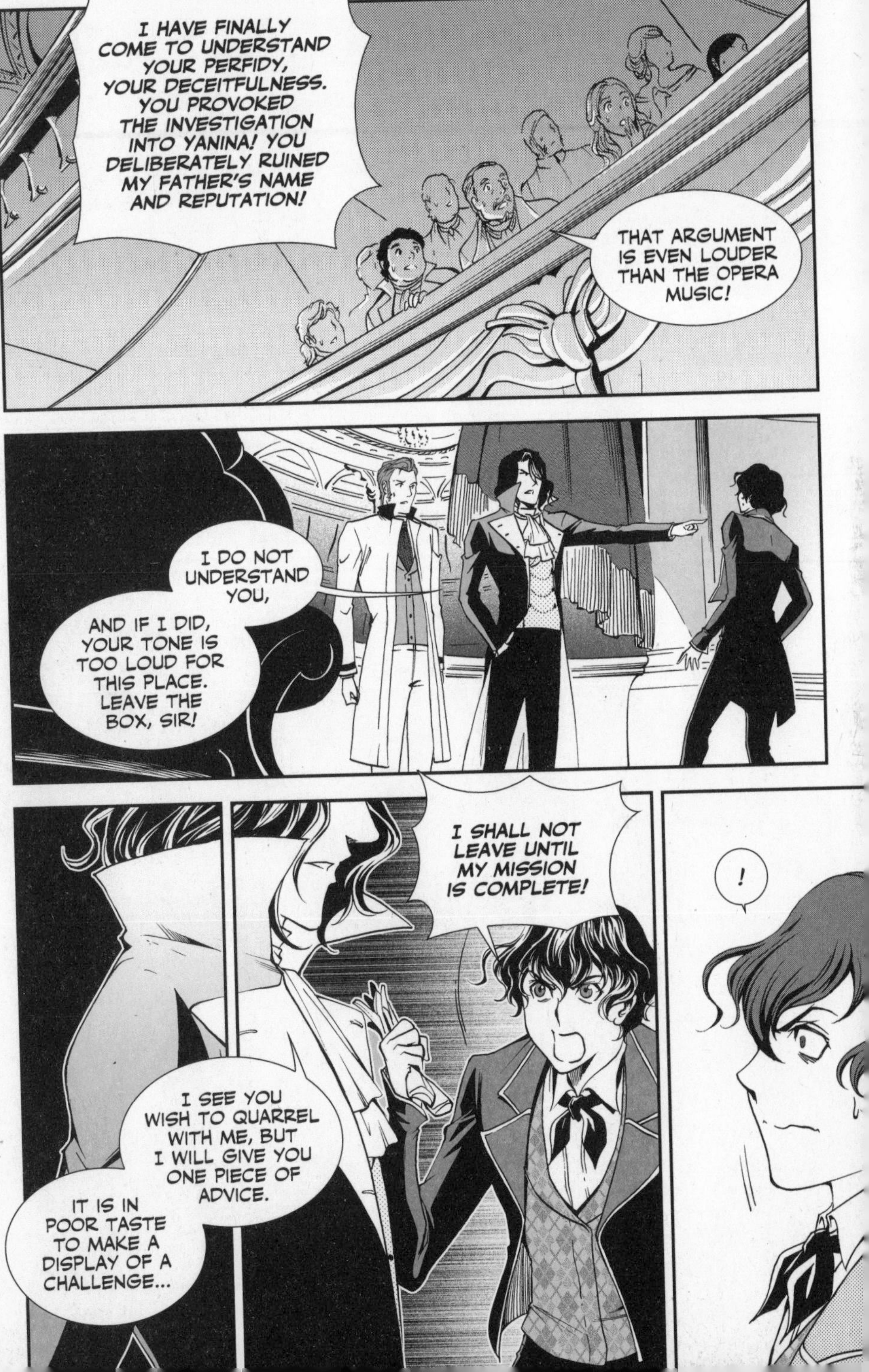
I HAVE FINALLY COME TO UNDERSTAND YOUR PERFIDY, YOUR DECEITFULNESS. YOU PROVOKED THE INVESTIGATION INTO YANINA! YOU DELIBERATELY RUINED MY FATHER'S NAME AND REPUTATION!
THAT ARGUMENT IS EVEN LOUDER THAN THE OPERA MUSIC!
I DO NOT UNDERSTAND YOU,
AND IF I DID, YOUR TONE IS TOO LOUD FOR THIS PLACE. LEAVE THE BOX, SIR!
!
I SHALL NOT LEAVE UNTIL MY MISSION IS COMPLETE!
I SEE YOU WISH TO QUARREL WITH ME, BUT I WILL GIVE YOU ONE PIECE OF ADVICE.
IT IS IN POOR TASTE TO MAKE A DISPLAY OF A CHALLENGE...

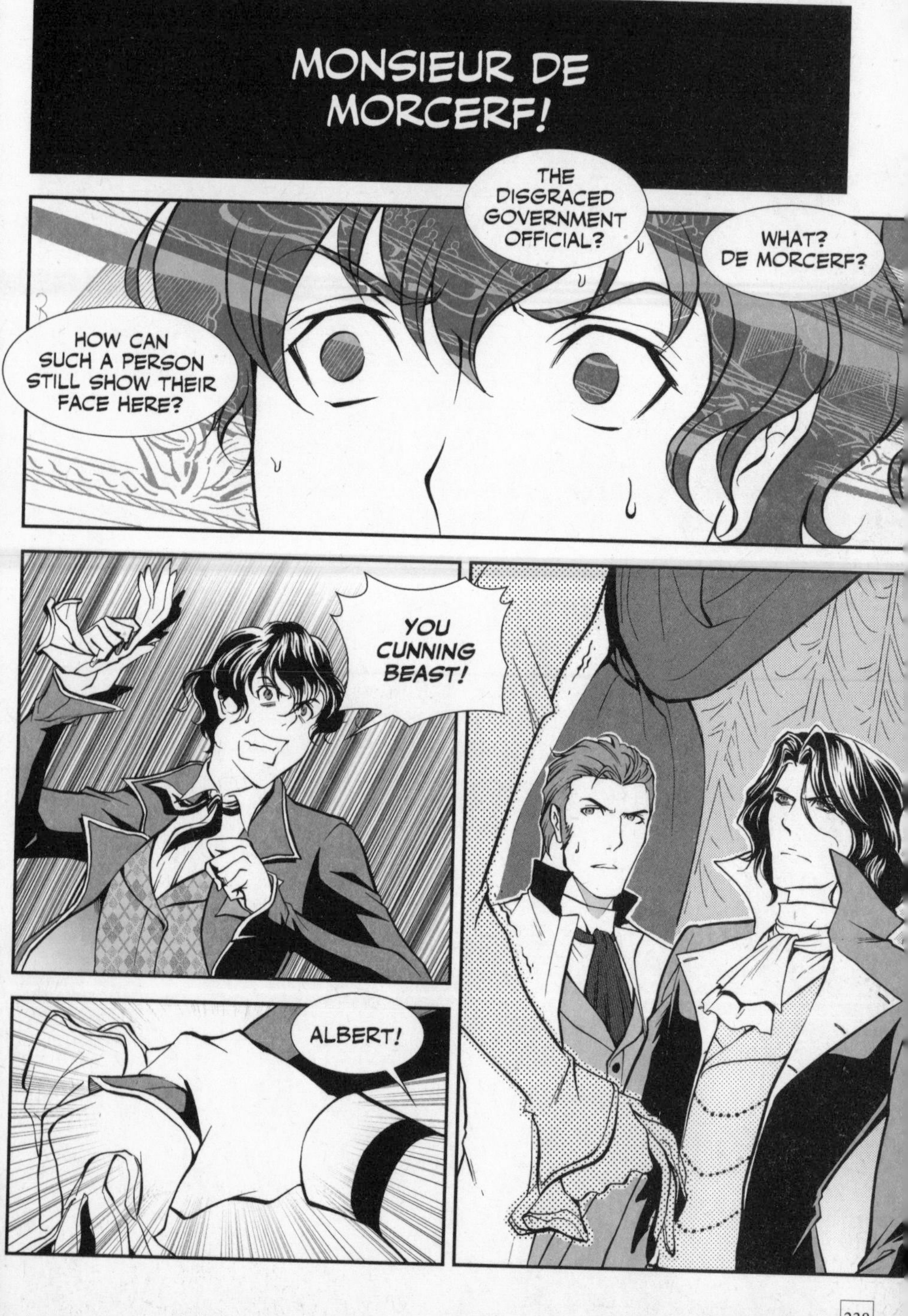
MONSIEUR DE MORCERF!
WHAT? DE MORCERF?
THE DISGRACED GOVERNMENT OFFICIAL?
HOW CAN SUCH A PERSON STILL SHOW THEIR FACE HERE?
YOU CUNNING BEAST!
ALBERT!

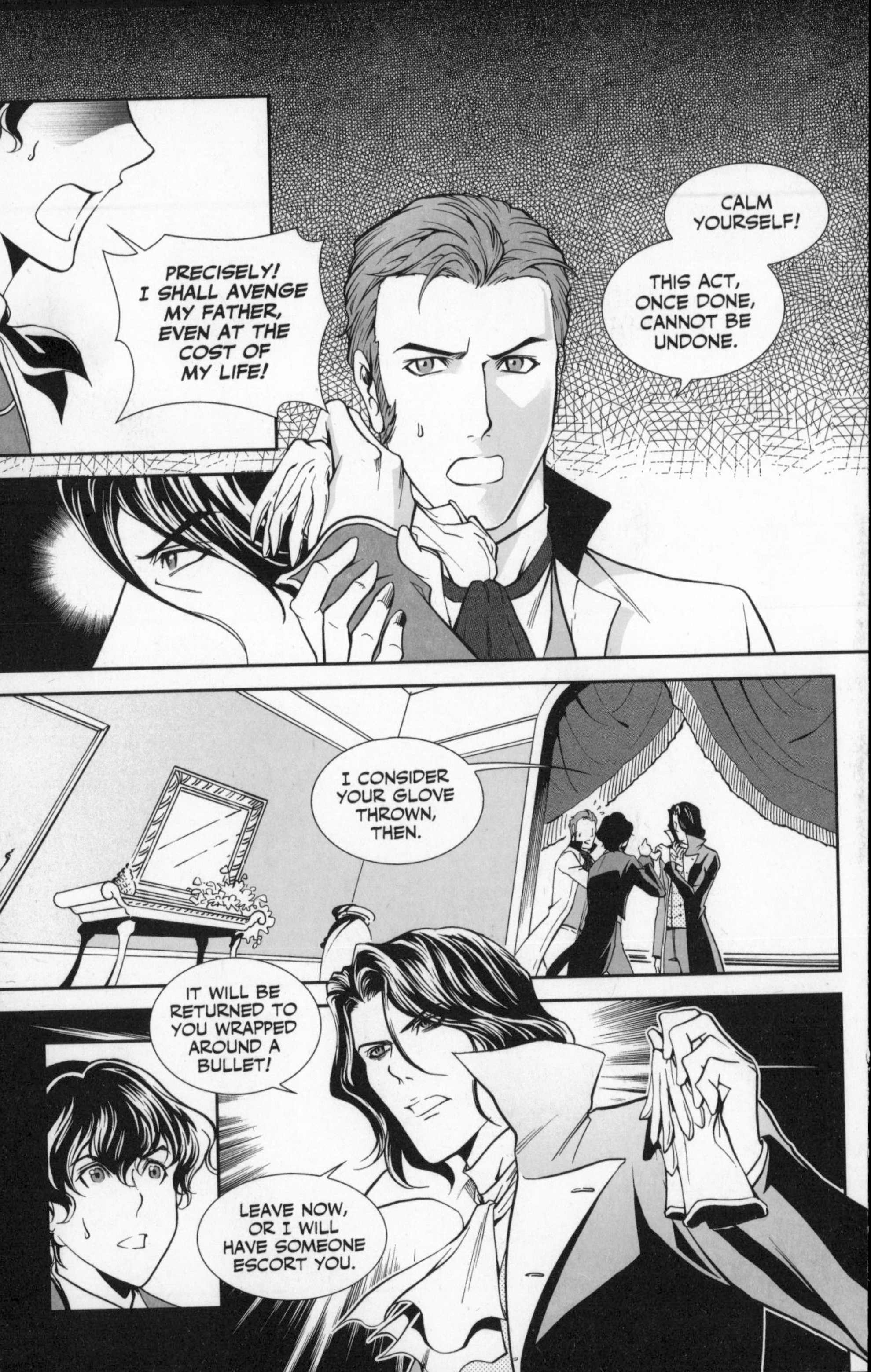
CALM YOURSELF!
THIS ACT, ONCE DONE, CANNOT BE UNDONE.
PRECISELY! I SHALL AVENGE MY FATHER, EVEN AT THE COST OF MY LIFE!
I CONSIDER YOUR GLOVE THROWN, THEN.
IT WILL BE RETURNED TO YOU WRAPPED AROUND A BULLET!
LEAVE NOW, OR I WILL HAVE SOMEONE ESCORT YOU.

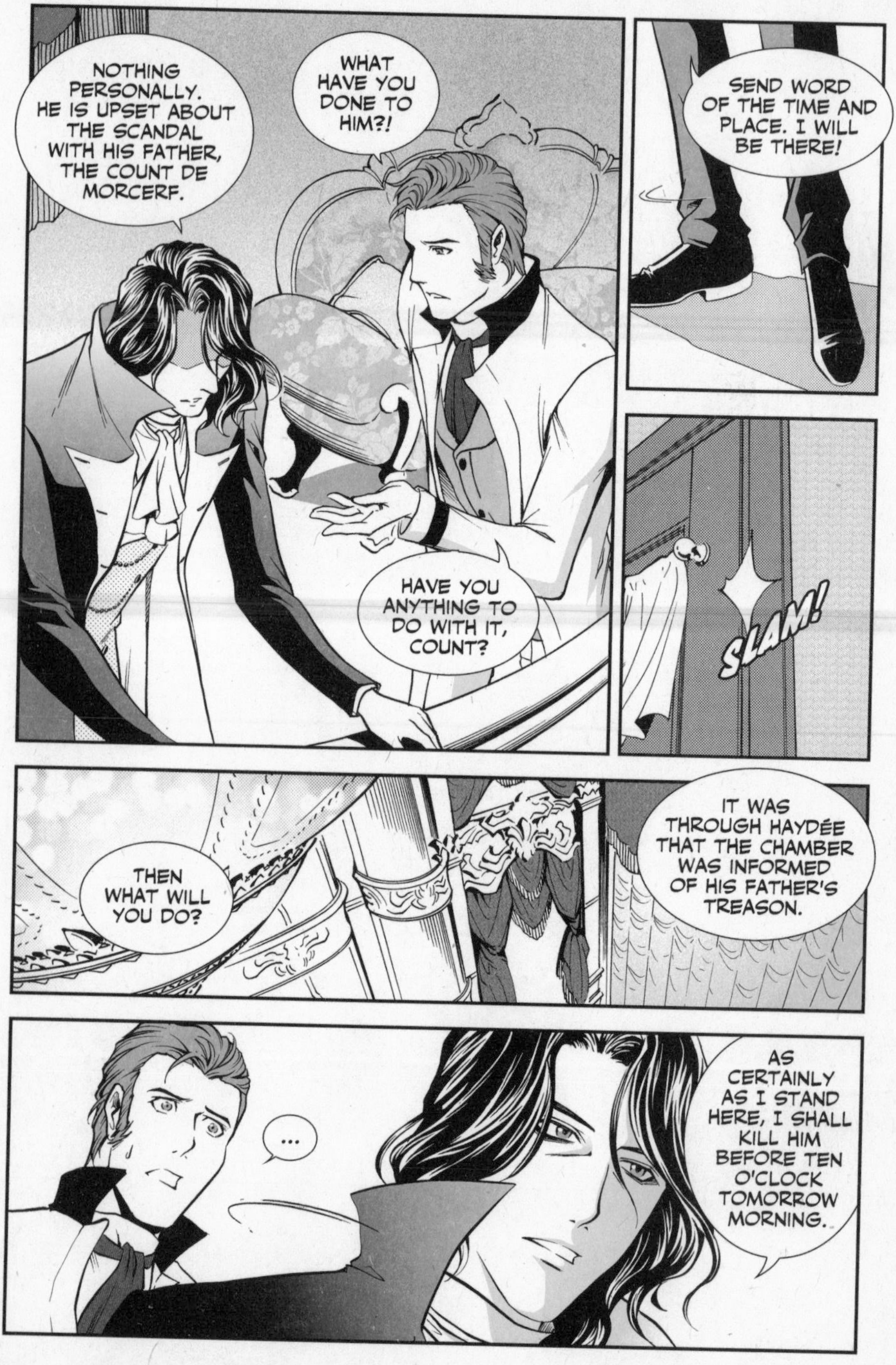
SEND WORD OF THE TIME AND PLACE. I WILL BE THERE!
SLAM!
WHAT HAVE YOU DONE TO HIM?!
NOTHING PERSONALLY. HE IS UPSET ABOUT THE SCANDAL WITH HIS FATHER, THE COUNT DE MORCERF.
HAVE YOU ANYTHING TO DO WITH IT, COUNT?
IT WAS THROUGH HAYDÉE THAT THE CHAMBER WAS INFORMED OF HIS FATHER'S TREASON.
THEN WHAT WILL YOU DO?
AS CERTAINLY AS I STAND HERE, I SHALL KILL HIM BEFORE TEN O'CLOCK TOMORROW MORNING.
...

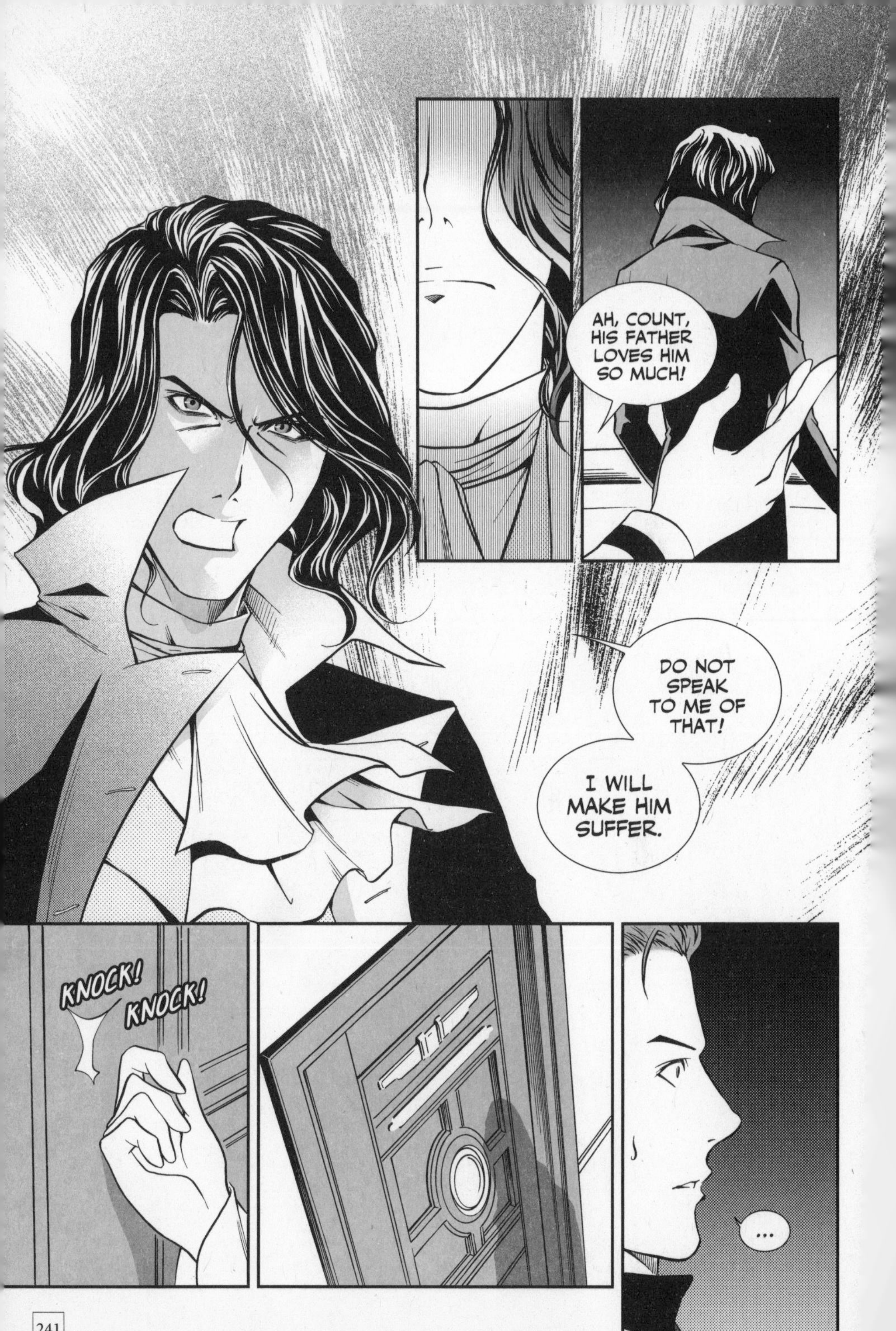
AH, COUNT, HIS FATHER LOVES HIM SO MUCH!
DO NOT SPEAK TO ME OF THAT!
I WILL MAKE HIM SUFFER.
...
KNOCK! KNOCK!

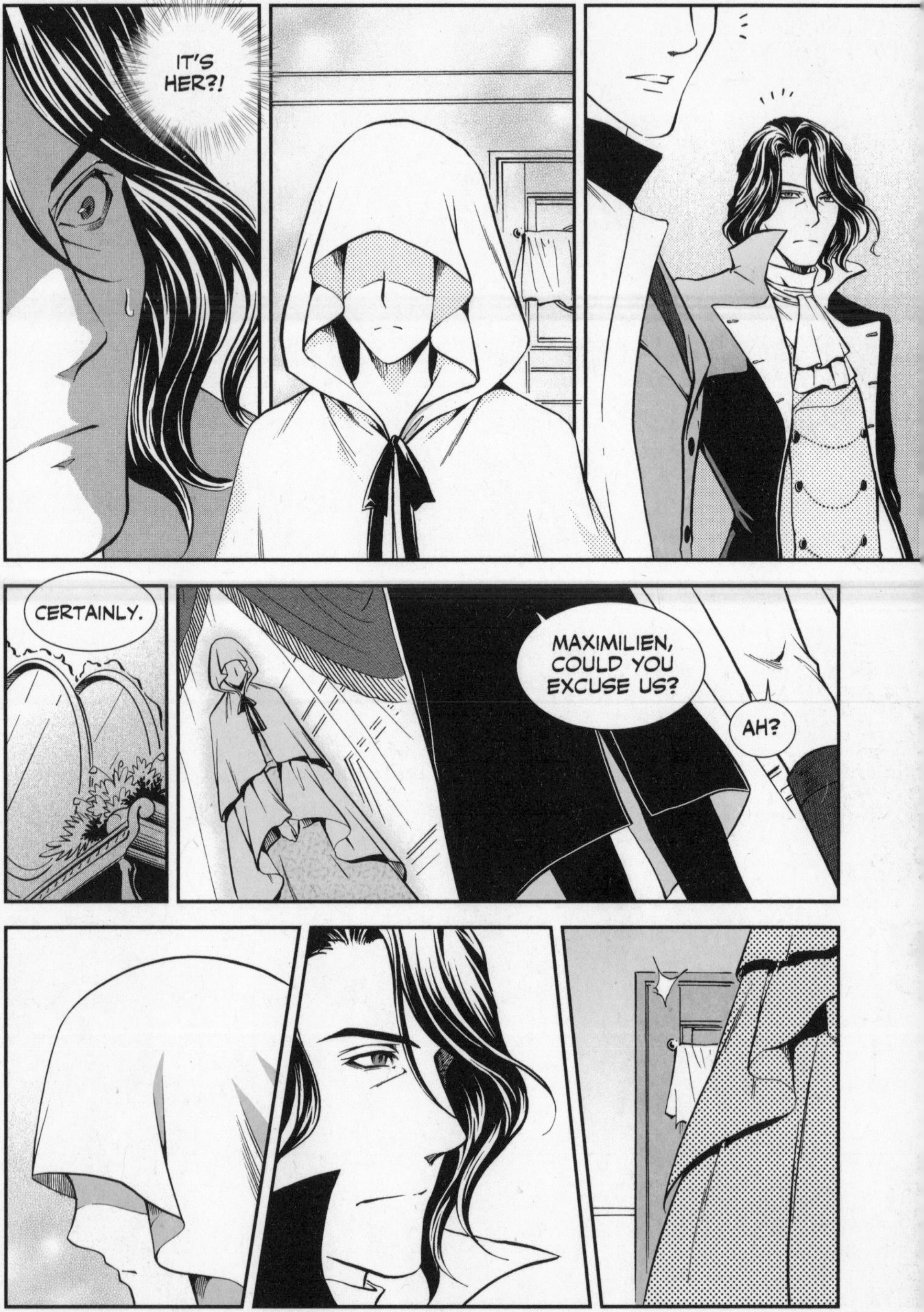
IT'S HER?!
MAXIMILIEN, COULD YOU EXCUSE US?
AH?
CERTAINLY.

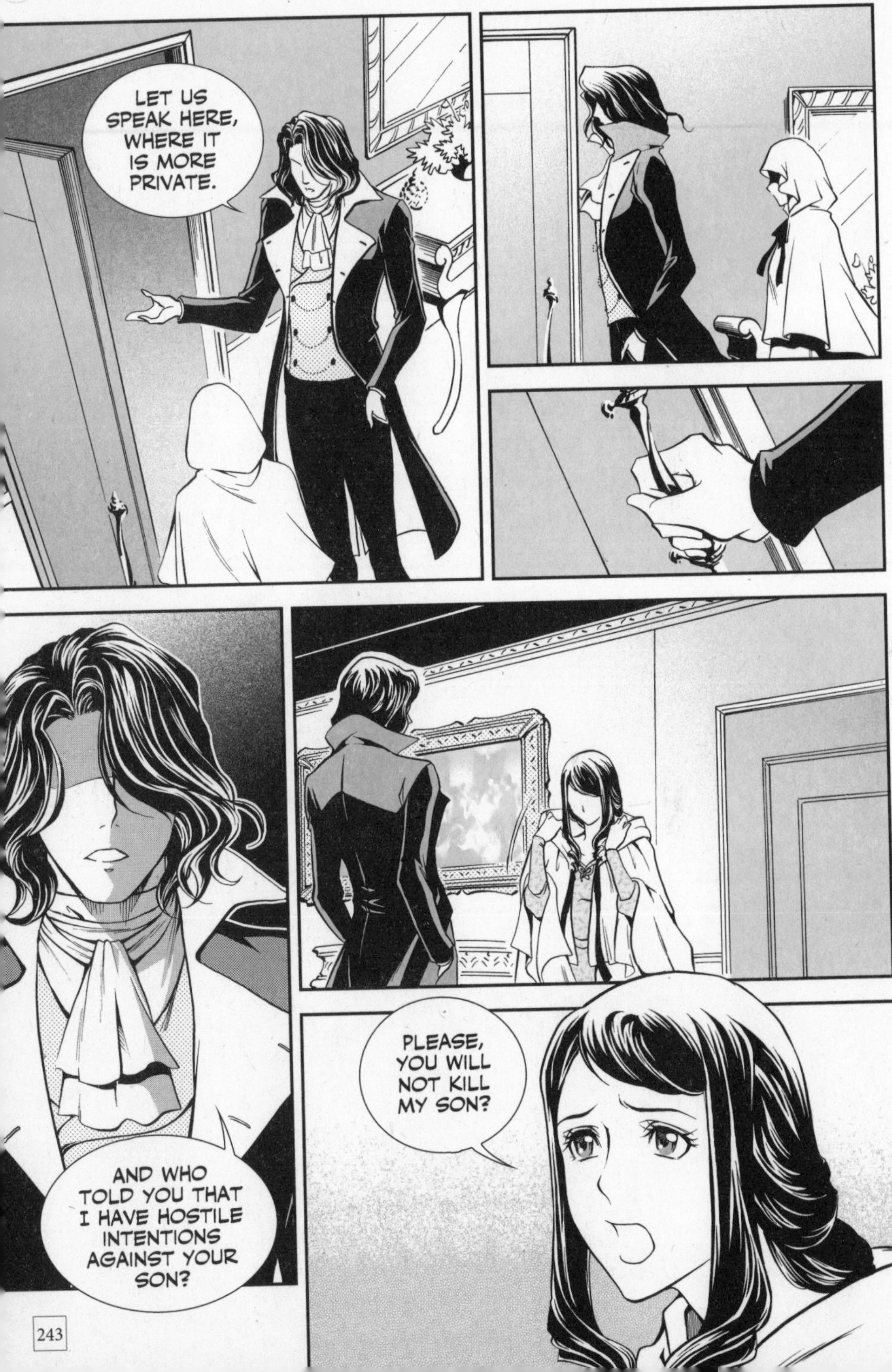
LET US SPEAK HERE, WHERE IT IS MORE PRIVATE.
PLEASE, YOU WILL NOT KILL MY SON?
AND WHO TOLD YOU THAT I HAVE HOSTILE INTENTIONS AGAINST YOUR SON?

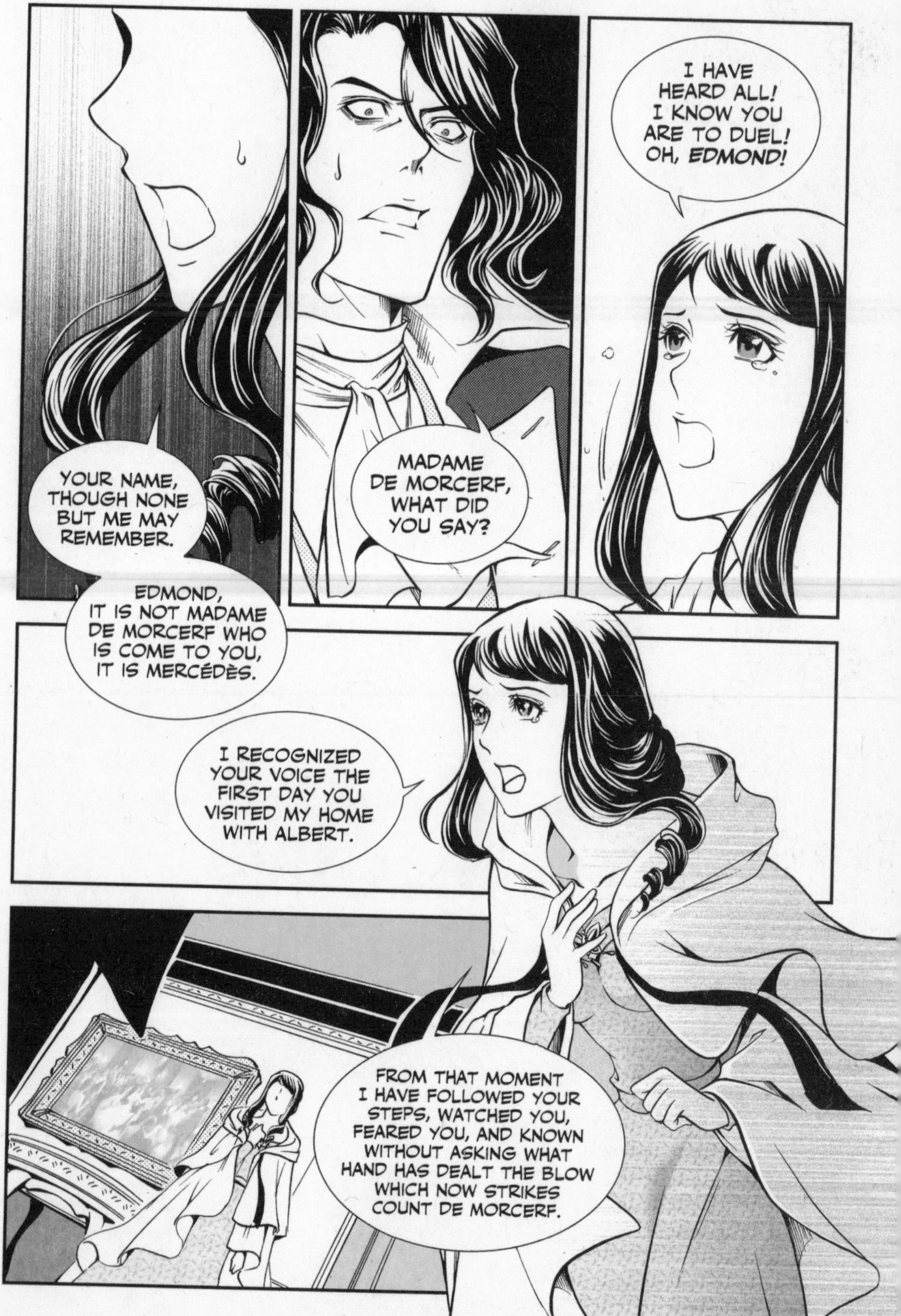
I HAVE HEARD ALL! I KNOW YOU ARE TO DUEL! OH, EDMOND!
MADAME DE MORCERF, WHAT DID YOU SAY?
YOUR NAME, THOUGH NONE BUT ME MAY REMEMBER.
EDMOND, IT IS NOT MADAME DE MORCERF WHO IS COME TO YOU, IT IS MERCÉDÈS.
I RECOGNIZED YOUR VOICE THE FIRST DAY YOU VISITED MY HOME WITH ALBERT.
FROM THAT MOMENT I HAVE FOLLOWED YOUR STEPS, WATCHED YOU, FEARED YOU, AND KNOWN WITHOUT ASKING WHAT HAND HAS DEALT THE BLOW WHICH NOW STRIKES COUNT DE MORCERF.

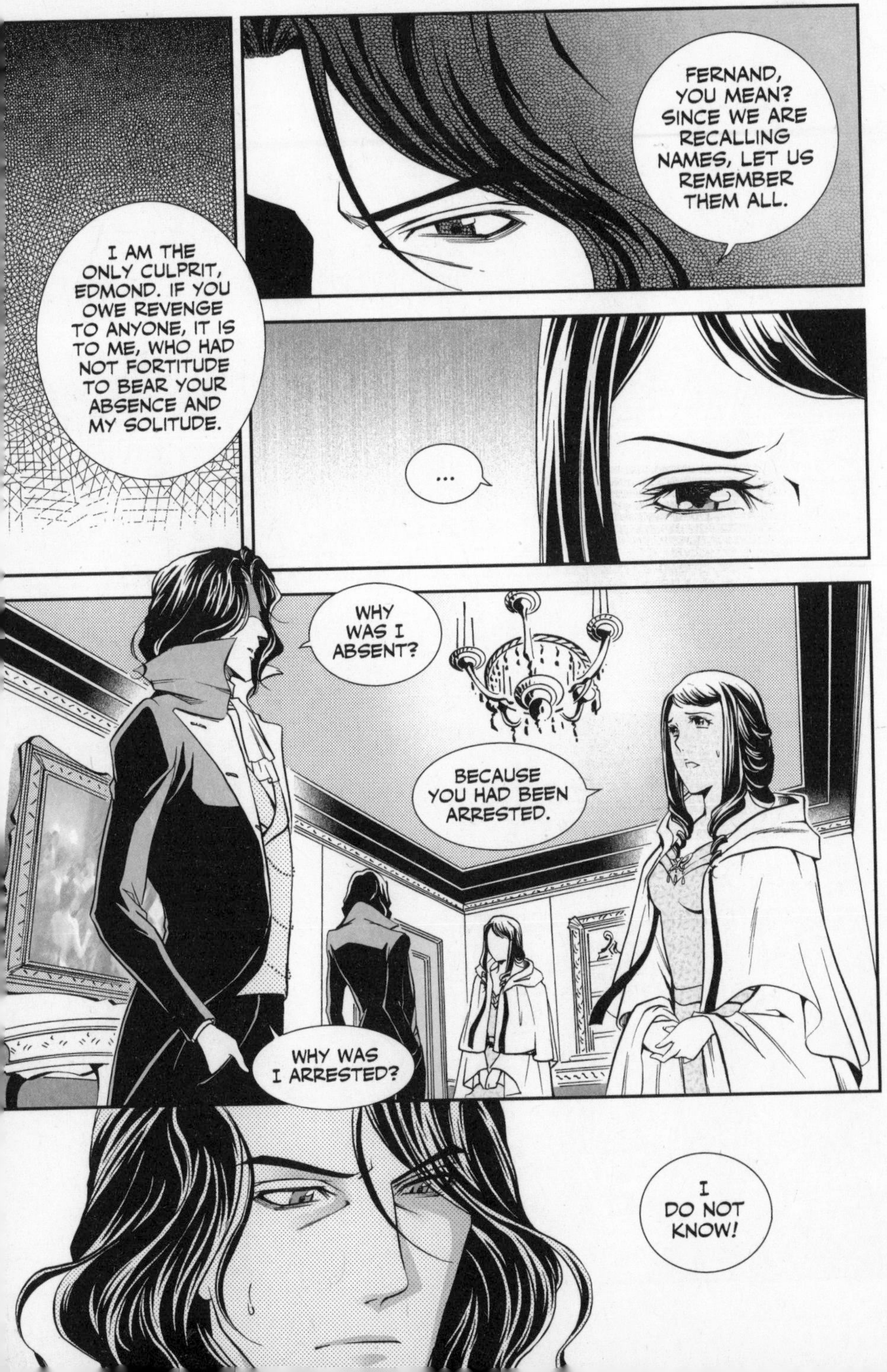
FERNAND, YOU MEAN? SINCE WE ARE RECALLING NAMES, LET US REMEMBER THEM ALL.
...
I AM THE ONLY CULPRIT, EDMOND. IF YOU OWE REVENGE TO ANYONE, IT IS TO ME, WHO HAD NOT FORTITUDE TO BEAR YOUR ABSENCE AND MY SOLITUDE.
WHY WAS I ABSENT?
BECAUSE YOU HAD BEEN ARRESTED.
WHY WAS I ARRESTED?
I DO NOT KNOW!

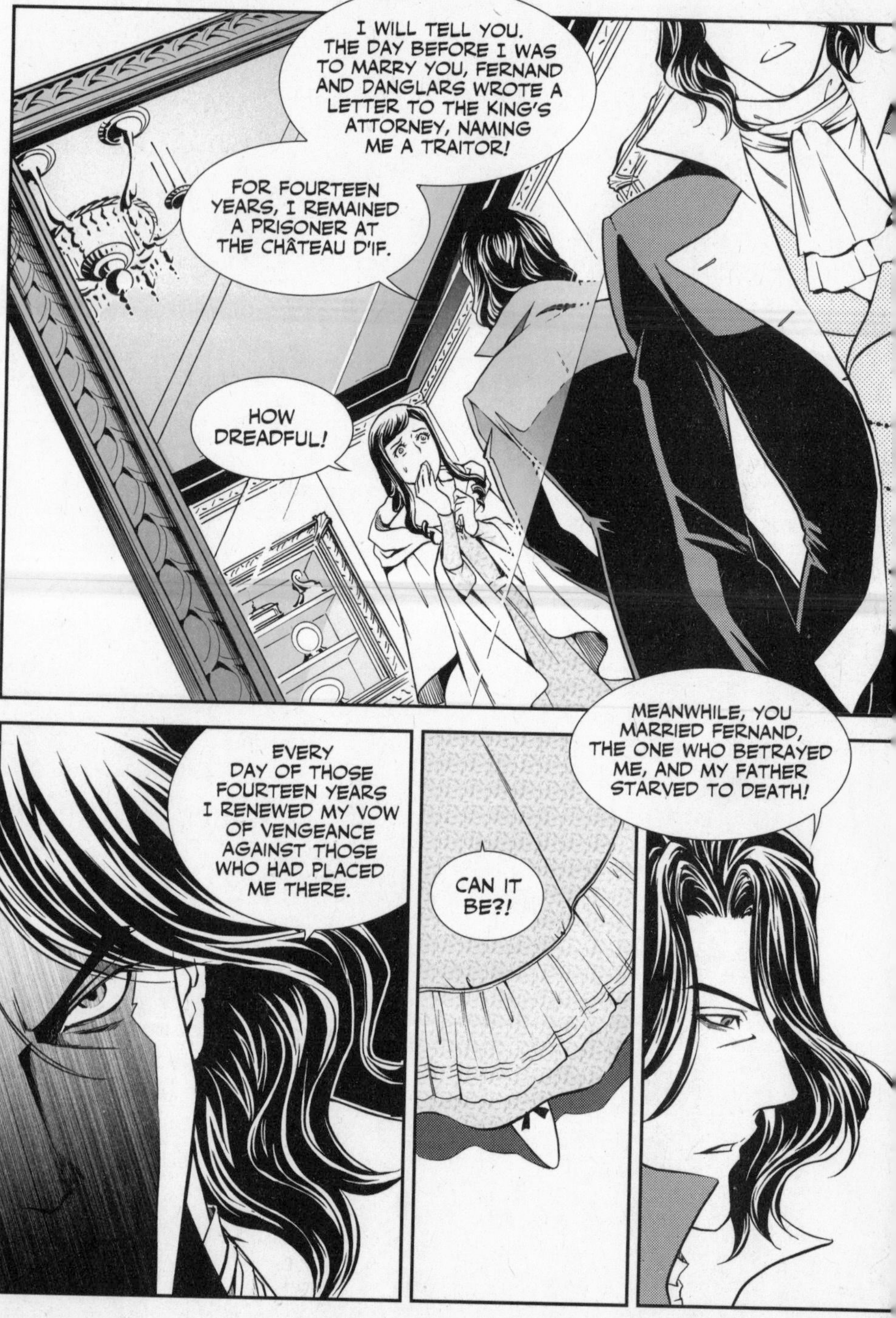
I WILL TELL YOU. THE DAY BEFORE I WAS TO MARRY YOU, FERNAND AND DANGLARS WROTE A LETTER TO THE KING'S ATTORNEY, NAMING ME A TRAITOR!
FOR FOURTEEN YEARS, I REMAINED A PRISONER AT THE CHÂTEAU D'IF.
HOW DREADFUL!
MEANWHILE, YOU MARRIED FERNAND, THE ONE WHO BETRAYED ME, AND MY FATHER STARVED TO DEATH!
CAN IT BE?!
EVERY DAY OF THOSE FOURTEEN YEARS I RENEWED MY VOW OF VENGEANCE AGAINST THOSE WHO HAD PLACED ME THERE.

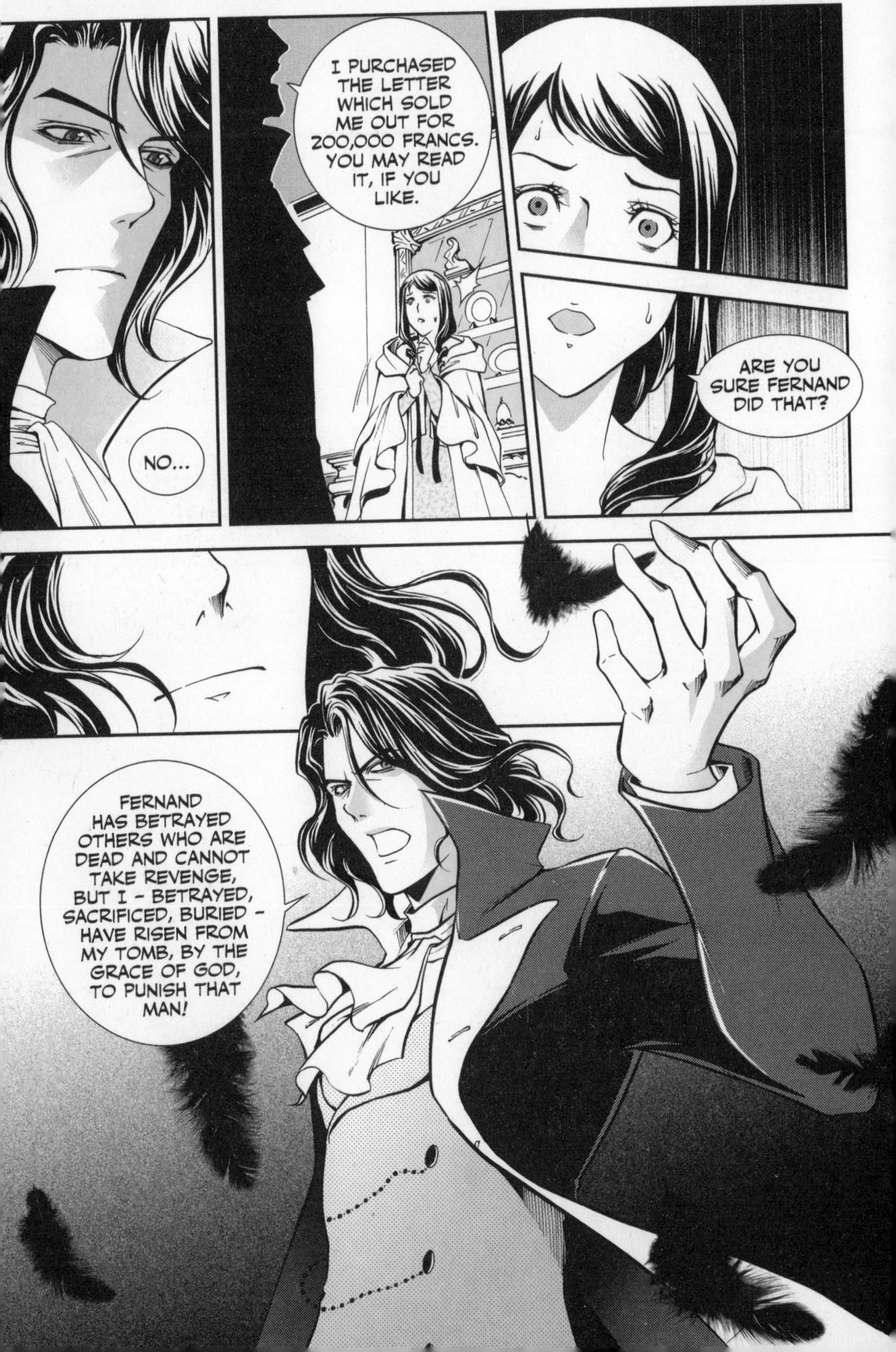
ARE YOU SURE FERNAND DID THAT?
I PURCHASED THE LETTER WHICH SOLD ME OUT FOR 200,000 FRANCS. YOU MAY READ IT, IF YOU LIKE.
NO...
FERNAND HAS BETRAYED OTHERS WHO ARE DEAD AND CANNOT TAKE REVENGE, BUT I - BETRAYED, SACRIFICED, BURIED - HAVE RISEN FROM MY TOMB, BY THE GRACE OF GOD, TO PUNISH THAT MAN!

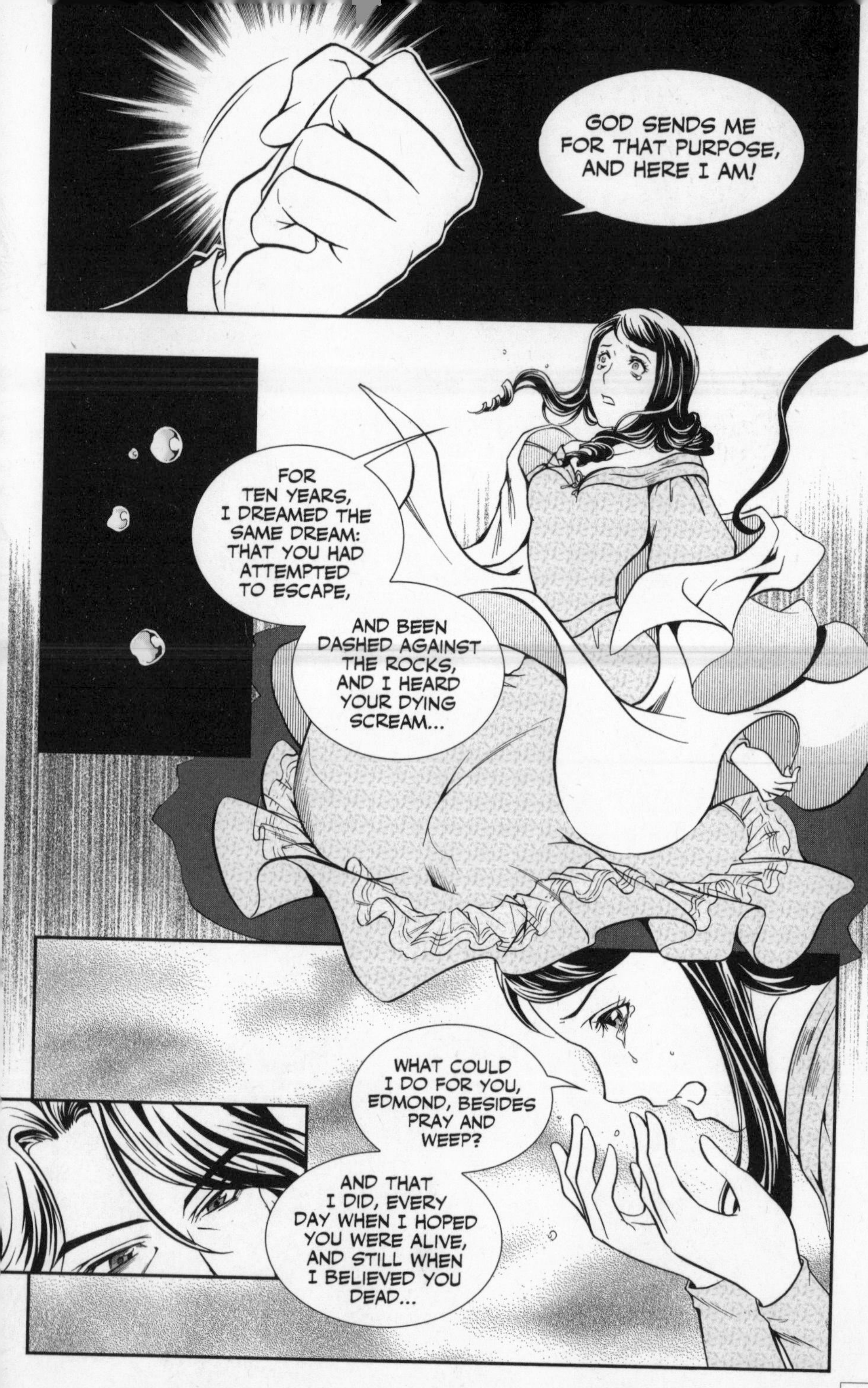
GOD SENDS ME FOR THAT PURPOSE, AND HERE I AM!
FOR TEN YEARS, I DREAMED THE SAME DREAM: THAT YOU HAD ATTEMPTED TO ESCAPE,
AND BEEN DASHED AGAINST THE ROCKS, AND I HEARD YOUR DYING SCREAM...
WHAT COULD I DO FOR YOU, EDMOND, BESIDES PRAY AND WEEP?
AND THAT I DID, EVERY DAY WHEN I HOPED YOU WERE ALIVE, AND STILL WHEN I BELIEVED YOU DEAD...

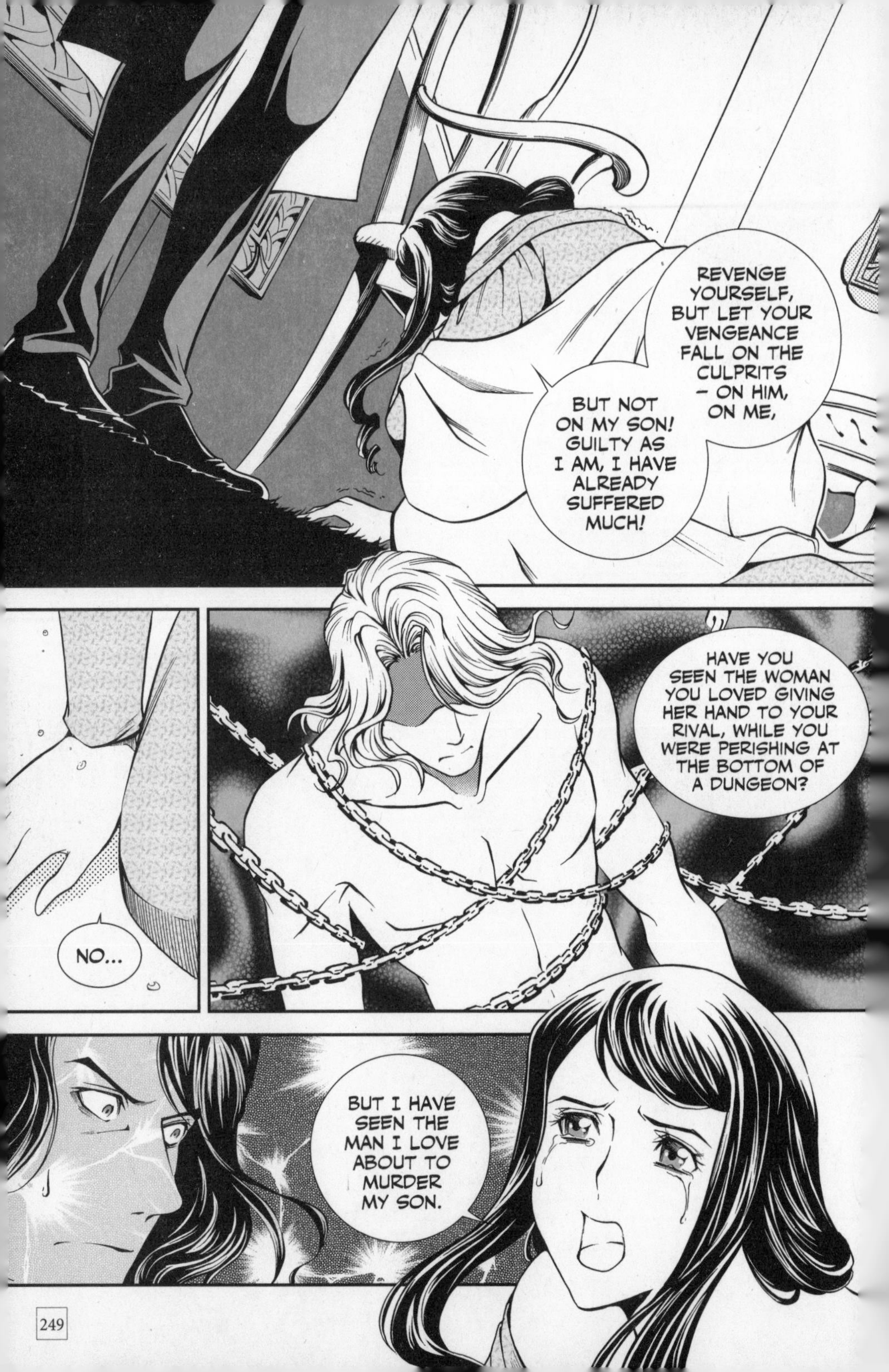
REVENGE YOURSELF, BUT LET YOUR VENGEANCE FALL ON THE CULPRITS – ON HIM, ON ME,
BUT NOT ON MY SON! GUILTY AS I AM, I HAVE ALREADY SUFFERED MUCH!
HAVE YOU SEEN THE WOMAN YOU LOVED GIVING HER HAND TO YOUR RIVAL, WHILE YOU WERE PERISHING AT THE BOTTOM OF A DUNGEON?
NO...
BUT I HAVE SEEN THE MAN I LOVE ABOUT TO MURDER MY SON.

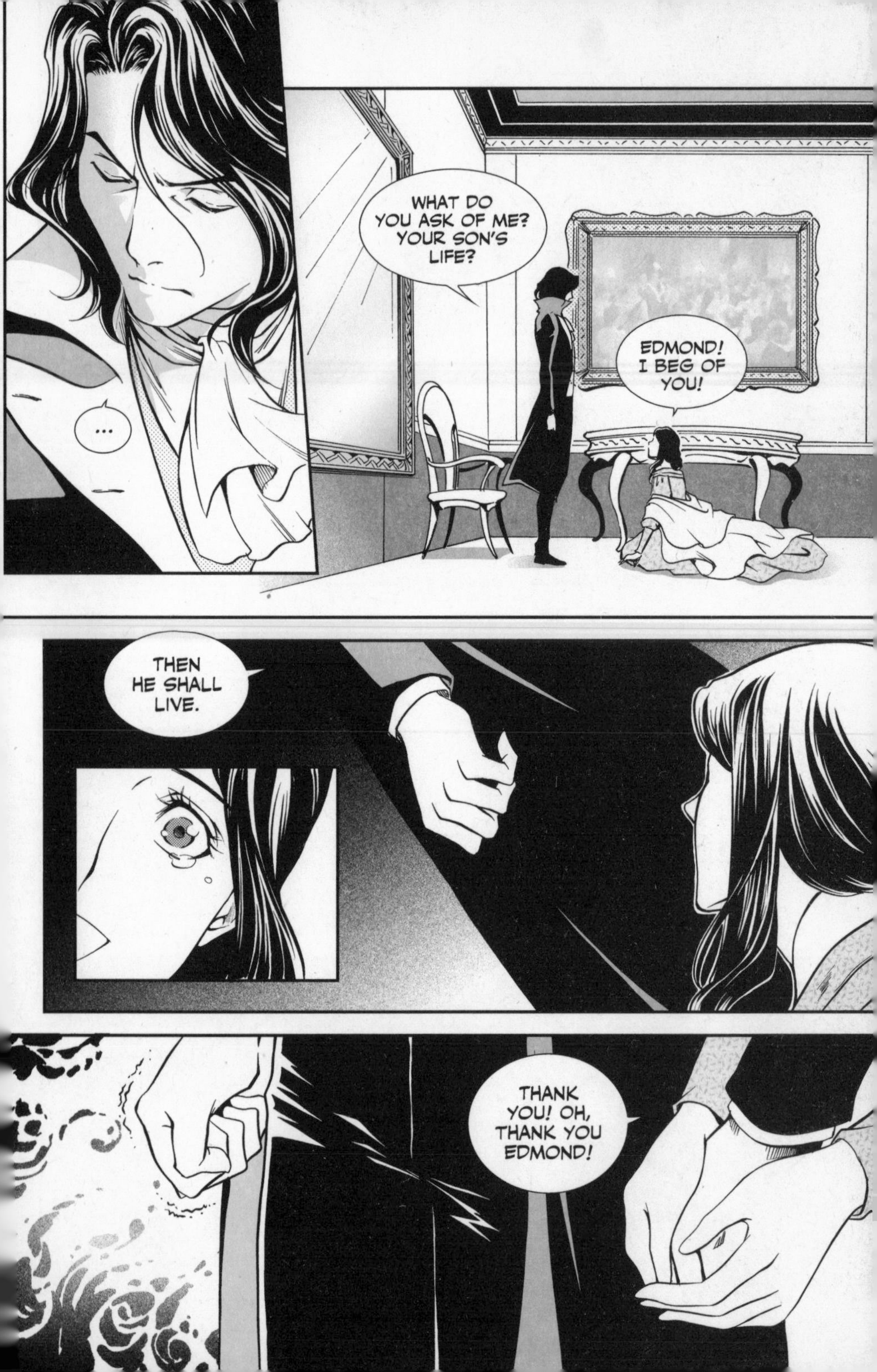
EDMOND! I BEG OF YOU!
WHAT DO YOU ASK OF ME? YOUR SON'S LIFE?
...
THEN HE SHALL LIVE.
THANK YOU! OH, THANK YOU EDMOND!

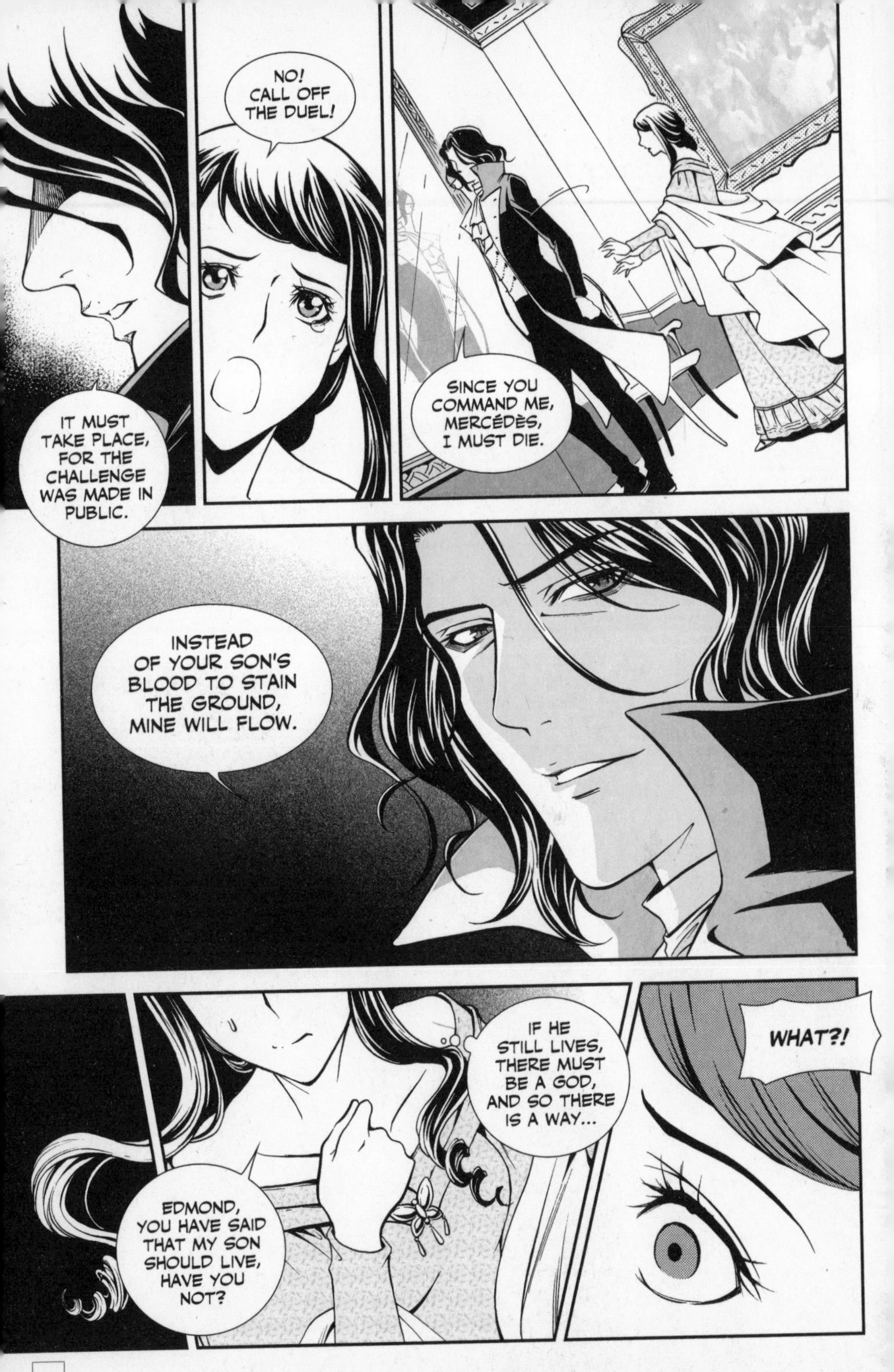
NO! CALL OFF THE DUEL!
IT MUST TAKE PLACE, FOR THE CHALLENGE WAS MADE IN PUBLIC.
SINCE YOU COMMAND ME, MERCÉDÈS, I MUST DIE.
INSTEAD OF YOUR SON'S BLOOD TO STAIN THE GROUND, MINE WILL FLOW.
IF HE STILL LIVES, THERE MUST BE A GOD, AND SO THERE IS A WAY...
EDMOND, YOU HAVE SAID THAT MY SON SHOULD LIVE, HAVE YOU NOT?
WHAT?!

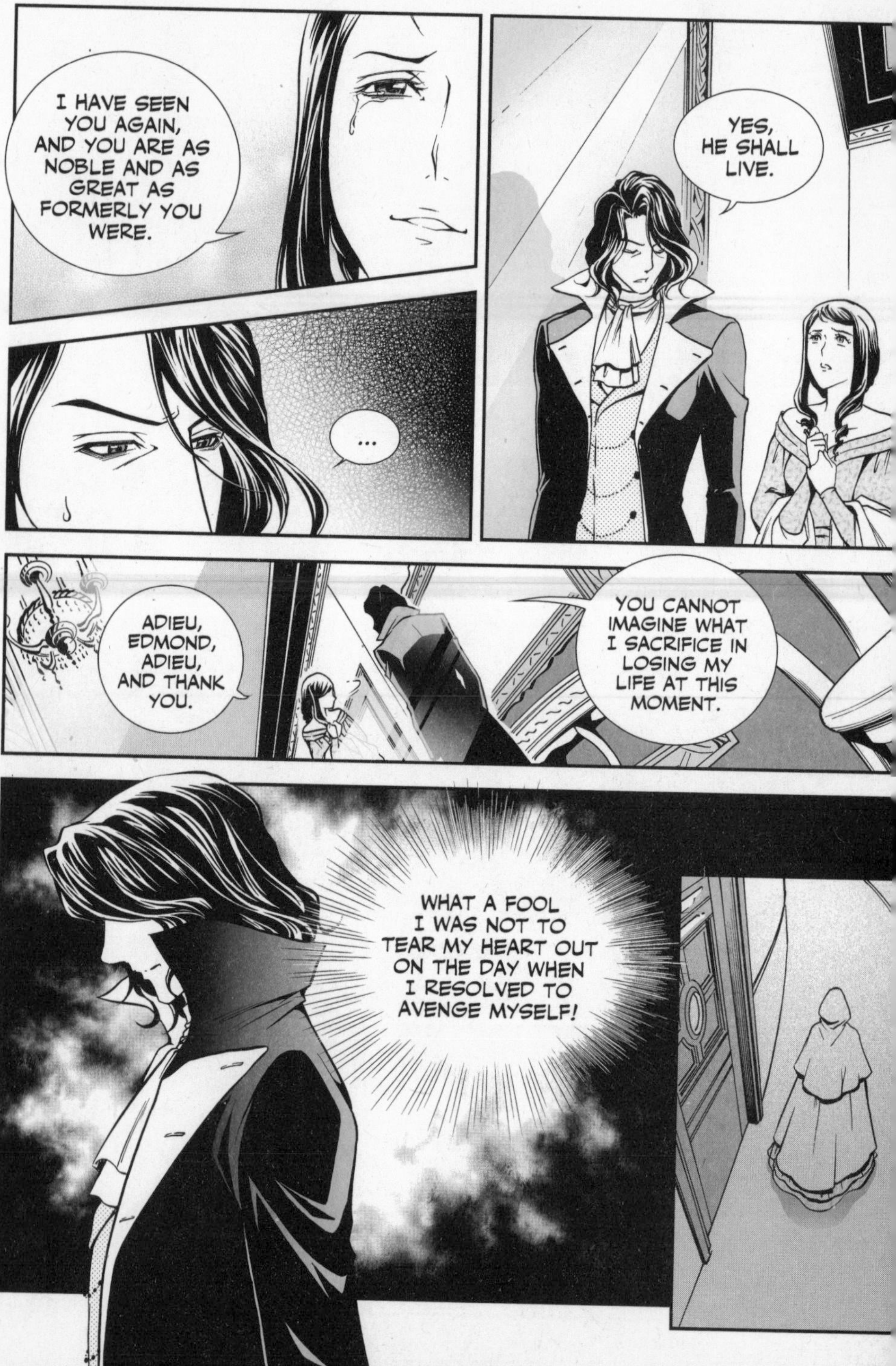
YES, HE SHALL LIVE.
I HAVE SEEN YOU AGAIN, AND YOU ARE AS NOBLE AND AS GREAT AS FORMERLY YOU WERE.
...
YOU CANNOT IMAGINE WHAT I SACRIFICE IN LOSING MY LIFE AT THIS MOMENT.
ADIEU, EDMOND, ADIEU, AND THANK YOU.
WHAT A FOOL I WAS NOT TO TEAR MY HEART OUT ON THE DAY WHEN I RESOLVED TO AVENGE MYSELF!

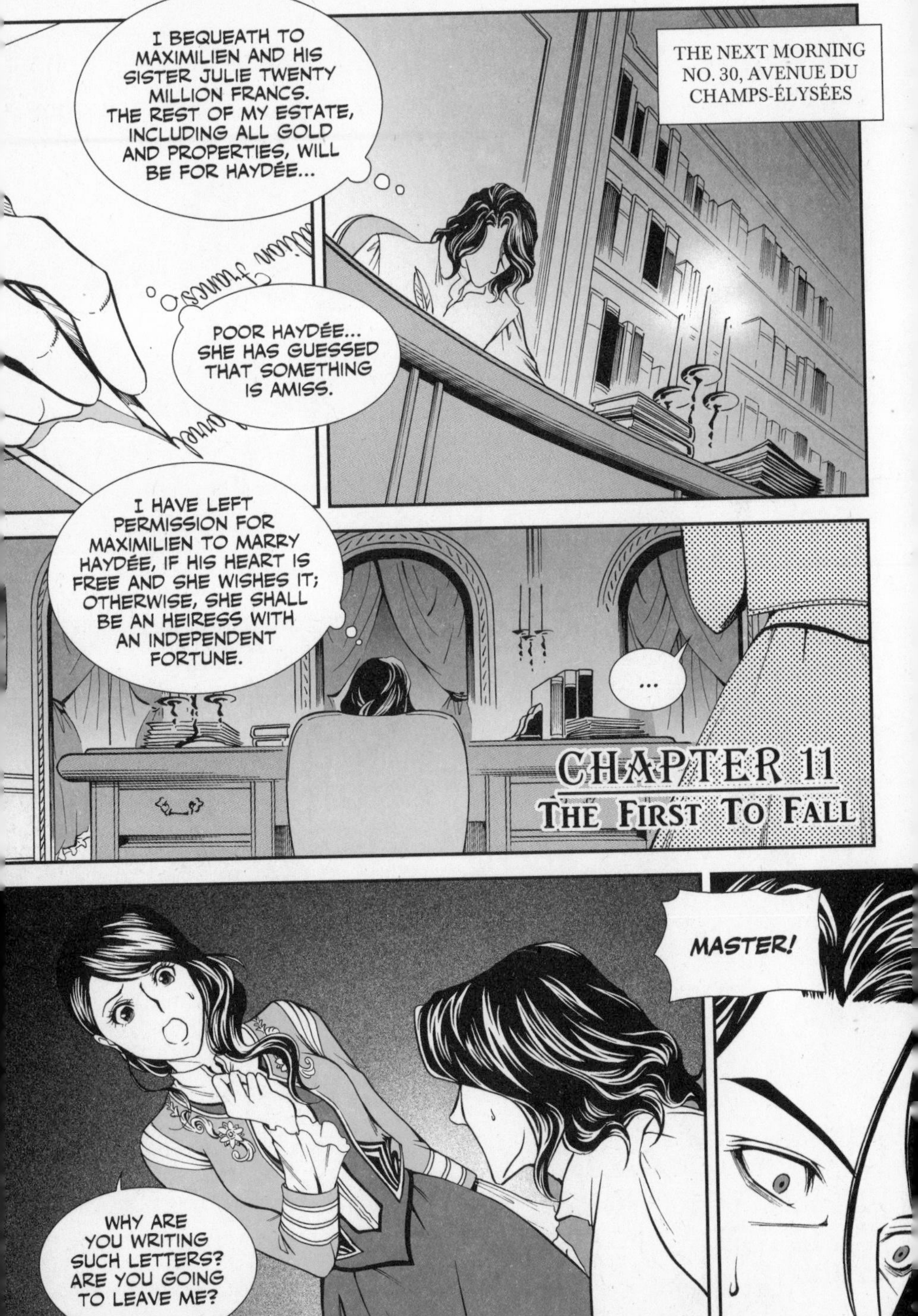
THE NEXT MORNING NO. 30, AVENUE DU CHAMPS-ÉLYSÉES
I BEQUEATH TO MAXIMILIEN AND HIS SISTER JULIE TWENTY MILLION FRANCS. THE REST OF MY ESTATE, INCLUDING ALL GOLD AND PROPERTIES, WILL BE FOR HAYDÉE...
POOR HAYDÉE... SHE HAS GUESSED THAT SOMETHING IS AMISS.
I HAVE LEFT PERMISSION FOR MAXIMILIEN TO MARRY HAYDÉE, IF HIS HEART IS FREE AND SHE WISHES IT; OTHERWISE, SHE SHALL BE AN HEIRESS WITH AN INDEPENDENT FORTUNE.
...
CHAPTER 11
THE FIRST TO FALL
MASTER!
WHY ARE YOU WRITING SUCH LETTERS? ARE YOU GOING TO LEAVE ME?

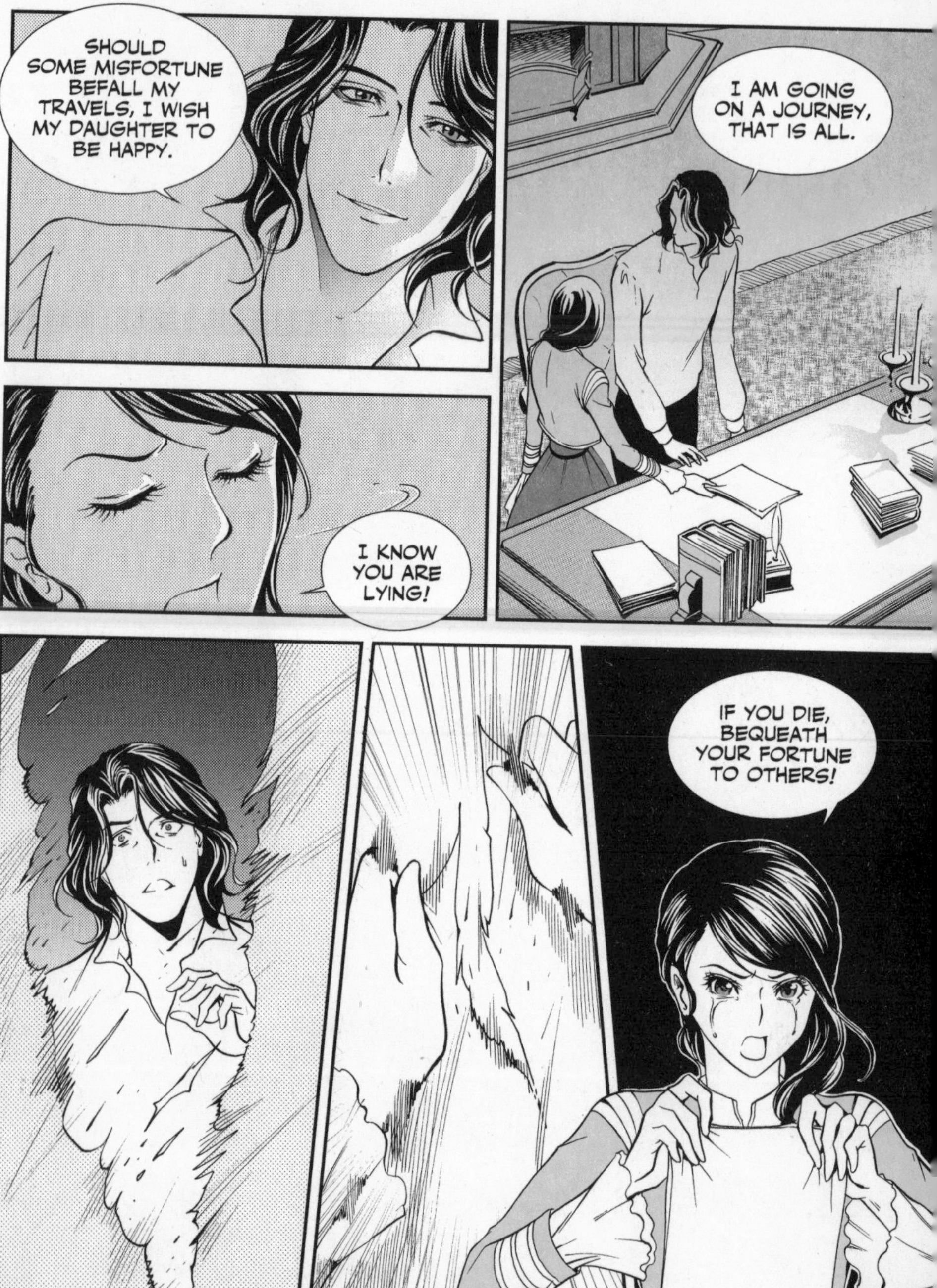
I AM GOING ON A JOURNEY, THAT IS ALL.
SHOULD SOME MISFORTUNE BEFALL MY TRAVELS, I WISH MY DAUGHTER TO BE HAPPY.
I KNOW YOU ARE LYING!
IF YOU DIE, BEQUEATH YOUR FORTUNE TO OTHERS!

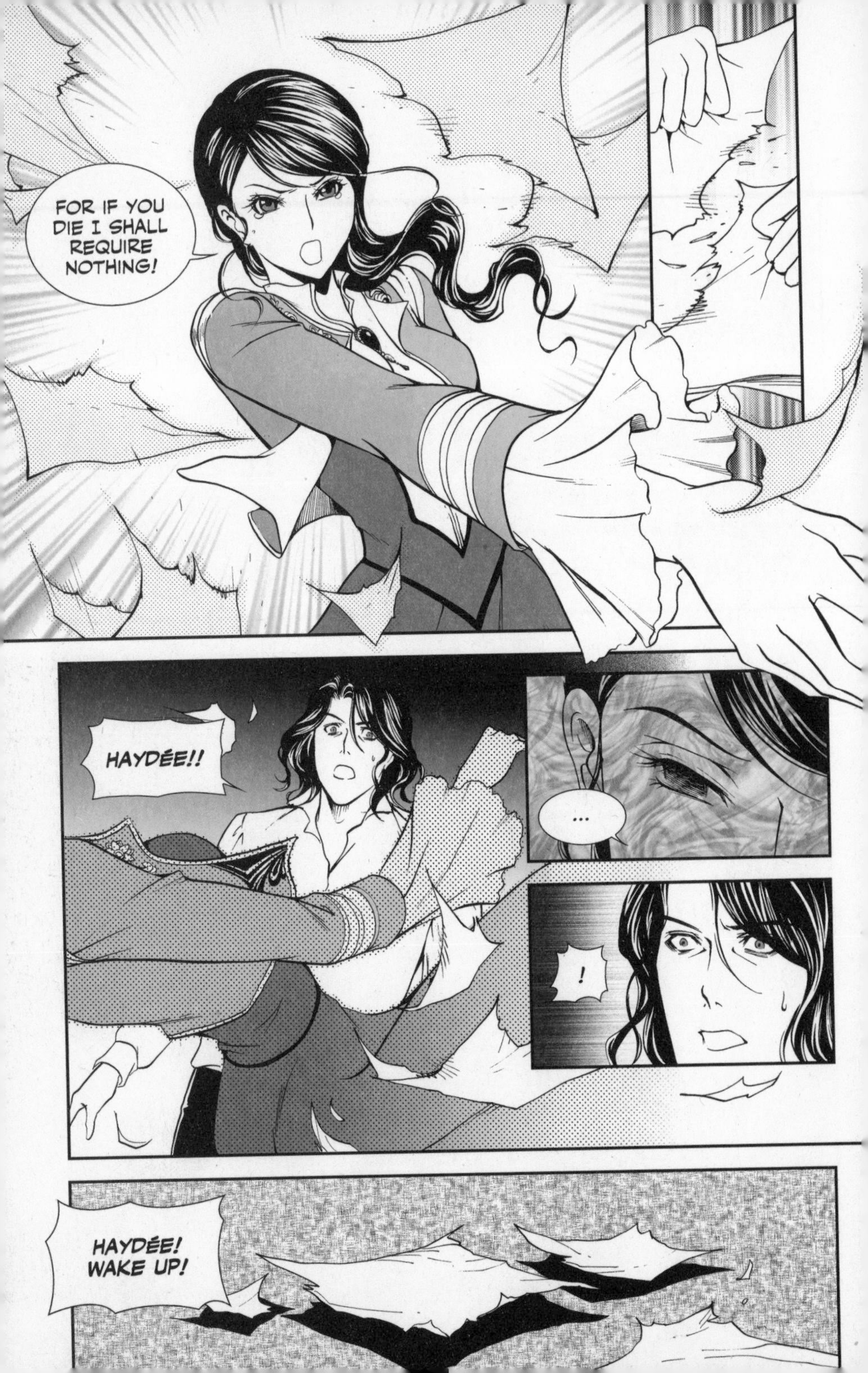
FOR IF YOU DIE I SHALL REQUIRE NOTHING!
...
!
HAYDÉE!!
HAYDÉE! WAKE UP!

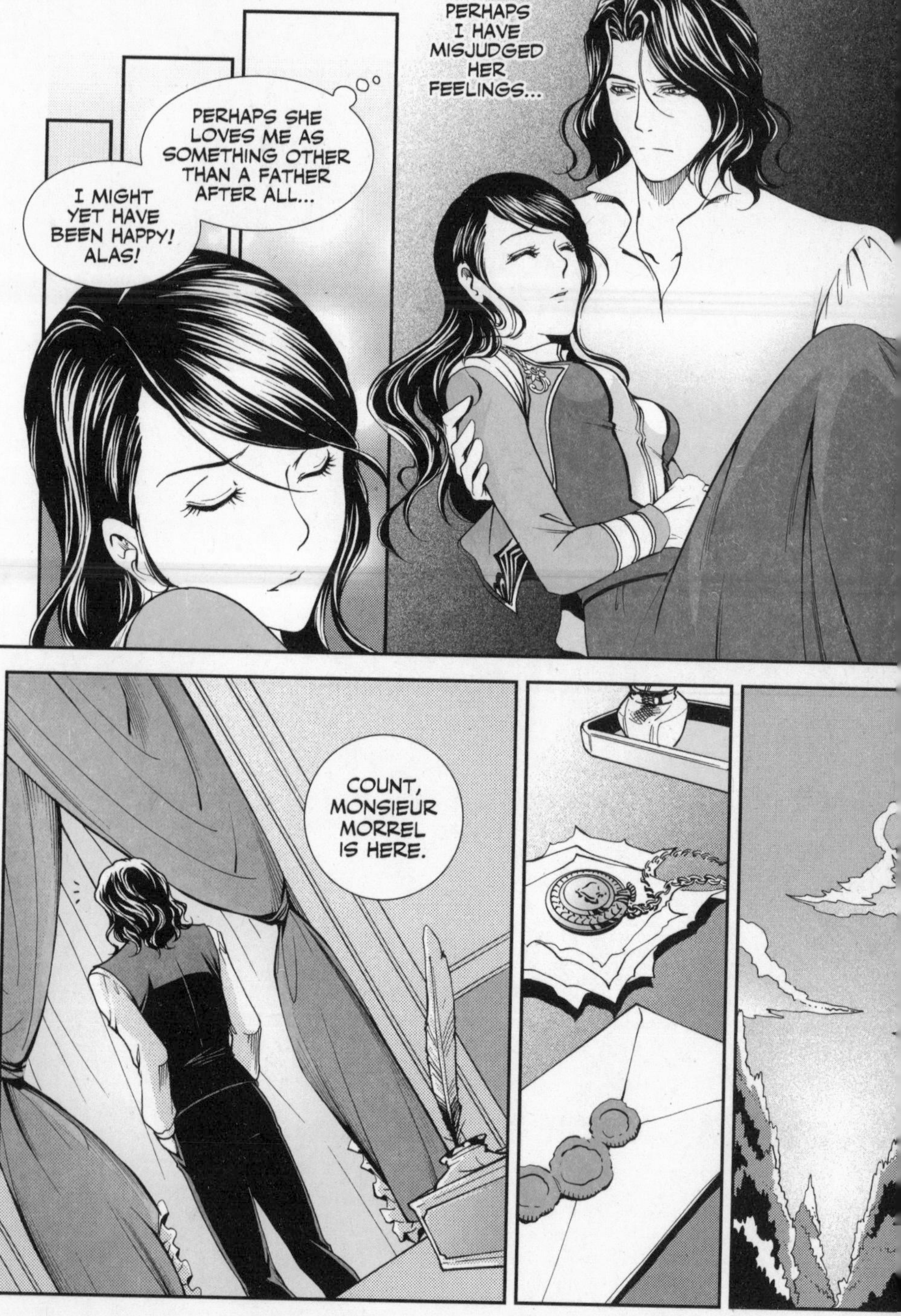
PERHAPS I HAVE MISJUDGED HER FEELINGS...
PERHAPS SHE LOVES ME AS SOMETHING OTHER THAN A FATHER AFTER ALL...
I MIGHT YET HAVE BEEN HAPPY! ALAS!
COUNT, MONSIEUR MORREL IS HERE.

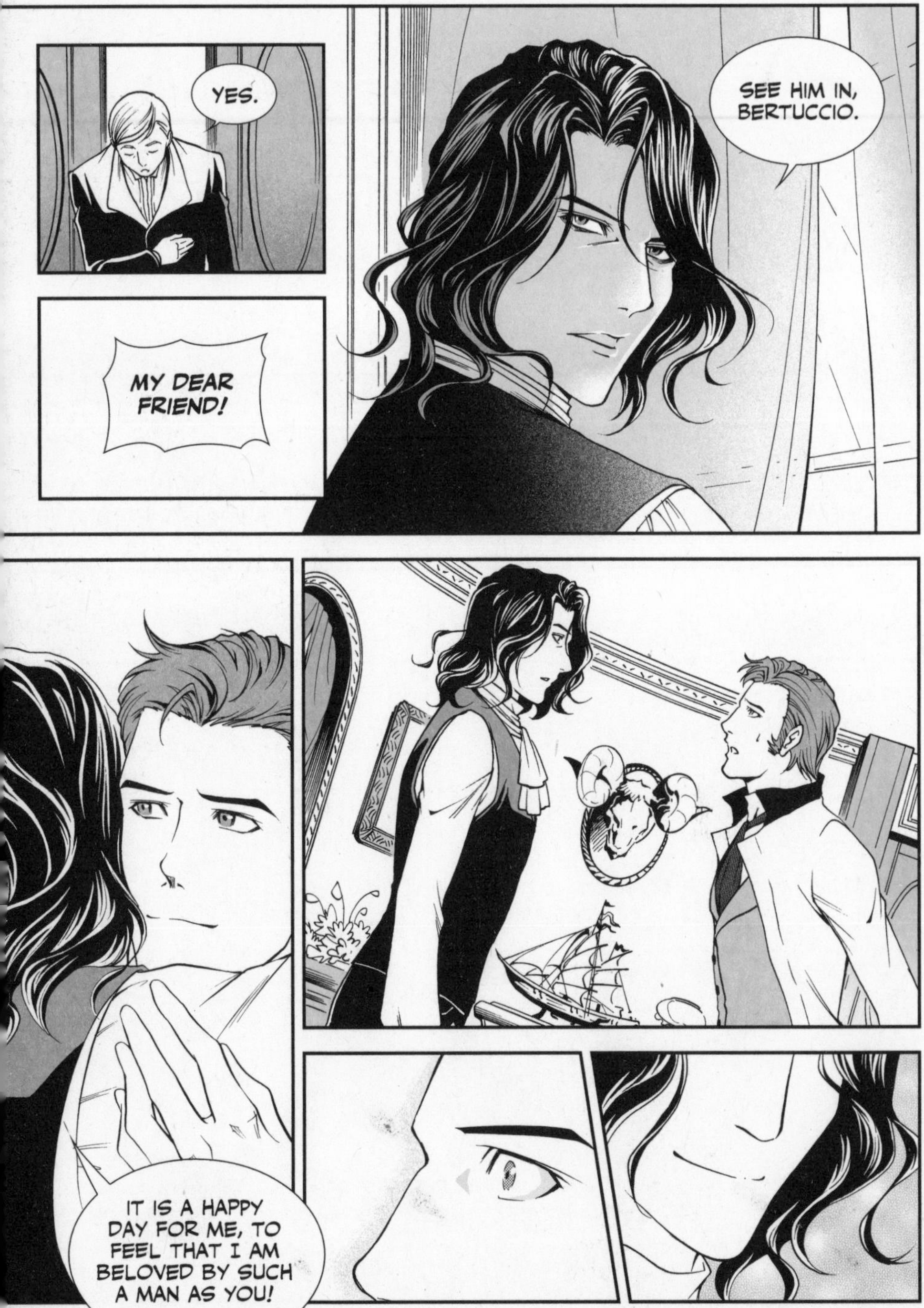
SEE HIM IN, BERTUCCIO.
YES.
MY DEAR FRIEND!
IT IS A HAPPY DAY FOR ME, TO FEEL THAT I AM BELOVED BY SUCH A MAN AS YOU!

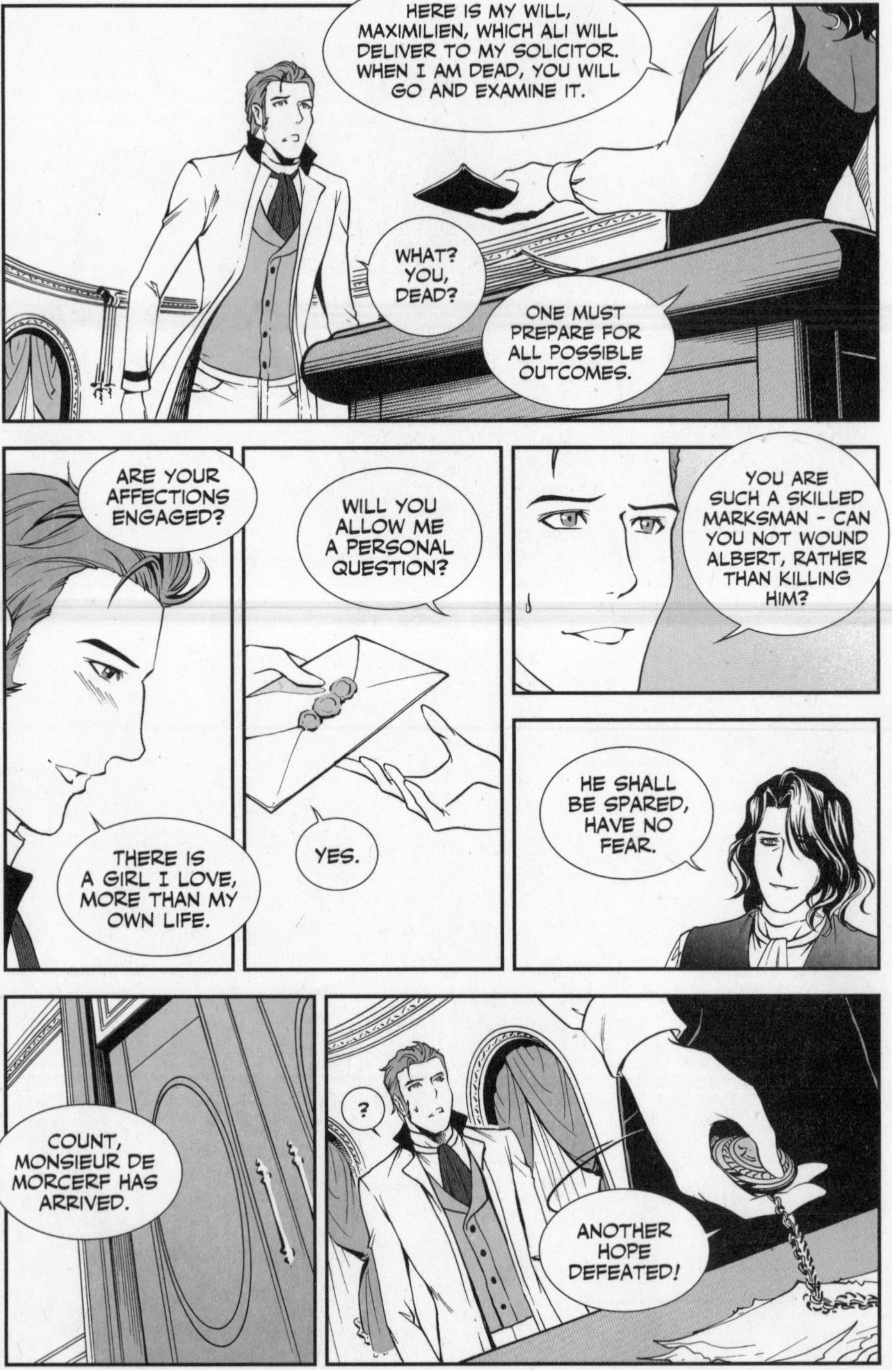
HERE IS MY WILL, MAXIMILIEN, WHICH ALI WILL DELIVER TO MY SOLICITOR. WHEN I AM DEAD, YOU WILL GO AND EXAMINE IT.
WHAT? YOU, DEAD?
ONE MUST PREPARE FOR ALL POSSIBLE OUTCOMES.
YOU ARE SUCH A SKILLED MARKSMAN - CAN YOU NOT WOUND ALBERT, RATHER THAN KILLING HIM?
HE SHALL BE SPARED, HAVE NO FEAR.
WILL YOU ALLOW ME A PERSONAL QUESTION?
YES.
ARE YOUR AFFECTIONS ENGAGED?
THERE IS A GIRL I LOVE, MORE THAN MY OWN LIFE.
?
ANOTHER HOPE DEFEATED!
COUNT, MONSIEUR DE MORCERF HAS ARRIVED.

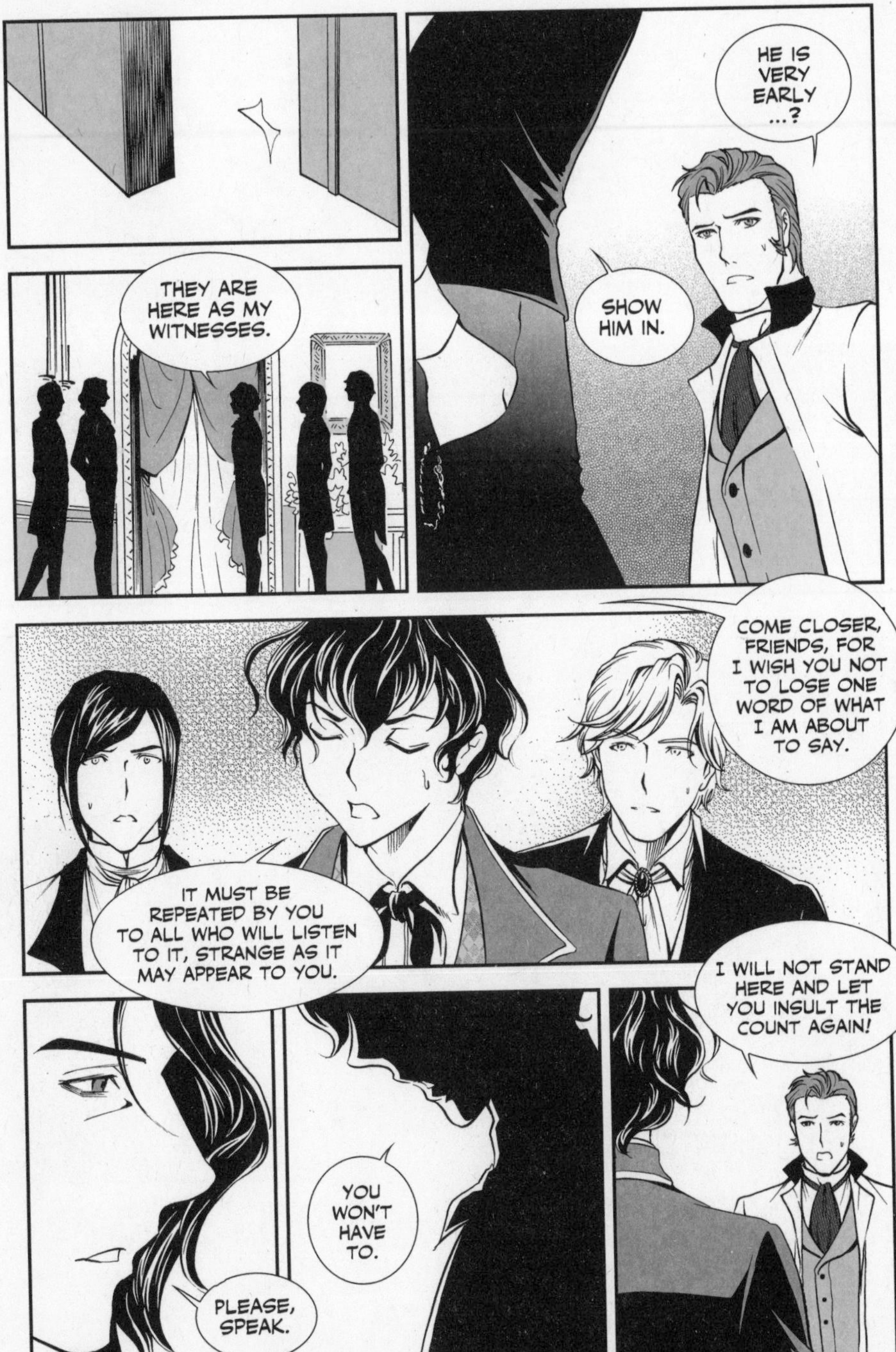
HE IS VERY EARLY ...?
SHOW HIM IN.
THEY ARE HERE AS MY WITNESSES.
COME CLOSER, FRIENDS, FOR I WISH YOU NOT TO LOSE ONE WORD OF WHAT I AM ABOUT TO SAY.
IT MUST BE REPEATED BY YOU TO ALL WHO WILL LISTEN TO IT, STRANGE AS IT MAY APPEAR TO YOU.
I WILL NOT STAND HERE AND LET YOU INSULT THE COUNT AGAIN!
YOU WON'T HAVE TO.
PLEASE, SPEAK.

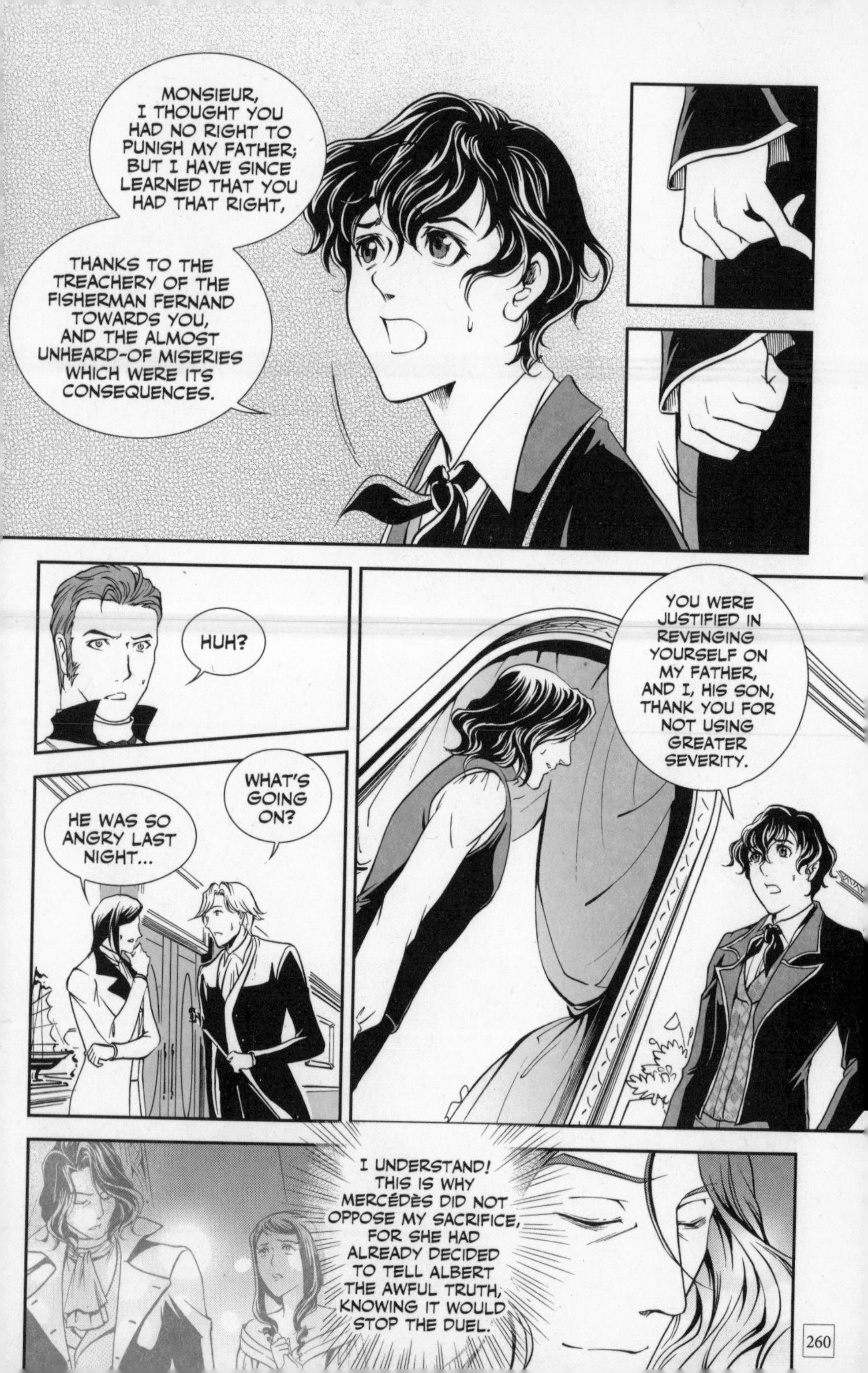
MONSIEUR, I THOUGHT YOU HAD NO RIGHT TO PUNISH MY FATHER; BUT I HAVE SINCE LEARNED THAT YOU HAD THAT RIGHT,
THANKS TO THE TREACHERY OF THE FISHERMAN FERNAND TOWARDS YOU, AND THE ALMOST UNHEARD-OF MISERIES WHICH WERE ITS CONSEQUENCES.
YOU WERE JUSTIFIED IN REVENGING YOURSELF ON MY FATHER, AND I, HIS SON, THANK YOU FOR NOT USING GREATER SEVERITY.
HUH?
WHAT'S GOING ON?
HE WAS SO ANGRY LAST NIGHT...
I UNDERSTAND! THIS IS WHY MERCÉDÈS DID NOT OPPOSE MY SACRIFICE, FOR SHE HAD ALREADY DECIDED TO TELL ALBERT THE AWFUL TRUTH, KNOWING IT WOULD STOP THE DUEL.

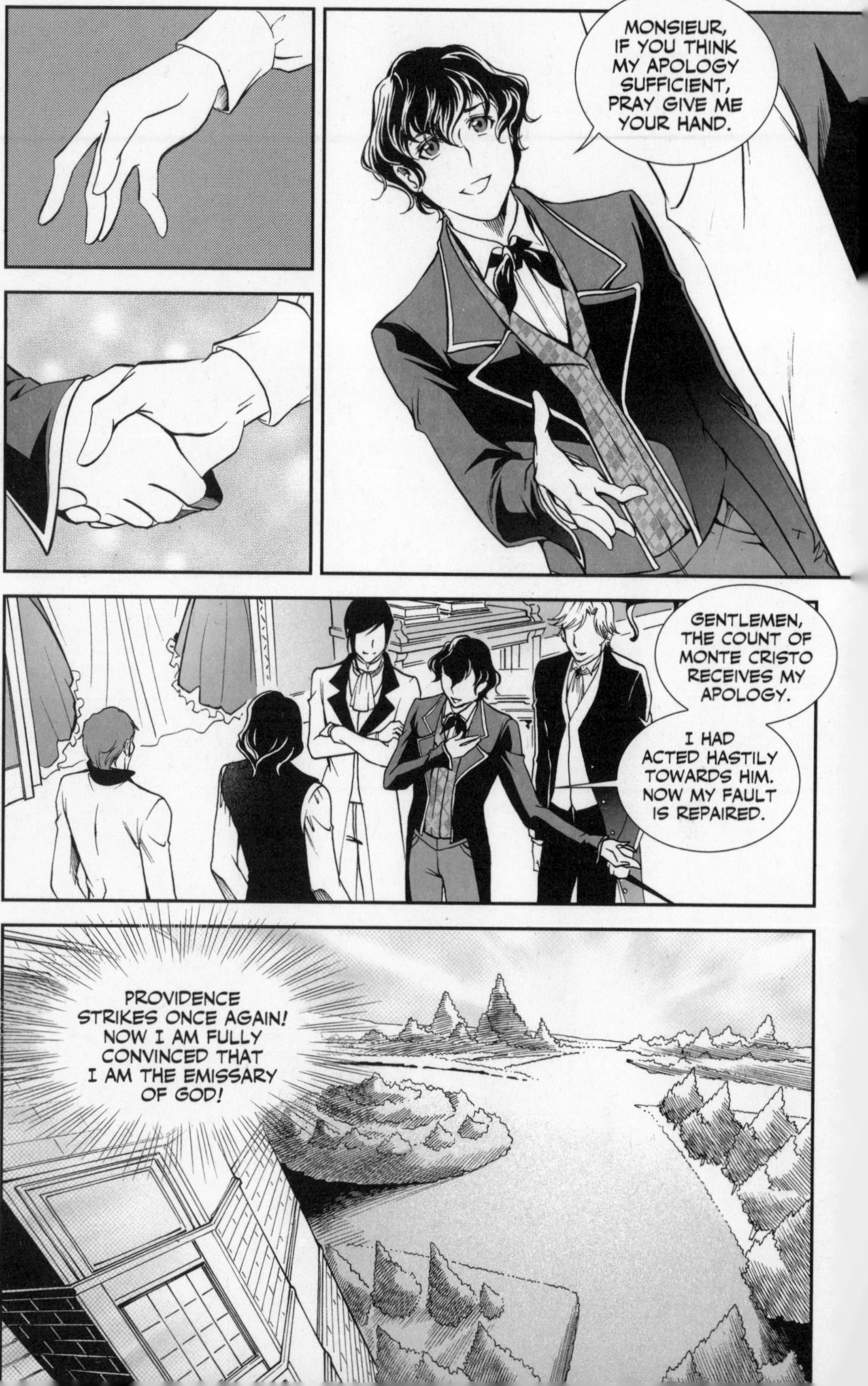
MONSIEUR, IF YOU THINK MY APOLOGY SUFFICIENT, PRAY GIVE ME YOUR HAND.
GENTLEMEN, THE COUNT OF MONTE CRISTO RECEIVES MY APOLOGY.
I HAD ACTED HASTILY TOWARDS HIM. NOW MY FAULT IS REPAIRED.
PROVIDENCE STRIKES ONCE AGAIN! NOW I AM FULLY CONVINCED THAT I AM THE EMISSARY OF GOD!

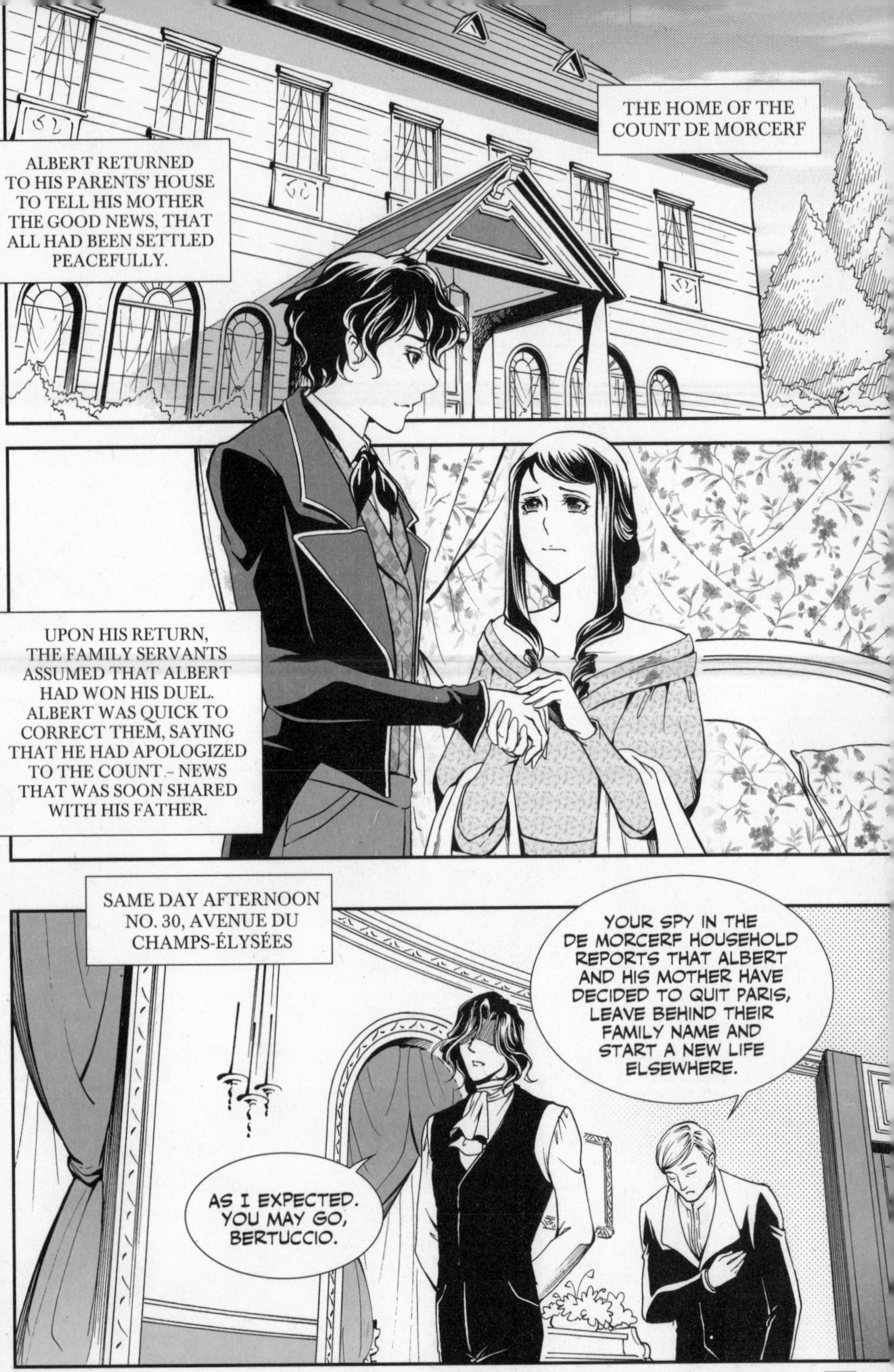
THE HOME OF THE COUNT DE MORCERF
ALBERT RETURNED TO HIS PARENTS' HOUSE TO TELL HIS MOTHER THE GOOD NEWS, THAT ALL HAD BEEN SETTLED PEACEFULLY.
UPON HIS RETURN, THE FAMILY SERVANTS ASSUMED THAT ALBERT HAD WON HIS DUEL. ALBERT WAS QUICK TO CORRECT THEM, SAYING THAT HE HAD APOLOGIZED TO THE COUNT – NEWS THAT WAS SOON SHARED WITH HIS FATHER.
SAME DAY AFTERNOON NO. 30, AVENUE DU CHAMPS-ÉLYSÉES
YOUR SPY IN THE DE MORCERF HOUSEHOLD REPORTS THAT ALBERT AND HIS MOTHER HAVE DECIDED TO QUIT PARIS, LEAVE BEHIND THEIR FAMILY NAME AND START A NEW LIFE ELSEWHERE.
AS I EXPECTED. YOU MAY GO, BERTUCCIO.

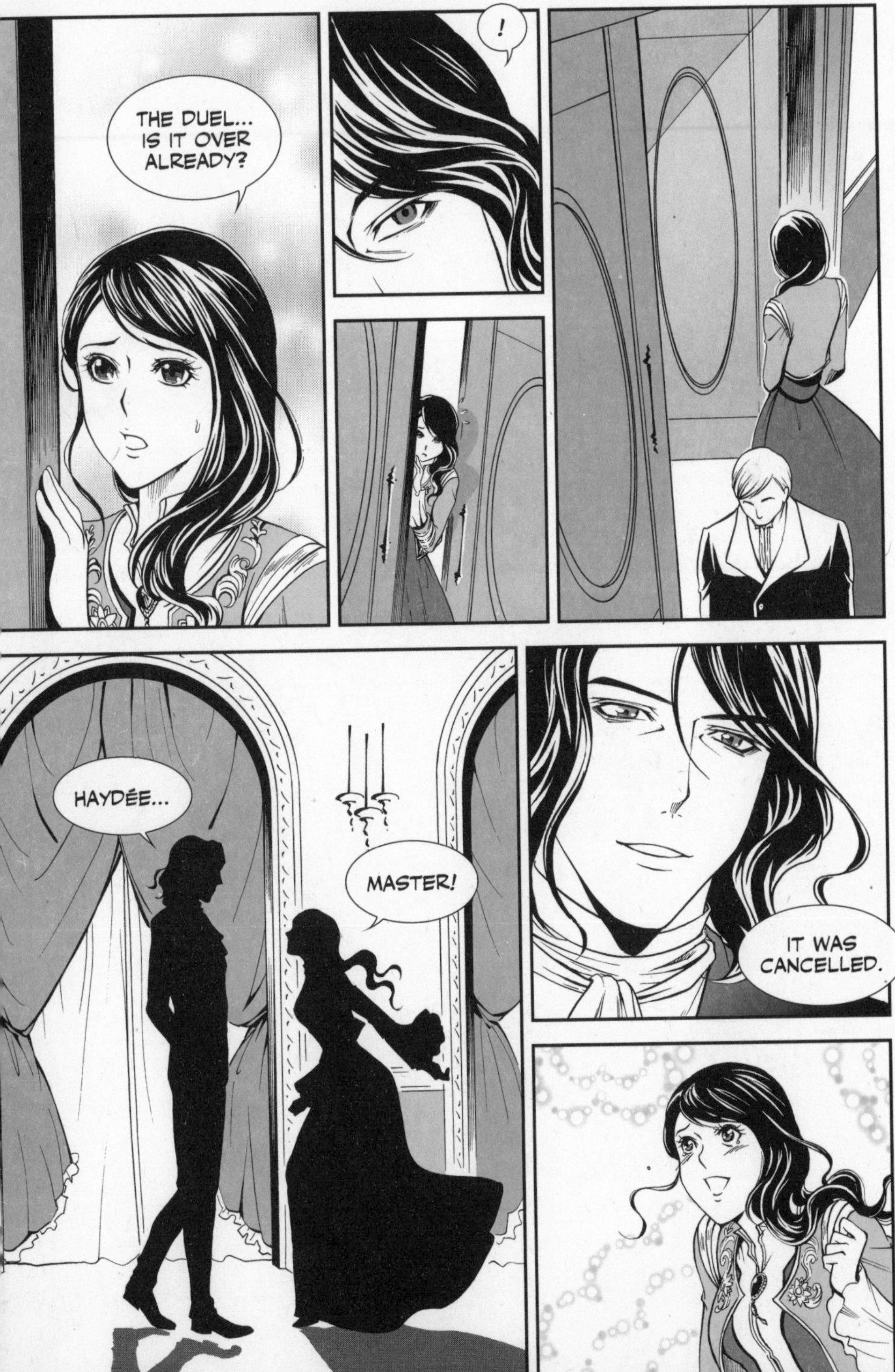
!
THE DUEL... IS IT OVER ALREADY?
IT WAS CANCELLED.
HAYDÉE...
MASTER!

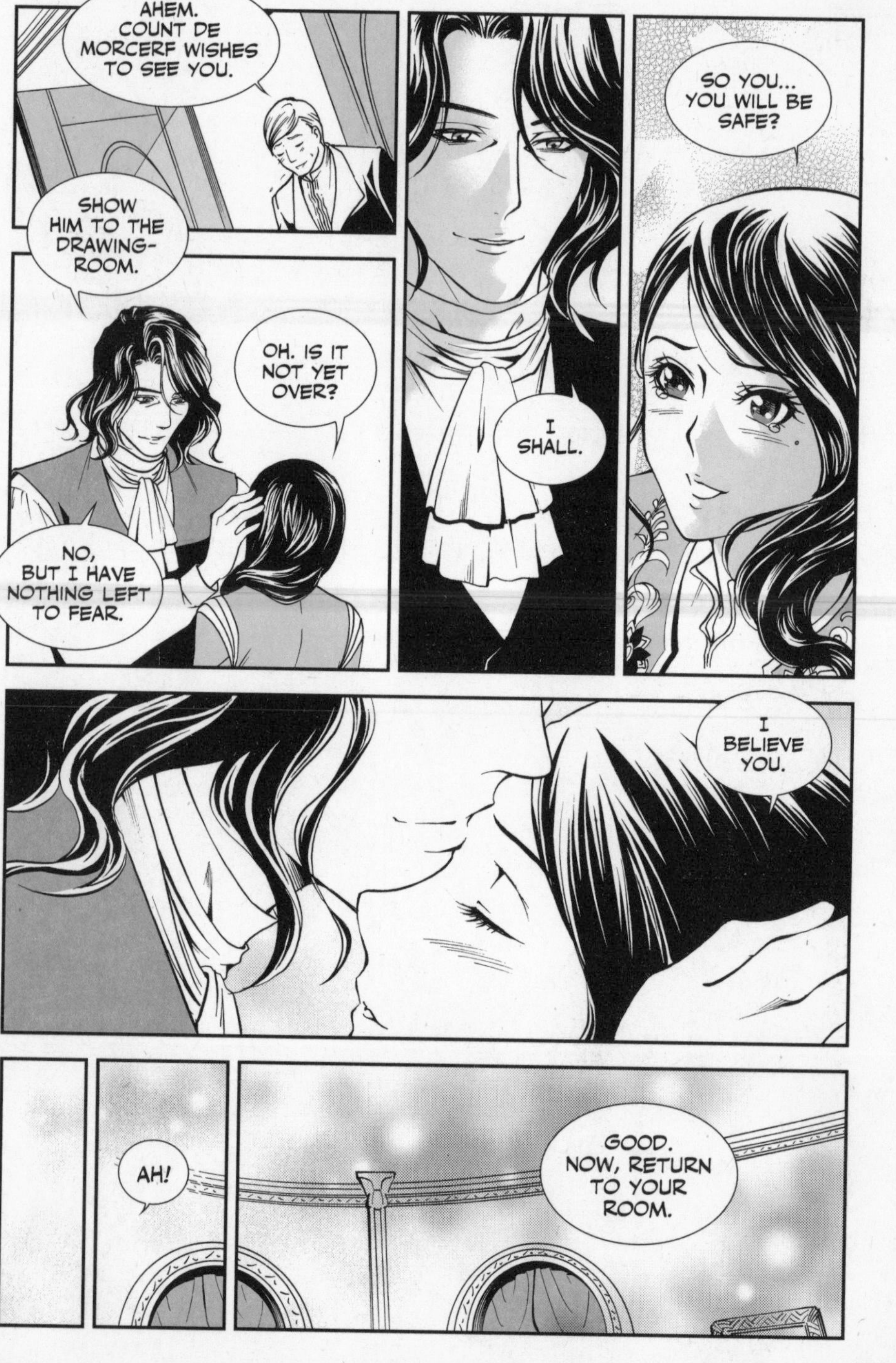
AHEM. COUNT DE MORCERF WISHES TO SEE YOU.
SHOW HIM TO THE DRAWING-ROOM.
OH. IS IT NOT YET OVER?
NO, BUT I HAVE NOTHING LEFT TO FEAR.
SO YOU... YOU WILL BE SAFE?
I SHALL.
I BELIEVE YOU.
AH!
GOOD. NOW, RETURN TO YOUR ROOM.

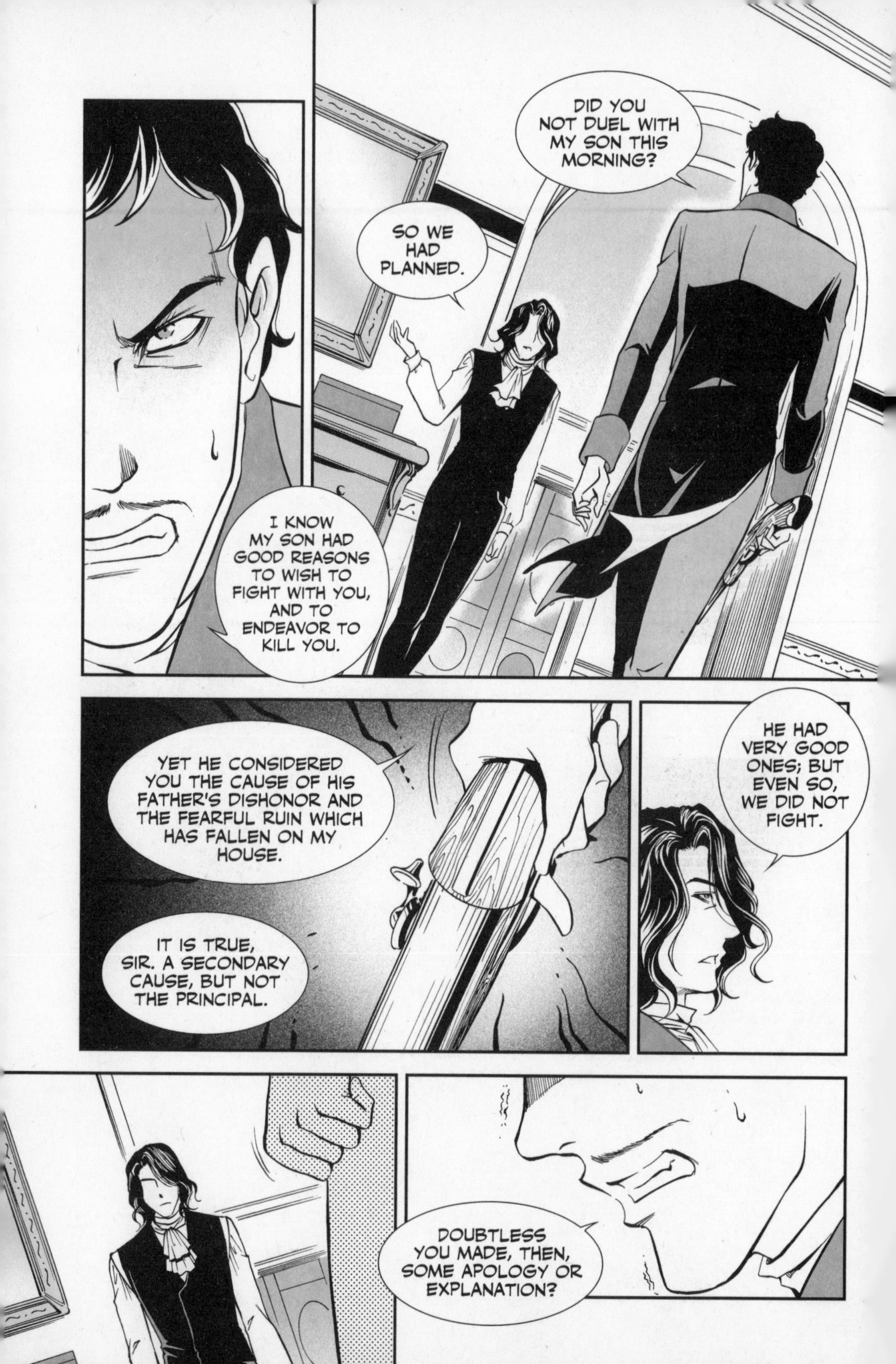
DID YOU NOT DUEL WITH MY SON THIS MORNING?
SO WE HAD PLANNED.
I KNOW MY SON HAD GOOD REASONS TO WISH TO FIGHT WITH YOU, AND TO ENDEAVOR TO KILL YOU.
HE HAD VERY GOOD ONES; BUT EVEN SO, WE DID NOT FIGHT.
YET HE CONSIDERED YOU THE CAUSE OF HIS FATHER'S DISHONOR AND THE FEARFUL RUIN WHICH HAS FALLEN ON MY HOUSE.
IT IS TRUE, SIR. A SECONDARY CAUSE, BUT NOT THE PRINCIPAL.
DOUBTLESS YOU MADE, THEN, SOME APOLOGY OR EXPLANATION?

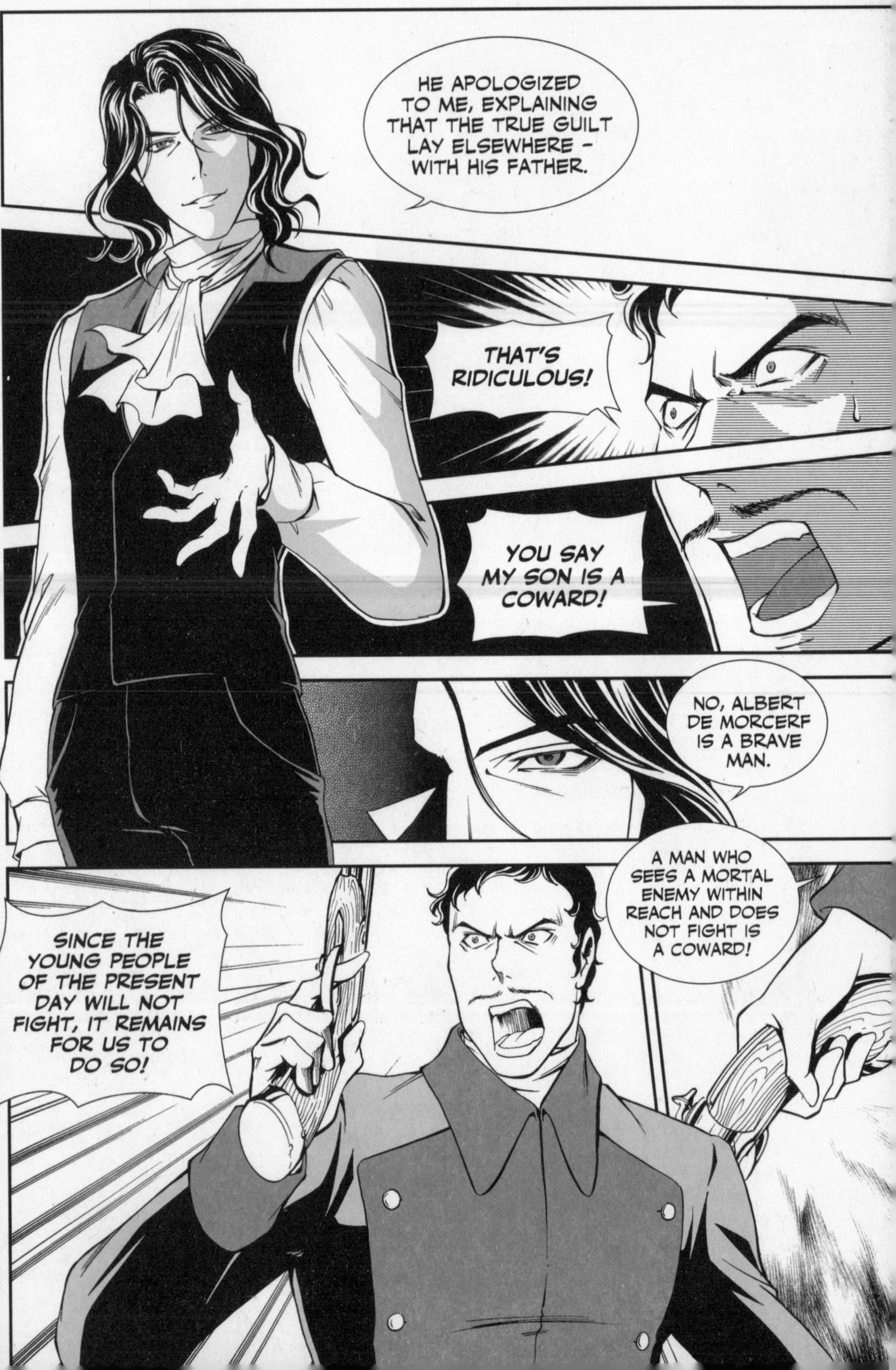
HE APOLOGIZED TO ME, EXPLAINING THAT THE TRUE GUILT LAY ELSEWHERE – WITH HIS FATHER.
THAT'S RIDICULOUS!
YOU SAY MY SON IS A COWARD!
NO, ALBERT DE MORCERF IS A BRAVE MAN.
A MAN WHO SEES A MORTAL ENEMY WITHIN REACH AND DOES NOT FIGHT IS A COWARD!
SINCE THE YOUNG PEOPLE OF THE PRESENT DAY WILL NOT FIGHT, IT REMAINS FOR US TO DO SO!

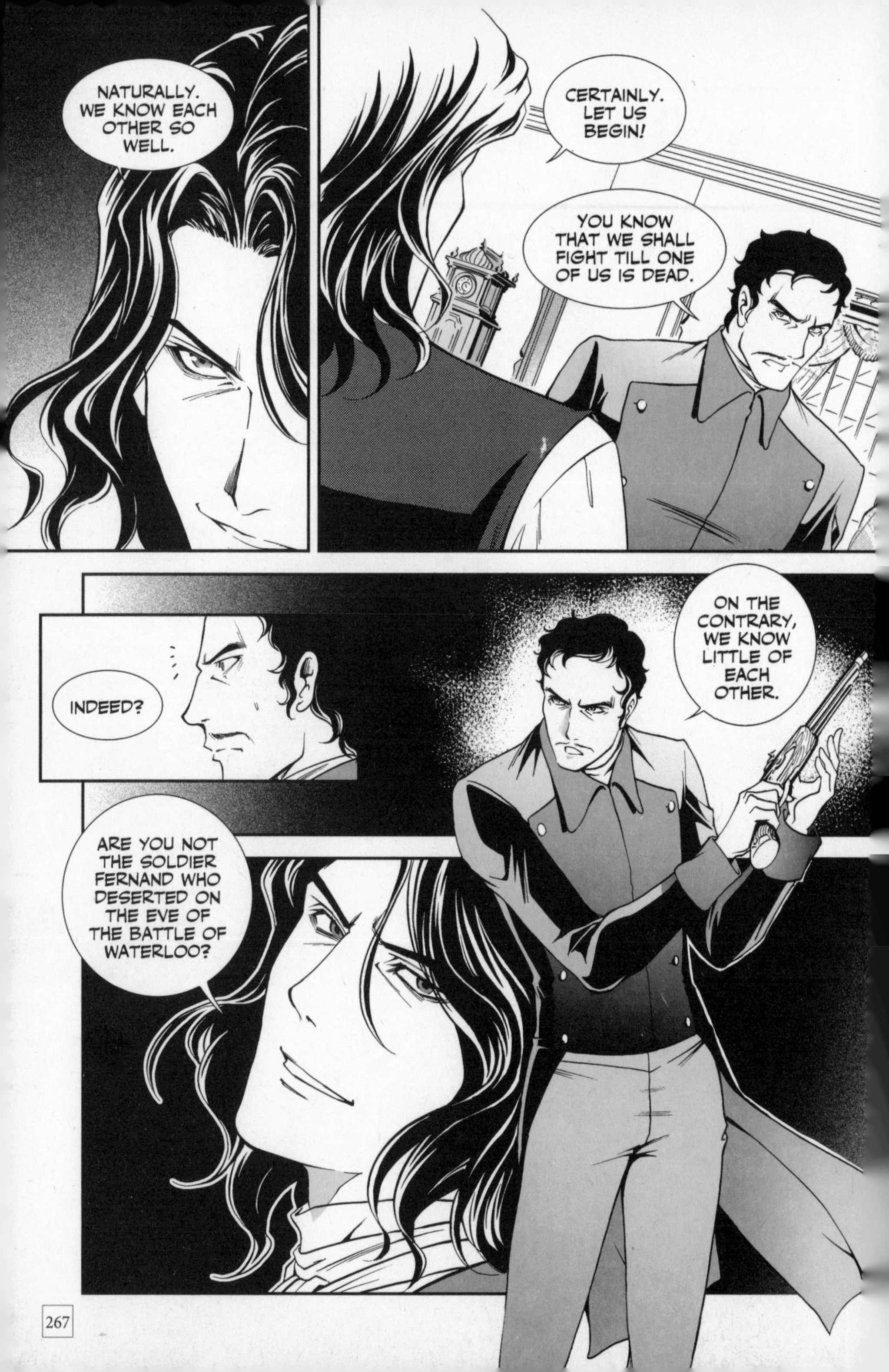
CERTAINLY. LET US BEGIN!
YOU KNOW THAT WE SHALL FIGHT TILL ONE OF US IS DEAD.
NATURALLY. WE KNOW EACH OTHER SO WELL.
ON THE CONTRARY, WE KNOW LITTLE OF EACH OTHER.
INDEED?
ARE YOU NOT THE SOLDIER FERNAND WHO DESERTED ON THE EVE OF THE BATTLE OF WATERLOO?

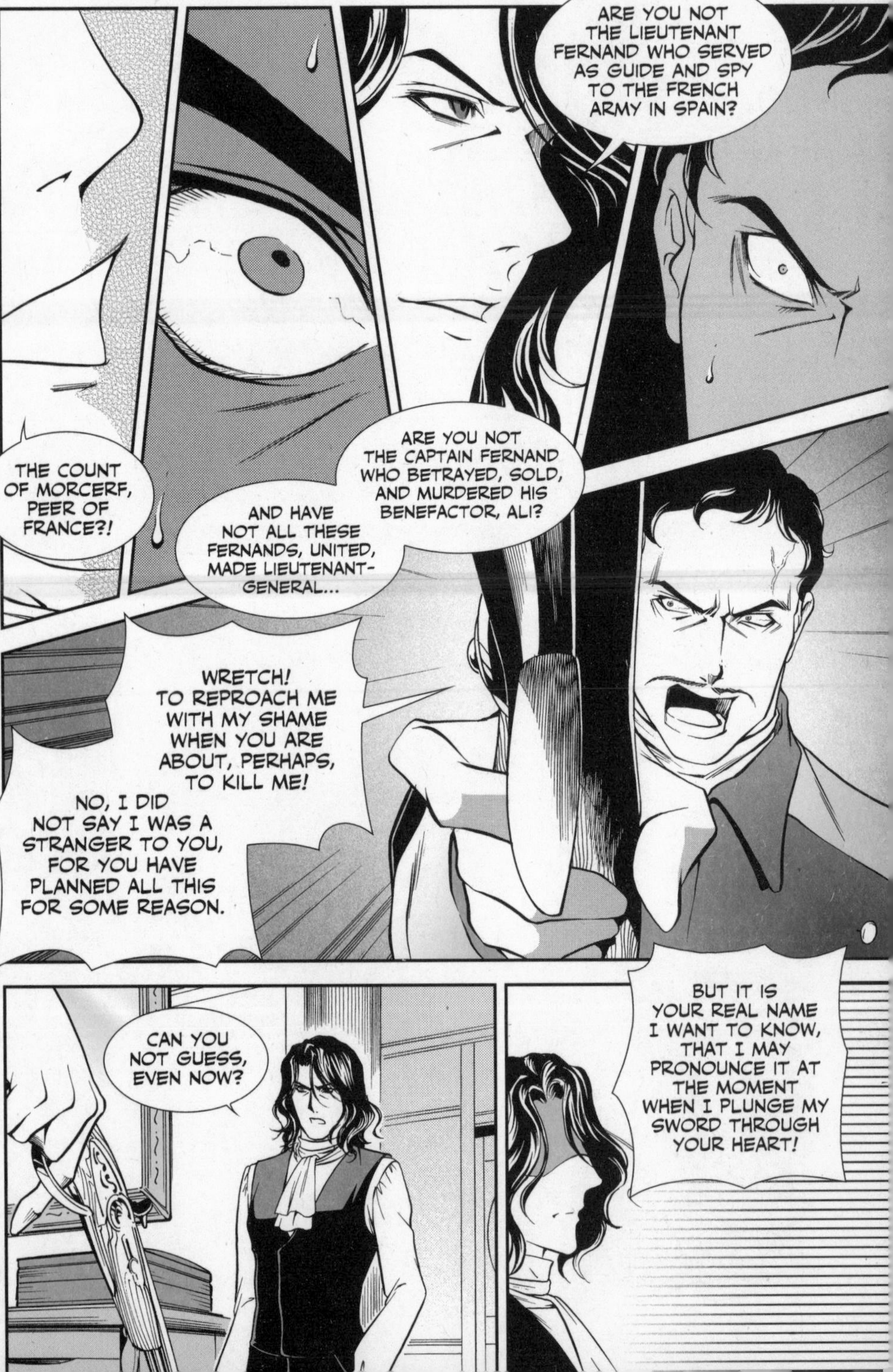
ARE YOU NOT THE LIEUTENANT FERNAND WHO SERVED AS GUIDE AND SPY TO THE FRENCH ARMY IN SPAIN?
ARE YOU NOT THE CAPTAIN FERNAND WHO BETRAYED, SOLD, AND MURDERED HIS BENEFACTOR, ALI?
AND HAVE NOT ALL THESE FERNANDS, UNITED, MADE LIEUTENANT-GENERAL...
THE COUNT OF MORCERF, PEER OF FRANCE?!
WRETCH! TO REPROACH ME WITH MY SHAME WHEN YOU ARE ABOUT, PERHAPS, TO KILL ME!
NO, I DID NOT SAY I WAS A STRANGER TO YOU, FOR YOU HAVE PLANNED ALL THIS FOR SOME REASON.
BUT IT IS YOUR REAL NAME I WANT TO KNOW, THAT I MAY PRONOUNCE IT AT THE MOMENT WHEN I PLUNGE MY SWORD THROUGH YOUR HEART!
CAN YOU NOT GUESS, EVEN NOW?

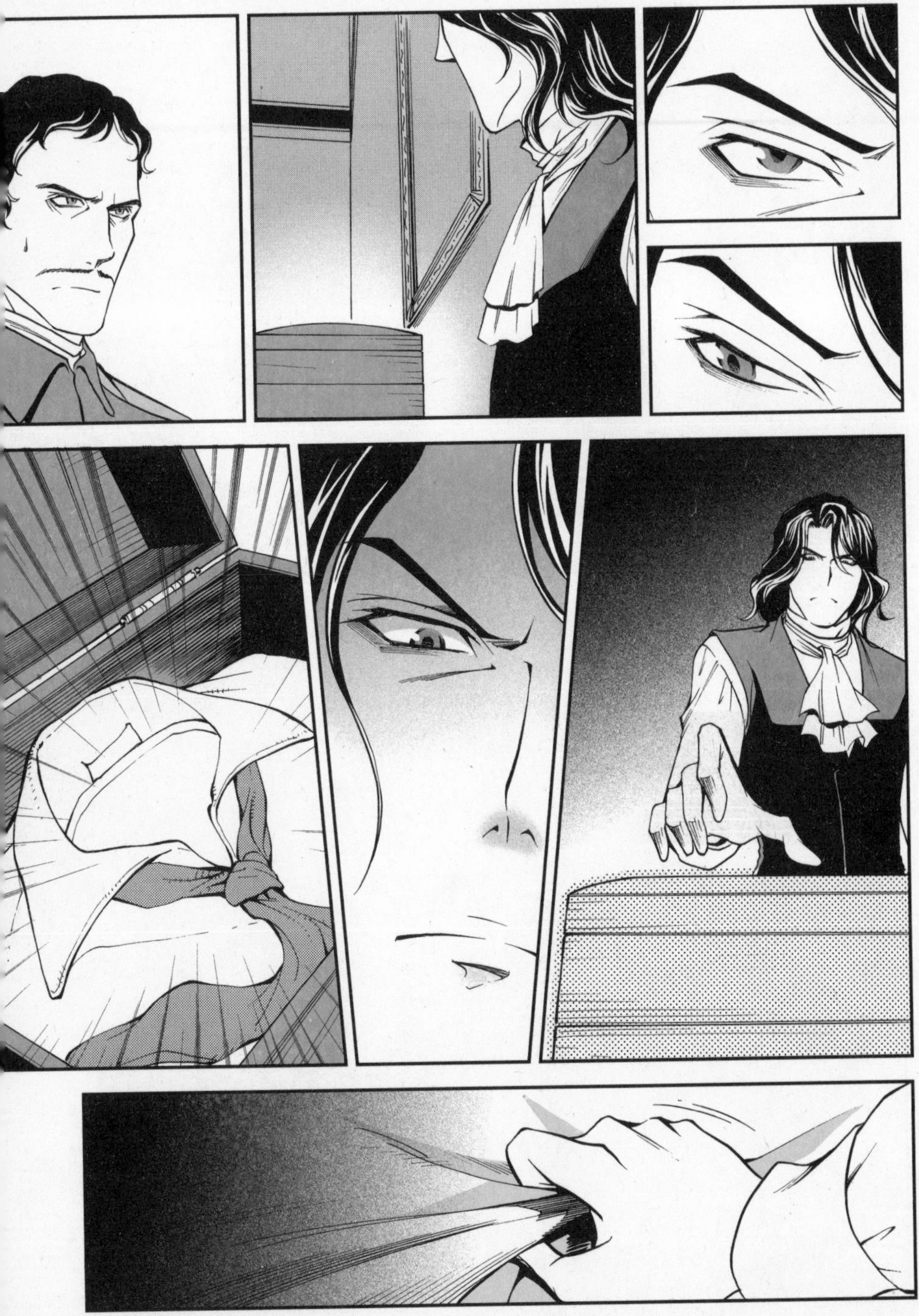

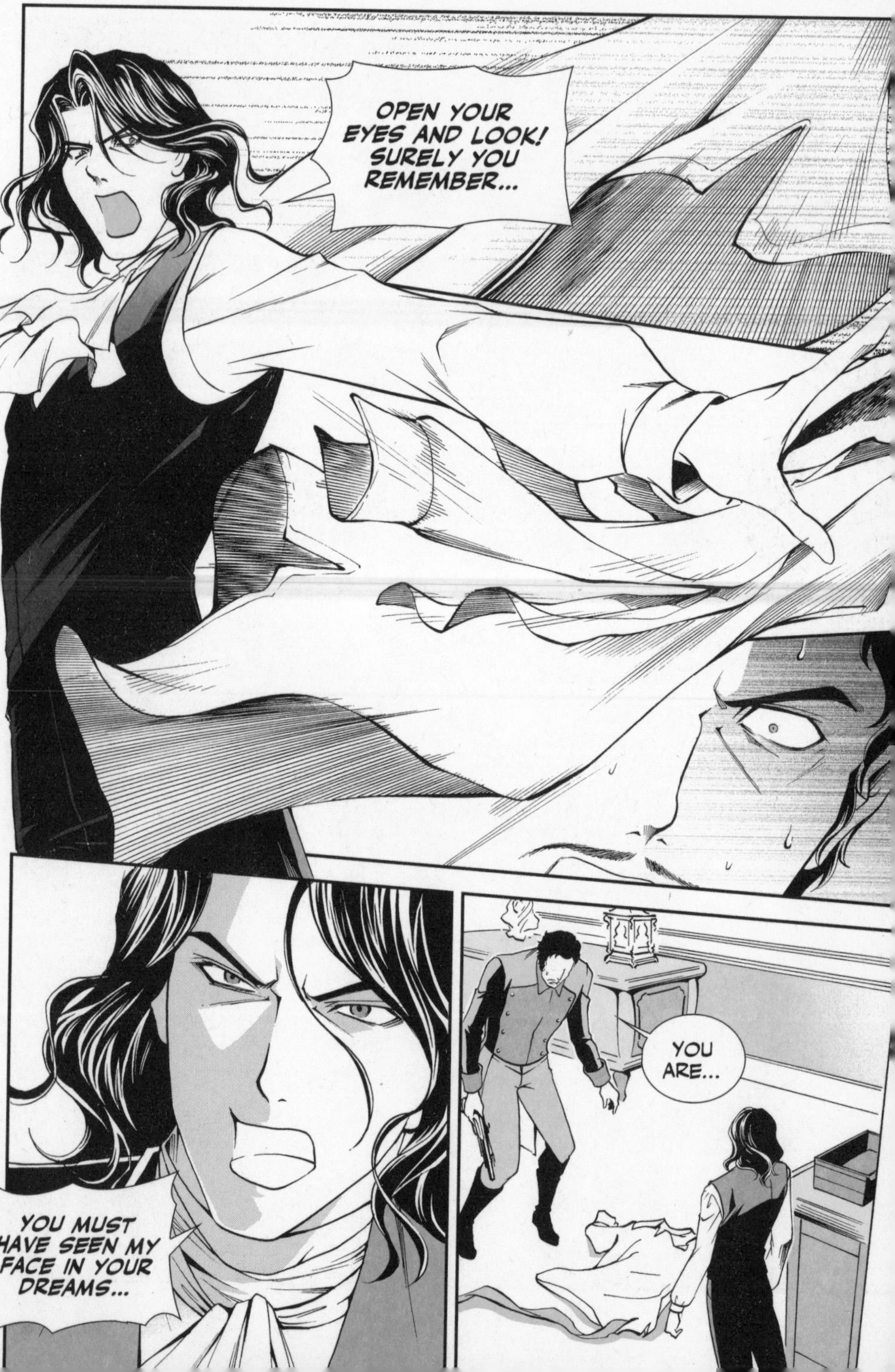
OPEN YOUR EYES AND LOOK! SURELY YOU REMEMBER...
YOU ARE...
YOU MUST HAVE SEEN MY FACE IN YOUR DREAMS...

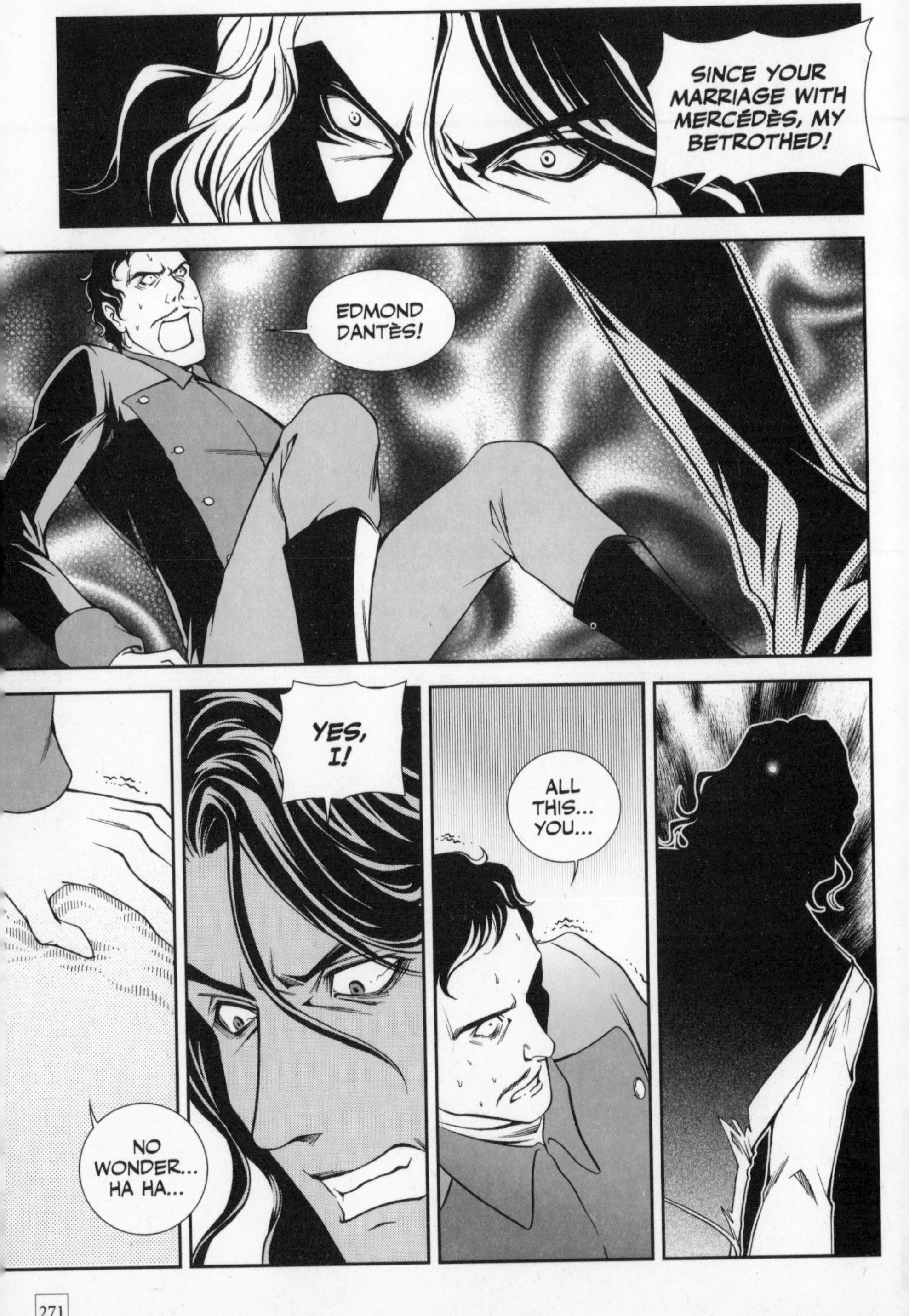
SINCE YOUR MARRIAGE WITH MERCÉDÈS, MY BETROTHED!
EDMOND DANTÈS!
ALL THIS... YOU...
YES, I!
NO WONDER... HA HA...

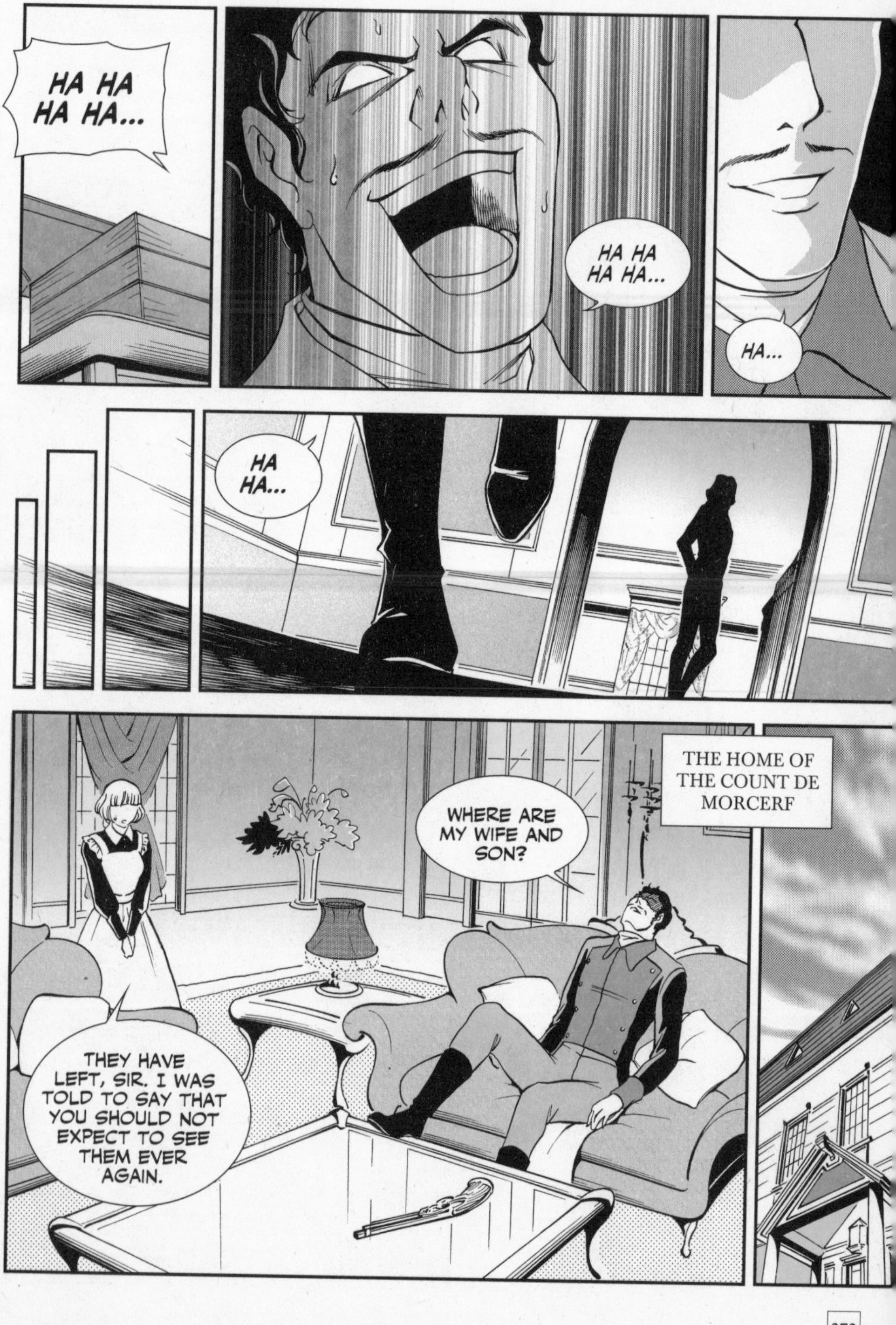
HA...
HA HA HA HA...
HA HA HA HA...
HA HA...
THE HOME OF THE COUNT DE MORCERF
WHERE ARE MY WIFE AND SON?
THEY HAVE LEFT, SIR. I WAS TOLD TO SAY THAT YOU SHOULD NOT EXPECT TO SEE THEM EVER AGAIN.

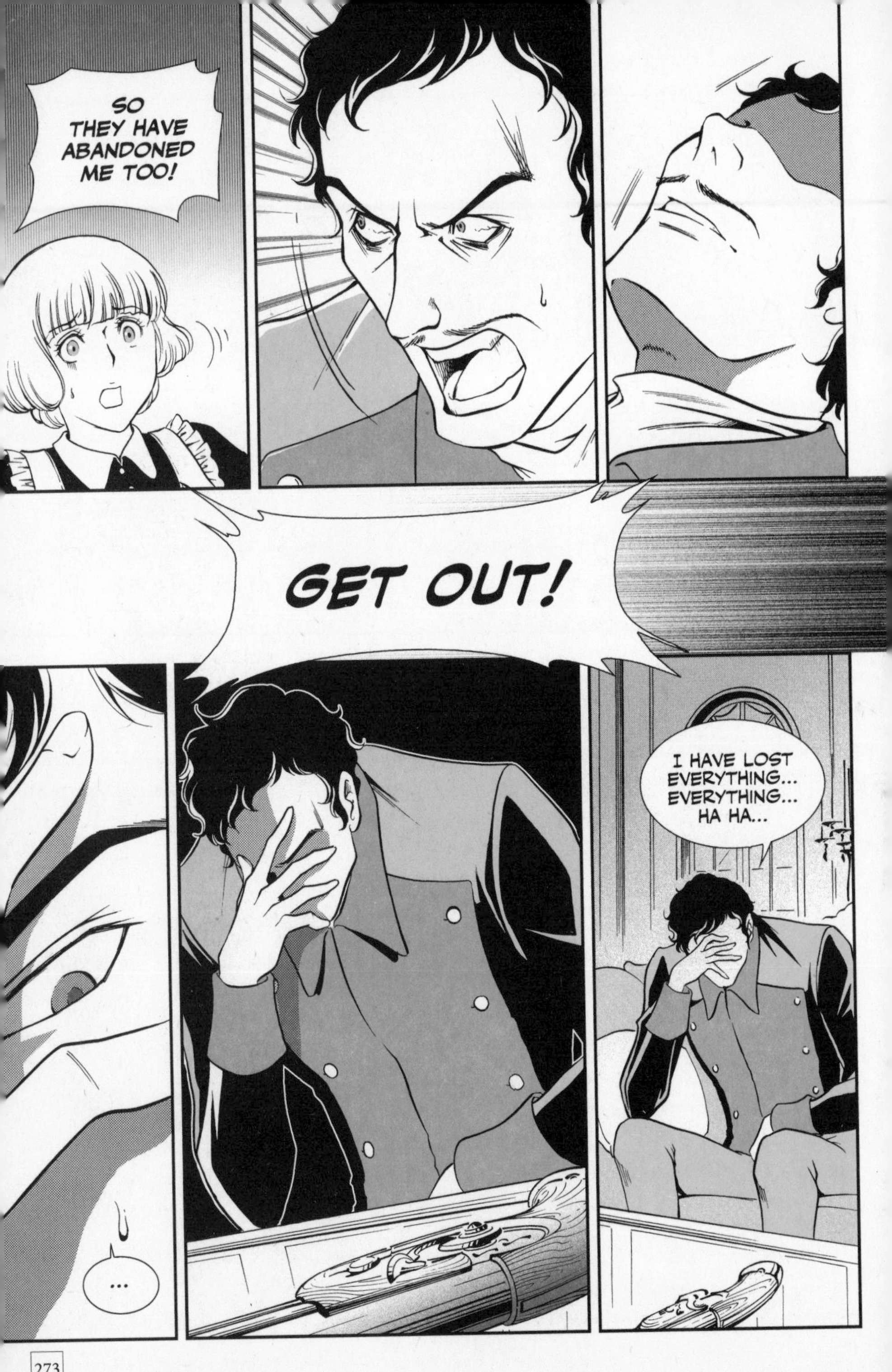
SO THEY HAVE ABANDONED ME TOO!
GET OUT!
I HAVE LOST EVERYTHING... EVERYTHING... HA HA...
...

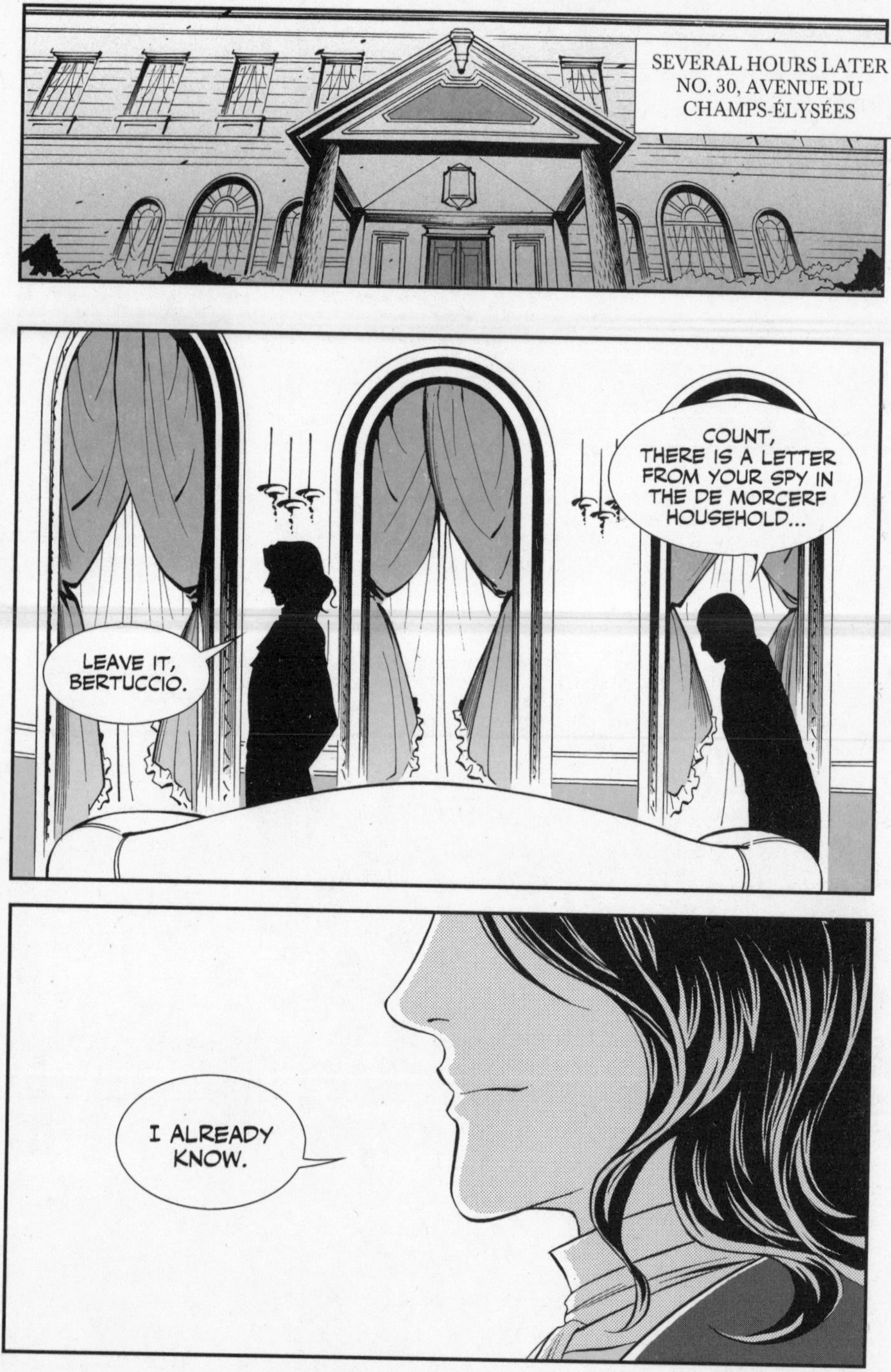
SEVERAL HOURS LATER NO. 30, AVENUE DU CHAMPS-ÉLYSÉES
COUNT, THERE IS A LETTER FROM YOUR SPY IN THE DE MORCERF HOUSEHOLD...
LEAVE IT, BERTUCCIO.
I ALREADY KNOW.

CHAPTER 12 That Accursed Line

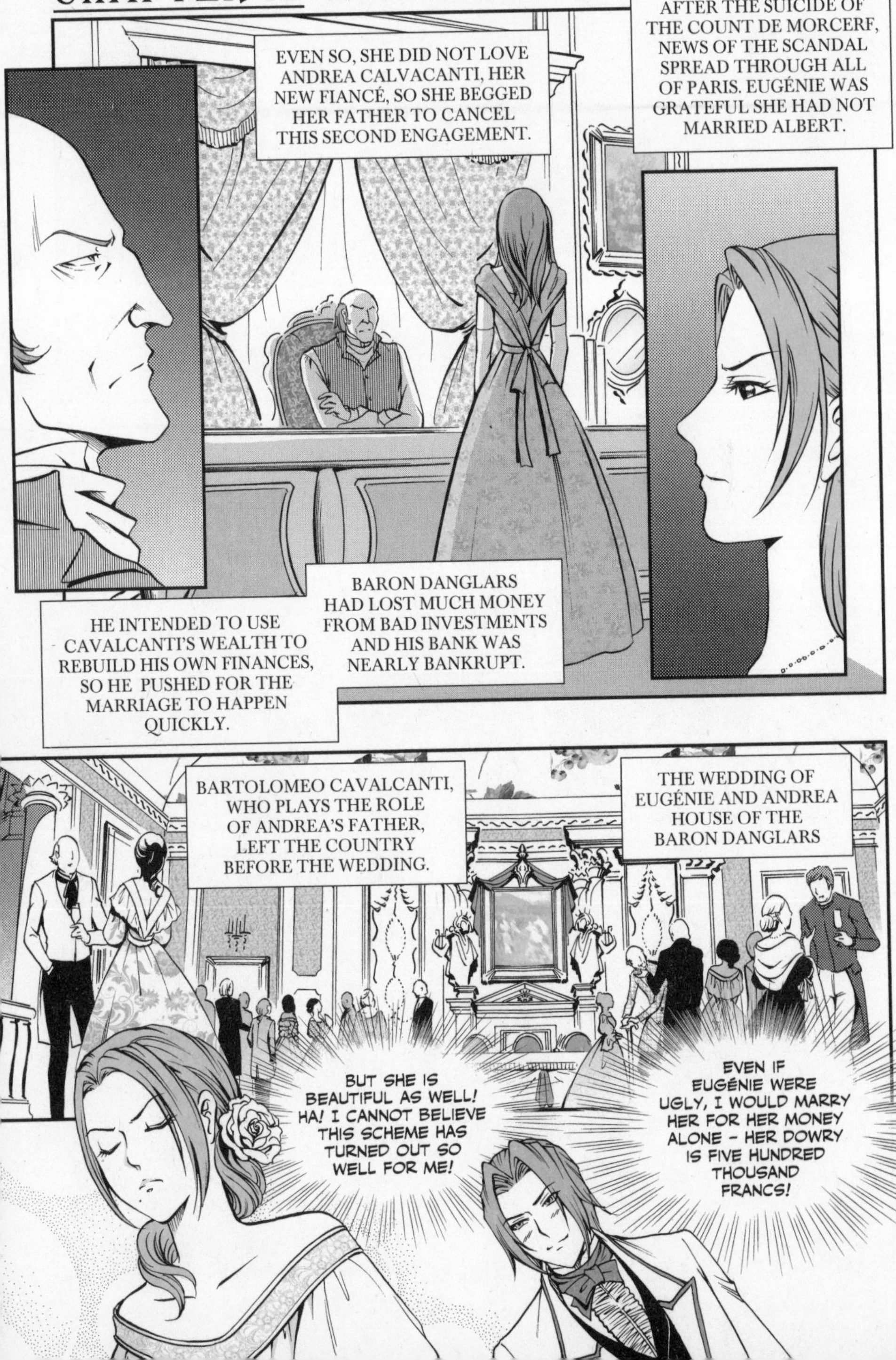
AFTER THE SUICIDE OF THE COUNT DE MORCERF, NEWS OF THE SCANDAL SPREAD THROUGH ALL OF PARIS. EUGÉNIE WAS GRATEFUL SHE HAD NOT MARRIED ALBERT.
EVEN SO, SHE DID NOT LOVE ANDREA CALVACANTI, HER NEW FIANCÉ, SO SHE BEGGED HER FATHER TO CANCEL THIS SECOND ENGAGEMENT.
BARON DANGLARS HAD LOST MUCH MONEY FROM BAD INVESTMENTS AND HIS BANK WAS NEARLY BANKRUPT.
HE INTENDED TO USE CAVALCANTI'S WEALTH TO REBUILD HIS OWN FINANCES, SO HE PUSHED FOR THE MARRIAGE TO HAPPEN QUICKLY.
THE WEDDING OF EUGÉNIE AND ANDREA HOUSE OF THE BARON DANGLARS
BARTOLOMEO CAVALCANTI, WHO PLAYS THE ROLE OF ANDREA'S FATHER, LEFT THE COUNTRY BEFORE THE WEDDING.
EVEN IF EUGÉNIE WERE UGLY, I WOULD MARRY HER FOR HER MONEY ALONE - HER DOWRY IS FIVE HUNDRED THOUSAND FRANCS!
BUT SHE IS BEAUTIFUL AS WELL! HA! I CANNOT BELIEVE THIS SCHEME HAS TURNED OUT SO WELL FOR ME!

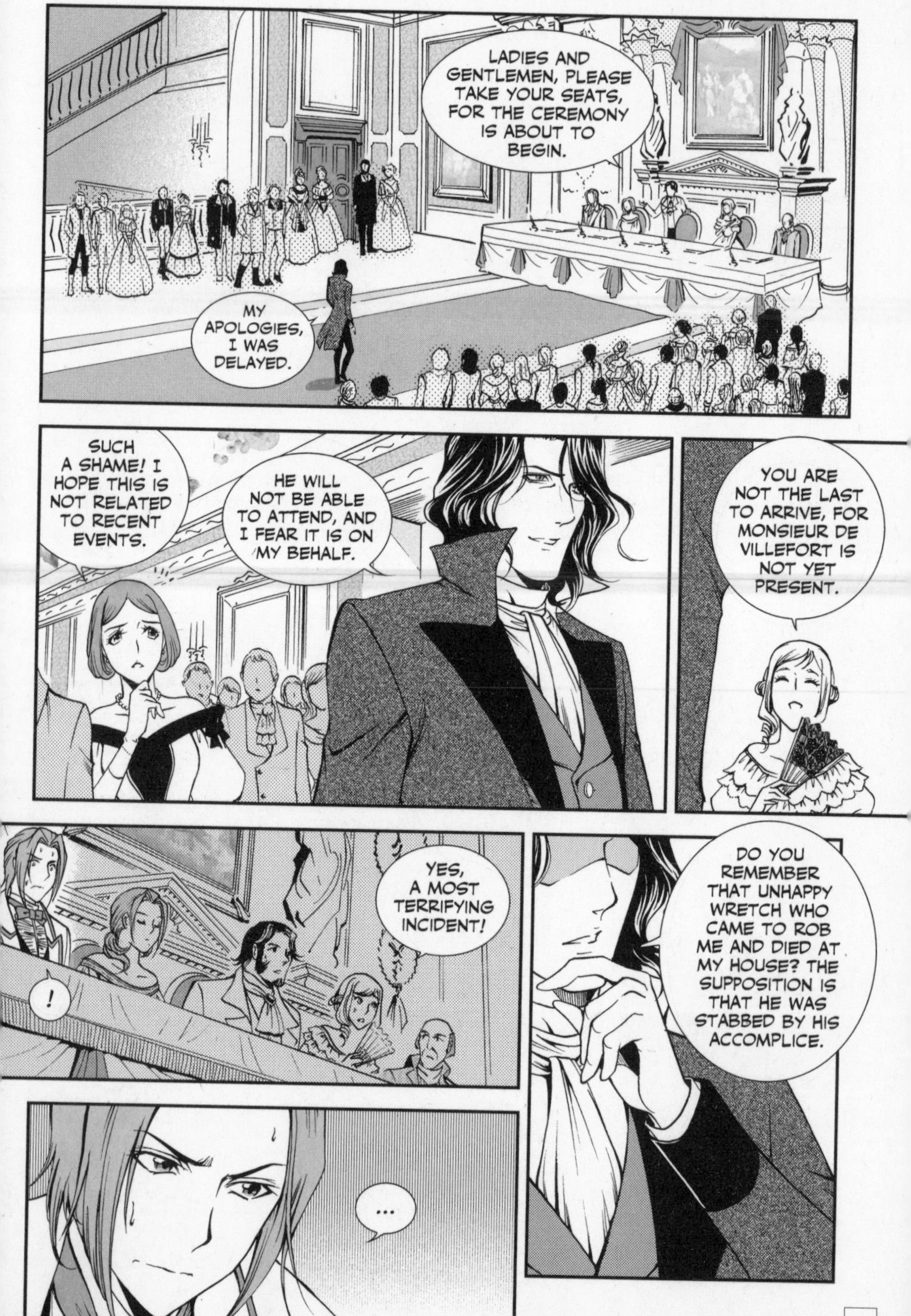
LADIES AND GENTLEMEN, PLEASE TAKE YOUR SEATS, FOR THE CEREMONY IS ABOUT TO BEGIN.
MY APOLOGIES, I WAS DELAYED.
YOU ARE NOT THE LAST TO ARRIVE, FOR MONSIEUR DE VILLEFORT IS NOT YET PRESENT.
HE WILL NOT BE ABLE TO ATTEND, AND I FEAR IT IS ON MY BEHALF.
SUCH A SHAME! I HOPE THIS IS NOT RELATED TO RECENT EVENTS.
DO YOU REMEMBER THAT UNHAPPY WRETCH WHO CAME TO ROB ME AND DIED AT MY HOUSE? THE SUPPOSITION IS THAT HE WAS STABBED BY HIS ACCOMPLICE.
YES, A MOST TERRIFYING INCIDENT!
!
...

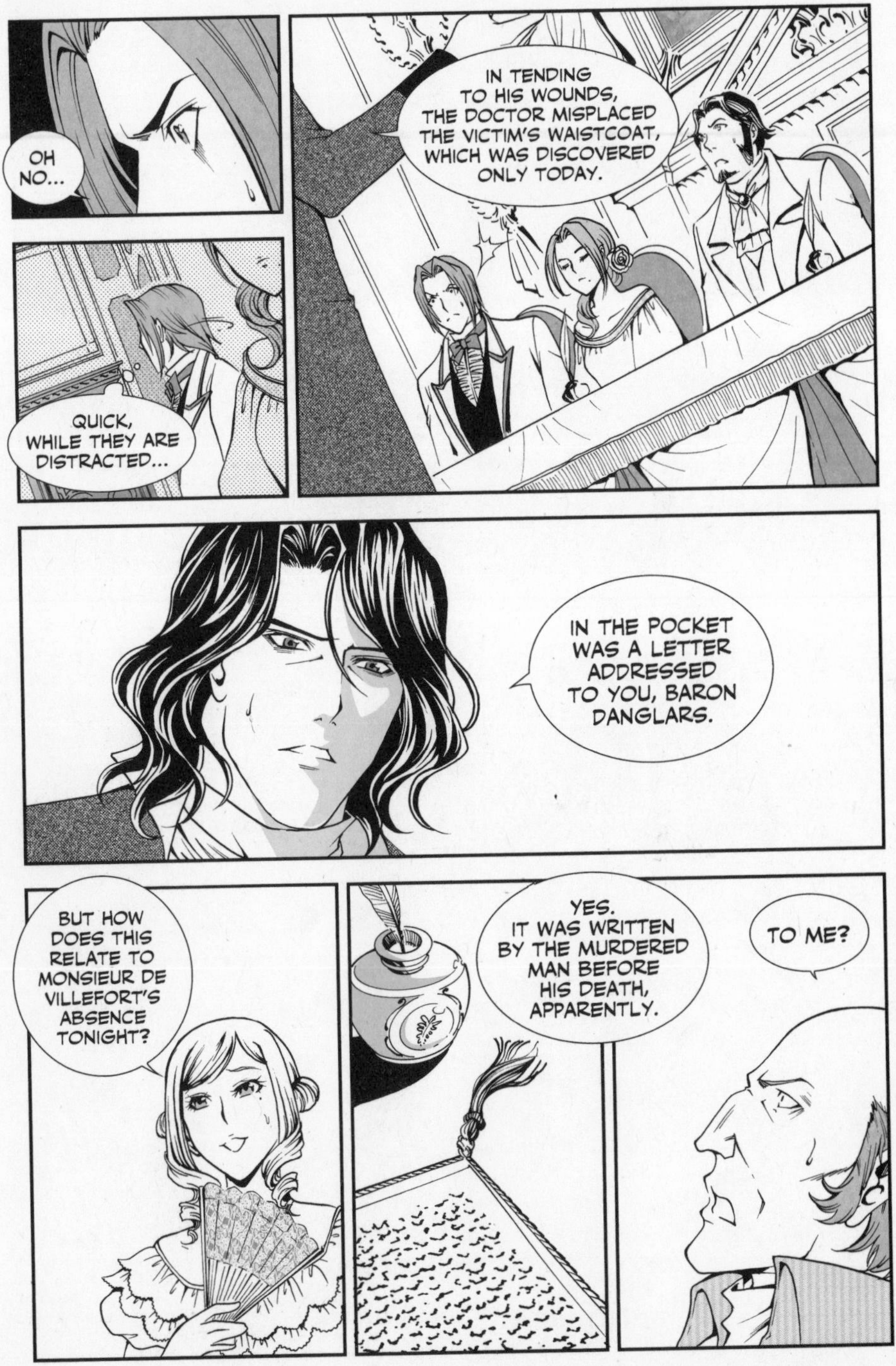
IN TENDING TO HIS WOUNDS, THE DOCTOR MISPLACED THE VICTIM'S WAISTCOAT, WHICH WAS DISCOVERED ONLY TODAY.
OH NO...
QUICK, WHILE THEY ARE DISTRACTED...
IN THE POCKET WAS A LETTER ADDRESSED TO YOU, BARON DANGLARS.
TO ME?
YES. IT WAS WRITTEN BY THE MURDERED MAN BEFORE HIS DEATH, APPARENTLY.
BUT HOW DOES THIS RELATE TO MONSIEUR DE VILLEFORT'S ABSENCE TONIGHT?

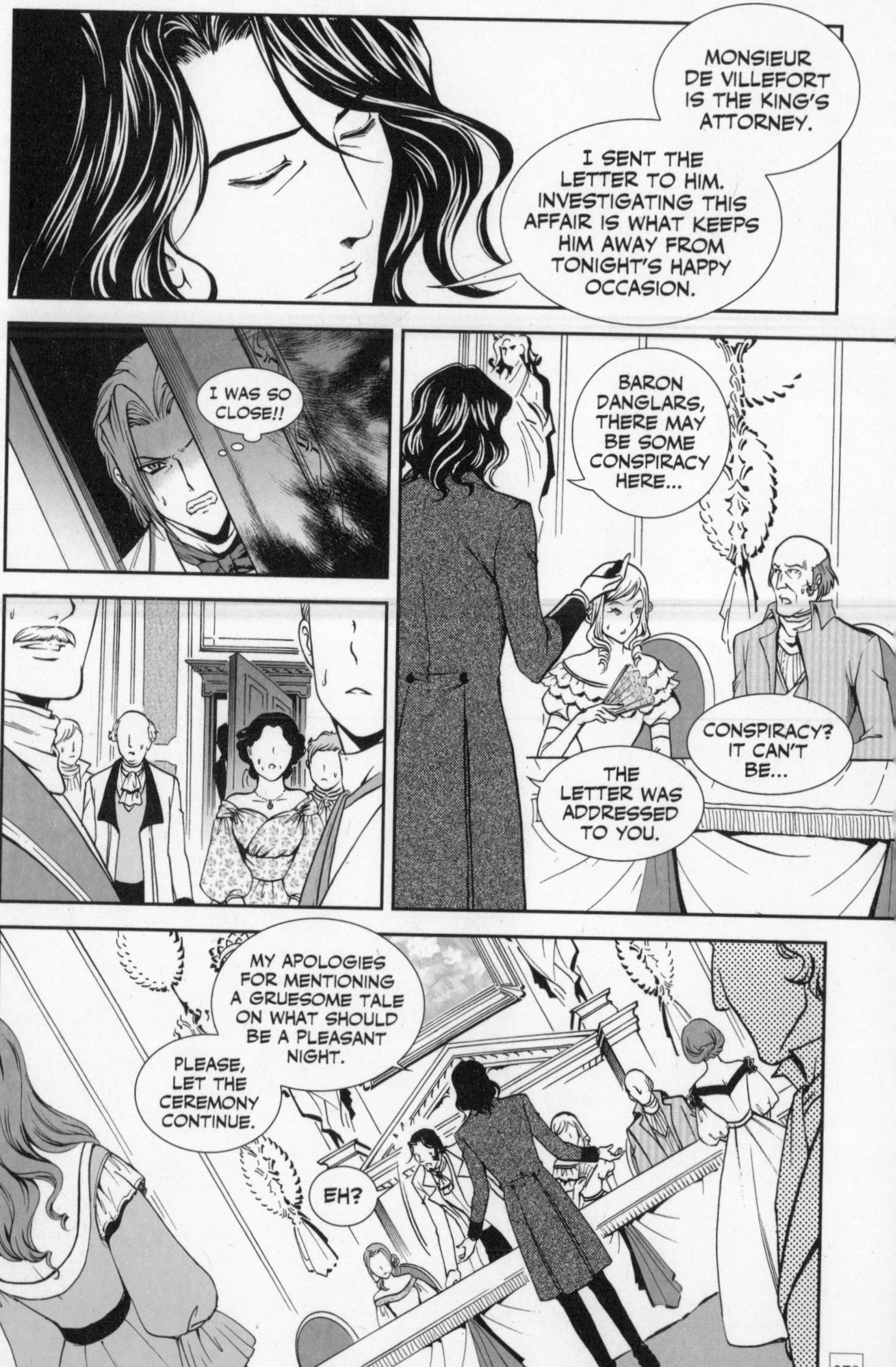
MONSIEUR DE VILLEFORT IS THE KING'S ATTORNEY.
I SENT THE LETTER TO HIM. INVESTIGATING THIS AFFAIR IS WHAT KEEPS HIM AWAY FROM TONIGHT'S HAPPY OCCASION.
BARON DANGLARS, THERE MAY BE SOME CONSPIRACY HERE...
CONSPIRACY? IT CAN'T BE...
THE LETTER WAS ADDRESSED TO YOU.
I WAS SO CLOSE!!
MY APOLOGIES FOR MENTIONING A GRUESOME TALE ON WHAT SHOULD BE A PLEASANT NIGHT.
PLEASE, LET THE CEREMONY CONTINUE.
EH?

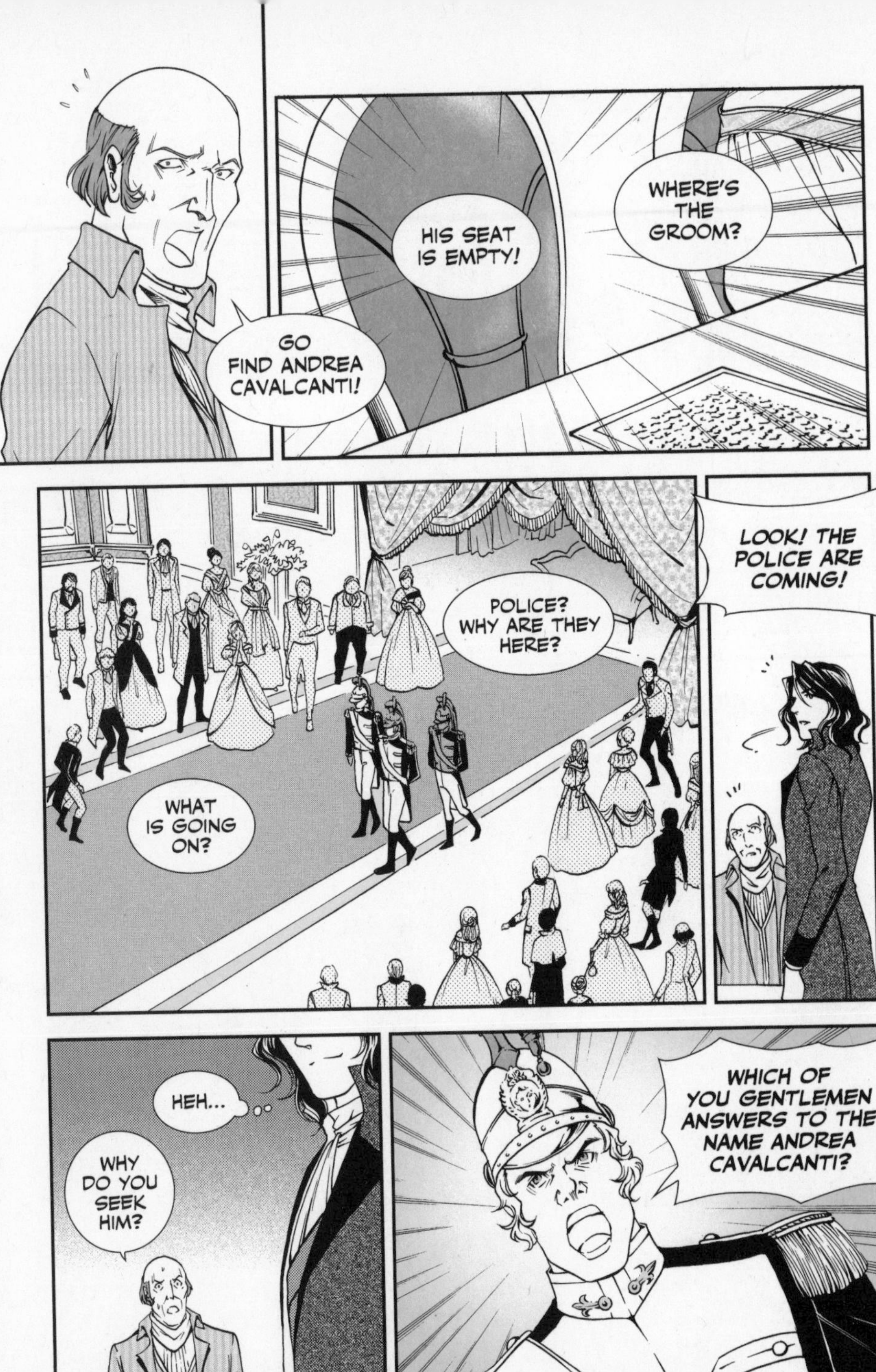
WHERE'S THE GROOM?
HIS SEAT IS EMPTY!
GO FIND ANDREA CAVALCANTI!
LOOK! THE POLICE ARE COMING!
POLICE? WHY ARE THEY HERE?
WHAT IS GOING ON?
WHICH OF YOU GENTLEMEN ANSWERS TO THE NAME ANDREA CAVALCANTI?
HEH...
WHY DO YOU SEEK HIM?

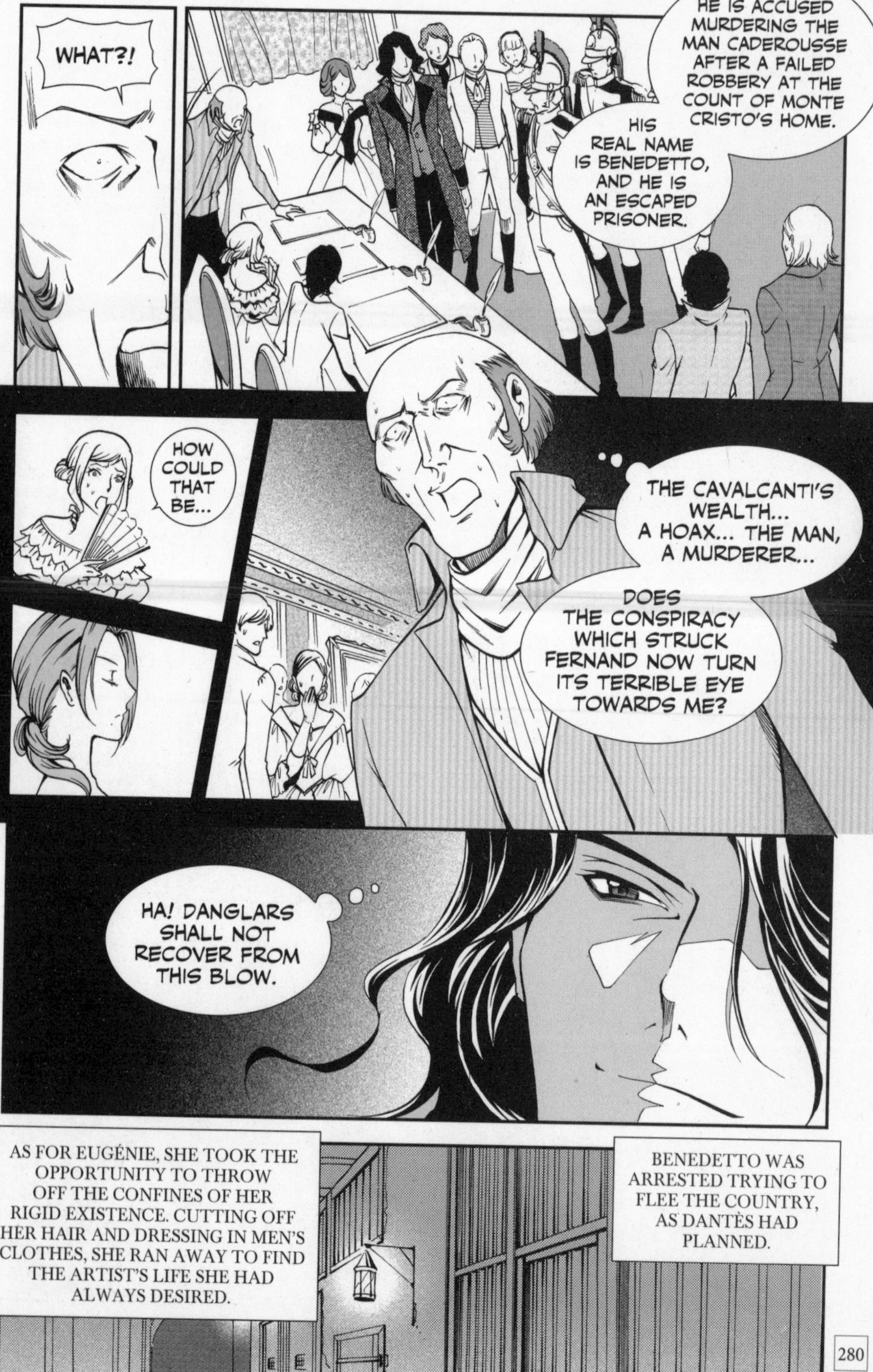

HE IS ACCUSED MURDERING THE MAN CADEROUSSE AFTER A FAILED ROBBERY AT THE COUNT OF MONTE CRISTO'S HOME.
HIS REAL NAME IS BENEDETTO, AND HE IS AN ESCAPED PRISONER.
WHAT?!
THE CAVALCANTI'S WEALTH... A HOAX... THE MAN, A MURDERER...
DOES THE CONSPIRACY WHICH STRUCK FERNAND NOW TURN ITS TERRIBLE EYE TOWARDS ME?
HOW COULD THAT BE...
HA! DANGLARS SHALL NOT RECOVER FROM THIS BLOW.
BENEDETTO WAS ARRESTED TRYING TO FLEE THE COUNTRY, AS DANTÈS HAD PLANNED.
AS FOR EUGÉNIE, SHE TOOK THE OPPORTUNITY TO THROW OFF THE CONFINES OF HER RIGID EXISTENCE. CUTTING OFF HER HAIR AND DRESSING IN MEN'S CLOTHES, SHE RAN AWAY TO FIND THE ARTIST'S LIFE SHE HAD ALWAYS DESIRED.

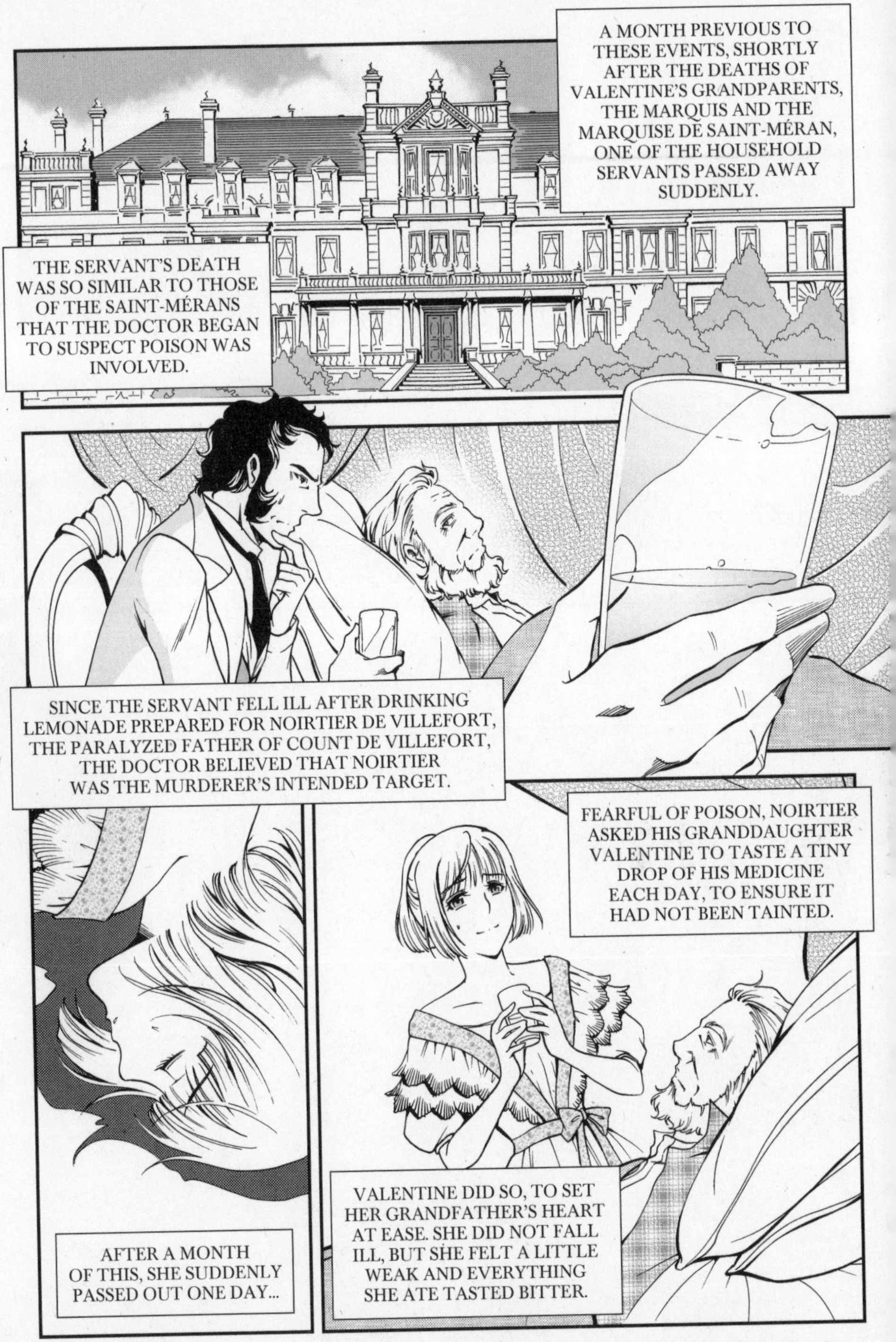
A MONTH PREVIOUS TO THESE EVENTS, SHORTLY AFTER THE DEATHS OF VALENTINE'S GRANDPARENTS, THE MARQUIS AND THE MARQUISE DE SAINT-MÉRAN, ONE OF THE HOUSEHOLD SERVANTS PASSED AWAY SUDDENLY.
THE SERVANT'S DEATH WAS SO SIMILAR TO THOSE OF THE SAINT-MÉRANS THAT THE DOCTOR BEGAN TO SUSPECT POISON WAS INVOLVED.
SINCE THE SERVANT FELL ILL AFTER DRINKING LEMONADE PREPARED FOR NOIRTIER DE VILLEFORT, THE PARALYZED FATHER OF COUNT DE VILLEFORT, THE DOCTOR BELIEVED THAT NOIRTIER WAS THE MURDERER'S INTENDED TARGET.
FEARFUL OF POISON, NOIRTIER ASKED HIS GRANDDAUGHTER VALENTINE TO TASTE A TINY DROP OF HIS MEDICINE EACH DAY, TO ENSURE IT HAD NOT BEEN TAINTED.
VALENTINE DID SO, TO SET HER GRANDFATHER'S HEART AT EASE. SHE DID NOT FALL ILL, BUT SHE FELT A LITTLE WEAK AND EVERYTHING SHE ATE TASTED BITTER.
AFTER A MONTH OF THIS, SHE SUDDENLY PASSED OUT ONE DAY...

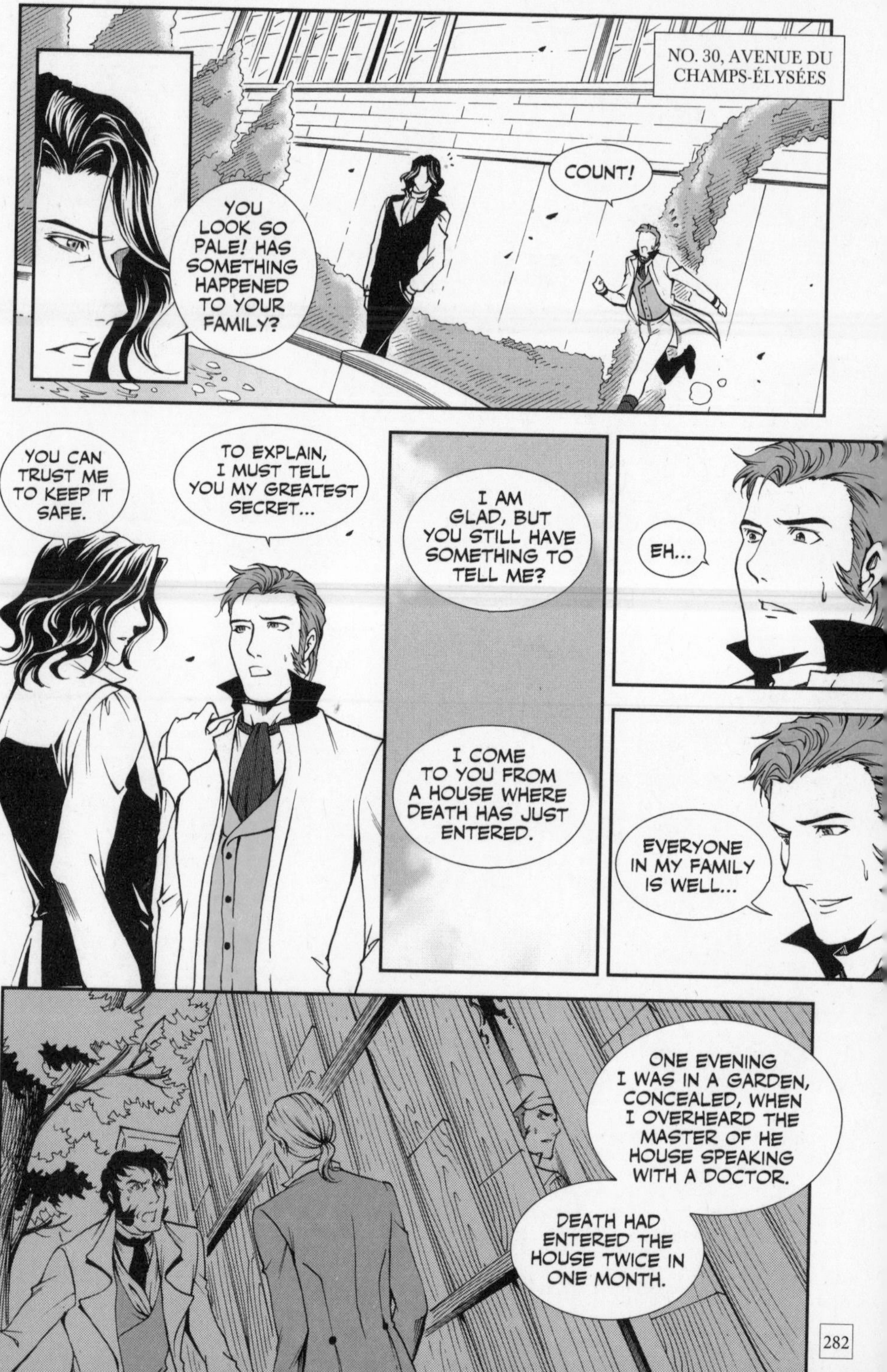
NO. 30, AVENUE DU CHAMPS-ÉLYSÉES
COUNT!
YOU LOOK SO PALE! HAS SOMETHING HAPPENED TO YOUR FAMILY?
EH...
EVERYONE IN MY FAMILY IS WELL...
I AM GLAD, BUT YOU STILL HAVE SOMETHING TO TELL ME?
I COME TO YOU FROM A HOUSE WHERE DEATH HAS JUST ENTERED.
TO EXPLAIN, I MUST TELL YOU MY GREATEST SECRET...
YOU CAN TRUST ME TO KEEP IT SAFE.
ONE EVENING I WAS IN A GARDEN, CONCEALED, WHEN I OVERHEARD THE MASTER OF HE HOUSE SPEAKING WITH A DOCTOR.
DEATH HAD ENTERED THE HOUSE TWICE IN ONE MONTH.

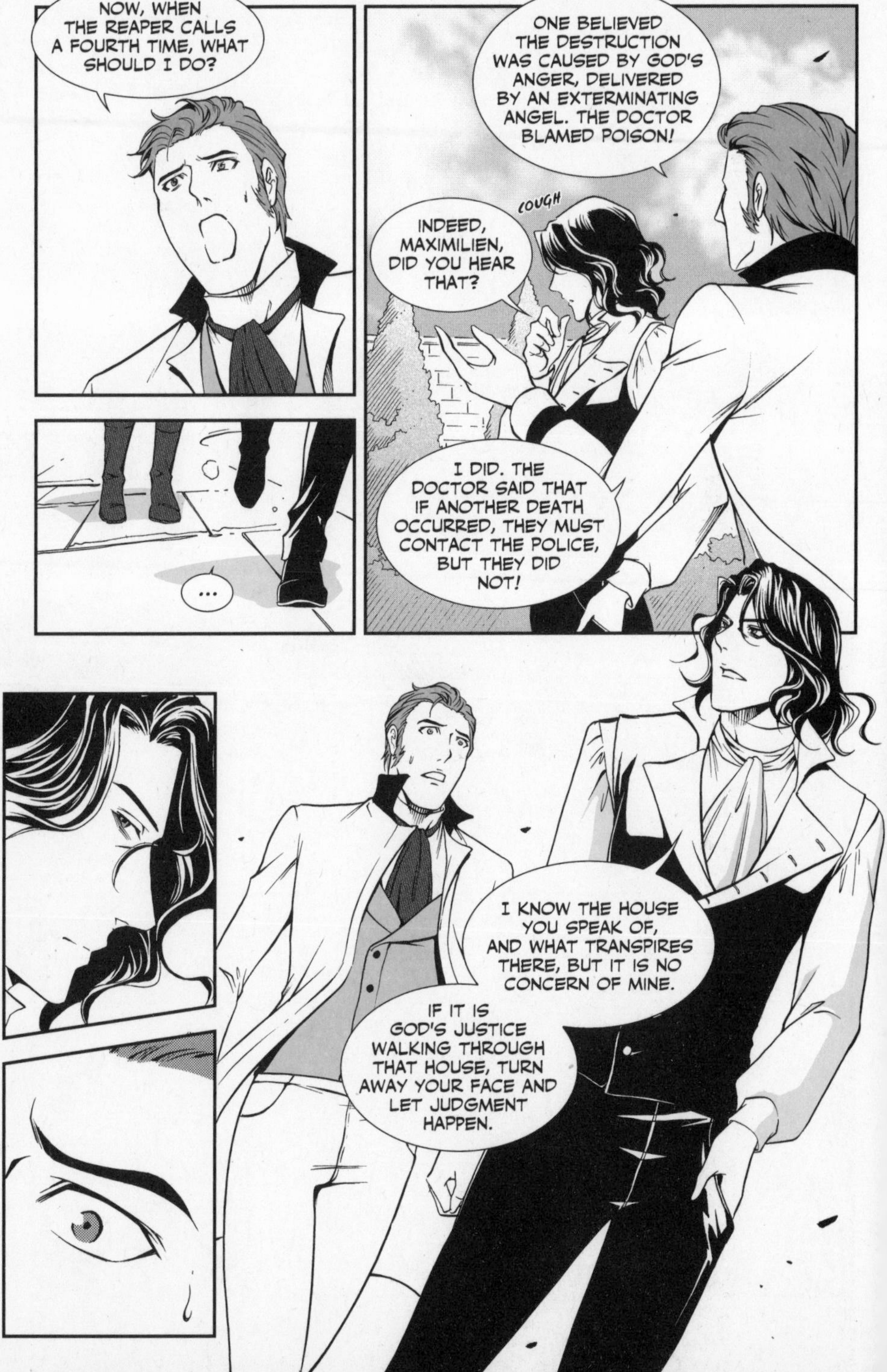
ONE BELIEVED THE DESTRUCTION WAS CAUSED BY GOD'S ANGER, DELIVERED BY AN EXTERMINATING ANGEL. THE DOCTOR BLAMED POISON!
COUGH
INDEED, MAXIMILIEN, DID YOU HEAR THAT?
I DID. THE DOCTOR SAID THAT IF ANOTHER DEATH OCCURRED, THEY MUST CONTACT THE POLICE, BUT THEY DID NOT!
NOW, WHEN THE REAPER CALLS A FOURTH TIME, WHAT SHOULD I DO?
...
I KNOW THE HOUSE YOU SPEAK OF, AND WHAT TRANSPIRES THERE, BUT IT IS NO CONCERN OF MINE.
IF IT IS GOD'S JUSTICE WALKING THROUGH THAT HOUSE, TURN AWAY YOUR FACE AND LET JUDGMENT HAPPEN.

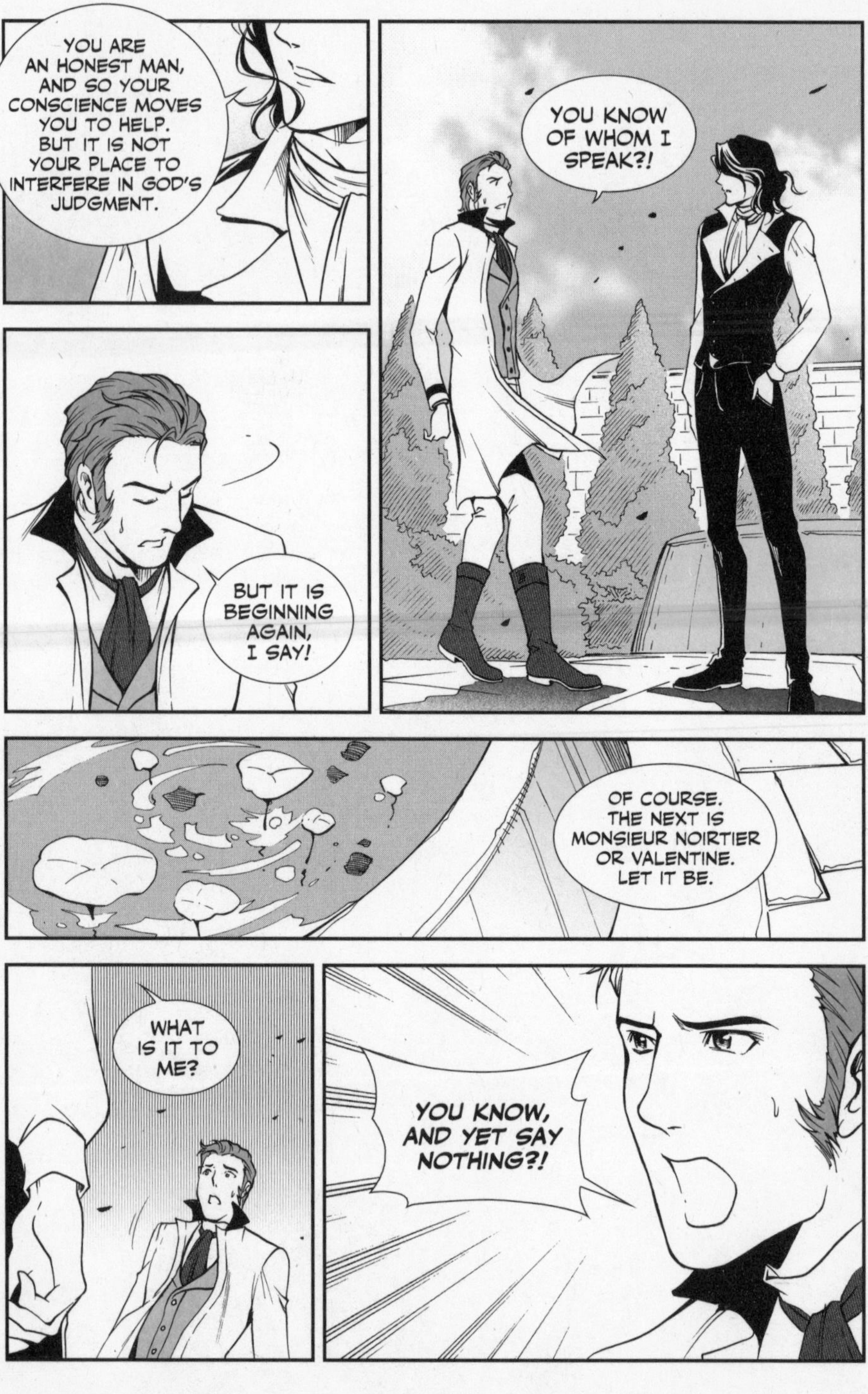
YOU KNOW OF WHOM I SPEAK?!
YOU ARE AN HONEST MAN, AND SO YOUR CONSCIENCE MOVES YOU TO HELP. BUT IT IS NOT YOUR PLACE TO INTERFERE IN GOD'S JUDGMENT.
BUT IT IS BEGINNING AGAIN, I SAY!
OF COURSE. THE NEXT IS MONSIEUR NOIRTIER OR VALENTINE. LET IT BE.
YOU KNOW, AND YET SAY NOTHING?!
WHAT IS IT TO ME?

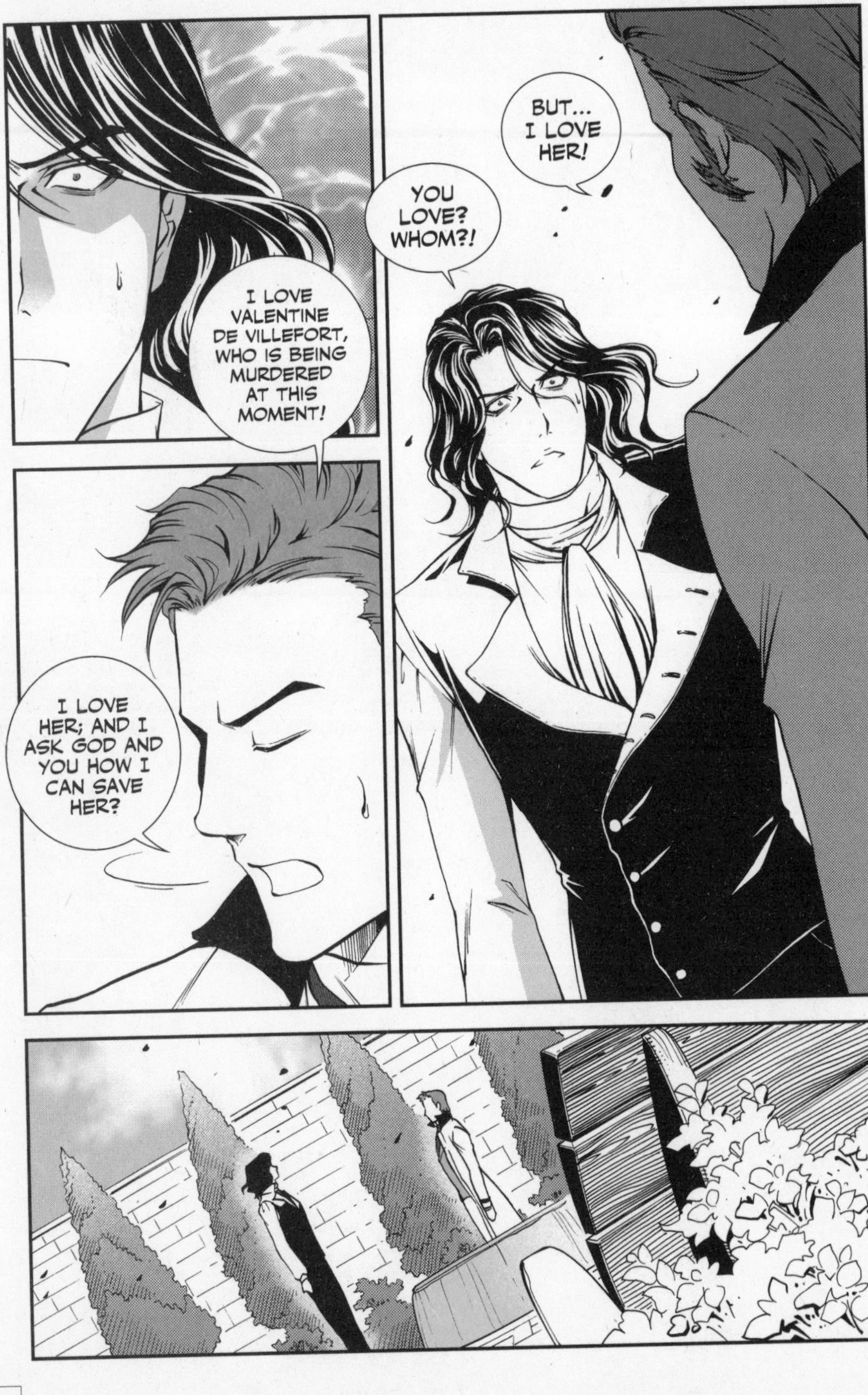
BUT... I LOVE HER!
YOU LOVE? WHOM?!
I LOVE VALENTINE DE VILLEFORT, WHO IS BEING MURDERED AT THIS MOMENT!
I LOVE HER; AND I ASK GOD AND YOU HOW I CAN SAVE HER?

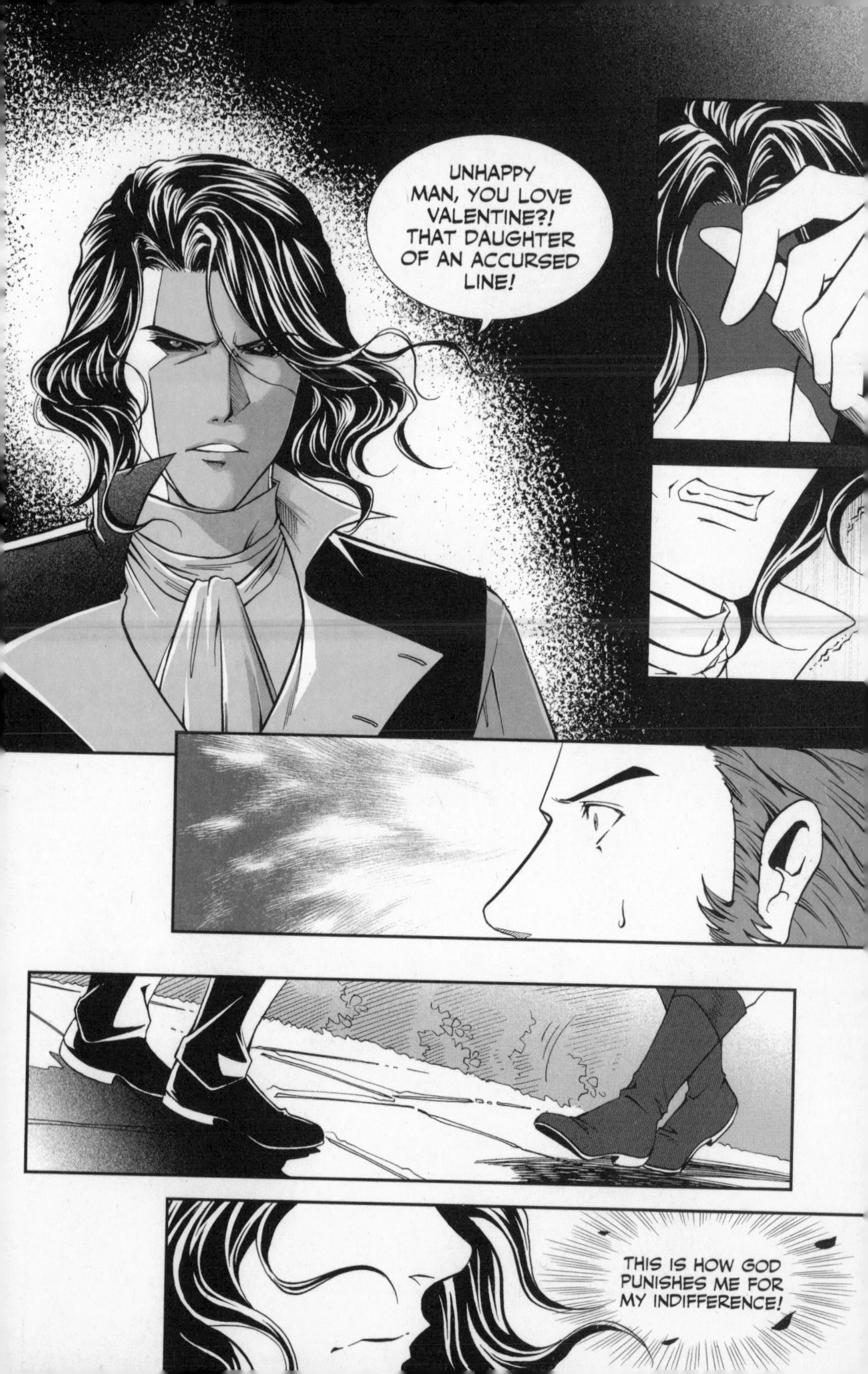
UNHAPPY MAN, YOU LOVE VALENTINE?! THAT DAUGHTER OF AN ACCURSED LINE!
THIS IS HOW GOD PUNISHES ME FOR MY INDIFFERENCE!

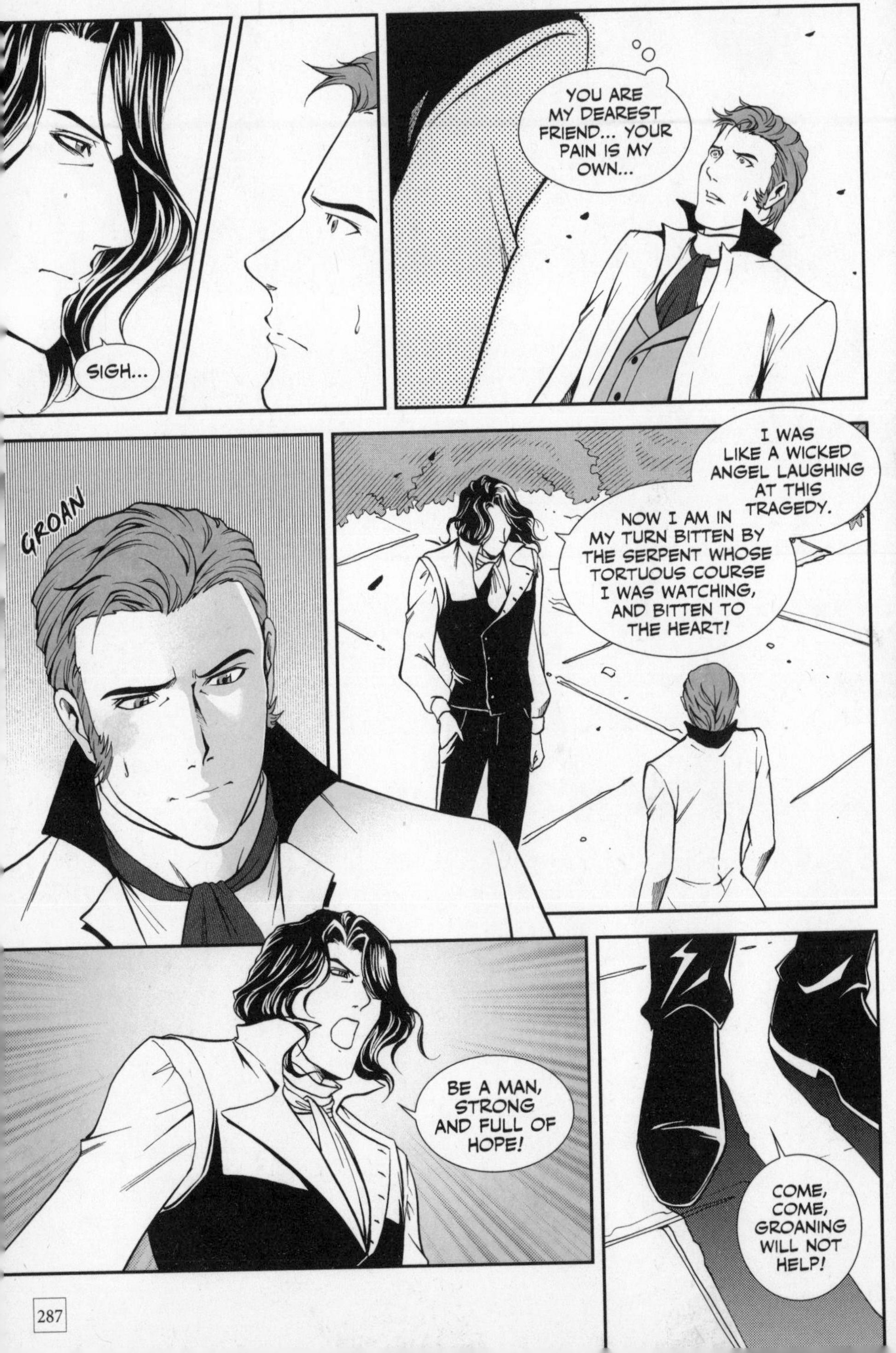
YOU ARE MY DEAREST FRIEND... YOUR PAIN IS MY OWN...
SIGH...
I WAS LIKE A WICKED ANGEL LAUGHING AT THIS TRAGEDY.
NOW I AM IN MY TURN BITTEN BY THE SERPENT WHOSE TORTUOUS COURSE I WAS WATCHING, AND BITTEN TO THE HEART!
GROAN
COME, COME, GROANING WILL NOT HELP!
BE A MAN, STRONG AND FULL OF HOPE!

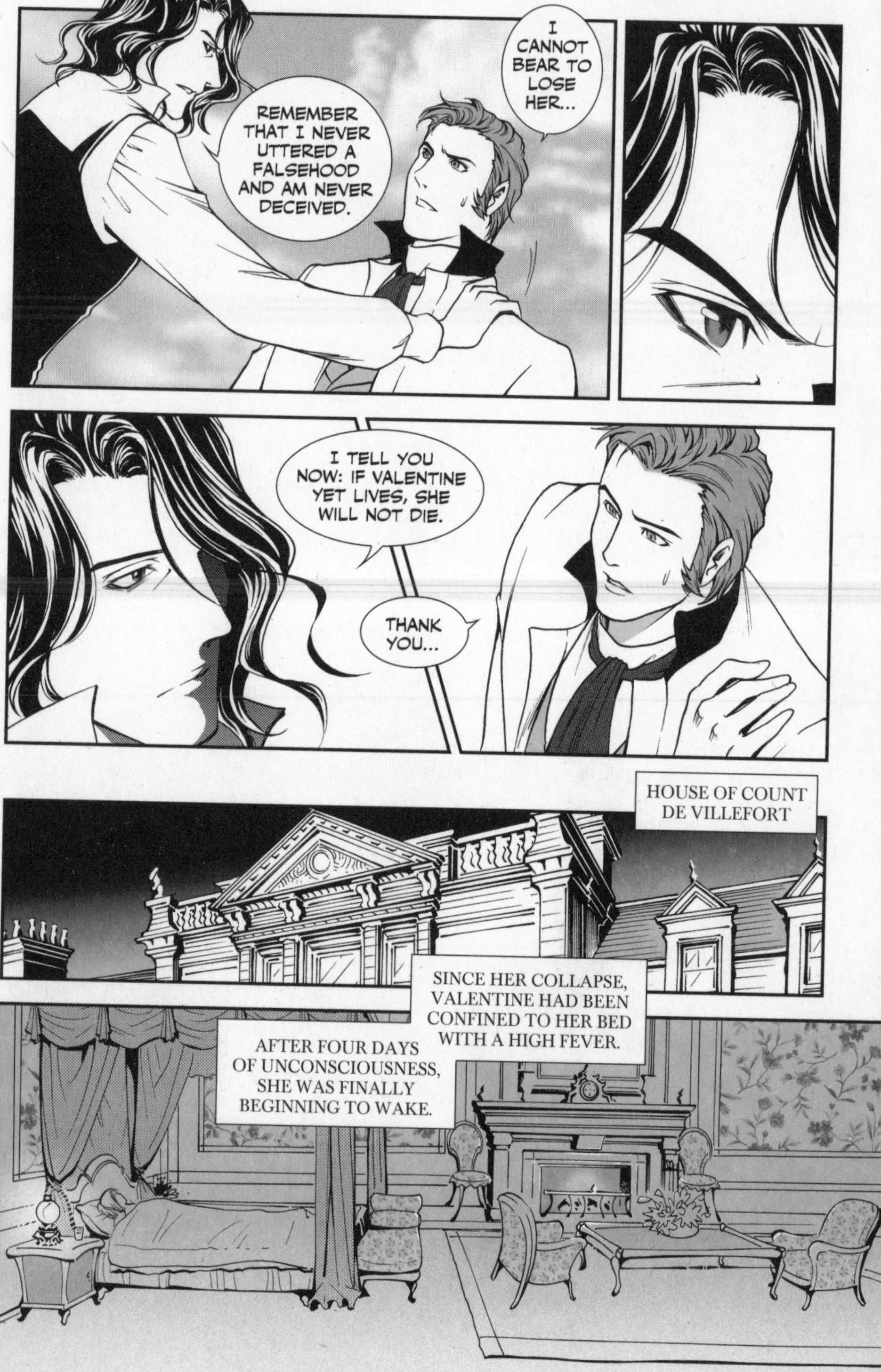
I CANNOT BEAR TO LOSE HER...
REMEMBER THAT I NEVER UTTERED A FALSEHOOD AND AM NEVER DECEIVED.
I TELL YOU NOW: IF VALENTINE YET LIVES, SHE WILL NOT DIE.
THANK YOU...
HOUSE OF COUNT DE VILLEFORT
SINCE HER COLLAPSE, VALENTINE HAD BEEN CONFINED TO HER BED WITH A HIGH FEVER.
AFTER FOUR DAYS OF UNCONSCIOUSNESS, SHE WAS FINALLY BEGINNING TO WAKE.

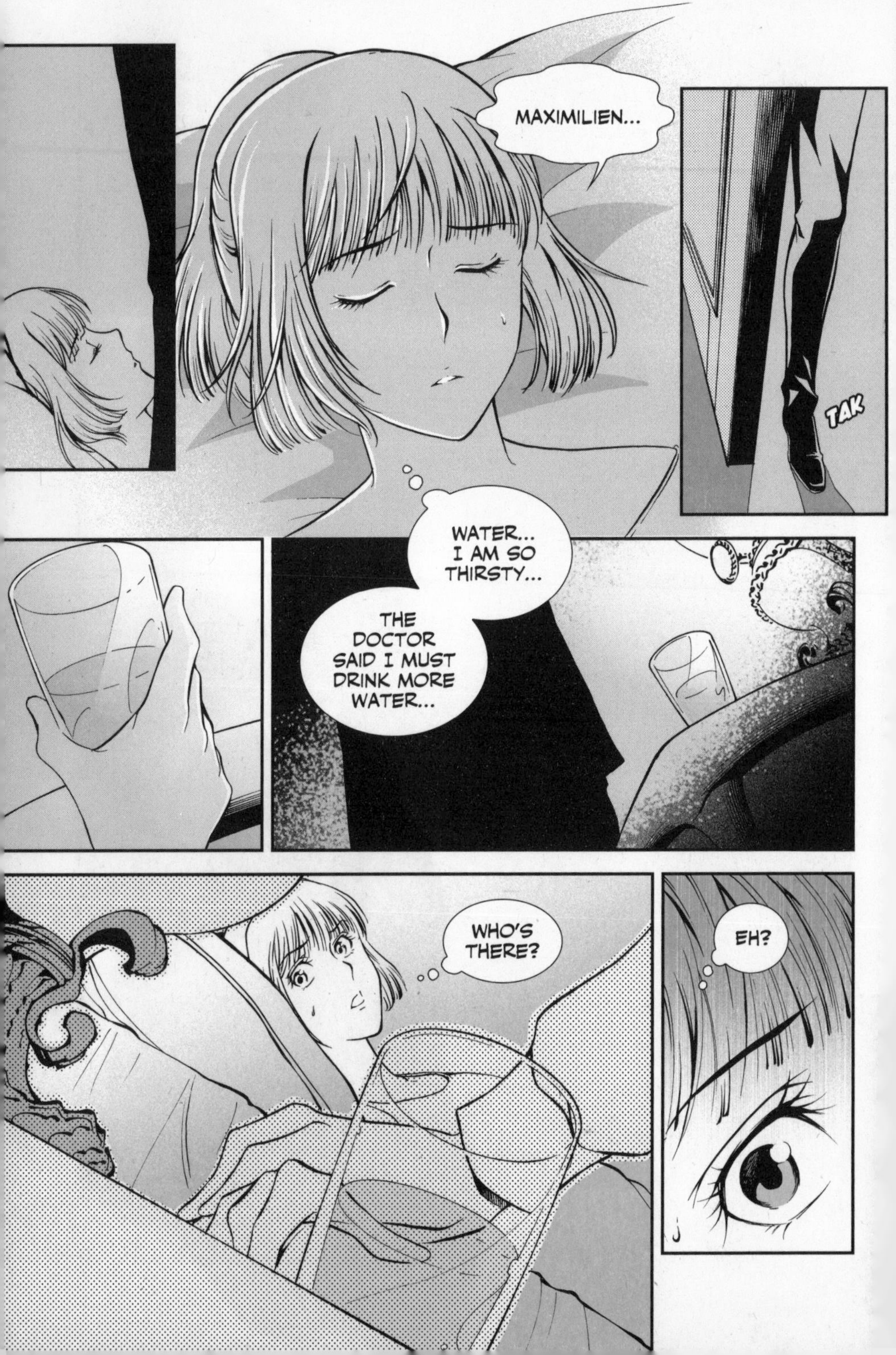
TAK
MAXIMILIEN...
WATER... I AM SO THIRSTY...
THE DOCTOR SAID I MUST DRINK MORE WATER...
EH?
WHO'S THERE?

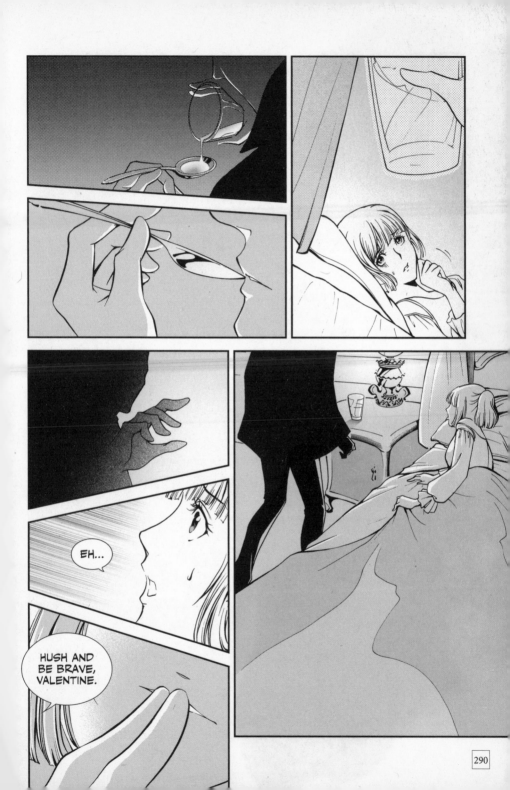

EH...

HUSH AND
BE BRAVE,
VALENTINE.

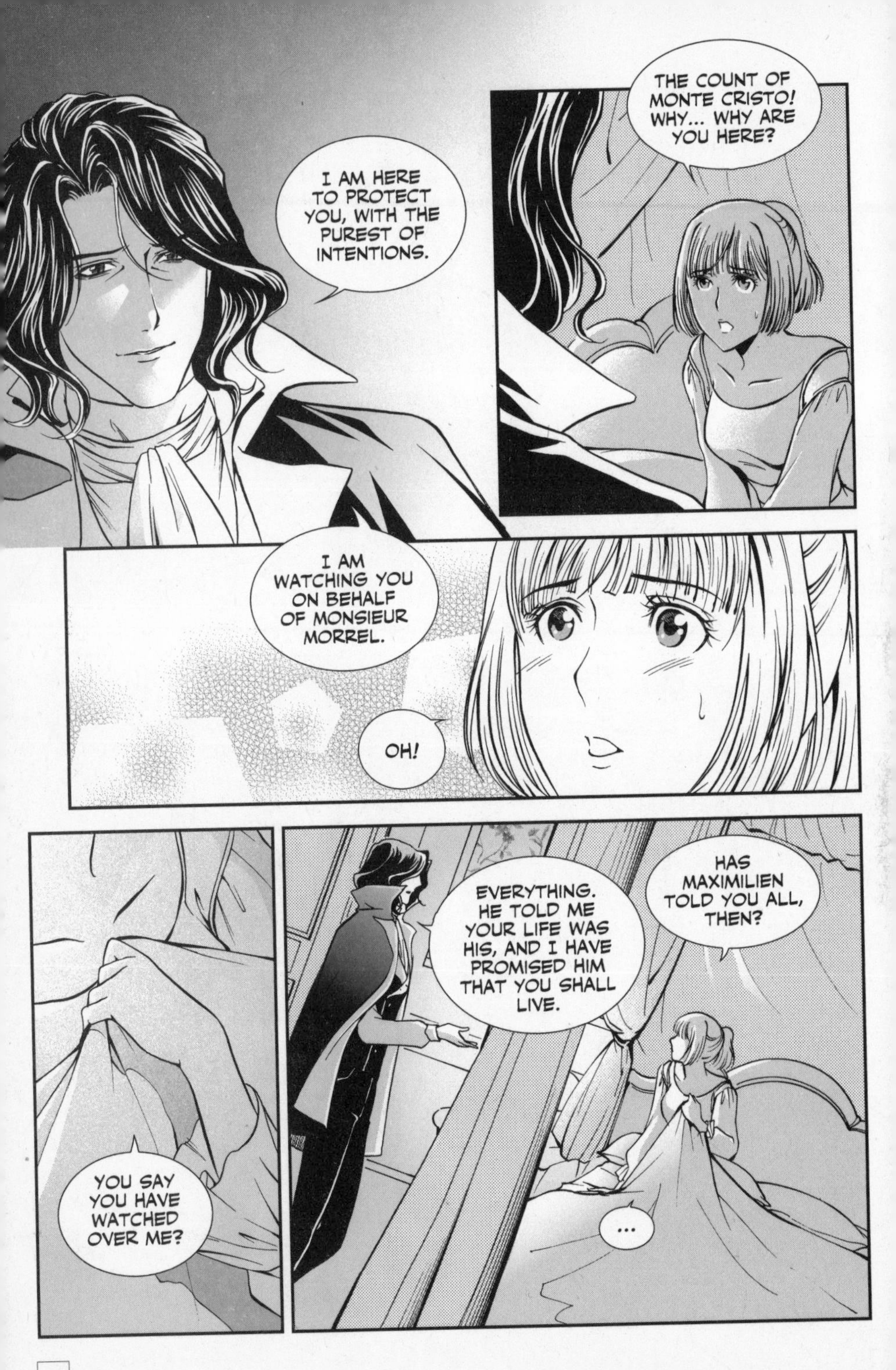
THE COUNT OF MONTE CRISTO! WHY... WHY ARE YOU HERE?
I AM HERE TO PROTECT YOU, WITH THE PUREST OF INTENTIONS.
I AM WATCHING YOU ON BEHALF OF MONSIEUR MORREL.
OH!
HAS MAXIMILIEN TOLD YOU ALL, THEN?
EVERYTHING. HE TOLD ME YOUR LIFE WAS HIS, AND I HAVE PROMISED HIM THAT YOU SHALL LIVE.
...
YOU SAY YOU HAVE WATCHED OVER ME?

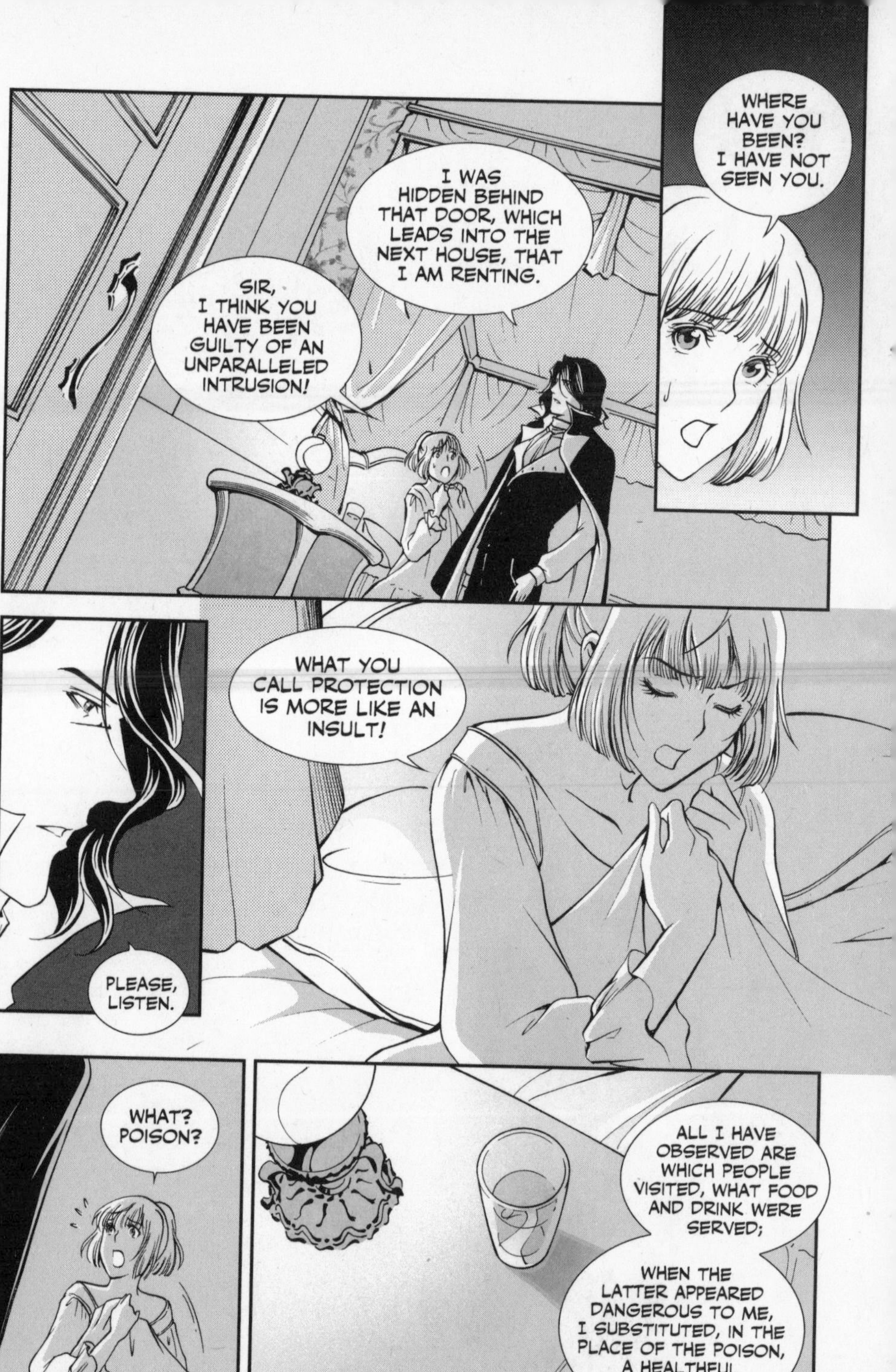
WHERE HAVE YOU BEEN? I HAVE NOT SEEN YOU.
I WAS HIDDEN BEHIND THAT DOOR, WHICH LEADS INTO THE NEXT HOUSE, THAT I AM RENTING.
SIR, I THINK YOU HAVE BEEN GUILTY OF AN UNPARALLELED INTRUSION!
WHAT YOU CALL PROTECTION IS MORE LIKE AN INSULT!
PLEASE, LISTEN.
ALL I HAVE OBSERVED ARE WHICH PEOPLE VISITED, WHAT FOOD AND DRINK WERE SERVED;
WHEN THE LATTER APPEARED DANGEROUS TO ME, I SUBSTITUTED, IN THE PLACE OF THE POISON, A HEALTHFUL DRAUGHT.
WHAT? POISON?

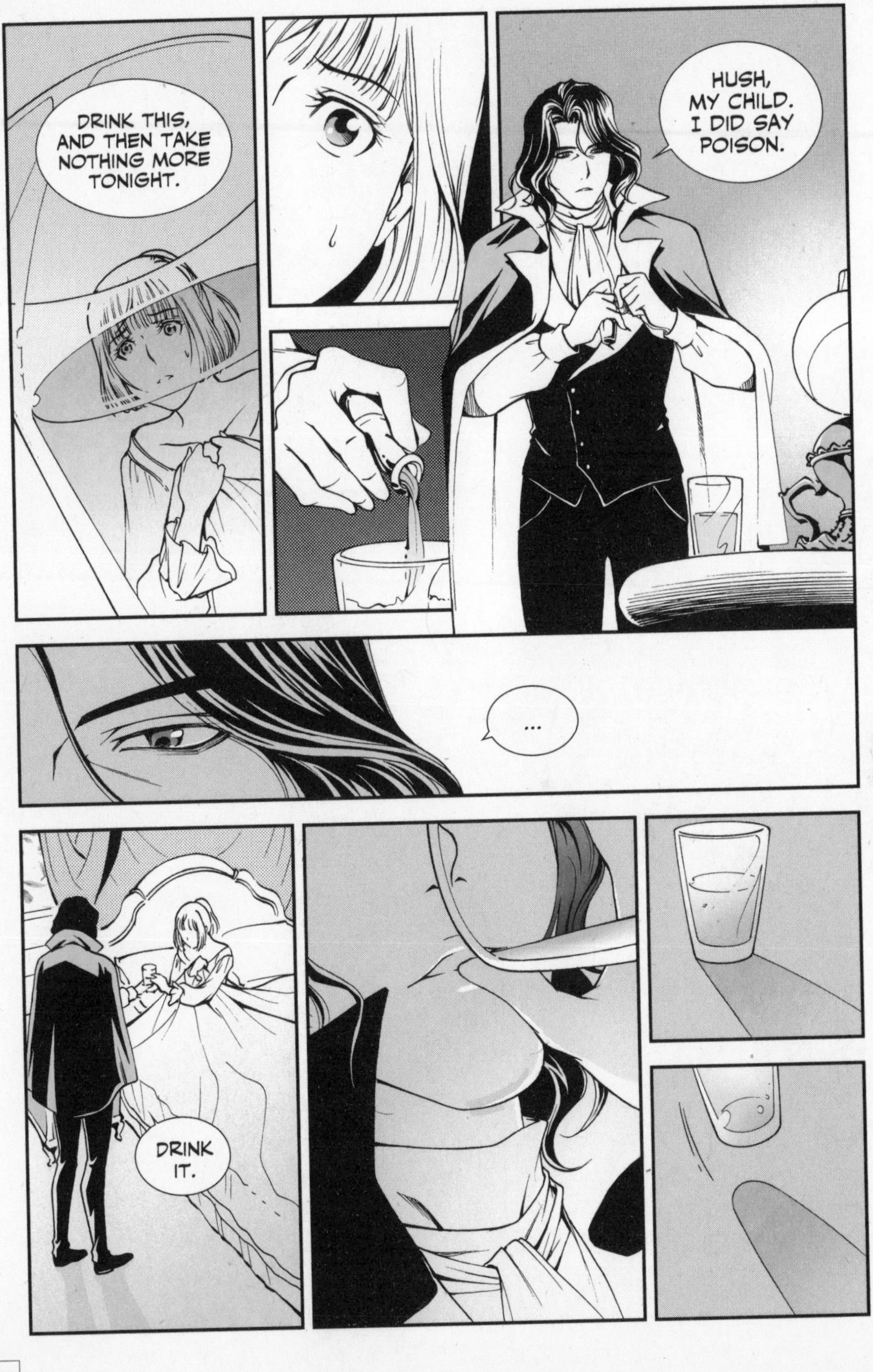
HUSH, MY CHILD. I DID SAY POISON.
DRINK THIS, AND THEN TAKE NOTHING MORE TONIGHT.
...
DRINK IT.

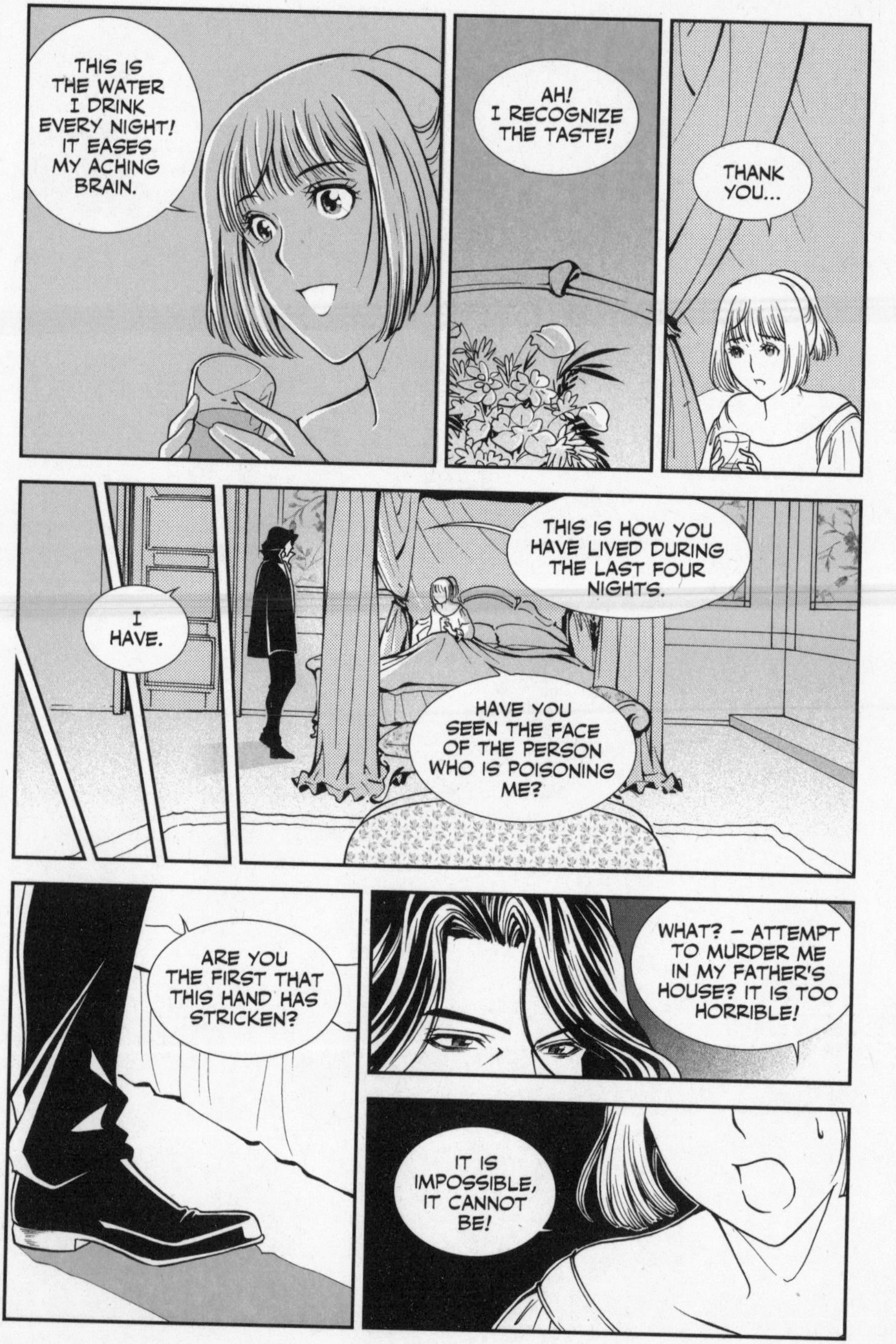
THANK YOU...
AH! I RECOGNIZE THE TASTE!
THIS IS THE WATER I DRINK EVERY NIGHT! IT EASES MY ACHING BRAIN.
THIS IS HOW YOU HAVE LIVED DURING THE LAST FOUR NIGHTS.
HAVE YOU SEEN THE FACE OF THE PERSON WHO IS POISONING ME?
I HAVE.
WHAT? – ATTEMPT TO MURDER ME IN MY FATHER'S HOUSE? IT IS TOO HORRIBLE!
IT IS IMPOSSIBLE, IT CANNOT BE!
ARE YOU THE FIRST THAT THIS HAND HAS STRICKEN?

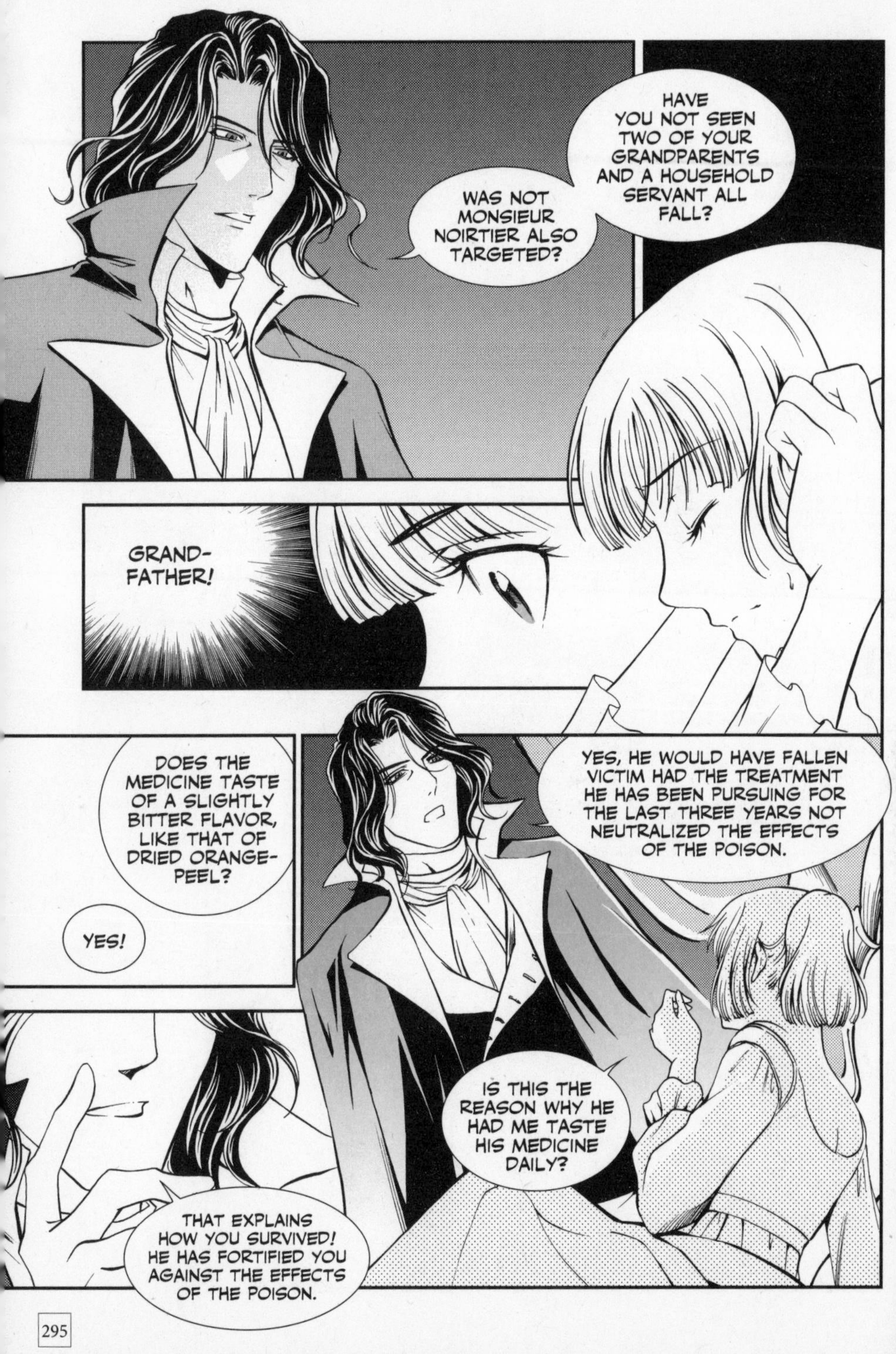
HAVE YOU NOT SEEN TWO OF YOUR GRANDPARENTS AND A HOUSEHOLD SERVANT ALL FALL?
WAS NOT MONSIEUR NOIRTIER ALSO TARGETED?
GRAND-FATHER!
YES, HE WOULD HAVE FALLEN VICTIM HAD THE TREATMENT HE HAS BEEN PURSUING FOR THE LAST THREE YEARS NOT NEUTRALIZED THE EFFECTS OF THE POISON.
IS THIS THE REASON WHY HE HAD ME TASTE HIS MEDICINE DAILY?
DOES THE MEDICINE TASTE OF A SLIGHTLY BITTER FLAVOR, LIKE THAT OF DRIED ORANGE-PEEL?
YES!
THAT EXPLAINS HOW YOU SURVIVED! HE HAS FORTIFIED YOU AGAINST THE EFFECTS OF THE POISON.

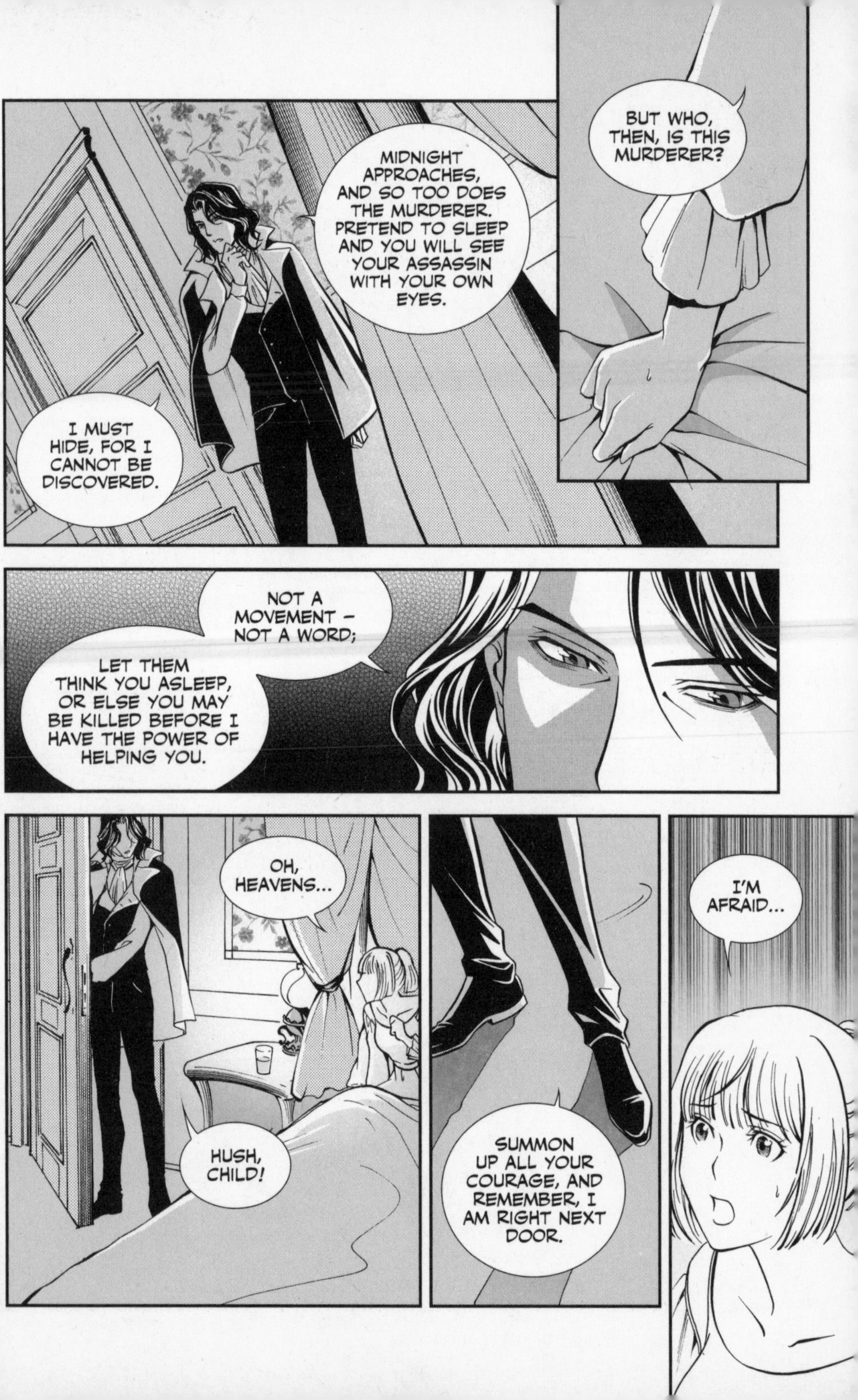
BUT WHO, THEN, IS THIS MURDERER?
MIDNIGHT APPROACHES, AND SO TOO DOES THE MURDERER. PRETEND TO SLEEP AND YOU WILL SEE YOUR ASSASSIN WITH YOUR OWN EYES.
I MUST HIDE, FOR I CANNOT BE DISCOVERED.
NOT A MOVEMENT – NOT A WORD;
LET THEM THINK YOU ASLEEP, OR ELSE YOU MAY BE KILLED BEFORE I HAVE THE POWER OF HELPING YOU.
I'M AFRAID...
SUMMON UP ALL YOUR COURAGE, AND REMEMBER, I AM RIGHT NEXT DOOR.
OH, HEAVENS...
HUSH, CHILD!

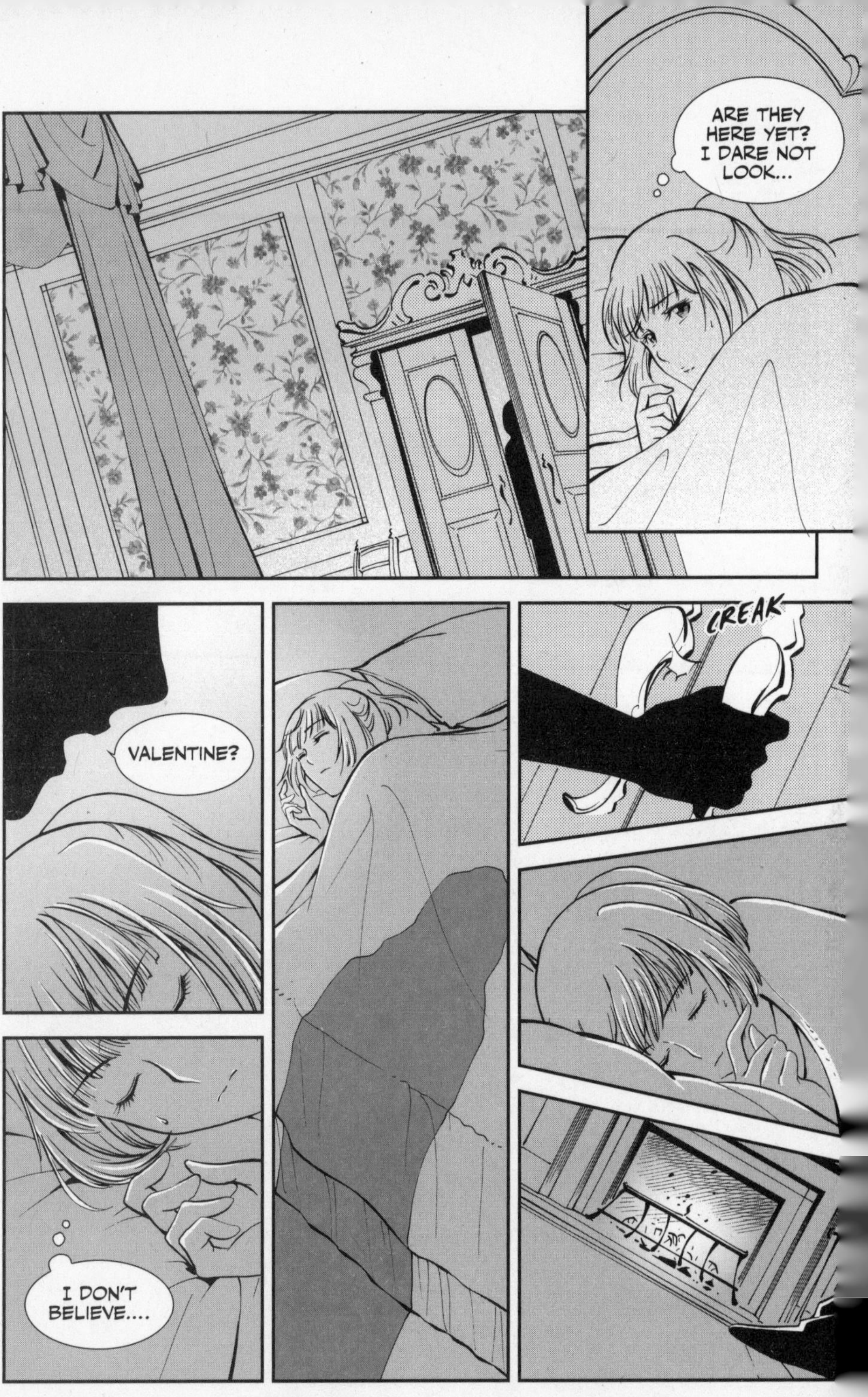
ARE THEY HERE YET? I DARE NOT LOOK...
CREAK
VALENTINE?
I DON'T BELIEVE....

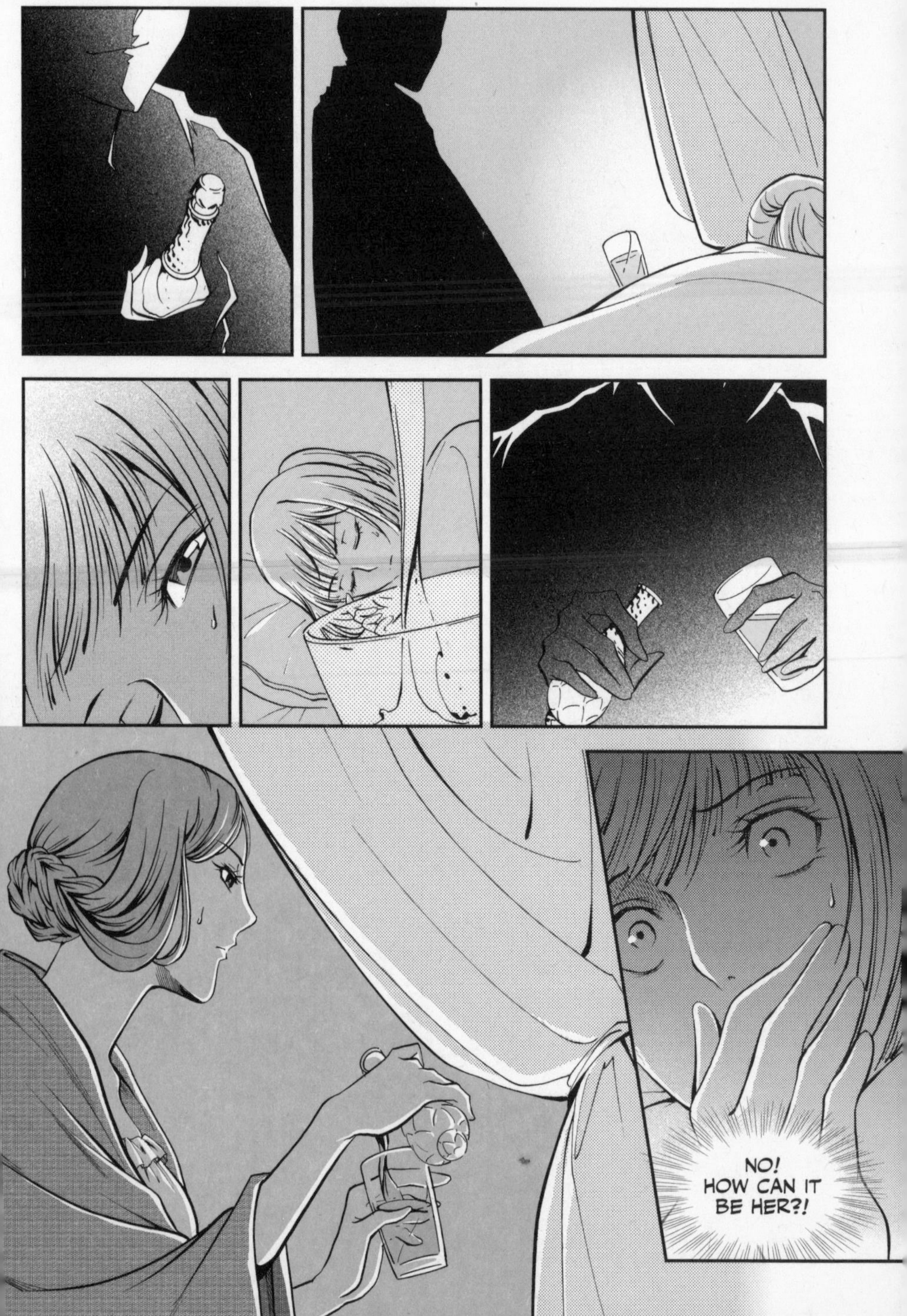
NO!
HOW CAN IT
BE HER?!

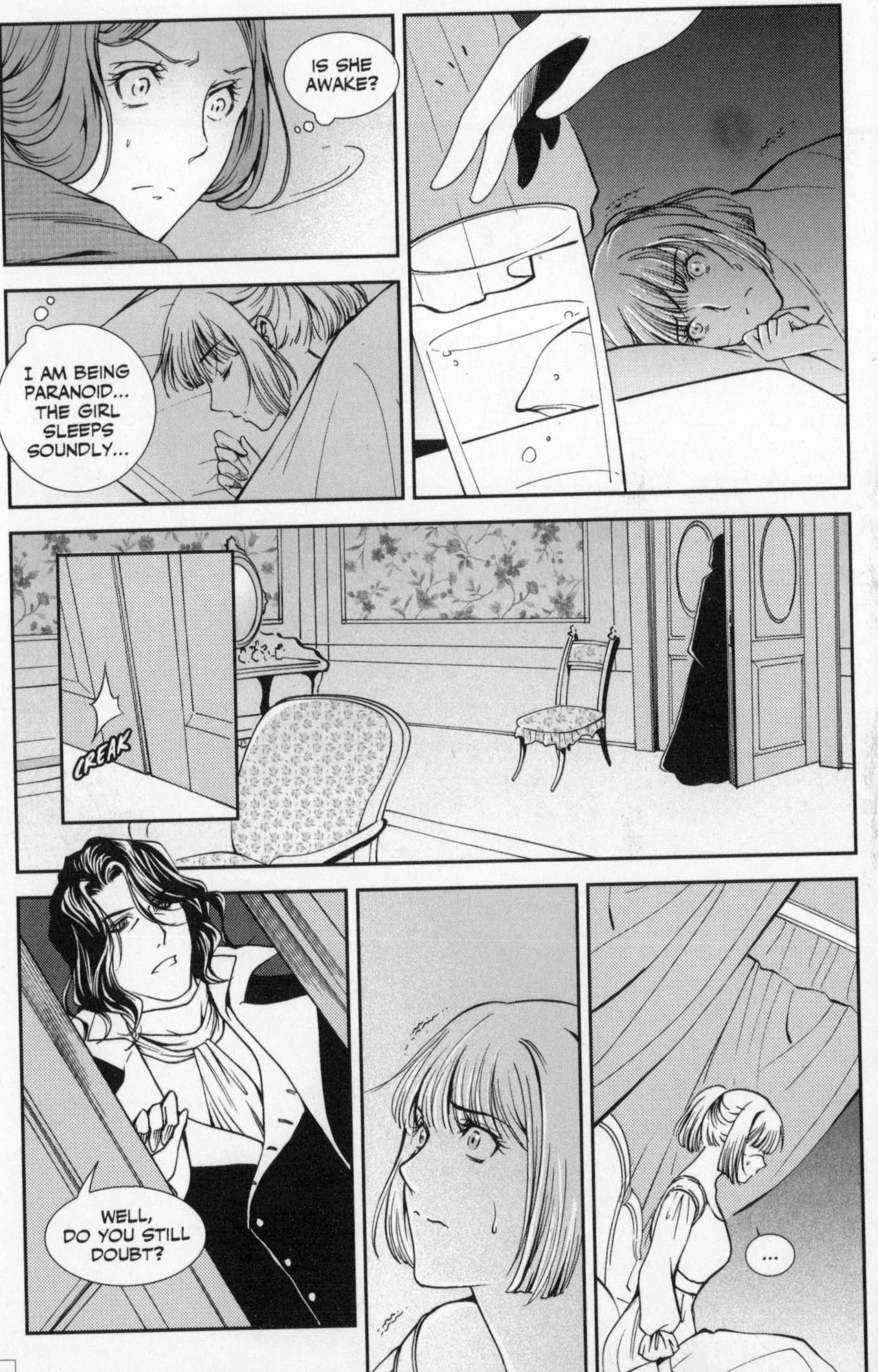
IS SHE AWAKE?
I AM BEING PARANOID... THE GIRL SLEEPS SOUNDLY...
CREAK
...
WELL, DO YOU STILL DOUBT?

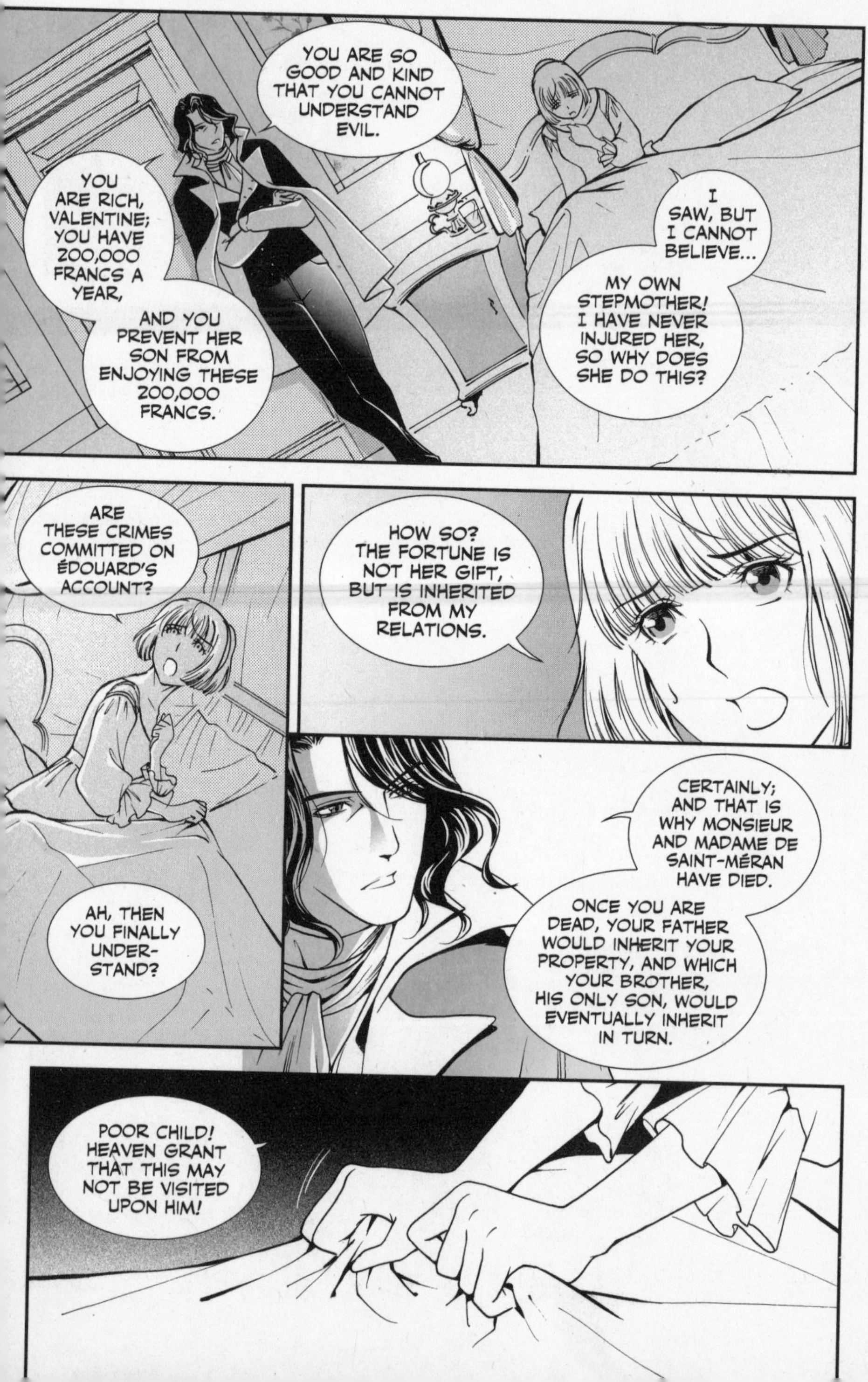
I SAW, BUT I CANNOT BELIEVE...
MY OWN STEPMOTHER! I HAVE NEVER INJURED HER, SO WHY DOES SHE DO THIS?
YOU ARE SO GOOD AND KIND THAT YOU CANNOT UNDERSTAND EVIL.
YOU ARE RICH, VALENTINE; YOU HAVE 200,000 FRANCS A YEAR,
AND YOU PREVENT HER SON FROM ENJOYING THESE 200,000 FRANCS.
HOW SO? THE FORTUNE IS NOT HER GIFT, BUT IS INHERITED FROM MY RELATIONS.
CERTAINLY; AND THAT IS WHY MONSIEUR AND MADAME DE SAINT-MÉRAN HAVE DIED.
ONCE YOU ARE DEAD, YOUR FATHER WOULD INHERIT YOUR PROPERTY, AND WHICH YOUR BROTHER, HIS ONLY SON, WOULD EVENTUALLY INHERIT IN TURN.
ARE THESE CRIMES COMMITTED ON ÉDOUARD'S ACCOUNT?
AH, THEN YOU FINALLY UNDER-STAND?
POOR CHILD! HEAVEN GRANT THAT THIS MAY NOT BE VISITED UPON HIM!

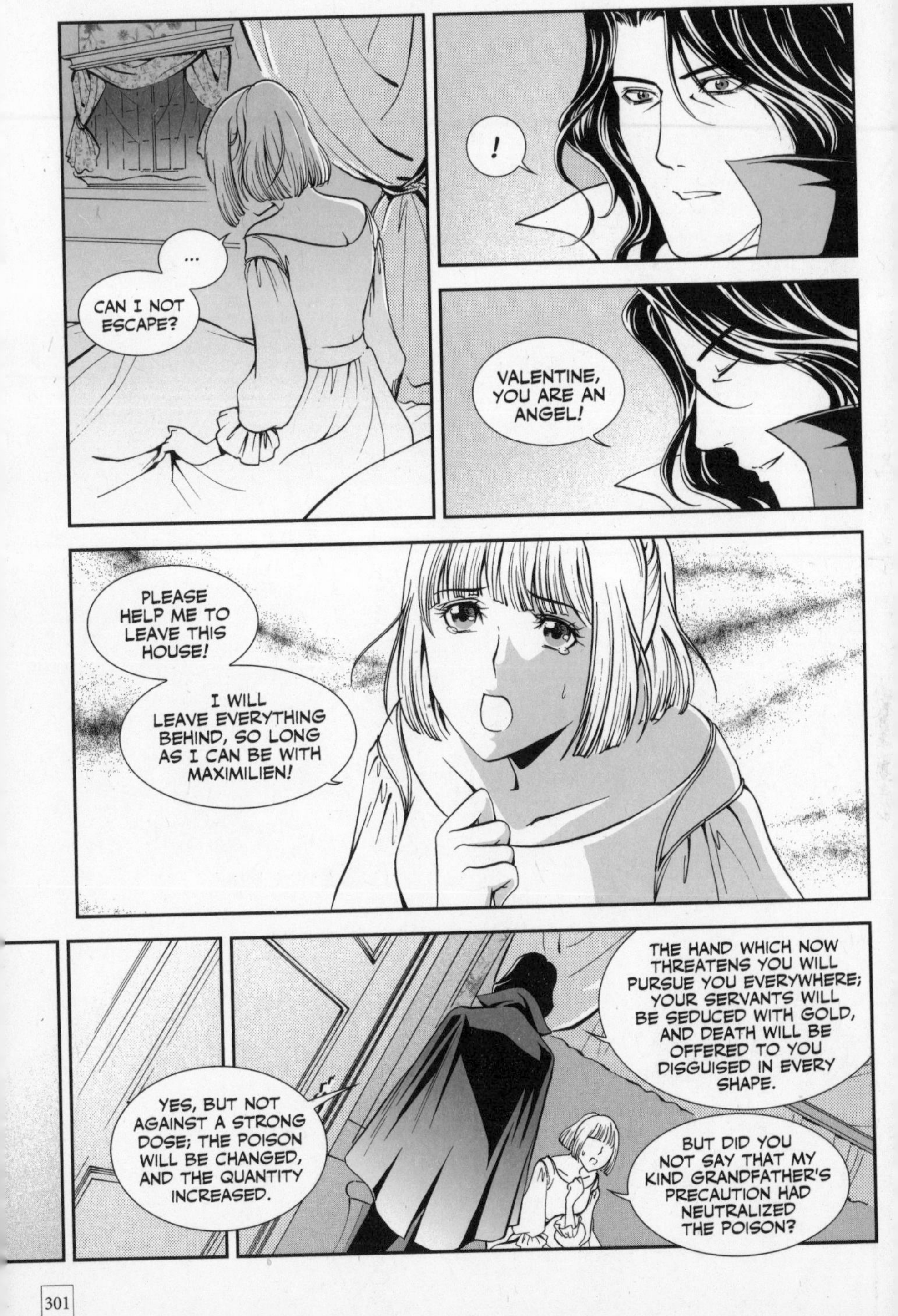
!
VALENTINE, YOU ARE AN ANGEL!
...
CAN I NOT ESCAPE?
PLEASE HELP ME TO LEAVE THIS HOUSE!
I WILL LEAVE EVERYTHING BEHIND, SO LONG AS I CAN BE WITH MAXIMILIEN!
THE HAND WHICH NOW THREATENS YOU WILL PURSUE YOU EVERYWHERE; YOUR SERVANTS WILL BE SEDUCED WITH GOLD, AND DEATH WILL BE OFFERED TO YOU DISGUISED IN EVERY SHAPE.
BUT DID YOU NOT SAY THAT MY KIND GRANDFATHER'S PRECAUTION HAD NEUTRALIZED THE POISON?
YES, BUT NOT AGAINST A STRONG DOSE; THE POISON WILL BE CHANGED, AND THE QUANTITY INCREASED.

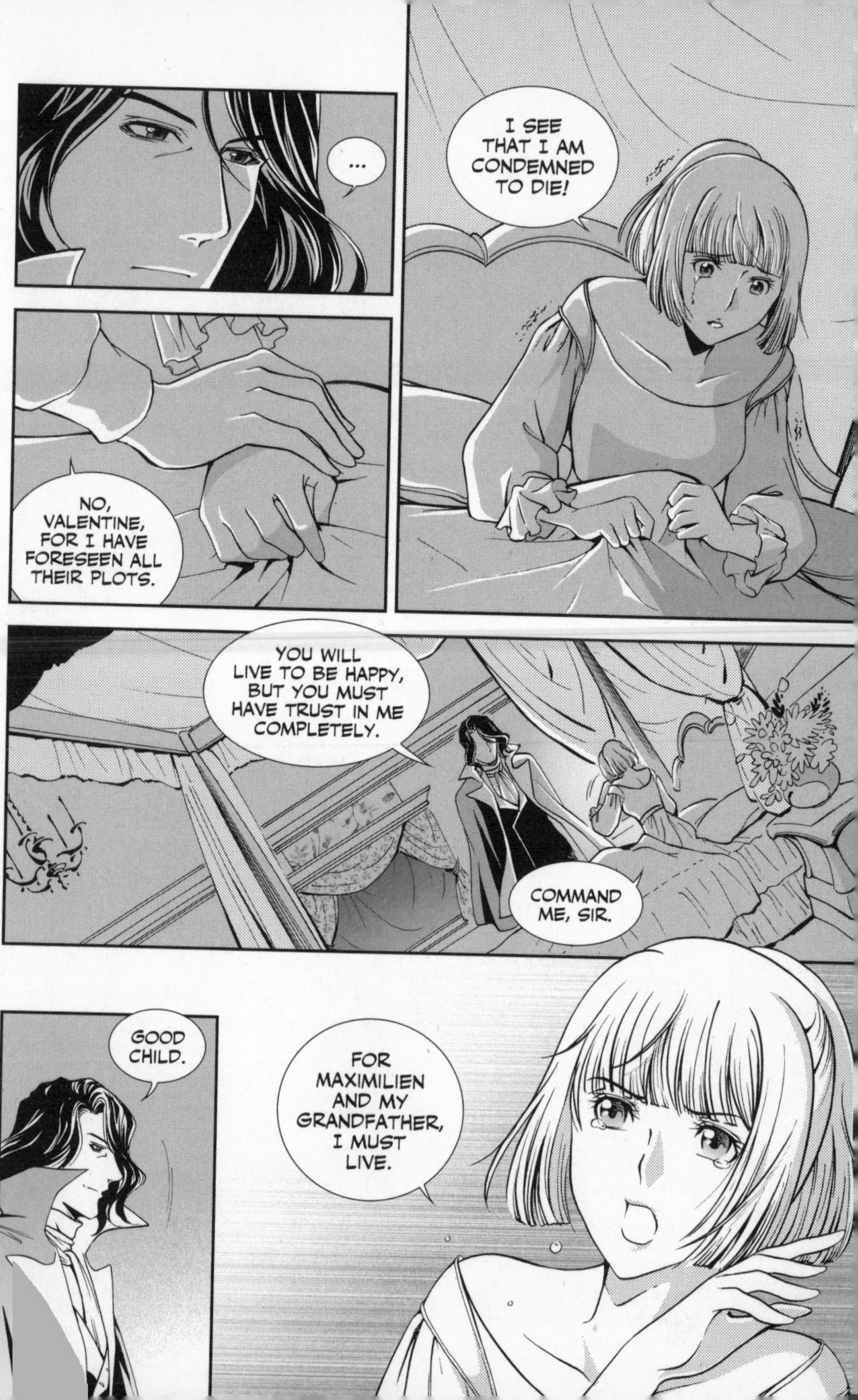
I SEE THAT I AM CONDEMNED TO DIE!
...
NO, VALENTINE, FOR I HAVE FORESEEN ALL THEIR PLOTS.
YOU WILL LIVE TO BE HAPPY, BUT YOU MUST HAVE TRUST IN ME COMPLETELY.
COMMAND ME, SIR.
FOR MAXIMILIEN AND MY GRANDFATHER, I MUST LIVE.
GOOD CHILD.

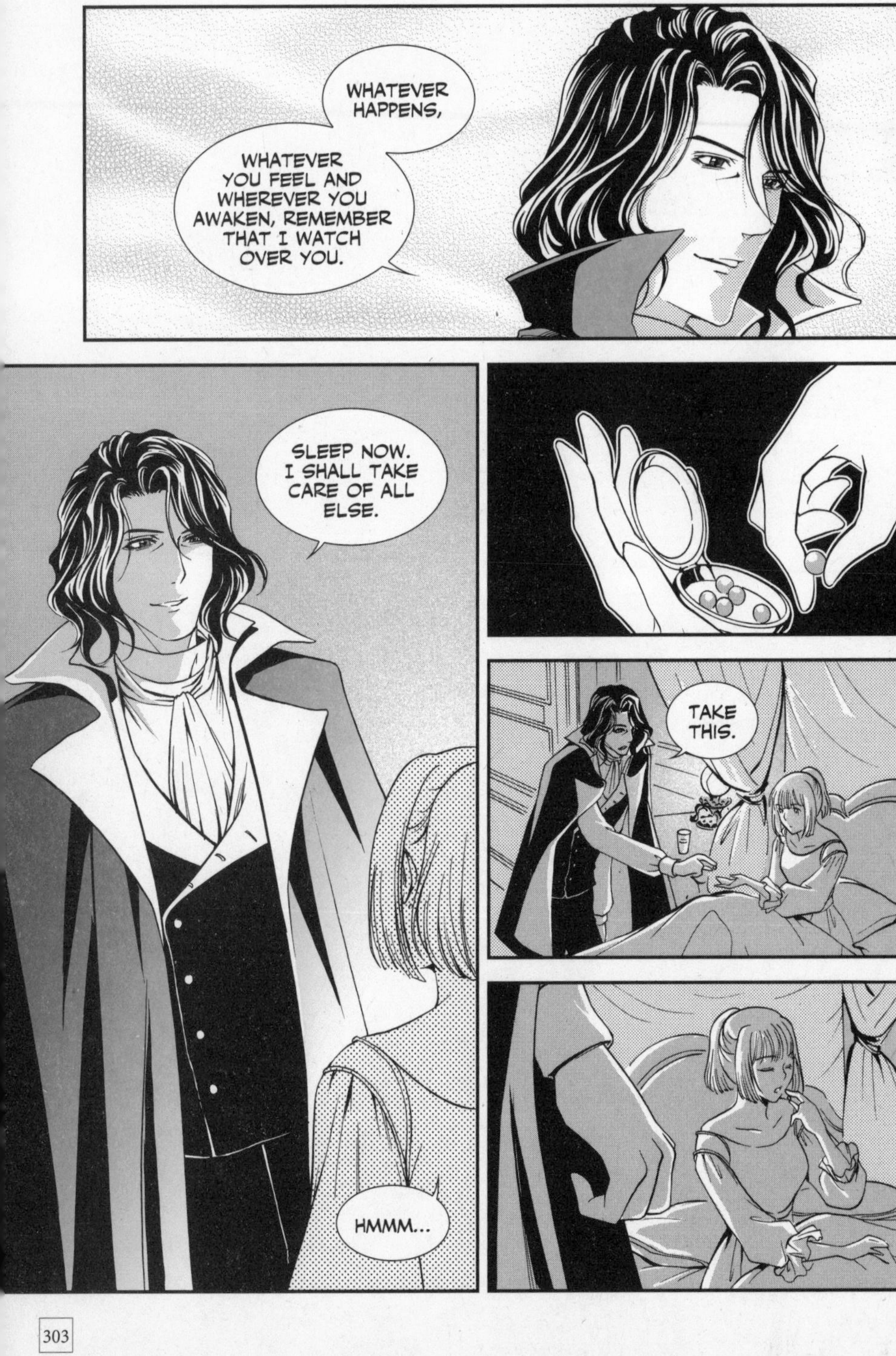
WHATEVER HAPPENS,
WHATEVER YOU FEEL AND WHEREVER YOU AWAKEN, REMEMBER THAT I WATCH OVER YOU.
TAKE THIS.
SLEEP NOW. I SHALL TAKE CARE OF ALL ELSE.
HMMM...

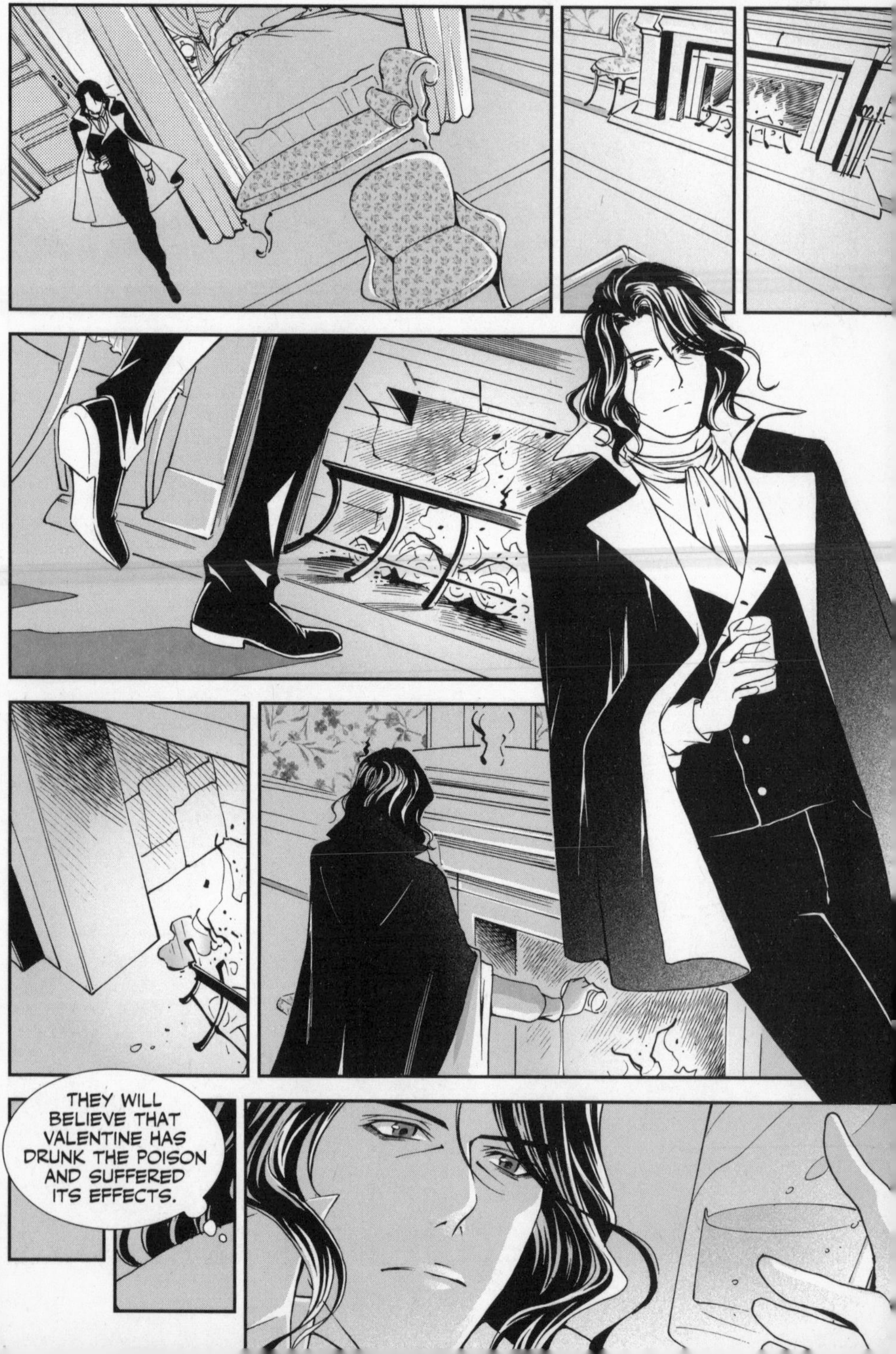
THEY WILL BELIEVE THAT VALENTINE HAS DRUNK THE POISON AND SUFFERED ITS EFFECTS.

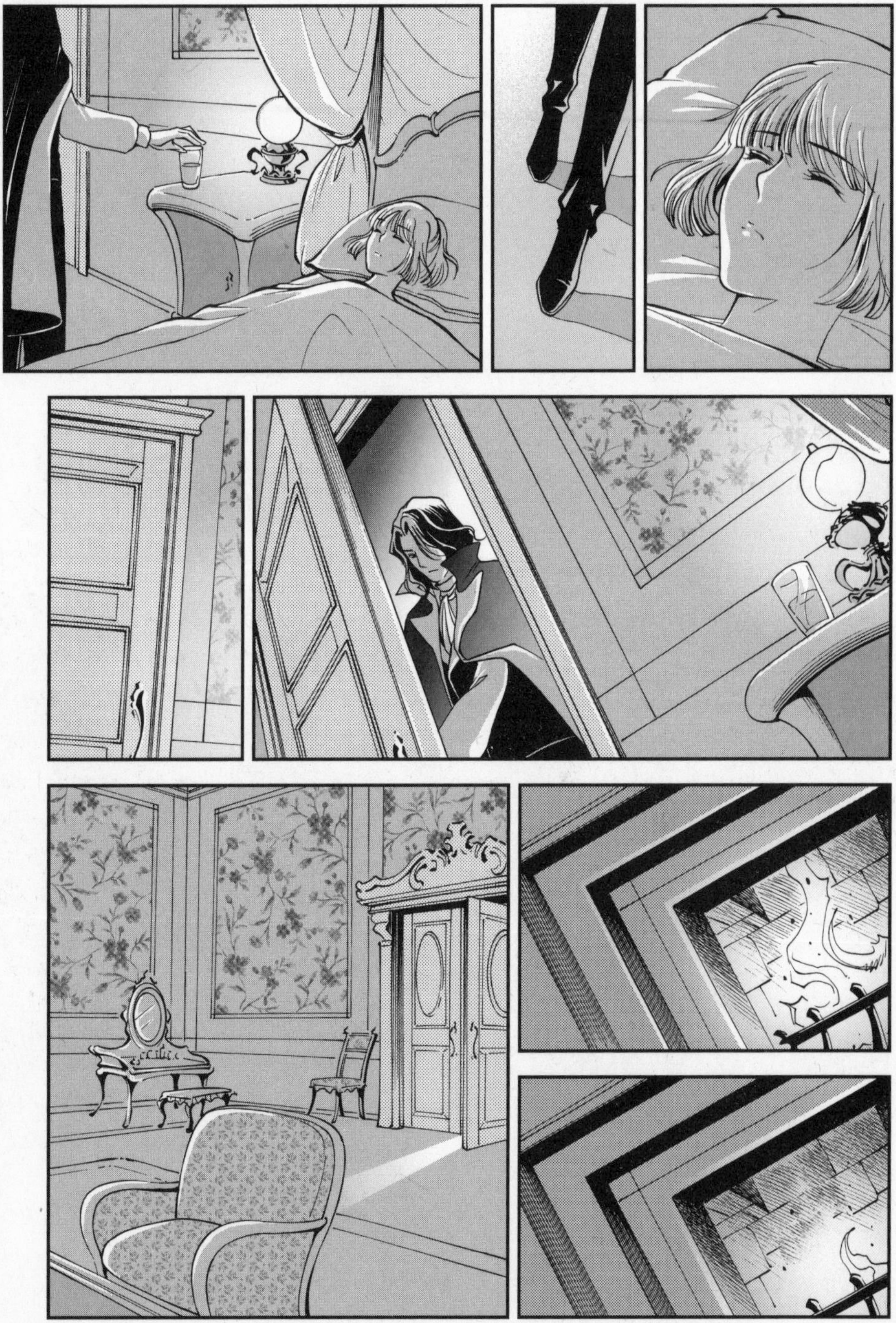

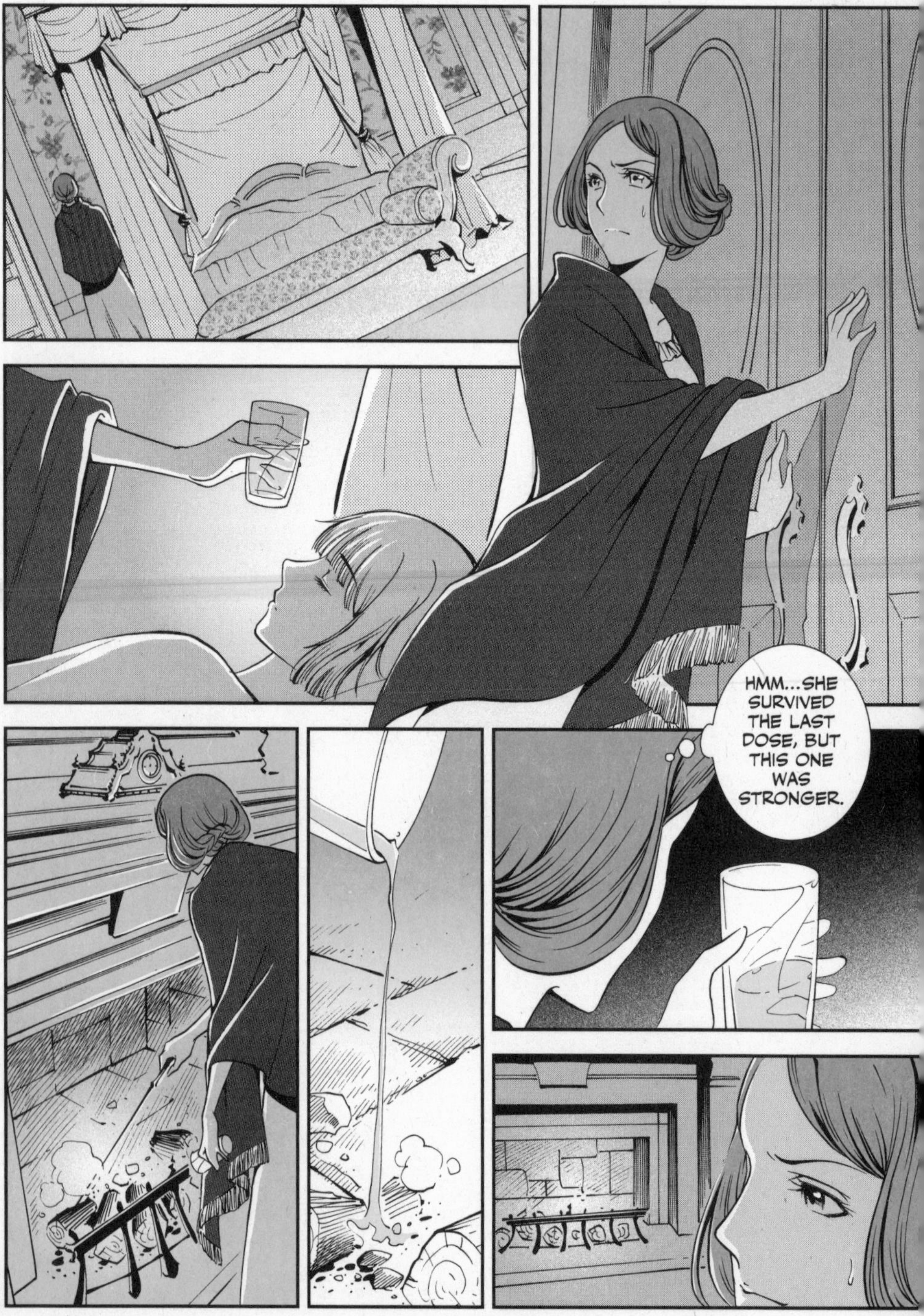
HMM...SHE SURVIVED THE LAST DOSE, BUT THIS ONE WAS STRONGER.

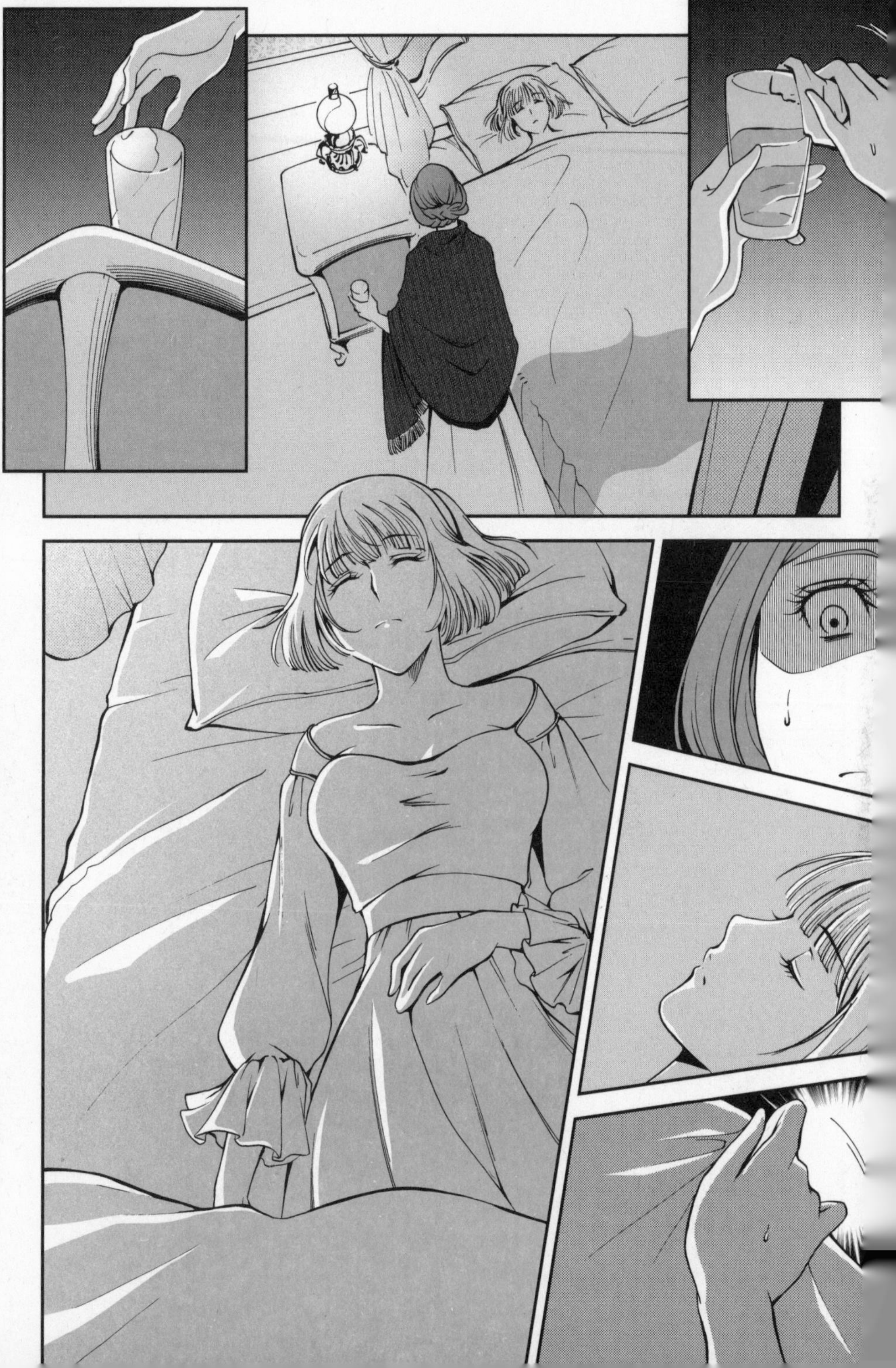

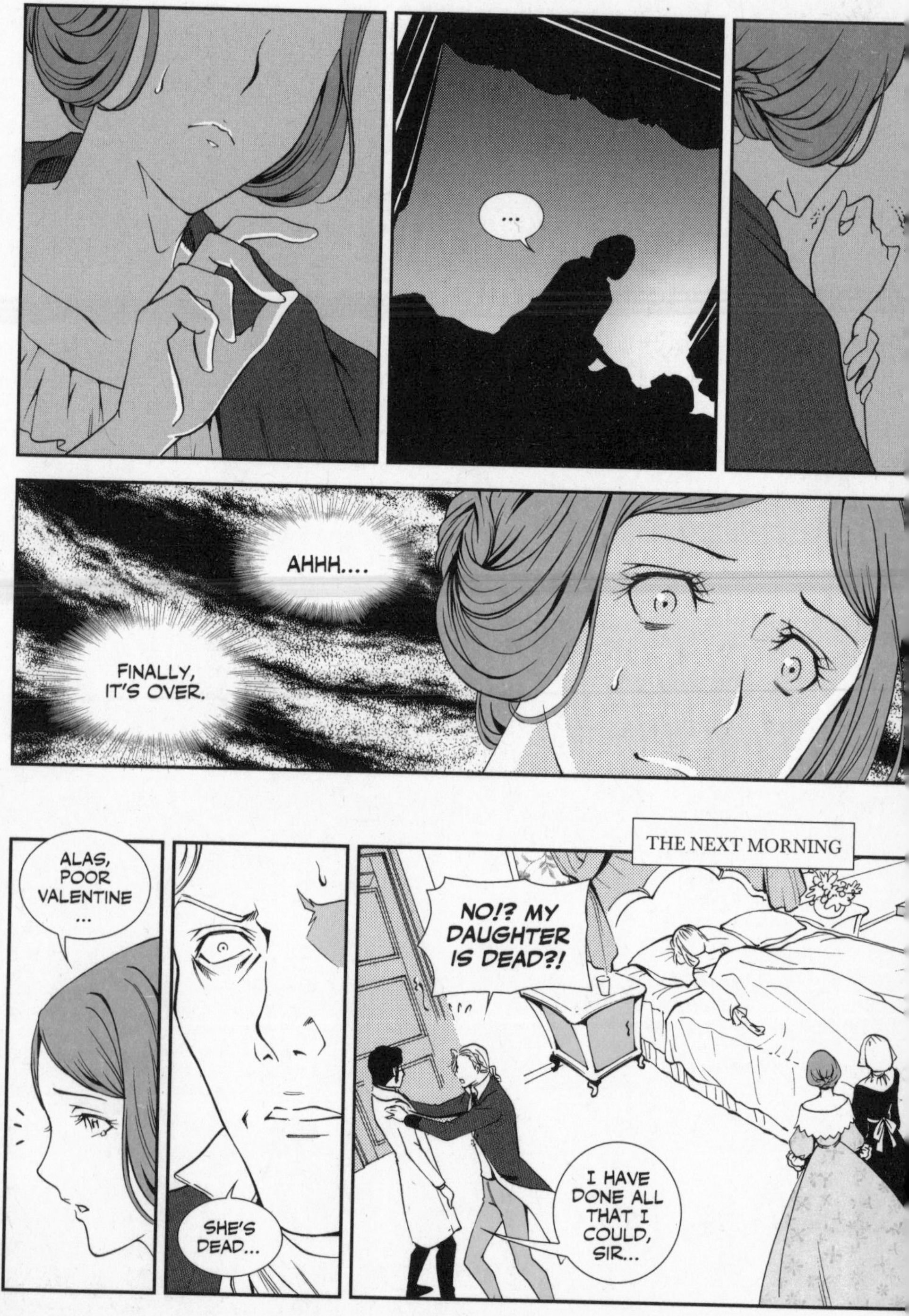
...
AHHH....
FINALLY, IT'S OVER.
THE NEXT MORNING
NO!? MY DAUGHTER IS DEAD?!
I HAVE DONE ALL THAT I COULD, SIR...
SHE'S DEAD...
ALAS, POOR VALENTINE ...

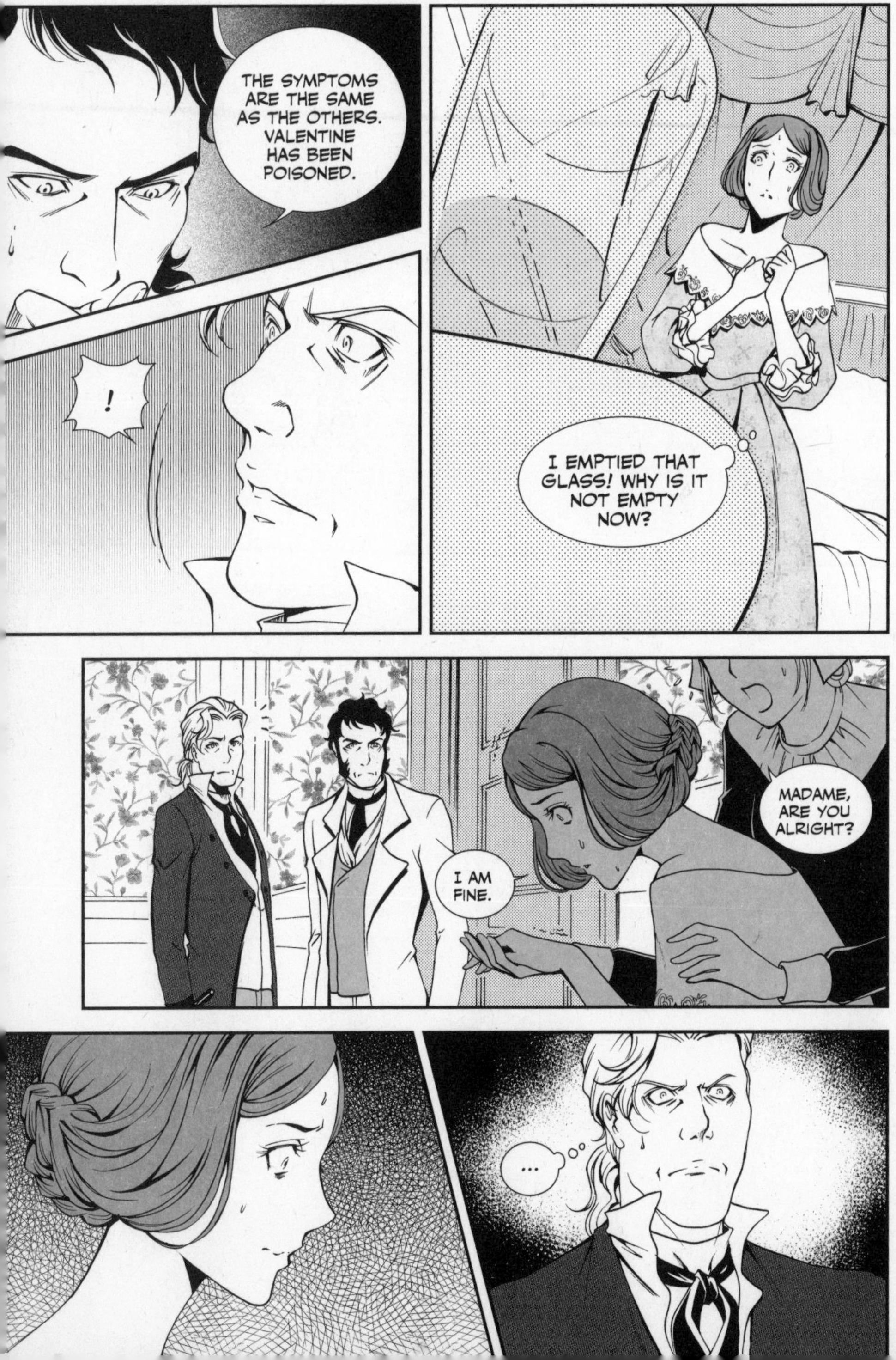
I EMPTIED THAT GLASS! WHY IS IT NOT EMPTY NOW?
THE SYMPTOMS ARE THE SAME AS THE OTHERS. VALENTINE HAS BEEN POISONED.
!
MADAME, ARE YOU ALRIGHT?
I AM FINE.
...

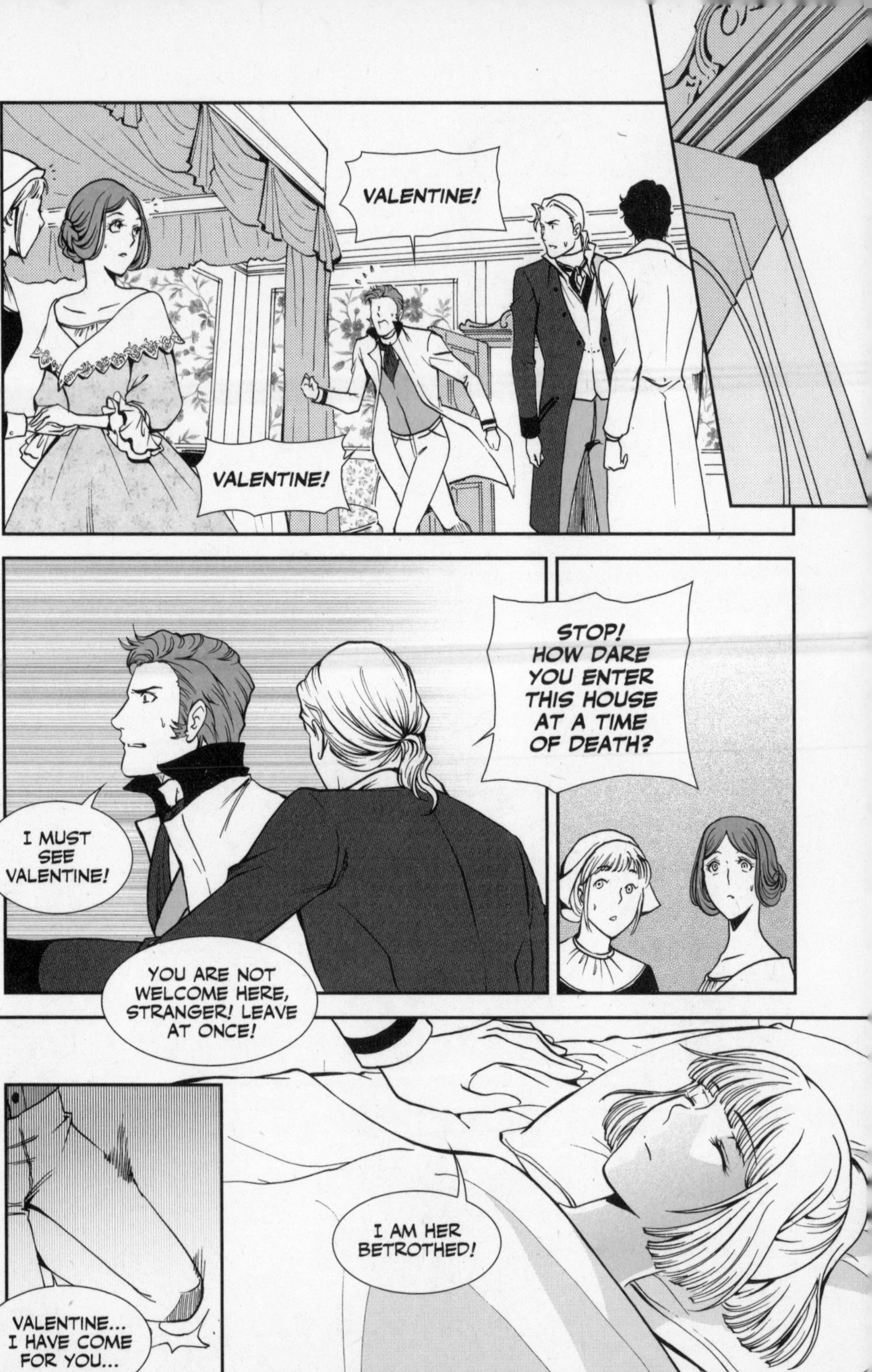
VALENTINE!
VALENTINE!
STOP! HOW DARE YOU ENTER THIS HOUSE AT A TIME OF DEATH?
I MUST SEE VALENTINE!
YOU ARE NOT WELCOME HERE, STRANGER! LEAVE AT ONCE!
I AM HER BETROTHED!
VALENTINE... I HAVE COME FOR YOU...

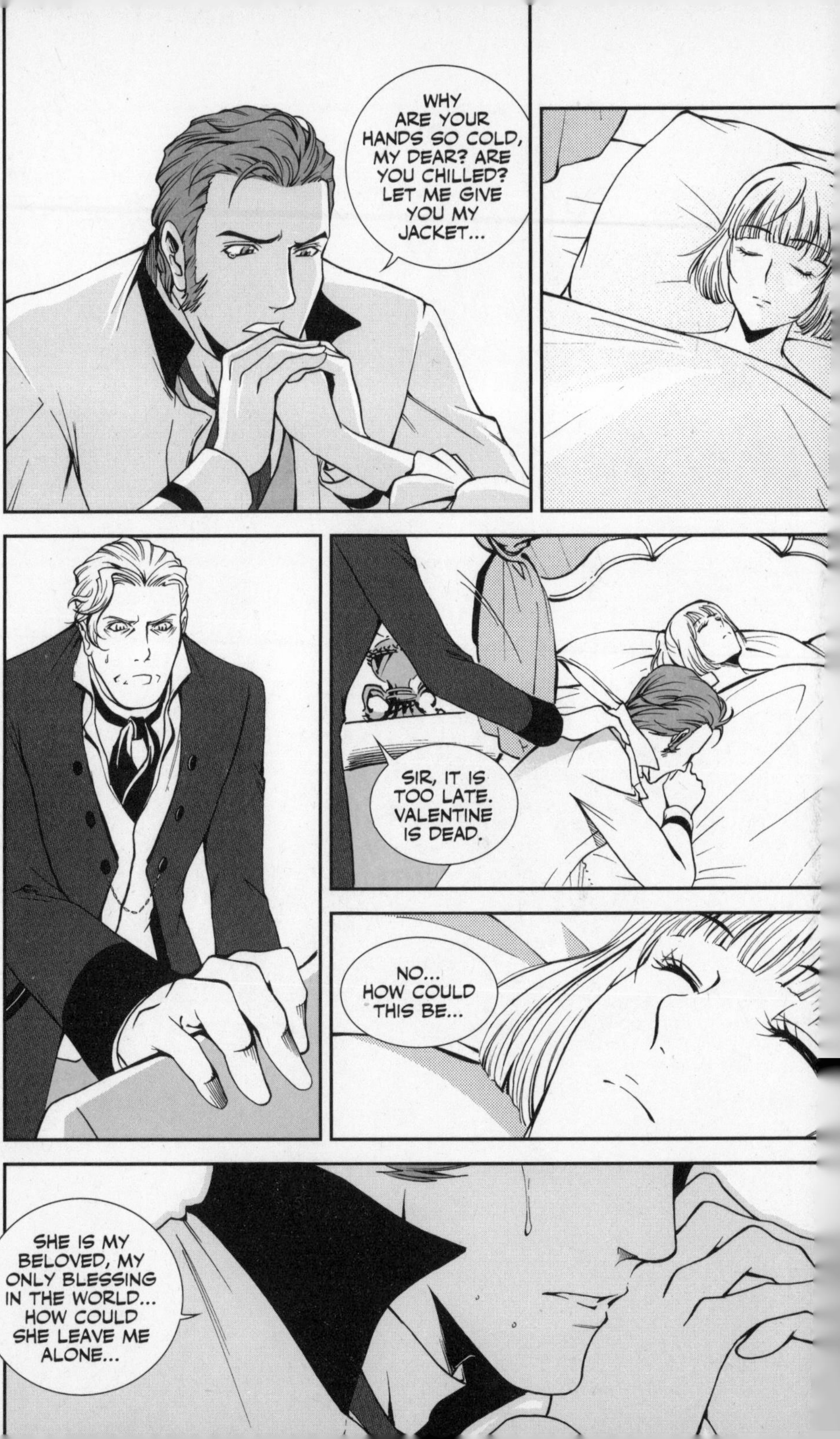
WHY ARE YOUR HANDS SO COLD, MY DEAR? ARE YOU CHILLED? LET ME GIVE YOU MY JACKET...
SIR, IT IS TOO LATE. VALENTINE IS DEAD.
NO... HOW COULD THIS BE...
SHE IS MY BELOVED, MY ONLY BLESSING IN THE WORLD... HOW COULD SHE LEAVE ME ALONE...

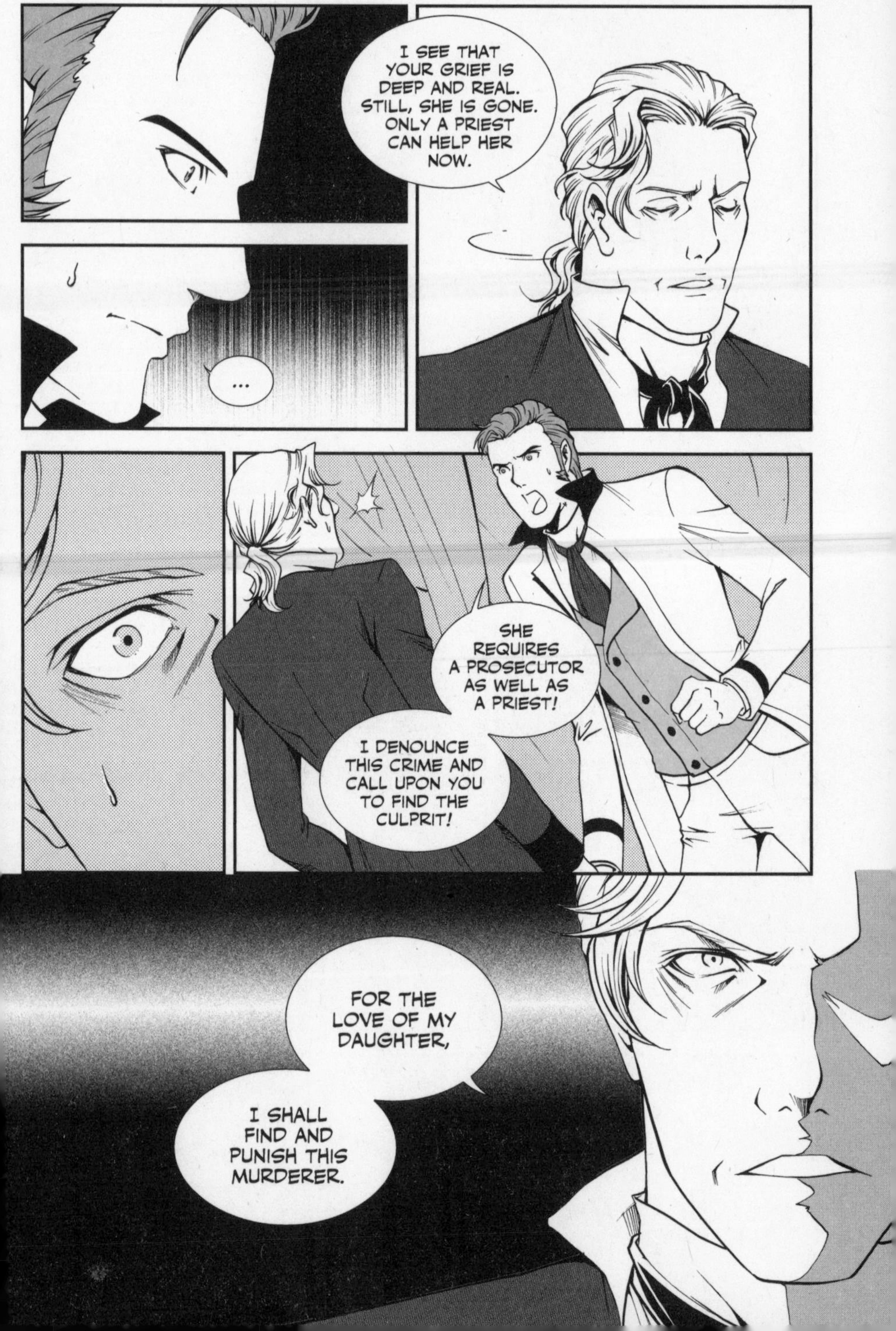
I SEE THAT YOUR GRIEF IS DEEP AND REAL. STILL, SHE IS GONE. ONLY A PRIEST CAN HELP HER NOW.
...
SHE REQUIRES A PROSECUTOR AS WELL AS A PRIEST!
I DENOUNCE THIS CRIME AND CALL UPON YOU TO FIND THE CULPRIT!
FOR THE LOVE OF MY DAUGHTER,
I SHALL FIND AND PUNISH THIS MURDERER.

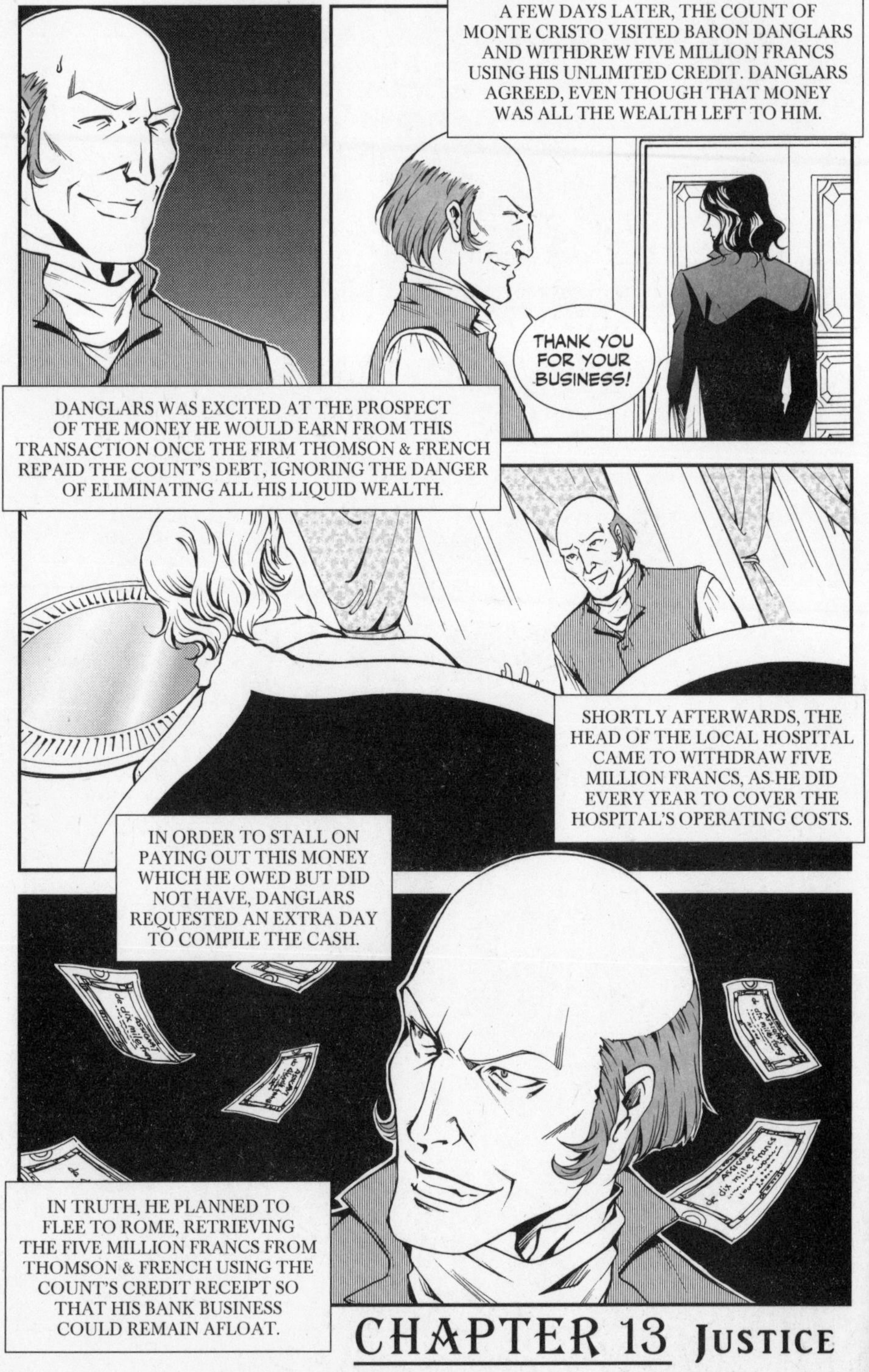
A FEW DAYS LATER, THE COUNT OF MONTE CRISTO VISITED BARON DANGLARS AND WITHDREW FIVE MILLION FRANCS USING HIS UNLIMITED CREDIT. DANGLARS AGREED, EVEN THOUGH THAT MONEY WAS ALL THE WEALTH LEFT TO HIM.
THANK YOU FOR YOUR BUSINESS!
DANGLARS WAS EXCITED AT THE PROSPECT OF THE MONEY HE WOULD EARN FROM THIS TRANSACTION ONCE THE FIRM THOMSON & FRENCH REPAID THE COUNT'S DEBT, IGNORING THE DANGER OF ELIMINATING ALL HIS LIQUID WEALTH.
SHORTLY AFTERWARDS, THE HEAD OF THE LOCAL HOSPITAL CAME TO WITHDRAW FIVE MILLION FRANCS, AS HE DID EVERY YEAR TO COVER THE HOSPITAL'S OPERATING COSTS.
IN ORDER TO STALL ON PAYING OUT THIS MONEY WHICH HE OWED BUT DID NOT HAVE, DANGLARS REQUESTED AN EXTRA DAY TO COMPILE THE CASH.
IN TRUTH, HE PLANNED TO FLEE TO ROME, RETRIEVING THE FIVE MILLION FRANCS FROM THOMSON & FRENCH USING THE COUNT'S CREDIT RECEIPT SO THAT HIS BANK BUSINESS COULD REMAIN AFLOAT.

CHAPTER 13 Justice

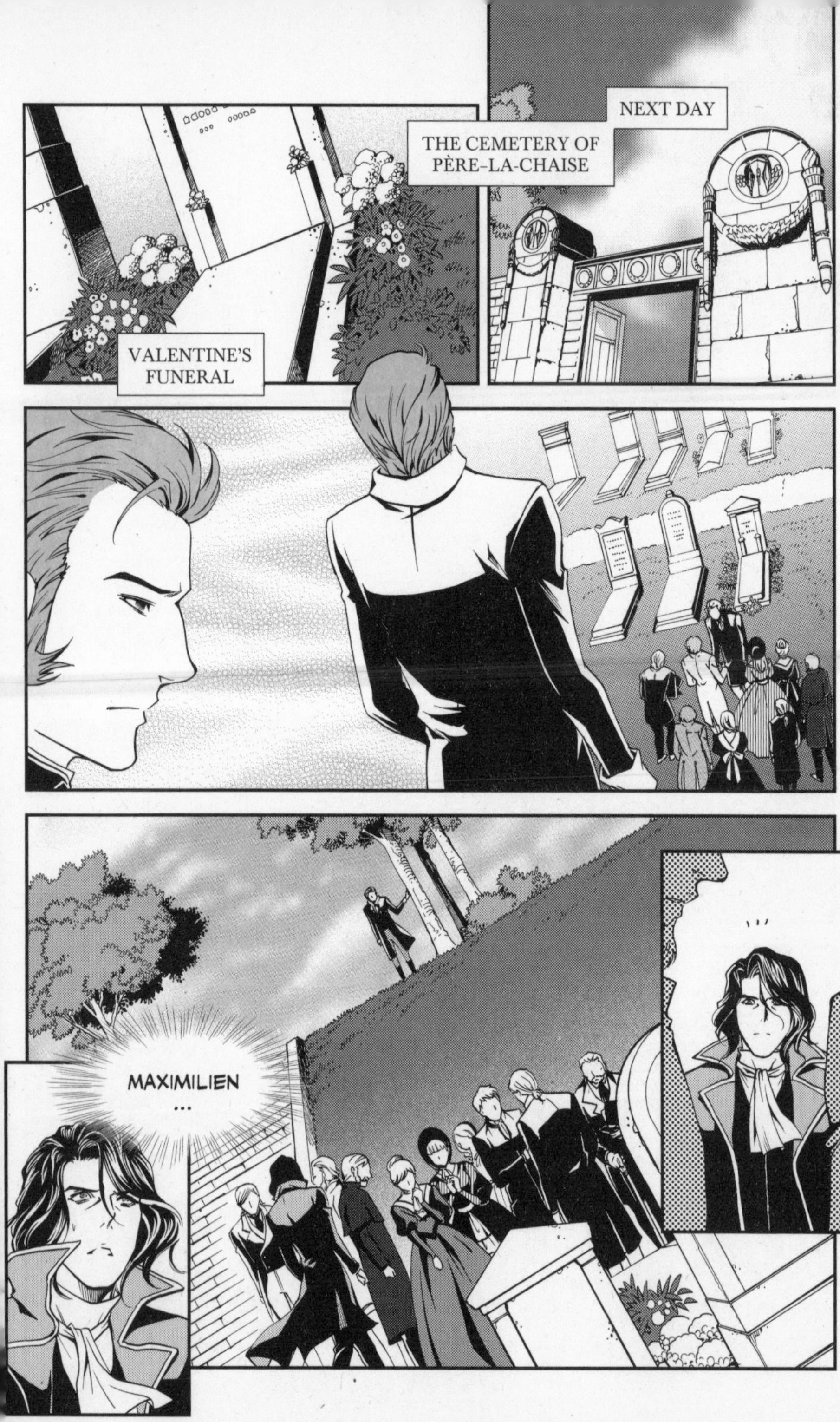
NEXT DAY
THE CEMETERY OF PÈRE-LA-CHAISE
VALENTINE'S FUNERAL
MAXIMILIEN ...

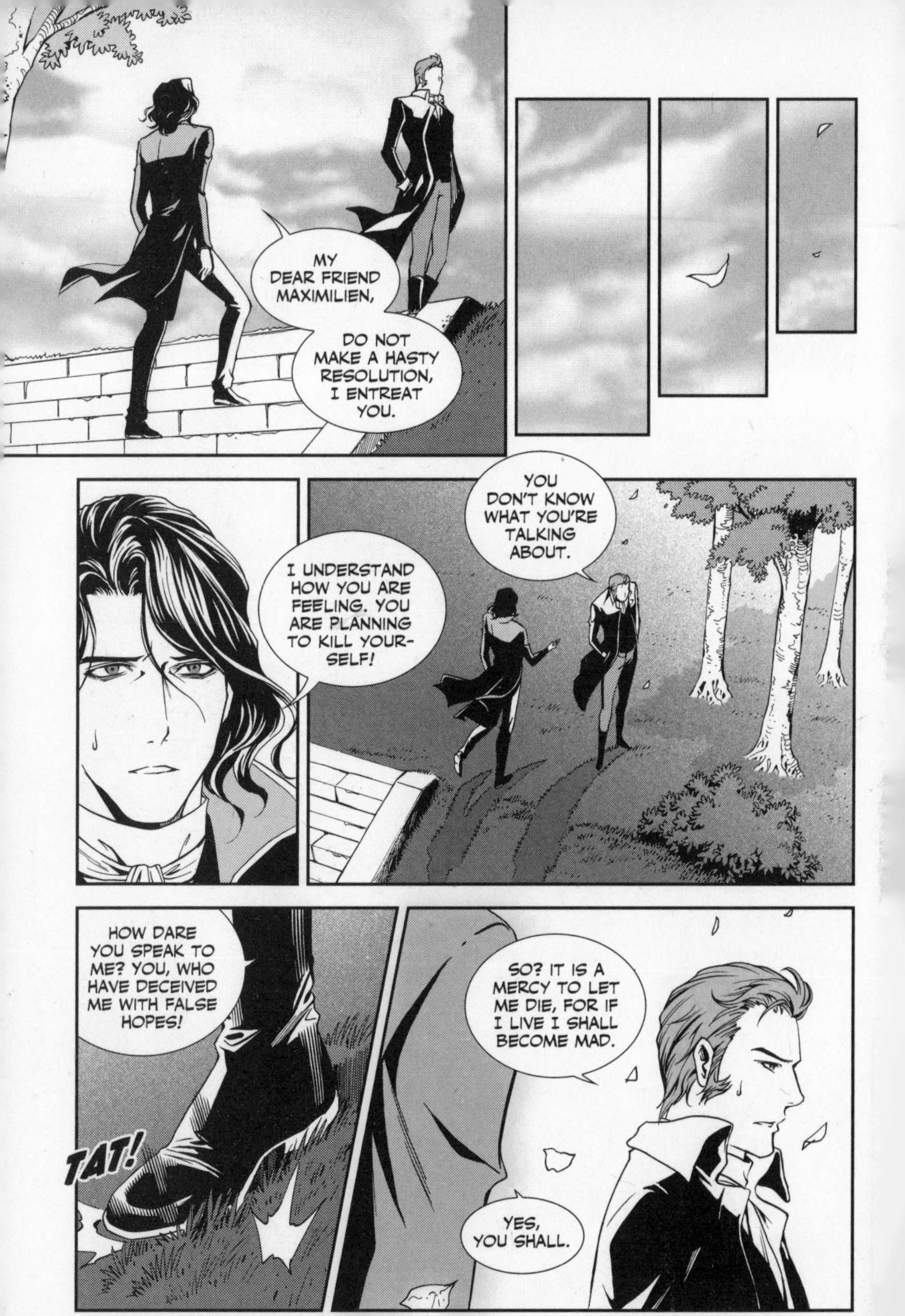
MY DEAR FRIEND MAXIMILIEN,
DO NOT MAKE A HASTY RESOLUTION, I ENTREAT YOU.
YOU DON'T KNOW WHAT YOU'RE TALKING ABOUT.
I UNDERSTAND HOW YOU ARE FEELING. YOU ARE PLANNING TO KILL YOUR-SELF!
SO? IT IS A MERCY TO LET ME DIE, FOR IF I LIVE I SHALL BECOME MAD.
YES, YOU SHALL.
HOW DARE YOU SPEAK TO ME? YOU, WHO HAVE DECEIVED ME WITH FALSE HOPES!
TAT!

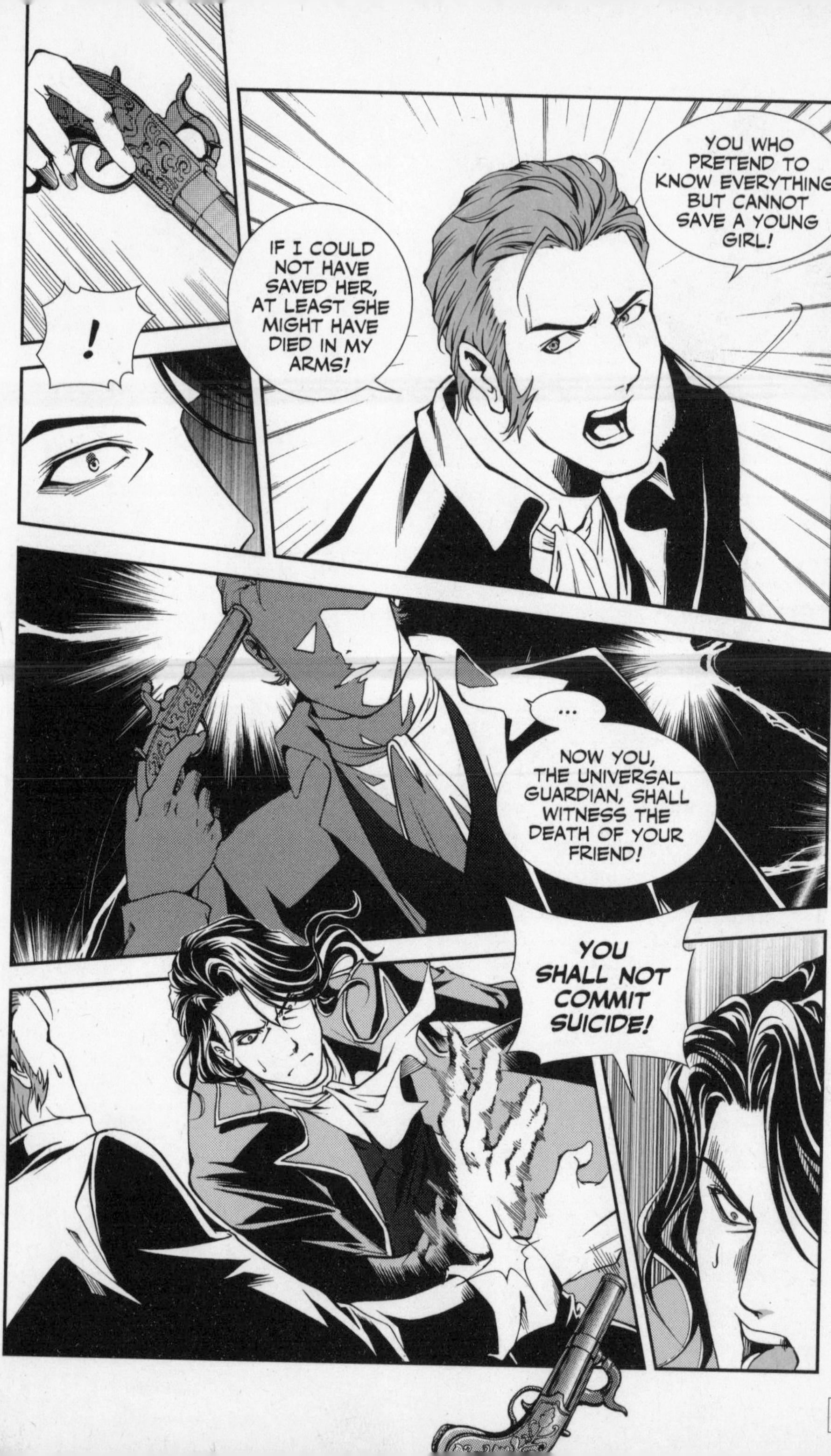
YOU WHO PRETEND TO KNOW EVERYTHING, BUT CANNOT SAVE A YOUNG GIRL!
IF I COULD NOT HAVE SAVED HER, AT LEAST SHE MIGHT HAVE DIED IN MY ARMS!
!
...
NOW YOU, THE UNIVERSAL GUARDIAN, SHALL WITNESS THE DEATH OF YOUR FRIEND!
YOU SHALL NOT COMMIT SUICIDE!

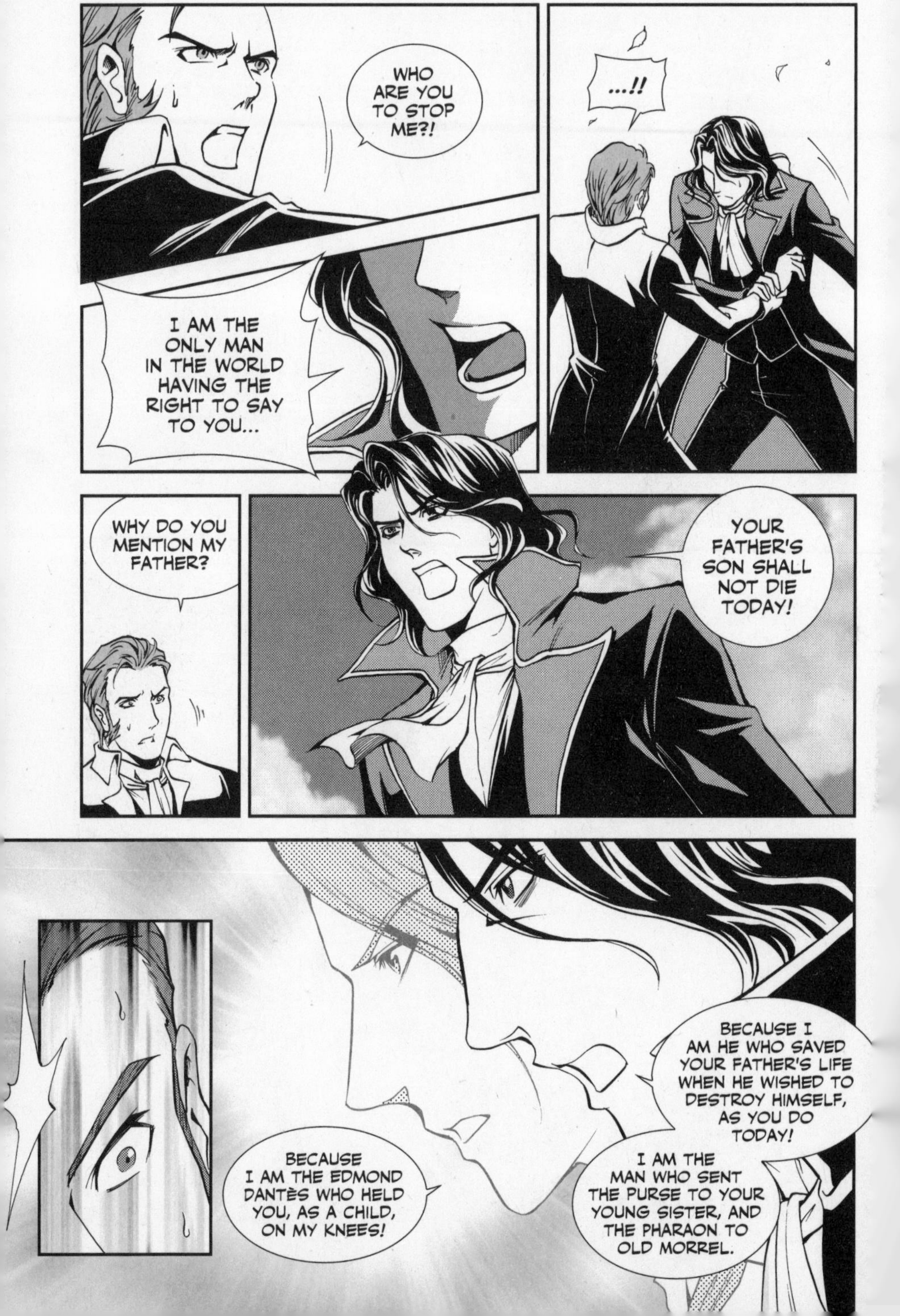
...!!
WHO ARE YOU TO STOP ME?!
I AM THE ONLY MAN IN THE WORLD HAVING THE RIGHT TO SAY TO YOU...
YOUR FATHER'S SON SHALL NOT DIE TODAY!
WHY DO YOU MENTION MY FATHER?
BECAUSE I AM HE WHO SAVED YOUR FATHER'S LIFE WHEN HE WISHED TO DESTROY HIMSELF, AS YOU DO TODAY!
I AM THE MAN WHO SENT THE PURSE TO YOUR YOUNG SISTER, AND THE PHARAON TO OLD MORREL.
BECAUSE I AM THE EDMOND DANTÈS WHO HELD YOU, AS A CHILD, ON MY KNEES!

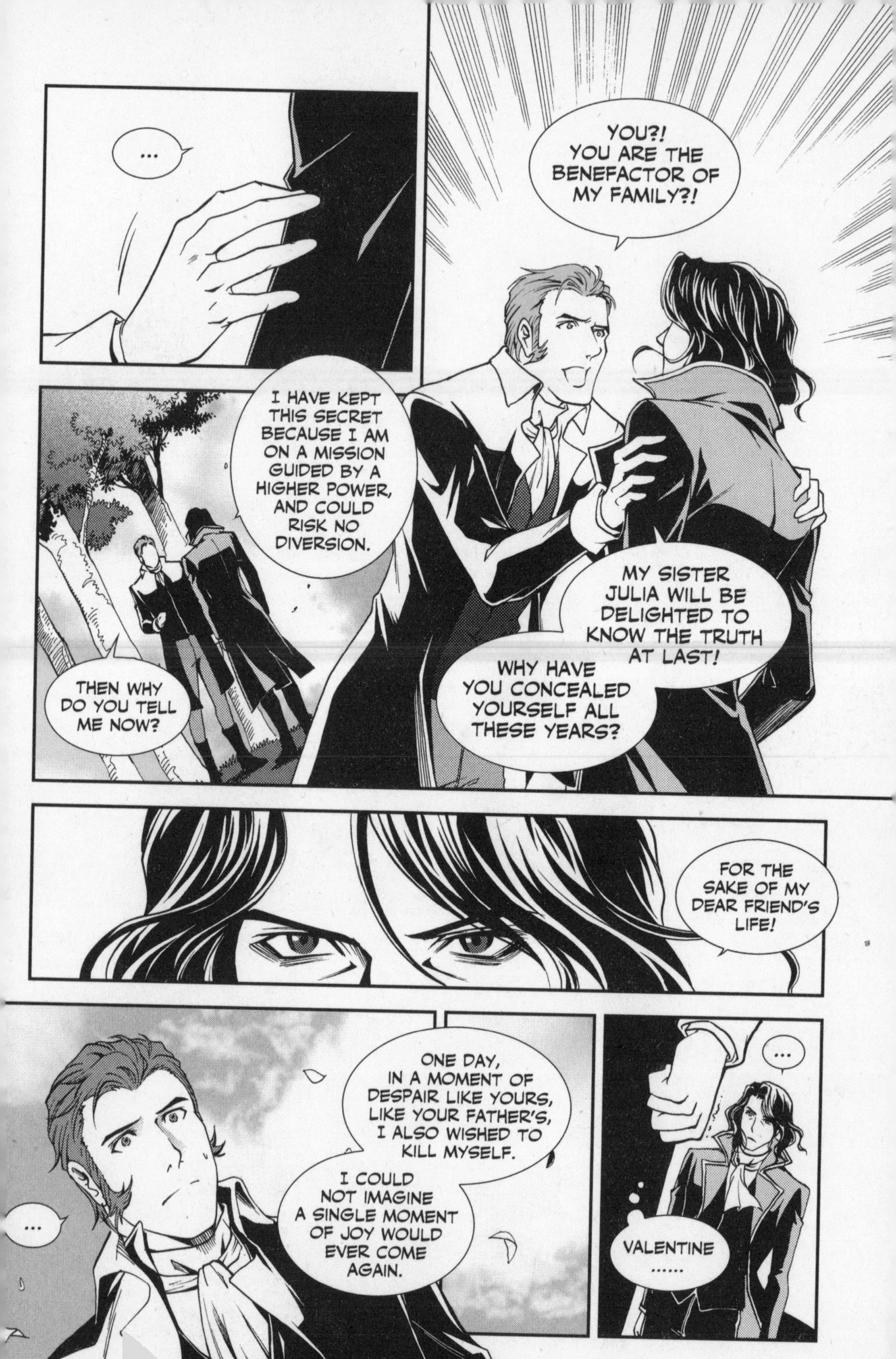
YOU?! YOU ARE THE BENEFACTOR OF MY FAMILY?!
MY SISTER JULIA WILL BE DELIGHTED TO KNOW THE TRUTH AT LAST!
WHY HAVE YOU CONCEALED YOURSELF ALL THESE YEARS?
...
I HAVE KEPT THIS SECRET BECAUSE I AM ON A MISSION GUIDED BY A HIGHER POWER, AND COULD RISK NO DIVERSION.
THEN WHY DO YOU TELL ME NOW?
FOR THE SAKE OF MY DEAR FRIEND'S LIFE!
...
VALENTINE ......
ONE DAY, IN A MOMENT OF DESPAIR LIKE YOURS, LIKE YOUR FATHER'S, I ALSO WISHED TO KILL MYSELF.
I COULD NOT IMAGINE A SINGLE MOMENT OF JOY WOULD EVER COME AGAIN.
...

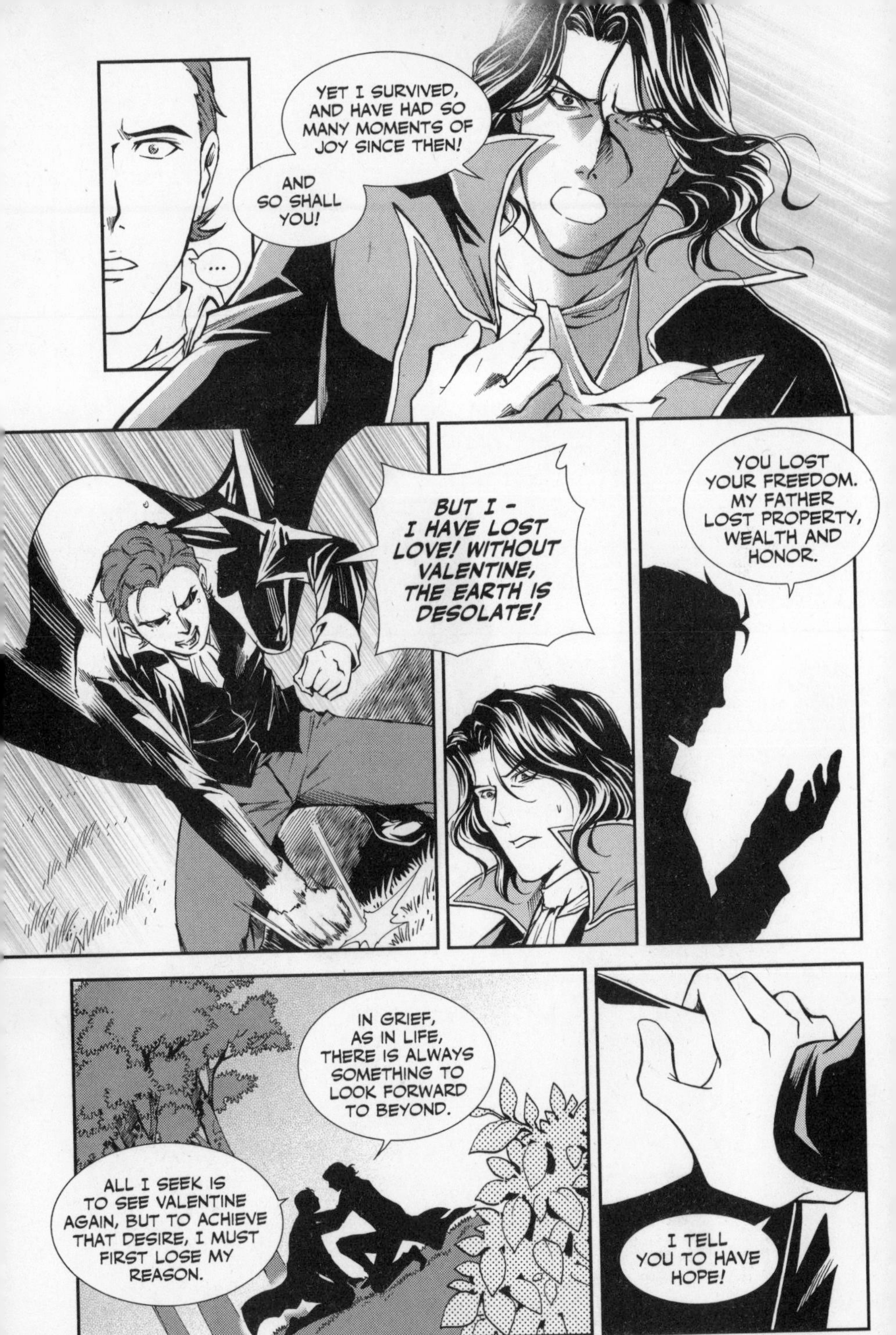
YET I SURVIVED, AND HAVE HAD SO MANY MOMENTS OF JOY SINCE THEN!
AND SO SHALL YOU!
...
YOU LOST YOUR FREEDOM. MY FATHER LOST PROPERTY, WEALTH AND HONOR.
BUT I - I HAVE LOST LOVE! WITHOUT VALENTINE, THE EARTH IS DESOLATE!
I TELL YOU TO HAVE HOPE!
IN GRIEF, AS IN LIFE, THERE IS ALWAYS SOMETHING TO LOOK FORWARD TO BEYOND.
ALL I SEEK IS TO SEE VALENTINE AGAIN, BUT TO ACHIEVE THAT DESIRE, I MUST FIRST LOSE MY REASON.

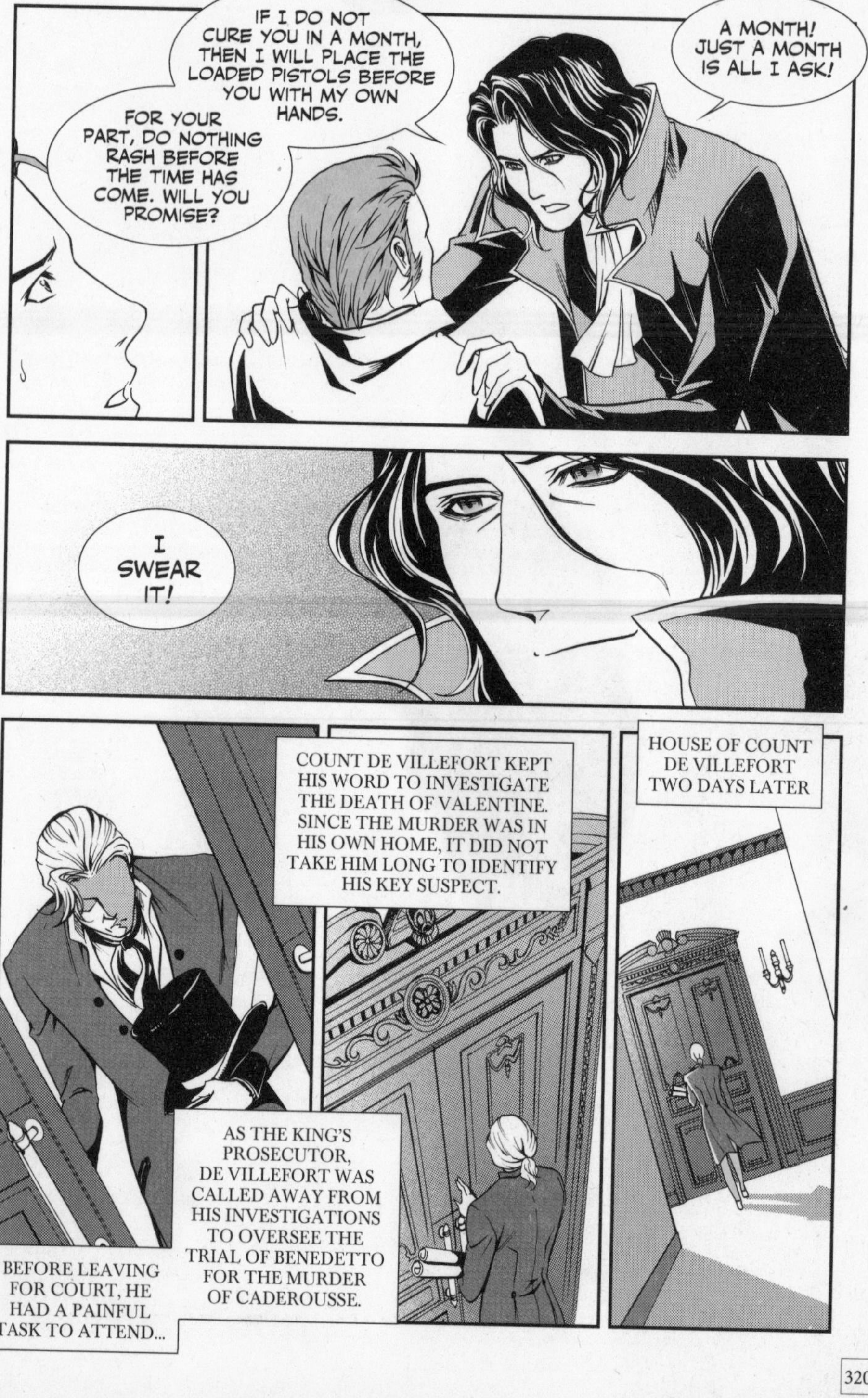
A MONTH! JUST A MONTH IS ALL I ASK!
IF I DO NOT CURE YOU IN A MONTH, THEN I WILL PLACE THE LOADED PISTOLS BEFORE YOU WITH MY OWN HANDS.
FOR YOUR PART, DO NOTHING RASH BEFORE THE TIME HAS COME. WILL YOU PROMISE?
I SWEAR IT!
HOUSE OF COUNT DE VILLEFORT TWO DAYS LATER
COUNT DE VILLEFORT KEPT HIS WORD TO INVESTIGATE THE DEATH OF VALENTINE. SINCE THE MURDER WAS IN HIS OWN HOME, IT DID NOT TAKE HIM LONG TO IDENTIFY HIS KEY SUSPECT.
AS THE KING'S PROSECUTOR, DE VILLEFORT WAS CALLED AWAY FROM HIS INVESTIGATIONS TO OVERSEE THE TRIAL OF BENEDETTO FOR THE MURDER OF CADEROUSSE.
BEFORE LEAVING FOR COURT, HE HAD A PAINFUL TASK TO ATTEND...

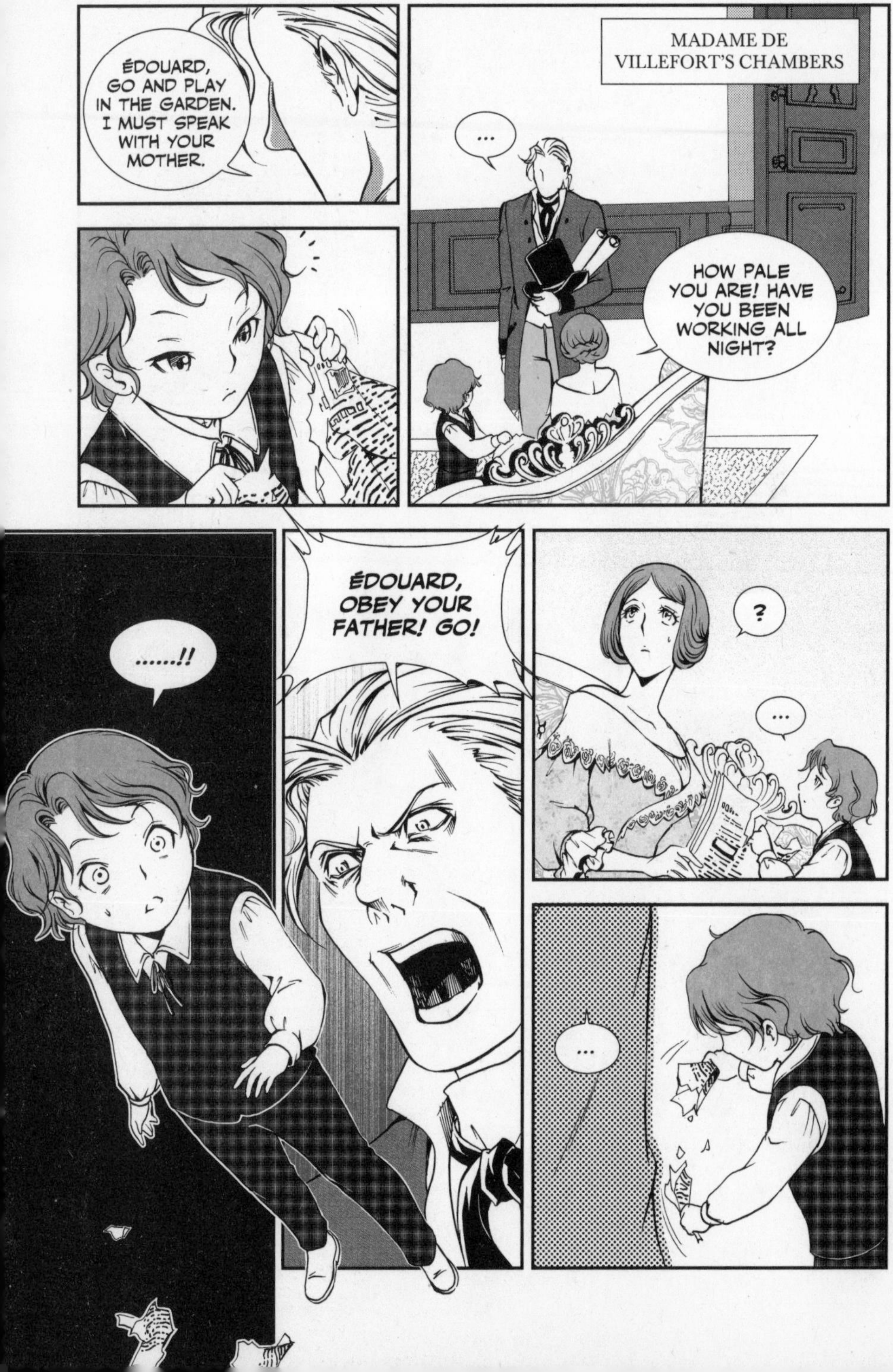
MADAME DE VILLEFORT'S CHAMBERS
...
HOW PALE YOU ARE! HAVE YOU BEEN WORKING ALL NIGHT?
ÉDOUARD, GO AND PLAY IN THE GARDEN. I MUST SPEAK WITH YOUR MOTHER.
?
...
...
ÉDOUARD, OBEY YOUR FATHER! GO!
......!!

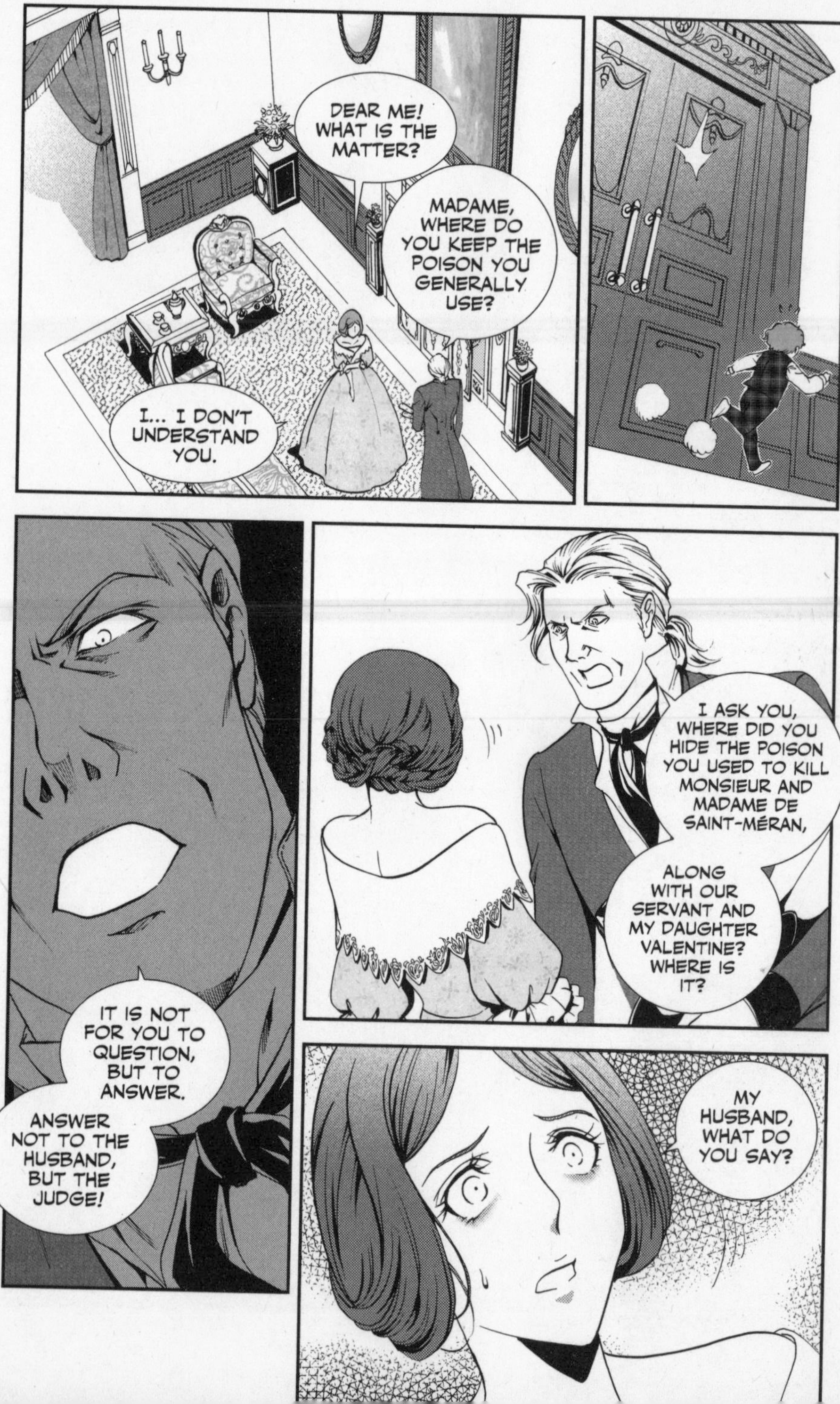
DEAR ME! WHAT IS THE MATTER?
MADAME, WHERE DO YOU KEEP THE POISON YOU GENERALLY USE?
I... I DON'T UNDERSTAND YOU.
I ASK YOU, WHERE DID YOU HIDE THE POISON YOU USED TO KILL MONSIEUR AND MADAME DE SAINT-MÉRAN,
ALONG WITH OUR SERVANT AND MY DAUGHTER VALENTINE? WHERE IS IT?
MY HUSBAND, WHAT DO YOU SAY?
IT IS NOT FOR YOU TO QUESTION, BUT TO ANSWER.
ANSWER NOT TO THE HUSBAND, BUT THE JUDGE!

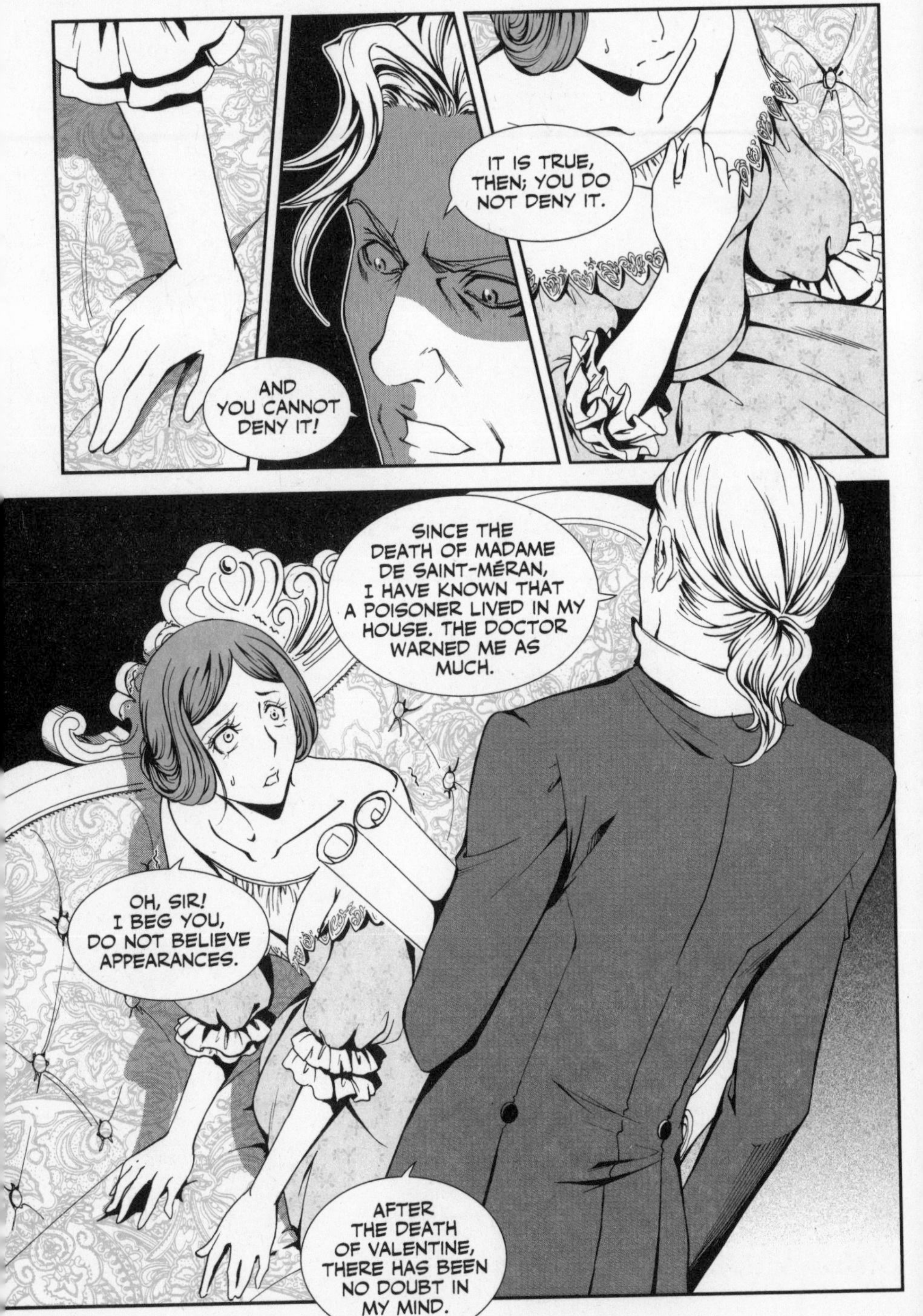
IT IS TRUE, THEN; YOU DO NOT DENY IT.
AND YOU CANNOT DENY IT!
SINCE THE DEATH OF MADAME DE SAINT-MÉRAN, I HAVE KNOWN THAT A POISONER LIVED IN MY HOUSE. THE DOCTOR WARNED ME AS MUCH.
OH, SIR! I BEG YOU, DO NOT BELIEVE APPEARANCES.
AFTER THE DEATH OF VALENTINE, THERE HAS BEEN NO DOUBT IN MY MIND.

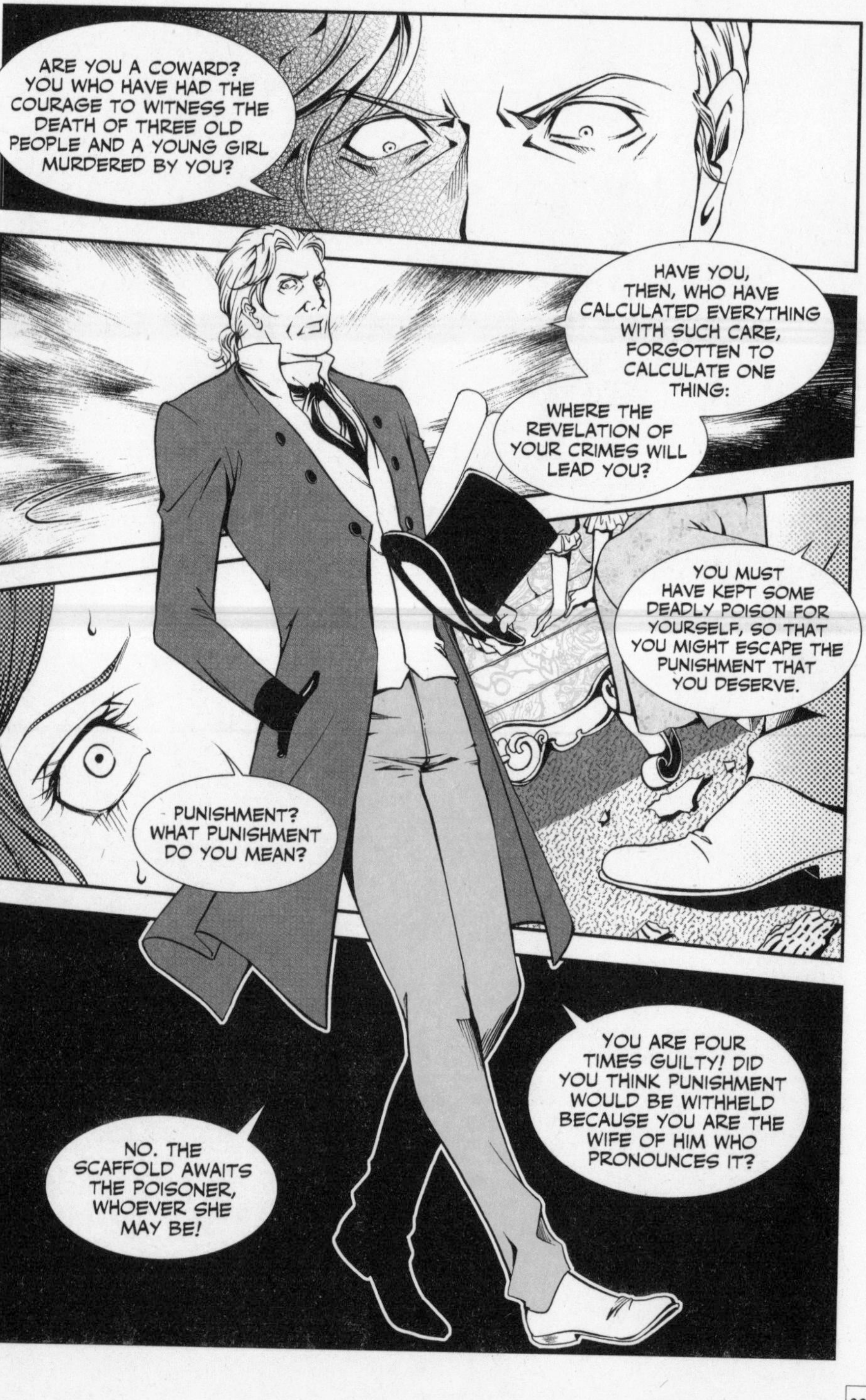

ARE YOU A COWARD? YOU WHO HAVE HAD THE COURAGE TO WITNESS THE DEATH OF THREE OLD PEOPLE AND A YOUNG GIRL MURDERED BY YOU?
HAVE YOU, THEN, WHO HAVE CALCULATED EVERYTHING WITH SUCH CARE, FORGOTTEN TO CALCULATE ONE THING:
WHERE THE REVELATION OF YOUR CRIMES WILL LEAD YOU?
YOU MUST HAVE KEPT SOME DEADLY POISON FOR YOURSELF, SO THAT YOU MIGHT ESCAPE THE PUNISHMENT THAT YOU DESERVE.
PUNISHMENT? WHAT PUNISHMENT DO YOU MEAN?
YOU ARE FOUR TIMES GUILTY! DID YOU THINK PUNISHMENT WOULD BE WITHHELD BECAUSE YOU ARE THE WIFE OF HIM WHO PRONOUNCES IT?
NO. THE SCAFFOLD AWAITS THE POISONER, WHOEVER SHE MAY BE!

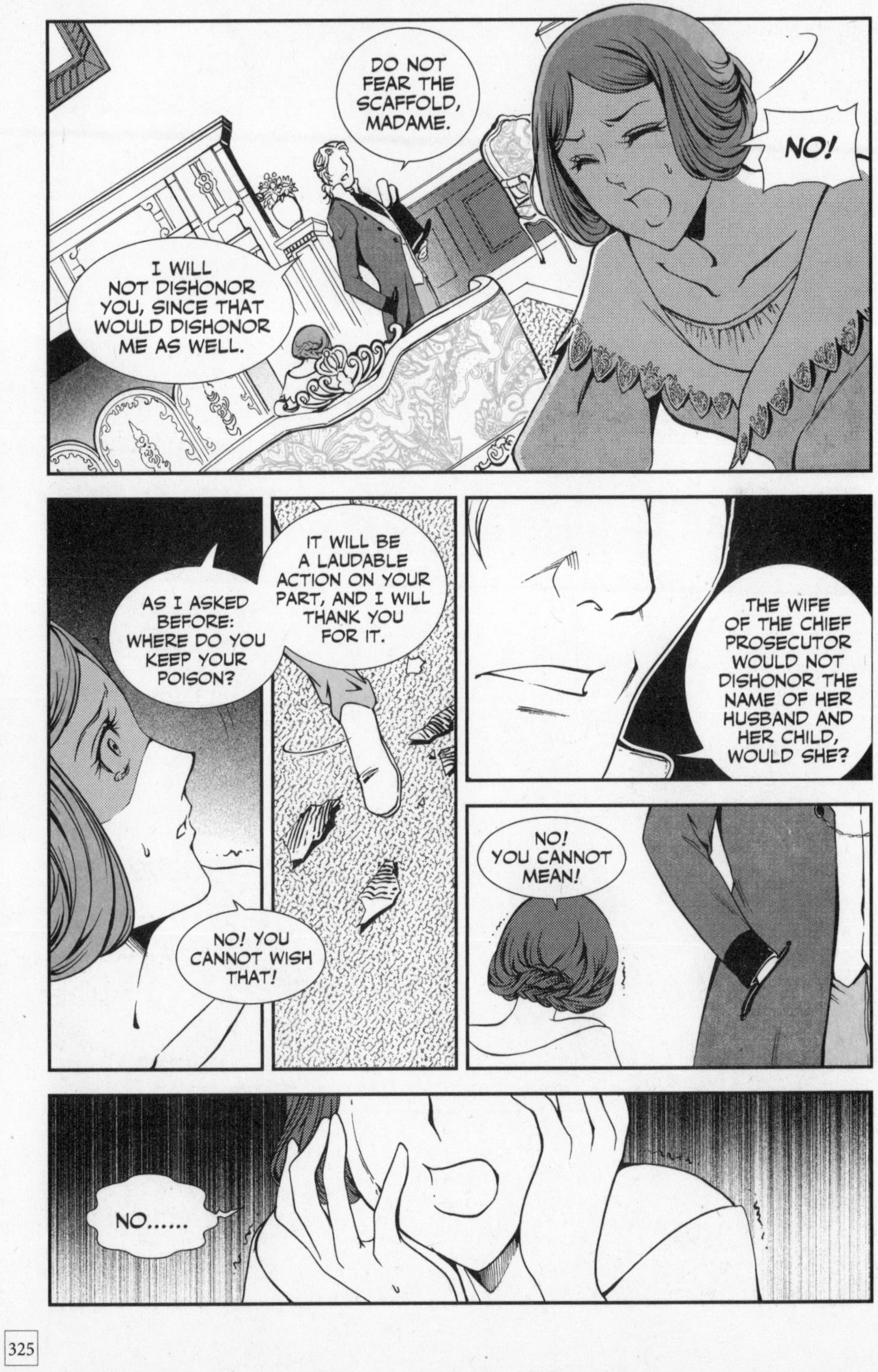
NO!
DO NOT FEAR THE SCAFFOLD, MADAME.
I WILL NOT DISHONOR YOU, SINCE THAT WOULD DISHONOR ME AS WELL.
THE WIFE OF THE CHIEF PROSECUTOR WOULD NOT DISHONOR THE NAME OF HER HUSBAND AND HER CHILD, WOULD SHE?
NO! YOU CANNOT MEAN!
IT WILL BE A LAUDABLE ACTION ON YOUR PART, AND I WILL THANK YOU FOR IT.
AS I ASKED BEFORE: WHERE DO YOU KEEP YOUR POISON?
NO! YOU CANNOT WISH THAT!
NO......

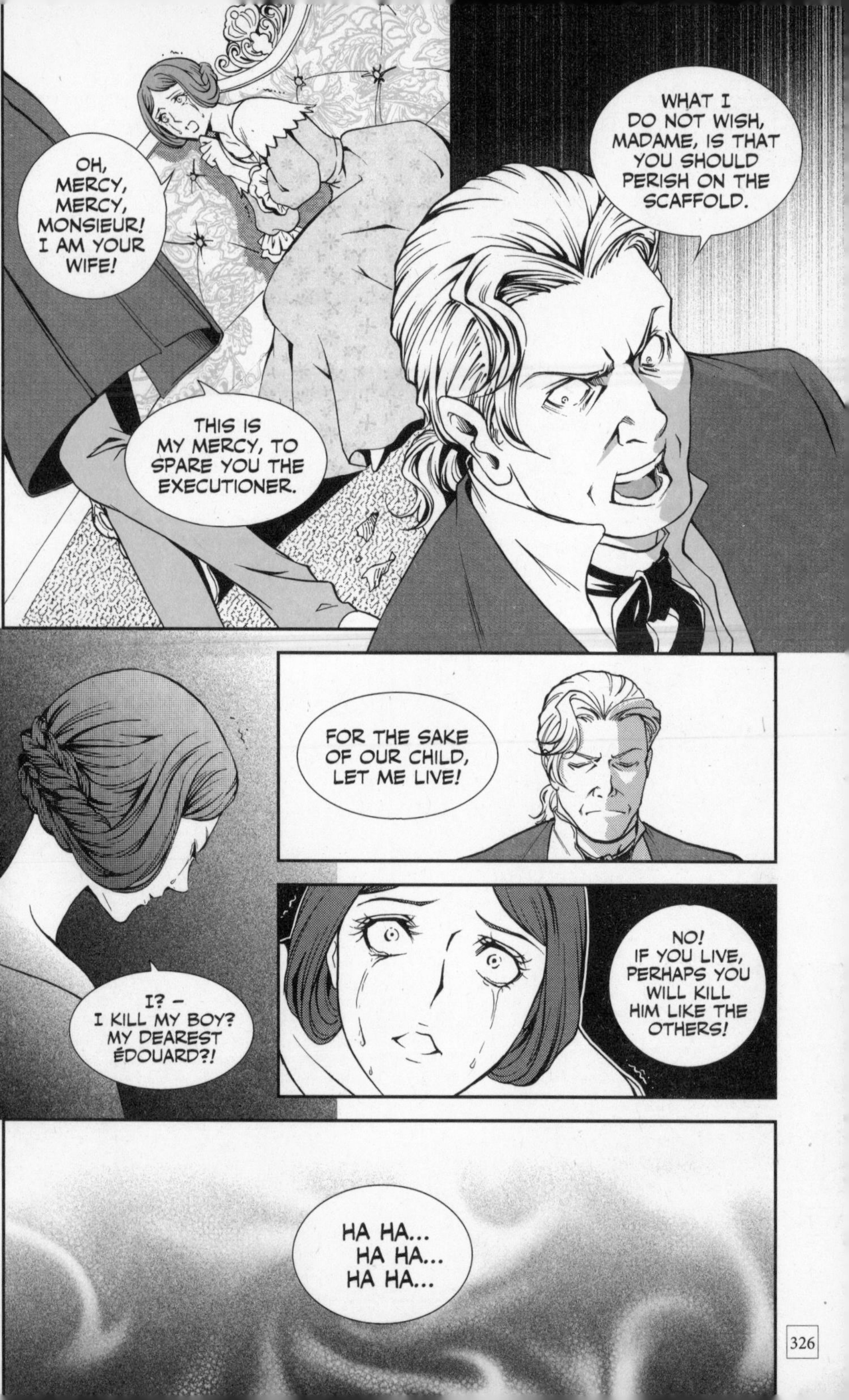
WHAT I DO NOT WISH, MADAME, IS THAT YOU SHOULD PERISH ON THE SCAFFOLD.
OH, MERCY, MERCY, MONSIEUR! I AM YOUR WIFE!
THIS IS MY MERCY, TO SPARE YOU THE EXECUTIONER.
FOR THE SAKE OF OUR CHILD, LET ME LIVE!
NO! IF YOU LIVE, PERHAPS YOU WILL KILL HIM LIKE THE OTHERS!
I? – I KILL MY BOY? MY DEAREST ÉDOUARD?!
HA HA... HA HA... HA HA...

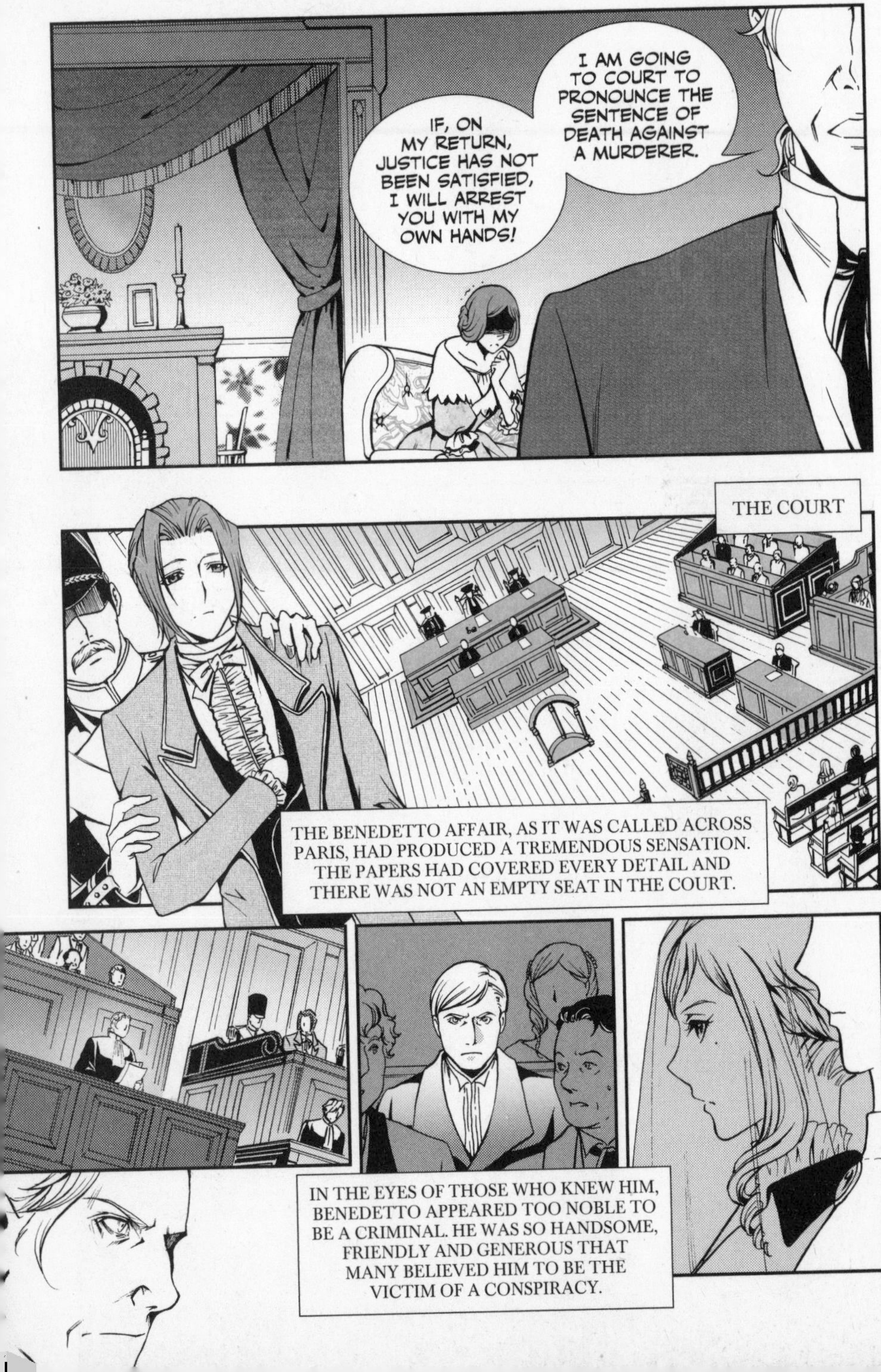

I AM GOING TO COURT TO PRONOUNCE THE SENTENCE OF DEATH AGAINST A MURDERER.
IF, ON MY RETURN, JUSTICE HAS NOT BEEN SATISFIED, I WILL ARREST YOU WITH MY OWN HANDS!
THE COURT
THE BENEDETTO AFFAIR, AS IT WAS CALLED ACROSS PARIS, HAD PRODUCED A TREMENDOUS SENSATION. THE PAPERS HAD COVERED EVERY DETAIL AND THERE WAS NOT AN EMPTY SEAT IN THE COURT.
IN THE EYES OF THOSE WHO KNEW HIM, BENEDETTO APPEARED TOO NOBLE TO BE A CRIMINAL. HE WAS SO HANDSOME, FRIENDLY AND GENEROUS THAT MANY BELIEVED HIM TO BE THE VICTIM OF A CONSPIRACY.

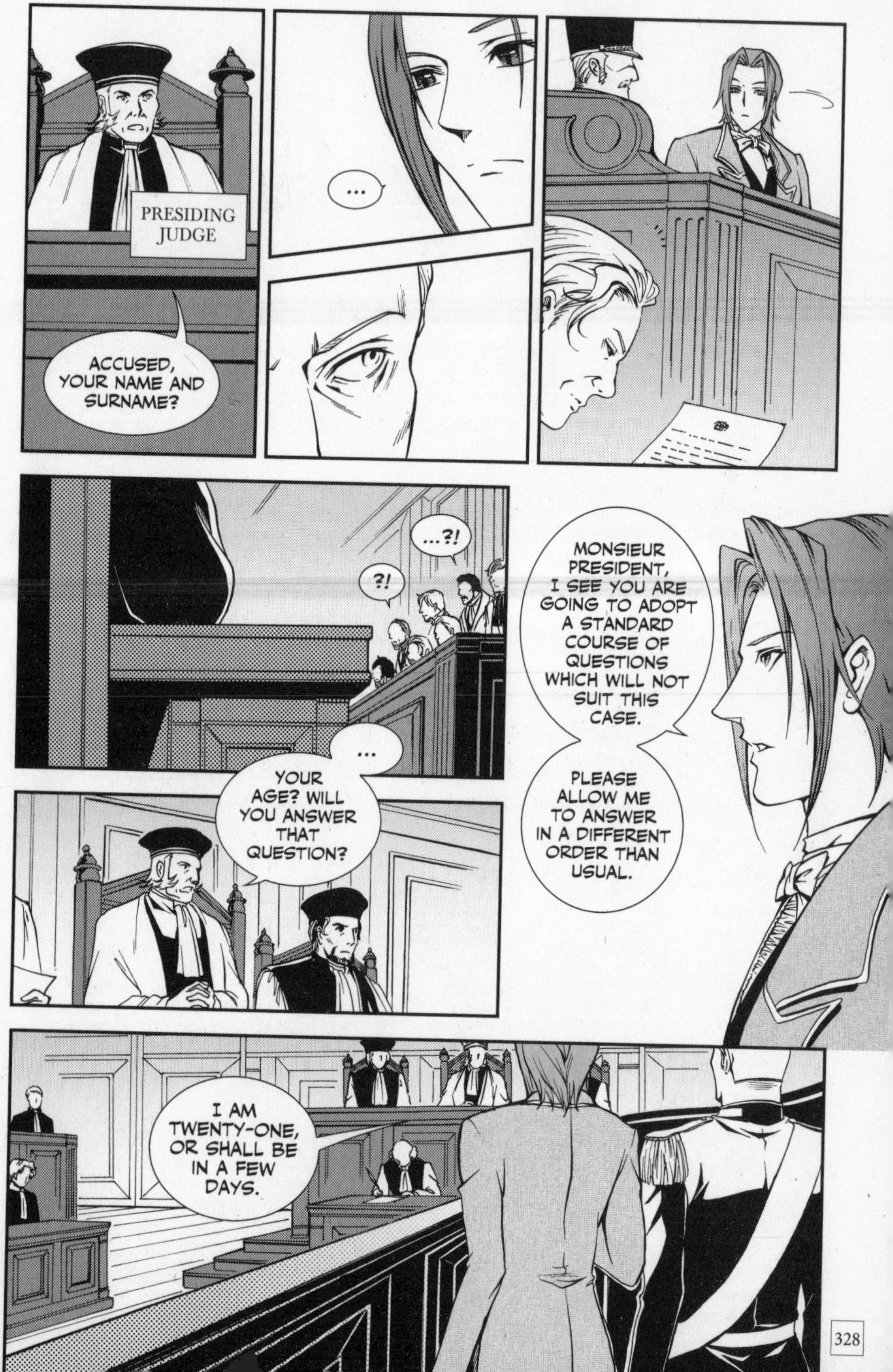
...
PRESIDING JUDGE
ACCUSED, YOUR NAME AND SURNAME?
MONSIEUR PRESIDENT, I SEE YOU ARE GOING TO ADOPT A STANDARD COURSE OF QUESTIONS WHICH WILL NOT SUIT THIS CASE.
PLEASE ALLOW ME TO ANSWER IN A DIFFERENT ORDER THAN USUAL.
...?!
?!
...
YOUR AGE? WILL YOU ANSWER THAT QUESTION?
I AM TWENTY-ONE, OR SHALL BE IN A FEW DAYS.

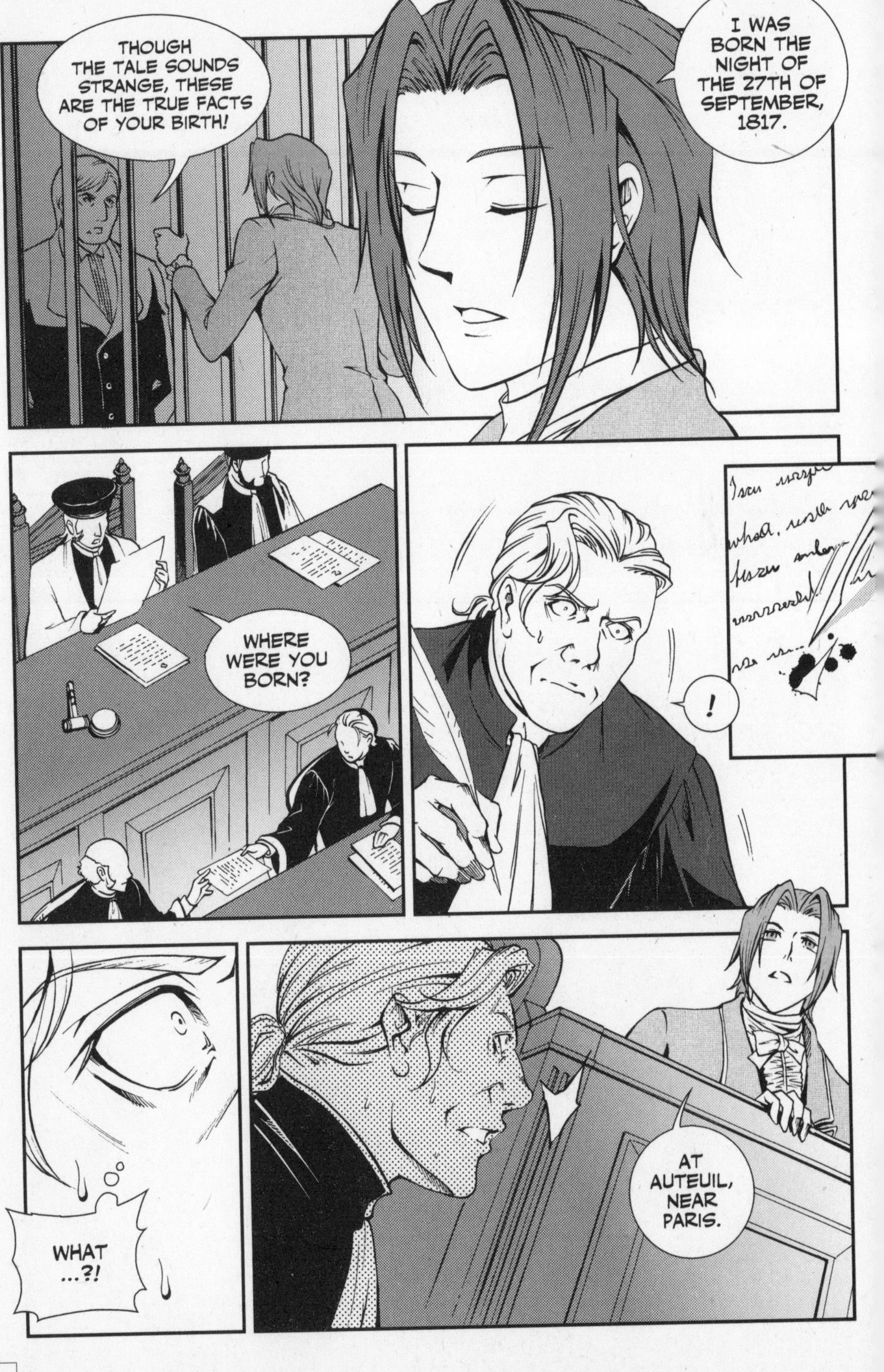
I WAS BORN THE NIGHT OF THE 27TH OF SEPTEMBER, 1817.
THOUGH THE TALE SOUNDS STRANGE, THESE ARE THE TRUE FACTS OF YOUR BIRTH!
!
WHERE WERE YOU BORN?
AT AUTEUIL, NEAR PARIS.
WHAT ...?!

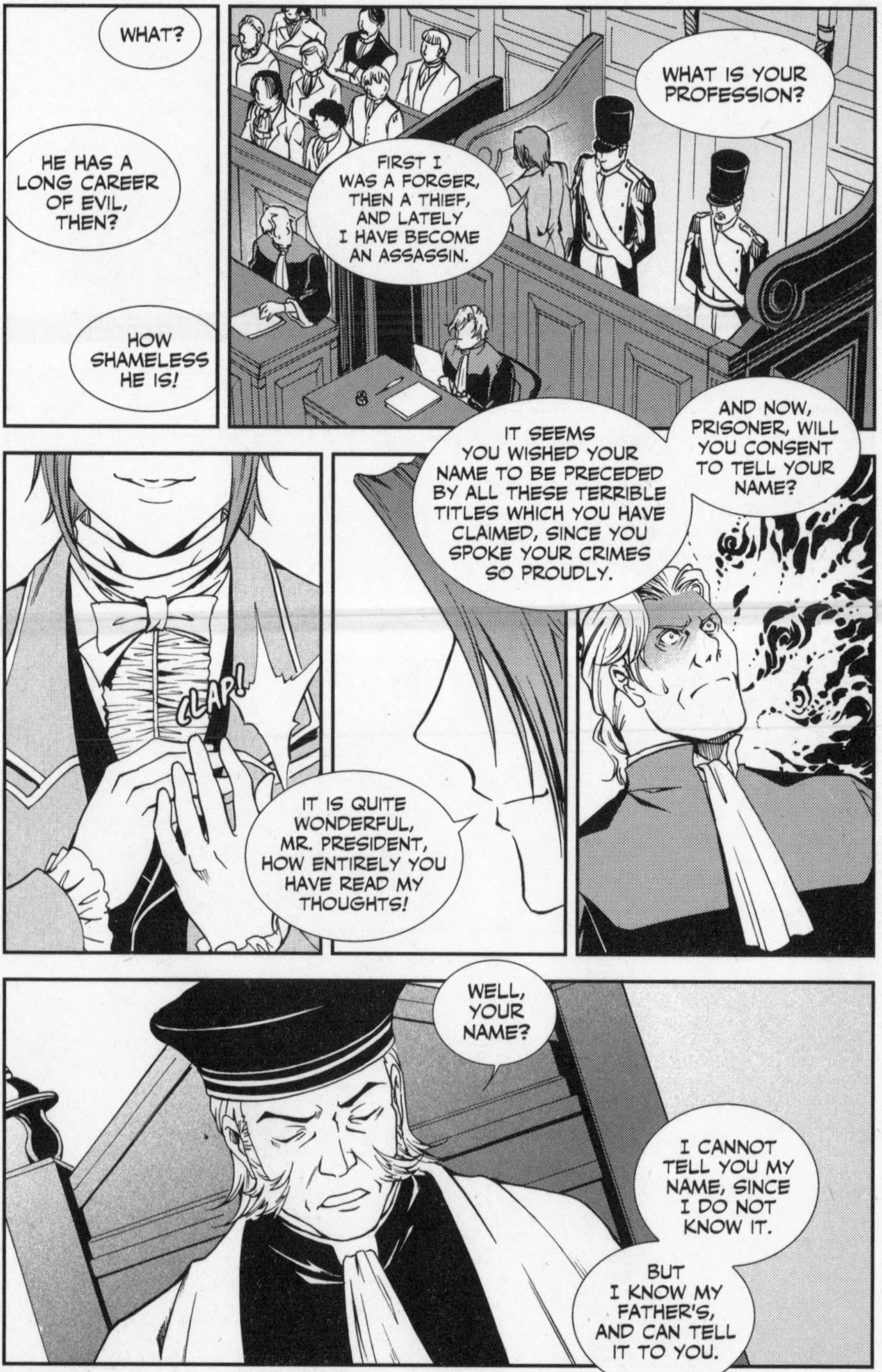
WHAT IS YOUR PROFESSION?
FIRST I WAS A FORGER, THEN A THIEF, AND LATELY I HAVE BECOME AN ASSASSIN.
WHAT?
HE HAS A LONG CAREER OF EVIL, THEN?
HOW SHAMELESS HE IS!
AND NOW, PRISONER, WILL YOU CONSENT TO TELL YOUR NAME?
IT SEEMS YOU WISHED YOUR NAME TO BE PRECEDED BY ALL THESE TERRIBLE TITLES WHICH YOU HAVE CLAIMED, SINCE YOU SPOKE YOUR CRIMES SO PROUDLY.
IT IS QUITE WONDERFUL, MR. PRESIDENT, HOW ENTIRELY YOU HAVE READ MY THOUGHTS!
CLAP!
WELL, YOUR NAME?
I CANNOT TELL YOU MY NAME, SINCE I DO NOT KNOW IT.
BUT I KNOW MY FATHER'S, AND CAN TELL IT TO YOU.

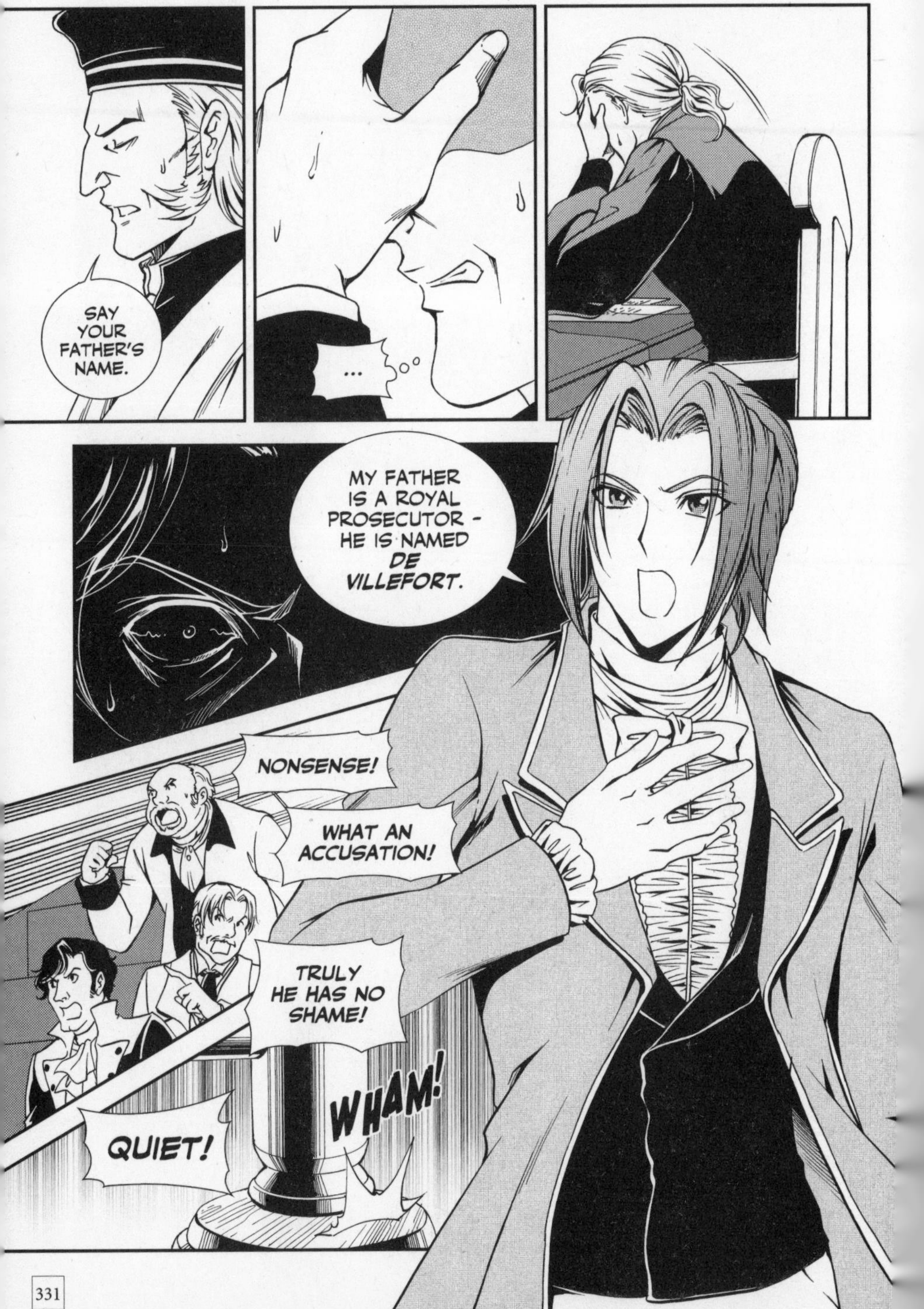
...
SAY YOUR FATHER'S NAME.
MY FATHER IS A ROYAL PROSECUTOR - HE IS NAMED DE VILLEFORT.
NONSENSE!
WHAT AN ACCUSATION!
TRULY HE HAS NO SHAME!
WHAM!
QUIET!

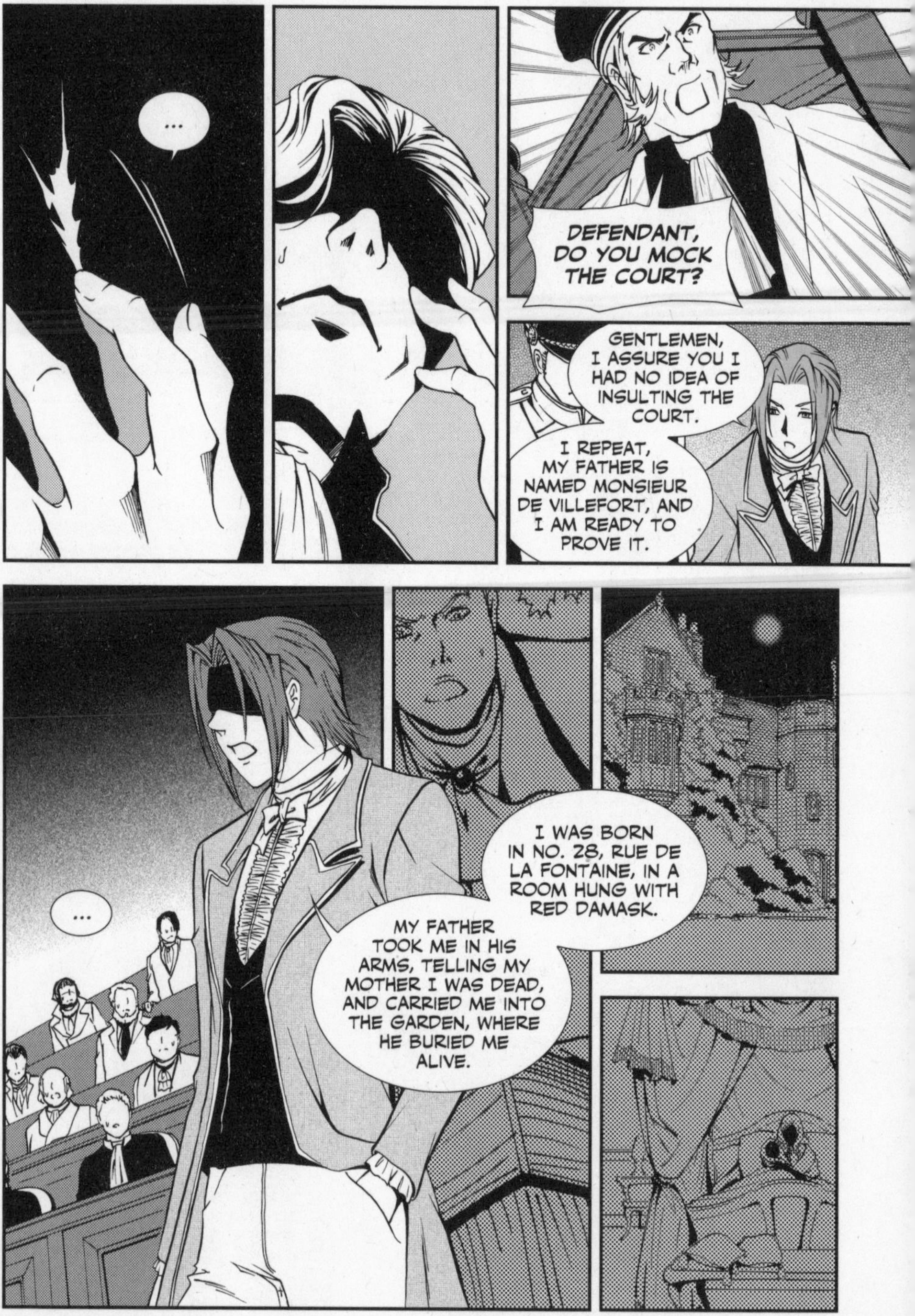
DEFENDANT, DO YOU MOCK THE COURT?
GENTLEMEN, I ASSURE YOU I HAD NO IDEA OF INSULTING THE COURT.
I REPEAT, MY FATHER IS NAMED MONSIEUR DE VILLEFORT, AND I AM READY TO PROVE IT.
...
I WAS BORN IN NO. 28, RUE DE LA FONTAINE, IN A ROOM HUNG WITH RED DAMASK.
MY FATHER TOOK ME IN HIS ARMS, TELLING MY MOTHER I WAS DEAD, AND CARRIED ME INTO THE GARDEN, WHERE HE BURIED ME ALIVE.
...

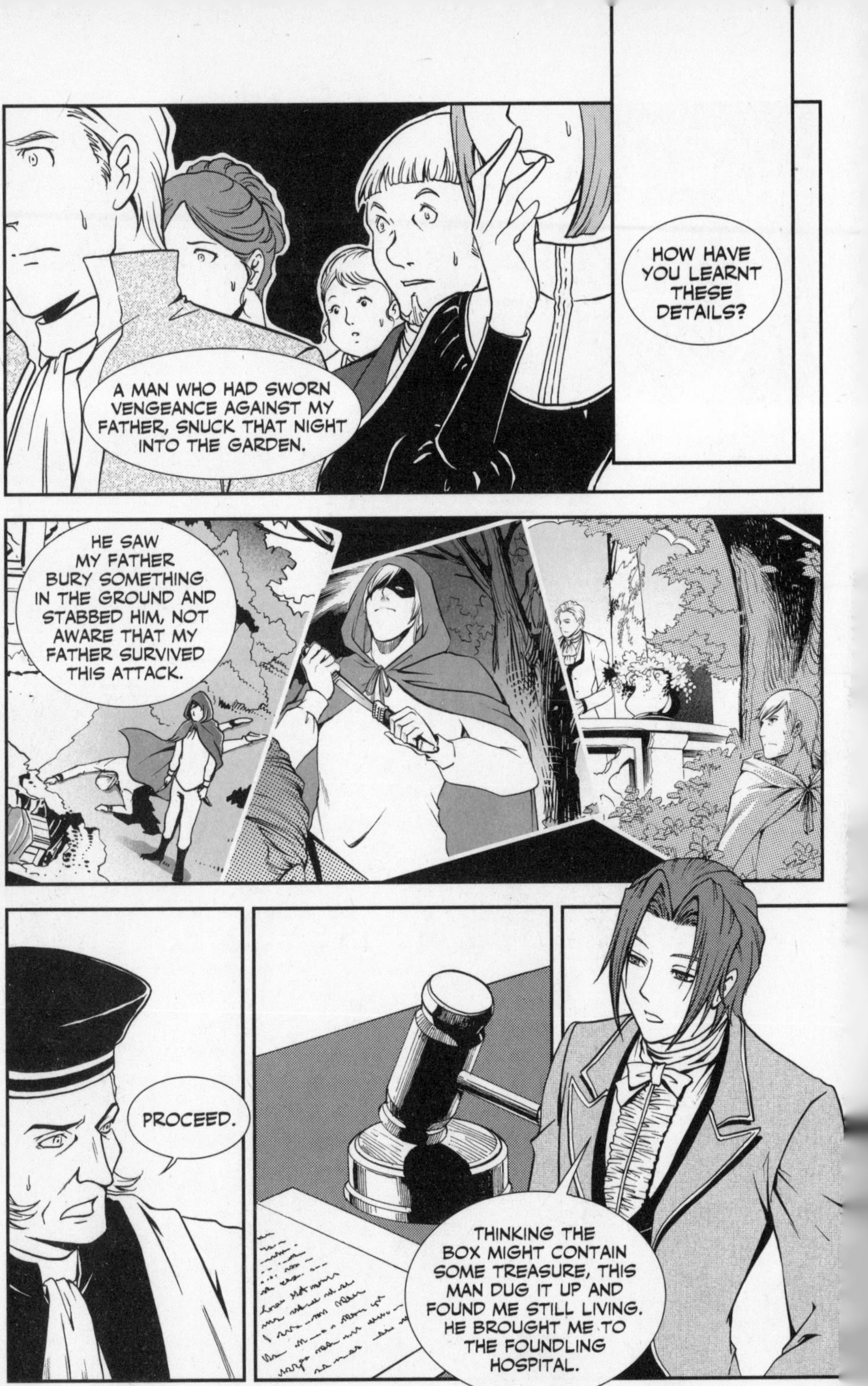
HOW HAVE YOU LEARNT THESE DETAILS?
A MAN WHO HAD SWORN VENGEANCE AGAINST MY FATHER, SNUCK THAT NIGHT INTO THE GARDEN.
HE SAW MY FATHER BURY SOMETHING IN THE GROUND AND STABBED HIM, NOT AWARE THAT MY FATHER SURVIVED THIS ATTACK.
THINKING THE BOX MIGHT CONTAIN SOME TREASURE, THIS MAN DUG IT UP AND FOUND ME STILL LIVING. HE BROUGHT ME TO THE FOUNDLING HOSPITAL.
PROCEED.

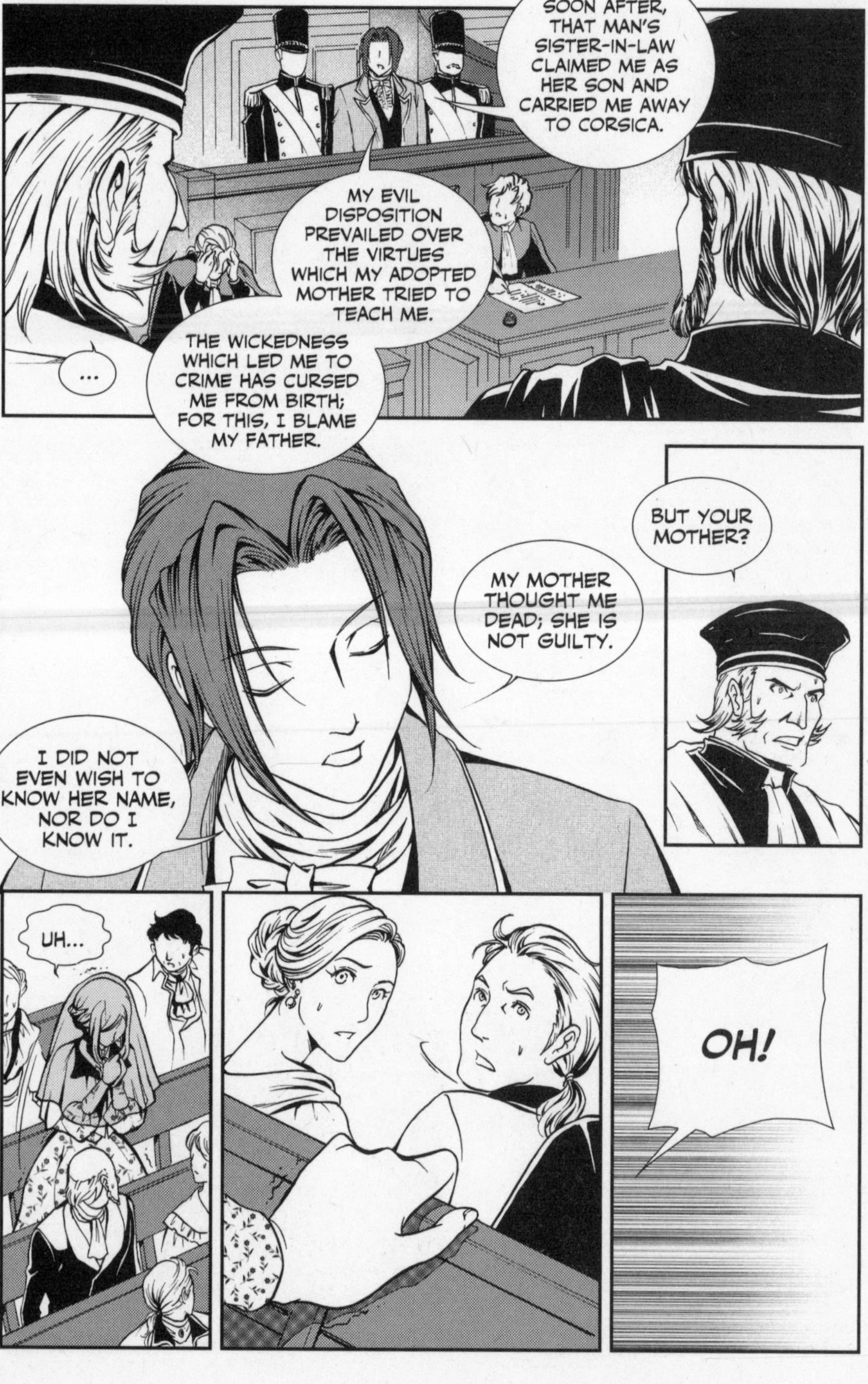
SOON AFTER, THAT MAN'S SISTER-IN-LAW CLAIMED ME AS HER SON AND CARRIED ME AWAY TO CORSICA.
MY EVIL DISPOSITION PREVAILED OVER THE VIRTUES WHICH MY ADOPTED MOTHER TRIED TO TEACH ME.
THE WICKEDNESS WHICH LED ME TO CRIME HAS CURSED ME FROM BIRTH; FOR THIS, I BLAME MY FATHER.
...
BUT YOUR MOTHER?
MY MOTHER THOUGHT ME DEAD; SHE IS NOT GUILTY.
I DID NOT EVEN WISH TO KNOW HER NAME, NOR DO I KNOW IT.
OH!
UH...

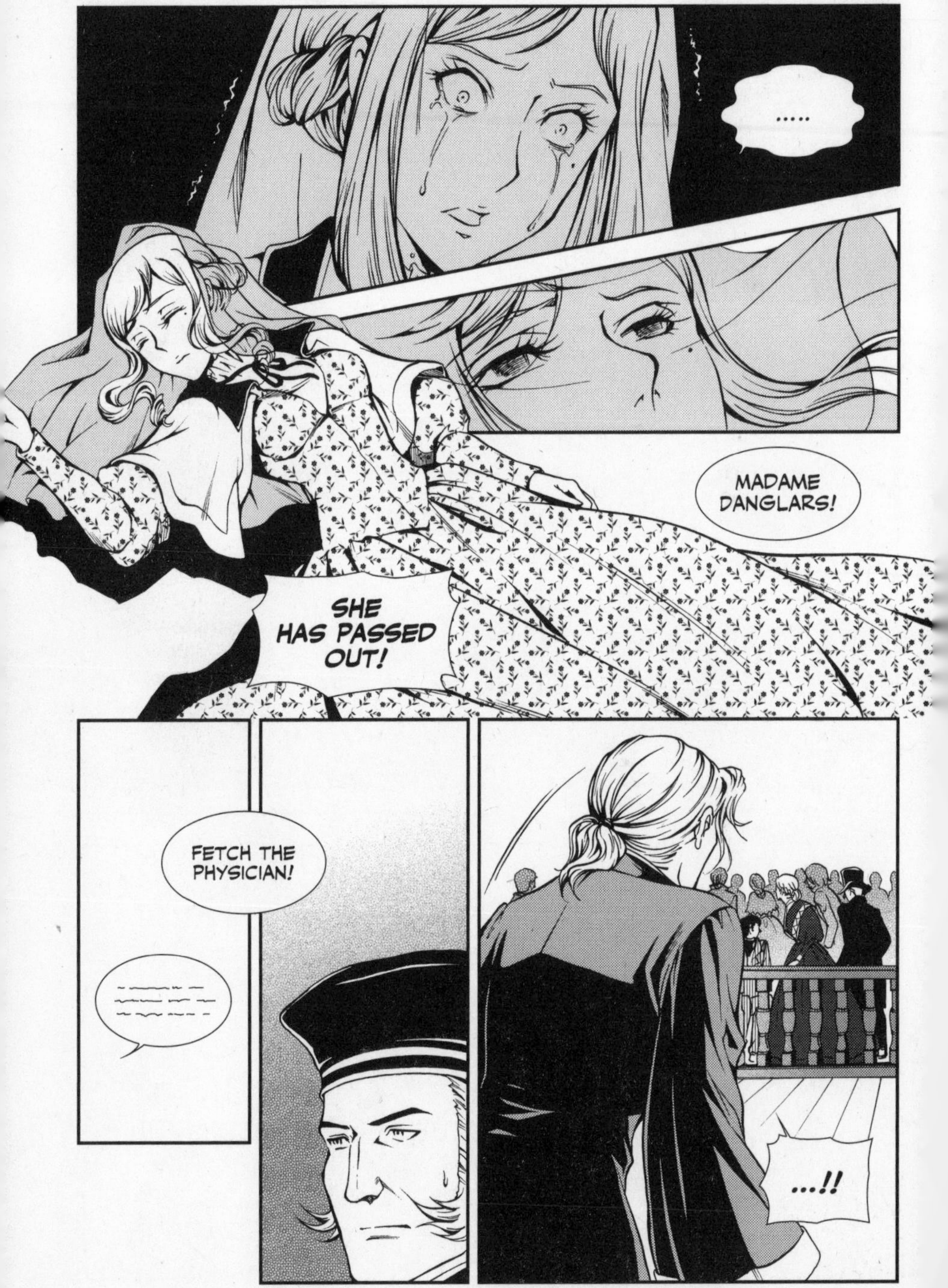
.....
MADAME DANGLARS!
SHE HAS PASSED OUT!
...!!
FETCH THE PHYSICIAN!

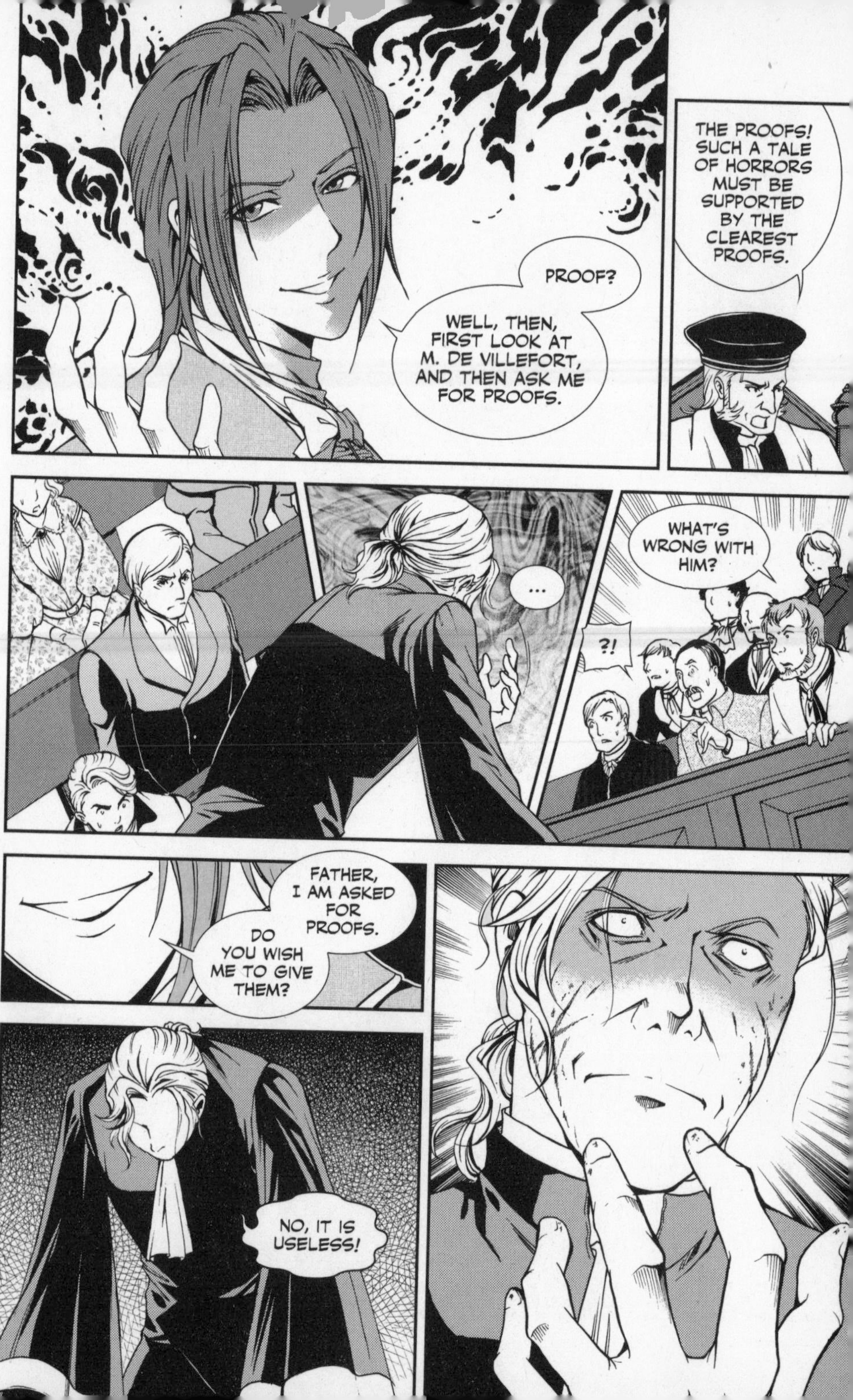
THE PROOFS! SUCH A TALE OF HORRORS MUST BE SUPPORTED BY THE CLEAREST PROOFS.
PROOF?
WELL, THEN, FIRST LOOK AT M. DE VILLEFORT, AND THEN ASK ME FOR PROOFS.
WHAT'S WRONG WITH HIM?
?!
...
FATHER, I AM ASKED FOR PROOFS.
DO YOU WISH ME TO GIVE THEM?
NO, IT IS USELESS!

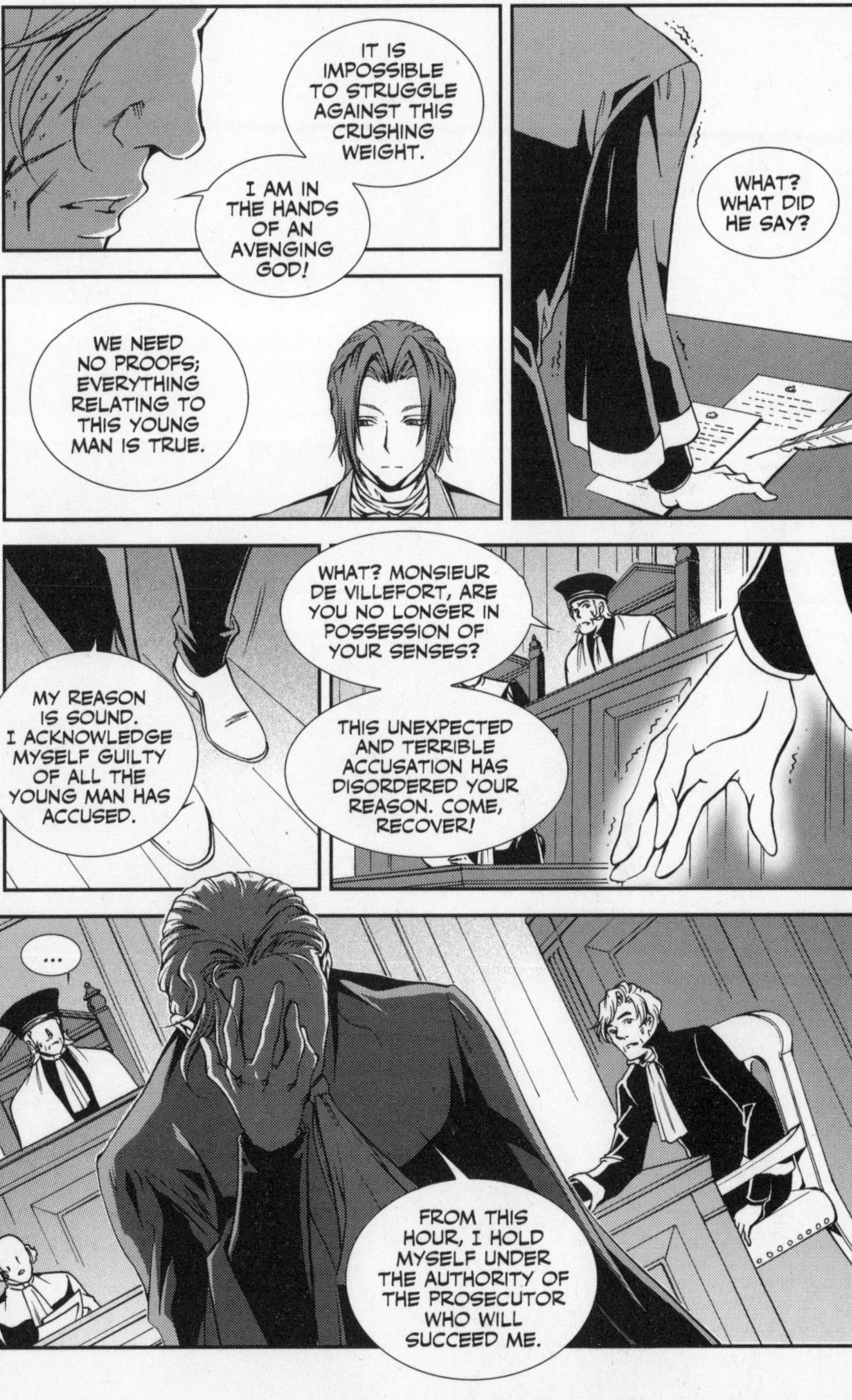
WHAT? WHAT DID HE SAY?
IT IS IMPOSSIBLE TO STRUGGLE AGAINST THIS CRUSHING WEIGHT.
I AM IN THE HANDS OF AN AVENGING GOD!
WE NEED NO PROOFS; EVERYTHING RELATING TO THIS YOUNG MAN IS TRUE.
WHAT? MONSIEUR DE VILLEFORT, ARE YOU NO LONGER IN POSSESSION OF YOUR SENSES?
THIS UNEXPECTED AND TERRIBLE ACCUSATION HAS DISORDERED YOUR REASON. COME, RECOVER!
MY REASON IS SOUND. I ACKNOWLEDGE MYSELF GUILTY OF ALL THE YOUNG MAN HAS ACCUSED.
...
FROM THIS HOUR, I HOLD MYSELF UNDER THE AUTHORITY OF THE PROSECUTOR WHO WILL SUCCEED ME.

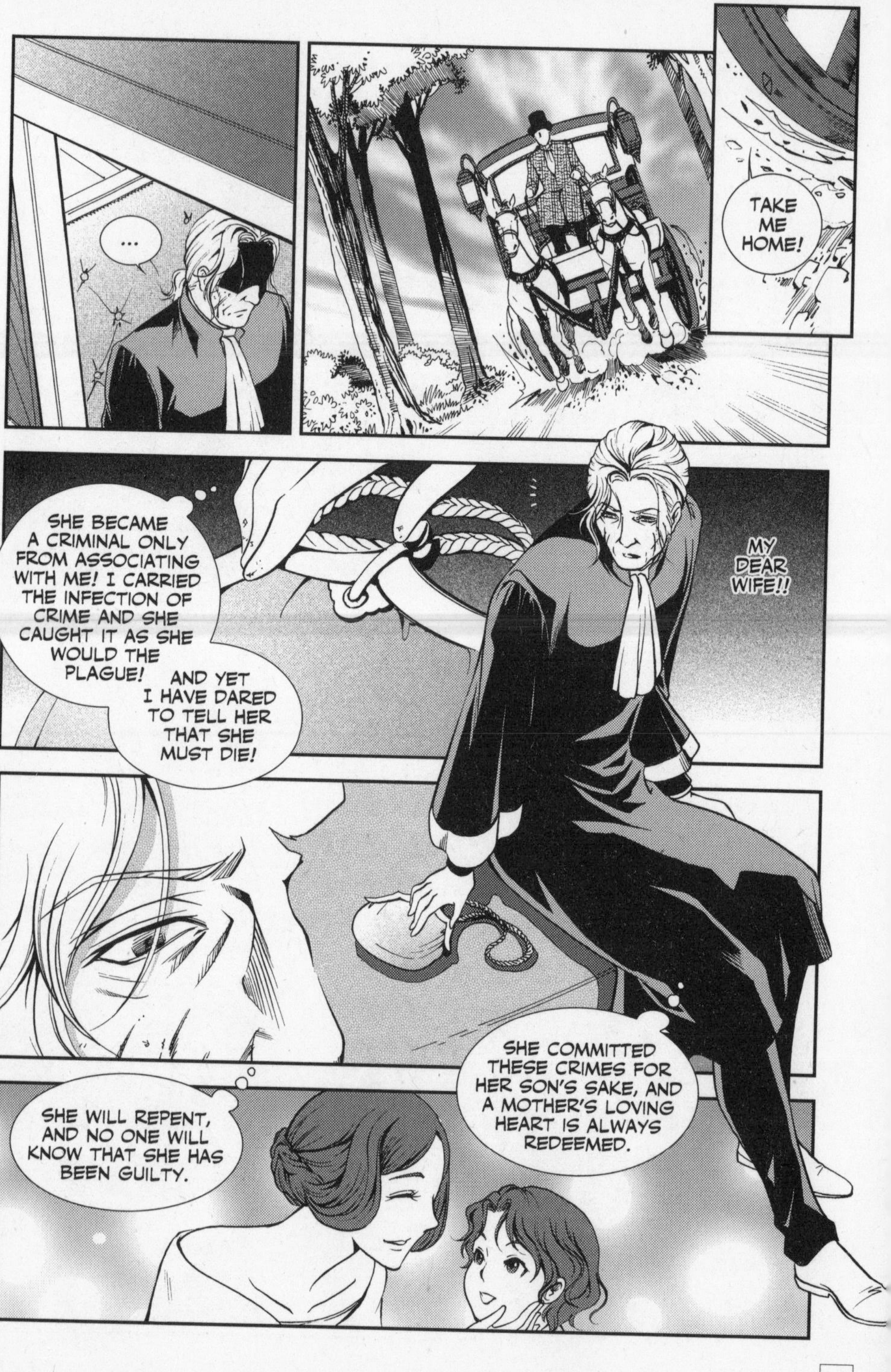
TAKE ME HOME!
...
MY DEAR WIFE!!
SHE BECAME A CRIMINAL ONLY FROM ASSOCIATING WITH ME! I CARRIED THE INFECTION OF CRIME AND SHE CAUGHT IT AS SHE WOULD THE PLAGUE!
AND YET I HAVE DARED TO TELL HER THAT SHE MUST DIE!
SHE COMMITTED THESE CRIMES FOR HER SON'S SAKE, AND A MOTHER'S LOVING HEART IS ALWAYS REDEEMED.
SHE WILL REPENT, AND NO ONE WILL KNOW THAT SHE HAS BEEN GUILTY.

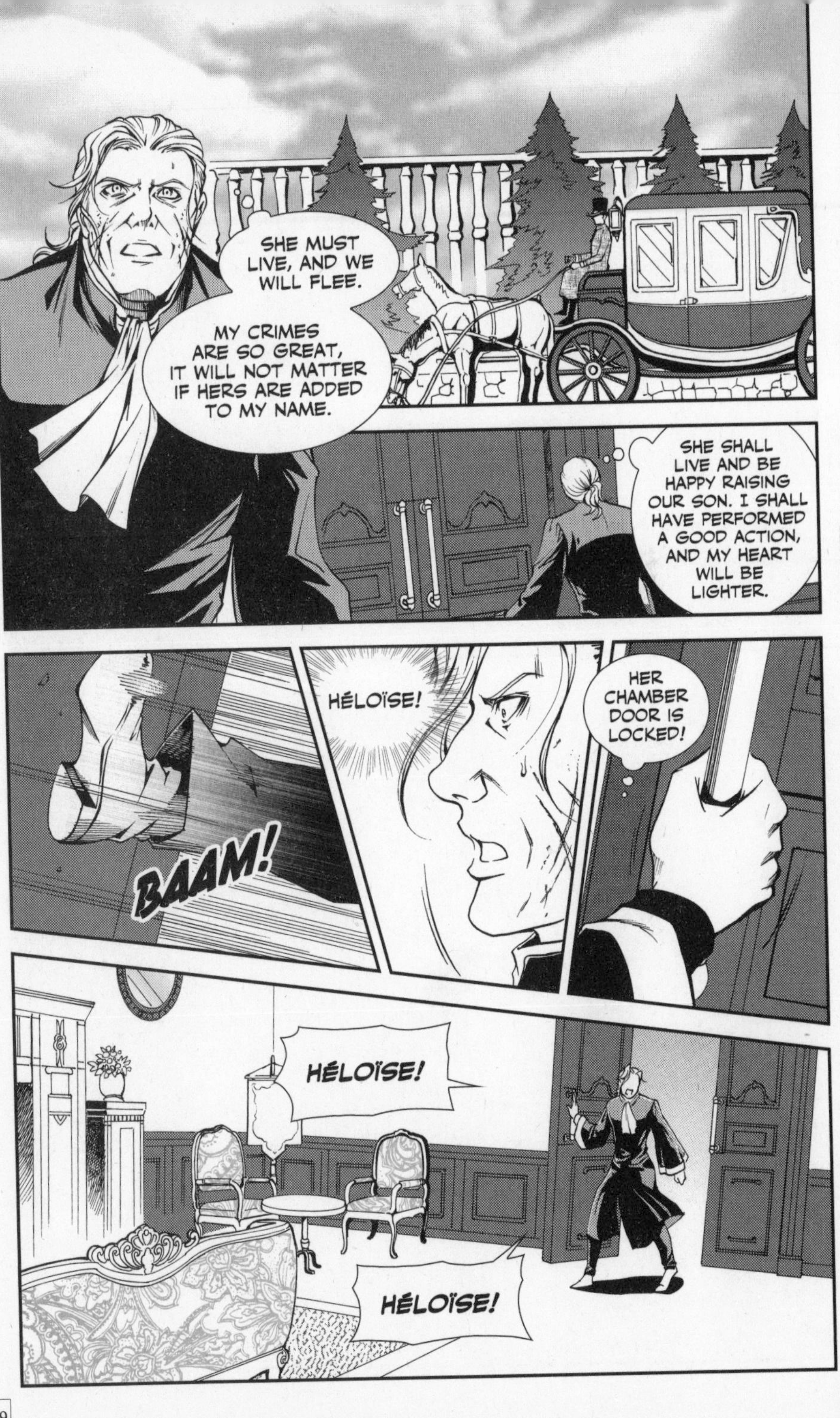
SHE MUST LIVE, AND WE WILL FLEE.
MY CRIMES ARE SO GREAT, IT WILL NOT MATTER IF HERS ARE ADDED TO MY NAME.
SHE SHALL LIVE AND BE HAPPY RAISING OUR SON. I SHALL HAVE PERFORMED A GOOD ACTION, AND MY HEART WILL BE LIGHTER.
HER CHAMBER DOOR IS LOCKED!
HÉLOÏSE!
BAAM!
HÉLOÏSE!
HÉLOÏSE!

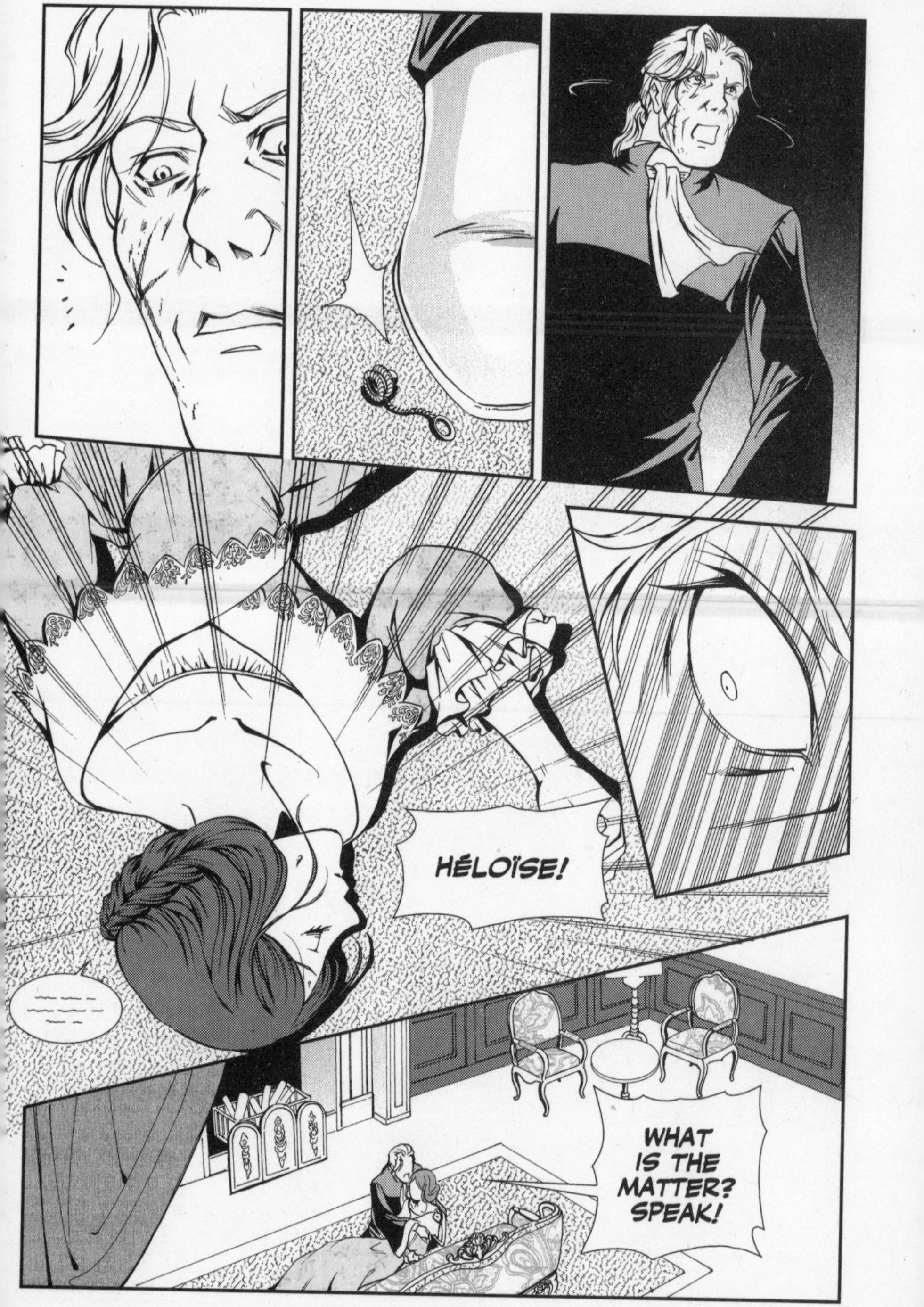
HÉLOÏSE!
WHAT IS THE MATTER? SPEAK!

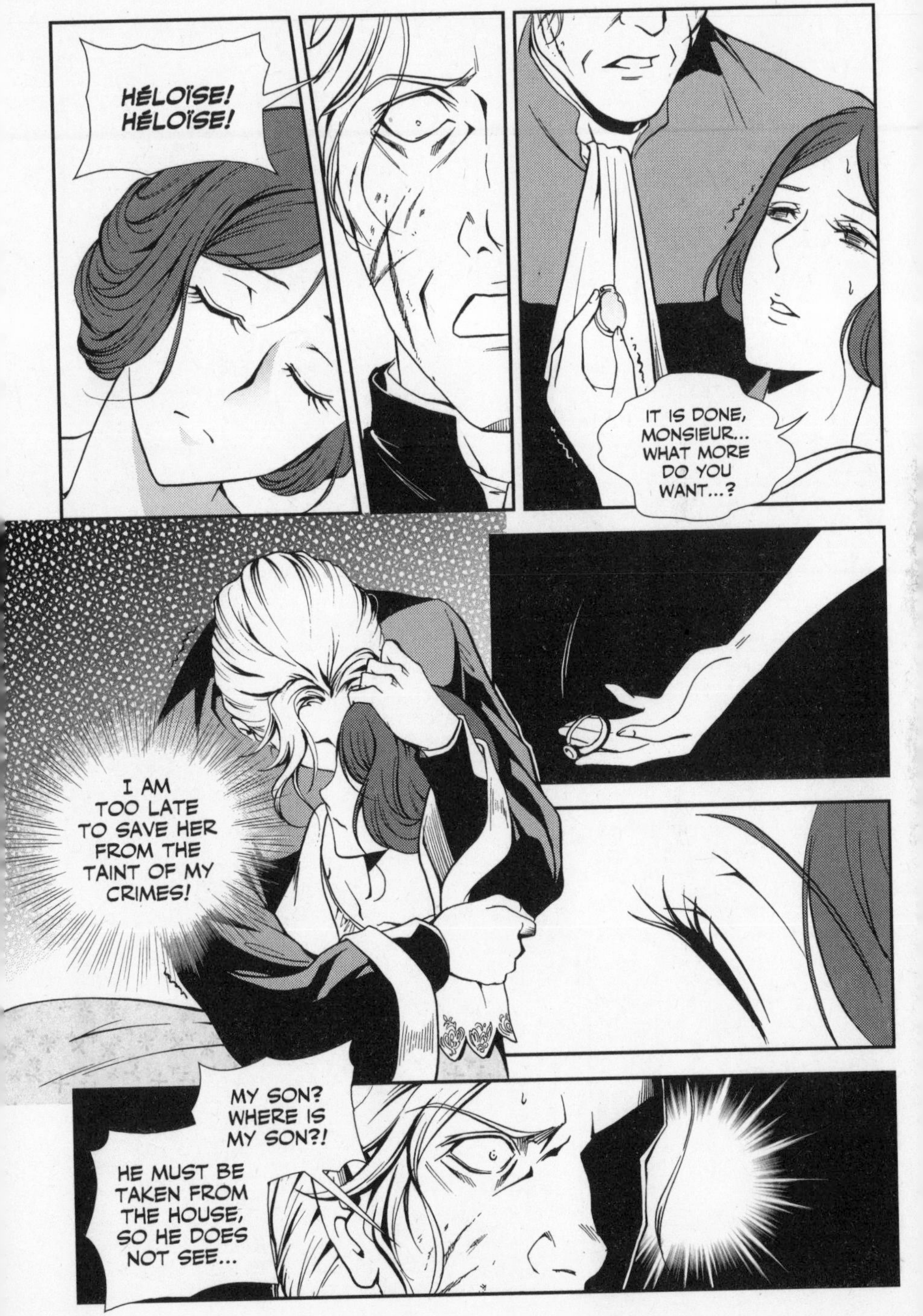
IT IS DONE, MONSIEUR... WHAT MORE DO YOU WANT...?
HÉLOÏSE! HÉLOÏSE!
I AM TOO LATE TO SAVE HER FROM THE TAINT OF MY CRIMES!
MY SON? WHERE IS MY SON?!
HE MUST BE TAKEN FROM THE HOUSE, SO HE DOES NOT SEE...

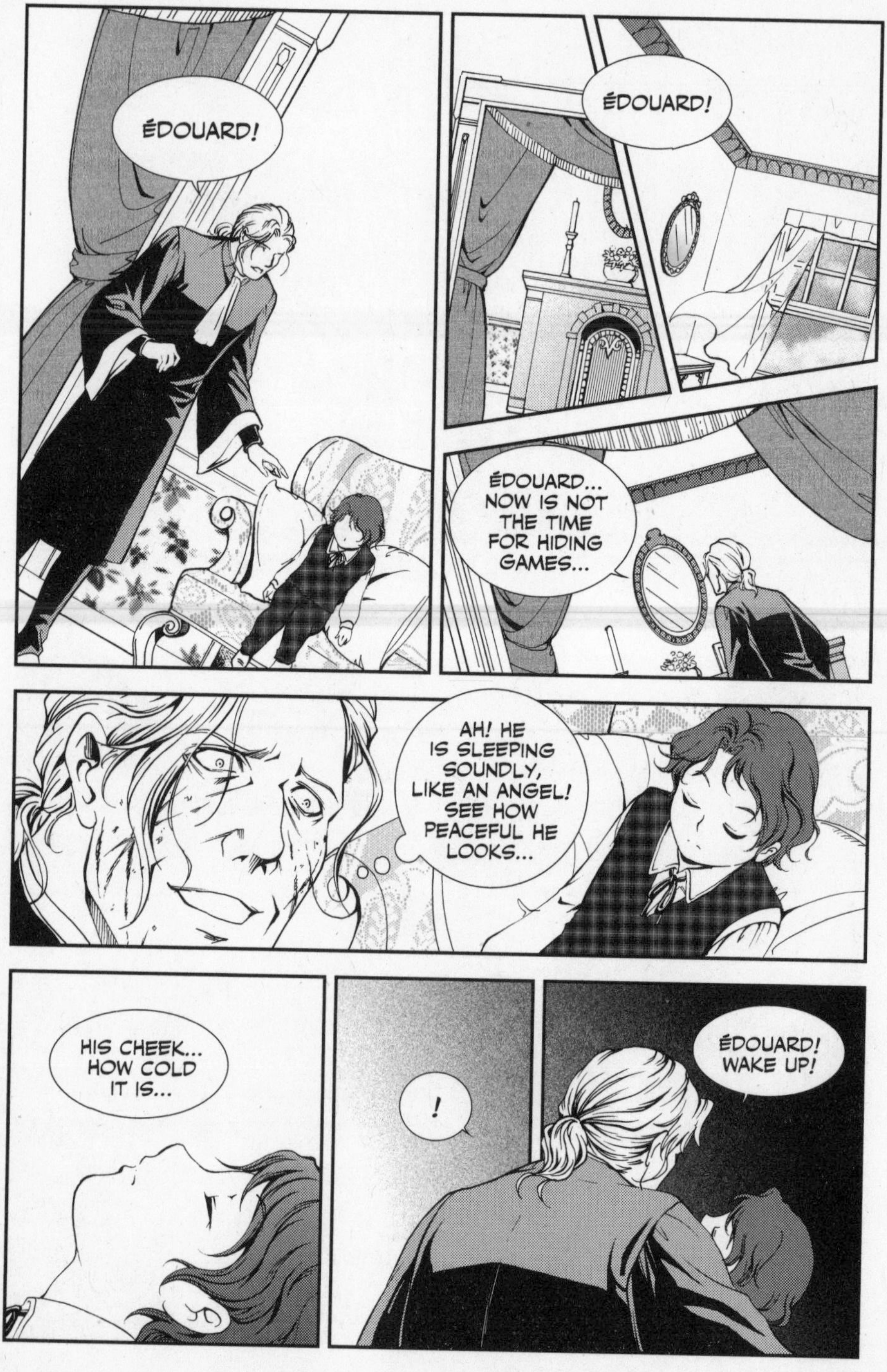
ÉDOUARD!
ÉDOUARD... NOW IS NOT THE TIME FOR HIDING GAMES...
ÉDOUARD!
AH! HE IS SLEEPING SOUNDLY, LIKE AN ANGEL! SEE HOW PEACEFUL HE LOOKS...
ÉDOUARD! WAKE UP!
!
HIS CHEEK... HOW COLD IT IS...

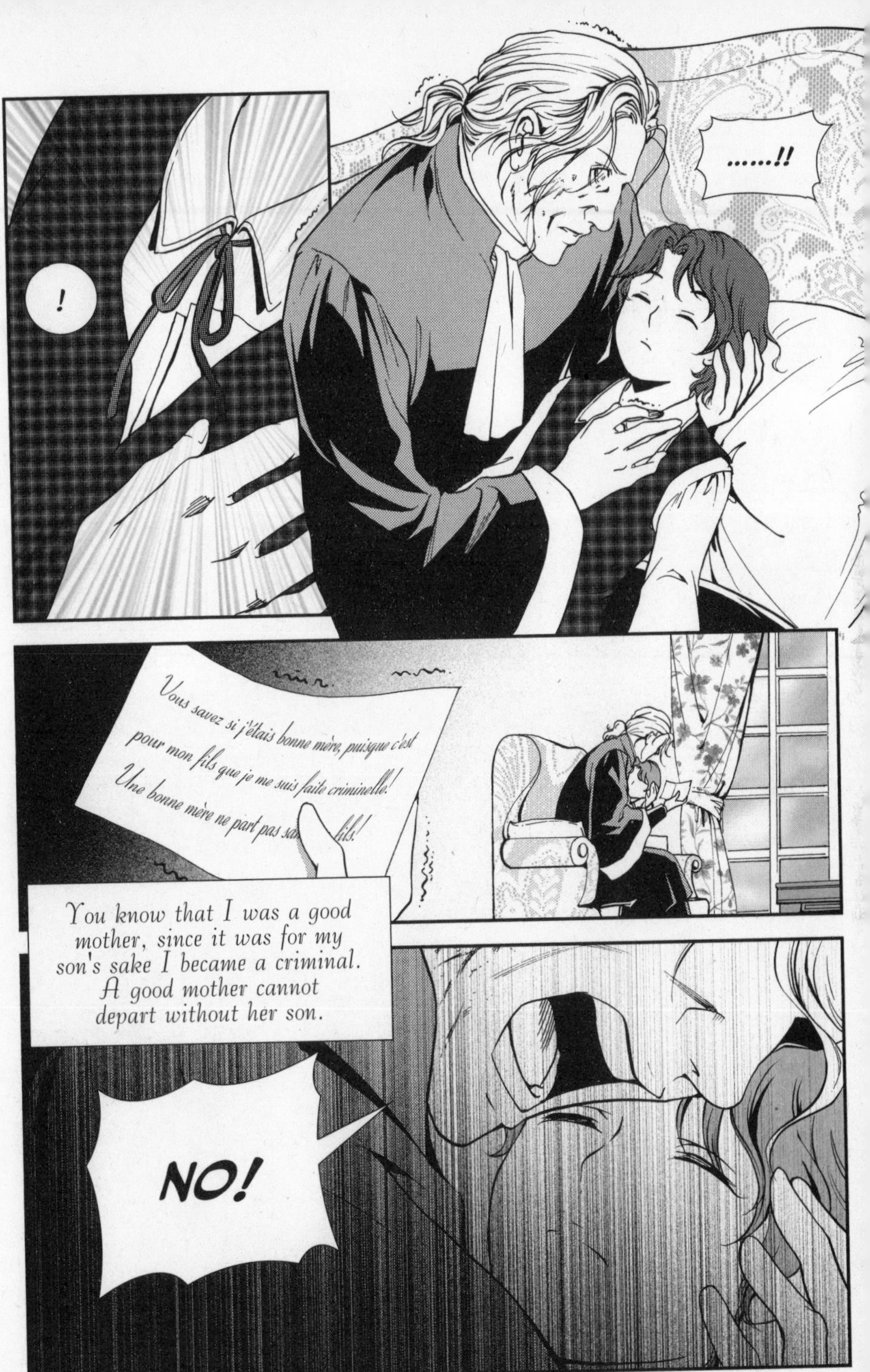
......!!
!
Vous savez si j'étais bonne mère, puisque c'est pour mon fils que je me suis faite criminelle!
Une bonne mère ne part pas sa fils!
You know that I was a good mother, since it was for my son's sake I became a criminal. A good mother cannot depart without her son.
NO!

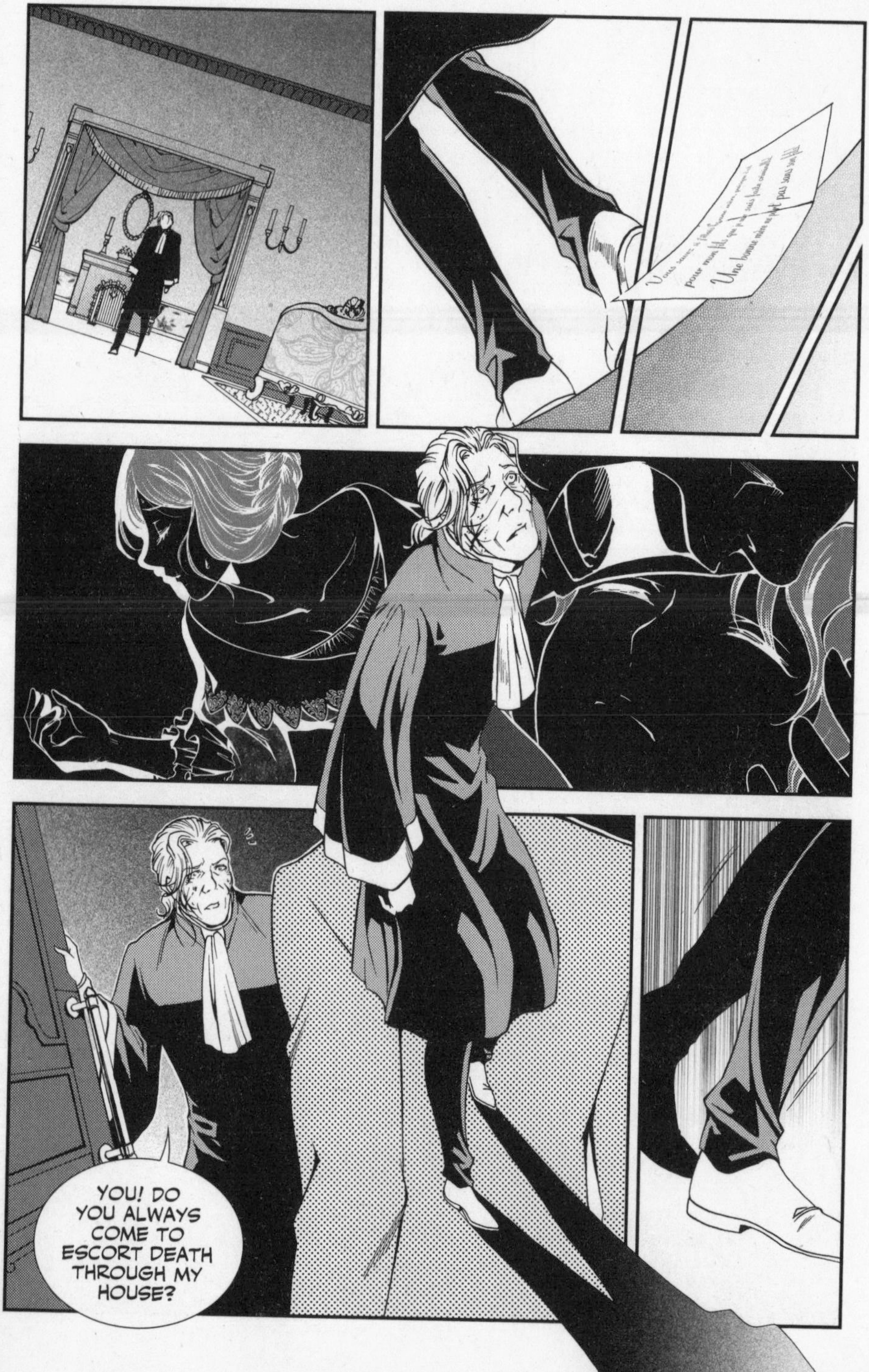
YOU! DO YOU ALWAYS COME TO ESCORT DEATH THROUGH MY HOUSE?

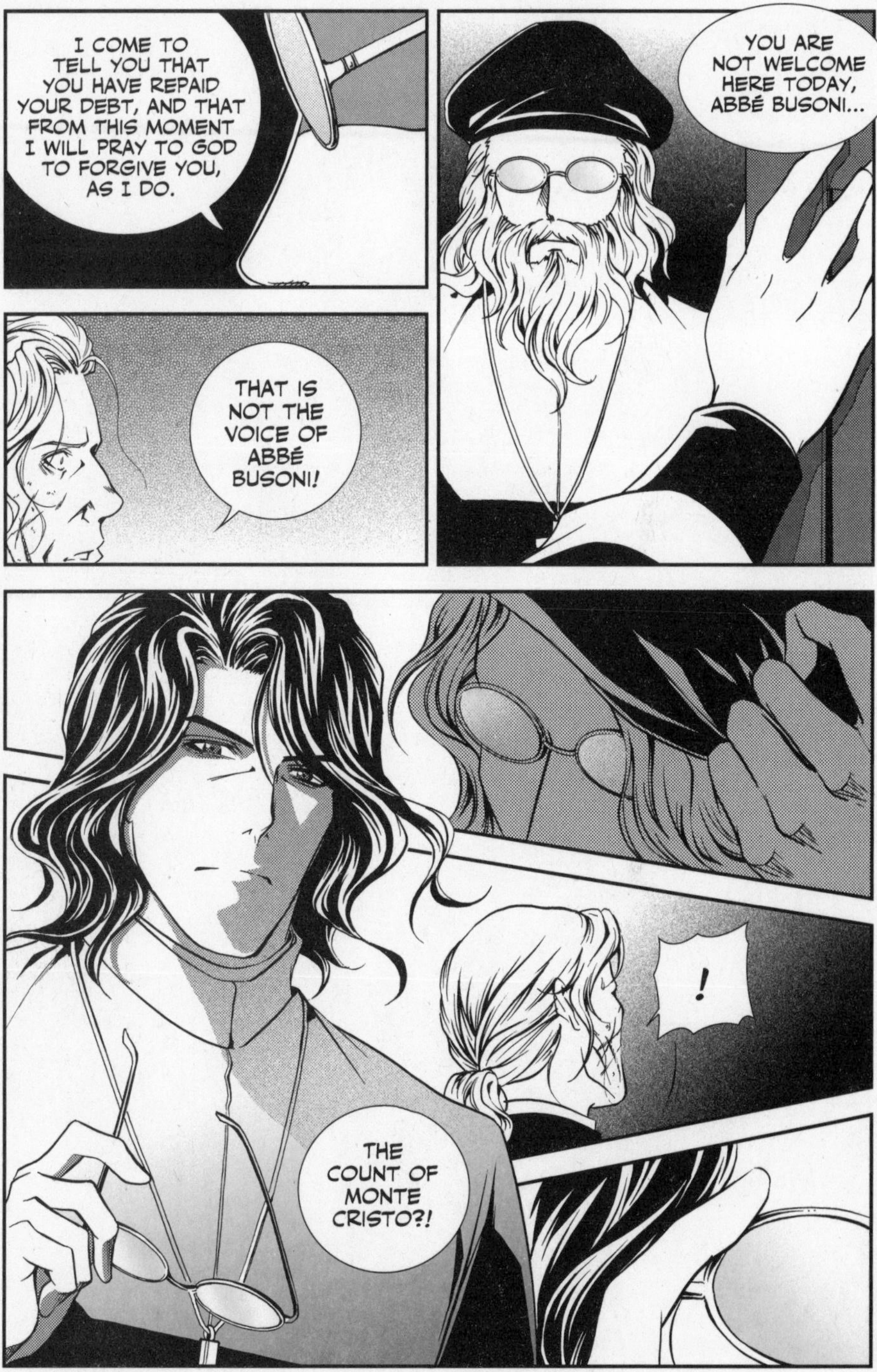
YOU ARE NOT WELCOME HERE TODAY, ABBÉ BUSONI...
I COME TO TELL YOU THAT YOU HAVE REPAID YOUR DEBT, AND THAT FROM THIS MOMENT I WILL PRAY TO GOD TO FORGIVE YOU, AS I DO.
THAT IS NOT THE VOICE OF ABBÉ BUSONI!
!
THE COUNT OF MONTE CRISTO?!

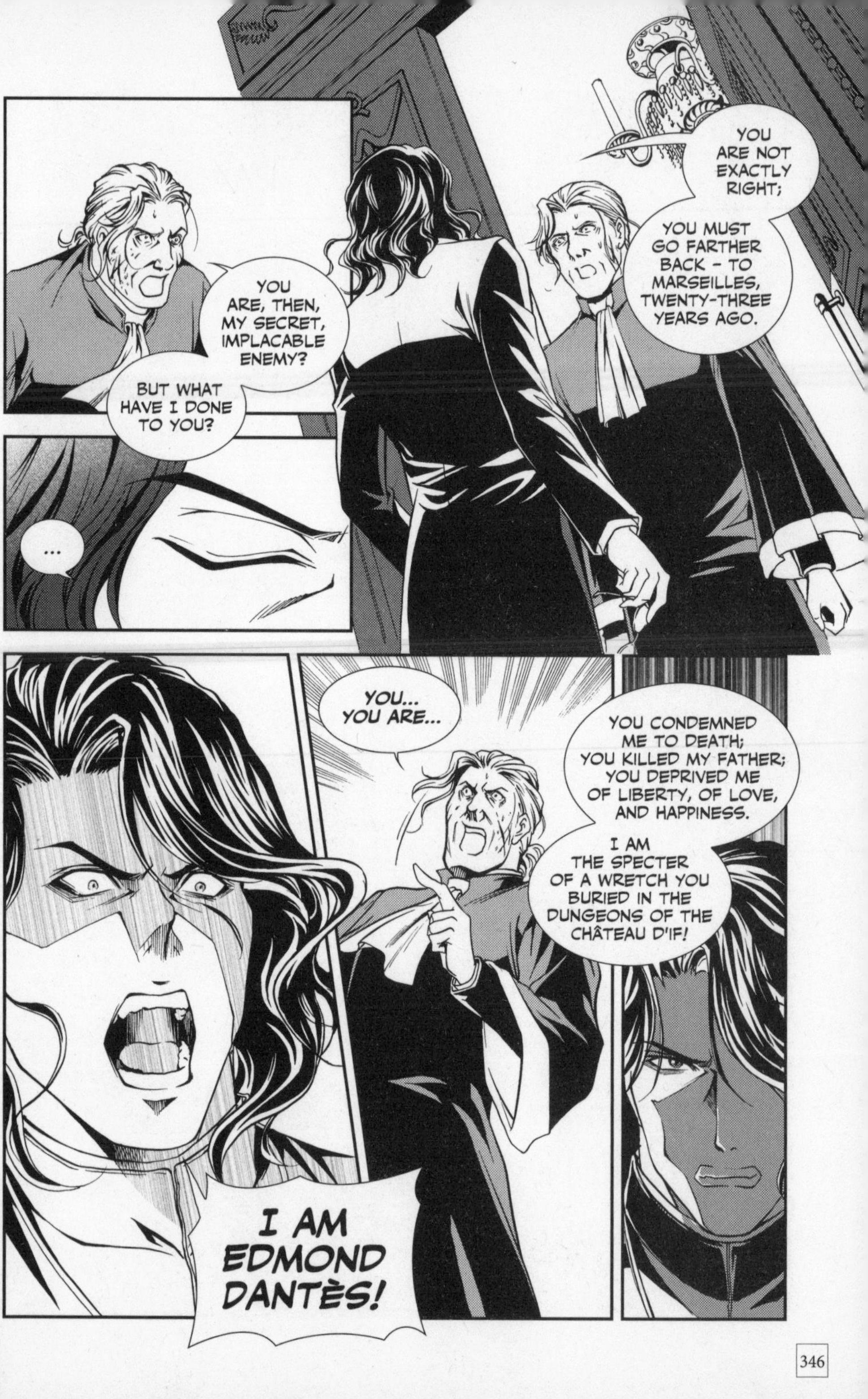
YOU ARE NOT EXACTLY RIGHT;
YOU MUST GO FARTHER BACK - TO MARSEILLES, TWENTY-THREE YEARS AGO.
YOU ARE, THEN, MY SECRET, IMPLACABLE ENEMY?
BUT WHAT HAVE I DONE TO YOU?
...
YOU CONDEMNED ME TO DEATH; YOU KILLED MY FATHER; YOU DEPRIVED ME OF LIBERTY, OF LOVE, AND HAPPINESS.
I AM THE SPECTER OF A WRETCH YOU BURIED IN THE DUNGEONS OF THE CHÂTEAU D'IF!
YOU... YOU ARE...
I AM EDMOND DANTÈS!

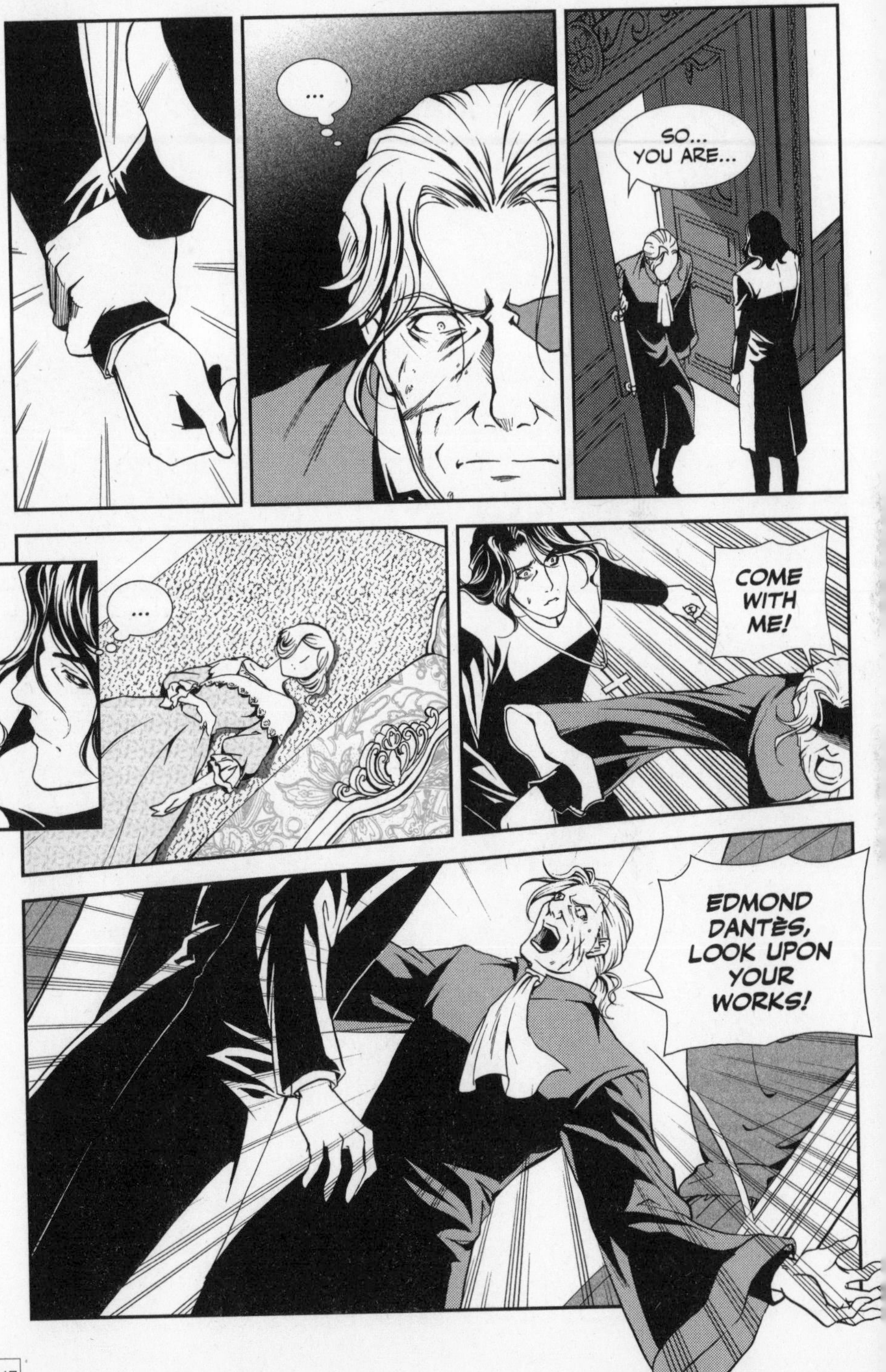
SO... YOU ARE...
...
COME WITH ME!
...
EDMOND DANTÈS, LOOK UPON YOUR WORKS!

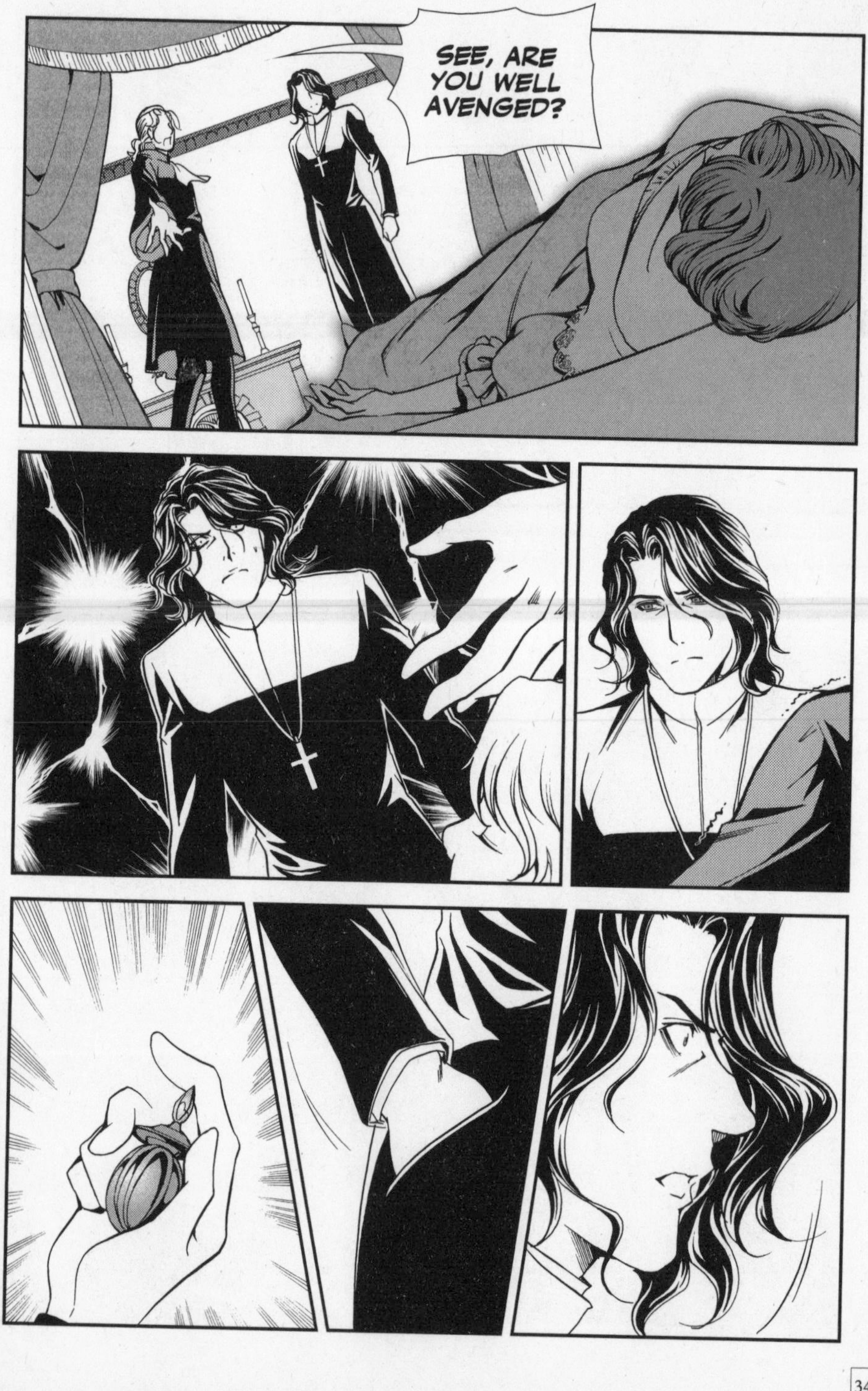
SEE, ARE YOU WELL AVENGED?

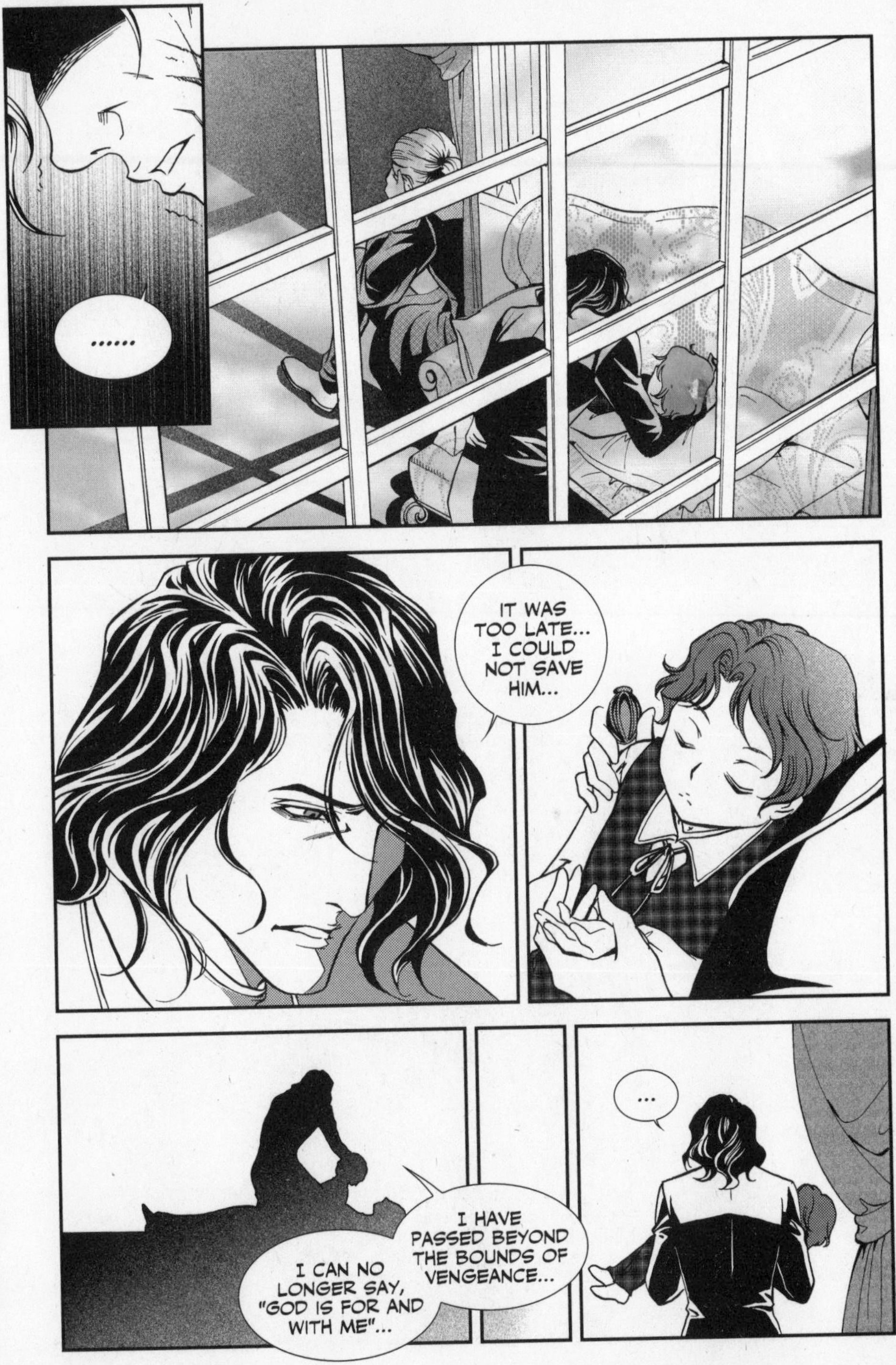
......
IT WAS TOO LATE... I COULD NOT SAVE HIM...
...
I HAVE PASSED BEYOND THE BOUNDS OF VENGEANCE...
I CAN NO LONGER SAY, "GOD IS FOR AND WITH ME"...

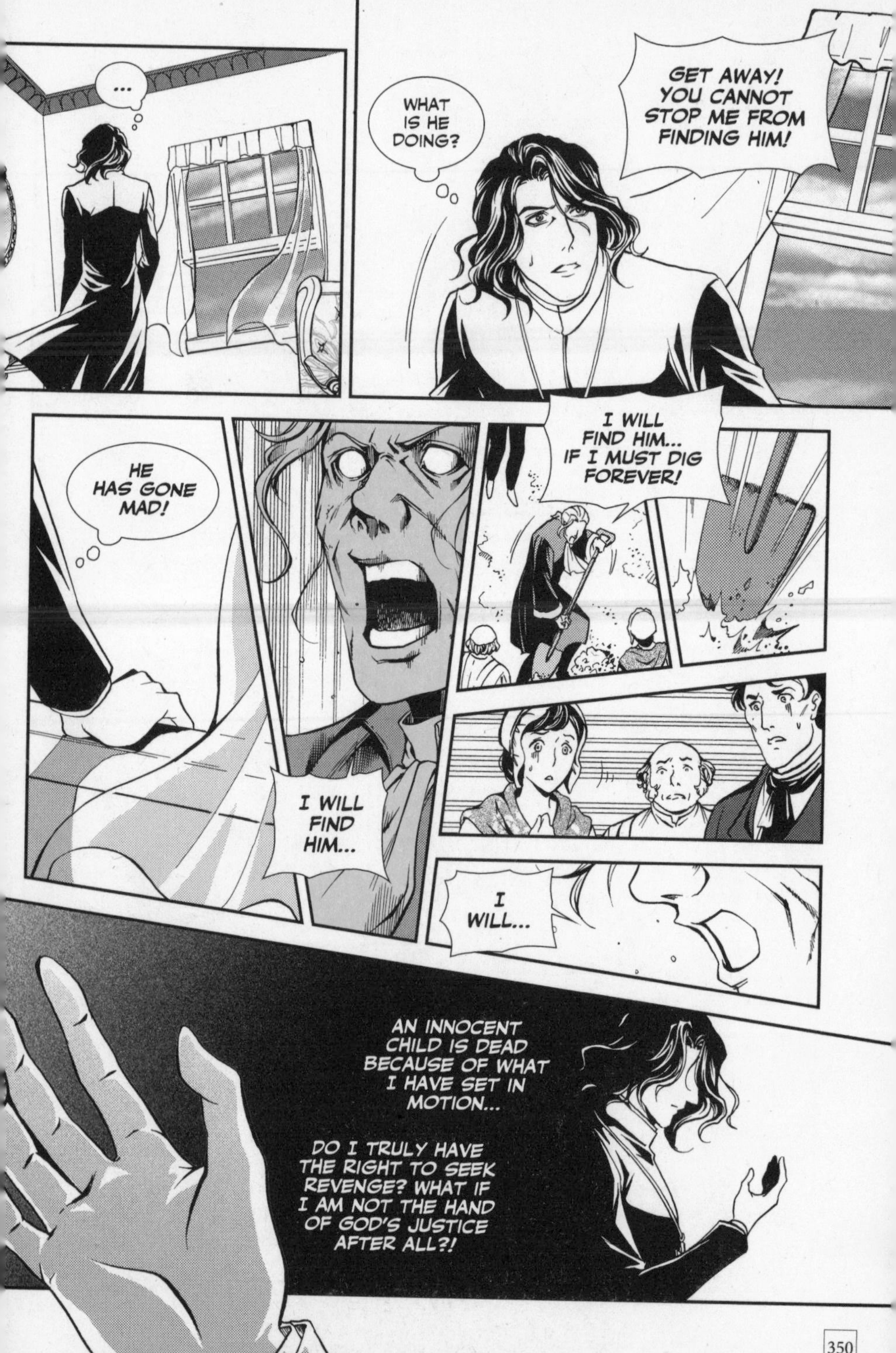
GET AWAY! YOU CANNOT STOP ME FROM FINDING HIM!
WHAT IS HE DOING?
...
I WILL FIND HIM... IF I MUST DIG FOREVER!
I WILL...
I WILL FIND HIM...
HE HAS GONE MAD!
AN INNOCENT CHILD IS DEAD BECAUSE OF WHAT I HAVE SET IN MOTION...
DO I TRULY HAVE THE RIGHT TO SEEK REVENGE? WHAT IF I AM NOT THE HAND OF GOD'S JUSTICE AFTER ALL?!

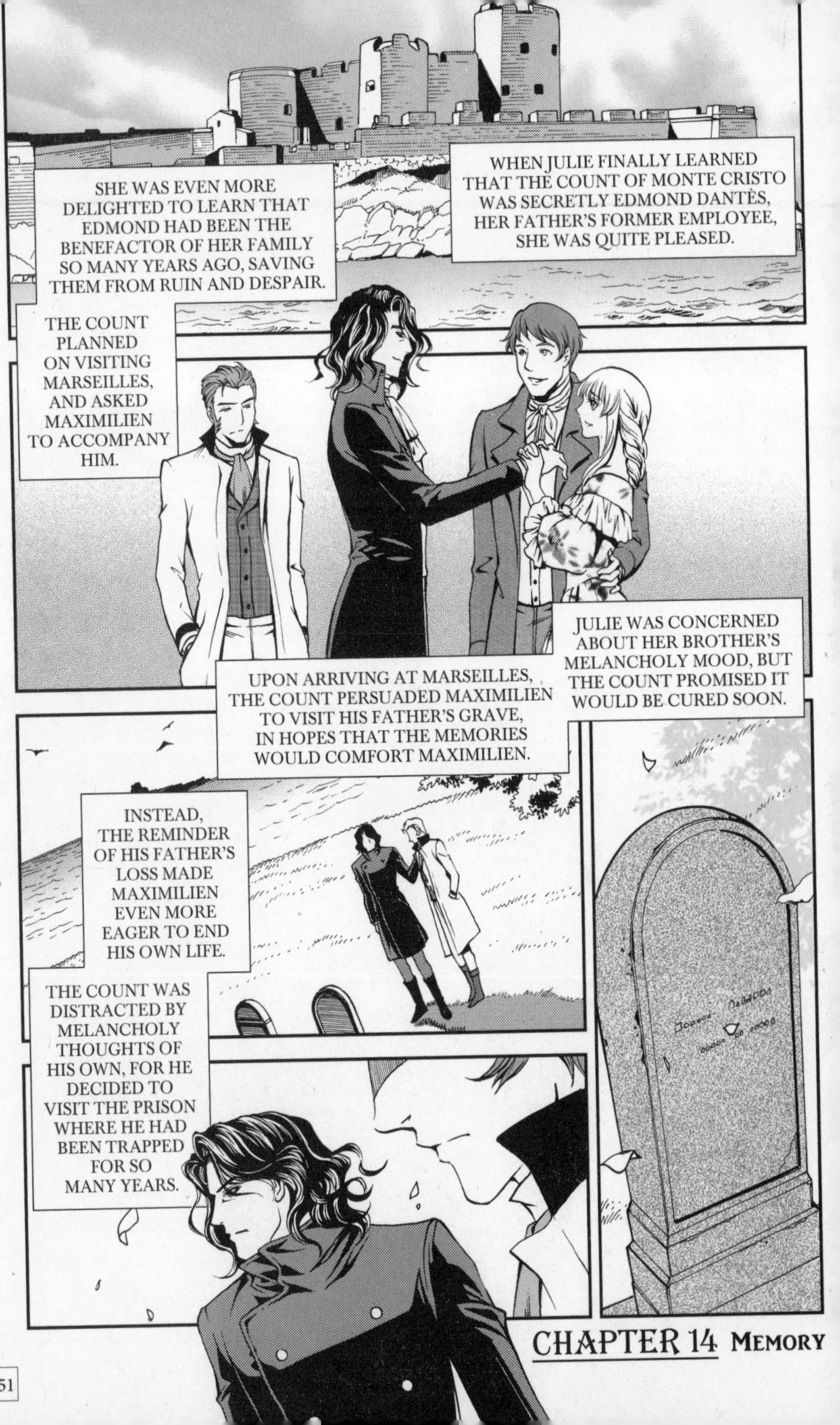
WHEN JULIE FINALLY LEARNED THAT THE COUNT OF MONTE CRISTO WAS SECRETLY EDMOND DANTÈS, HER FATHER'S FORMER EMPLOYEE, SHE WAS QUITE PLEASED.
SHE WAS EVEN MORE DELIGHTED TO LEARN THAT EDMOND HAD BEEN THE BENEFACTOR OF HER FAMILY SO MANY YEARS AGO, SAVING THEM FROM RUIN AND DESPAIR.
THE COUNT PLANNED ON VISITING MARSEILLES, AND ASKED MAXIMILIEN TO ACCOMPANY HIM.
JULIE WAS CONCERNED ABOUT HER BROTHER'S MELANCHOLY MOOD, BUT THE COUNT PROMISED IT WOULD BE CURED SOON.
UPON ARRIVING AT MARSEILLES, THE COUNT PERSUADED MAXIMILIEN TO VISIT HIS FATHER'S GRAVE, IN HOPES THAT THE MEMORIES WOULD COMFORT MAXIMILIEN.
INSTEAD, THE REMINDER OF HIS FATHER'S LOSS MADE MAXIMILIEN EVEN MORE EAGER TO END HIS OWN LIFE.
THE COUNT WAS DISTRACTED BY MELANCHOLY THOUGHTS OF HIS OWN, FOR HE DECIDED TO VISIT THE PRISON WHERE HE HAD BEEN TRAPPED FOR SO MANY YEARS.

CHAPTER 14 Memory

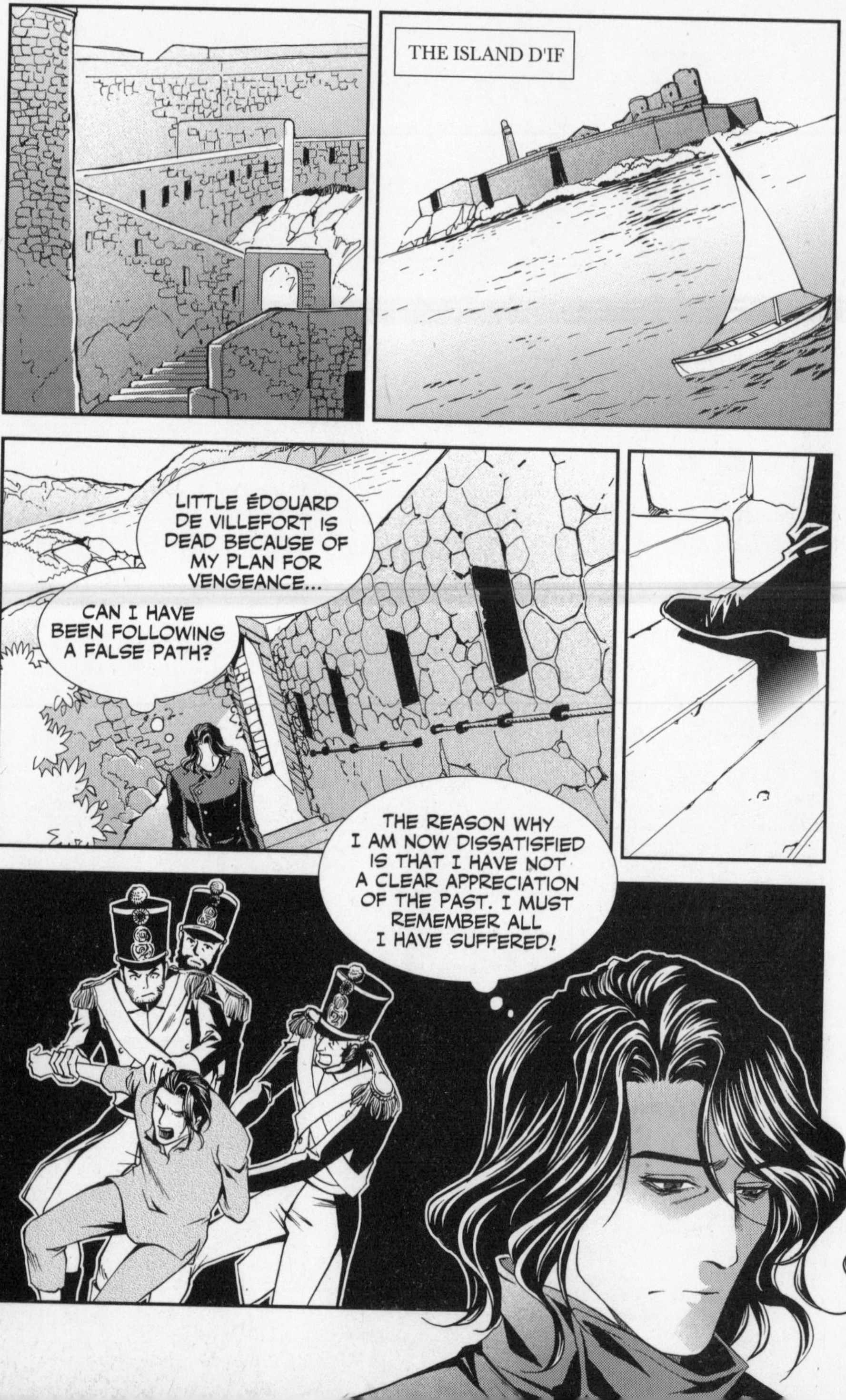
THE ISLAND D'IF
LITTLE ÉDOUARD DE VILLEFORT IS DEAD BECAUSE OF MY PLAN FOR VENGEANCE...
CAN I HAVE BEEN FOLLOWING A FALSE PATH?
THE REASON WHY I AM NOW DISSATISFIED IS THAT I HAVE NOT A CLEAR APPRECIATION OF THE PAST. I MUST REMEMBER ALL I HAVE SUFFERED!

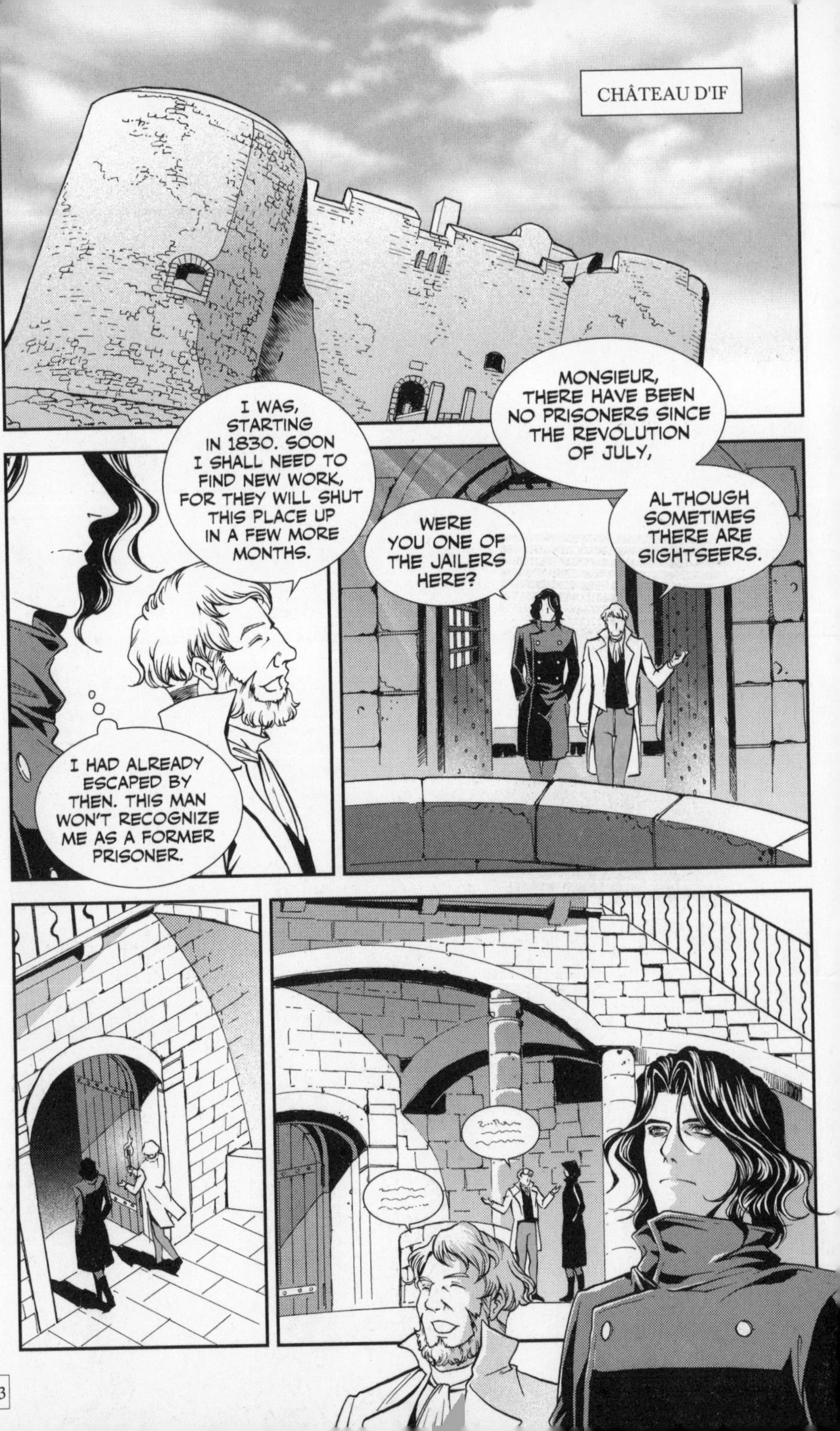
CHÂTEAU D'IF
MONSIEUR, THERE HAVE BEEN NO PRISONERS SINCE THE REVOLUTION OF JULY,
ALTHOUGH SOMETIMES THERE ARE SIGHTSEERS.
WERE YOU ONE OF THE JAILERS HERE?
I WAS, STARTING IN 1830. SOON I SHALL NEED TO FIND NEW WORK, FOR THEY WILL SHUT THIS PLACE UP IN A FEW MORE MONTHS.
I HAD ALREADY ESCAPED BY THEN. THIS MAN WON'T RECOGNIZE ME AS A FORMER PRISONER.

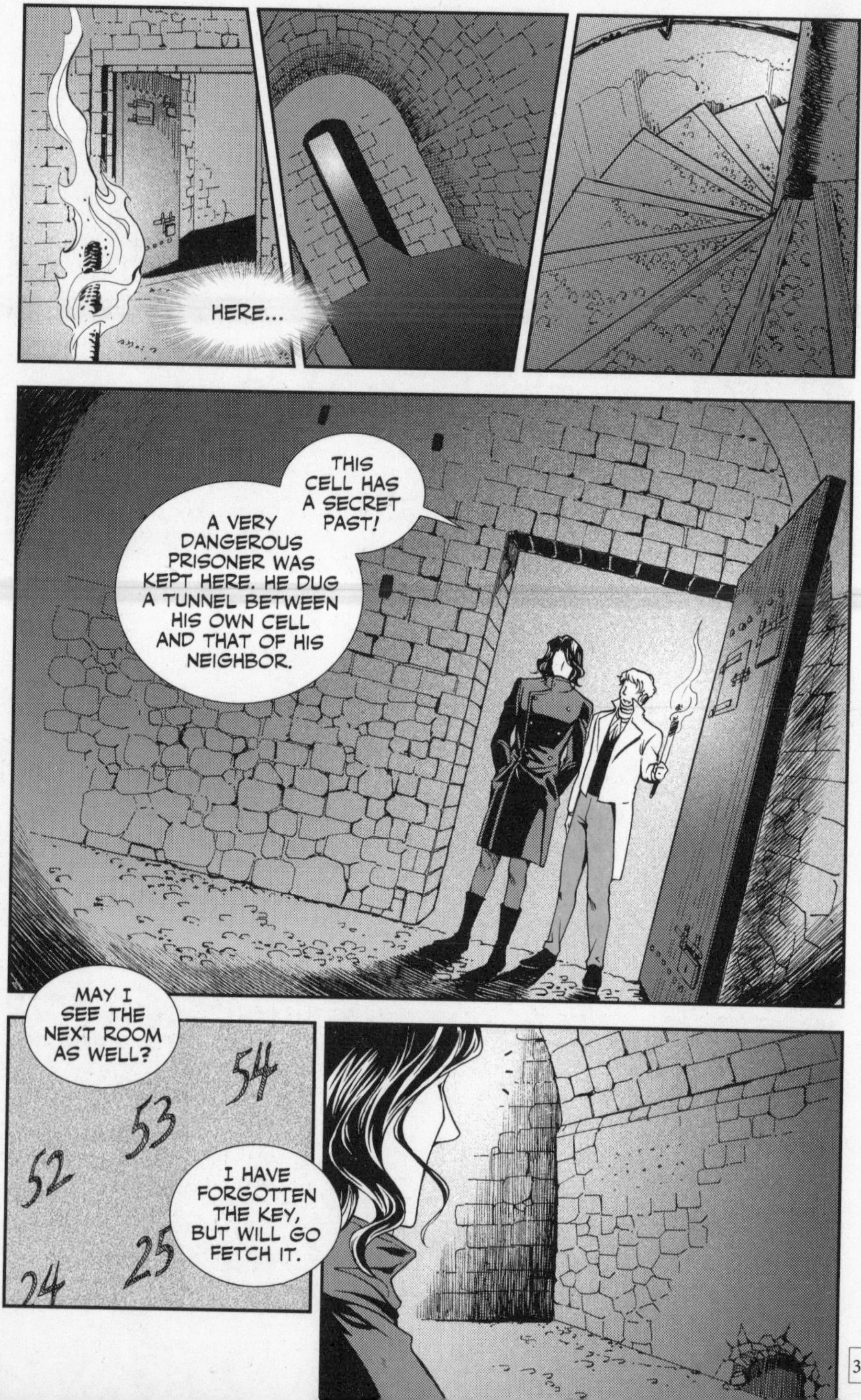
HERE...
THIS CELL HAS A SECRET PAST!
A VERY DANGEROUS PRISONER WAS KEPT HERE. HE DUG A TUNNEL BETWEEN HIS OWN CELL AND THAT OF HIS NEIGHBOR.
MAY I SEE THE NEXT ROOM AS WELL?
54
53
52
I HAVE FORGOTTEN THE KEY, BUT WILL GO FETCH IT.
25
24

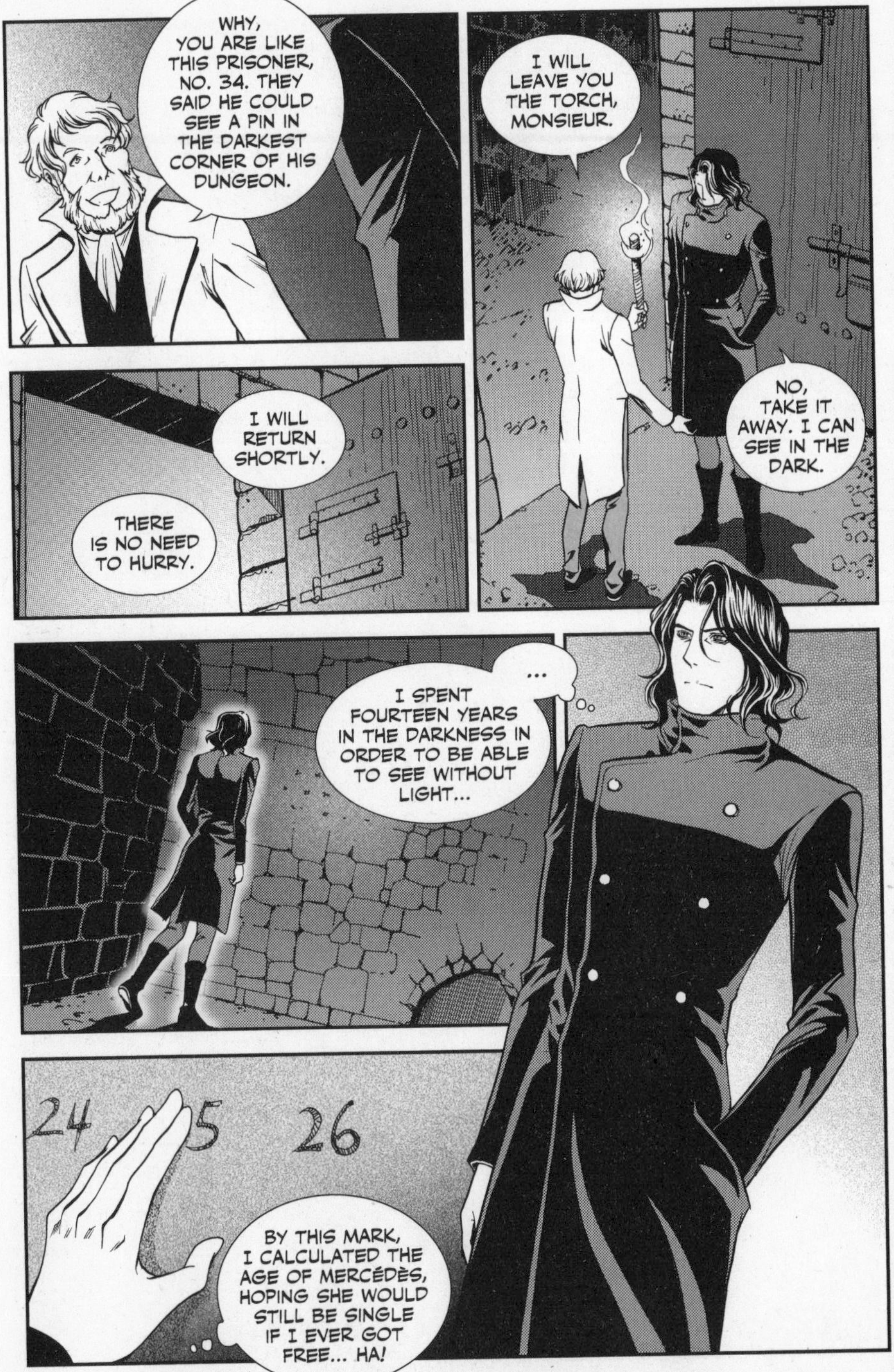
I WILL LEAVE YOU THE TORCH, MONSIEUR.
NO, TAKE IT AWAY. I CAN SEE IN THE DARK.
WHY, YOU ARE LIKE THIS PRISONER, NO. 34. THEY SAID HE COULD SEE A PIN IN THE DARKEST CORNER OF HIS DUNGEON.
I WILL RETURN SHORTLY.
THERE IS NO NEED TO HURRY.
...
I SPENT FOURTEEN YEARS IN THE DARKNESS IN ORDER TO BE ABLE TO SEE WITHOUT LIGHT...
24
5
26
BY THIS MARK, I CALCULATED THE AGE OF MERCÉDÈS, HOPING SHE WOULD STILL BE SINGLE IF I EVER GOT FREE... HA!

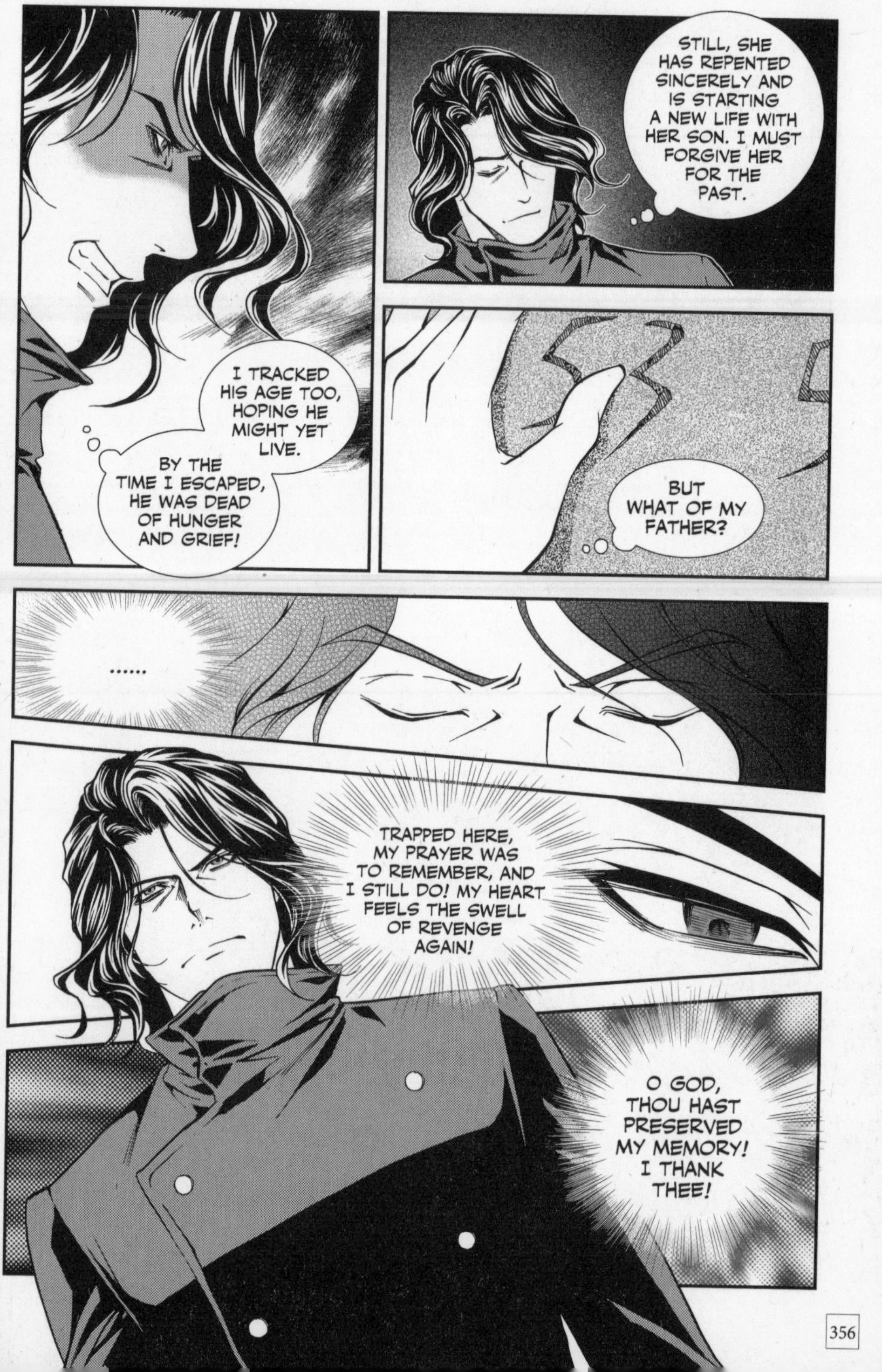
STILL, SHE HAS REPENTED SINCERELY AND IS STARTING A NEW LIFE WITH HER SON. I MUST FORGIVE HER FOR THE PAST.
BUT WHAT OF MY FATHER?
I TRACKED HIS AGE TOO, HOPING HE MIGHT YET LIVE.
BY THE TIME I ESCAPED, HE WAS DEAD OF HUNGER AND GRIEF!
......
TRAPPED HERE, MY PRAYER WAS TO REMEMBER, AND I STILL DO! MY HEART FEELS THE SWELL OF REVENGE AGAIN!
O GOD, THOU HAST PRESERVED MY MEMORY! I THANK THEE!

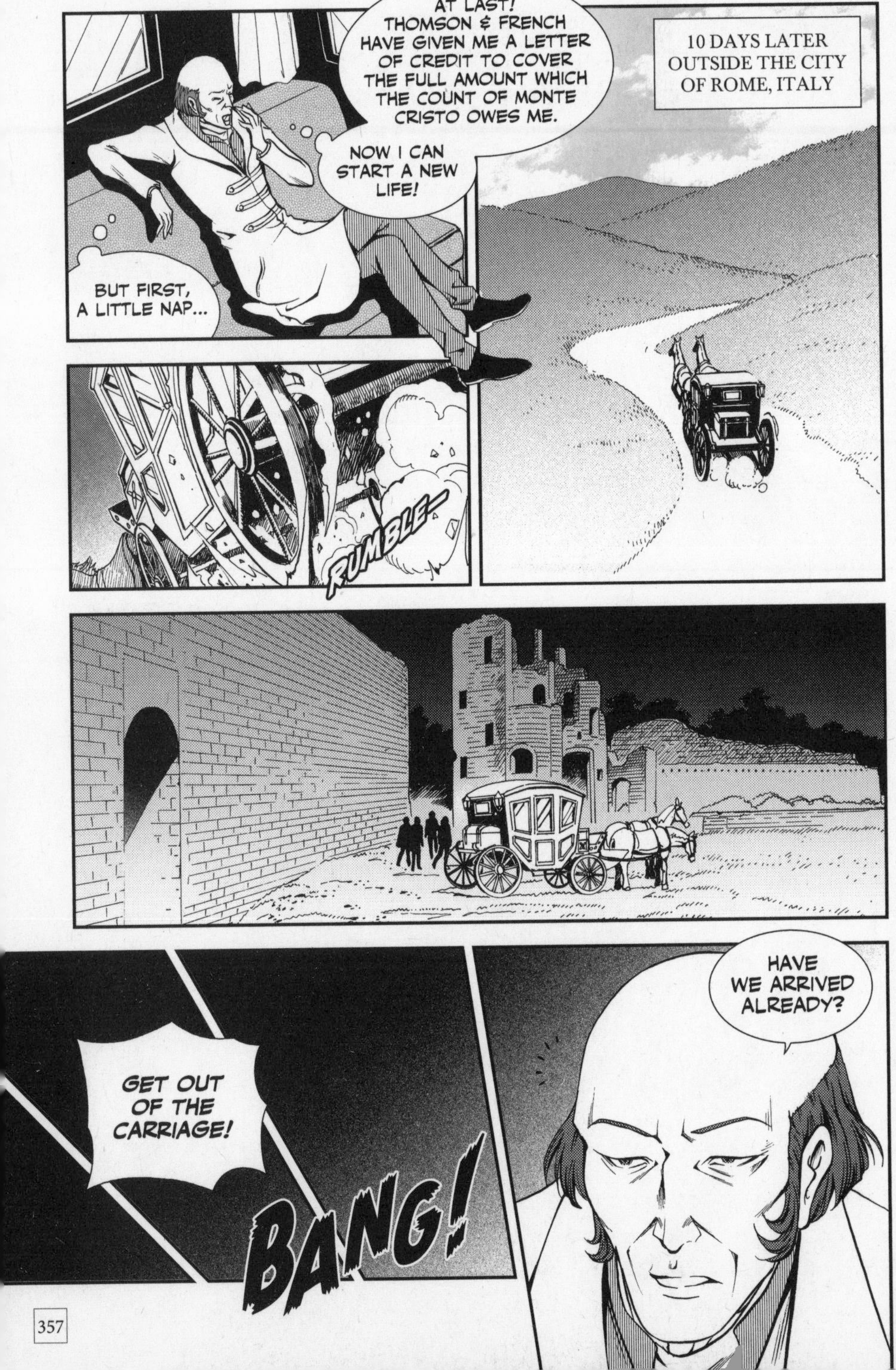

10 DAYS LATER OUTSIDE THE CITY OF ROME, ITALY
AT LAST! THOMSON & FRENCH HAVE GIVEN ME A LETTER OF CREDIT TO COVER THE FULL AMOUNT WHICH THE COUNT OF MONTE CRISTO OWES ME.
NOW I CAN START A NEW LIFE!
BUT FIRST, A LITTLE NAP...
RUMBLE
HAVE WE ARRIVED ALREADY?
GET OUT OF THE CARRIAGE!
BANG!

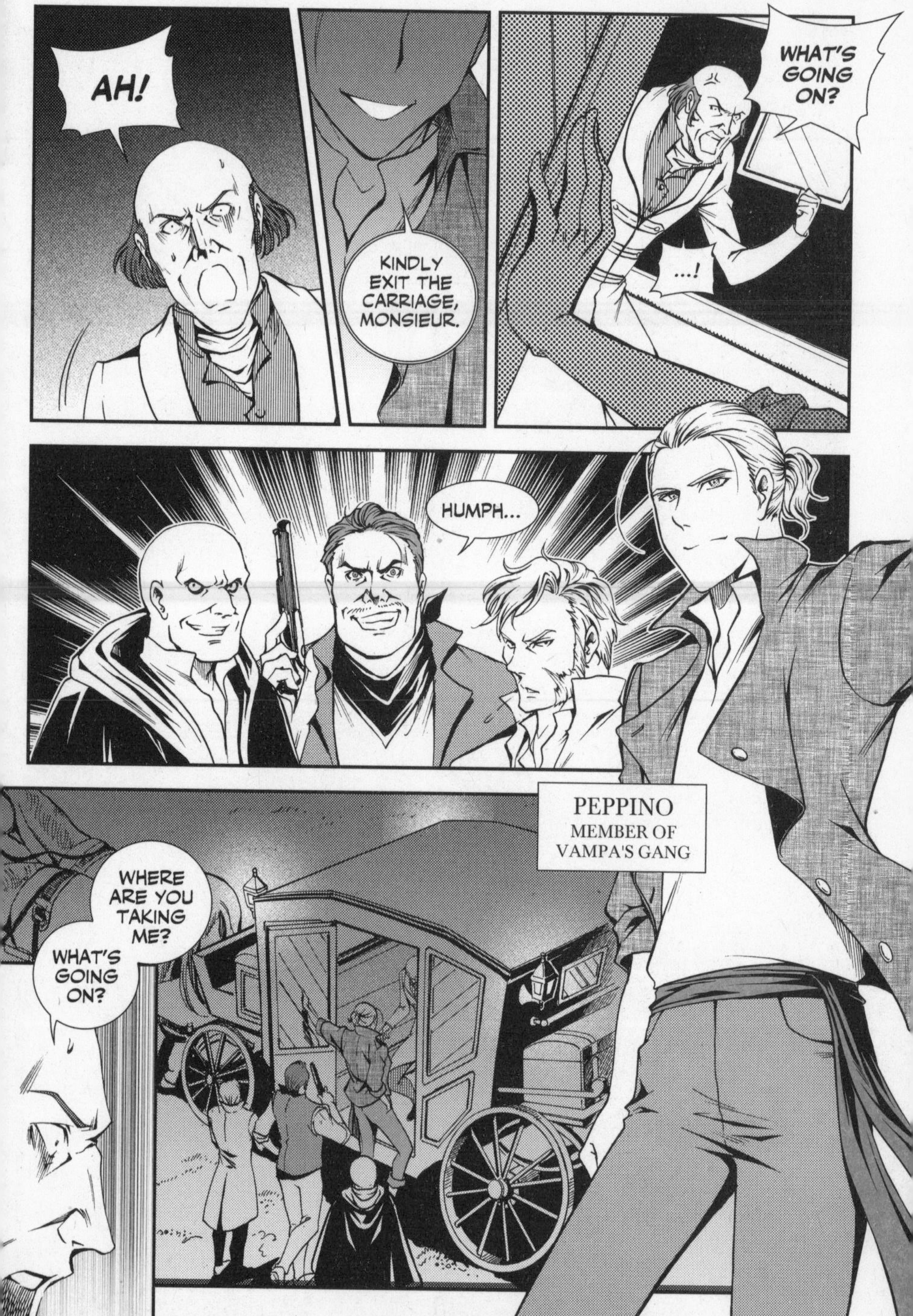
WHAT'S GOING ON?
...!
KINDLY EXIT THE CARRIAGE, MONSIEUR.
AH!
HUMPH...
PEPPINO
MEMBER OF VAMPA'S GANG
WHERE ARE YOU TAKING ME?
WHAT'S GOING ON?

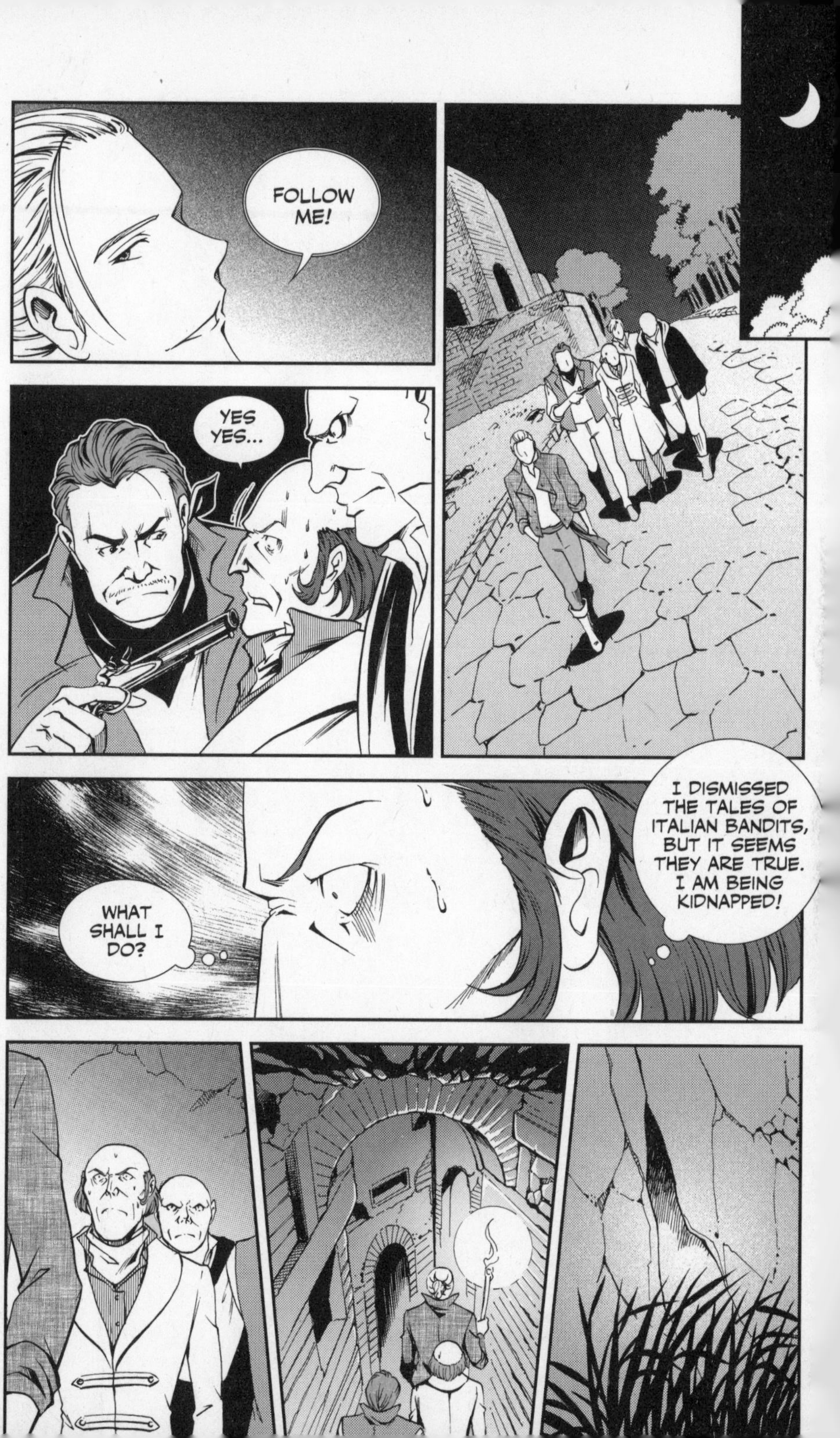
FOLLOW ME!
YES YES...
I DISMISSED THE TALES OF ITALIAN BANDITS, BUT IT SEEMS THEY ARE TRUE. I AM BEING KIDNAPPED!
WHAT SHALL I DO?

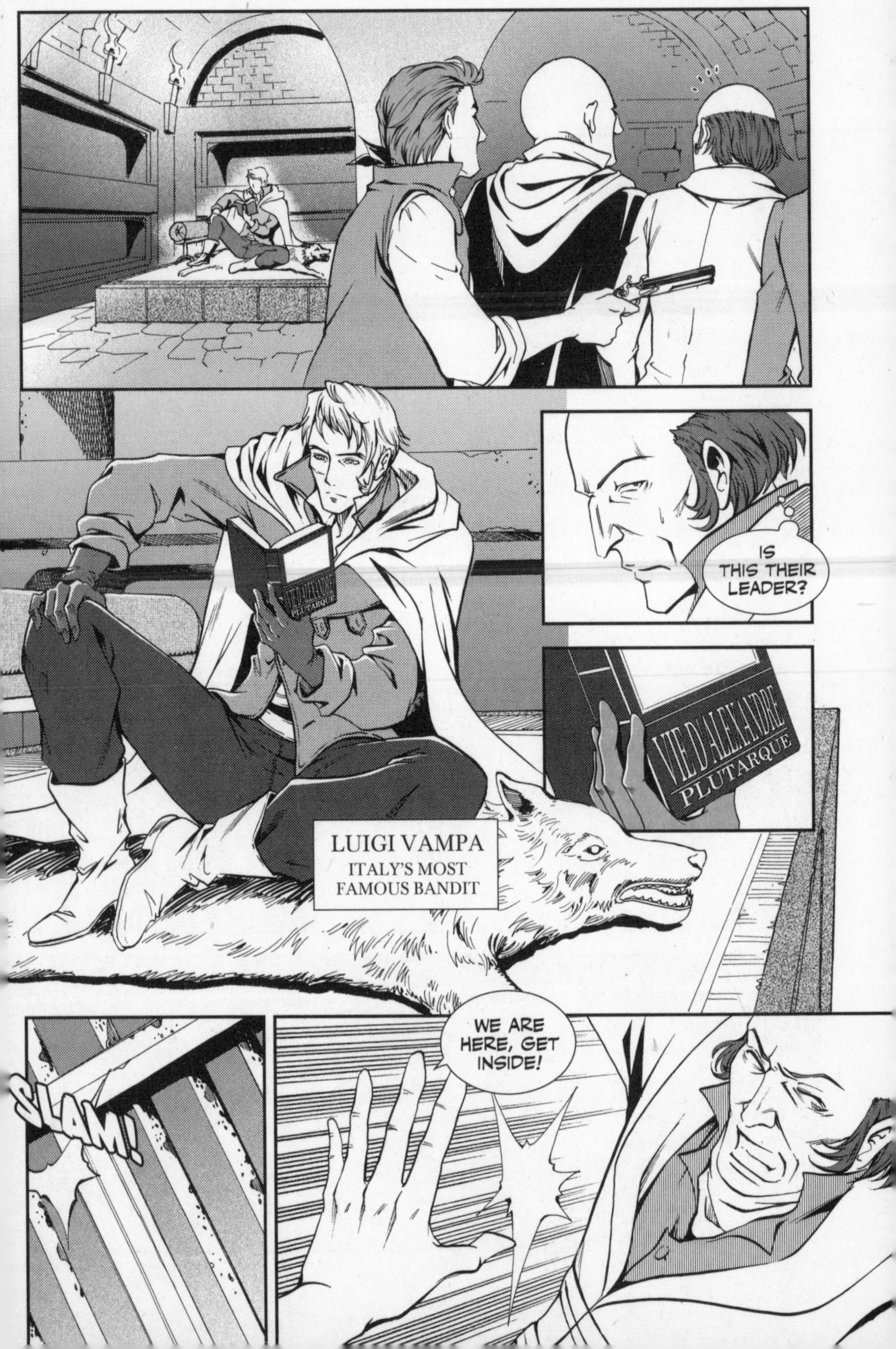
IS THIS THEIR LEADER?
VIE D'ALEXANDRE
PLUTARQUE
VIE D'ALEXANDRE
PLUTARQUE
LUIGI VAMPA
ITALY'S MOST FAMOUS BANDIT
WE ARE HERE, GET INSIDE!
SLAM!

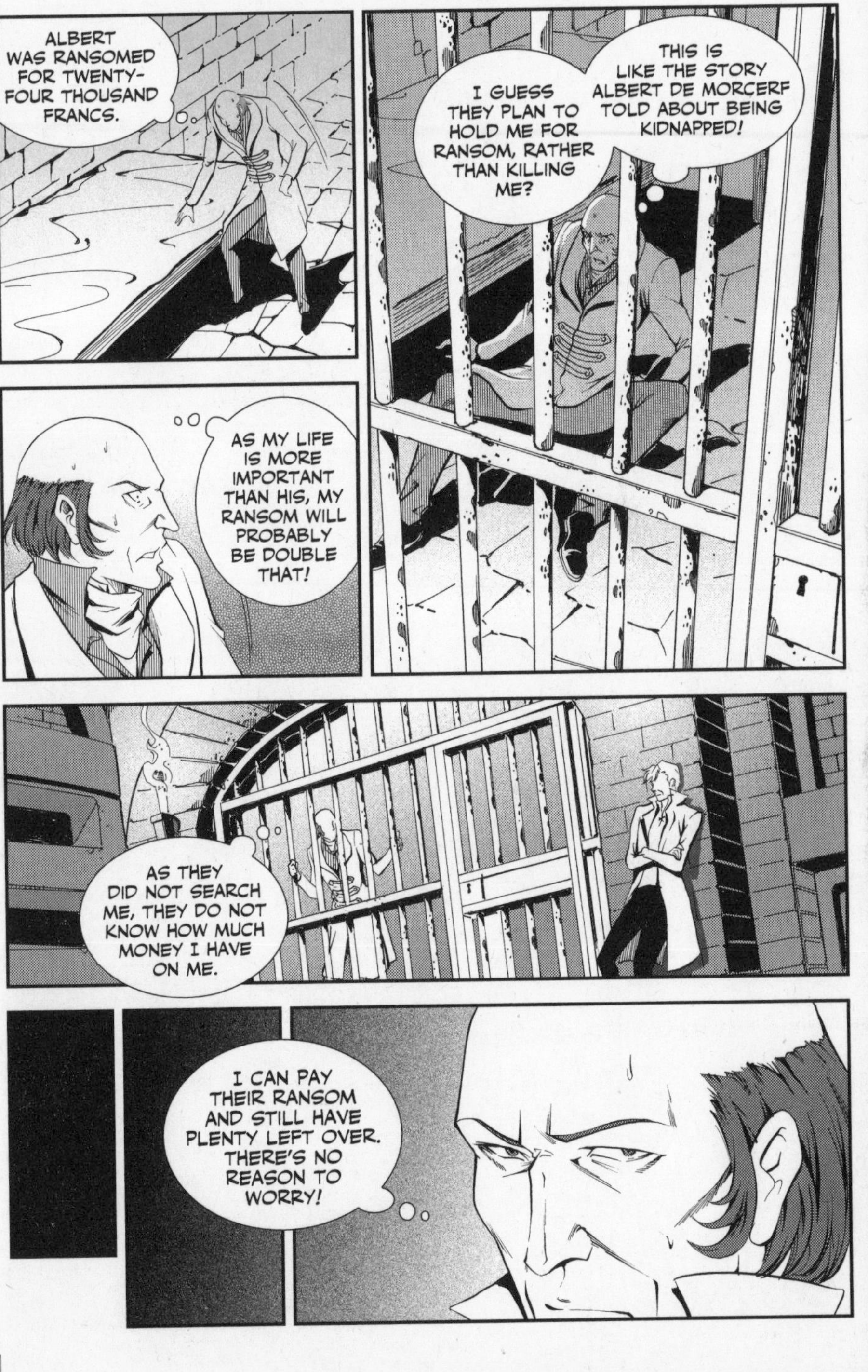
THIS IS LIKE THE STORY ALBERT DE MORCERF TOLD ABOUT BEING KIDNAPPED!
I GUESS THEY PLAN TO HOLD ME FOR RANSOM, RATHER THAN KILLING ME?
ALBERT WAS RANSOMED FOR TWENTY-FOUR THOUSAND FRANCS.
AS MY LIFE IS MORE IMPORTANT THAN HIS, MY RANSOM WILL PROBABLY BE DOUBLE THAT!
AS THEY DID NOT SEARCH ME, THEY DO NOT KNOW HOW MUCH MONEY I HAVE ON ME.
I CAN PAY THEIR RANSOM AND STILL HAVE PLENTY LEFT OVER. THERE'S NO REASON TO WORRY!

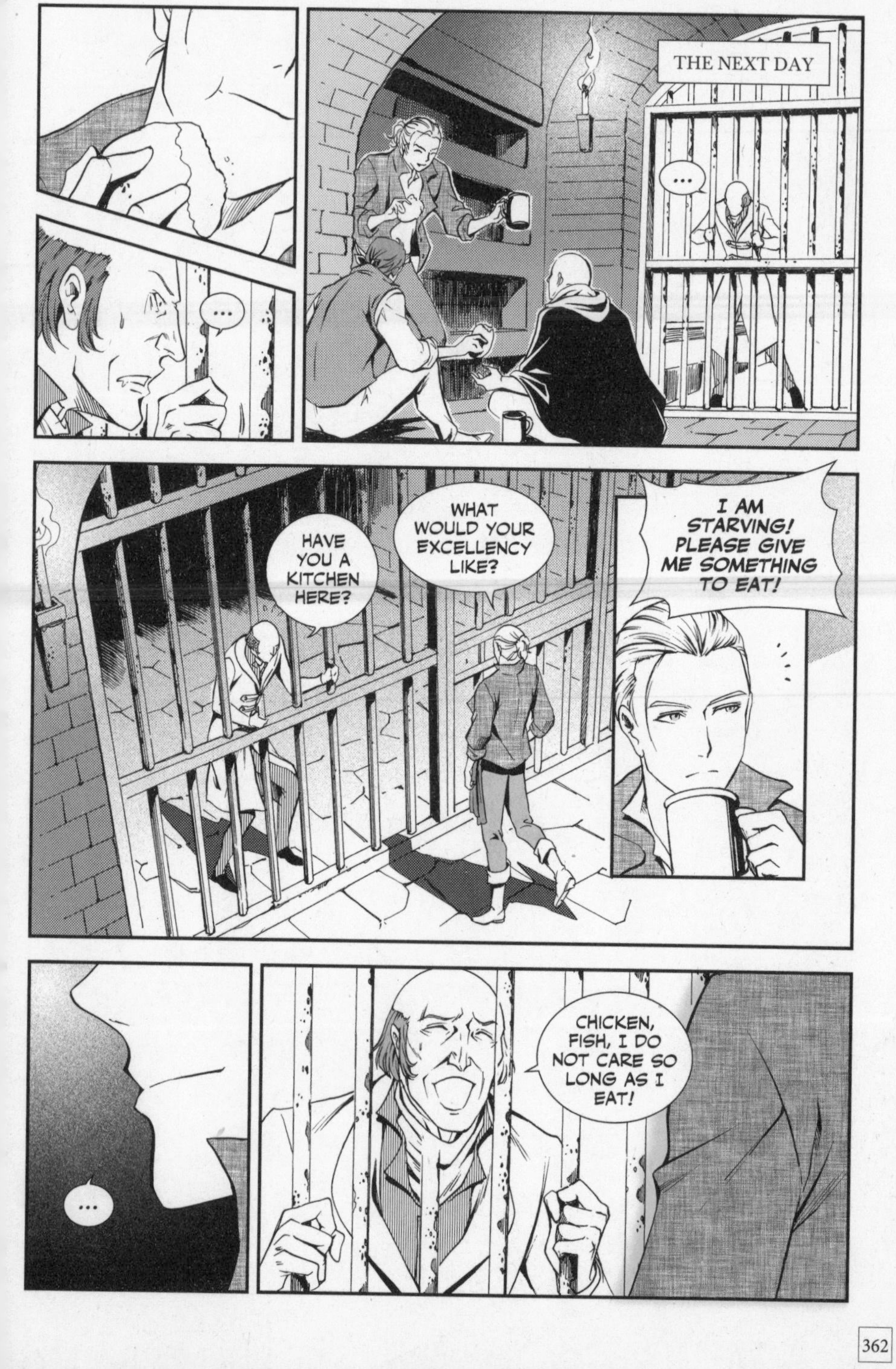
THE NEXT DAY
...
...
I AM STARVING! PLEASE GIVE ME SOMETHING TO EAT!
WHAT WOULD YOUR EXCELLENCY LIKE?
HAVE YOU A KITCHEN HERE?
CHICKEN, FISH, I DO NOT CARE SO LONG AS I EAT!
...

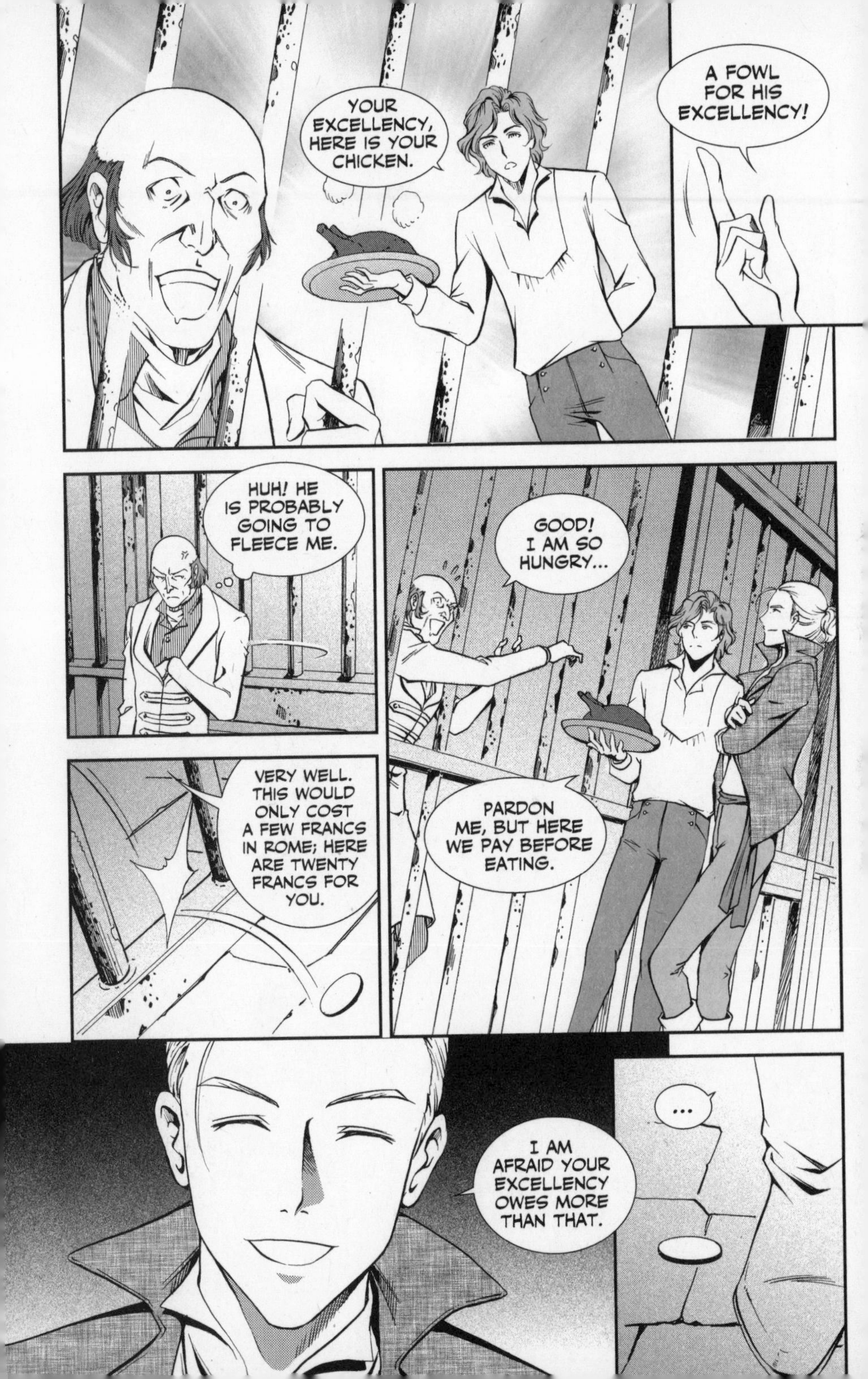
A FOWL FOR HIS EXCELLENCY!
YOUR EXCELLENCY, HERE IS YOUR CHICKEN.
GOOD! I AM SO HUNGRY...
PARDON ME, BUT HERE WE PAY BEFORE EATING.
HUH! HE IS PROBABLY GOING TO FLEECE ME.
VERY WELL. THIS WOULD ONLY COST A FEW FRANCS IN ROME; HERE ARE TWENTY FRANCS FOR YOU.
...
I AM AFRAID YOUR EXCELLENCY OWES MORE THAN THAT.

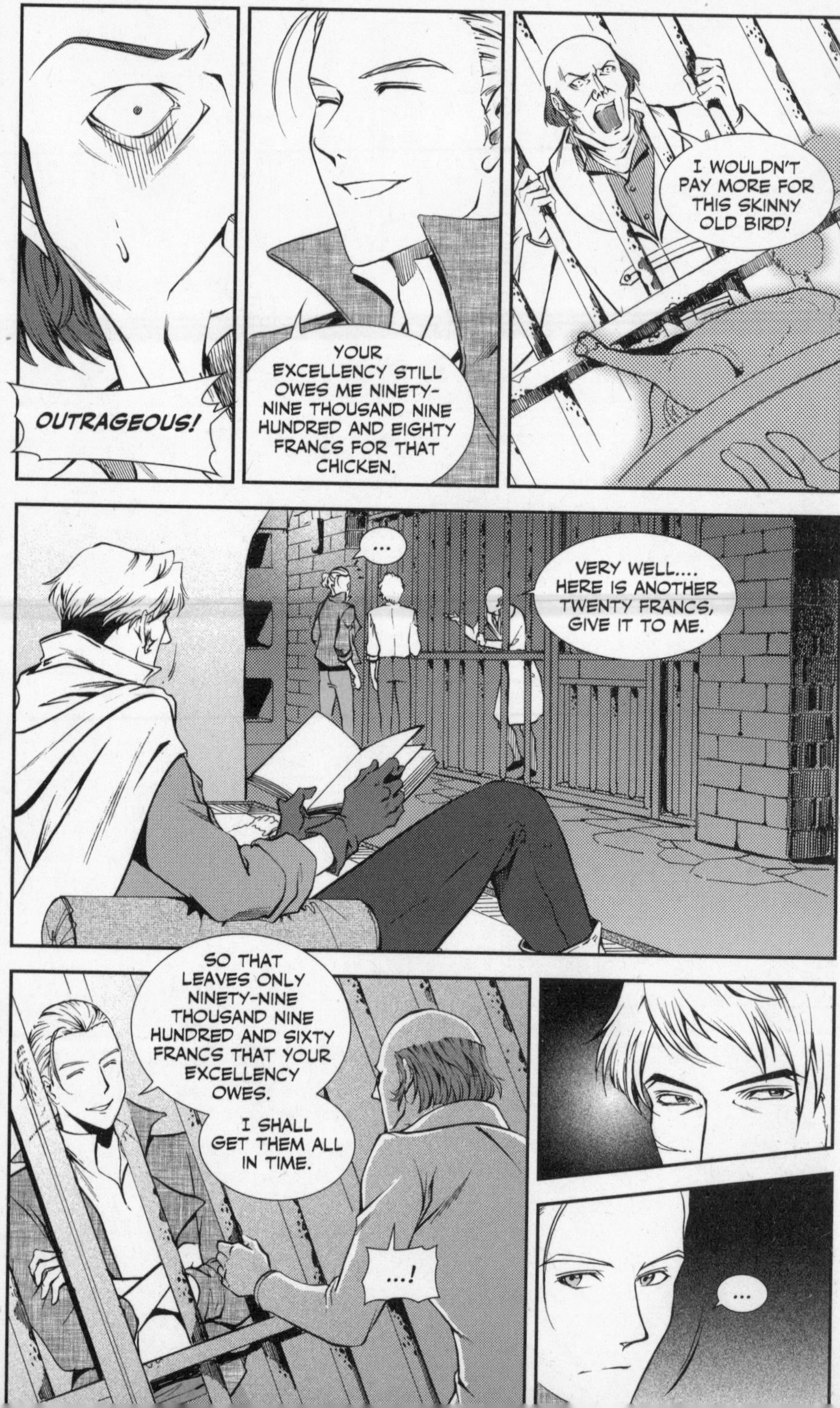
I WOULDN'T PAY MORE FOR THIS SKINNY OLD BIRD!
YOUR EXCELLENCY STILL OWES ME NINETY-NINE THOUSAND NINE HUNDRED AND EIGHTY FRANCS FOR THAT CHICKEN.
OUTRAGEOUS!
VERY WELL.... HERE IS ANOTHER TWENTY FRANCS, GIVE IT TO ME.
...
...
SO THAT LEAVES ONLY NINETY-NINE THOUSAND NINE HUNDRED AND SIXTY FRANCS THAT YOUR EXCELLENCY OWES.
I SHALL GET THEM ALL IN TIME.
...!

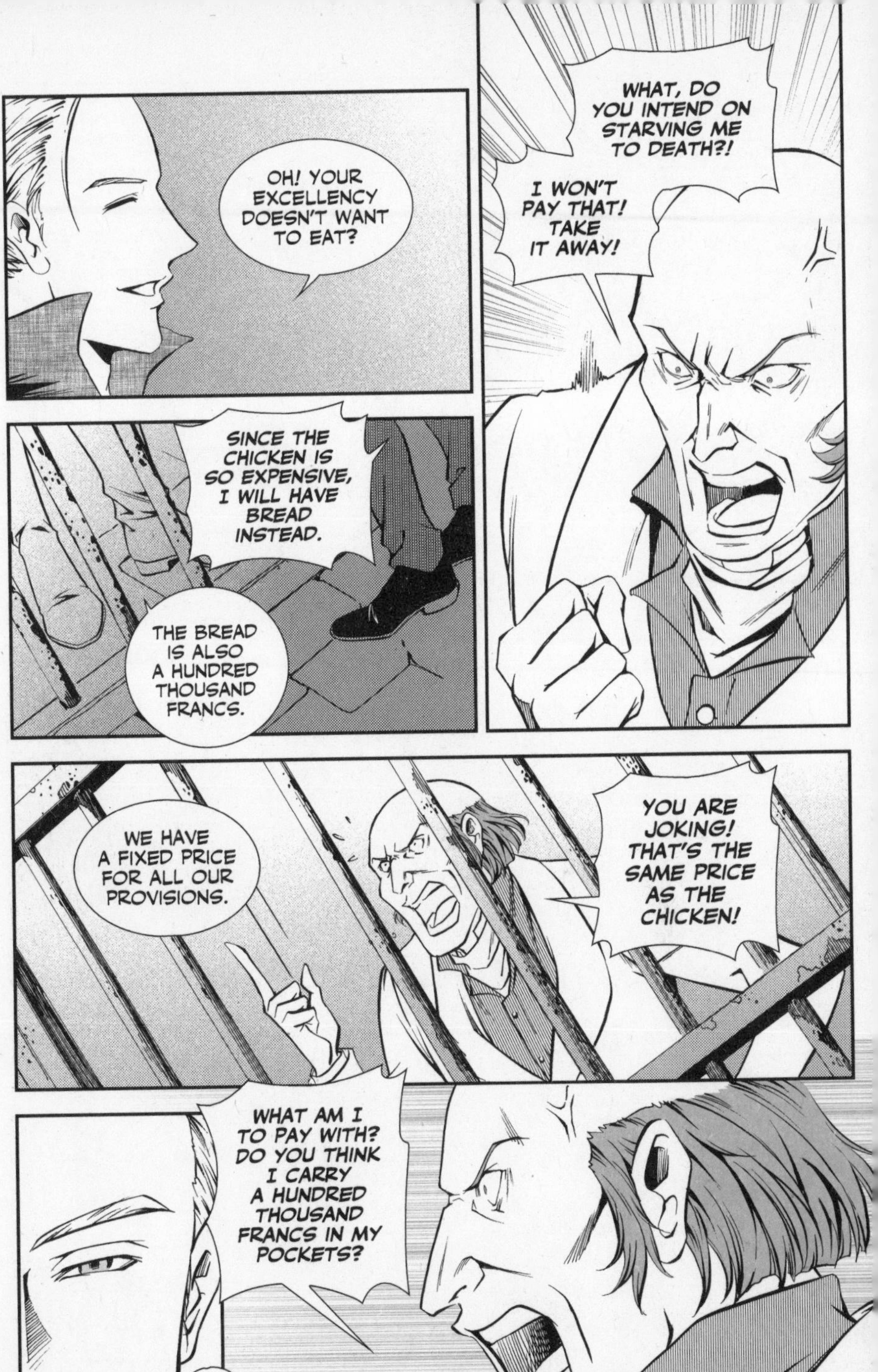
WHAT, DO YOU INTEND ON STARVING ME TO DEATH?!
I WON'T PAY THAT! TAKE IT AWAY!
OH! YOUR EXCELLENCY DOESN'T WANT TO EAT?
SINCE THE CHICKEN IS SO EXPENSIVE, I WILL HAVE BREAD INSTEAD.
THE BREAD IS ALSO A HUNDRED THOUSAND FRANCS.
YOU ARE JOKING! THAT'S THE SAME PRICE AS THE CHICKEN!
WE HAVE A FIXED PRICE FOR ALL OUR PROVISIONS.
WHAT AM I TO PAY WITH? DO YOU THINK I CARRY A HUNDRED THOUSAND FRANCS IN MY POCKETS?
...

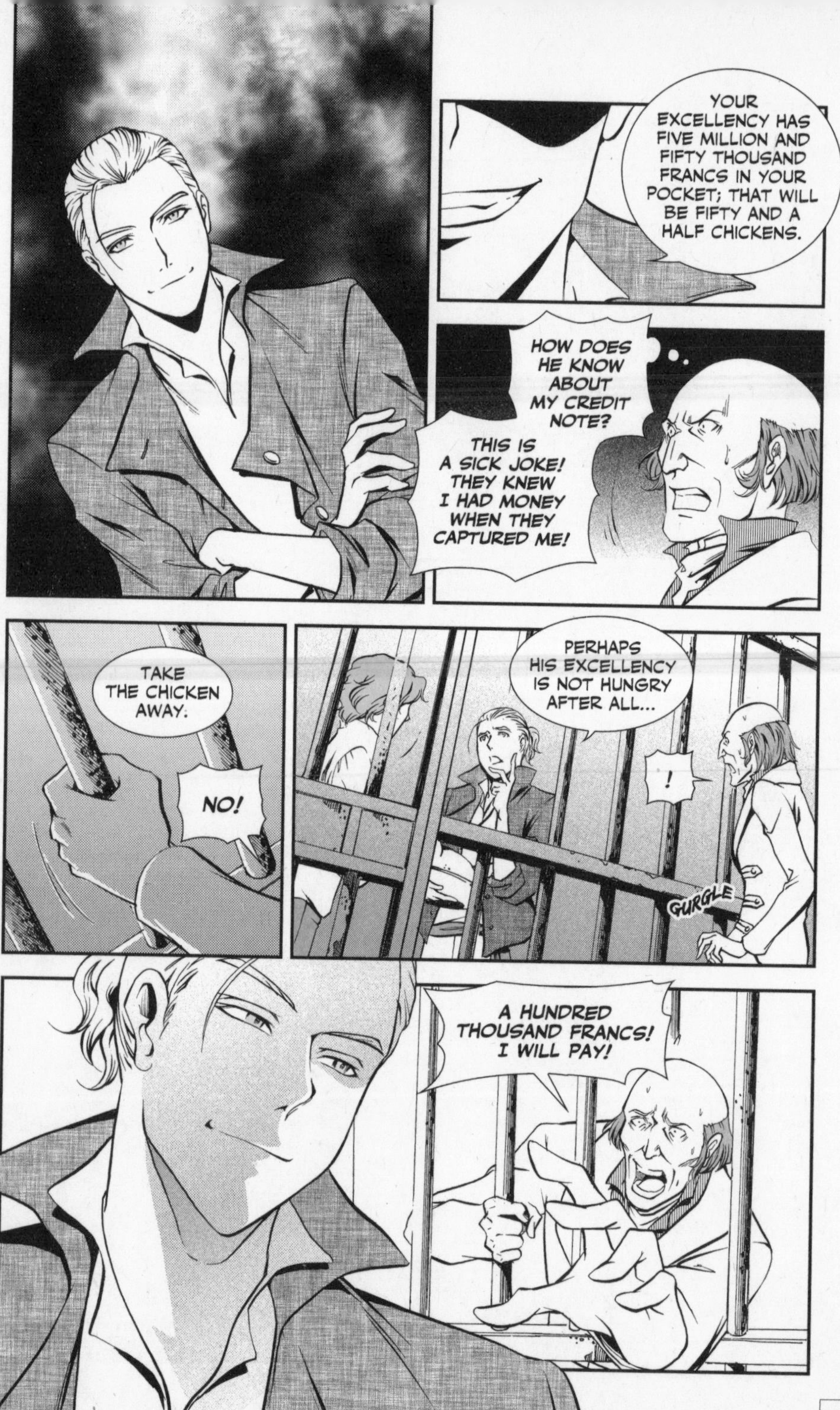
YOUR EXCELLENCY HAS FIVE MILLION AND FIFTY THOUSAND FRANCS IN YOUR POCKET; THAT WILL BE FIFTY AND A HALF CHICKENS.
HOW DOES HE KNOW ABOUT MY CREDIT NOTE?
THIS IS A SICK JOKE! THEY KNEW I HAD MONEY WHEN THEY CAPTURED ME!
PERHAPS HIS EXCELLENCY IS NOT HUNGRY AFTER ALL...
!
GURGLE
TAKE THE CHICKEN AWAY.
NO!
A HUNDRED THOUSAND FRANCS! I WILL PAY!

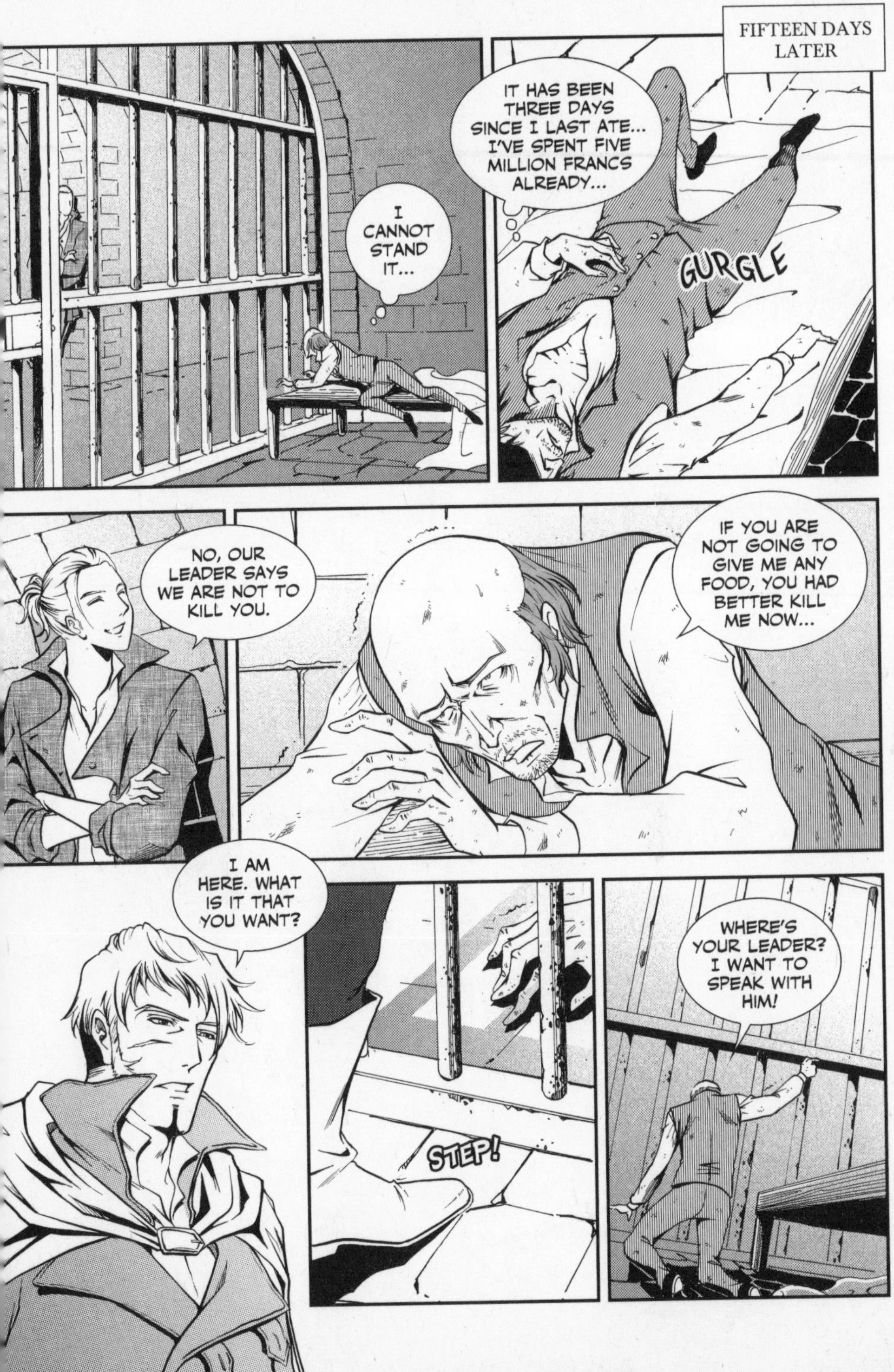
FIFTEEN DAYS LATER
IT HAS BEEN THREE DAYS SINCE I LAST ATE... I'VE SPENT FIVE MILLION FRANCS ALREADY...
GURGLE
I CANNOT STAND IT...
IF YOU ARE NOT GOING TO GIVE ME ANY FOOD, YOU HAD BETTER KILL ME NOW...
NO, OUR LEADER SAYS WE ARE NOT TO KILL YOU.
WHERE'S YOUR LEADER? I WANT TO SPEAK WITH HIM!
STEP!
I AM HERE. WHAT IS IT THAT YOU WANT?

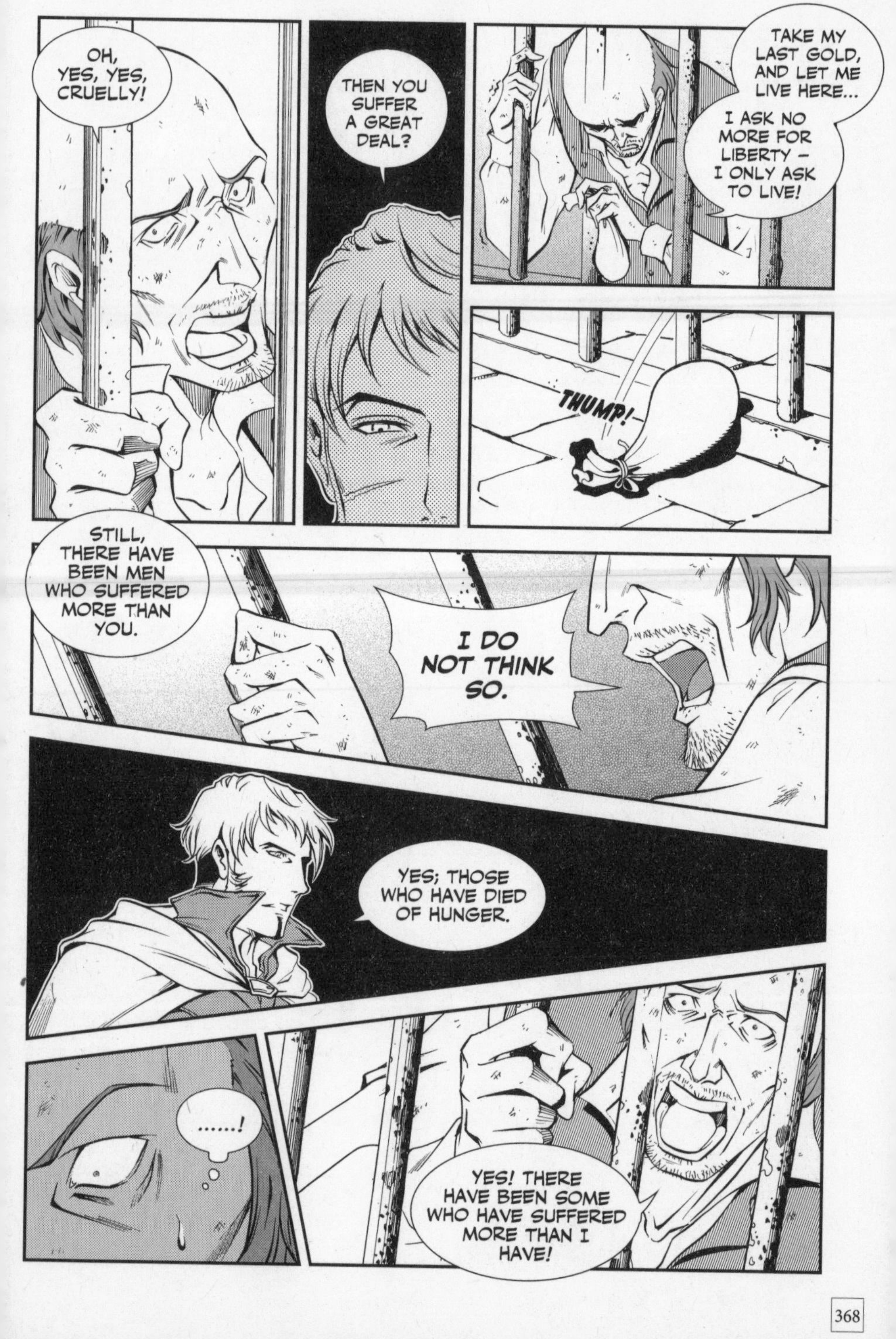
OH, YES, YES, CRUELLY!
THEN YOU SUFFER A GREAT DEAL?
TAKE MY LAST GOLD, AND LET ME LIVE HERE...
I ASK NO MORE FOR LIBERTY – I ONLY ASK TO LIVE!
THUMP!
STILL, THERE HAVE BEEN MEN WHO SUFFERED MORE THAN YOU.
I DO NOT THINK SO.
YES; THOSE WHO HAVE DIED OF HUNGER.
......!
YES! THERE HAVE BEEN SOME WHO HAVE SUFFERED MORE THAN I HAVE!

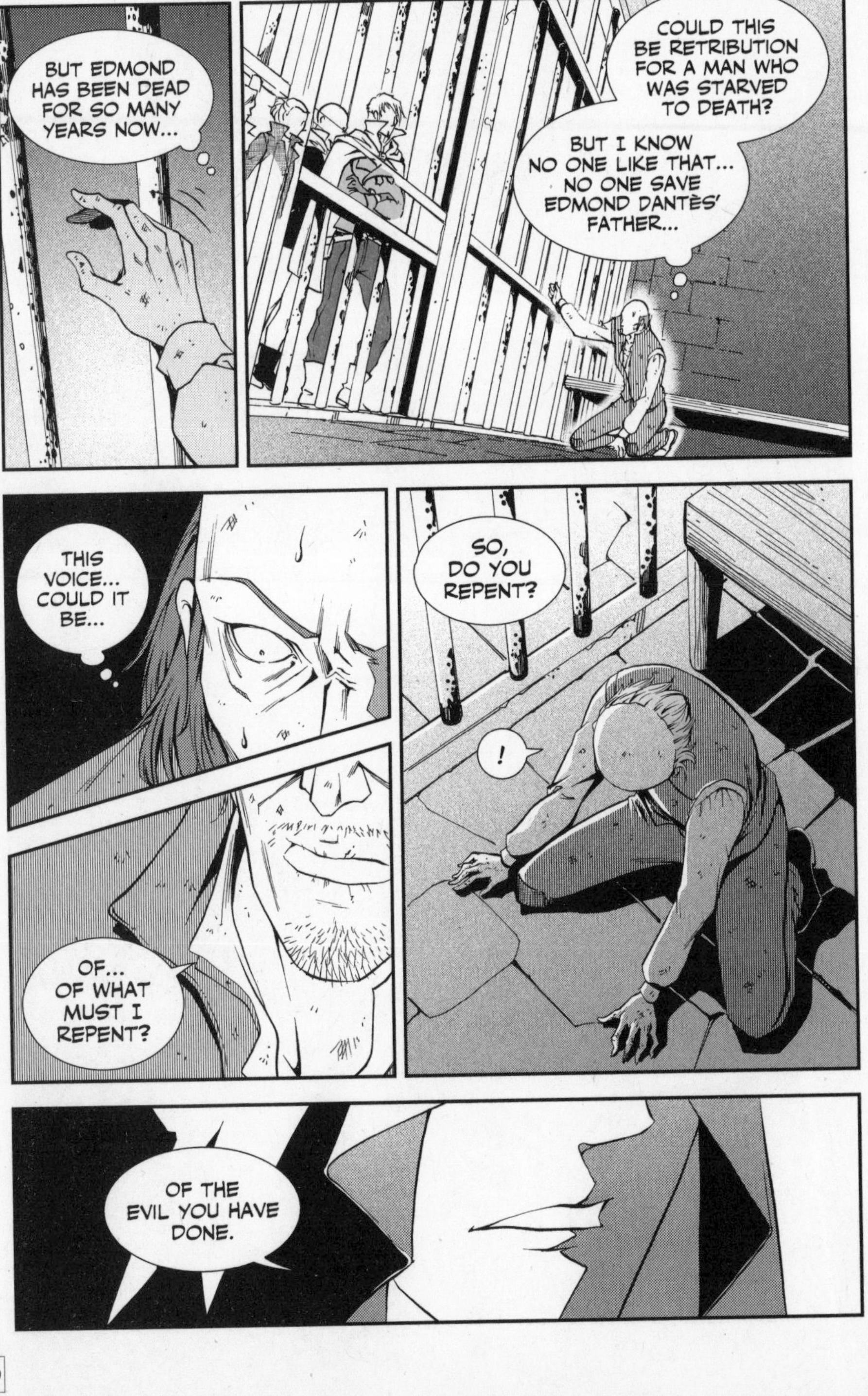
COULD THIS BE RETRIBUTION FOR A MAN WHO WAS STARVED TO DEATH?
BUT I KNOW NO ONE LIKE THAT... NO ONE SAVE EDMOND DANTÈS' FATHER...
BUT EDMOND HAS BEEN DEAD FOR SO MANY YEARS NOW...
SO, DO YOU REPENT?
!
THIS VOICE... COULD IT BE...
OF... OF WHAT MUST I REPENT?
OF THE EVIL YOU HAVE DONE.

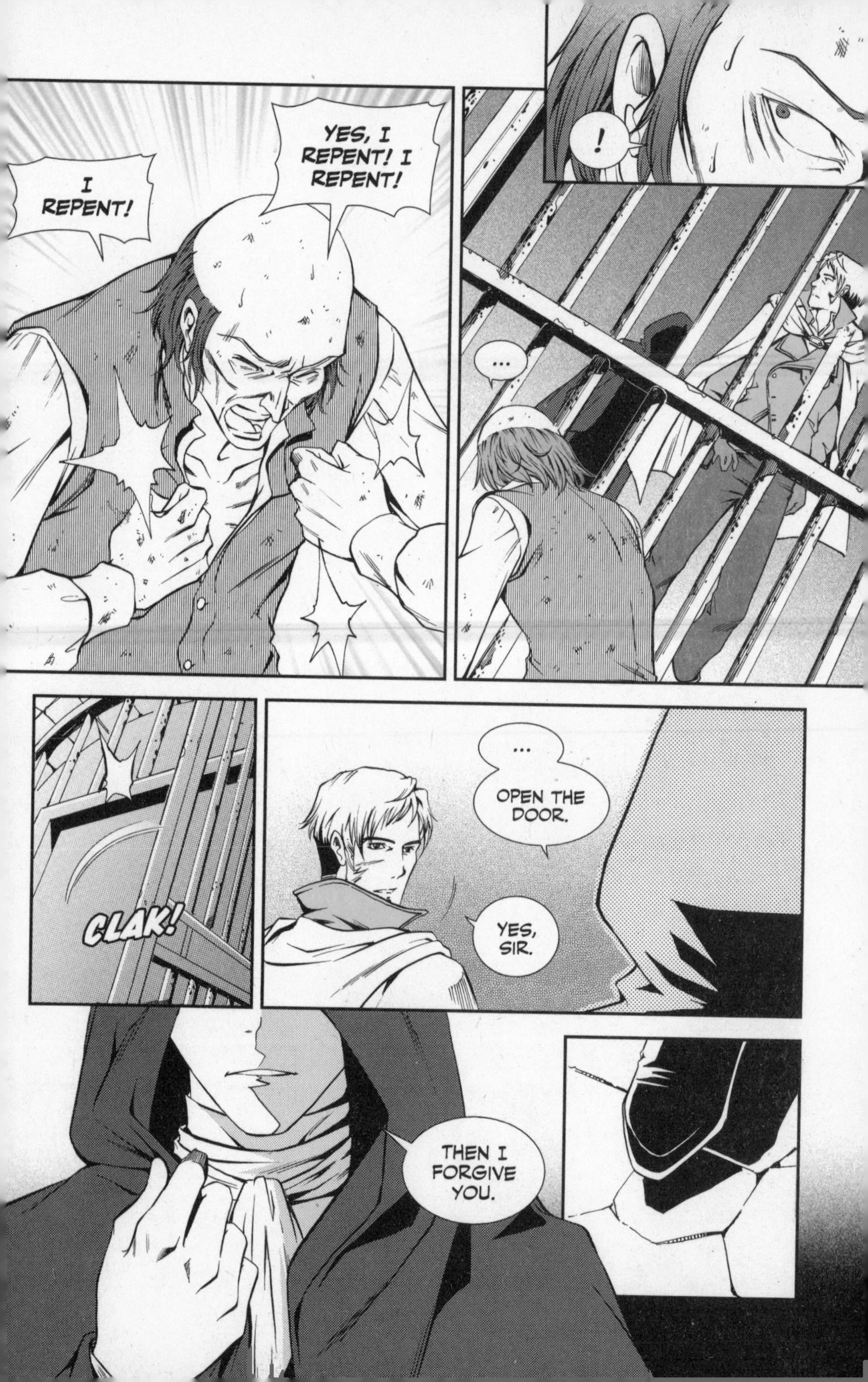
!
...
YES, I REPENT! I REPENT!
I REPENT!
... OPEN THE DOOR.
YES, SIR.
CLAK!
THEN I FORGIVE YOU.

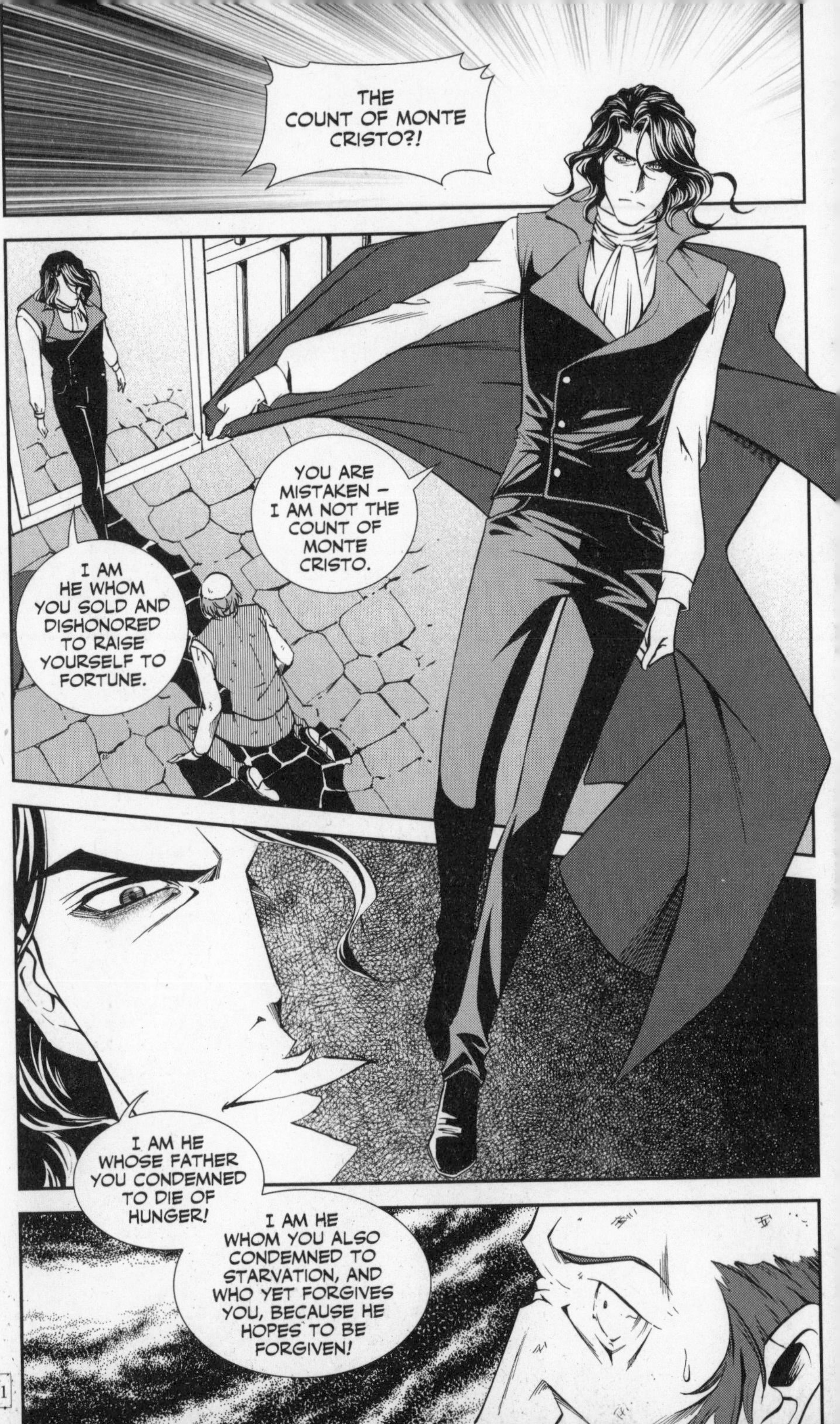
THE COUNT OF MONTE CRISTO?!
YOU ARE MISTAKEN – I AM NOT THE COUNT OF MONTE CRISTO.
I AM HE WHOM YOU SOLD AND DISHONORED TO RAISE YOURSELF TO FORTUNE.
I AM HE WHOSE FATHER YOU CONDEMNED TO DIE OF HUNGER!
I AM HE WHOM YOU ALSO CONDEMNED TO STARVATION, AND WHO YET FORGIVES YOU, BECAUSE HE HOPES TO BE FORGIVEN!

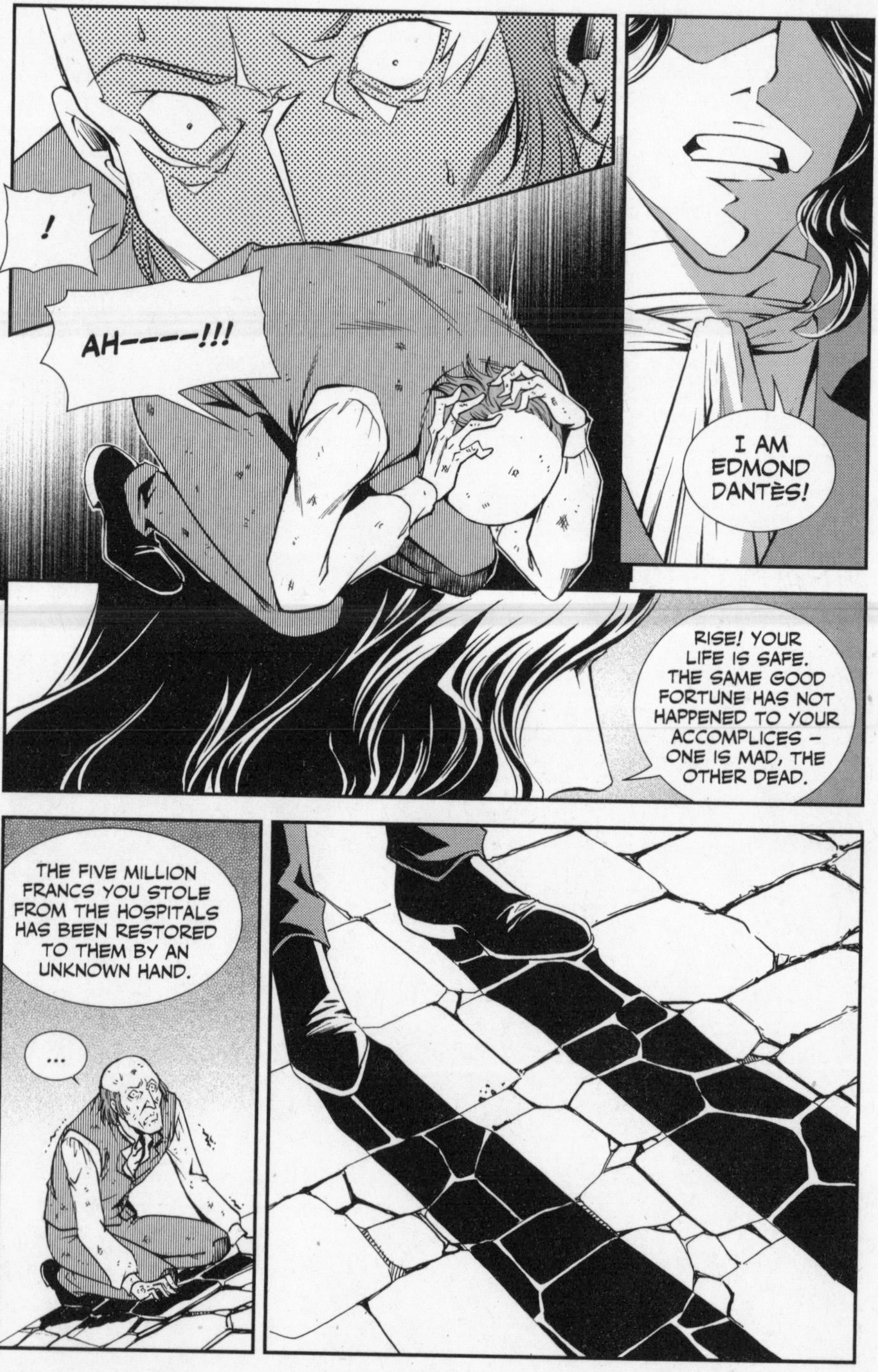
I AM EDMOND DANTÈS!
!
AH----!!!
RISE! YOUR LIFE IS SAFE. THE SAME GOOD FORTUNE HAS NOT HAPPENED TO YOUR ACCOMPLICES - ONE IS MAD, THE OTHER DEAD.
THE FIVE MILLION FRANCS YOU STOLE FROM THE HOSPITALS HAS BEEN RESTORED TO THEM BY AN UNKNOWN HAND.
...

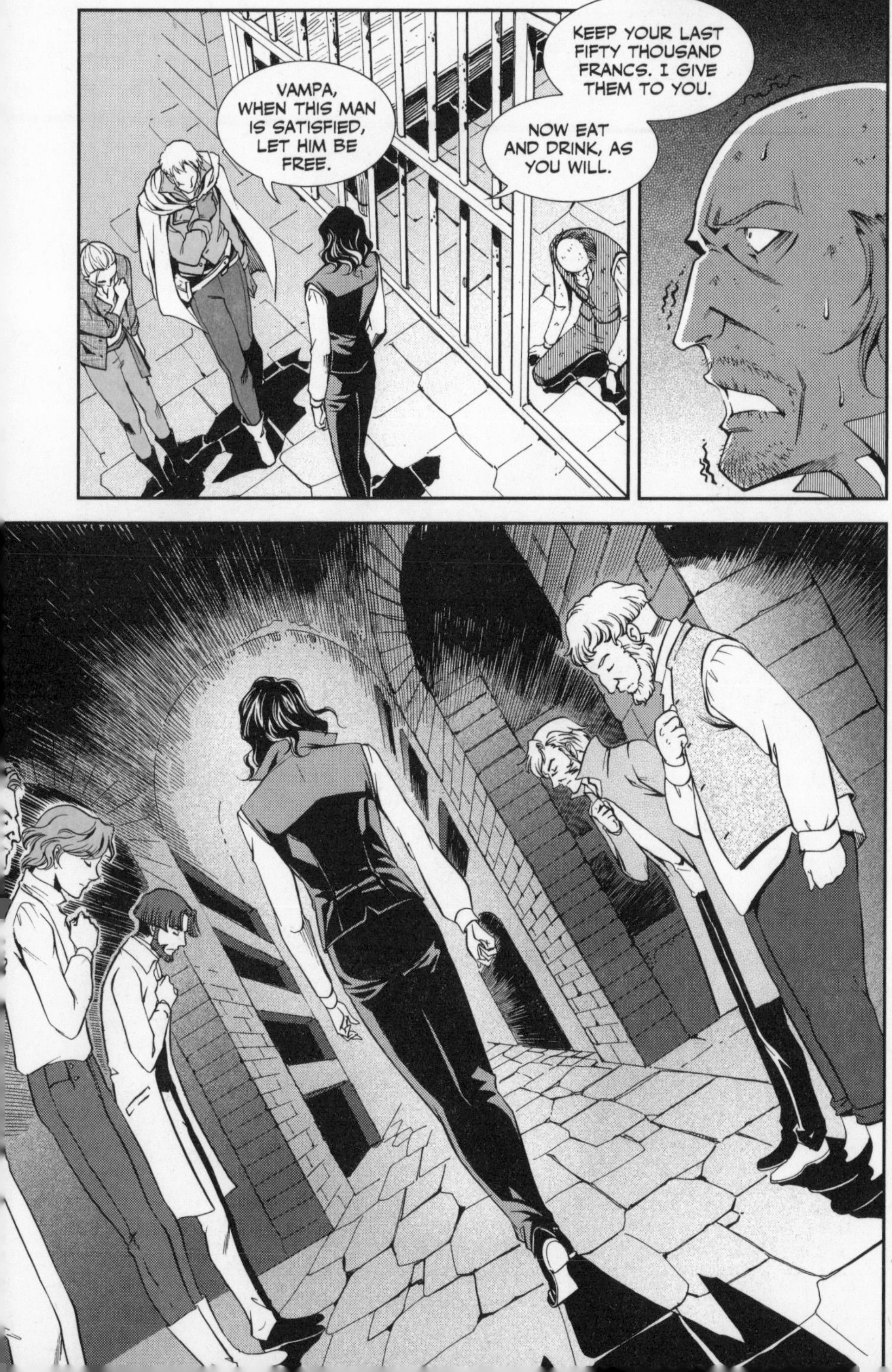
KEEP YOUR LAST FIFTY THOUSAND FRANCS. I GIVE THEM TO YOU.
NOW EAT AND DRINK, AS YOU WILL.
VAMPA, WHEN THIS MAN IS SATISFIED, LET HIM BE FREE.

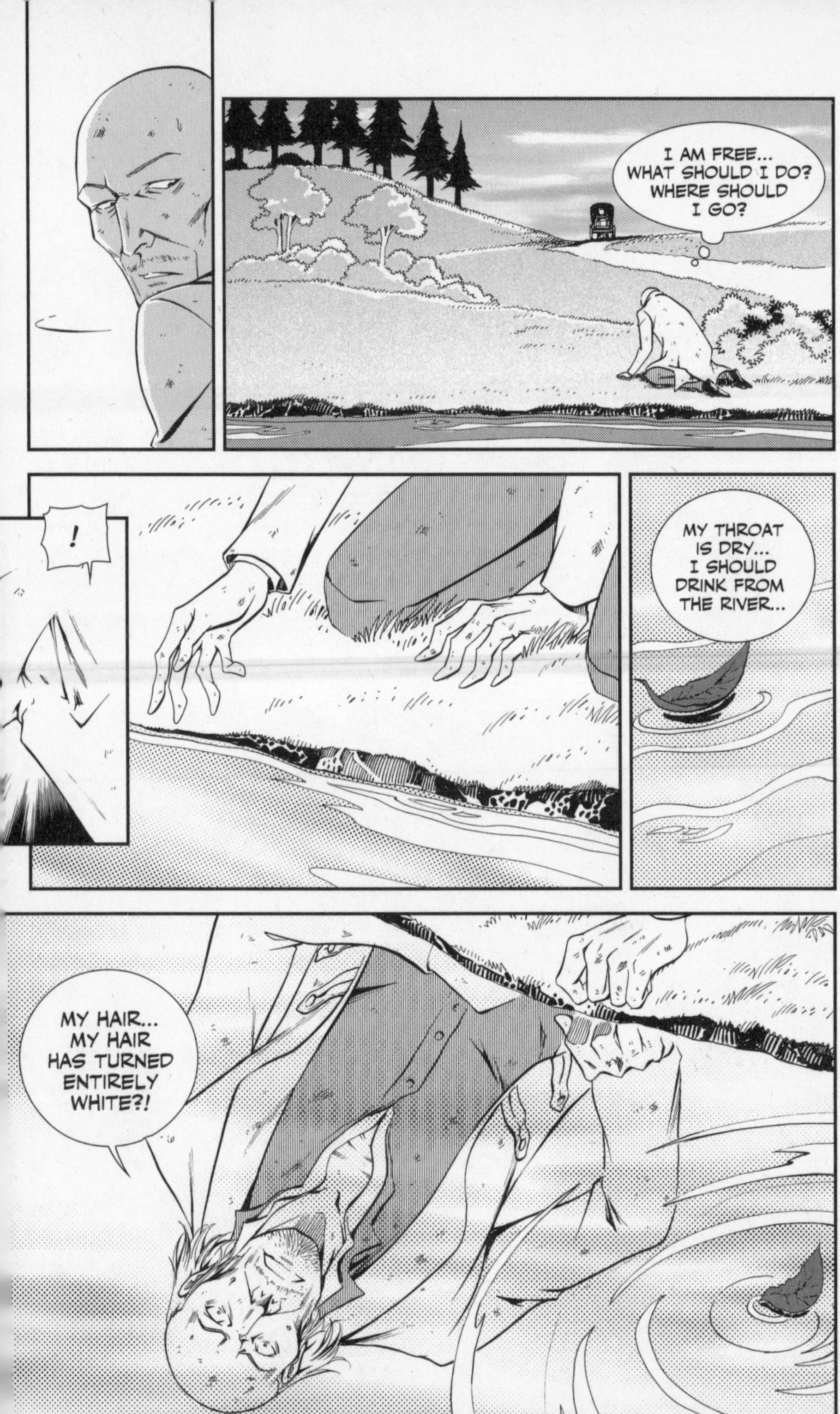
I AM FREE... WHAT SHOULD I DO? WHERE SHOULD I GO?
MY THROAT IS DRY... I SHOULD DRINK FROM THE RIVER...
!
MY HAIR... MY HAIR HAS TURNED ENTIRELY WHITE?!

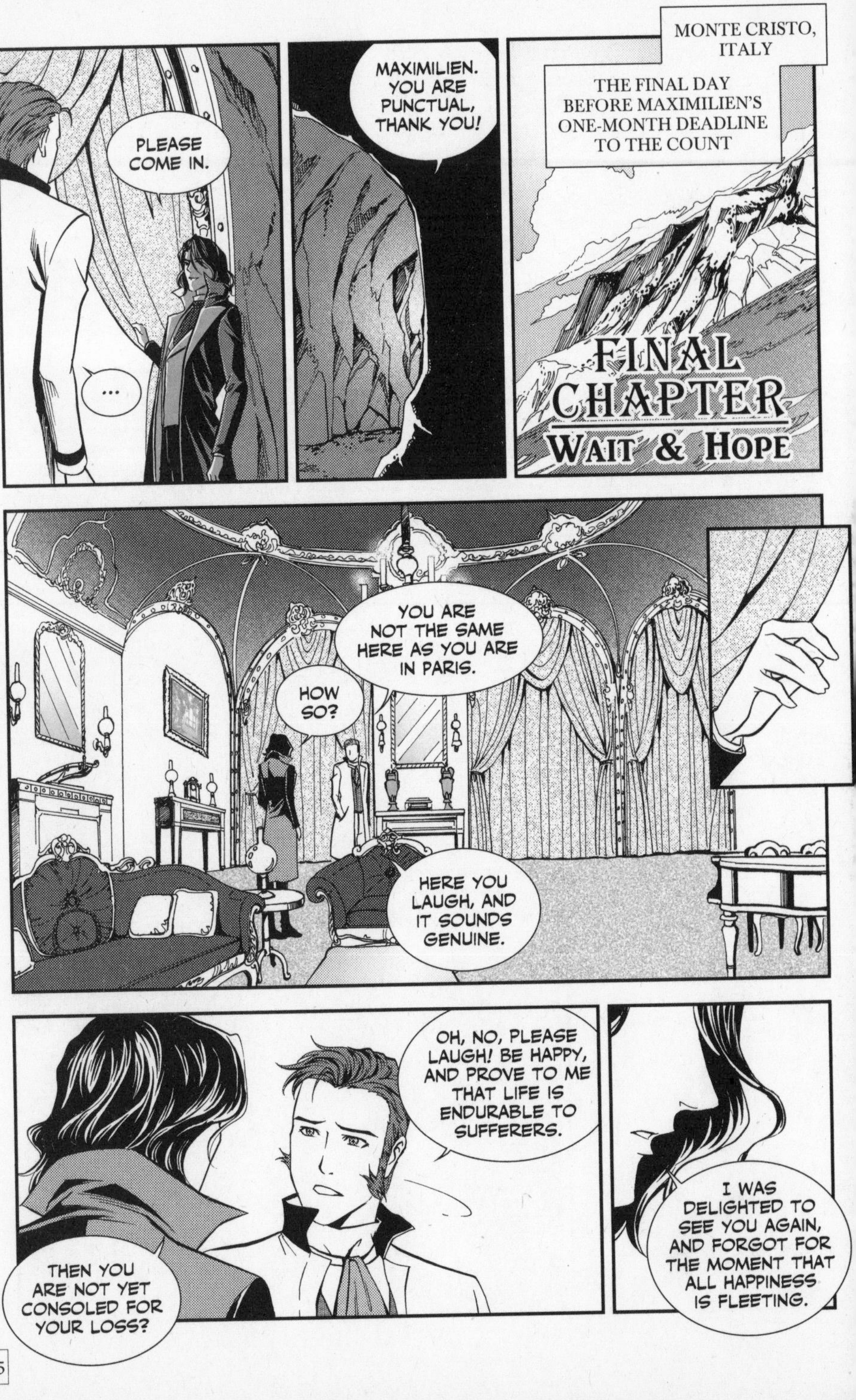
MONTE CRISTO, ITALY
THE FINAL DAY BEFORE MAXIMILIEN'S ONE-MONTH DEADLINE TO THE COUNT
FINAL CHAPTER
WAIT & HOPE
MAXIMILIEN. YOU ARE PUNCTUAL, THANK YOU!
PLEASE COME IN.
...
YOU ARE NOT THE SAME HERE AS YOU ARE IN PARIS.
HOW SO?
HERE YOU LAUGH, AND IT SOUNDS GENUINE.
I WAS DELIGHTED TO SEE YOU AGAIN, AND FORGOT FOR THE MOMENT THAT ALL HAPPINESS IS FLEETING.
OH, NO, PLEASE LAUGH! BE HAPPY, AND PROVE TO ME THAT LIFE IS ENDURABLE TO SUFFERERS.
THEN YOU ARE NOT YET CONSOLED FOR YOUR LOSS?

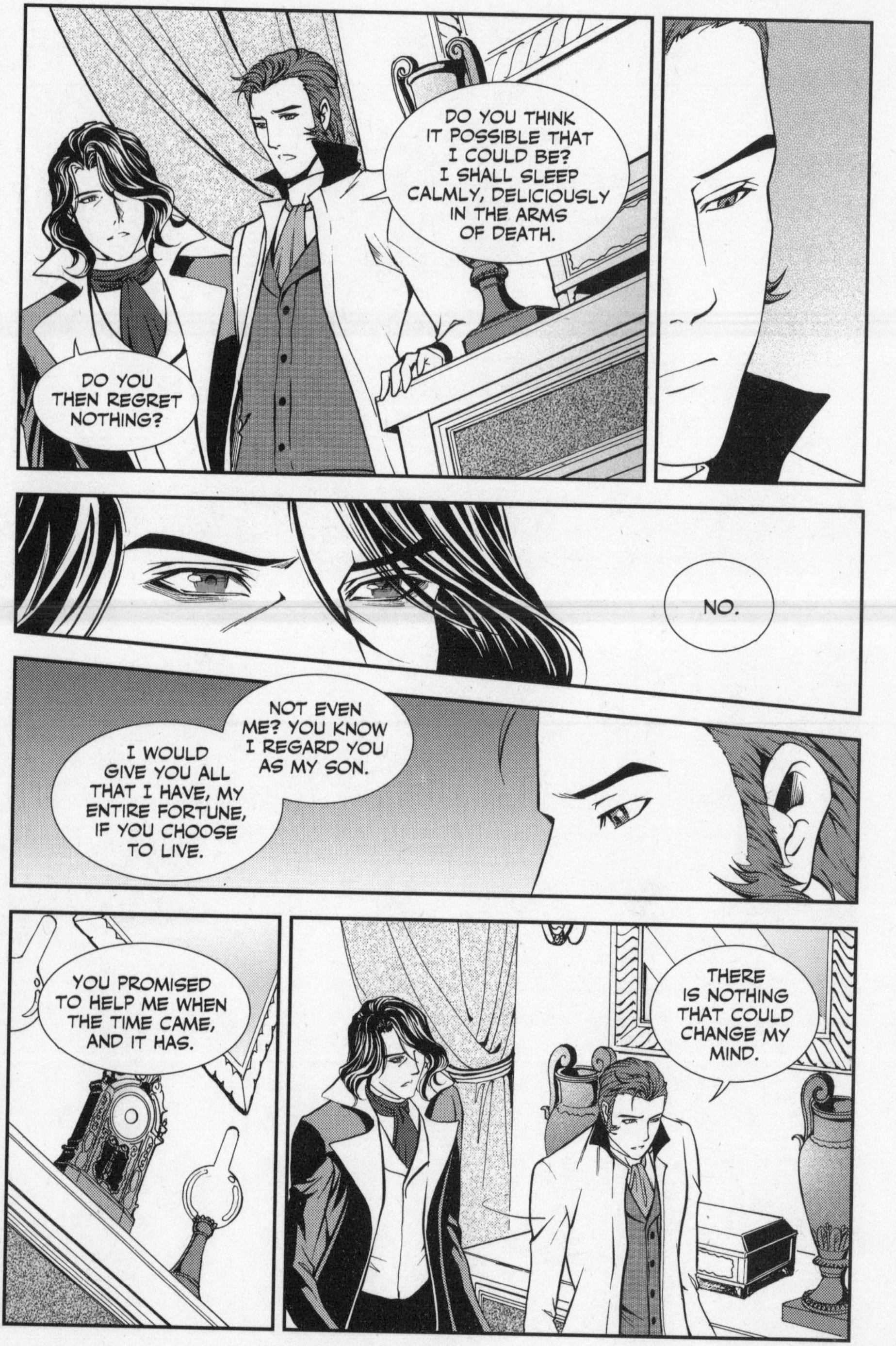
DO YOU THINK IT POSSIBLE THAT I COULD BE? I SHALL SLEEP CALMLY, DELICIOUSLY IN THE ARMS OF DEATH.
DO YOU THEN REGRET NOTHING?
NO.
NOT EVEN ME? YOU KNOW I REGARD YOU AS MY SON.
I WOULD GIVE YOU ALL THAT I HAVE, MY ENTIRE FORTUNE, IF YOU CHOOSE TO LIVE.
THERE IS NOTHING THAT COULD CHANGE MY MIND.
YOU PROMISED TO HELP ME WHEN THE TIME CAME, AND IT HAS.

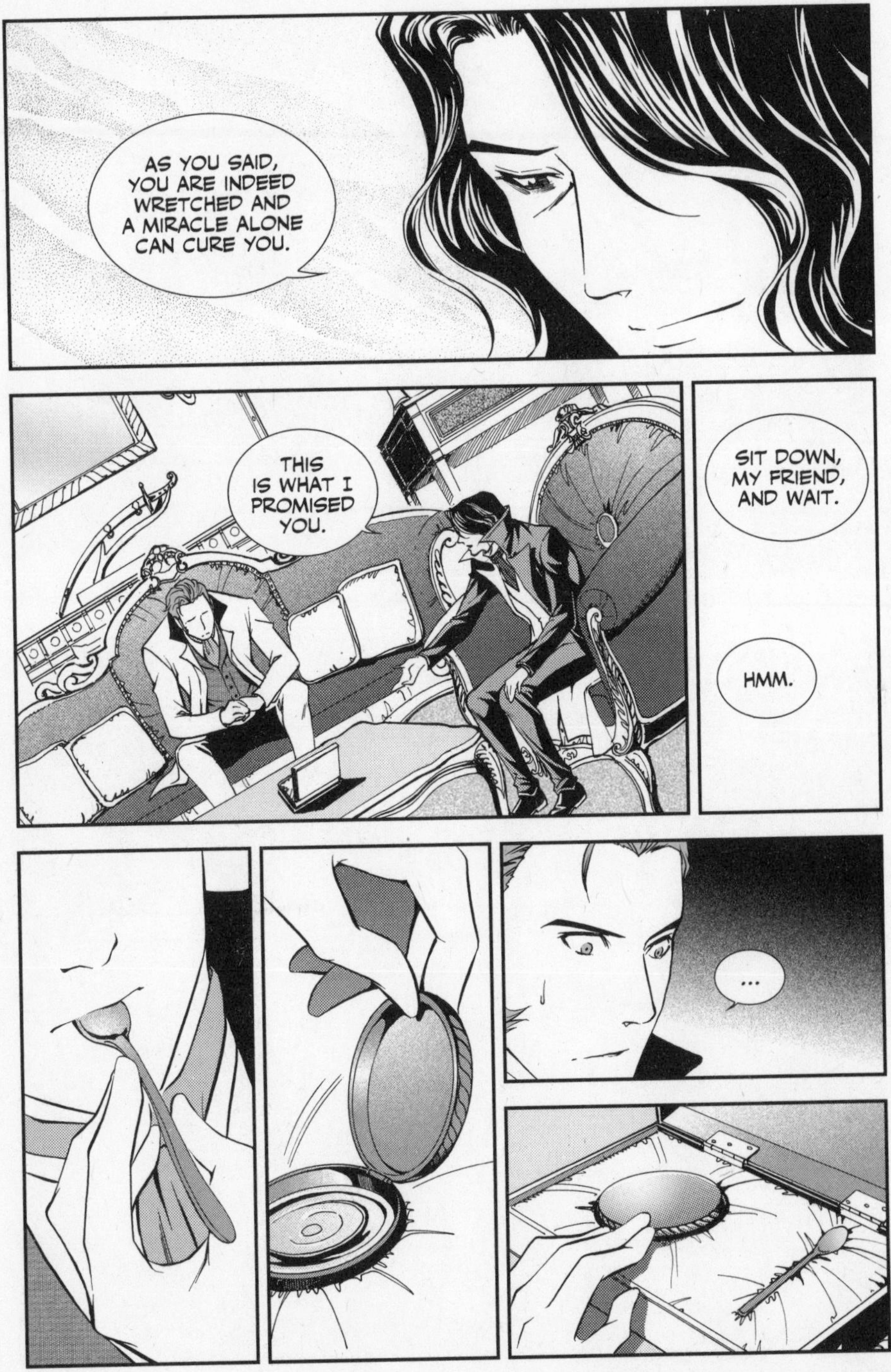
AS YOU SAID, YOU ARE INDEED WRETCHED AND A MIRACLE ALONE CAN CURE YOU.
SIT DOWN, MY FRIEND, AND WAIT.
HMM.
THIS IS WHAT I PROMISED YOU.
...

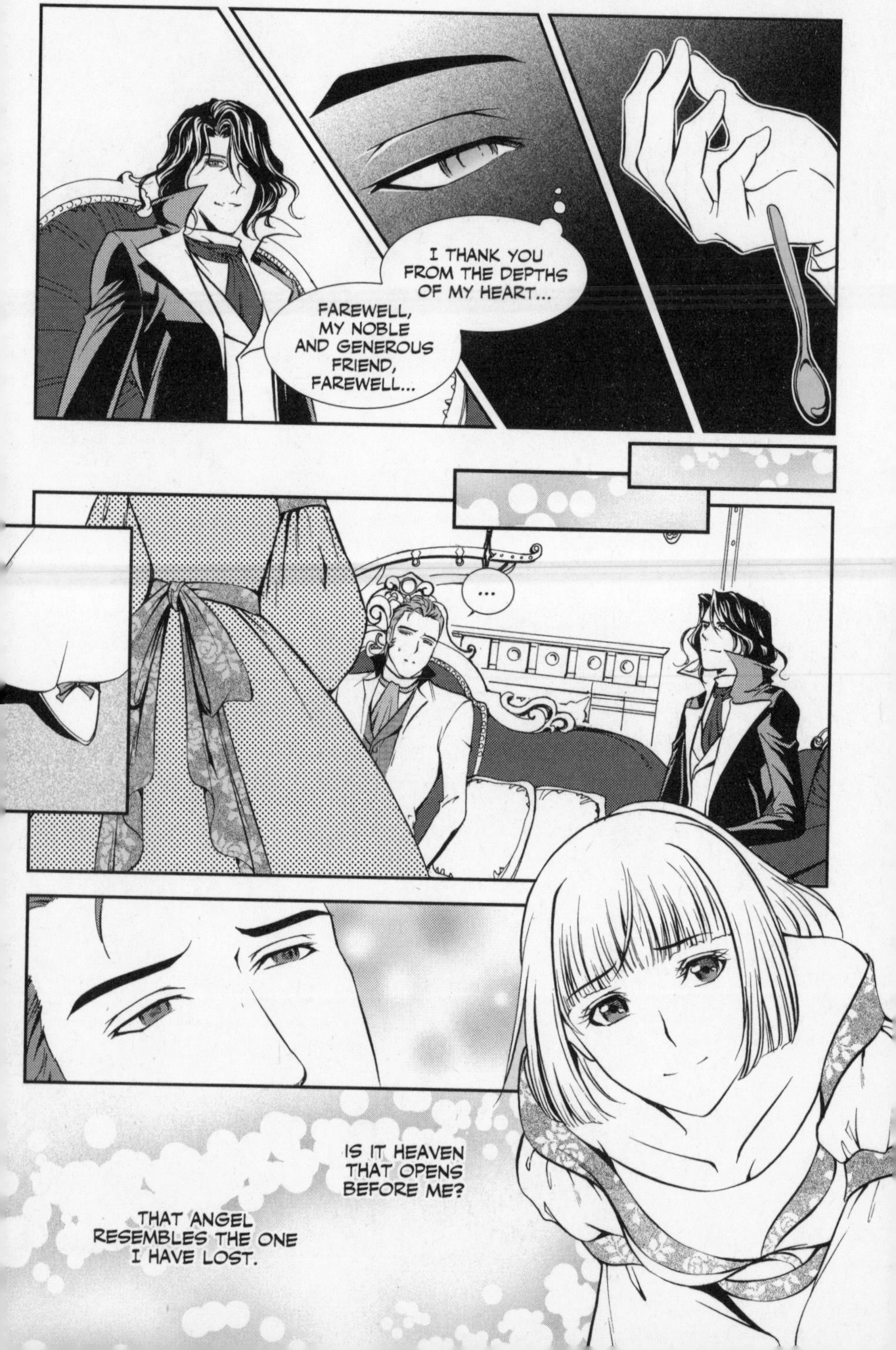
I THANK YOU FROM THE DEPTHS OF MY HEART...
FAREWELL, MY NOBLE AND GENEROUS FRIEND, FAREWELL...
...
IS IT HEAVEN THAT OPENS BEFORE ME?
THAT ANGEL RESEMBLES THE ONE I HAVE LOST.

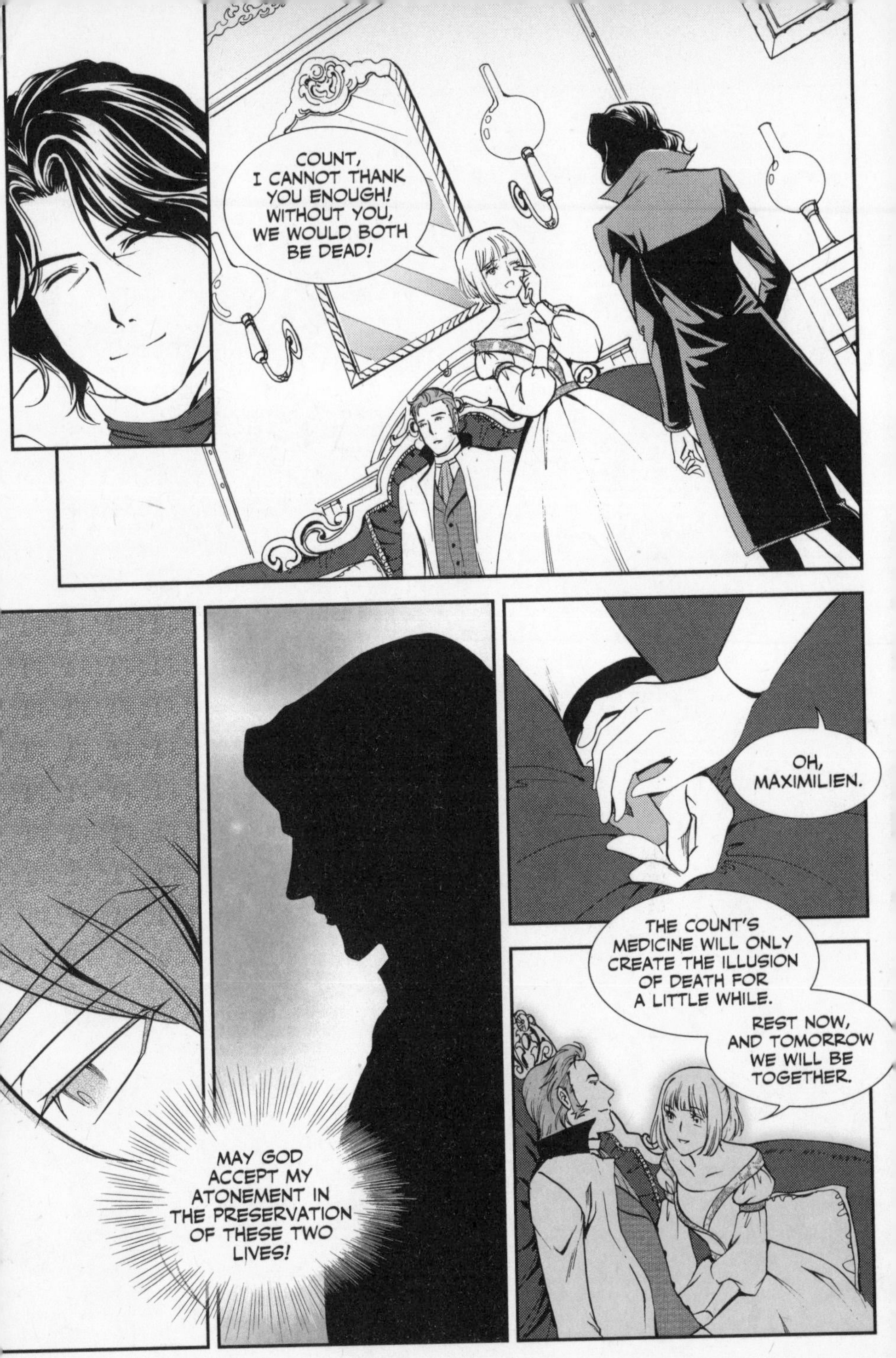
COUNT, I CANNOT THANK YOU ENOUGH! WITHOUT YOU, WE WOULD BOTH BE DEAD!
OH, MAXIMILIEN.
THE COUNT'S MEDICINE WILL ONLY CREATE THE ILLUSION OF DEATH FOR A LITTLE WHILE.
REST NOW, AND TOMORROW WE WILL BE TOGETHER.
MAY GOD ACCEPT MY ATONEMENT IN THE PRESERVATION OF THESE TWO LIVES!

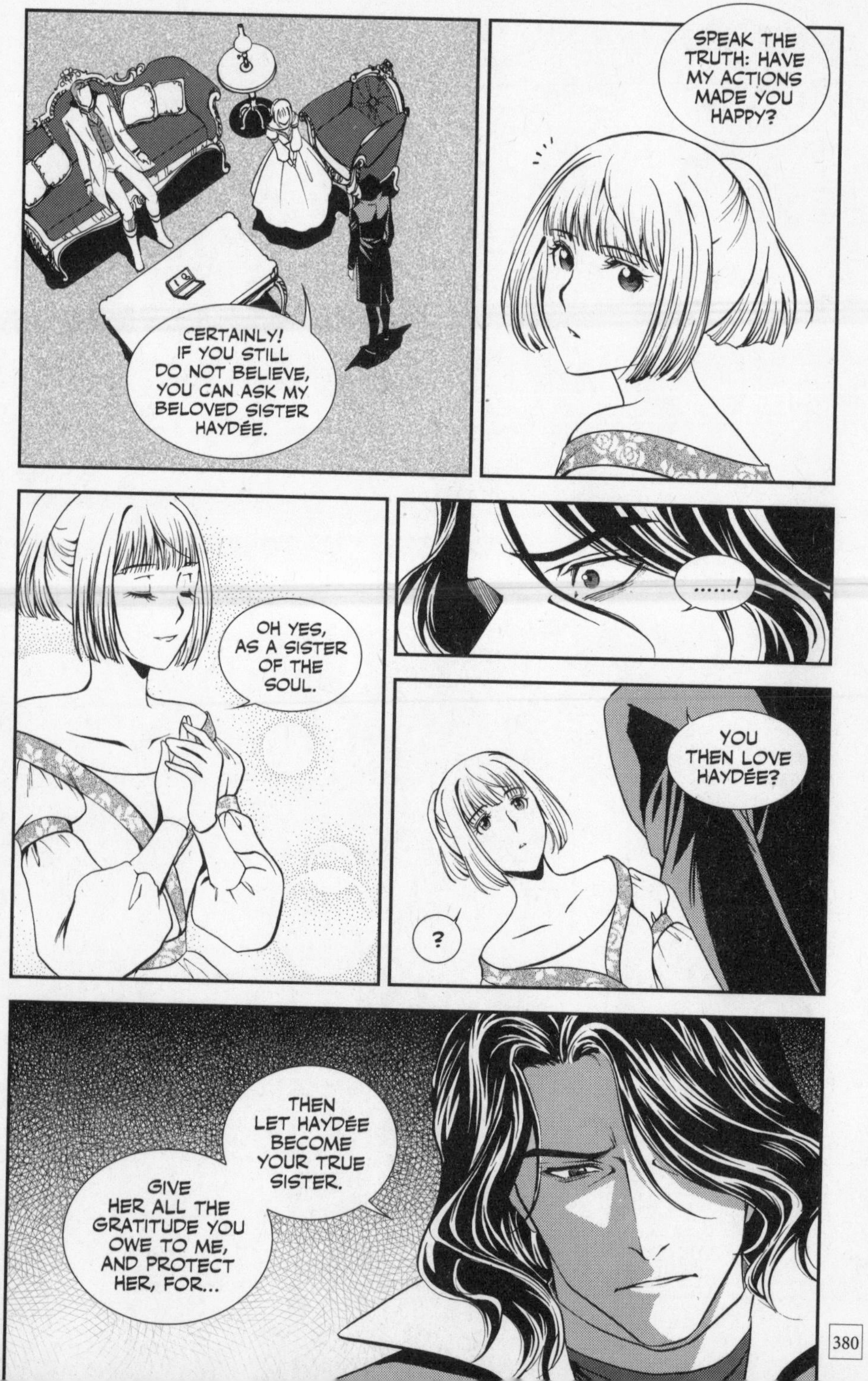
SPEAK THE TRUTH: HAVE MY ACTIONS MADE YOU HAPPY?
CERTAINLY! IF YOU STILL DO NOT BELIEVE, YOU CAN ASK MY BELOVED SISTER HAYDÉE.
......!
YOU THEN LOVE HAYDÉE?
?
OH YES, AS A SISTER OF THE SOUL.
THEN LET HAYDÉE BECOME YOUR TRUE SISTER.
GIVE HER ALL THE GRATITUDE YOU OWE TO ME, AND PROTECT HER, FOR...

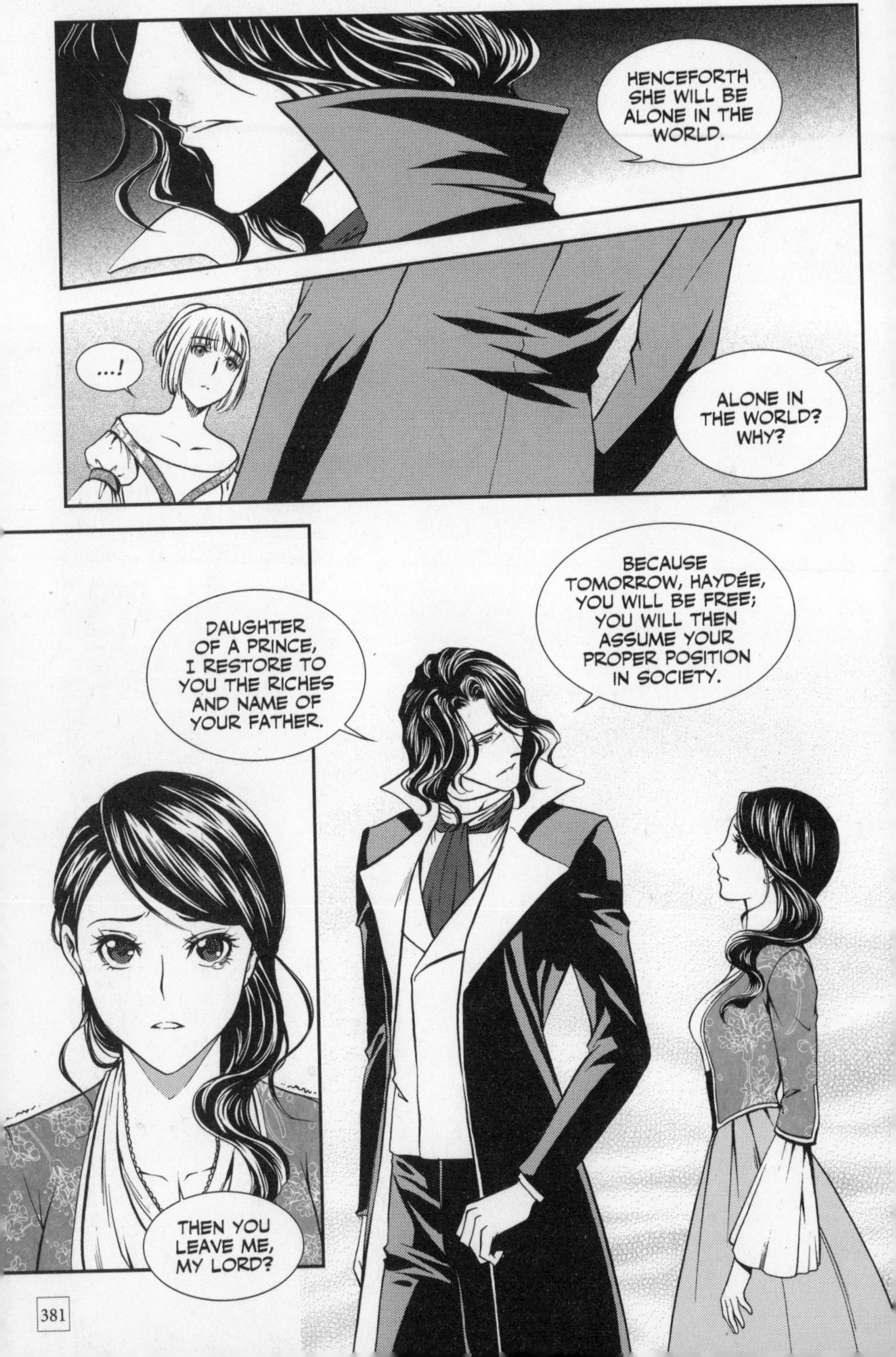
HENCEFORTH SHE WILL BE ALONE IN THE WORLD.
ALONE IN THE WORLD? WHY?
...!
BECAUSE TOMORROW, HAYDÉE, YOU WILL BE FREE; YOU WILL THEN ASSUME YOUR PROPER POSITION IN SOCIETY.
DAUGHTER OF A PRINCE, I RESTORE TO YOU THE RICHES AND NAME OF YOUR FATHER.
THEN YOU LEAVE ME, MY LORD?

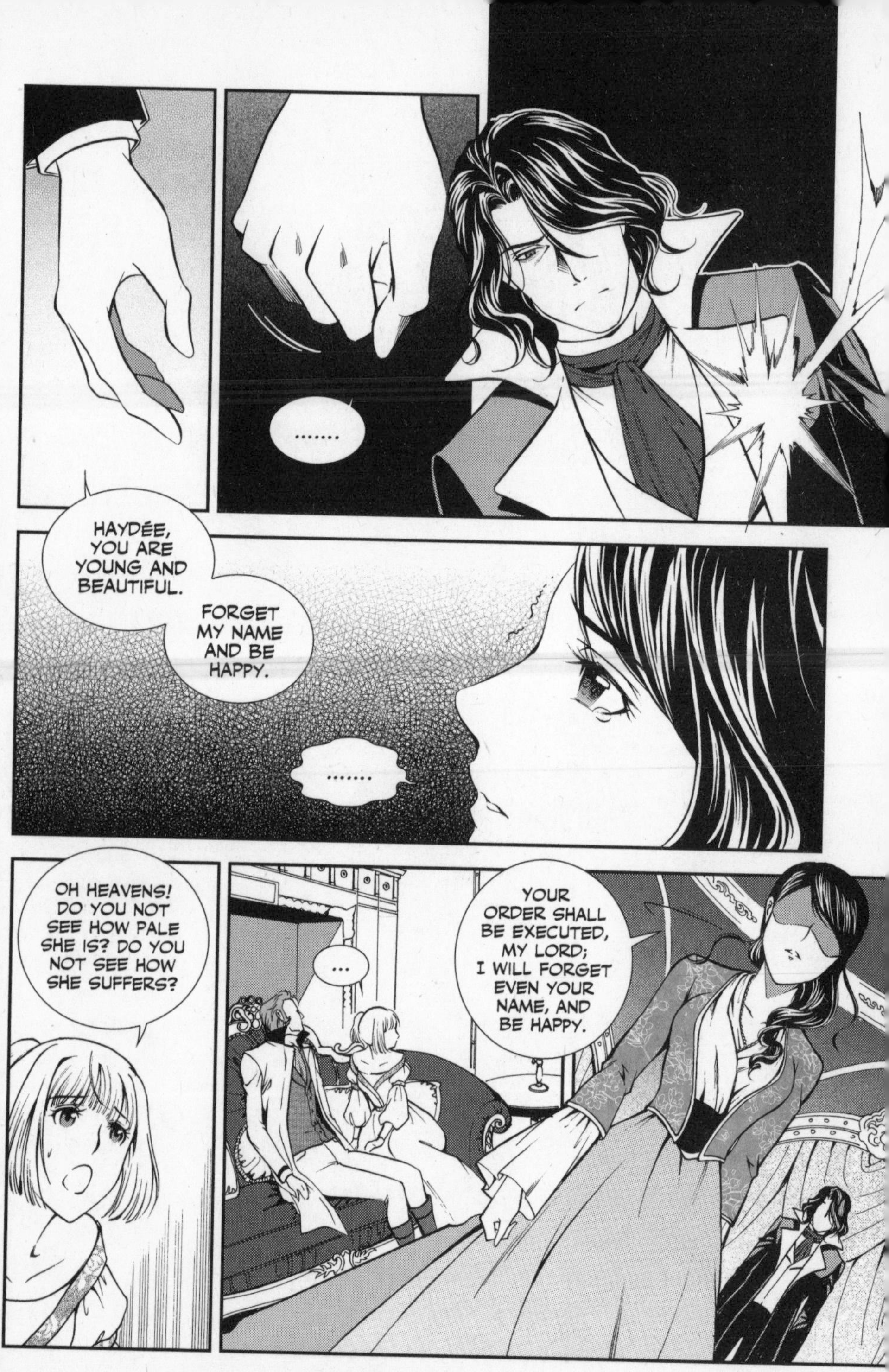
....
HAYDÉE, YOU ARE YOUNG AND BEAUTIFUL.
FORGET MY NAME AND BE HAPPY.
....
YOUR ORDER SHALL BE EXECUTED, MY LORD; I WILL FORGET EVEN YOUR NAME, AND BE HAPPY.
...
OH HEAVENS! DO YOU NOT SEE HOW PALE SHE IS? DO YOU NOT SEE HOW SHE SUFFERS?

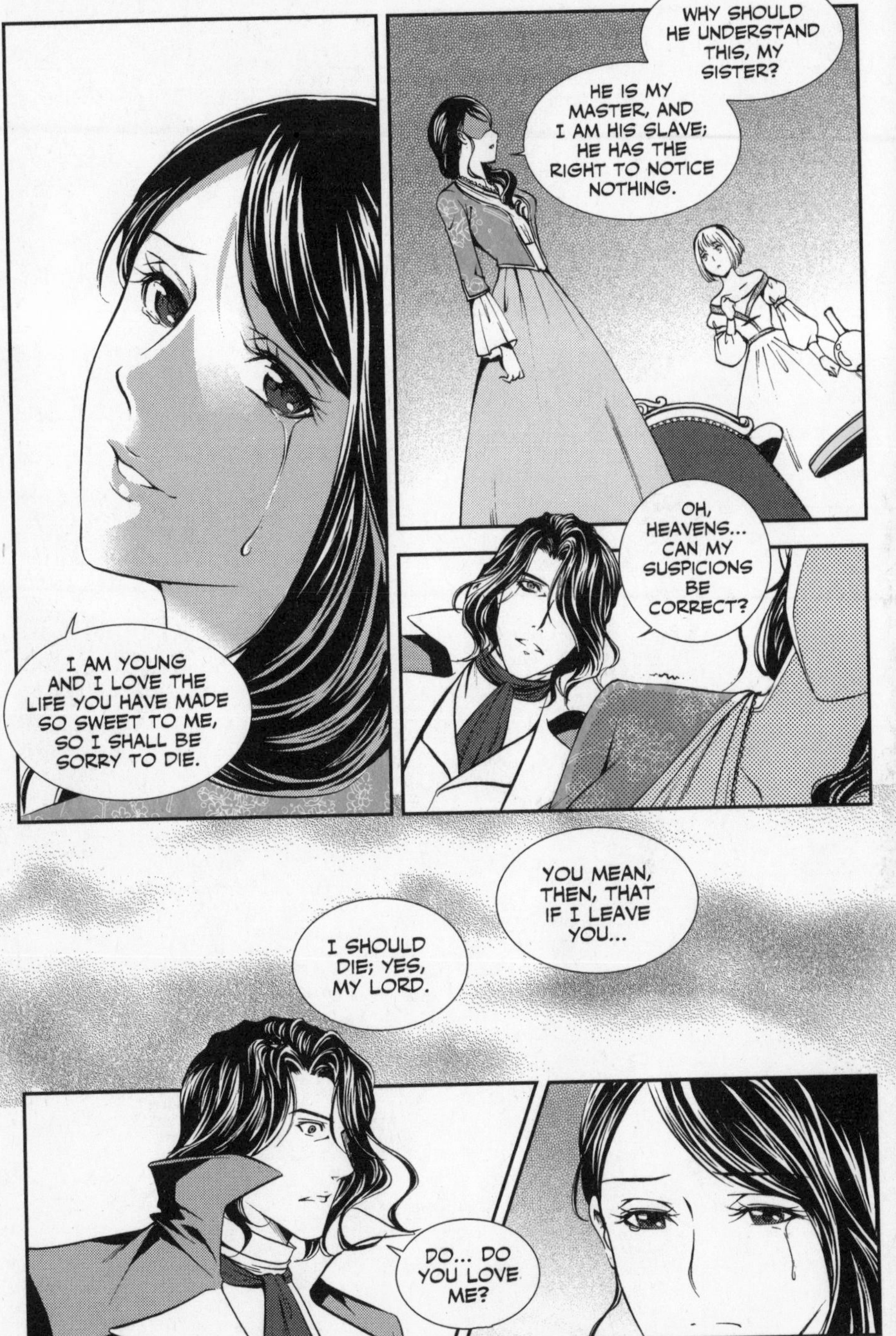
WHY SHOULD HE UNDERSTAND THIS, MY SISTER?
HE IS MY MASTER, AND I AM HIS SLAVE; HE HAS THE RIGHT TO NOTICE NOTHING.
OH, HEAVENS... CAN MY SUSPICIONS BE CORRECT?
I AM YOUNG AND I LOVE THE LIFE YOU HAVE MADE SO SWEET TO ME, SO I SHALL BE SORRY TO DIE.
YOU MEAN, THEN, THAT IF I LEAVE YOU...
I SHOULD DIE; YES, MY LORD.
DO... DO YOU LOVE ME?

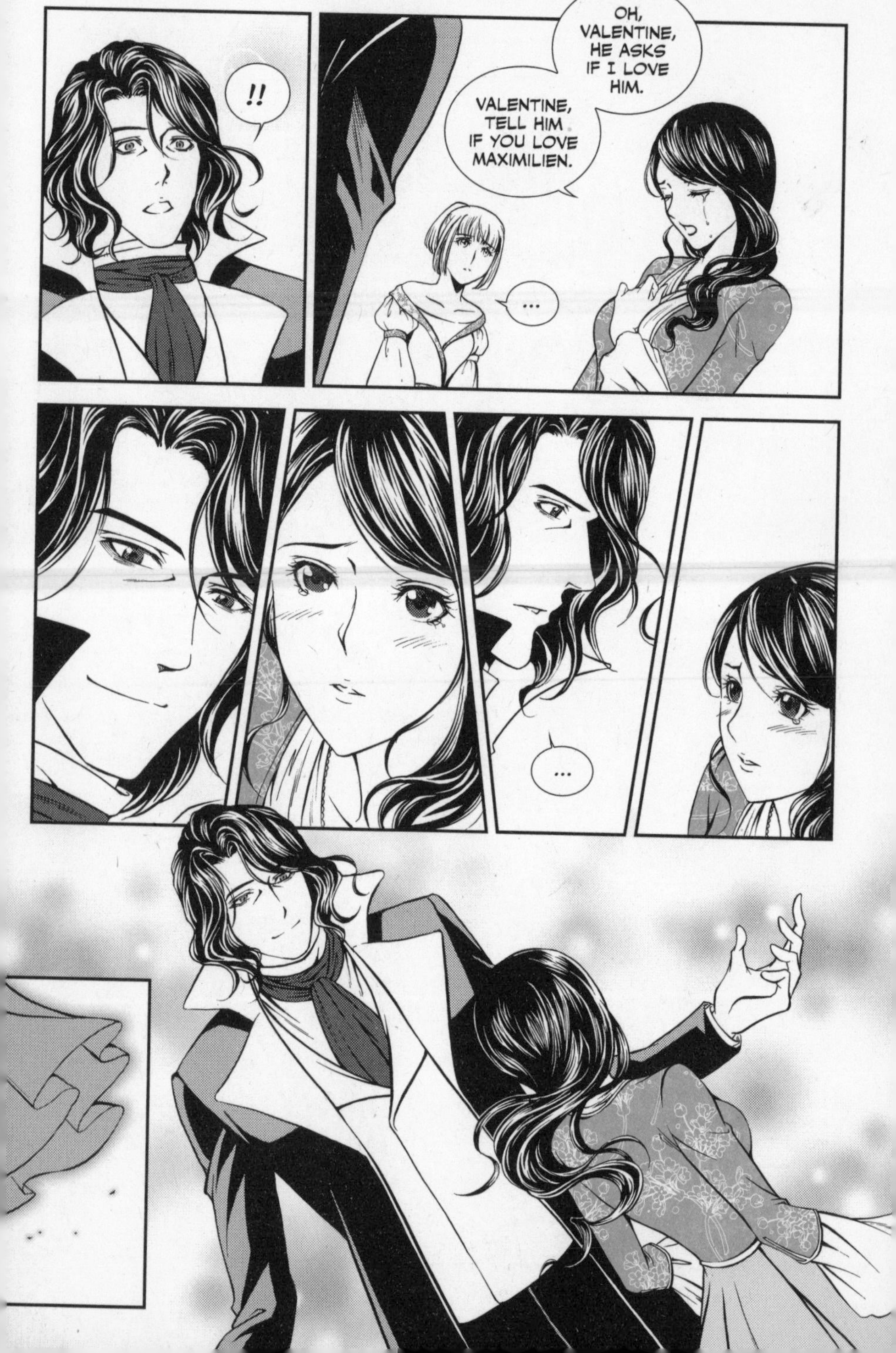
OH, VALENTINE, HE ASKS IF I LOVE HIM.
VALENTINE, TELL HIM IF YOU LOVE MAXIMILIEN.
...
!!
...

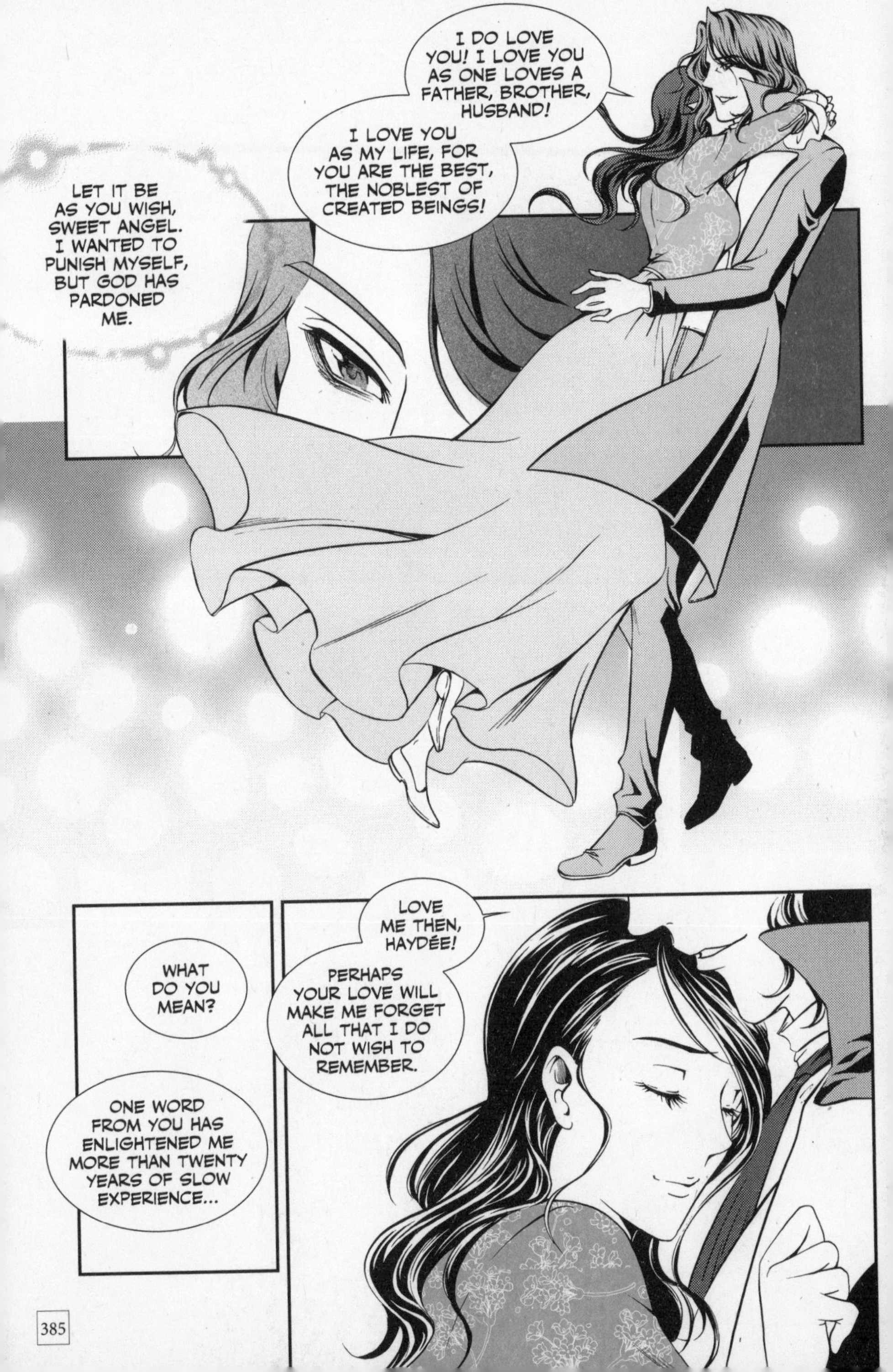
I DO LOVE YOU! I LOVE YOU AS ONE LOVES A FATHER, BROTHER, HUSBAND!
I LOVE YOU AS MY LIFE, FOR YOU ARE THE BEST, THE NOBLEST OF CREATED BEINGS!
LET IT BE AS YOU WISH, SWEET ANGEL. I WANTED TO PUNISH MYSELF, BUT GOD HAS PARDONED ME.
LOVE ME THEN, HAYDÉE!
PERHAPS YOUR LOVE WILL MAKE ME FORGET ALL THAT I DO NOT WISH TO REMEMBER.
WHAT DO YOU MEAN?
ONE WORD FROM YOU HAS ENLIGHTENED ME MORE THAN TWENTY YEARS OF SLOW EXPERIENCE...

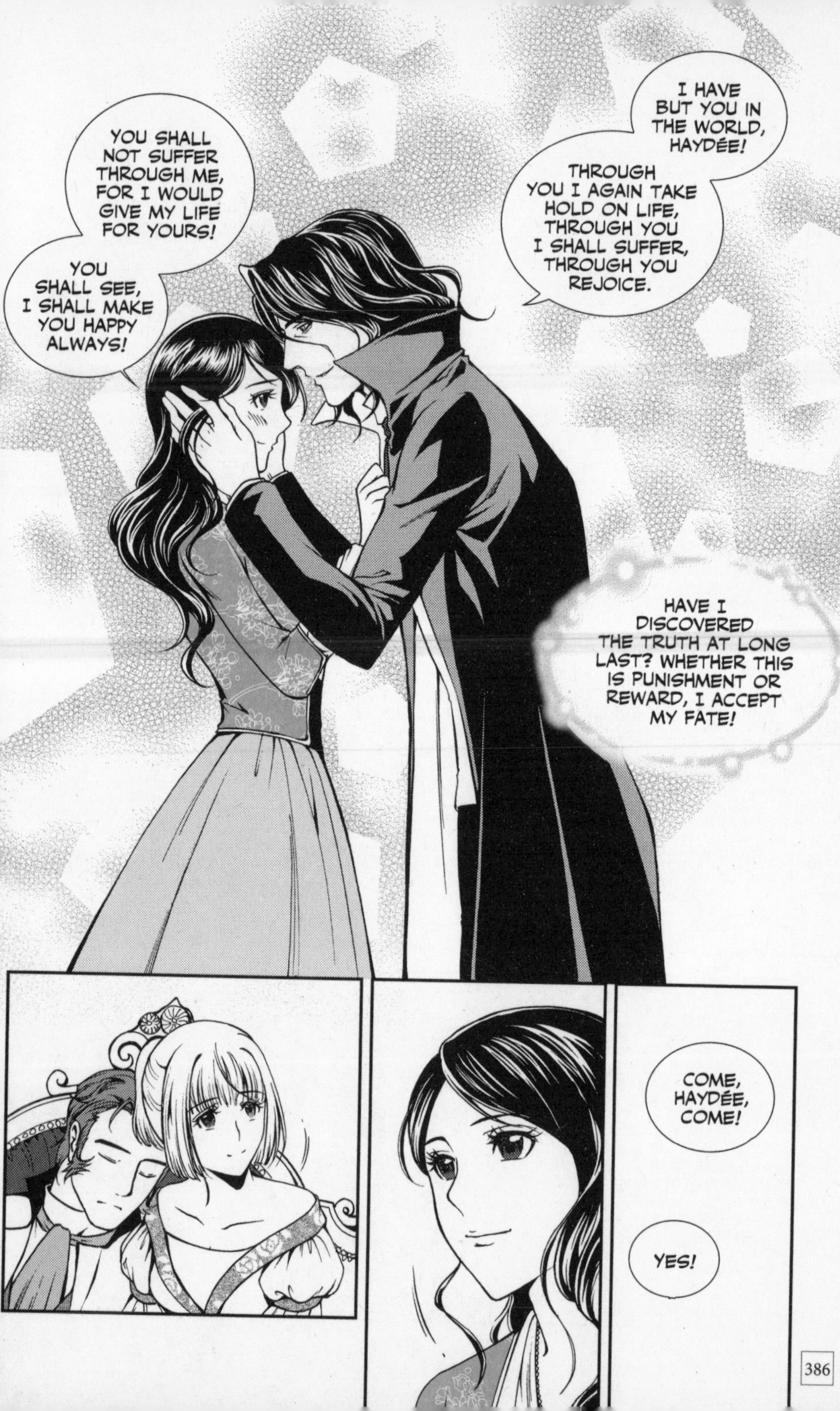
I HAVE BUT YOU IN THE WORLD, HAYDÉE!
THROUGH YOU I AGAIN TAKE HOLD ON LIFE, THROUGH YOU I SHALL SUFFER, THROUGH YOU REJOICE.
YOU SHALL NOT SUFFER THROUGH ME, FOR I WOULD GIVE MY LIFE FOR YOURS!
YOU SHALL SEE, I SHALL MAKE YOU HAPPY ALWAYS!
HAVE I DISCOVERED THE TRUTH AT LONG LAST? WHETHER THIS IS PUNISHMENT OR REWARD, I ACCEPT MY FATE!
COME, HAYDÉE, COME!
YES!

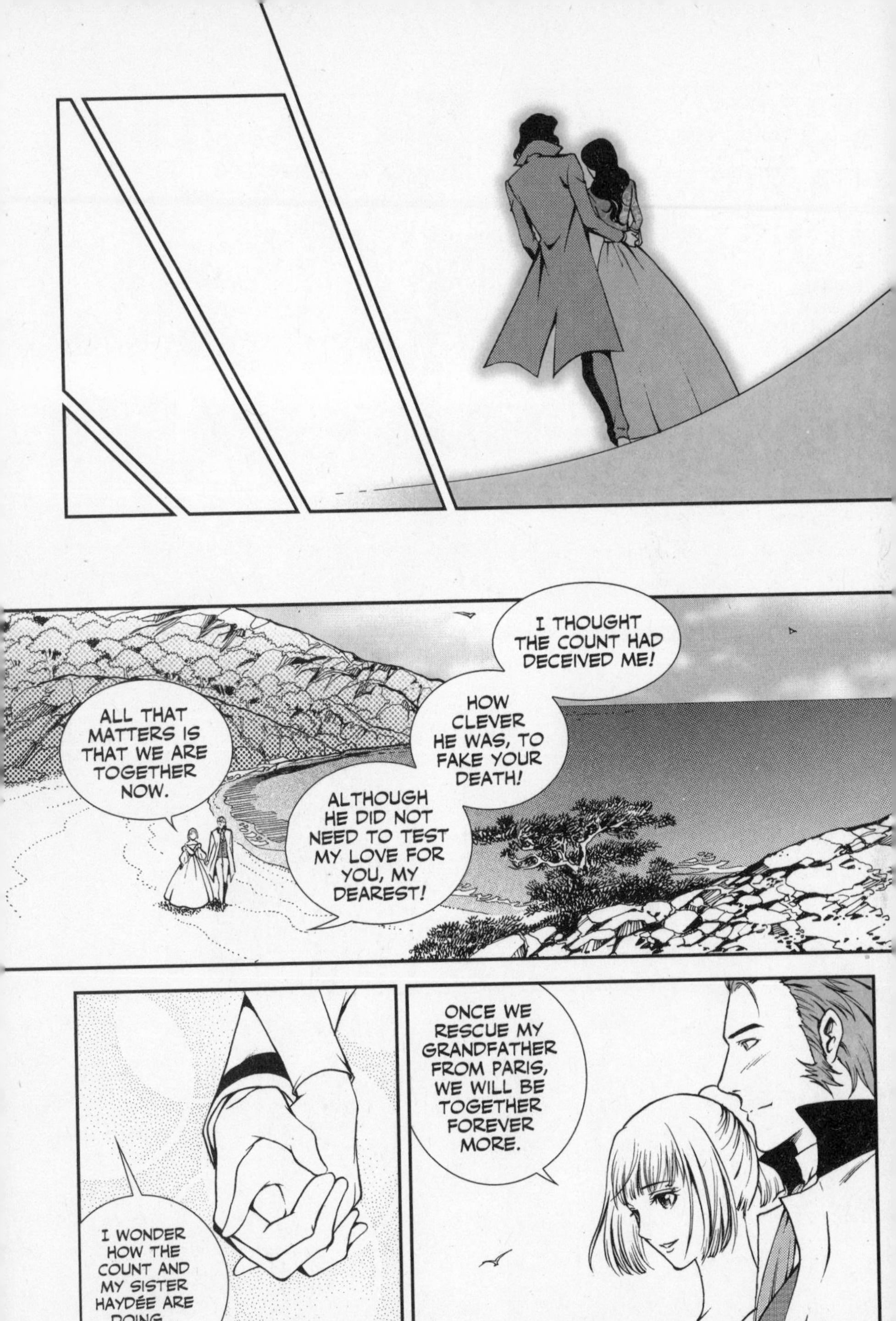
I THOUGHT THE COUNT HAD DECEIVED ME!
HOW CLEVER HE WAS, TO FAKE YOUR DEATH!
ALTHOUGH HE DID NOT NEED TO TEST MY LOVE FOR YOU, MY DEAREST!
ALL THAT MATTERS IS THAT WE ARE TOGETHER NOW.
ONCE WE RESCUE MY GRANDFATHER FROM PARIS, WE WILL BE TOGETHER FOREVER MORE.
I WONDER HOW THE COUNT AND MY SISTER HAYDÉE ARE DOING...

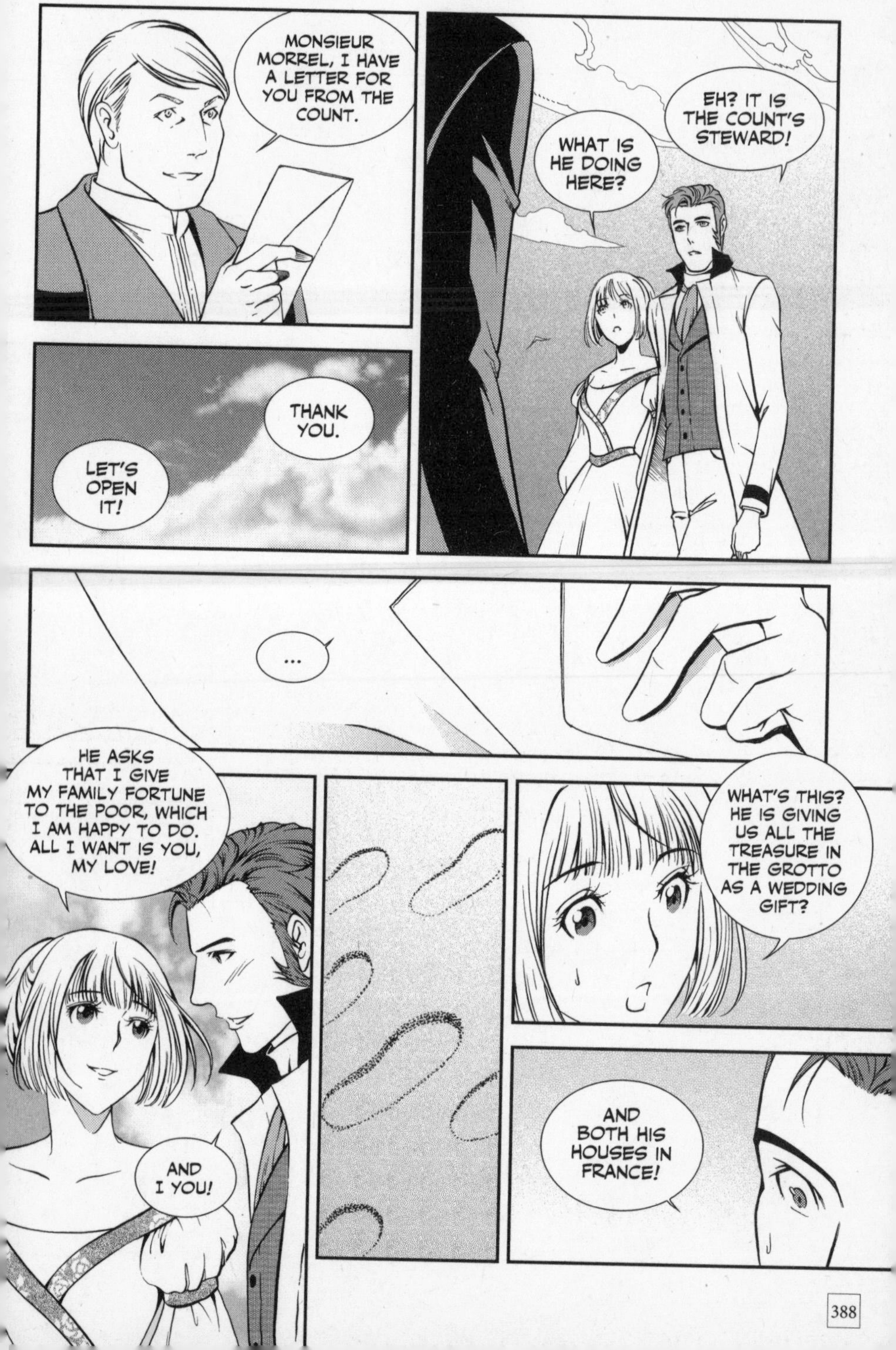
EH? IT IS THE COUNT'S STEWARD!
WHAT IS HE DOING HERE?
MONSIEUR MORREL, I HAVE A LETTER FOR YOU FROM THE COUNT.
THANK YOU.
LET'S OPEN IT!
...
WHAT'S THIS? HE IS GIVING US ALL THE TREASURE IN THE GROTTO AS A WEDDING GIFT?
AND BOTH HIS HOUSES IN FRANCE!
HE ASKS THAT I GIVE MY FAMILY FORTUNE TO THE POOR, WHICH I AM HAPPY TO DO. ALL I WANT IS YOU, MY LOVE!
AND I YOU!

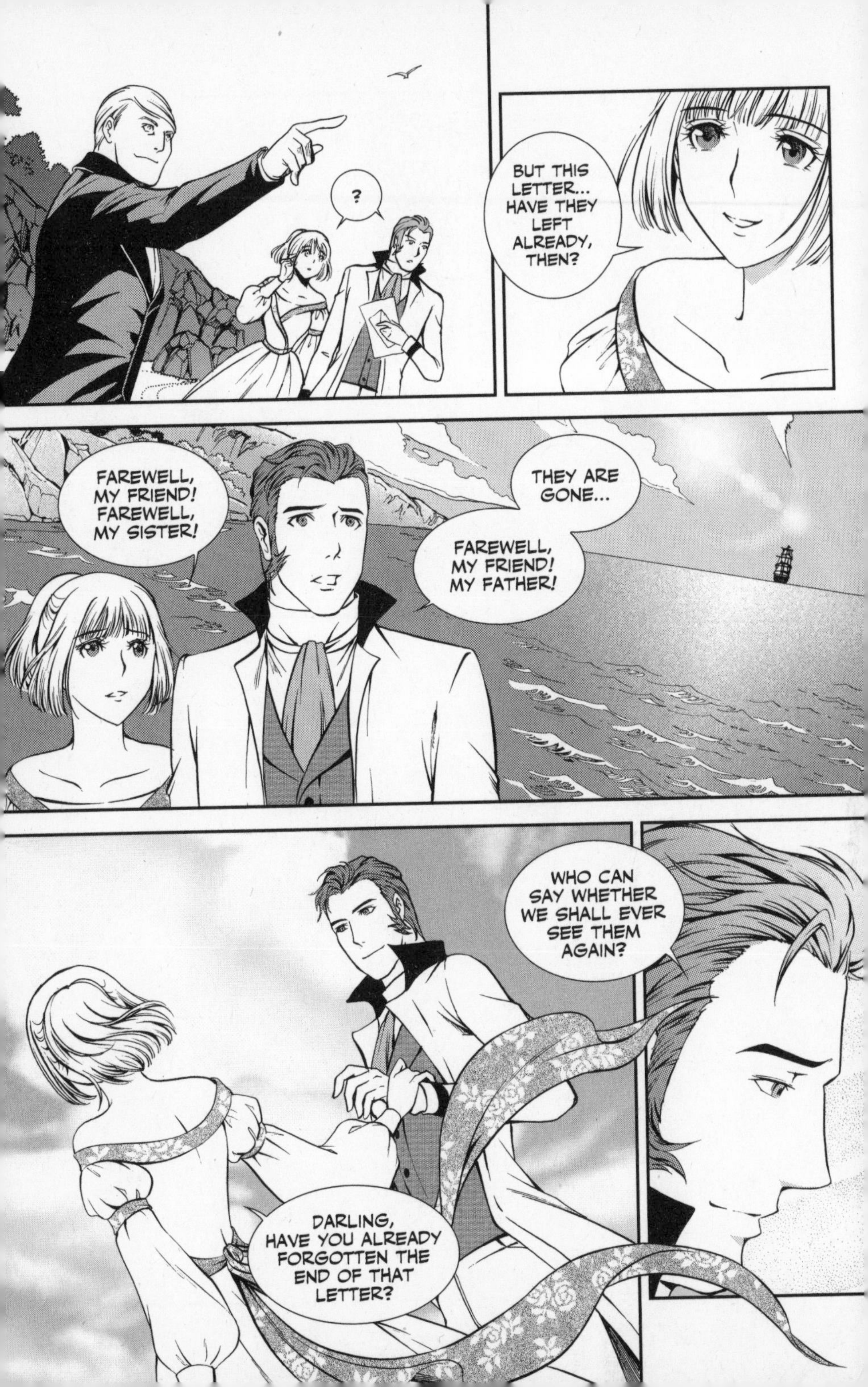
BUT THIS LETTER... HAVE THEY LEFT ALREADY, THEN?
?
THEY ARE GONE...
FAREWELL, MY FRIEND! MY FATHER!
FAREWELL, MY FRIEND! FAREWELL, MY SISTER!
WHO CAN SAY WHETHER WE SHALL EVER SEE THEM AGAIN?
DARLING, HAVE YOU ALREADY FORGOTTEN THE END OF THAT LETTER?

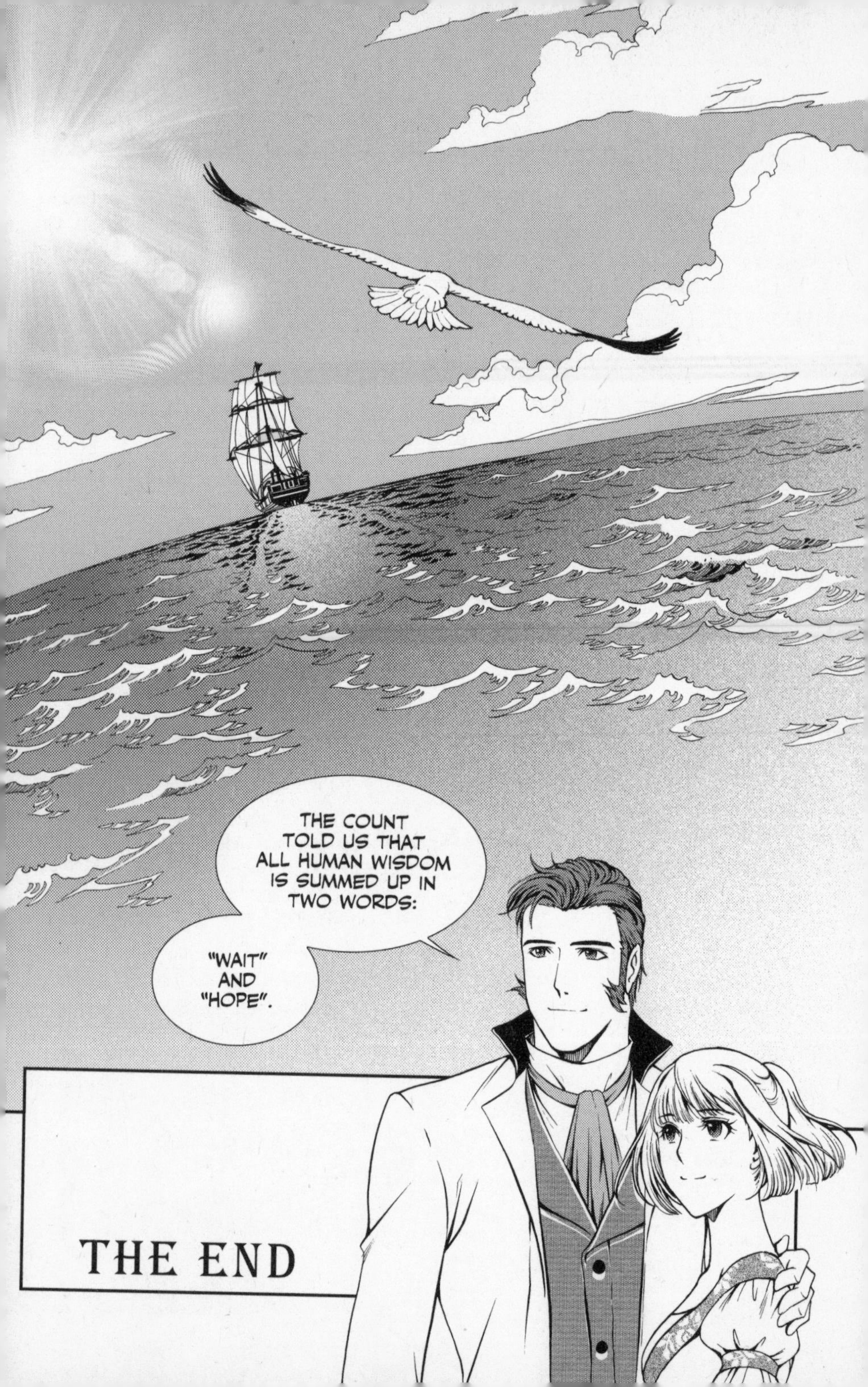
THE COUNT TOLD US THAT ALL HUMAN WISDOM IS SUMMED UP IN TWO WORDS:
"WAIT" AND "HOPE".
THE END

CRYSTAL S. CHAN:
THE ADAPTATION OF MONTE CRISTO

The Count of Monte Cristo is one of Alexandre Dumas' greatest works. Its huge and complex plot and vast ensemble of characters make it the most complex story that *Manga Classics* has taken on to date! Our biggest challenge, then, was figuring out how to trim the story while still staying true to the spirit of the original, and our team worked hard to fit as much plot into every panel as we possibly could. Let me share my process with you!

RULES OF TRIMMING:

The original book has a rich plot, full of twists and turns - and it's huge, even compared to other books of the time! Our priority was to make the main storyline both easy to understand and interesting to read. Based on this, we decided to remove all the details and digressions that did not fit into the main story. Since the book is called *The Count of Monte Cristo*, our focus was very clear: it is about the Count of Monte Cristo. More to the point, it is about how he took his revenge on those who did him wrong while also repaying the man who helped him. Therefore, some readers may be curious as to why there are stories about people besides the Count in the manga version of the story.

For example, take Maximilien Morrel and Valentine de Villefort. Their secret relationship did not seem to have much to do with the Count at first, but soon we discover that they were tied to him by their backgrounds: Valentine was the daughter of his hated enemy, Gérard de Villefort, while Maximilien was the son of his benefactor, Pierre Morrel. When Maximilien realized that someone was trying to kill Valentine, he went to the Count for help, unwittingly forcing the Count into a conundrum: should he repay Morrel by helping his son, or should he revenge himself on de Villefort by letting his daughter die? This is a fascinating subplot, and it develops into an important part of the main plot - so we foreshadowed the relationship at the beginning of the story in order to enhance the decisive moment in which the Count is driven to decide.

On the other hand, Edmond Dantès' escape from prison and his finding of the treasure are both crucial elements of his vengeance - so why did I simplify these details? In the end, I decided that what was important was not how he escaped and found the treasure, but how he used his newfound riches to take his revenge. I simplified these parts because they were less important to the main story, which is ultimately about vengeance.

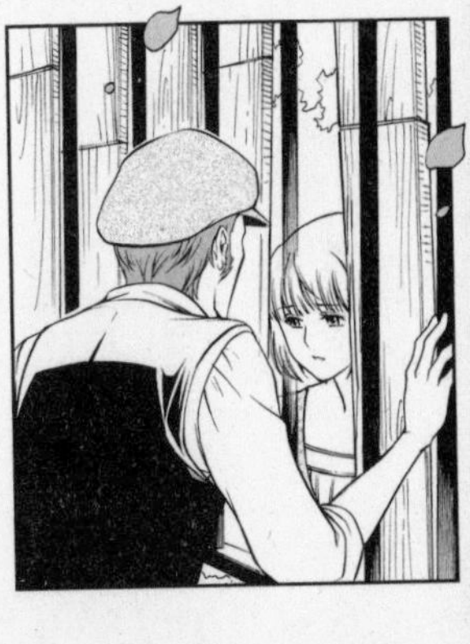

Continues on Page 2...

2. Madame Danglars knows that de Villefort has checked the Count's background and does not think it to be suspicious at all. Therefore, we learn that she believes that she does not have to worry that their affair has been discovered.

3. When Albert introduces Maximilien to Valentine's stepmother Héloïse, she treats him coldly, implying that she does not accept him as a potential son-in-law. This makes it easy to see why Maximilien and Valentine have to keep their relationship a secret.

4. Maximilien and Valentine are thrilled to see each other at the ball because of their love for one another; this helps to prepare readers for the moment when Maximilien begs the Count to help his beloved, and sets up parts of the ending as well.

5. When Andrea Cavalcanti first meets Eugénie Danglars, he tries very hard to flatter her, demonstrating his desire for her and setting up his eventual request for her hand in marriage. Since she is engaged to Albert, it is easy for the Count to incite Andrea to look into de Morcerf's betrayal of Ali Tebelen.

6. Related to point five, when the Count implies to Danglars that de Morcerf's secret was to be found in Greece, Danglars is pointed in the right direction to further the Count's revenge.

7. Lastly, Mercédès' reaction to the Count's presence makes it very clear that she still has feelings for him, despite everything that has happened.

This scene at the Morcerfs' ball seems so short and quiet, but it is so full of important details! Many other scenes in the manga are similarly packed full of information, too many for me to detail here – if you're interested in all these hidden details, we hope you'll look for them in the original book as well!

Continues on Page 4...

...Continued from Page 1

Foreshadowing is also important in helping plot elements fit into the story. If a plot element suddenly appears with no warning, it feels odd, so I foreshadowed those elements as needed. Why did I spend seven pages having Haydée tell the story of her birth to Albert? Because Haydée would be testifying against Fernand in a later chapter, and waiting until that point to have her reveal her background would make it feel like that plot element came out of nowhere. Since Fernand's hearing is very important to the Count's revenge, I decided to have Haydée talk about herself earlier in the story in order to make the plot flow well.

There is one other simple way to trim a plot, of course: you can remove a character. While we were preparing this adaptation, the production team suggested cutting out one of the Count's three enemies to make more room for the other two. The artist and I disagreed with this suggestion, since the stories of those three characters were all densely interwoven (and also because the goal of *Manga Classics* is to be as faithful to the original work as possible). It would have been difficult to remove one of these three enemies without creating obvious plot holes, so we insisted that they all be included, and they were.

CONDENSING THE PLOTS:

The Count of Monte Cristo is far too complex to be adapted for manga without some trimming. We could use narration, of course, but it isn't really manga if we rely too much on boxes full of narrative! Fortunately, thanks to the nature of manga, we were able to combine many chapters full of digression into short yet complex scenes, like the one at the Morcerfs' ball in chapter five. In this instance, we were able to condense three chapters of the original book into just seven pages! Since all of the main characters were present, I was also able to foreshadow many of the events to come:

1. We learn that it is well known that Albert has a good relationship with the Count. Thus, when Albert learns that it was the Count who ruined his father's reputation, it is easier to see why he is so furious.

The scenes of Edmond in prison had already been drawn when I went to visit the Château. We had done our best using pictures available online, but we were forced to invent some of the details ourselves. Once I visited the Château, however, I realized how different the real thing is. I took a lot of pictures and showed them to the team, and we decided to fix the relevant scenes accordingly. A lot of backgrounds had to be redrawn, but that's how much attention we pay to the details here at *Manga Classics*!

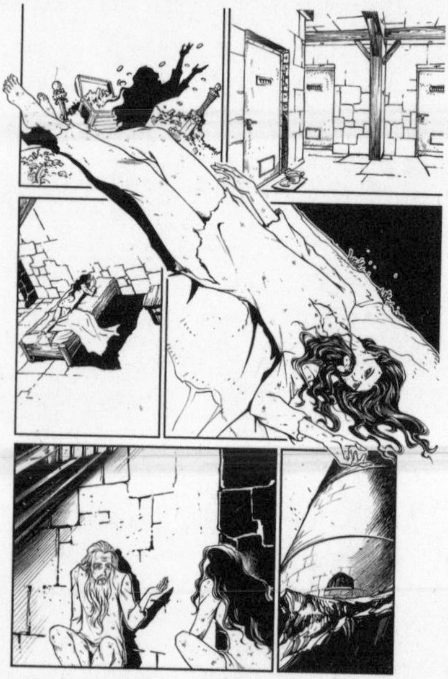

OLD VERSION

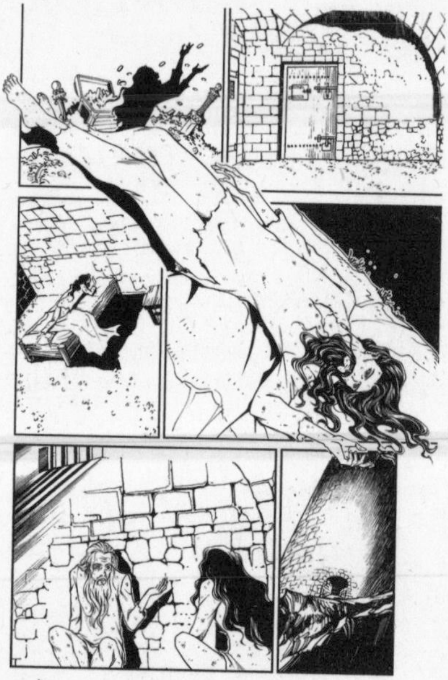

NEW VERSION

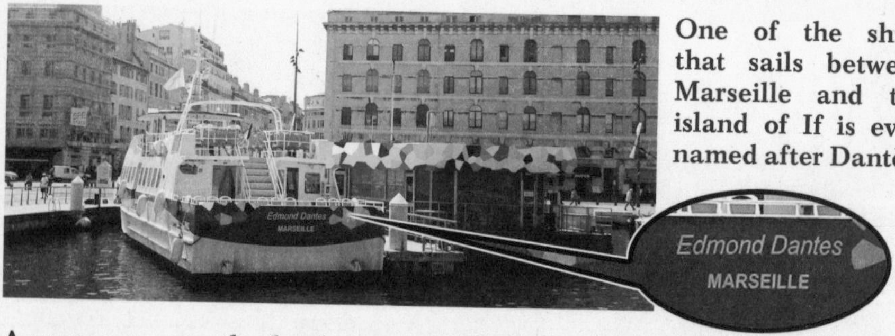
Edmond Dantes
MARSEILLE

One of the ships that sails between Marseille and the island of If is even named after Dantès!

As you can see, the book was a challenge to adapt to manga, with its complicated plot and hundreds of small - but important! - details. I tried my best to tell the story in a limited amount of space without removing any important characters or plot elements, which took a lot of effort. I hope everyone enjoys this condensed version of *The Count of Monte Cristo*!

Crystal (Silvermoon) Chan

...Continued from Page 3

ON LOCATION!!

Many of the locations in *The Count of Monte Cristo* are real places, and some even became popular tourist destinations because of the book. It made the preliminary research fun for me, and eventually sparked my interest in visiting those spots in person.

In order to satisfy this desire, I traveled to France and visited a few of the book's locations. They're much more impressive in person than they are in pictures. I could almost feel the presence of the characters!

The place that impacted me the most was the Château d'If. The prison plays an important role in the story, and - just like in the book - it became a big tourist spot in reality. When I arrived I felt just like the Count, visiting it at the end of the book! As I followed in his footsteps, imagining how he must have felt as he was stripped of his freedoms, I came to really comprehend how furiously revenge must have burned in the Count's heart. It became clear to me why he was willing to enact his revenge at all costs, even if it meant taking down an innocent child in the process.

CHARACTER RELATIONSHIP GUIDE

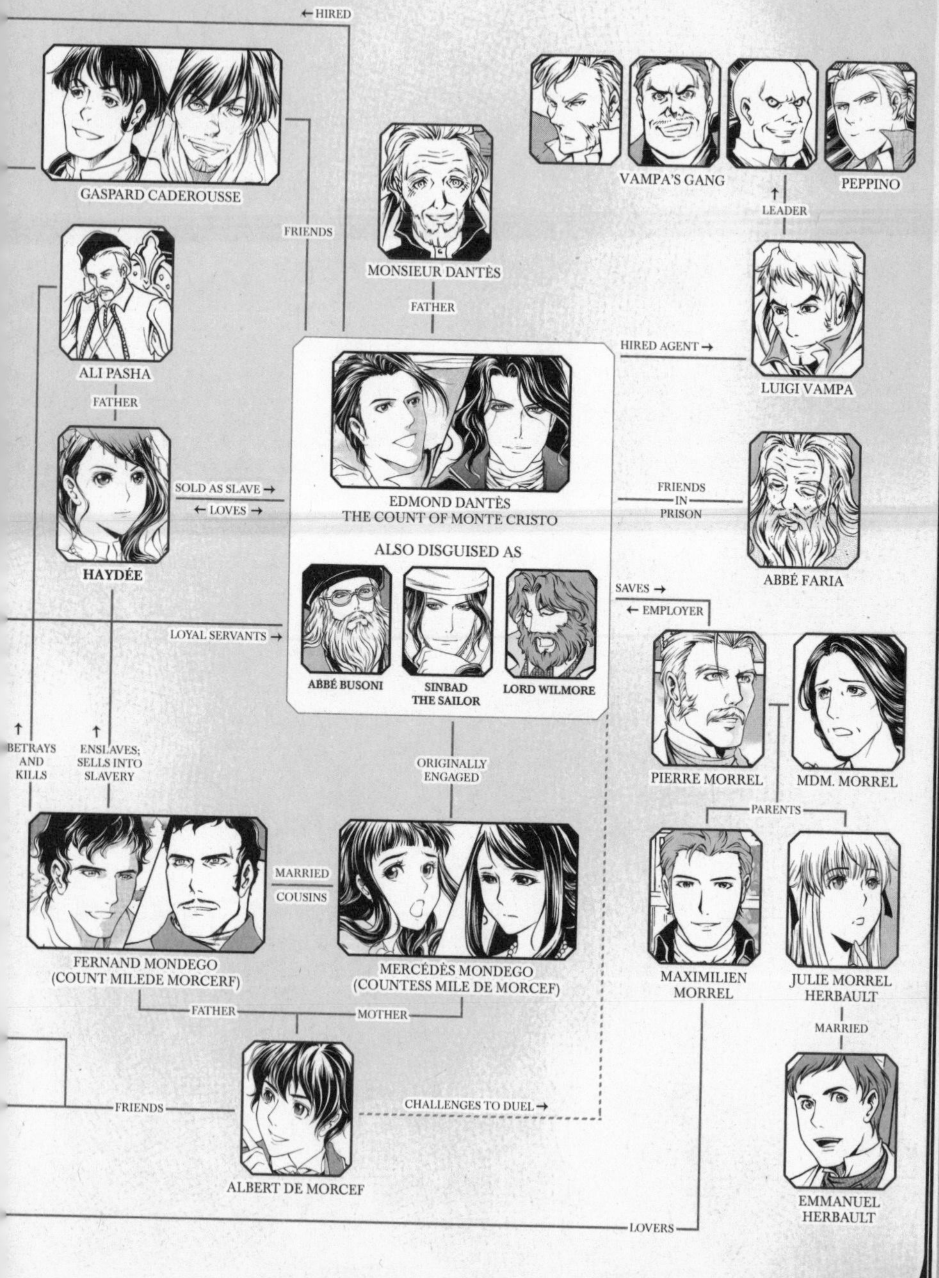

← HIRED
GASPARD CADEROUSSE
FRIENDS
MONSIEUR DANTÈS
FATHER
VAMPA'S GANG
PEPPINO
LEADER
HIRED AGENT →
LUIGI VAMPA
ALI PASHA
FATHER
EDMOND DANTÈS
THE COUNT OF MONTE CRISTO
SOLD AS SLAVE →
← LOVES →
HAYDÉE
FRIENDS IN PRISON
ABBÉ FARIA
ALSO DISGUISED AS
ABBÉ BUSONI
SINBAD THE SAILOR
LORD WILMORE
SAVES →
← EMPLOYER
LOYAL SERVANTS →
BETRAYS AND KILLS
ENSLAVES; SELLS INTO SLAVERY
ORIGINALLY ENGAGED
PIERRE MORREL
MDM. MORREL
PARENTS
MARRIED
COUSINS
FERNAND MONDEGO
(COUNT MILEDE MORCERF)
MERCÉDÈS MONDEGO
(COUNTESS MILE DE MORCEF)
MAXIMILIEN MORREL
JULIE MORREL HERBAULT
FATHER
MOTHER
MARRIED
FRIENDS
CHALLENGES TO DUEL →
ALBERT DE MORCEF
EMMANUEL HERBAULT
LOVERS

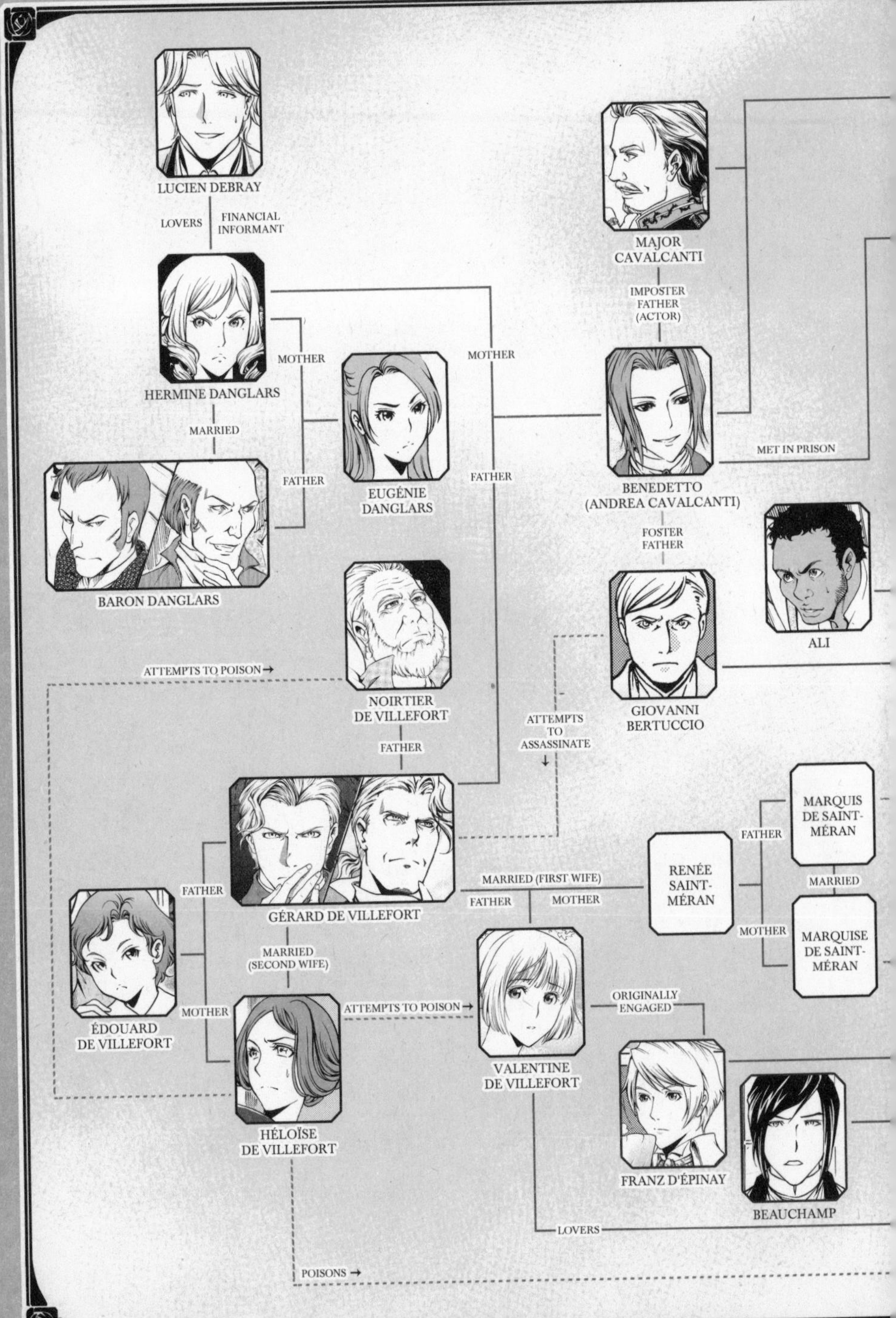

LUCIEN DEBRAY
LOVERS
FINANCIAL INFORMANT
HERMINE DANGLARS
MARRIED
BARON DANGLARS
MOTHER
FATHER
EUGÉNIE DANGLARS
MOTHER
FATHER
MAJOR CAVALCANTI
IMPOSTER FATHER (ACTOR)
BENEDETTO (ANDREA CAVALCANTI)
MET IN PRISON
FOSTER FATHER
GIOVANNI BERTUCCIO
ALI
NOIRTIER DE VILLEFORT
ATTEMPTS TO POISON →
ATTEMPTS TO ASSASSINATE ↓
FATHER
GÉRARD DE VILLEFORT
MARRIED (FIRST WIFE)
FATHER
MOTHER
RENÉE SAINT-MÉRAN
FATHER
MARQUIS DE SAINT-MÉRAN
MARRIED
MOTHER
MARQUISE DE SAINT-MÉRAN
FATHER
MOTHER
ÉDOUARD DE VILLEFORT
MARRIED (SECOND WIFE)
HÉLOÏSE DE VILLEFORT
ATTEMPTS TO POISON →
VALENTINE DE VILLEFORT
ORIGINALLY ENGAGED
FRANZ D'ÉPINAY
BEAUCHAMP
LOVERS
POISONS →

HAYDÉE

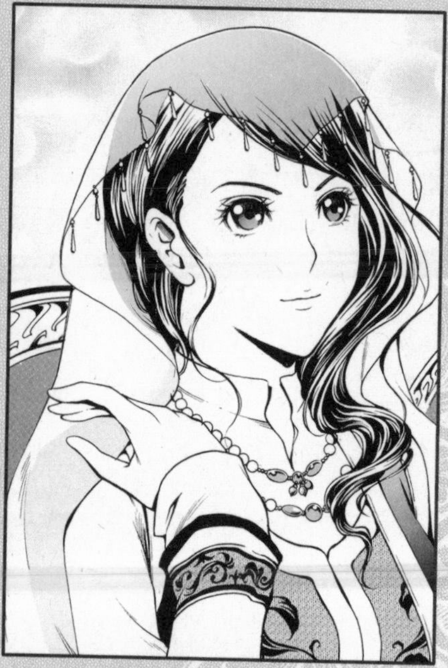

Haydée is also one of my favorite characters. A woman with a sad past, she is strong and courageous as well as beautiful; I was the most impressed by the scene where she testifies against Count de Morcerf. She was deeply in love with the Count, who did not realize this at all - he was so unaware that he kept trying to find someone else to marry her! I felt a lot of pity for Haydée and I am glad that she got her happy ending at last.

She was the hardest character to draw because there were so few photographic references for her outfit, which was very important, as she wore the clothes of her homeland all the time in the original book. She was also hard to draw because I worked so hard to make her as beautiful as possible every time!

ALBERT DE MORCERF

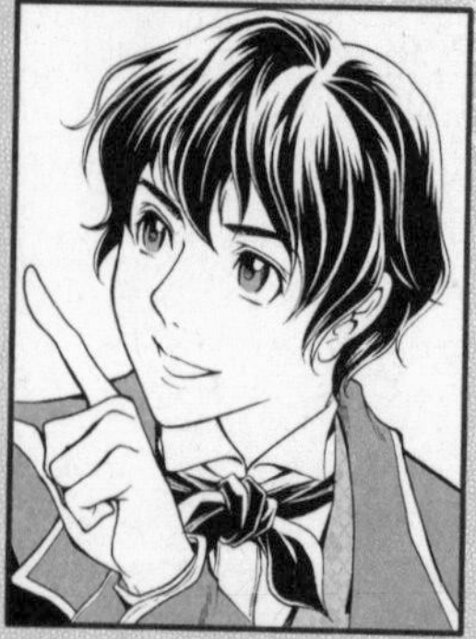

I did not come up with a satisfying design for this character until I was almost ready to start drawing the manga. His face was like his mother's, and his curly hair was like his father's, and that was that. I did not like him at first because he was frivolous, but I learned to like him by the end, as he was also kind and sincere.

VALENTINE DE VILLEFORT

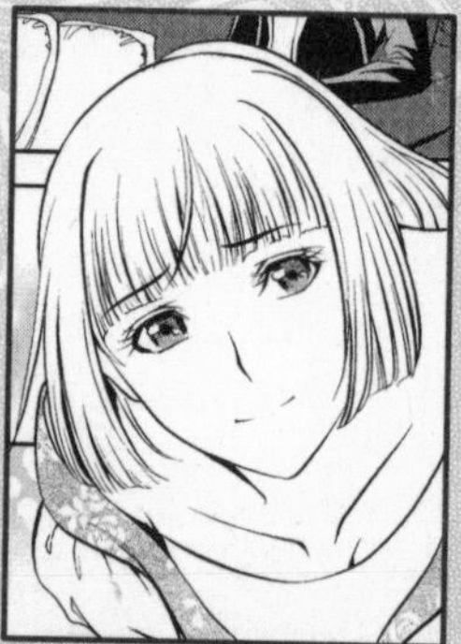

Valentine is another of my favorite characters. She seems so fragile, but at heart, she is very strong - even stronger than her lover Maximilien! I thought that her disposition was similar to Haydée's, which explains why they became good friends at the end.

I seldom draw hair cut like hers, but it was pretty handy to draw~!

Nokman Poon

DESIGNING THE CHARACTERS

Hello! This is Nokman, artist of this Manga Classics book! I would like to take this chance to share with you my thoughts about desiging some of the key characters!

EDMOND DANTÈS / THE COUNT OF MONTE CRISTO

Edmond was my favorite character in the book: very cool and a little bit evil, with the bearing of an emperor. He started life as a kind person, but his terrible experiences twisted him into a calculating, vengeful man.

Designing the characters for this manga was indeed a challenge, and I went through lots of pictures of good-looking actors and models to find the proper look for Edmond. Finally, I realized that the perfect model was one of the princes of Monaco, who has been described as the most handsome man in the world. My design for Edmond is based on this man, along with a healthy amount of my own imagination.

In the original book, the Count had a beard. He used fake beards in a number of his disguises, though, and he had a long beard while he was in jail, so I made him clean-shaven to make him look visually distinct. (Also, having the Count tear a fake beard off his real beard did not look cool enough – and it was painful for me to imagine.) I hope you like his design!

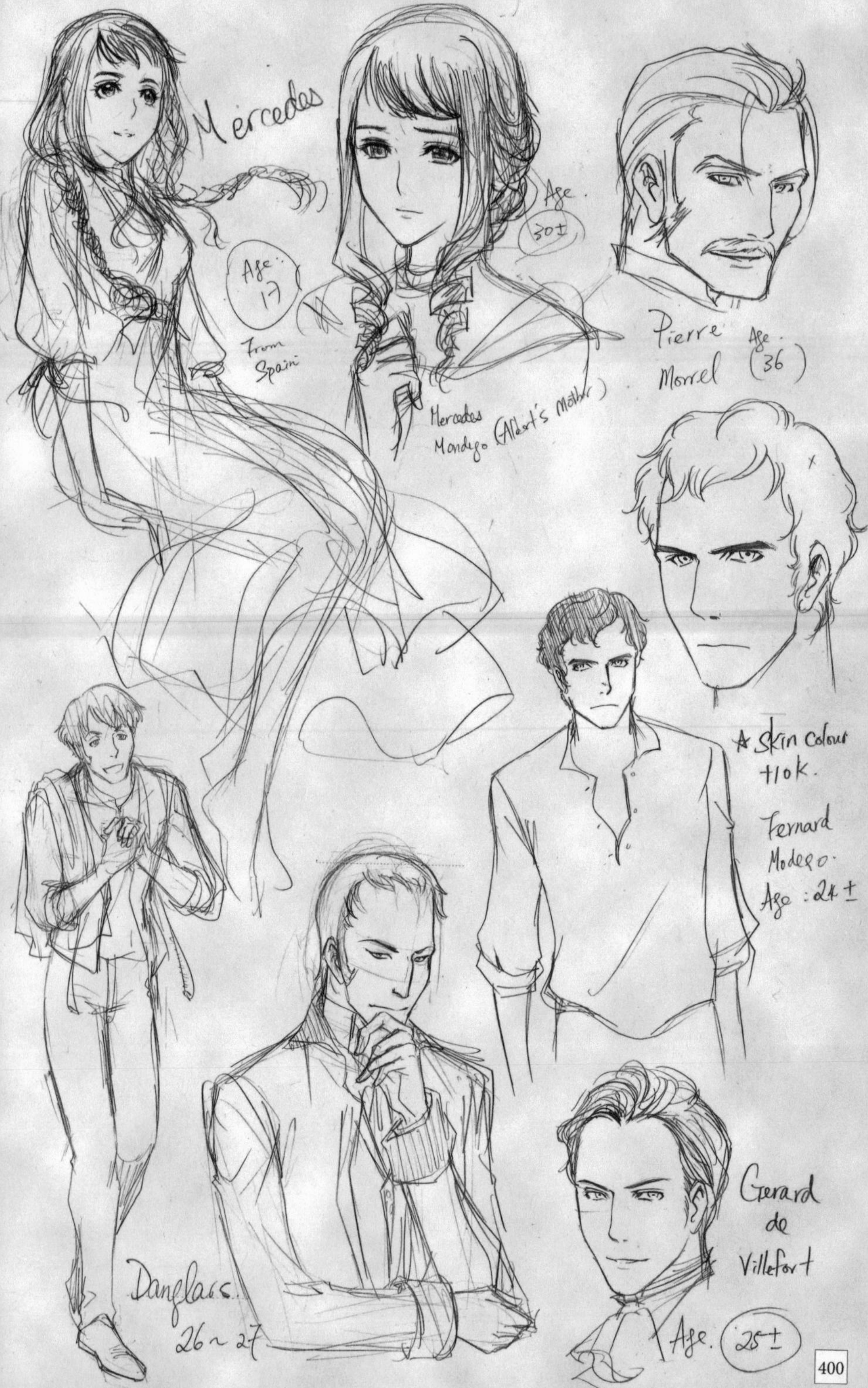
Mercedes
Age: 17
From Spain
Age. 30±
Mercedes Mondego (Albert's Mother)
Pierre Morrel
Age. (36)
★ skin colour +10k.
Fernard Modego.
Age: 24±
Danglars
26~27
Gerard de Villefort
Age. 25±

NOKMAN'S CHARACTER DESIGN SKETCH BOOK

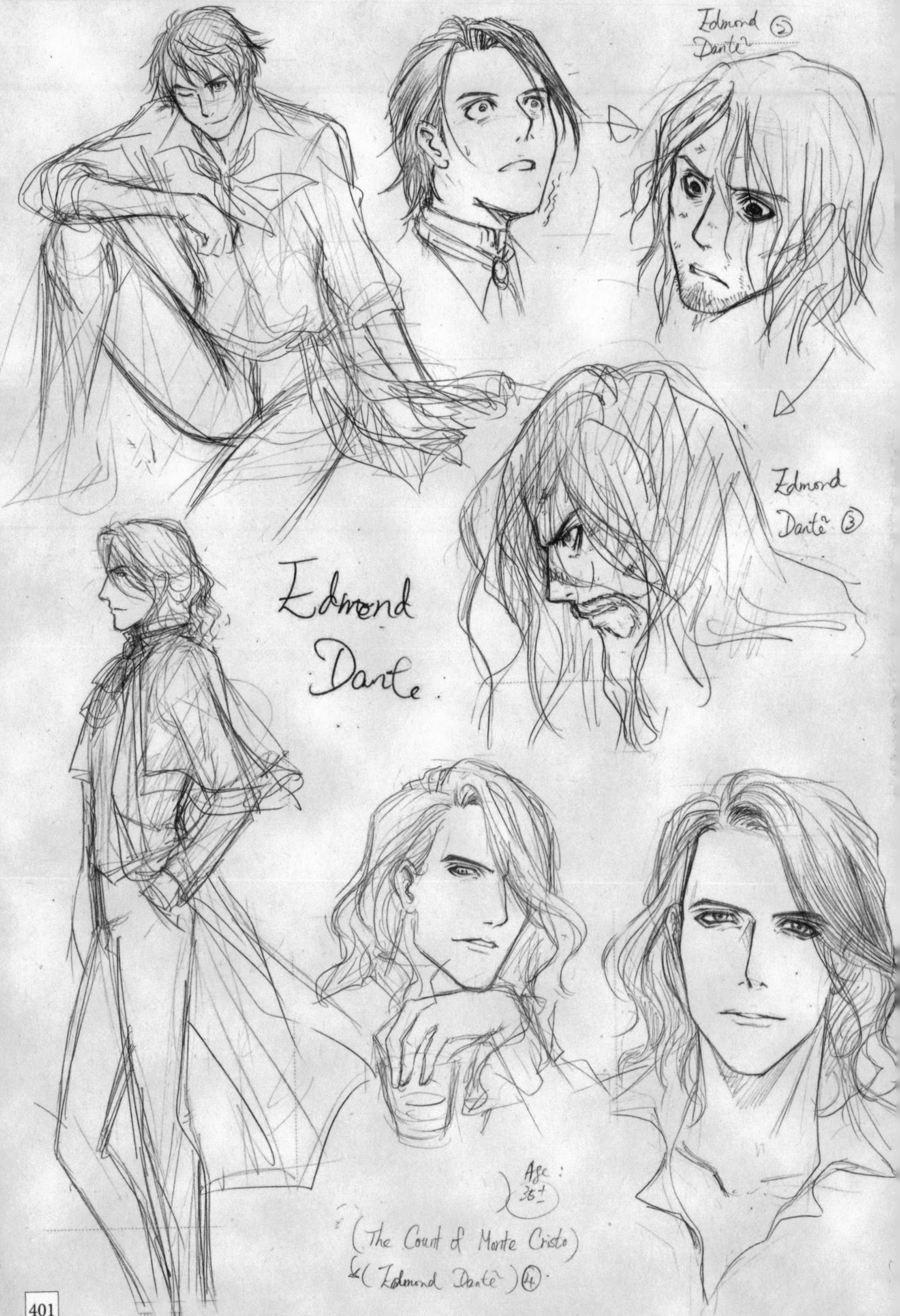

Edmond Dante 5
Edmond Dante 3
Edmond Dante
Age: 35±
(The Count of Monte Cristo)
&(Edmond Dante) 4

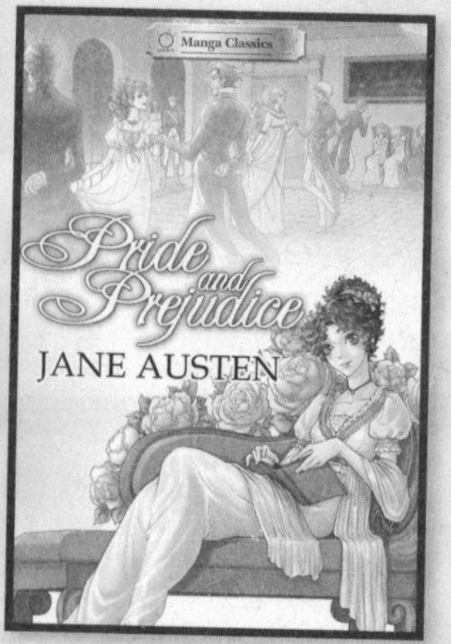
Manga Classics
Pride and Prejudice
JANE AUSTEN

**Manga Classics:
Pride and Prejudice**
Hard Cover $24.99
ISBN #978-1-927925-17-1
Soft Cover $17.99
ISBN #978-1-927-925-18-8

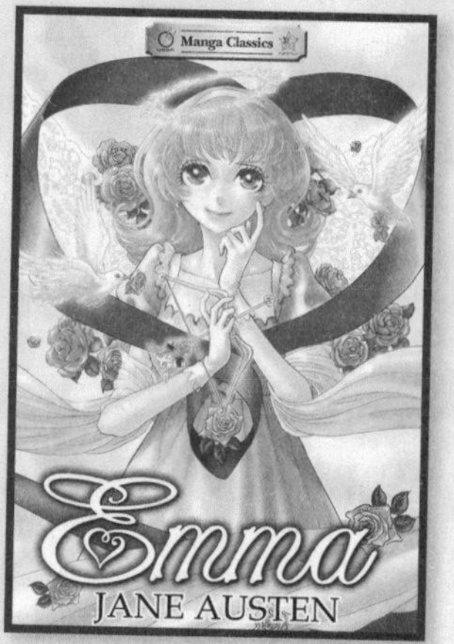
Manga Classics
Emma
JANE AUSTEN

**Manga Classics:
Emma**
Hard Cover $24.99
ISBN #978-1-927925-36-2
Soft Cover $17.99
ISBN #978-1-927-925-35-5

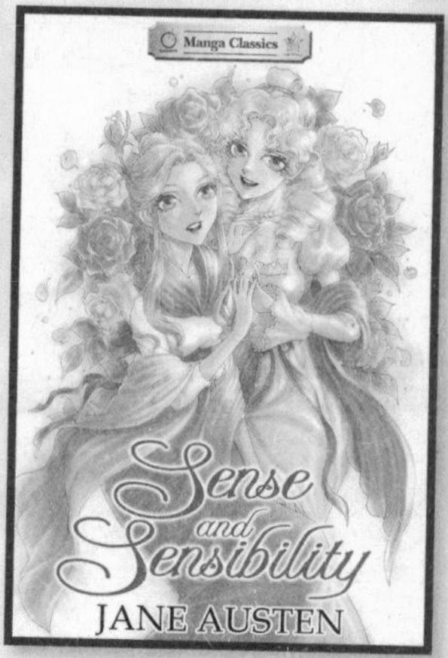
Manga Classics
Sense and Sensibility
JANE AUSTEN

**Manga Classics:
Sense and Sensibility**
Hard Cover $24.99
ISBN #978-1-927925-62-1
Soft Cover $17.99
ISBN #978-1-927925-63-8

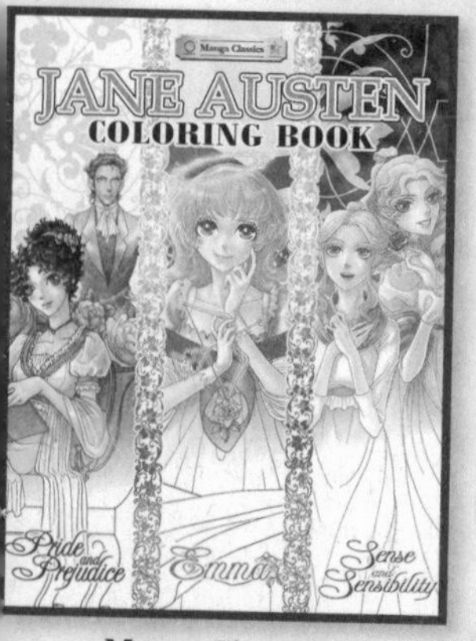
Manga Classics
JANE AUSTEN
COLORING BOOK
Pride and Prejudice
Emma
Sense and Sensibility

**Manga Classics:
Jane Austen Coloring Book**
Soft Cover $12.99
ISBN #978-1-927925-78-2

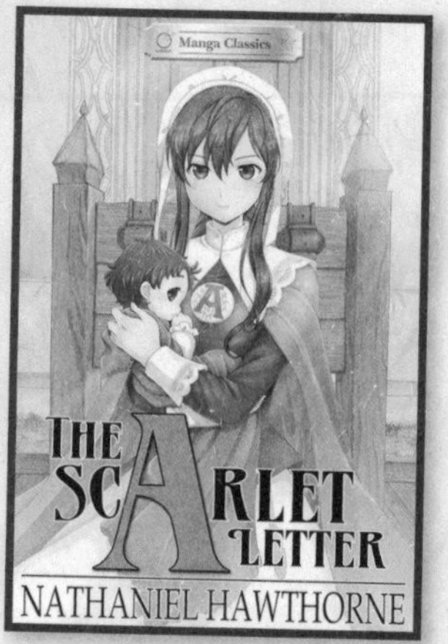
Manga Classics
THE SCARLET LETTER
NATHANIEL HAWTHORNE

**Manga Classics:
The Scarlet Letter**
Hard Cover $24.99
ISBN #978-1-927925-34-8
Soft Cover $17.99
ISBN #978-1-927925-33-1

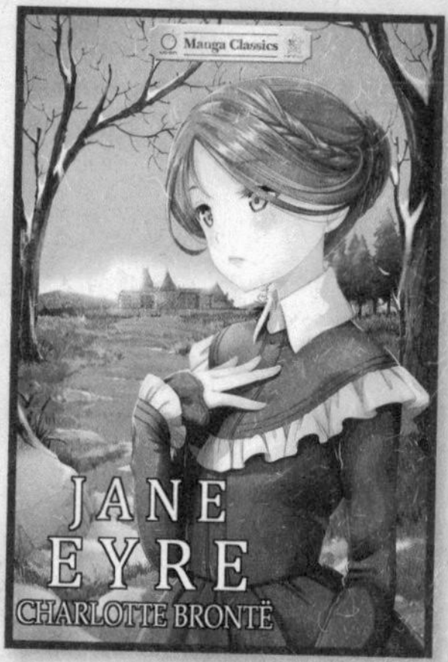
Manga Classics
JANE EYRE
CHARLOTTE BRONTË

**Manga Classics:
Jane Eyre**
Hard Cover $24.99
ISBN #978-1-927925-64-5
Soft Cover $17.99
ISBN #978-1-9279256-5-2

Check out more MANGA CLASSICS titles !!

◆ ! ◆ WHOOPS ◆ ! ◆
This is the back of the book!

UDON's Manga Classics books follow the Japanese comic (aka Manga!) reading order. Traditional manga is read in a "reversed" format starting on the right and heading towards the left. The story begins where English readers expect to find the last page because the spine of the book is on the opposite side. Flip to the other end of the book and start reading your Manga Classics!

THE COUNT OF MONTE CRISTO
ALEXANDRE DUMAS

Art by: Nokman Poon
Story Adaptation by: Crystal S. Chan
Lettering: Morpheus Studios
Lettering Assist: Jeannie Lee

UDON STAFF:

UDON Chief: Erik Ko
Manga Classics Group Editor: Stacy King
Senior Editor: Ash Paulsen
Associate Editor: M. Chandler
VP of Sales: John Shableski
Senior Producer: Long Vo
Marketing Manager: Jenny Myung
Production Manager: Janice Leung
Copy Editing Assistant: Michelle Lee
Japanese Liaison: Steven Cummings

MORPHEUS STAFF:

Morpheus Chief: Andy Hung
Production Manager: Yuen Him Tai
Production Assistant: Sei
Art Assistants: KK
 Man Yiu
 Touyu
 VIP 96neko
 Shougo
 Ron
 Stoon

AGE: YOUNG ADULT 12+
BISAC CAT: YAF010010 YAF01000 YAF009000 NOVELS/Manga/General
SUBJECT CATEGORIES: Comics, Graphic Novels, Manga,
Adventure/Intrigue, Revenge, France-Fiction, Fiction-General

Manga Classics: The Count of Monte Cristo. Published by UDON Entertainment Inc. 118 Tower Hill Road, C1, PO Box 20008, Richmond Hill, Ontario, L4K 0K0, Canada. Any similarities to persons living or dead are purely coincidental. No portion of this publication may be used or reproduced by any means (digital or print) without written permission from UDON Entertainment Inc. and Morpheus Publishing Limited except for review purposes. All artwork © UDON Entertainment Inc. and Morpheus Publishing Limited. **Printed in Canada**

First Printing April 2017
HARD COVER EDITION ISBN # 978-1-972925-60-7   PAPERBACK EDITION ISBN # 978-927925-61-4

www.mangaclassics.com

UDON
An UDON Entertainment Production, in association with Morpheus Publishing Limited.
www.udonentertainment.com www.morpheuspublishing.com

morpheus